Data Mining: Opportunities and Challenges

John Wang
Montclair State University, USA

IDEA GROUP PUBLISHING
Hershey • London • Melbourne • Singapore • Beijing

Acquisition Editor:	Mehdi Khosrow-Pour
Senior Managing Editor:	Jan Travers
Managing Editor:	Amanda Appicello
Development Editor:	Michele Rossi
Copy Editor:	Jane Conley
Typesetter:	Amanda Appicello
Cover Design:	Integrated Book Technology
Printed at:	Integrated Book Technology

Published in the United States of America by
Idea Group Publishing (an imprint of Idea Group Inc.)
701 E. Chocolate Avenue, Suite 200
Hershey PA 17033
Tel: 717-533-8845
Fax: 717-533-8661
E-mail: cust@idea-group.com
Web site: http://www.idea-group.com

and in the United Kingdom by
Idea Group Publishing (an imprint of Idea Group Inc.)
3 Henrietta Street
Covent Garden
London WC2E 8LU
Tel: 44 20 7240 0856
Fax: 44 20 7379 3313
Web site: http://www.eurospan.co.uk

Library of Congress Cataloging-in-Publication Data

Wang, John, 1955-
    Data mining : opportunities and challenges / John Wang.
        p. cm.
    ISBN 1-59140-051-1
 1. Data mining. I. Title.
    QA76.9.D343 W36 2002
    006.3--dc21

                                                            2002014190

eISBN 1-59140-095-3

British Cataloguing in Publication Data
A Cataloguing in Publication record for this book is available from the British Library.

NEW from Idea Group Publishing

- **Digital Bridges: Developing Countries in the Knowledge Economy**, John Senyo Afele/ ISBN:1-59140-039-2; eISBN 1-59140-067-8, © 2003
- **Integrative Document & Content Management: Strategies for Exploiting Enterprise Knowledge**, Len Asprey and Michael Middleton/ ISBN: 1-59140-055-4; eISBN 1-59140-068-6, © 2003
- **Critical Reflections on Information Systems: A Systemic Approach**, Jeimy Cano/ ISBN: 1-59140-040-6; eISBN 1-59140-069-4, © 2003
- **Web-Enabled Systems Integration: Practices and Challenges**, Ajantha Dahanayake and Waltraud Gerhardt ISBN: 1-59140-041-4; eISBN 1-59140-070-8, © 2003
- **Public Information Technology: Policy and Management Issues**, G. David Garson/ ISBN: 1-59140-060-0; eISBN 1-59140-071-6, © 2003
- **Knowledge and Information Technology Management: Human and Social Perspectives**, Angappa Gunasekaran, Omar Khalil and Syed Mahbubur Rahman/ ISBN: 1-59140-032-5; eISBN 1-59140-072-4, © 2003
- **Building Knowledge Economies: Opportunities and Challenges**, Liaquat Hossain and Virginia Gibson/ ISBN: 1-59140-059-7; eISBN 1-59140-073-2, © 2003
- **Knowledge and Business Process Management**, Vlatka Hlupic/ISBN: 1-59140-036-8; eISBN 1-59140-074-0, © 2003
- **IT-Based Management: Challenges and Solutions**, Luiz Antonio Joia/ISBN: 1-59140-033-3; eISBN 1-59140-075-9, © 2003
- **Geographic Information Systems and Health Applications**, Omar Khan/ ISBN: 1-59140-042-2; eISBN 1-59140-076-7, © 2003
- **The Economic and Social Impacts of E-Commerce**, Sam Lubbe/ ISBN: 1-59140-043-0; eISBN 1-59140-077-5, © 2003
- **Computational Intelligence in Control**, Masoud Mohammadian, Ruhul Amin Sarker and Xin Yao/ISBN: 1-59140-037-6; eISBN 1-59140-079-1, © 2003
- **Decision-Making Support Systems: Achievements and Challenges for the New Decade**, M.C. Manuel Mora, Guisseppi Forgionne and Jatinder N.D. Gupta/ISBN: 1-59140-045-7; eISBN 1-59140-080-5, © 2003
- **Architectural Issues of Web-Enabled Electronic Business**, Nansi Shi and V.K. Murthy/ ISBN: 1-59140-049-X; eISBN 1-59140-081-3, © 2003
- **Adaptive Evolutionary Information Systems**, Nandish V. Patel/ISBN: 1-59140-034-1; eISBN 1-59140-082-1, © 2003
- **Managing Data Mining Technologies in Organizations: Techniques and Applications**, Parag Pendharkar/ ISBN: 1-59140-057-0; eISBN 1-59140-083-X, © 2003
- **Intelligent Agent Software Engineering**, Valentina Plekhanova/ ISBN: 1-59140-046-5; eISBN 1-59140-084-8, © 2003
- **Advances in Software Maintenance Management: Technologies and Solutions**, Macario Polo, Mario Piattini and Francisco Ruiz/ ISBN: 1-59140-047-3; eISBN 1-59140-085-6, © 2003
- **Multidimensional Databases: Problems and Solutions**, Maurizio Rafanelli/ISBN: 1-59140-053-8; eISBN 1-59140-086-4, © 2003
- **Information Technology Enabled Global Customer Service**, Tapio Reponen/ISBN: 1-59140-048-1; eISBN 1-59140-087-2, © 2003
- **Creating Business Value with Information Technology: Challenges and Solutions**, Namchul Shin/ISBN: 1-59140-038-4; eISBN 1-59140-088-0, © 2003
- **Advances in Mobile Commerce Technologies**, Ee-Peng Lim and Keng Siau/ ISBN: 1-59140-052-X; eISBN 1-59140-089-9, © 2003
- **Mobile Commerce: Technology, Theory and Applications**, Brian Mennecke and Troy Strader/ ISBN: 1-59140-044-9; eISBN 1-59140-090-2, © 2003
- **Managing Multimedia-Enabled Technologies in Organizations**, S.R. Subramanya/ISBN: 1-59140-054-6; eISBN 1-59140-091-0, © 2003
- **Web-Powered Databases**, David Taniar and Johanna Wenny Rahayu/ISBN: 1-59140-035-X; eISBN 1-59140-092-9, © 2003
- **E-Commerce and Cultural Values**, Theerasak Thanasankit/ISBN: 1-59140-056-2; eISBN 1-59140-093-7, © 2003
- **Information Modeling for Internet Applications**, Patrick van Bommel/ISBN: 1-59140-050-3; eISBN 1-59140-094-5, © 2003
- **Data Mining: Opportunities and Challenges**, John Wang/ISBN: 1-59140-051-1; eISBN 1-59140-095-3, © 2003
- **Annals of Cases on Information Technology** – vol 5, Mehdi Khosrowpour/ ISBN: 1-59140-061-9; eISBN 1-59140-096-1, © 2003
- **Advanced Topics in Database Research** – vol 2, Keng Siau/ISBN: 1-59140-063-5; eISBN 1-59140-098-8, © 2003
- **Advanced Topics in End User Computing** – vol 2, Mo Adam Mahmood/ISBN: 1-59140-065-1; eISBN 1-59140-100-3, © 2003
- **Advanced Topics in Global Information Management** – vol 2, Felix Tan/ ISBN: 1-59140-064-3; eISBN 1-59140-101-1, © 2003
- **Advanced Topics in Information Resources Management** – vol 2, Mehdi Khosrowpour/ ISBN: 1-59140-062-7; eISBN 1-59140-099-6, © 2003

Data Mining: Opportunities and Challenges

Table of Contents

Preface

Data mining (DM) is the extraction of hidden predictive information from large databases (DBs). With the automatic discovery of knowledge implicit within DBs, DM uses sophisticated statistical analysis and modeling techniques to uncover patterns and relationships hidden in organizational DBs. Over the last 40 years, the tools and techniques to process structured information have continued to evolve from DBs to data warehousing (DW) to DM. DW applications have become business-critical. DM can extract even more value out of these huge repositories of information.

Approaches to DM are varied and often confusing. This book presents an overview of the state of art in this new and multidisciplinary field. DM is taking off for several reasons: organizations are gathering more data about their businesses, costs of storage have dropped drastically, and competitive business pressures have increased. Other factors include the emergence of pressures to control existing IT investments, and last, but not least, the marked reduction in the cost/performance ratio of computer systems. There are four basic mining operations supported by numerous mining techniques: predictive model creation supported by supervised induction techniques; link analysis supported by association discovery and sequence discovery techniques; DB segmentation supported by clustering techniques; and deviation detection supported by statistical techniques.

Although DM is still in its infancy, companies in a wide range of industries - including retail, banking and finance, heath care, manufacturing, telecommunication, and aerospace - as well as government agencies are already using DM tools and techniques to take advantage of historical data. By using pattern-recognition technologies and statistical and mathematical techniques to sift through warehoused information, DM helps analysts recognize significant facts, relationships, trends, patterns, exceptions, and anomalies that might otherwise go unnoticed.

In my February 2001 call for chapters, I sought contributions to this book that would address a vast number of issues ranging from the breakthrough of new theories to case studies of firms' experiences with their DM. After spending one and a half years of preparation on the book and a strict peer-refereed process, I am delighted to see it appearing on the market. The primary objective of this book is to explore the myriad issues regarding DM, specifically focusing on those areas that explore new methodologies or examine case studies. A broad spectrum of scientists, practitioners, graduate students, and managers, who perform research and/or implement the discoveries, are the envisioned readers of this book.

The book contains a collection of twenty chapters written by a truly international team of forty-four experts representing the leading scientists and talented young scholars from seven countries (or areas): Argentina, Canada, Italy, South Africa, Sweden, Taiwan, and the United States.

Chapter 1 by Arnborg reviews the fundamentals of inference and gives a motivation for Bayesian analysis. The method is illustrated with dependency tests in data sets with categorical data variables, and the Dirichlet prior distributions. Principles and problems for deriving causality conclusions are reviewed and illustrated with Simpson's paradox. Selection of decomposable and directed graphical models illustrates the Bayesian approach. Bayesian and Expectation Maximization (EM) classification is described briefly. The material is illustrated by two cases, one in personalization of media distribution, and one in schizophrenia research. These cases are illustrations of how to approach problems that exist in many other application areas.

Chapter 2 by Hsu discusses the problem of Feature Selection (also called Variable Elimination) in supervised inductive learning approaches to DM, in the context of controlling Inductive Bias - i.e., any preference for one (classification or regression) hypothesis other than pure consistency with training data. Feature selection can be achieved using combinatorial search and optimization approaches. This chapter focuses on data-driven validation-based techniques, particularly the WRAPPER approach. Hsu presents a wrapper that uses Genetic Algorithms for the search component and a validation criterion, based upon model accuracy and problem complexity, as the Fitness Measure. This method is related to the Classifier System of Booker, Golderberg and Holland (1989). Current research relates the Model Selection criterion in the fitness to the Minimum Description Length (MDL) family of learning criteria. Hsu presents two case studies in large-scale commercial DM and decision support: crop condition monitoring, and loss prediction for insurance pricing. Part of these case studies includes a synopsis of the general experimental framework, using the Machine Learning in Java (MLJ) and Data to Knowledge (D2K) Java-based visual programming systems for DM and information visualization.

Chapter 3 by Herna Viktor, Eric Paquet, and Gys le Roux explores the use of visual DM and virtual reality-based visualization in a cooperative learning environment. The chapter introduces a cooperative learning environment in which multiple DM tools reside and describes the ViziMine DM tool used to visualize the cooperative DM process. The aim of the ViziMine tool is twofold. Firstly, the data repository is visualized during data preprocessing and DM. Secondly, the knowledge, as obtained through DM, is assessed and modified through the interactive visualization of the cooperative DM process and its results. In this way, the user is able to assess and possibly improve the results of DM to reflect his or her domain expertise. Finally, the use of three-dimensional visualization, virtual reality-based visualization, and multimedia DM is discussed. The chapter shows how these leading-edge technologies can be used to visualize the data and its descriptors.

Feature subset selection is an important problem in knowledge discovery, not only for the insight gained from determining relevant modeling variables but also for the improved understandability, scalability, and possibly, accuracy of the resulting models. The purpose of Chapter 4 is to provide a comprehensive analysis of feature selection via evolutionary search in supervised and unsupervised learning. To achieve this purpose, Kim, Street, and Menczer first discuss a general framework for feature selection based on a new search algorithm, Evolutionary Local Selection Algorithm (ELSA). The search is formulated as a multi-objective optimization problem to examine the trade-off between the complexity of the generated solutions against their quality. ELSA considers multiple objectives efficiently while avoiding computationally expensive global comparison. The authors combine ELSA with Artificial Neural Networks (ANNs) and the EM algorithm for feature selection in supervised and unsupervised learning, respectively. Further, they show a new two-level evolutionary algorithm, Meta-Evolutionary Ensembles (MEE), in which feature selection is used to promote diversity among classifiers for ensemble classification.

Coppola and Vanneschi consider the application of parallel programming environments to develop portable and efficient high-performance DM tools. They discuss the main issues in exploiting parallelism in DM applications to improve the scalability of several mining techniques to large or geographically distributed DBs. The main focus of Chapter 5 is on parallel software engineering, showing that the skeleton-based, high-level approach can be effective both in developing portable high-performance DM kernels, and in easing their integration with other data management tools. Three test cases are described that present parallel algorithms for association rules, classification, and clustering, starting from the problem and going up to a concrete implementation. Experimental results are discussed with respect to performance and software costs. To help the integration of high-level application with existing environments, an object-oriented interface is proposed. This interface complements the parallel skeleton approach and allows the use of a number of external libraries and software modules as *external objects*, including shared-memory-distributed objects.

Rough set theory, originated by Z. Pawlak in 1982, among other applications, is a methodological tool for DM and machine learning. The main advantage of rough set theory is that it does not need any preliminary or additional information about data (such as probability distribution assumptions in probability classifier theory, grade of membership in fuzzy set theory, etc.). Numerical estimates of uncertainty of rough set theory have immediate interpretation in evidence theory (Dempster-Shafer theory). The chapter "Data Mining Based on Rough Sets" by Grzymala-Busse and Ziarko starts from fundamentals of rough set theory. Then two generalizations of rough set theory are presented: Variable Precision Rough Set Model (VPRSM) and Learning from Examples using Rough Sets (LERS). The prime concern of VPRSM is forming decision tables, while LERS produces rule sets. The two generalizations of rough set theory are independent and neither can be reduced to the other. Among many applications of LERS, those related to medical area and natural language are briefly described.

DM is based upon searching the concatenation of multiple DBs that usually contain some amount of missing data along with a variable percentage of inaccurate data, pollution, outliers, and noise. During the last four decades, statisticians have attempted to address the impact of missing data on IT. Chapter 7 by Brown and Kros commences with a background analysis, including a review of both seminal and current literature. Reasons for data inconsistency along with definitions of various types of missing data are discussed. The chapter mainly focuses on methods of addressing missing data and the impact that missing data has on the knowledge discovery process via prediction, estimation, classification, pattern recognition, and association rules. Finally, trends regarding missing data and DM are discussed, in addition to future research opportunities and concluding remarks.

In Chapter 8, Yang and Lee use a self-organizing map to cluster documents and form two feature maps. One of the map, namely the document cluster map, clusters documents according to the co-occurrence patterns of terms appeared in the documents. The other map, namely the word cluster map, is obtained by selecting the words of common interest for those documents in the same cluster. They then apply an iterative process to these maps to discover the main themes and generate hierarchies of the document clusters. The hierarchy generation and theme discovery process both utilize the synaptic weights developed after the clustering process using the self-organizing map. Thus, their technique incorporates the knowledge from the neural networks and may provide promising directions in other knowledge-discovery applications. Although this work was originally designed for text categorization tasks, the hierarchy mining process developed by these authors also poses an interesting direction in discovering and organizing unknown knowledge.

Although DM may often seem a highly effective tool for companies to be using in their business endeavors, there are a number of pitfalls and/or barriers that may impede these firms from properly budgeting for DM projects in the short term. In Chapter 9, Wang and Oppenheim indicate that the pitfalls of DM can be categorized into several distinct categories. The authors explore the issues of accessibility and usability, affordability and efficiency, scalability and adaptability, systematic patterns vs. sample-specific patterns, explanatory factors vs. random variables, segmentation vs. sampling, accuracy and cohesiveness, and standardization and verification. Finally, they present the technical challenges regarding the pitfalls of DM.

Chapter 10 by Troutt, Gribbin, Shanker, and Zhang proposes the principle of Maximum Performance Efficiency (MPE) as a contribution to the DM toolkit. This principle seeks to estimate optimal or boundary behavior, in contrast to techniques like regression analysis that predict average behavior. This MPE principle is explained and used to estimate best-practice cost rates in the context of an activity-based costing situation where the authors consider multiple activities contributing to a single cost pool. A validation approach for this estimation method is developed in terms of what the authors call normal-like-or-better performance effectiveness. Extensions to time series data on a single unit, and marginal cost-oriented basic cost models are also briefly described.

One of the major problems faced by DM technologies is how to deal with uncertainty. Bayesian methods provide an explicit way of using probability for quantifying uncertainty. The purpose of Chapter 11 by Lauria and Tayi is twofold: to provide an overview of the theoretical framework of Bayesian methods and its application to DM, with special emphasis on statistical modeling and machine learning techniques. Topics covered include Bayes Theorem and its implications, Bayesian classifiers, Bayesian belief networks, statistical computing, and an introduction to Markov Chain Monte Carlo techniques. The coverage of these topics has been augmented by providing numerical examples.

Knowledge of the structural organization of information in documents can be of significant assistance to information systems that use documents as their knowledge bases. In particular, such knowledge is of use to information retrieval systems that retrieve documents in response to user queries. Chapter 12 by Kulyukin and Burke presents an approach to mining free-text documents for structure that is qualitative in nature. It complements the statistical and machine learning approaches insomuch as the structural organization of information in documents is discovered through mining free text for content markers left behind by document writers. The ultimate objective is to find scalable DM solutions for free-text documents in exchange for modest knowledge engineering requirements.

Chapter 13 by Johnson, Fotouhi, and Draghici presents three systems that incorporate document structure information into a search of the Web. These systems extend existing Web searches by allowing the user to not only request documents containing specific search words, but also to specify that documents be of a certain type. In addition to being able to search a local DB, all three systems are capable of dynamically querying the Web. Each system applies a *query-by-structure* approach that captures and utilizes structure information as well as content during a query of the Web. Two of the systems also employ Neural Networks (NNs) to organize the information based on relevancy of both the content and structure. These systems utilize a supervised Hamming NN and an unsupervised competitive NN, respectively. Initial testing of these systems has shown promising result when compared to straight keyword searches.

Chapter 14 seeks to evaluate the feasibility of using self-organizing maps (SOMs) for financial benchmarking of companies. Eklund, Back, Vanharanta, and Visa collected a number of annual reports from companies in the international pulp and paper industry, for the period 1995-2000. They then create a financial DB consisting of a number of financial ratios, calculated based on the values from the income and balance sheets of the annual reports. The financial ratios used were selected based on their reliability and validity in international comparisons. The authors also briefly discuss issues related to the use of SOMs, such as data pre-processing, and the training of the map. The authors then perform a financial benchmarking of the companies by visualizing them on a SOM. This benchmarking includes finding the best and poorest performing companies, illustrating the effects of the Asian financial crisis, and comparing the performance of the five largest pulp and paper companies. The findings are evaluated using existing domain knowledge, i.e., information from the textual parts of the annual reports. The authors found the SOM to be a feasible tool for financial benchmarking.

In Chapter 15, general insight into DM with emphasis on the health care industry is provided by Payton. The discussion focuses on earlier electronic commerce health care initiatives, namely community health information networks (CHINs). CHINs continue to be widely debated by leading industry groups, such as The Healthy Cities Organization and The IEEE-USA Medical Technology and Policy Committee. These applications raise issues about how patient information can be mined to enable fraud detection, profitability analysis, patient profiling, and retention management. Withstanding these DM capabilities, social issues abound.

In Chapter 16, Long and Troutt discuss the potential contributions DM could make within the Human Resource (HR) function. They provide a basic introduction to DM techniques and processes and survey the literature on the steps involved in successfully mining this information. They also discuss the importance of DW and datamart considerations. A discussion of the contrast between DM and more routine statistical studies is given. They examine the value of HR information to support a firm's competitive position and for support of decision-making in organizations. Examples of potential applications are outlined in terms of data that is ordinarily captured in HR information systems. They note that few DM applications have been reported to date in the literature and hope that this chapter will spur interest among upper management and HR professionals.

The banking industry spends a large amount of IT budgets with the expectation that the investment will result in higher productivity and improved financial performance. However, bank managers make decisions on how to spend large IT budgets without accurate performance measurement systems on the business value of IT. It is a challenging DM task to investigate banking performance as a result of IT investment, because numerous financial and banking performance measures are present with the new IT cost category. Chapter 17 by Chen and Zhu presents a new DM approach that examines the impact of IT investment on banking performance, measures the financial performance of banking, and extracts performance patterns. The information obtained will provide banks with the most efficient and effective means to conduct business while meeting internal operational performance goals.

Chapter 18 by Cook and Cook highlights both the positive and negative aspects of DM. Specifically, the social, ethical, and legal implications of DM are examined through recent case law, current public opinion, and small industry-specific examples. There are many issues concerning this topic. Therefore, the purpose of this chapter is to expose the reader to some of the more interesting ones and provide insight into how information systems (ISs) professionals and businesses may protect themselves from the negative ramifications associated with improper use of data. The more experience with and exposure to social, ethical, and legal concerns with respect to DM, the better prepared the reader will be to prevent trouble in the future.

Chapter 19 by Böhm, Galli, and Chiotti presents a DM application to software engineering. Particularly, it describes the use of DM in different parts of the design process of a dynamic decision-support system agent-based architecture. By using DM techniques, a discriminating function to classify the system domains is defined. From this discriminating function, a system knowledge base is designed that stores the values of the parameters required by such a function. Also, by using DM, a data structure for analyzing the system operation results is defined. According to that, a case base to store the information of performed searches quality is designed. By mining this case base, rules to infer possible causes of domains classification error are specified. Based on these rules, a learning mechanism to update the knowledge base is designed.

DM is a field that is experiencing rapid growth and change, and new applications and developments are constantly being introduced. While many of the traditional statistical approaches to DM are still widely used, new technologies and uses for DM are coming to the forefront. The purpose of Chapter 20 is to examine and explore some of the newer areas of DM that are expected to have much impact not only for the present, but also for the future. These include the expanding areas of Web and text mining, as well as ubiquitous, distributed/collective, and phenomenal DM. From here, the discussion turns to the dynamic areas of hypertext, multimedia, spatial, and geographic DM. For those who love numbers and analytical work, constraint-based and time-eries mining are useful ways to better understand complex data. Finally, some of the most critical applications are examined, including bioinformatics.

References

Booker, L.B., Goldberg, D.E., & Holland, J.H. (1989). Classifier Systems and Genetic Algorithms. *Artificial Intelligence*, 40, 235-282.

Pawlak, Z. (1982). Rough Sets. *International Journal of Computer and Information Sciences,* 11, 341-356.

Acknowledgments

The editor would like to acknowledge the help of all involved in the development and review process of the book, without whose support the project could not have been satisfactorily completed. Thanks go to all those who provided constructive and comprehensive reviews. However, some of the reviewers must be mentioned as their reviews set the benchmark. Reviewers who provided the most comprehensive, critical, and constructive comments include: Nick Street of University of Iowa; Marvin D. Troutt of Kent State University; Herna Viktor of University of Ottawa; William H. Hsu of Kansas State University; Jack S. Cook of Rochester Institute of Technology; and Massimo Coppola of University of Pisa.

The support of the Office of Research and Sponsored Programs at Montclair State University is hereby graciously acknowledged for awarding me a Career Development Project Fund in 2001.

A further special note of thanks goes also to the publishing team at Idea Group Publishing, whose contributions throughout the whole process— from inception of the idea to final publication— have been invaluable. In particular, thanks to Michelle Rossi, whose continuous prodding via e-mail kept the project on schedule, and to Mehdi Khosrowpour, whose enthusiasm motivated me to initially accept his invitation to take on this project. In addition, Amanda Appicello at Idea Group Publishing made numerous corrections, revisions, and beautifications. Also, Carrie Stull Skovrinskie helped lead the book to the market.

In closing, I wish to thank all of the authors for their insights and excellent contributions to this book. I also want to thank a group of anonymous reviewers who assisted me in the peer-review process. In addition, I want to thank my parents (Houde Wang & Junyan Bai) for their encouragement, and last but not least, my wife Hongyu Ouyang for her unfailing support and dedication during the long development period, which culminated in the birth of both this book and our first boy, Leigh Wang, almost at the same time. Like a baby, DM has a bright and promising future.

John Wang, Ph.D.
Montclair State University
March 31, 2002

Chapter I

A Survey of Bayesian Data Mining

Stefan Arnborg
Royal Institute of Technology and
Swedish Institute of Computer Science, Sweden

ABSTRACT

This chapter reviews the fundamentals of inference, and gives a motivation for Bayesian analysis. The method is illustrated with dependency tests in data sets with categorical data variables, and the Dirichlet prior distributions. Principles and problems for deriving causality conclusions are reviewed, and illustrated with Simpson's paradox. The selection of decomposable and directed graphical models illustrates the Bayesian approach. Bayesian and EM classification is shortly described. The material is illustrated on two cases, one in personalization of media distribution, one in schizophrenia research. These cases are illustrations of how to approach problem types that exist in many other application areas.

INTRODUCTION

Data acquired for analysis can have many different forms. We will describe the analysis of data that can be thought of as samples drawn from a population, and the conclusions will be phrased as properties of this larger population. We will focus on very simple models. As the investigator's understanding of a problem area improves, the statistical models tend to become complex. Some examples of such areas are genetic linkage studies, ecosystem studies, and functional MRI investigations, where the signals extracted from measurements are very weak but potentially extremely useful for the application area. Experiments are typically analyzed using a combination of visualization, Bayesian analysis, and conventional test- and confidence-based statistics. In engineering and commercial applications of data mining, the goal is not normally to arrive at eternal truths, but to support decisions in design and business. Nevertheless, because of the competitive nature of these activities, one can expect well-founded analytical methods and understandable models to provide more useful answers than ad hoc ones.

This text emphasizes characterization of data and the population from which it is drawn with its statistical properties. Nonetheless, the application owners have typically very different concerns: they want to understand; they want to be able to predict and ultimately to control their objects of study. This means that the statistical investigation is a first phase that must be accompanied by activities extracting meaning from the data. There is relatively little theory on these later activities, and it is probably fair to say that their outcome depends mostly on the intellectual climate of the team—of which the analyst is only one member.

Summary

Our goal is to explain some advantages of the Bayesian approach and to show how probability models can display the information or knowledge we are after in an application. We will see that, although many computations of Bayesian data-mining are straightforward, one soon reaches problems where difficult integrals have to be evaluated, and presently only Markov Chain Monte Carlo (MCMC) and expectation maximization (EM) methods are available. There are several recent books describing the Bayesian method from both a theoretical (Bernardo & Smith, 1994) and an application-oriented (Carlin & Louis, 1997) perspective. Particularly, Ed Jaynes' unfinished lecture notes, now available in (Jaynes, 2003) have provided inspiration for me and numerous students using them all over the world. A current survey of MCMC methods, which can solve many complex evaluations required in advanced Bayesian modeling, can be found in the book *Markov Chain Monte Carlo in Practice* (Gilks, Richardson, & Spiegelhalter 1996). Theory and use of graphical models have been explained by Lauritzen (1996) and Cox and Wermuth (1996). A tutorial on Bayesian network approaches to data mining is found in Heckerman (1997). We omit, for reasons of space availability, a discussion of linear and generalized linear models, which are described, e.g., by Hand, Mannila, and Smyth (2001). Another recent technique we omit is optimal recursive Bayesian estimation with particle filters, which is an important new application of MCMC (Doucet, de Freitas & Gordon 2001).

SCHOOLS OF STATISTICS

Statistical inference has a long history, and one should not assume that all scientists and engineers analyzing data have the same expertise and would reach the same type of conclusion using the objectively "right" method in the analysis of a given data set. Probability theory is the basis of statistics, and it links a probability model to an outcome. But this linking can be achieved by a number of different principles. A pure mathematician interested in *mathematical probability* would only consider abstract spaces equipped with a probability measure. Whatever is obtained by analyzing such mathematical structures has no immediate bearing on how we should interpret a data set collected to give us knowledge about the world. When it comes to inference about real-world phenomena, there are two different and complementary views on probability that have competed for the position of "the" statistical method. With both views, we consider models that tell how data is generated in terms of probability. The models used for analysis reflect our - or the application owner's - understanding of the problem area. In a sense they are hypotheses, and in inference a hypothesis is often more or less equated with a probability model. Inference is concerned with saying something about which probability model generated our data — for this reason inference was sometimes called *inverse probability* (Dale, 1991).

Bayesian Inference

The first applications of inference used Bayesian analysis, where we can directly talk about the probability that a hypothesis H generated our observed data D. Using probability manipulation and treating both data D and hypotheses H_1 and H_2 as events we find:

$$\frac{P(H_1 \mid D)}{P(H_2 \mid D)} = \frac{P(D \mid H_1)}{P(D \mid H_2)} \frac{P(H_1)}{P(H_2)}$$

This rule says that the odds we assign to the choice between H_1 and H_2, the *prior odds* $P(H_1)/P(H_2)$, are changed to the *posterior odds* $P(H_1 \mid D)/P(H_2 \mid D)$, by multiplication with the *Bayes factor* $P(D \mid H_1)/P(D \mid H_2)$. In other words, the Bayes factor contains all information provided by the data relevant for choosing between the two hypotheses. The rule assumes that probability is *subjective*, dependent on information the observer holds, e.g., by having seen the outcome D of an experiment. If we have more than two hypotheses, or a parameterized hypothesis, similar calculations lead to formulas defining a posterior probability distribution that depends on the prior distribution:

$$P(H_i \mid D) = \frac{P(D \mid H_i) P(H_i)}{\sum_j P(D \mid H_j) P(H_j)} \tag{1}$$

$$f(\lambda \mid D) \propto P(D \mid H_\lambda) f(\lambda) \tag{2}$$

where $f(\lambda)$ is the prior density and $f(\lambda \mid D)$ is the posterior density, and $\propto$ is a sign that indicates that a normalization constant (independent of λ but not of D) has been omitted. For posteriors of parameter values the concept of *credible set* is important. A q-credible set is a set of parameter values among which the parameter has a high and known probability q of lying, according to the posterior distribution. The Bayes factor estimates the support given by the data to the hypotheses. Inevitably, random variation can give support to the "wrong" hypothesis. A useful rule is the following: if the Bayes factor is k in favor of H_1, then the probability of getting this factor or larger from an experiment where H_2 was the true hypothesis is less than $1/k$. For most specific hypothesis pairs, the bound is much better (Royall, 2000).

A Small Bayesian Example

We will see how Bayes' method works with a small example, in fact the same example used by Thomas Bayes(1703 — 1762). Assume we have found a coin among the belongings of a notorious gambling shark. Is this coin fair or unfair? The data we can obtain are a sequence of outcomes in a tossing experiment, represented as a binary string. Let one hypothesis be that the coin is fair, H_f. Then $P(D |H_f) = 2^{-n}$, where $n=|D|$ is the number of tosses made. We must also have another hypothesis that can fit better or worse to an outcome. Bayes used a parameterized model where the parameter is the unknown probability, p, of getting a one in a toss. For this model H_p, we have $P(D |H_p) = p^s (1-p)^f$ for a sequence D with s successes and f failures. The probability of an outcome under H_p is clearly a function of p. If we assume, with Bayes, that the prior distribution of p is uniform in the interval from 0 to 1, we get by Equation (2) a posterior distribution $f(p |D) = cp^s (1-p)^f$, a Beta distribution where the normalization constant is $c = (n+1)!/(s!f!)$. This function has a maximum at the observed frequency s/n. We cannot say that the coin is unfair just because s is not the same as f, since the normal variation makes inequality very much more likely than equality for a large number of tosses even if the coin is fair.

If we want to decide between fairness and unfairness we must introduce a composite hypothesis by specifying a probability distribution for the parameter p in H_p. A conventional choice is again the uniform distribution. Let H_u be the hypothesis of unfairness, expressed as H_p with a uniform distribution on the parameter p. By integration we find $P(D|H_u) = s!f! / (n+1)!$. In other words, the number of ones in the experiment is uniformly distributed. Suppose now that we toss the coin twelve times and obtain the sequence 000110000001, three successes and nine failures. The Bayes factor in favor of unfairness is 1.4. This is a too small value to be of interest. Values above 3 are worth mentioning, above 30 significant, and factors above 300 would give strong support to the first hypothesis. In order to get strong support to fairness or unfairness in the example we would need much more than 12 tosses.

Bayesian Decision Theory and Multiple Hypothesis Comparisons

The posterior gives a numerical measure of belief in the two hypotheses compared. Suppose our task is to decide by choosing one of them. If the Bayes factor is greater than one, H_1 is more likely than H_2, assuming no prior preference of either. But this does not necessarily mean that H_1 is true, since the data can be misleading by natural random fluctuation. The recipe for choosing is to make the choice with smallest expected cost (Berger, 1985). This rule is also applicable when simultaneously making many model comparisons.

When making inference for the parameter value of a parameterized model, equation (2) gives only a distribution over the parameter value. If we want a point estimate l of the parameter value λ, we should also use Bayesian decision theory. We want to minimize the loss incurred by stating the estimate l when the true value is λ, $L(l, \lambda)$. But we do not know λ. As with a discrete set of decision alternatives, we minimize the expected loss over the posterior for λ, by integration. If the loss function is the squared error, the optimal estimator is the mean of $f(\lambda |D)$; if the loss is the absolute value of the error, the optimal estimator is the median; with a discrete parameter space, minimizing the probability of an error (no matter how small) gives the *Maximum A Posteriori* (MAP) estimate. As an example, when tossing a coin gives s heads and f tails, the posterior with a uniform prior is $f(p \mid s, f) = cp^s (1 - p)^f$, the MAP estimate for p is the observed frequency $s/(s+f)$, the mean estimate is the Laplace estimator $(s+1)/(s+f+2)$ and the median is a fairly complicated quantity expressible, when s and f are known, as the solution to an algebraic equation of high degree.

Test-Based Inference

The irrelevance of long run properties of hypothesis probabilities made one school of statistics reject subjective probability altogether. This school works with what is usually known as *objective probability*. Data is generated in repeatable experiments with a fixed distribution of the outcome. The device used by a practitioner of objective probability is testing. For a single hypothesis *H*, a *test statistic* is designed as a mapping *f* of the possible outcomes to an ordered space, normally the real numbers. The data probability function $P(D|H)$ will now induce a distribution of the test statistic on the real line. We continue by defining a *rejection region*, an interval with low probability, typically 5% or 1%. Next, the experiment is performed or the data *D* is obtained, and if the test statistic $f(D)$ falls in the rejection region, the hypothesis *H* is rejected. For a parameterized hypothesis, rejection depends on the value of the parameter. In objective probability inference, we use the concept of a confidence interval, whose definition is unfortunately rather awkward and is omitted (it is discussed in all elementary statistics texts). Unfortunately, there is no strong reason to accept the null hypothesis just because it could not be rejected, and there is no strong reason to accept the alternative just because the null was rejected. But this is how testing is usually applied. The *p*-value is the probability of obtaining a test statistic not less extreme than the one obtained, under the null hypothesis, so that a *p*-value less than 0.01 allows one to reject the null hypothesis on the 1% level.

A Small Hypothesis Testing Example

Let us analyze coin tossing again. We have the two hypotheses H_f and H_u. Choose H_f, the coin is fair, as the null hypothesis. Choose the number of successes as test statistic. Under the null hypothesis we can easily compute the *p*-value, the probability of obtaining nine or more failures with a fair coin tossed 12 times, which is .075. This is 7.5%, so the experiment does not allow us to reject fairness at the 5% level. On the other hand, if the testing plan was to toss the coin until three heads have been seen, the *p*-value should be computed as the probability of seeing nine or more failures before the third success, which is .0325. Since this is 3.25%, we can now reject the fairness hypothesis at 5%. The result of a test depends thus not only on the choice of hypothesis and significance level, but also on the experimental design, i.e., on data we did not see but could have seen.

Discussion: Objective vs. Subjective Probability

Considering that both types of analysis are used heavily in practical applications by the most competent analysts, it would be somewhat optimistic if one thought that one of these approaches could be shown right and the other wrong. Philosophically, Bayesianism has a strong normative claim in the sense that every method that is not equivalent to Bayesianism can give results that are irrational in some circumstances, for example if one insists that inference should give a numerical measure of belief in hypotheses that can be translated to a fair betting odds (de Finetti, 1974; Savage, 1954). Among stated problems with Bayesian analysis the most important is probably a non-robustness sometimes observed with respect to choice of prior. This has been countered by introduction of families of priors in robust Bayesian analysis (Berger, 1994). Objective probability should not be identified with objective science;good scientific practice means that all assumptions made, like model choice, significance levels, choice of experiment, as well as choice of priors, are openly described and discussed.

Interpretation of observations is fundamental for many engineering applications and is studied under the heading of *uncertainty management*. Designers have often found statistical methods unsatisfactory for such applications, and invented a considerable battery of alternative methods claimed to be better in some or all applications. This has caused significant problems in applications like tracking in command and control, where different tracking systems with different types of uncertainty management cannot easily be integrated to make optimal use of the available plots and bearings. Among alternative uncertainty management methods are Dempster-Shafer Theory (Shafer, 1976) and many types of non-monotonic reasoning. These methods can be explained as robust Bayesian analysis and Bayesian analysis with infinitesimal probabilities, respectively (Wilson, 1996; Benferhat, Dubois, & Prade, 1997). We have shown that under weak assumptions, uncertainty management where belief is expressed with families of probability distributions that can contain infinitesimal probabilities is the most general method,satisfying compelling criteria on rationality (Arnborg & Sjödin, 2001). Most alternative approaches to uncertainty like Fuzzy sets and case-based reasoning can be explained as robust extended Bayesianism with unconventional model families.

DATA MODEL

We consider a data matrix where rows are cases and columns are variables. In a medical research application, the row could be associated with a person or an investigation (patient and date). In an Internet use application, the case could be an interaction session. The columns describe a large number of variables that could be recorded, such as background data (occupation, gender, age, etc.), and numbers extracted from investigations made, like sizes of brain regions, receptor densities and blood flow by region, etc. Categorical data can be equipped with a confidence (probability that the recorded datum is correct), and numerical data with an error bar. Every datum can be recorded as missing, and the reason for missing data can be related to patient condition or external factors (like equipment unavailability or time and cost constraints). Only the latter type of missing data is (at least approximately) unrelated to the domain of investigation. On the level of exploratory analysis, we confine ourselves to discrete distributions, with Dirichlet priors. If the data do not satisfy the conditions following this approach, (e.g., non-discreteness for real valued variable), they may do so after suitable transformation, discretization, and/or segmentation.

In many applications the definition of the data matrices is not obvious. For example, in text-mining applications, the character sequences of information items are not directly of interest, but a complex coding of their meaning must be done, taking into account the (natural) language used and the purpose of the application.

Multivariate Data Models

Given a data matrix, the first question that arises concerns the relationships between its variables (columns). Could some pairs of variables be considered independent, or do the data indicate that there is a connection between them — either directly causal, mediated through another variable, or introduced through sampling bias? These questions are analyzed using graphical models, directed or decomposable (Madigan & Raftery, 1994). As an example, in Figure 1, *M1* indicates a model where *A* and *B* are dependent, whereas they are independent in model *M2*. In Figure 2, we describe a directed graphical model *M4"* indicating that variables *A* and *B* are independently determined, but the value of *C* will be dependent on the values for *A* and *B*. The similar decomposable model *M4* indicates that the dependence of *A* and *B* is completely explained by the mediation of variable *C*.

Bayesian analysis of graphical models involves selecting all or some graphs on the variables, dependent on prior information, and comparing their posterior probabilities with respect to the data matrix. A set of highest posterior probability models usually gives many clues to the data dependencies, although one must — as always in statistics — constantly remember that dependencies are not necessarily causalities.

A second question that arises concerns the relationships between rows (cases) in the data matrix. Are the cases built up from distinguishable classes, so that each class has its data generated from a simpler graphical model than that of the whole data set? In the simplest case,

Figure 1: Graphical models, dependence or independence?

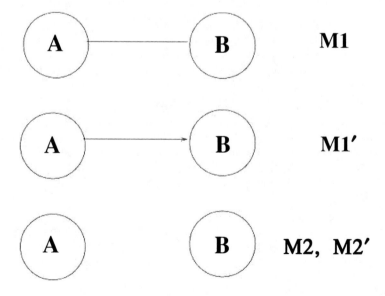

Figure 2: Graphical models, conditional independence?

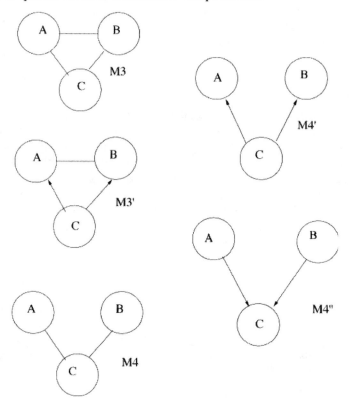

these classes can be directly read off in the graphical model. In a data matrix where intervariable dependencies are well explained by the model *M4*, if *C* is a categorical variable taking only few values, splitting the rows by the value of *C* could give a set of data matrices in each of which *A* and *B* are independent. However, the interesting cases are those in which the classes cannot be directly seen in a graphical model. If the data matrix of the example contained only variables *A* and *B*, because *C* was unavailable or unknown to interfere with *A* and *B*, the highest posterior probability graphical model is one with a link from *A* to *B*. The classes would still be there, but since C would be latent or hidden, the classes would have to be derived from only the A and B variables. A different case of classification is one in which the values of one numerical variable are drawn from several normal distributions with different means and variances. The full column would fit very badly to any single normal distribution, but after classification, each class could have a set of values fitting well to a class-specific normal distribution. The problem of identifying classes is known as *unsupervised classification*. A comprehensive system for classification based on Bayesian methodology is described in Cheeseman and Stutz (1995). A third question —often the one of highest practical concern — is whether some designated variable can be reliably predicted in the sense that it is well related to combinations of values of other variables, not only in the data matrix, but also with high confidence in new cases that are presented. Consider a data matrix well described by model *M4* in Figure 2. It is conceivable that the value of *C* is a good predictor of variable *B*, and better than *A*. It also seems likely that knowing both *A* and *C* is of little help compared to knowing only *C*, because the influence of *A* on *B* is completely mediated by *C*. On the other hand, if we want to predict *C*, it is very conceivable that knowing both *A* and *B* is better than knowing only one of them.

Bayesian Analysis and Over-Fitting

A natural procedure for estimating dependencies among categorical variables is by means of conditional probabilities estimated as frequencies in the data matrix. Such procedures usually lead to selection of more detailed models and give poor generalizing performance, in the sense that new sets of data are likely to have completely different dependencies. Various penalty terms have been tried to avoid over-fitting. However, the Bayesian method has a built-in mechanism that favors the simplest models compatible with the data, and also selects more detailed models as the amount of data increases. This effect appears, e.g., in the coin tossing example, where few tosses cannot give a verdict that the coin is unfair. The procedure is to compare posterior model probabilities, where the posterior probability of a model is obtained by combining its prior distribution of parameters with the probability of the data as a function of the parameters, using Bayes' rule. Thus, if $p(\Theta)$ is the prior pdf of the parameter (set) Θ of model *M*, and the probability of obtaining the case (row of data matrix) d is $p(d|M, \Theta)$, then the probability in model *M* of the data matrix *D* containing the ordered cases d_i is:

$$p(D \mid M) = \int \prod_i p(d_i \mid M\theta) p(\theta) d\theta,$$

and the posterior probability of model *M* given the data *D* is, by Bayes' rule:

$$p(M \mid D) = p(D \mid M) p(M) / p(D)$$

Two models *M1* and *M2* can now be related with respect to the data by the Bayes factor $p(D| M1)/p(D|M2)$ used to go from the prior to the posterior odds. With the Bayesian method, there is no need to penalize more detailed models to avoid over-fitting — if *M2* is more detailed than *M1* in the sense of having more parameters to fit, then the parameter dimension is larger in *M2*, and $p(\Theta1)$ is larger than $p(\Theta2)$, which automatically penalizes *M2* against *M1* when the parameters are integrated out. This automatic penalization has been found appropriate in most application cases, and should be complemented by explicit prior model probabilities only when there is concrete prior information that justifies it or when the data is too abundant to select a model simple enough to comprehend. When the more detailed model is the true one, Bayes factor in favor of it will increase exponentially with sample size, but in the other case the Bayes factor in favor of the less detailed model will only increase polynomially.

LOCAL GRAPHICAL MODEL CHOICE

We will analyze a number of models involving two or three variables of categorical type, as a preparation to the task of determining likely decomposable or directed graphical models. First, consider the case of two variables, A and B, and our task is to determine whether or not these variables are dependent. We must define one model $M2$ that captures the concept of independence, and one model $M1$ that captures the concept of dependence, and ask which one produced our data. The Bayes factor is $p(D|M2)/p(D|M1)$ in favor of independence, and it will be multiplied with the prior odds (which, lacking prior information in this general setting, we assume is one) to get the posterior odds. There is some latitude in defining the data model for dependence and independence, but it leads us to quite similar computations, as we shall see.

Let d_A and d_B be the number of possible values for A and B, respectively. It is natural to regard categorical data as produced by a discrete probability distribution, and then it is convenient to assume Dirichlet distributions for the parameters (probabilities of the possible outcomes) of the distribution. We will find that this analysis is the key step in determining a full graphical model for the data matrix. For a discrete distribution over d values, the parameter set is a sequence of probabilities $\bar{x} = (x_1, . . x_d)$ constrained by $0 \leq x_i$ and $\sum x_i = 1$ (often the last parameter x_d is omitted — it is determined by the first $d-1$ ones). A prior distribution over $\bar{x}$ is the conjugate Dirichlet distribution with a sequence of non-negative parameters $\bar{\alpha} = (\alpha_1, . . \alpha_d)$. Then the Dirichlet distribution is $\mathrm{Di}(\bar{x}|\bar{\alpha}) = \Gamma(\sum \alpha_i)/\prod \Gamma(\alpha_i) \times \prod x_i^{(\alpha_i - 1)}$, where $\Gamma(n+1) = n!$ for natural number n. The normalizing constant gives a useful mnemonic for integrating $\prod x_i^{(\alpha_i - 1)}$ over the $d-1$-dimensional unit cube (with $x_d = 1 - \sum_1^{d-1} x_i$). It is very convenient to use Dirichlet priors, for the posterior is also a Dirichlet distribution. After having obtained data with frequency count $\bar{n}$ we just add it to the prior parameter vector to get the posterior parameter vector $\bar{\alpha} + \bar{n}$. It is also easy to handle priors that are mixtures of Dirichlets, because the mixing propagates through and we only need to mix the posteriors of the components to get the posterior of the mixture.

With no specific prior information for x, it is necessary from symmetry considerations to assume all Dirichlet parameters equal to some value α. A convenient prior is the uniform prior ($\alpha = 1$). This is, e.g., the prior used by Bayes and Laplace to derive the rule of succession (see Chapter 18 of Jaynes 2003). Other priors have been used, but experiments have shown little difference between these choices. In many cases, an expert's delivered prior information can be expressed as an equivalent sample that is just added to the data matrix, and then this modified matrix can be analyzed with the uniform prior. Likewise, a number of experts can be mixed to form a mixture prior. If the data has occurrence vector n_i for the d possible data values in a case, and $n = n_+ = \sum_i n_i$, then the probability for these data given the discrete distribution parameters x, is

$$p(\bar{n} \, |\bar{x}) = \binom{n}{n_1, . \, n_d} \prod_i x_i^{n_i} .$$

Integrating out the x_i with the uniform prior gives the probability of the data given model M (M is characterized by a probability distribution and a Dirichlet prior on its parameters):

$$p(\bar{n}|M) = \int p(\bar{n}|\bar{x})d\bar{x}$$

$$= \int \binom{n}{n_1, \ldots n_d} \prod_i x_i^{n_i} \prod_i x_i^{\alpha_i - 1} \frac{\Gamma(\alpha_+)}{\prod_i \Gamma(\alpha_i)} d\bar{x}$$

$$= \frac{\Gamma(n+1)\Gamma(d)}{\Gamma(n+d)}.$$

(3)

Thus, the probability for each sample size is independent of the actual data with the uniform Dirichlet prior. Consider now the data matrix over A and B. Let $n_{i.}$ be the number of rows with value i for A and value j for B. Let n_{+j} and n_{i+} be the marginal counts where we have summed over the 'dotted' index, and $n = n_{++}$. Let model $M1$ (figure 1) be the model where the A and B value for a row is combined to a categorical variable ranging over $d_A d_B$ different values. The probability of the data given $M1$ is obtained by replacing the products and replacing d by $d_A d_B$ in equation (3):

$$p(\bar{n}|M_1) = \frac{\Gamma(n+1)\Gamma(d_A d_B)}{\Gamma(n+d_A d_B)}$$

(4)

We could also consider a different model $M1'$, where the A column is generated first and then the B column is generated for each value of A in turn. With uniform priors we get:

$$p(\bar{n}|M_1') = \frac{\Gamma(n+1)\Gamma(d_A)\Gamma(d_B)^{dA}}{\Gamma(n+d_A)} \prod_i \frac{\Gamma(n_{i+}+1)}{\Gamma(n_{i+}+d_B)}$$

(5)

Observe that we are not allowed to decide between the undirected $M1$ and the directed model $M1'$ based on Equations (4) and (5). This is because these models define the same set of pdfs involving A and B. In the next model $M2$, we assume that the A and B columns are independent, each having its own discrete distribution. There are two different ways to specify prior information in this case. We can either consider the two columns separately, each being assumed to be generated by a discrete distribution with its own prior. Or we could follow the style of $M1'$ above, with the difference that each A value has the same distribution of B values. Now the first approach: assuming parameters $\bar{x}^A$ and $\bar{x}^B$ for the two distributions, a row with values i for A and j for B will have probability $x_i^A x_j^B$. For discrete distribution parameters $\bar{x}^A \bar{x}^B$, the probability of the data matrix $\bar{n}$ will be:

$$p(\bar{n}\,|\bar{x}^A,\bar{x}^B) = \binom{n}{n_1,..n_{dAdB}}\prod_{i,j=1}^{dA,dB}(x_i^A x_j^B)^{n_{ij}} = \binom{n}{n_1,..n_{dAdB}}\prod_{i=1}^{dA}(x_i^A)^{n_{i+}}\prod_{j=1}^{dB}(x_j^B)^{n_{+j}}.$$

Integration over the uniform priors for A and B gives the data probability given model $M2$:

$$p(\bar{n}\,|M_2) = \int p(\bar{n}\,|\bar{x}^A\bar{x}^B)p(\bar{x}^A)p(\bar{x}^B)d\bar{x}^A d\bar{x}^B =$$

$$\int \binom{n}{n_{11},..n_{dAdB}}\prod_{i=1}^{dA}(x_i^A)^{n_{i+}}\prod_{j=1}^{dB}(x_j^B)^{n_{+j}} \times \Gamma(d_A)\Gamma(d_B)d\bar{x}^A d\bar{x}^B =$$

$$\frac{\Gamma(n+1)\Gamma(d_A)\Gamma(d_B)}{\Gamma(n+d_A)\Gamma(n+d_B)}\frac{\prod_i \Gamma(n_{i+}+1)\prod_j \Gamma(n_{+j}+1)}{\prod_{ij}\Gamma(n_{ij}+1)}.$$

From this and Equation (4) we obtain the Bayes factor for the undirected data model:

$$\frac{p(\bar{n}\,|M_2)}{p(\bar{n}\,|M_1)} = \frac{\Gamma(n+d_A d_B)\Gamma(d_A)\Gamma(d_B)}{\Gamma(n+d_A)\Gamma(n+d_B)\Gamma(d_A d_B)}\frac{\prod_j \Gamma(n_{+j}+1)\prod_i \Gamma(n_{i+}+1)}{\prod_{ij}\Gamma(n_{ij}+1)}. \tag{6}$$

The second approach to model independence between A and B gives the following:

$$p(\bar{n}\,|M_2') = \frac{\Gamma(n+1)\Gamma(d_A)}{\Gamma(n+d_A)}\int\left(\prod_i\binom{n_{i+}}{n_{i1},..n_{idB}}\right)\prod_j x_j^{n_{ij}}\Gamma(d_B)d\bar{x}^B =$$

$$\frac{\Gamma(n+1)\Gamma(d_A)\Gamma(d_B)}{\Gamma(n+d_A)\Gamma(n+d_B)}\frac{\prod_i \Gamma(n_{i+}+1)\prod_j \Gamma(n_{+j}+1)}{\prod_{ij}\Gamma(n_{ij}+1)}. \tag{7}$$

We can now find the Bayes factor relating models $M1'$ (Equation 5) and $M2'$ (Equation 7), with no prior preference of either:

$$\frac{p(M_2'|D)}{p(M_1'|D)} = \frac{p(D\,|M_2')}{p(D\,|M_1')} = \frac{\prod_j \Gamma(n_{+j}+1)\prod_i \Gamma(n_{i+}+d_B)}{\Gamma(d_B)^{dA-1}\Gamma(n+d_B)\prod_{ij}\Gamma(n_{ij}+1)}. \tag{8}$$

Consider now a data matrix with three variables, A, B and C (Figure 2). The analysis of the model $M3$ where full dependencies are accepted is very similar to $M1$ above (Equation 4). For the model $M4$ without the link between A and B, we should partition the data matrix by the value of C and multiply the probabilities of the blocks with the probability of the partitioning defined by C. Since we are ultimately after the Bayes factor relating $M4$ and $M3$

(respectively *M4'* and *M3'*), we can simply multiply the Bayes factors relating *M2* and *M1* (Equation 6) (respectively *M2'* and *M1'*) for each block of the partition to get the Bayes factors sought:

$$\frac{p(M_4 \mid D)}{p(M_3 \mid D)} = \frac{p(\bar{n} \mid M_4)}{p(\bar{n} \mid M_3)} =$$

$$\frac{\Gamma(d_A)^{dC}\Gamma(d_B)^{dC}}{\Gamma(d_A d_B)^{dC}} \prod_c \frac{\Gamma(n_{++c} + d_A d_B) \prod_j \Gamma(n_{+jc} + 1)\Gamma(n_{i+c} + 1)}{\Gamma(n_{++c} + d_A)\Gamma(n_{++c} + d_B)\prod_{ij}\Gamma(n_{ijc} + 1)} . \tag{9}$$

The directed case is similar (Heckerman, 1997). The value of the gamma function is rather large even for moderate values of its argument. For this reason, the formulas in this section are always evaluated in logarithm form, where products like in Formula 9 translate to sums of logarithms.

Causality and Direction in Graphical Models

Normally, the identification of cause and effect must depend on one's understanding of the mechanisms that generated the data. There are several claims or semi-claims that purely computational statistical methods can identify causal relations among a set of variables. What is worth remembering is that these methods create suggestions, and that even the concept of cause is not unambiguously defined but a result of the way the external world is viewed. The claim that causes can be found is based on the observation that directionality can in some instances be identified in graphical models. Consider the models *M4"* and *M4'* of Figure 2. In *M4'*, variables *A* and *B* could be expected to be marginally dependent, whereas in *M4"* they would be independent. On the other hand, conditional on the value of *C*, the opposite would hold: dependence between *A* and *B* in *M4"* and independence in *M4'*! This means that it is possible to identify the direction of arrows in some cases in directed graphical models. It is difficult to believe that the causal influence should not follow the direction of arrows in those cases. Certainly, this is a potentially useful idea, but it should not be applied in isolation from the application expertise, as the following example illustrates. It is known as *Simpson's Paradox*, although it is not paradoxical at all.

Consider the application of drug testing. We have a new wonder drug that we hope cures an important disease. We find a population of 800 subjects who have the disease; they are asked to participate in the trial and given a choice between the new drug and the alternative treatment currently assumed to be best. Fortunately, half the subjects, 400, choose the new drug. Of these, 200 recover. Of those 400 who chose the traditional treatment, only 160 recovered. Since the test population seems large enough, we can conclude that the new drug causes recovery in 50% of patients, whereas the traditional treatment only cures 40%. But the drug may not be advantageous for men. Fortunately, it is easy to find the gender of each subject and to make separate judgments for men and women. So when men and women are separated, we find the following table:

Table 1: Outcomes for men, women, and men+women in a clinical trial

	recovery	no recovery	Total	rec. rate
Men treated	180	120	300	60%
not treated	70	30	100	70%
Women treated	20	80	100	20%
not treated	90	210	300	30%
Tot treated	200	200	400	50%
not treated	240	160	400	40%

Obviously, the recovery rate is lower for the new treatment, both for women and men. Examining the table reveals the reason, which is not paradoxical at all: the disease is more severe for women, and the explanation for the apparent benefits of the new treatment is simply that it was tried by more men. The gender influences both the severity of the disease and the willingness to test the new treatment; in other words, gender is a confounder. This situation can always occur in studies of complex systems like living humans and most biological, engineering, or economic systems that are not entirely understood, and the confounder can be much more subtle than gender. When we want to find the direction of causal links, the same effect can occur. In complex systems of nature, and even in commercial databases, it is unlikely that we have at all measured the variable that will ultimately become the explanation of a causal effect. Such an unknown and unmeasured causal variable can easily turn the direction of causal influence indicated by the comparison between models $M4''$ and $M4'$, even if the data is abundant. Nevertheless, the new theories of causality have attracted a lot of interest, and if applied

Figure 3: Symptoms and causes relevant to heart problem.

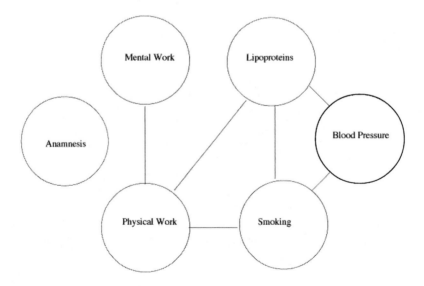

with caution they should be quite useful (Glymour & Cooper, 1999; Pearl, 2000). Their philosophical content is that a mechanism, causality, that could earlier not or only with difficulty be formalized, has become available for analysis in observational data, whereas it could earlier only be accessed in controlled experiments.

GLOBAL GRAPHICAL MODEL CHOICE

If we have many variables, their interdependencies can be modeled as a graph with vertices corresponding to the variables. The example in Fgure 3 is from Madigan and Raftery(1994) and shows the dependencies in a data matrix related to heart disease. Of course, a graph of this kind can give a data probability to the data matrix in a way analogous to the calculations in the previous section, although the formulas become rather involved and the number of possible graphs increases dramatically with the number of variables. It is completely infeasible to list and evaluate all graphs if there is more than a handful of variables. An interesting possibility to simplify the calculations would use some kind of separation, so that an edge in the model could be given a score independent of the inclusion or exclusion of most other potential edges. Indeed, the derivations of last section show how this works. Let C in that example be a compound variable, obtained by merging columns $c1, \dots cd$. If two models G and G' differ only by the presence and absence of the edge (A, B), and if there is no path between A and B except through vertex set C, then the expressions for $p(\bar{n}|M_4)$ and $p(\bar{n}|M_3)$ above will become factors of the expressions for $p(\bar{n}|G)$ and $p(\bar{n}|G')$, respectively, and the other factors will be the same in the two expressions. Thus, the Bayes factor relating the probabilities of G and G' is the same as that relating $M4$ and $M3$. This result is independent of the choice of distributions and priors of the model, since the structure of the derivation follows the structure of the graph of the model — it is equally valid for Gaussian or other data models, as long as the parameters of the participating distributions are assumed independent in the prior assumptions.

We can now think of various "greedy"methods for building high probability interaction graphs relating the variables (columns in the data matrix). It is convenient and customary to restrict attention to either decomposable (chordal) graphs or directed acyclic graphs. *Chordal graphs* are fundamental in many applications of describing relationships between variables (typically variables in systems of equations or inequalities). They can be characterized in many different but equivalent ways(see Rose, 1970). One simple way is to consider a decomposable graph as consisting of the union of a number of maximally connected complete graphs (*cliques*, or maximally connected subgraphs), in such a way that (i) there is at least one vertex that appears in only one clique (a *simplicial vertex*), and (ii) if an edge to a simplicial vertex is removed, another decomposable graph remains, and (iii) the graph without any edges is decomposable. A characteristic feature of a simplicial vertex is that its neighbors are completely connected by edges. If the graph G' obtained by adding an edge between s and n to G is also decomposable, we will call such an edge a *permissible edge* of G. This concept implies a generation structure (a directed acyclic graph whose vertices are decomposable graphs on the set of vertices) containing all decomposable graphs on the variable set. An interesting feature of this generation process is that it is easy to compute the Bayes factor comparing the posterior probabilities of the graphs G and G' as graphical models of the data: let s correspond to A, n to B, and the compound variable obtained by fusing the neighbors of s to C in the analysis of Section 5. Without explicit prior model probabilities we have:

$$\frac{p(G \mid D)}{p(G' \mid D)} = \frac{p(\bar{n} \mid M_3)}{p(\bar{n} \mid M_4)}$$

A search for high probability graphs can now be organized as follows:
1.   Start from the graph $G0$ without edges.
2.   Repeat: find a number of permissible edges that give the highest Bayes factor, and add the edge if the factor is greater than 1. Keep a set of highest probability graphs encountered.
3.   Then repeat: For the high probability graphs found in the previous step, find simplicial edges whose removal increases the Bayes factor the most.

For each graph kept in this process, its Bayes factor relative to $G0$ can be found by multiplying the Bayes factors in the generation sequence. A procedure similar to this one is reported by Madigan and Raftery (1994), and its results on small variable sets was found good, in that it found the best graphs reported in other approaches. For directed graphical models, a similar method of obtaining high probability graphs is known as the K2 algorithm (Berthold & Hand, 1999).

NON-CATEGORICAL VARIABLES

We will now consider data matrices made up from ordinal and real valued data, and then matrices consisting of ordinal, real, and categorical data. The standard choice for a real valued data model is the univariate or multivariate Gaussian or normal distribution. It has nice theoretical properties manifesting themselves in such forms as the central limit theorem, the least squares method, principal components, etc. It is possible to formulate the theory of the model choice section using inverse Wishart distributions as conjugate priors for multivariate normal distributions, but this is leads to fairly complex formulas and is seldom implemented (Bernardo & Smith, 1994). The normal distribution is also unsatisfactory for many data sets occurring in practice, because of its thin tail and because many real life distributions deviate terribly from it. Several approaches to solve this problem are available. One is to consider a variable as being obtained by mixing several normal distributions. Another is to disregard the distribution over the real line, and considering the variable as just being made up of an ordered set of values. A quite useful and robust method is to discretize the variables. This is equivalent to assuming that their probability distribution functions are piecewise constant. Discretized variables can be treated as categorical variables by the methods described above. The methods waste some information, but are quite simple and robust. Typically, the granularity of the discretization is chosen so that a reasonably large number of observations fall in each level. A compromise between discretization and use of continuous distributions is analyses of the *rankings* of the variables occurring in data tables. When considering the association between a categorical and a continuous variable one would thus investigate the ranks of the continuous variable, which are uniformly distributed over their range for every category if there is no association. Using a model where the ranks are non-uniformly distributed (e.g., with a linearly varying density), we can build the system of model comparisons of the model choice section. The difficulty is that the nuisance parameters cannot be analytically integrated out, so a numerical or MCMC quadrature procedure must be used.

A review of distributions used by statisticians and their parameter estimation methods is found in Chapter 11.

Missing Values in Data Matrix

Data collected from experiments are seldom perfect. The problem of missing and erroneous data is a vast field in the statistics literature. First of all, there is a possibility that "missingness" of data values are significant for the analysis, in which case missingness should be modeled as an ordinary data value. Then the problem has been internalized, and the analysis can proceed as usual, with the important difference being that the missing values are not available for analysis. A more skeptical approach was developed by Ramoni and Sebastiani(1998), who consider an option to regard the missing values as adversaries (the conclusions on dependence structure would then be true, no matter what the missing values are – but with lots of missing data, conclusions will become very weak). A third possibility is that missingness is known to have nothing to do with the objectives of the analysis – data are missing completely at random. For example, in a medical application, if data is missing because of the bad condition of the patient, missingness is significant if the investigation is concerned with patients. But if data is missing because of unavailability of equipment, it is probably not - unless maybe if the investigation is related to hospital quality.

Assuming that data is missing completely at random, it is relatively easy to get an adequate analysis. It is not necessary to waste entire cases just because they have a missing item. Most of the analyses made refer only to a small number of columns, and these columns can be compared for all cases that have no missing data in these particular columns. In this way it is, for example, possible to make a graphical model for a data set even if every case has some missing item, since all computations of the graphical model choice section refer to a small number of columns. In this situation, it is even possible to impute the values missing, because the graphical model obtained shows which variables most influence the missing one. So every missing value for a variable can be predicted from values of the case for neighbors of the variable in the graph of the model. When this is done, one must always remember that the value is a guess. It can thus never be used to create a formal significance measure - that would be equivalent to using the same data twice, which is not permitted in formal inference. A comprehensive review of the missing data problem can be found in Chapter 7.

The method of imputing missing values has a nice formalization in the Expectation Maximization (EM) method. This method is used to create values for missing data items by using a parameterized statistical model of the data. In the first step, the non-missing data is used to create an approximation of the parameters. Then the missing data values are defined (given imputed values) to give highest probability to the imputed data matrix. We can then refine the parameter estimates by maximization of probability over parameters with the now imputed data, then over the missing data, etc., until convergence results. This method is recommended for use in many situations, despite the fact that it is not strictly Bayesian and it violates the principle of not creating significance from guessed (imputed) values. The most spectacular use of the EM algorithm is for automatic (unsupervised) classification in the AUTOCLASS model (see next subsection).

Segmentation - Latent Variables

Segmentation and latent variable analysis aims at describing the data set as a collection of subsets, each having simpler descriptions than the full data matrix. The related technique of cluster analysis, although not described here, can also be given a Bayesian interpretation as an effort to describe a data set as a collection of clusters with small variation around the center of each cluster. Suppose data set D is partitioned into d_c classes $\{D^{(i)}\}$, and each of these has a high posterior probability $p(D^{(i)} | M_i)$ wrt some model set M_i. Then we think that the classification is a good model for the data. However, some problems remain to consider. First, what is it that we compare the classification against, and second, how do we accomplish the partitioning of the data cases into classes? The first question is the simplest to answer: we compare a classification model against some other model, based on classification or not. The second is trickier, since the introduction of this section is somewhat misleading. The prior information for a model based on classification must have some information about classes, but it does not have an explicit division of the data into classes available. Indeed, if we were allowed to make this division into classes on our own, seeking the highest posterior class model probabilities, we would probably over-fit by using the same data twice — once for class assignment and once for posterior model probability computation. The statistical model generating segmented data could be the following: a case is first assigned to a class by a discrete distribution obtained from a suitable uninformative Dirichlet distribution, and then its visible attributes are assigned by a class-dependent distribution. This model can be used to compute a probability of the data matrix, and then, via Bayes' rule, a Bayes factor relating the model with another one, e.g., one without classes or with a different number of classes. One can also have a variable number of classes and evaluate by finding the posterior distribution of the number of classes. The data probability is obtained by integrating, over the Dirichlet distribution, the sum over all assignments of cases to classes, of the assignment probability times the product of all resulting case probabilities according to the respective class model. Needless to say, this integration is feasible only for a handful of cases where the data is too meager to permit any kind of significant conclusion on the number of classes and their distributions. The most well-known procedures for automatic classification are built on expectation maximization. With this technique, a set of class parameters are refined by assigning cases to classes probabilistically, with the probability of each case membership determined by the likelihood vector for it in the current class parameters (Cheeseman & Stutz, 1995). After this likelihood computation, a number of cases are moved to new classes to which they belong with high likelihood. This procedure converges to a local maximum, where each case with highest likelihood belongs to its current class. But there are many local maxima, and the procedure must be repeated a number of times with different starting configurations.

Basic Classification

We assume that rows are generated as a finite mixture with a uniform Dirichlet prior for the component (class) probabilities, and each mixture component has its rows generated independently, according to a discrete distribution also with a uniform Dirichet prior for each column and class. Assume that the number of classes C is given, the number of rows is n and the number of columns is K, and that there are d_k different values that can occur in column k. For a given classification, the data probability can be computed; let $n_i^{(c,k)}$ be the number of occurrences of value i in column k of rows belonging to class c. Let $x_i^{(c,k)}$ be the probability of class c having the value i in column k. Let $n_{\bar{i}}^{(c)}$ be the number of occurences in class c of the row $\bar{i}$, and $n^{(c)}$ the number of rows of class c. By equation (3) the probability of the class assignment depends only on the number of classes and the table size, $\Gamma(n+1)\Gamma(C)/\Gamma(n+C)$. The probability of the data in class c is, if $\bar{i} = (i_1, \ldots i_K)$:

$$\int \prod_{k,\bar{i}} (x_{\bar{i}_k}^{(c,k)})^{n_{\bar{i}}^{(c)}} \, d\bar{x} = \prod_{k=1}^{K} \int \prod_{\bar{i}=1}^{d_k} (x_{\bar{i}}^{(c,k)})^{n_{\bar{i}}^{(c,k)}} \, d\bar{x}^{(c,k)} \ .$$

The right side integral can be evaluated using the normalization constant of the Dirichlet distribution, giving the total data probability of a classification:

$$\frac{\Gamma(n+1)\Gamma(C)}{\Gamma(n+C)} \prod_{c,k} \frac{\prod_i \Gamma(n_i^{(c,k)}+1)}{\Gamma(n^{(c)}+d_k)}$$

The posterior class assignment distribution is obtained normalizing over all class assignments. This distribution is intractable, but can be approximated by searching for a number of local maxima and estimating the weight of the neighborhood of each maximum. Here the EM algorithm is competitive to MCMC calculations in many cases, because of the difficulty of tuning the proposal distribution of MCMC computations to avoid getting stuck in local minima. The procedure is to randomly assign a few cases to classes, estimate parameters $x_i^{(c,k)}$, assign remaining cases to optimum classes, recomputing the distribution of each case over classes, reclassifying each case to optimum class, and repeating until convergence. After repeating this procedure for a while, one typically finds a single, most probable class assignment for each number of classes. The set of local optima so obtained can be used to guide a MCMC simulation giving more precise estimates of the probabilities of the classifications possible. But in practice, a set of high-probability classifications is normally a starting point for application specialists trying to give application meaning to the classes obtained.

CASE 1: PERSONALIZED MEDIA DISTRIBUTION

The application concerns personalized presentation of news items. A related area is recommendation systems (Kumar, Raghavan, Rajagopalan, & Tomkins 2001). The data used are historical records of individual subscribers to an electronic news service. The purpose of the investigation is to design a presentation strategy where an individual is first treated as the "average customer," then as his record increases, he can be included in one of a set of "customer types," and finally he can also get a profile of his own. Only two basic mechanisms are available for evaluating an individual's interest in an item: to which degree has he been interested in similar items before, and to which degree have similar individuals been interested in this item? This suggests two applications of the material of this chapter: segmentation or classification of customers into types, and evaluating a customer record against a number of types to find out whether or not he can confidently be said to differ. We will address these problems here, and we will leave out many practical issues in the implementation.

The data base consists of a set of news items with coarse classification; a set of customers, each with a type, a "profile" and a list of rejected and accepted items; and a set of customer types, each with a list of members. Initially, we have no types or profiles, but only classified news items and the different individuals' access records. The production of customer types is a fairly manual procedure; even if many automatic classification programs can make a reasonable initial guess, it is inevitable that the type list will be scrutinized and modified by media professionals — the types are normally also used for direct marketing.

The assignment of new individuals to types cannot be done manually because of the large volumes. Our task is thus to say, for a new individual with a given access list, to which type he belongs. The input to this problem is a set of tables, containing for each type as well as for the new individual, the number of rejected and accepted offers of items from each class. The modeling assumptionrequired is that for each news category, there is a probability of accepting the item for the new individual or for an average member of a type. Our question is now do these data support the conclusion that the individual has the same probability table as one of the types, or is he different from every type (and thus should get a profile of his own)? We can formulate the model choice problem by a transformation of the access tables to a dependency problem for data tables that we have already treated in depth. For a type t with a_i accepts and r_i rejects for a news category i, we imagine a table with three columns and $\sum (a_i + r_i)$ rows: a t in Column 1 to indicate an access of the type, the category number i in Column 2 of $a_i + r_i$ rows, a_i of which contain 1 (for accept) and r_i a 0 (for reject) in Column 3. We add a similar set of rows for the access list of the individual, marked with 0 in Column 1. If the probability of a 0 (or

1) in Column 3 depends on the category (Column 2) but not on Column 1, then the user cannot be distinguished from the type. But Columns 1 and 2 may be dependent if the user has seen a different mixture of news categories compared to the type. In graphical modeling terms, we could use the model choice algorithm. The probability of the customer belonging to type t is thus equal to the probability of model $M4$ against $M3$, where variable C in Figure 2 corresponds to the category variable (Column 2). In a prototype implementation we have the following customer types described by their accept probabilities:

Table 2: Customer types in a recommender system

Category	Typ1	Typ2	Typ3	Typ4
News-int	0.9	0.06	0.82	0.23
News-loc	0.88	0.81	0.34	0.11
Sports-int	0.16	0	0.28	0.23
Sports-loc	0.09	0.06	0.17	0.21
Cult-int	0.67	0.24	0.47	0.27
Cult-loc	0.26	0.7	0.12	0.26
Tourism-int	0.08	0.2	0.11	0.11
Tourism-loc	0.08	0.14	0.2	0.13
Entertainment	0.2	0.25	0.74	0.28

Three new customers have arrived, with the following access records of presented (accepted) offers:

Table 3: Individual's access records

Category	Ind1	Ind2	Ind3
News-int	3(3)	32(25)	17(8)
News-loc	1(1)	18(9)	25(14)
Sports-int	1(1)	7(2)	7(3)
Sports-loc	0(0)	5(5)	6(1)
Cult-int	2(2)	11(4)	14(6)
Cult-loc	1(1)	6(2)	10(3)
Tourism-int	0(0)	4(4)	8(8)
Tourism-loc	1(1)	5(1)	8(3)
Entertainment	1(1)	17(13)	15(6)

The results in our example, if the types are defined by a sample of 100 items of each category, are:

Table 4: Probabilities of assignments of types to customers

	Typ1	Typ2	Typ3	Typ4
Ind1	0.2500	0.2500	0.2500	0.2500
Ind2	0.0000	0.0000	1.0000	0.0000
Ind3	0.0000	0.0001	0.9854	.0145

It is now clear that the access record for Individual 1 is inadequate, and that the third individual is not quite compatible with any type. It should be noted that throughout this example we have worked with uniform priors. These priors have no canonic justification but should be regarded as conventional. If specific information justifying other priors is available, they can easy be used, but this is seldom the case. The choice of prior will affect the assignment of individual to type in rare cases, but only when the access records are very short and when the individual does not really fit to any type.

CASE 2: SCHIZOPHRENIA RESEARCH – CAUSALITY IN COMPLEX SYSTEMS

This application is directed at understanding a complex system – the human brain (Hall, Larsson, & Sedvall 1999). Similar methods have been applied to undestanding complex engineered systems like paper mills, and economic systems. Many investigations on normal subjects have brought immense new knowledge about the normal function of the human brain, but mental disorders still escape understanding of their causes and cures (despite a large number of theories, it is not known why mental disorders develop except in special cases, and it is not known which physiological and/or psychological processes cause them). In order to get handles on the complex relationships between psychology, psychiatry, and physiology of the human brain, a data base is being built with many different types of variables measured for a large population of schizophrenia patients and control subjects. For each volunteering subject, a large number of variables are obtained or measured, like age, gender, age of admission to psychiatric care; volumes of gray and white matter and cerebrospinal fluid in several regions of the brain (obtained from MR images), genetic characterization, and measurements of concentrations in the blood of large numbers of substances and metabolites. For the affected subjects, a detailed clinical characterization is recorded.

In this application, one can easily get lost. There is an enormous amount of relatively unorganized knowledge in the medical profession on the relationships and possible significances of these many variables. At the same time, the data collection process is costly, so the total number of subjects is very small compared, for example, with national registers that have millions of persons but relatively few variables for each of them. This means that statistical significance problems become important. A test set of 144 subjects, 83 controls, and 61 affected by schizophrenia was obtained. This set was investigated with most methods described in this chapter, giving an understanding of the strongest relationships (graphical model), possible classifications into different types of the disease, etc. In order to find possible causal chains, we tried to find variables and variable pairs with a significant difference in co-variation with the disease, i.e., variables and tuples of variables whose joint distribution is significantly different for affected person relative to control subjects. This exercise exhibited a very large number of such variables and tuples, many of which were known before, others not. All these associations point to possible mechanisms involved in the disease, which seems to permeate every part of the organism. Using the methods finding directions of arrows in directed graphical models, it turns out that in several cases independent variables like subject's genotype or age come out as caused by variables that are dependent, like blood tests or brain region sizes. This shows that application of causality methods give misleading results in a case like this, where it is known that many important variables cannot be measured, and are even not known. Thus it is not generally possible to see which is the effect and what is the cause, and many of the effects can be related to the strong medication given to all schizophrenic patients. In order to single out the more promising effects, an undirected graphical model approach was tried: Each variable was standardized around its mean, separately for affected and controls, and discretized. Then the pairs of variables were detected giving the highest probability to the left graph in Figure 4. Here D stands for the diagnosis (classification of the subject as affected or control), and A and B are the two variables compared. In the next graph, the relationship can be described as affecting the two variables independently, whereas in the next model where variables A and D are swapped, the relationship can be described as the disease affecting one of them but with a relationship to the other that is the same for affected and for controls. Many of the pairs selecting the first graph involved some parts of the vermis (a part of cerebellum). Particularly important was the subject age and posterior superior vermis volume pair. As shown in Figure 5, this part of the brain decreases in size with age for normal subjects. But for the affected persons the size is smaller and does not change with age. Neither does the size depend significantly on the duration of the disease or the medication received. Although these findings could be explained by confounding effects, the more likely explanation presently is that the size reduction occured before outbreak of the disease and that processes leading to the disease involve disturbing the development of this part of the brain. Several other variables were linked to the vermis in the same way; there was an association for control subjects but not for the affected ones, indicating that the normal co-variation is broken by the mechanisms of the disease. For variables that were

Figure 4: Graphical models detecting co-variation.

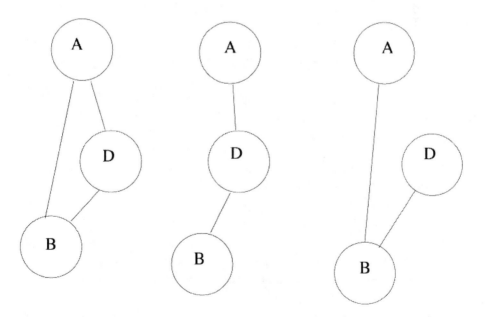

Figure 5: Association between age and posterior superior vermis volume depends on diagnosis. The principal directions of variation for controls(o) and affected subjects (+) are shown.

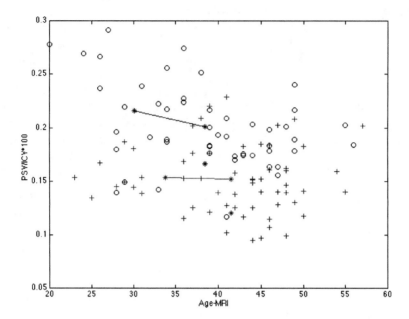

similarly co-varying with the vermis for controls and affected, there is a possibility that these regions are also affected by the disease similarly to the vermis.

CONCLUSIONS

This chapter emphasized the statistical approach to data mining. Meaning of data is therefore linked to its properties relative to statistical models. It also emphasizes a Bayesian approach, mainly because of its intellectual appeal. The techniques proposed for analytical models and EM classification can be applied to very large data sets, possibly after small tunings of the "obvious" algorithm. On the other hand, Markov Chain Monte Carlo methods are not used today on gigantic data sets. The methods described here are easy to apply using general-purpose software like C, Matlab, Octave, R, etc. An ongoing development is the adaptation of the simple family of models described here to large and complex applications. This leads to increased complexity. In the Bayesian paradigm, increasing complexity means using more detailed models and more application-specific assumptions in prior distributions. But this is also a complete description of what can be done, besides improving performance by careful implementation and integration, and carefully selected approximate computational methods.

ACKNOWLEDGMENTS

Discussions with students in my courses and Master of Science thesis writers are acknowledged. The media application was discussed with Erik Wallin, Tomas Olsson, and Henrik Dyberg. The schizophrenia case was produced in the HUBIN project (Hall et al., 1999).

REFERENCES

Arnborg, S. & Sjödin, G. (2001). On the foundations of Bayesianism. In A. Mohammad-Djarafi (ed.),*Bayesian inference and maximum entropy methods in science and engineering, 20th International Workshop Gif-sur-Yvette, 2000*. pp. 61-71. College Park, MD: AIP Press.

Benferhat, S., Dubois, D.,& H. Prade,(1997). Nonmonotonic reasoning, conditional objects and possibility theory. *Artificial Intelligence* 92, 259–276.

Berger, J. O. (1985). *Statistical decision theory and Bayesian Analysis*. New York: Springer-Verlag.

Berger, J. O. (1994).An overview of robust Bayesian analysis (with discussion). *Test,* 3, 5-124.

Bernardo, J. M. & Smith, A. F. (1994). *Bayesian theory.* New York: Wiley.

Berthold, M. &. Hand, D. (eds.).(1999). *Intelligent data analysis, An introduction.* New York: Springer-Verlag.

Carlin, B. P. & Louis, T. A. (1997). *Bayes and empirical Bayes methods for data analysis.* London: Chapman and Hall.

Cheeseman, P. & Stutz, J. (1995). Bayesian classification (AUTOCLASS): Theory and results. In U. M. Fayyad, G. Piatetsky-Shapiro, P. Smyth, and R. Uthurusamy (Eds.), *Advances in Knowledge Discovery and Data Mining*. Menlo Park: AAAI Press, ISBN: 0-262-56097-6.

Cox, D. R. & Wermuth, N. (1996). *Multivariate dependencies*. London:Chapman and Hall.

Dale, A. 1991. *A history of inverse probability: From Thomas Bayes to Karl Pearson.* Berlin: Springer.

de Finetti, B. (1974). *Theory of probability*. London: Wiley.

Doucet, A., de Freitas, N.,& Gordon, N. (2001). *Sequential Monte Carlo Methods in practice*. New York: Springer.

Gilks, W.R., Richardson, S., & Spiegelhalter, D.J. (1996). *Markov Chain Monte Carlo in practice*. London: Chapman and Hall.Glymour, C. & Cooper, G. (eds.). (1999). *Computation, causation and discovery*. Cambridge, MA: MIT Press.

Hall, H., Larsson, S. & Sedvall, G.(1999). HUBIN Web page, http://hubin.org.

Hand, D., Mannila, H.& Smyth, P. (2001). *Principles of data mining*. Cambridge, MA: MIT Press.

Heckerman, D. (1997). Bayesian networks for data mining. *Data Mining and Knowledge Discovery* 1, 79-119.

Jaynes, E. T. (2003). *Probability theory: The logic of science*. Cambridge University Press, ISBN: 0521592712.

Kumar, R., Raghavan, P., Rajagopalan, S., & Tomkins, A. (2001). Recommendation systems: A probabilistic analysis. *JCSS: Journal of Computer and System Sciences* 63(1): 42–61.

Lauritzen, S. L. (1996), *Graphical models*. Oxford, UK: Clarendon Press.

Madigan, D. & Raftery, A.E. (1994). Model selection and accounting for model uncertainty in graphical models using Occam's window. *J. American Statistical Ass.* 428, 1535–1546.

Pearl, J. (2000). *Causality: Models, reasoning, and inference*. Cambridge, UK: Cambridge University Press.

Ramoni, M. & Sebastiani,P. (1998). Parameter estimation in Bayesian networks from incomplete databases. *Intelligent Data Analysis,* 2(1).

Rose, D. J. (1970). Triangulated graphs and the elimination process. *J. Math. Anal. Appl.* 32, 597–609.

Royall, R. (2000). On the probability of observing misleading statistical evidence (with discussion). *J. American Statistical Ass.* 95, 760–780.

Savage, L. (1954). *Foundations of statistics*. New York: John Wiley & Sons.

Shafer, G. (1976. *A mathematical theory of evidence*. Princeton, NJ: Princeton University Press.

Wilson, N. (1996).Extended probability. In *Proceedings of the 12th European Conference on Artificial Intelligence, Budapest, Hungary*. Chichester: John Wiley and Sons, pp. 667–671.

Chapter II

Control of Inductive Bias in Supervised Learning Using Evolutionary Computation: A Wrapper-Based Approach

William H. Hsu
Kansas State University, USA

ABSTRACT

In this chapter, I discuss the problem of feature subset selection for supervised inductive learning approaches to knowledge discovery in databases (KDD), and examine this and related problems in the context of controlling inductive bias. I survey several combinatorial search and optimization approaches to this problem, focusing on data-driven, validation-based techniques. In particular, I present a wrapper approach that uses genetic algorithms for the search component, using a validation criterion based upon model accuracy and problem complexity, as the fitness measure. Next, I focus on design and configuration of high-level optimization systems (wrappers) for relevance determination and constructive induction, and on integrating these wrappers with elicited knowledge on attribute relevance and synthesis. I then discuss the relationship between this model selection criterion and those from the minimum description length (MDL) family of learning criteria. I then present results on several synthetic problems on task-decomposable machine learning and on two large-scale commercial data-mining and decision-support projects: crop condition monitoring, and loss prediction for insurance pricing. Finally, I report experiments using the Machine Learning in Java (MLJ) *and* Data to Knowledge (D2K) *Java-based visual programming systems for data mining and information visualization, and several commercial and research tools. Test set accuracy using a genetic wrapper is significantly higher than that of decision tree inducers alone and is comparable to that of the best extant search-space based wrappers.*

INTRODUCTION

This chapter introduces the problems for change of representation (Benjamin, 1990) in supervised inductive learning. I address the focal problem of inductive learning in data mining and present a multi-strategy framework for automatically improving the representation of learning problems. This framework incorporates methodological aspects of *feature subset selection and feature (attribute) partitioning, automated problem decomposition*, and *model selection*. The focus is on *wrapper-based* methods as studied in recent and continuing research.

As an example, I present a new metric-based model selection approach (composite learning) for decomposable learning tasks. The type of data for which this approach is best suited is heterogeneous, time series data – that arising from multiple sources of data (as in sensor fusion or multimodal human-computer interaction tasks, for example). The rationale for applying multi-strategy learning to such data is that, by systematic analysis and transformation of learning tasks, both the efficiency and accuracy of classifier learning may be improved for certain time series problems. Such problems are referred to in this chapter as *decomposable*; the methods addressed are: task decomposition and subproblem definition, quantitative model selection, and construction of hierarchical mixture models for data fusion. This chapter presents an integrated, multi-strategy system for decomposition of time series classifier learning tasks.

A typical application for such a system is learning to predict and classify hazardous and potentially catastrophic conditions. This prediction task is also known as *crisis monitoring*, a form of pattern recognition that is useful in decision support or *recommender* systems (Resnick & Varian, 1997) for many time-critical applications. Examples of crisis monitoring problems in the industrial, military, agricultural, and environmental sciences are numerous. They include: crisis control automation (Hsu *et al.*, 1998), online medical diagnosis (Hayes-Roth *et al.*, 1996), simulation-based training and critiquing for crisis management (Gaba *et al.*, 1992; Grois, Hsu, Voloshin, & Wilkins *et al.*, 1998), and intelligent data visualization for *real-time decision-making* (Horvitz & Barry, 1995).

Motivation: Control of Inductive Bias

The broad objectives of the approach I present here are to increase the robustness of inductive machine learning algorithms and develop learning systems that can be automatically tuned to meet the requirements of a knowledge discovery (KD) performance element. When developers of learning systems can map a KD application to a set of automatic higher-order parameter-turning problems, the reuse of design and code embodied by this generalization over traditional learning can reduce development costs. When addressing KD problems in computational science and engineering, the time required to develop an effective representation and to tune these hyperparameters using training and validation data sets can be a significant fraction of the development time of the KD system, exceeding the time required to apply traditional learning algorithms with fixed hyperparameters and bias parameters. This setting introduces new flexibility and complexity into the learning problem and may extend the expected useful lifetime of the system. For example, if the learning component is made more adaptable through automated performance tuning, then the overall system, not merely the learning algorithms it uses, may last longer than one tailored to a specific data set or problem domain. Thus it becomes subject to traditional maintenance and evolution. On the other hand, performance tuning may reduce the development time of highly specialized KD systems as well, by identifying and constructing relevant variables. In this case, reducing the cost of developing the more limited-use software can, in turn, significantly reduce that of solving the intended scientific or engineering problem. In many real-world KD applications, it is preferable to automatically tune some but not all of the available bias parameters to prevent overfitting of training data. This is because the computational time savings for the performance element (e.g., prediction, classification, or pattern detection function) and marginal gains in solution quality (e.g., utility or accuracy) do not make it worthwhile to fine-tune some bias parameters that are less significant for the learning problem. A significant component of development costs is related to reducing wasted development time and computation time by making the entire programming systems product (Brooks, 1995) responsive and adaptable to end-user needs. Combinatorial search and statistical validation over representations, visualization of the models and their relation to quantitative inductive bias (Benjamin, 1990; Mitchell, 1997), and high-level user interfaces for KD can be applied to achieve these goals.

A major motivation for the automation of problem transformation is *transparency*. The end user of a KD system is often a specialist in scientific, engineering, or business-related technical fields other than intelligent systems and machine learning. He or she knows the requirements of the application in terms of the performance element, an analytical function that can: predict the continuation of a historical time series; detect anomalous conditions in a time annotated episodic log; classify, diagnose, or explain set of database records; make a recommendation for a business or medical decision; or generate a plan, schedule, or design. These predictors, anomaly detectors, classifiers, diagnostic and recommender systems, policies, and other problem solvers have their own performance measures, perhaps including real-time requirements, which in turn dictate those of the learning system. This suggests that more robust KD may be achieved by letting the end user specify requirements pertaining to the performance element and automatically generating specifications for the desired representation and higher-order parameters to be tuned. In this way, the improvement of problem representation by automated transformation can be driven by users' specified time and resource constraints.

The research covered in this chapter focuses on demonstrating, through development of a learning enhancement framework and through empirical evaluation, that these broad objectives can be achieved for a wide variety of real-world KD applications. This research thrust has two main objectives: assessing the breadth of applicability of automatic transformation of learning problems by training the resultant models and applying them to large-scale KD problems over real-world data sets, and developing information visualization techniques to help users understand this process of improving problem representations.

Attribute-Driven Problem Decomposition: Subset Selection and Partition Search

Many techniques have been studied for decomposing learning tasks, to obtain more tractable subproblems, and to apply multiple models for reduced variance. This section examines *attribute-based* approaches for problem reformulation, especially *partitioning* of input attributes in order to define *intermediate concepts* (Fu & Buchanan, 1985) in problem decomposition. This mechanism produces multiple subproblems for which appropriate models must be selected; the trained models can then be combined using *classifier fusion* models adapted from bagging (Breiman, 1996), boosting (Freund & Schapire, 1996), stacking (Wolpert, 1992), and hierarchical mixture models (Jordan & Jacobs, 1994).

One of the approaches we shall examine in this chapter uses partitioning to *decompose* a learning task into parts that are individually useful (using *aggregation* as described in the background section of this chapter), rather than to *reduce* attributes to a single useful group. This permits new intermediate concepts to be formed by unsupervised learning methods such as conceptual clustering (Michalski & Stepp, 1983) or cluster formation using self-organizing algorithms (Kohonen, 1990; Hsu *et al.*, 2002). The newly defined problem or problems can then be mapped to one or more appropriate hypothesis languages (model specifications). In our new system, the subproblem definitions obtained by partitioning of attributes also specify a mixture estimation problem (i.e., data fusion step occurs after training of the models for all the subproblems).

Subproblem Definition

The purpose of attribute partitioning is to define intermediate concepts and subtasks of decomposable time series learning tasks, which can be mapped to the appropriate submodels. In both attribute subset selection and partitioning, attributes are grouped into subsets that are relevant to a particular task: the overall learning task or a subtask. Each subtask for a partitioned attribute set has its own inputs (the attribute subset) and its own *intermediate concept*. This intermediate concept can be discovered using unsupervised learning methods, such as self-organizing feature maps (Kohonen, 1990; Hsu *et al.*, 2002) and *k-means clustering* (Duda *et al.*, 2000). Other methods, such as *competitive clustering* or *vector quantization* using radial basis functions (Haykin, 1999), *neural trees* (Li *et al.*, 1993) and similar models (Ray & Hsu, 1998; Duda *et al.*, 2000), *principal components analysis* (Watanabe, 1985; Haykin, 1999), *Karhunen-Loève transforms* (Watanabe, 1985), or *factor analysis* (Watanabe, 1985), can also be used.

Attribute partitioning is used to control the formation of intermediate concepts in this system. Whereas attribute subset selection yields a *single*, reformulated learning problem (whose intermediate concept is neither necessarily nor intentionally different from the original concept), attribute partitioning yields *multiple learning subproblems* (whose intermediate concepts may or may not differ, but are simpler by design when they do). The goal of this approach is to find a natural and principled way to specify *how* intermediate concepts should be simpler than the overall concept.

Metric-Based Model Selection and Composite Learning

Model selection is the problem of choosing a hypothesis class that has the appropriate complexity for the given training data (Stone, 1977; Schuurmans, 1997). Quantitative methods for model selection have previously been used to learn using highly flexible *nonparametric* models with many degrees of freedom, but with no particular assumptions on the structure of decision surfaces.

The ability to decompose a learning task into simpler subproblems prefigures a need to map these subproblems to the appropriate models. The general mapping problem, broadly termed *model selection*, can be addressed at very minute to very coarse levels. This chapter examines quantitative, metric-based approaches for model selection at a coarse level. This approach is a direct extension of the *problem definition and technique selection* process (Engels *et al.*, 1998). We will henceforth use the term *model selection* to refer to both traditional model selection and the metric-based methods for technique selection as presented here. We begin with background on the general framework of inductive bias control and then survey time series learning architectures, their *representation biases* (Witten & Frank, 2000), and methods for selecting them from a collection of model components.

BACKGROUND
Key Problem: Automated Control of Inductive Bias

We first focus on development of a new learning system for spatiotemporal KD. The KD performance element in this problem is not just analytical but includes decision support through model visualization and anomaly detection.

The problems we face are threefold and are surveyed in the above sections on current and related work. First, we must address *relevance determination* to determine what sensor data channels are useful for a particular KD objective and data set. This problem is related to the so-called *curse of dimensionality* wherein an overabundance of input variables makes it difficult to learn the prediction, classification, or pattern recognition element. Second, the task of identifying hyperparameters of the KD system is subject to deceptivity and instability because bias optimization in general introduces a new level of combinatorial complexity to the problem of inductive learning. Third, the very large spatiotemporal databases we are dealing with are highly heterogeneous, arising from many disparate sources such as global positioning systems (GPS), surveying, sensors such as radar, and historical databases; this heterogeneity presents the advantage of type information that can help constrain dimensionality but also aggra-

Figure 1: A composite learning framework.

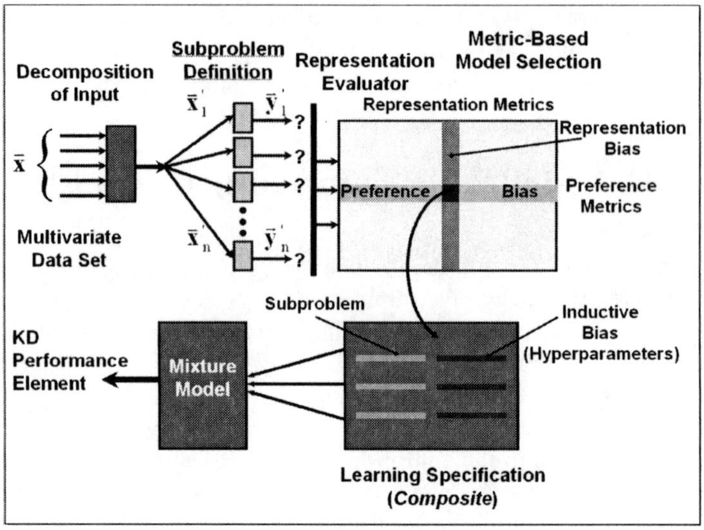

vates the problem of relevance determination because including irrelevant sensors can lead to severe inefficiencies in data acquisition, interpretation of visual results, and the learning component.

In Hsu, Ray, and Wilkins *et al.*(2000), we address these problems through a framework called *composite learning* that is depicted in Figure 1. We define a composite learning system to be a committee machine (Haykin, 1999) designed to improve the performance of a collection of supervised inductive learning algorithms with specific parameters for representation and preference bias (Mitchell, 1997), over multivariate – possibly heterogeneous – data. The open research problem I discuss is how composite learning systems can be applied to automatically improve representations of complex learning problems.

Composite learning provides a search-based and validation-based procedure for controlling the inductive bias, specifically the total problem specification, of systems for learning from decomposable, multi-attribute data sets. The central elements of this system are: *decomposition of input, metric-based model selection*, and a *mixture model* for integration of multiple submodels. In recent research, I applied composite learning to audio signal classification (Ray & Hsu, 1998) and crop condition prediction, the central component of a monitoring problem (Hsu, 1998; Hsu *et al.*, 2000). Given a specification for decomposed – i.e., selected or partitioned – subsets of input variables, new intermediate concepts $\bar{\mathbf{y}}_1$ can be formed by unsupervised learning. For this step we have used Gaussian *radial-basis functions* or RBFs (Ray & Hsu, 1998) and *self-organizing maps* (Kohonen, 1990). The newly defined problem or problems can then be mapped to one or more appropriate hypothesis languages (model specifications). We have developed a high-level algorithm for tuning explicit parameters that control representation and preference bias, to generate this specification of a composite. This algorithm is used by Hsu *et al.*, (2000) to select components for a hierarchical mixture network (specialist-moderator network) and train them for multi-strategy learning. A data fusion step occurs after individual training of each model. The system incorporates attribute partitioning into constructive induction to obtain multiple problem definitions (decomposition of learning tasks); applies metric-based model selection over subtasks to *search for efficient hypothesis preferences*; and integrates these techniques in a data fusion (mixture estimation) framework.

The metrics we have derived for controlling preference bias in hierarchical mixture models are positively correlated with learning performance by a particular learning method (for a learning problem defined on a particular partitioning of a time series). This makes them approximate indicators of the suitability of the corresponding mixture model and the assumption that the learning problem adheres to its characteristics (with respect to interaction among subproblems). Thus, preference bias metrics may be used for partial model selection.

Although this approach has yielded positive results from applying composite learning to KD, the breadth of domains for which this framework has been tested is still limited. A STETchallenge and opportunity is the application of composite learning to learning problems in precision agriculture, specifically the illustrative example in and the problem of *soil fertility mapping*, which generates a map of quantitative fertility estimates from remotely sensed, hydrological, meteorological, wind erosion, and pedological data. One purpose of generating such maps is to control variable-rate fertilizer application to increase yield with minimal environmental impact. Test bed for heterogeneous data mining abound in the literature and are becoming freely available.

In past and current research, we have achieved empirical improvement in constructive induction in several ways in which we propose to further generalize and systematically validate. First, we found that decomposition of learning tasks using techniques such as attribute partitioning or ensemble selection can help reduce variance when computational resources are limited. We conjecture that this may be useful in domains such as real-time intelligent systems, where deadlines are imposed on training and inference time.

Current techniques such as *automated relevance determination, feature selection*, and *clustering* tend to address the problem of constructive induction in isolated stages rather than as an integrative mechanism for transforming the data – input and output schemata – into a more tractable and efficient form. As outlined in the previous section, we address this by combining search-based combinatorial optimization, statistical validation, and hierarchical abstraction into the coherent framework of composite learning.

Furthermore, many complex KDD problems can be decomposed on the basis of spatial, temporal, logical, and functional organization in their performance element. Techniques such as *model selection* and *ensemble learning* have been used to systematically identify and break down these problems, and, given a specification of a modular learning system, *hierarchical mixture estimation* techniques have been used to build pattern recognition models by parts and integrate them. The challenge is how to isolate prediction or classification models. The author has identified several low-order Box-Jenkins (autoregressive integrated moving average, also known as ARMA or ARIMA) process models (Box *et al.*, 1994) that can be isolated from heterogeneous historical data, based on quantitative metrics (Hsu, 1998). Composite learning can be applied to derive a complete committee machine specification from data to learn intermediate predictors (e.g., temporal artificial neural networks such as simple recurrent networks and time-delay neural networks). We believe that this approach can discover other hierarchical organization such as embedded clusters (Hsu *et al.*, 2002), factorial structure (Ray & Hsu, 1998), and useful behavioral structure, which we shall outline in the next section on evolutionary computation for KD. The proposed research is therefore not specific to time series.

The line of research that we have described in this section shall lead to the development of techniques for making inductive learning more robust by controlling inductive bias to increase generalization accuracy. We propose to use my framework, composite learning, for specifying high-level characteristics of the problem representation to be tuned in a systematic way. The next section presents a specific combinatorial optimization technique for tuning these hyperparameters using validation and other criteria.

Evolutionary Computation Wrappers for Enhanced KD

Over the past three years, we have been engaged in the development of a novel system for combinatorial optimization in KD from complex domains, which uses evolutionary computation – genetic algorithms (GA) and genetic programming (GP) – to enhance the machine learning process. Mechanisms for KD enhancement that use the empirical performance of a learning function as feedback are referred to in the intelligent systems literature as *wrappers* (Kohavi & John, 1997). Our objective at this stage of the research is to relax assumptions we have previously made regarding two aspects of automatically improving the representation of learning problems. First, we seek to generalize the *structure* of the mapping between the original and improved representations, not restricting it merely to feature selection or construction. Second, we seek to design a framework for automatic discovery of hierarchical structure in learning problems, both from data and from reinforcements in problem solving environments. The key contribution of this component of the research is to make the automatic search for representations more systematic and reproducible by putting it into an engineering framework.

Problems: Attribute Subset Selection and Partitioning

This section introduces the *attribute partitioning* problem and a method for subproblem definition in multi-attribute inductive learning.

Attribute-Driven Problem Decomposition for Composite Learning

Many techniques have been studied for decomposing learning tasks to obtain more tractable subproblems and to apply multiple models for reduced variance. This section examines *attribute-based* approaches for problem reformulation, which start with restriction of the set of input attributes on which the supervised learning algorithms will focus. First, this chapter presents a new approach to problem decomposition that is based on finding a good *partitioning* of input attributes. Previous research on attribute subset selection (Kohavi & John, 1997), is highly relevant ,though directed toward a different goal for problem reformulation; this section outlines differences between subset selection and partitioning and how partitioning may be applied to task decomposition. Second, this chapter compares top-down, bottom-up, and hybrid approaches for attribute partitioning, and considers the role of partitioning in feature extraction from heterogeneous time series. Third, it discusses how grouping of input attributes leads naturally to the problem of forming *intermediate concepts* in problem decomposition. This mechanism defines different subproblems for which appropriate models must be selected; the trained models can then be combined using *classifier fusion* models adapted from bagging (Breiman, 1996), boosting (Freund & Schapire, 1996), stacking (Wolpert, 1992), and hierarchical mixture models (Jordan & Jacobs, 1994).

Overview of Attribute-Driven Decomposition

Figure 2 depicts two alternative systems for attribute-driven reformulation of learning tasks (Benjamin, 1990; Donoho, 1996). The left-hand side, shown with dotted lines, is based on the traditional method of attribute *subset selection* (Kohavi & John, 1997). The right-hand side, shown with solid lines, is based on attribute *partitioning*, which is adapted in this chapter to decomposition of time series learning tasks. Given a specification for reformulated (reduced or partitioned) input, new intermediate concepts can be formed by unsupervised learning (e.g., conceptual clustering); the newly defined problem or problems can then be mapped to one or more appropriate hypothesis languages (model specifications). The new models are selected for a reduced problem or for multiple subproblems obtained by partitioning of attributes; in the latter case, a data fusion step occurs after individual training of each model.

Figure 2: Systems for attribute-driven unsupervised learning and model selection.

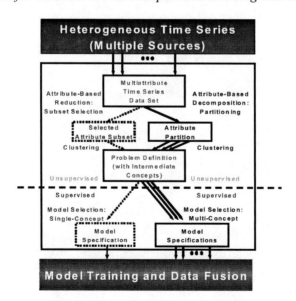

Subset Selection and Partitioning

Attribute subset selection, also called *feature subset selection*, is the task of focusing a learning algorithm's attention on some subset of the given input attributes, while ignoring the rest (Kohavi & John, 1997). In this research, subset selection is adapted to the systematic decomposition of learning problems over heterogeneous time series. Instead of focusing a single algorithm on a single subset, the set of all input attributes is partitioned, and a specialized algorithm is focused on *each* subset. While subset selection is designed for refinement of attribute sets for single-model learning, attribute partitioning is designed specifically for multiple-model learning. This new approach adopts the role of feature construction in constructive induction (Michalski, 1983; Donoho, 1996), as depicted in Figure 2. It uses subset partitioning to *decompose* a learning task into parts that are individually useful, rather than to *reduce* attributes to a single useful group. This permits multiple-model methods such as *bagging* (Breiman, 1996), *boosting* (Freund & Schapire, 1996), and *hierarchical mixture models* (Jordan & Jacobs, 1994) to be adapted to multi-strategy learning.

Partition Search

For clarity, I review the basic combinatorial problem of *attribute partitioning*. First, consider that the state space for attribute subset selection grows exponentially in the number of attributes n: its size is simply 2^n. The size of the state space for n attributes is B_n, the nth Bell number, defined as follows[1]:

$$B_n = \sum_{k=0}^{n} S(n,k)$$

$$S(n,k) = \begin{cases} 0 & if\ n < k\ or\ k = 0, n \neq 0 \\ 1 & if\ n = k \\ S(n-1,k-1) + kS(n-1,k) & otherwise \end{cases}$$

Thus, it is impractical to search the space exhaustively, even for moderate values of n. The function B_n is $\omega(2^n)$ and $o(n!)$, i.e., its asymptotic growth is strictly *faster* than that of 2^n and strictly *slower* than that of $n!$. It thus results in a highly intractable evaluation problem if all partitions are considered. Instead, a heuristic evaluation function is used so that informed search methods (Russell & Norvig, 1995) may be applied. This evaluation function is identical to the one used to prescribe the *multi-strategy hierarchical mixture of experts* (*MS-HME*) model; therefore, its definition is deferred until the next section.

The state space for of a set of five attributes consists of 52 possible partitions. We shall examine a simple synthetic problem learning problem, *modular parity*, that can be used to test search algorithms for the optimum partition. As the parity problem, a generalization of *XOR* to many variables, demonstrates the expressiveness of a representation for models or hypotheses in inductive learning (and was thus used to illustrate the limitations of the perceptron), the modular parity problem tests the expressiveness and flexibility of a learning system when dealing with heterogeneous data.

Subproblem Definition

This section summarizes the role of attribute partitioning in defining intermediate concepts and subtasks of decomposable time series learning tasks, which can be mapped to the appropriate submodels.

Intermediate Concepts and Attribute-Driven Decomposition

In both attribute subset selection and partitioning, attributes are grouped into subsets that are relevant to a particular task: the overall learning task or a subtask. Each subtask for a partitioned attribute set has its own inputs (the attribute subset) and its own *intermediate concept*. This intermediate concept can be discovered using unsupervised learning algorithms, such as *k-means clustering*. Other methods, such as competitive clustering or vector quantization (using radial basis functions (Lowe, 1995; Hassoun, 1995; Haykin, 1999), neural trees (Li *et al.*, 1993), and similar models (Duda *et al.*, 2000; Ray & Hsu, 1998), principal components analysis (Watanabe, 1985; Hassoun, 1995; Haykin, 1999), Karhunen-Loève transforms (Watanabe, 1985, Hassoun, 1995), or factor analysis (Watanabe, 1985; Duda *et al.*, 2000), can also be used.

Attribute partitioning is used to control the formation of intermediate concepts in this system. Attribute subset selection yields a single, reformulated learning problem (whose intermediate concept is neither necessarily different from the original concept, nor intended to differ). By contrast, attribute partitioning yields multiple learning *subproblems* (whose intermediate concepts may or may not differ, but are simpler by design when they do differ).

The goal of this approach is to find a natural and principled way to specify *how* intermediate concepts should be simpler than the overall concept. In the next section, two mixture models are presented: the *Hierarchical Mixture of Experts* (HME) of Jordan and Jacobs (1994), and the *Specialist-Moderator* (SM) network of Ray and Hsu (Ray & Hsu, 1998; Hsu *et al.*, 2000). The following sections explain and illustrate why this design choice is a critically important consideration in how a hierarchical learning model is built, and how it affects the performance of multi-strategy approaches to learning from heterogeneous time series. The mechanisms by which HME and SM networks perform data fusion, and how this process is affected by attribute partitioning, are examined in both theoretical and experimental terms in this chapter. Finally, a survey of experiments by the author investigates the empirical effects of attribute partitioning on learning performance, including its indirect effects through intermediate concept formation.

Role of Attribute Partitioning in Model Selection

Model selection, the process of choosing a hypothesis class that has the appropriate complexity for the given training data (Geman *et al.*, 1992; Schuurmans, 1997), is a consequent of attribute-driven problem decomposition. It is also one of the original directives for performing decomposition (i.e., to apply the appropriate learning algorithm to each homogeneous subtask). Attribute partitioning is a determinant of subtasks, because it specifies new (restricted) views of the input and new target outputs for each model. Thus, it also determines, indirectly, what models are called for. This system organization may be described as a *wrapper* system *cf.* (Kohavi & John, 1997) whose primary adjustable parameter is the attribute partition. A second parameter is a high-level model descriptor (the architecture and type of hierarchical *classifier fusion* model).

Machine Learning Methodologies: Models and Algorithms

Recurrent Neural Networks and Statistical Time Series Models

SRNs, TDNNs, and gamma networks (Mehrotra *et al.*, 1997) are all temporal varieties of artificial neural networks (ANNs). A *temporal naïve Bayesian network* is a restricted type of Bayesian network called a *global knowledge map* as defined by Heckerman (1991), which has two stipulations. The first is that some random variables may be temporal (e.g., they may denote the durations or rates of change of original variables). The second is that the topological structure of the Bayesian network is learned by naïve Bayes. A hidden Markov model (HMM) is a stochastic state transition diagram whose transitions are also annotated with probability distributions over output symbols (Lee, 1989).

The primary criterion used to characterize a stochastic process in my multi-strategy time series learning system is its *memory form*. To determine the memory form for temporal ANNs, two properties of statistical time series models are exploited. The first property is that the temporal pattern represented by a memory form can be described as a *convolutional code*. That is, past values of a time series are stored by a particular type of recurrent ANN, which transforms the original data into its internal representation. This transformation can be formally defined in terms of a *kernel function* that is convolved over the time series. This convolutional or functional definition is important because it yields a general mathematical characterization for individually weighted "windows" of past values (time delay or *resolution*) and nonlinear memories that "fade" smoothly (attenuated decay, or *depth*) (Mozer, 1994; Principé & Lefebvre, 2001; Principé & deVries, 1992). It is also important to metric-based model selection, because it concretely describes the transformed time series that we should evaluate in order to compare memory forms and choose the most effective one. The second property is that a transformed time series can be evaluated by measuring the change in *conditional entropy* (Cover & Thomas, 1991) for the stochastic process of which the training data is a sample. The entropy of the next value conditioned on past values of the *original* data should, in general, be higher than that of the next value conditioned on past values of the *transformed* data. This indicates that the memory form yields an improvement in predictive capability, which is ideally proportional to the expected performance of the model being evaluated.

Given an input sequence $\mathbf{x}(t)$ with components $\{\hat{\mathbf{x}}_i(t), 1 \leq i \leq n\}$, its convolution $\hat{\mathbf{x}}_i(t)$ with a kernel function $c_i(t)$ (specific to the ith component of the model) is defined as follows:

$$\hat{\mathbf{x}}_i(t) = \sum_{k=0}^{t} c_i(t-k)\mathbf{x}(k)$$

(Each $\mathbf{x}$ or $\mathbf{x}_i$ value contains all the attributes in *one subset* of a partition.)

Kernel functions for simple recurrent networks, Gamma memories, and are presented in the context of convolutional codes and time series learning by Mozer (1994), Mehrotra *et al.* (1997), and Hsu (1998). The interested reader may also refer to data sets such as the Santa Fe corpus (Gershenfeld & Weigend, 1994) and ANN simulation software for additional information; readers new to this family of learning models are encouraged to experiment with such test corpora and codes in order to gain basic experience.

Evolutionary Computation: Genetic Algorithms and Genetic Programming

The notion of using evolutionary computation to improve the representation of learning problems in KD draws from foundational work on controlling genetic algorithms and finds applications in evolutionary control and data mining using genetic algorithms as inducers.

In the field of evolutionary computation, many aspects of the genetic coding and evolutionary system can be tuned automatically. Much of the recent research has focused on this meta-optimization problem and has led to both theoretical and empirical results on population sizing (Horn, 1997), probability of selection, crossover, and mutation (Goldberg, 1998), and parallel, distributed load balancing in genetic algorithms (Cantu-Paz, 1999). Genetic algorithms that tune some of their own hyperparameters are referred to in the literature as *parameterless* (Harik & Lobo, 1997). This idea has also been used to develop genetic wrappers for performance enhancement in KD, an innovation dating back to the first applications of genetic algorithms to inductive learning (Booker, Goldberg, & Holland, 1989; Dejong *et al.*, 1993; Goldberg, 1989).

We seek to optimize the representation and preference biases of a learning system for KD. Therefore, we are interested in four kinds of hyperparameter: input descriptors, output descriptors, specifications for what kind of committee machine or ensemble architecture to use, and control variables for the search algorithm (the choice of search algorithm itself, heuristic coefficients, and hyperparameters in various learning frameworks). The first three kinds of hyperparameter control are representation bias, the fourth, preference bias. (Witten & Frank, 2000) This distinction is important in our study of evolutionary computation because it generates requirements for coding and fitness evaluation in our specification of combinatorial optimization problems. For example, finding intermediate learning targets can be formulated as an unsupervised learning problem, and the gene expression of an evolved selector, partition, or construction rule or program for describing these target outputs shall differ from that for inputs.

Koza (1992) defines five specification components for a GP system: determining the terminal set, function set, fitness cases or evaluation function, termination conditions, and result. The process of determining these drives the design of a GP-based wrapper. In data mining with evolutionary algorithms, many direct approaches have been made toward constructive induction; selecting and extracting features is very natural with a genetic algorithm because the hyperparameters (e.g., feature subsets) can be encoded as bit strings and, provided the proper parallel and distributed computing system is used, the task of evaluating fitness based upon model criteria and statistical validation data is trivially parallelizable. Similarly, with the proper encoding of synthetic variables as symbolic (e.g., logical or arithmetic) expressions over the original ground variables, GP is well suited to performing feature construction by combinatorial optimization.

There is a extensive but diffuse literature on hierarchical learning(especially in areas of biologically inspired computing where it is studied in contexts of neural modularity and hierarchy; niching, speciation, and demes) and artificial societies. In contrast, the concept of divide-and-conquer algorithms is pervasively and thoroughly studied. This line of research aims toward raising the understanding of layered learning in soft computing to such a level, particularly for evolutionary computation in KD and reinforcement learning over large spatial and temporal databases.

METHODOLOGIES
Metric-Based Model Selection in Time Series Learning

For time series, we are interested in actually identifying a stochastic process from the training data (i.e., a process that generates the observations). The performance element, time series classification, will then apply a model of this process to a continuation of the input (i.e., "test" data) to generate predictions. The question addressed in this section is: "To what degree does the training data (or a restriction of that data to a subset of attributes) probabilistically match a prototype of some known stochastic process?" This is the purpose of metric-based model selection— to estimate the degree of match between a subset of the observed data and a known prototype. Prototypes, in this framework, are memory forms (Mozer, 1994), and manifest as embedded patterns generated by the stochastic process that the memory form describes. For example, an exponential trace memory form can express certain types of $MA(1)$ processes. The kernel function for this process is given in Hsu (1998). The more precisely a time series can be described in terms of exponential processes (wherein future values depend on exponential growth or decay of previous values), the more strongly it will match this memory form. The stronger this match, the better the expected performance of an $MA(1)$ learning model, such as an input recurrent (IR) network. Therefore, a metric that measures this degree of match on an arbitrary time series is a useful predictor of IR network performance.

Control of Representation Bias: A Time-Series Learning Example

Table 1 lists five learning representations, each exemplifying a type of *representation* or *restriction bias* for inductive learning from time series, and the metrics corresponding to their strengths. These are referred to as representation metrics because, as documented in the first section (see Figure 1), the choice of representation is local to each

Table 1: Five time series representations and their prescriptive metrics

(Time Series) Representation Bias	Representation Metric
Simple recurrent network (SRN)	Exponential trace (AR) score
Time delay neural network (TDNN)	Moving average (MA) score
Gamma network	Autoregressive moving average (ARMA) score
Temporal naïve Bayesian network	Relevance score
Hidden Markov model (HMM)	Test set perplexity

node (subnetwork) in the hierarchy, corresponding to a single set within an attribute partition.   The choice of hierarchical model is global over the partition, and the corresponding metrics are therefore called *representation metrics*. Note that this set may be an abstraction, or "merge," of the lowest-level partition used, and is likely to be a refinement, or "split," of the top-level (unpartitioned) set.   The metrics are called *prescriptive* because each one provides evidence in favor of a particular architecture.

The design rationale is that each metric is based on an attribute chosen to *correlate positively* (and, to the extent feasible, *uniquely*) with the *characteristic memory form* of a time series. A *memory form* as defined by Mozer (1994) is the representation of some specific temporal pattern, such as a limited-depth buffer, exponential trace, gamma memory (Principé & Lefebvre, 2001), or state transition model.

To model a time series as a stochastic process, one assumes that there is some mechanism that generates a random variable at each point in time. The random variables $X(t)$ can be univariate or multivariate (corresponding to single and multiple attributes or *channels* of input per exemplar) and can take discrete or continuous values, and time can be either discrete or continuous.   For clarity of exposition, the experiments focus on discrete classification problems with discrete time. The classification model is *generalized linear regression* (Neal, 1996), also known as a *1-of-C coding* (Sarle, 2002), or *local coding* (Kohavi & John, 1997).

Following the parameter estimation literature (Duda *et al.*, 2000), time series learning can be defined as finding the parameters $\Theta = \{\theta_1, ..., \theta_n\}$ that describe the stochastic mechanism, typically by maximizing the likelihood that a set of realized or *observable* values, $\{x(t_1), x(t_2), ..., x(t_k)\}$, were actually generated by that mechanism. This corresponds to the backward, or maximization, step in the *expectation-maximization (EM)* algorithm (Duda *et al.*, 2000). Forecasting with time series is accomplished by calculating the conditional density $P(X(t) \mid \{\Theta, \{X(t-1), ..., X(t-m)\}\})$, when the stochastic mechanism and the parameters have been identified by the observable values $\{x(t)\}$. The order m of the stochastic mechanism can, in some cases, be infinite; in this case, one can only approximate the conditional density.

Despite recent developments with nonlinear models, some of the most common stochastic models used in time series learning are parametric linear models called *autoregressive (AR), moving average (MA),* and *autoregressive moving average (ARMA)* processes.

MA or moving average processes are the most straightforward to understand. First, let *{Z(t)}* be some fixed zero-mean, unit-variance "white noise" or "purely random" process (i.e., one for which $Cov[Z(t_i), Z(t_j)] = 1$ *iff* $t_i = t_j$, 0otherwise). $X(t)$ is an *MA(q)* process, or "moving average process of order q," if $X(t) = \sum_{\tau=0}^{q} \beta_\tau Z(t-\tau)$, where the β_τ are constants. It follows that $E[X(t)] = 0$ and $Var[X(t)] = \sum_{\tau=0}^{q} \beta_\tau$. Moving average processes are used to capture "exponential traces" in a time series (Mehrotra *et al.*, 1997; Mozer, 1994; Principé & Lefebvre, 2001). For example, input recurrent neural networks (Ray & Hsu, 1998) are a restricted form of nonlinear *MA* process model.

AR or autoregressive processes are processes in which the values at time *t* depend linearly on the values at previous times. With *{Z(t)}* as defined above, *X(t)* is an *AR(p)* process, or "autoregressive process of order *p*", if $\sum_{\upsilon=0}^{p}\alpha_{\upsilon}X(t-\upsilon)=Z(t)$, where the α_{υ} are constants. In this case, $E[X(t)]=0$, but the calculation of $Var[X(t)]$ depends upon the relationship among the α_{υ}; in general, if $|\alpha_{\upsilon}|\ge 1$, then *X(t)* will quickly diverge. Autoregressive processes are often used to describe stochastic mechanisms that have a finite, short-term, linear "memory"; they are equivalent to infinite-length *MA* processes constants. Both *Jordan recurrent neural networks* (Mozer, 1994) and *time-delay neural networks* (Lang, Waibel, & Hinton., 1990), also known as *tapped delay-line neural networks* or *TDNNs*, are a restricted form of nonlinear *AR* process model (Mehrotra *et al.*, 1997, Principé & Lefebvre, 2001).

ARMA is a straightforward combination of *AR* and *MA* processes. With the above definitions, an *ARMA(p, q)* process is a stochastic process *X(t)* in which $\sum_{\upsilon=0}^{p}\alpha_{\upsilon}X(t-\upsilon)=\sum_{\tau=0}^{q}\beta_{\tau}Z(t-\tau)$, where the $\{\alpha_{\upsilon},\beta_{\tau}\}$ are constants (Mozer, 1994). Because it can be shown that *AR* and *MA* are of equal expressive power, that is, because they can both represent the same linear stochastic processes, possibly with infinite *p* or *q* (Box *et al.*, 1994), *ARMA* model selection and parameter fitting should be done with specific criteria in mind. For example, it is typically appropriate to balance the roles of the *AR(p)* and *MA(q)*, and to limit *p* and *q* to small constant values (typically 4 or 5) for tractability (Box *et al.*, 1994; Principé & Lefebvre, 2001). The Gamma memory (Principé & deVries, 1992; Principé & Lefebvre, 2001) is a restricted, nonlinear *ARMA* process model with a neural network architecture and learning rules.

In *heterogeneous* time series, the embedded temporal patterns belong to different categories of statistical models, such as *MA(1)* and *AR(1)*. Examples of such embedded processes are presented in the discussion of the experimental test beds. A multichannel time series learning problem can be decomposed into homogeneous subtasks by aggregation or synthesis of attributes. *Aggregation* occurs in multimodal sensor fusion (e.g., for medical, industrial, and military monitoring), where each group of input attributes represents the bands of information available to a sensor (Stein & Meredith, 1993). In geospatial data mining, these groupings may be topographic. Complex attributes may be *synthesized* explicitly by constructive induction, as in causal discovery of latent (hidden) variables (Heckerman, 1996); or implicitly by preprocessing transforms (Haykin, 1999; Mehrotra *et al.*, 1997; Ray & Hsu, 1998).

Control of Preference Bias: A Data Fusion Example

The learning methods being evaluated define the hierarchical model used to perform multi-strategy learning in the integrated, or composite, learning system. Examples of these are listed in Table 2. Continuing research (Hsu, 1998) also considers the training algorithm to use but is beyond the scope of this chapter. This section presents the metrics for preference bias (the *combiner* type) and presents hierarchical models for classifier fusion in greater detail.

The expected performance of a hierarchical model is a *holistic* measurement; that is, it involves all of the subproblem definitions, the learning architecture used for each one, and even the training algorithm used. It must therefore take into account at least the subproblem definitions. Hence, the metrics used to select a hierarchical model are referred to as *preference metrics*. Preference metrics in this case are designed to evaluate only the subproblem definitions. This criterion has three benefits: first, it is consistent with the holistic function of hierarchical models; second, it is minimally complex, in that it omits less relevant issues such as the learning architecture for each subproblem from consideration; and third, it measures the quality of an attribute partition. The third property is very useful in heuristic search over attribute partitions; the tree metric can thus serve double duty as an evaluation function for a partition (given a hierarchical model to be used) and for mixture model (given a partitioned data set). As a convention, the choice of *partition* is committed first; next, the hierarchical model type; then, the learning architectures for each subset, with each selection being made subject to the previous choices.

The preference metric for specialist-moderator networks is the *factorization score*. The interested reader is referred to Hsu (1998) and Hsu *et al.* (2000).

Multi-strategy Hierarchical Mixture of Experts (MS-HME) Network

The tree metric for HME-type networks is the *modular mutual information score*. This score measures mutual information across subsets of a partition[2]. It is directly proportional to the conditional mutual information of the desired output given each subset *by itself* (i.e., the mutual information between one subset and the target class, *given* all other subsets). It is inversely proportional to the difference between joint and total conditional mutual information (i.e., shared information among all subsets). Let the first quantity be denoted I_i for each subset a_i, and the second quantity as I_∇ for an entire partition.

The mutual information between discrete random variables X and Y is defined (Cover & Thomas, 1991) as the Kullback-Leibler distance between joint and product distributions:

$$
\begin{aligned}
I(X;Y) =_{def} & \ D(p(x,y) \| p(x)p(y)) \\
= & \ H(X) - H(X \mid Y) \\
= & \ H(X) + H(Y) - H(X,Y) \qquad \text{(chain rule)} \\
= & \ H(Y) - H(Y \mid X)
\end{aligned}
$$

Table 2: Hierarchical committee machines (combiners) and their prescriptive metrics

Preference Bias (Combiner Type)	Preference Metric
Specialist-Moderator (SM) Network	Factorization score
Multi-strategy Hierarchical Mixture of Experts (MS-HME) Network	Modular mutual information score

The conditional mutual information of X and Y given Z is defined (Cover & Thomas, 1991) as the change in conditional entropy when the value of Z is known:

$$I(X;Y|Z) =_{def} H(X \mid Z) - H(X \mid Y, Z)$$
$$= H(Y \mid Z) - H(Y \mid X, Z)$$

The *common information* of X, Y, and Z (the analogue of k-way intersection in set theory, except that it can have negative value) can now be defined:

$$I(X;Y;Z) =_{def} I(X;Y) - I(X;Y|Z)$$
$$= I(X;Z) - I(X;Z|Y)$$
$$= I(Y;Z) - I(Y;Z|Y)$$
$$= I(X;Z) - I(X;Z|Y)$$
$$= I(Y;Z) - I(Y;Z|Y)$$

The idea behind the modular mutual information score is that it should reward high conditional mutual information between an attribute subset and the desired output given other subsets (i.e., each expert subnetwork will be allotted a large share of the work). It should also penalize high common information (i.e., the gating network is allotted more work relative to the experts). Given these dicta, we can define the modular mutual information for a partition as follows:

$$I(\mathbf{X}; \mathbf{Y}) =_{def} D(p(x_1, x_2, \ldots, x_n, y) \| p(x_1)p(x_2) \ldots p(x_n)p(y))$$
$$\mathbf{X} = \{\mathbf{X}_1, \ldots, \mathbf{X}_k\}$$
$$\bigcap_{i=1}^{k} \mathbf{X}_i = \varnothing$$
$$\bigcup_{i=1}^{k} \mathbf{X}_i = \{X_1, X_2, \ldots, X_n\}$$

which leads to the definition of I_i (modular mutual information) and I_∇ (modular common information):

$$I_i =_{def} I(\mathbf{X}_i; \mathbf{Y} \mid \mathbf{X}_{\neq i})$$
$$=_{def} H(\mathbf{X}; \mathbf{Y}) - H(\mathbf{X}_i \mid \mathbf{Y}, \mathbf{X}_1, \ldots, \mathbf{X}_{i-1}, \mathbf{X}_{i+1}, \ldots, \mathbf{X}_k)$$
$$I_\nabla =_{def} I(\mathbf{X}_1; \mathbf{X}_2; \ldots; \mathbf{X}_k; \mathbf{Y})$$
$$=_{def} I(\mathbf{X}; \mathbf{Y}) - \sum_{i=1}^{k} I_i$$

Because the desired metric rewards high I_i and penalizes high I_∇, we can define:

$$M_{MS\text{-}HME} = \left(\sum_{i=1}^{k} I_i \right) - I_\nabla$$
$$= \left(\sum_{i=1}^{k} I_i \right) - I(\mathbf{X}; \mathbf{Y}) - \sum_{i=1}^{k} I_i$$
$$= 2 \left(\sum_{i=1}^{k} I_i \right) - I(\mathbf{X}; \mathbf{Y})$$

Model Selection and Composite Learning

As explained in the introduction, being able to decompose a learning problem into simpler subproblems still leaves the task of mapping each to its appropriate model – the hypothesis language or *representation bias* (Mitchell, 1997; Witten & Frank, 2000). In the above methodology section, we have just formulated a rationale for using quantitative metrics to accumulate evidence in favor of particular models. This leads to the design presented here, a metric-based selection system for *time series learning architectures* and *general learning methods*. Next, we have studied specific time series learning architectures that populate part of a collection of model components, along with the metrics that correspond to each. We then addressed the problem of determining a preference bias (data fusion algorithm) for multi-strategy learning by examining two hierarchical mixture models to see how they can be converted into classifier fusion models that also populate this collection. Finally, we surveyed metrics that correspond to each.

I pause to justify this coarse-grained approach to model selection. As earlier defined, *model selection* is the problem of choosing a hypothesis class that has the appropriate complexity for the given training data (Hjorth, 1994; Schuurmans, 1997; Stone, 1977). Quantitative or *metric-based* methods for model selection have previously been used to learn using highly flexible models with many degrees of freedom (Schuurmans, 1997), but with no particular assumptions on the structure of decision surfaces, e.g., that they are linear or quadratic (Geman *et al.*, 1992). Learning without this characterization is known in the statistics literature as *model-free estimation* or *nonparametric statistical inference*. A premise of this chapter is that, for learning from heterogeneous time series, indiscriminate use of such models is too unmanageable. This is especially true in diagnostic monitoring applications such as crisis monitoring, because decision surfaces are more sensitive to error when the target concept is a catastrophic event (Hsu *et al.*, 1998).

The purpose of using model selection in *decomposable* learning problems is to *fit* a suitable hypothesis language (model) to each subproblem (Engels, Verdenius, & Aha,1998). A subproblem is defined in terms of a subset of the input and an intermediate concept, formed by unsupervised learning from that subset. Selecting a model entails three tasks. The first is *finding partitions* that are consistent enough to admit at most one "suitable" model per subset. The second is *building a collection of models* that is flexible enough so that some partition can have at least one model matched to each of its subsets. The third is to *derive a principled quantitative system for model evaluation* so that exactly one model can be correctly chosen per subset of the acceptable partition or partitions. These tasks indicate that a model selection system *at the level of subproblem definition* is desirable, because this corresponds to the granularity of problem decomposition, the design choices for the collection of models, and the evaluation function. This is a more comprehensive optimization problem than traditional model selection typically adopts (Geman *et al.*, 1992; Hjorth, 1994), but it is also approached from a less precise perspective, hence the term *coarse-grained*.

RESULTS
Synthetic and Small-Scale Data Mining Problems

This section presents experimental results with comparisons to existing inductive learning systems (Kohavi, Sommerfield & Dougherty, 1996): decision trees, traditional regression-based methods as adapted to time series prediction, and non-modular probabilistic networks (both atemporal and ARIMA-type ANNs).

The Modular Parity Problem

Figure 3 shows the classification accuracy in percent for specialist and moderator output for the concept:

$$\mathbf{Y} = \prod_{i=1}^{k} Y_i$$
$$= Y_1 \times Y_2 \times \ldots \times Y_k$$
$$Y_i = X_{i1} \oplus X_{i2} \oplus \ldots \oplus X_{in_i}$$
$$X_{ij} \in \mathbf{H} \equiv \{0, 1\}$$

All mixture models are trained using 24 hidden units, distributed across all specialists and moderators. When used as a heuristic evaluation function for partition search, the HME metric documented in the previous section finds the best partition for the 5-attribute problem (shown below) as well as 6, 7, and 8, with no backtracking, and indicates that an MS-HME model should be used.

This section documents improvements in classification accuracy as achieved by attribute partitioning. Figure 3 shows how the optimum partition {{1,2,3}{4,5}} for the concept:

$$parity(x_1, x_2, x_3) \times parity(x_4, x_5)$$

achieves the best specialist performance for any size-2 partition.

Figure 3 shows how this allows it to achieve the best moderator performance overall. Empirically, "good splits" – especially descendants and ancestors of the optimal one, i.e., members of its schema (Goldberg, 1989) – tend to perform well.

As documented in the background section, partition search is able to find Partition #16, {{1,2,3}{4,5}} (the optimum partition) after expanding all of the 2-subset partitions. This reduces B_n evaluations to $\Theta(2^n)$; attribute partitioning therefore remains an intractable problem, but is more feasible for small to moderate numbers of attributes (30-40 can be handled by high-performance computers, instead of 15-20 using exhaustive search). Approximation algorithms for polynomial-time evaluation (Cormen *et al.*, 2001) are currently being investigated by the author.

For experiments using specialist-moderator networks on a musical tune classification problem – synthetic data quantized from real-world audio recordings – the interested reader is referred to Hsu *et al.* (2000).

Application: Crop Condition Monitoring

Figure 4 visualizes a heterogeneous time series. The lines shown are phased *autocorrelograms*, or plots of autocorrelation shifted in time, for (subjective) weekly *crop condition* estimates, averaged from 1985-1995 for the state of Illinois. Each *point* represents the correlation between one week's mean estimate and the mean estimate for a subsequent week. Each *line* contains the correlation between values for a particular

Figure 3:   Mean classification accuracy of specialists vs. moderators for all (52) partitions of 5-attribute modular parity problem.

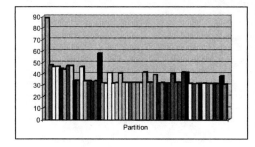 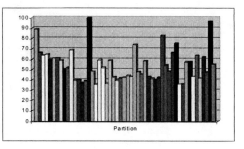

week and all subsequent weeks. The data is heterogeneous because it contains both an autoregressive pattern (the linear increments in autocorrelation for the first ten weeks) and a moving average pattern (the larger, unevenly spaced increments from 0.4 to about 0.95 in the rightmost column). The autoregressive process, which can be represented by a time-delay model, expresses weather "memory" (correlating early and late drought); the moving average process, which can be represented by an exponential trace model, physiological damage from drought. Task decomposition can improve performance here by isolating the AR and MA components for identification and application of the correct specialized architecture – a time delay neural network (Haykin, 1999; Lang *et al.*, 1990) or simple recurrent network (Principé & Lefebvre, 2001), respectively.

We applied a simple mixture model to reduce variance in ANN-based classifiers. A paired *t*-test with 10 degrees of freedom (for 11-*year* cross-validation over the weekly predictions) indicates significance at the level of $p < 0.004$ for the moderator versus TDNN and at the level of $p < 0.0002$ for the moderator versus IR. The null hypothesis is rejected at the 95% level of confidence for TDNN outperforming IR ($p < 0.09$), which is consistent with the hypothesis that an MS-HME network yields a performance boost over either network type alone. This result, however, is based on relatively few samples (in terms of weeks per year) and very coarse spatial granularity (statewide averages).

Table 3 summarizes the performance of an MS-HME network versus that of other induction algorithms from *MLC++* (Kohavi *et al.*, 1996) on the crop condition monitoring problem. This experiment illustrates the usefulness of learning task decomposition over heterogeneous time series. The improved learning results due to application of multiple models (TDNN and IR specialists) and a mixture model (the Gamma network moderator). Reports from the literature on common statistical models for time series (Box *et al.*, 1994; Gershenfeld & Weigend, 1994; Neal, 1996) and experience with the (highly heteroge-

Figure 4: Phased autocorrelogram (plot of autocorrelation shifted over time) for crop condition (average quantized estimates).

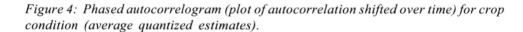

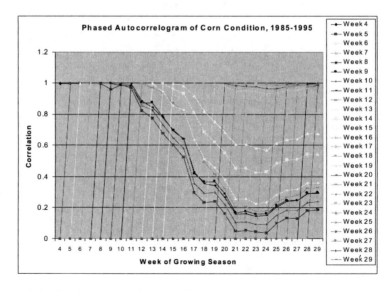

neous) test bed domains documented here bears out the idea that "fitting the right tool to each job" is critical.

Application: Loss Ratio Prediction in Automobile Insurance Pricing

Table 4 summarizes the performance of the *ID3* decision tree induction algorithm and the state-space search-based feature subset selection (FSS) wrapper in *MLC++* (Kohavi *et al.*, 1996) compared to that of a *genetic wrapper* for feature selection. This system is documented in detail in Hsu, Welge, Redman, and Clutter (2002). We used a version of *ALLVAR-2*, a data set for decision support in automobile insurance policy pricing. This data set was used for clustering and classification and initially contained 471-attribute record for each of over 300,000 automobile insurance policies, with five bins of *loss ratio* as a prediction target. Wall clock time for the *Jenesis* and *FSS-ID3* wrappers was comparable. As the table shows, both the *Jenesis* wrapper and the *MLC++* wrapper (using *ID3* as the wrapped inducer) produce significant improvements over unwrapped *ID3* in classification accuracy and very large reductions in the number of attributes used. The test set accuracy and the number of selected attributes are averaged over five cross validation folds (70 aggregate test cases each). Results for data sets from the Irvine database repository that are known to contain irrelevant attributes are also positive. Table 10 presents more descriptive statistics on the five-way cross-validated performance of ID3, FSS-ID3 (the *MLC++* implementation of *ID3* with its feature subset selection wrapper), and *Jenesis*. Severe overfitting is quite evident for *ID3*, based on the

Table 3: Performance of a HME-type mixture model compared with compared with that of other inducers on the crop condition monitoring problem

Classification Accuracy, Crop Condition Monitoring (%)								
	Training				Cross Validation			
Inducer	Min	Mean	Max	StdDev	Min	Mean	Max	StdDev
ID3	100.0	100.0	100.0	0.00	33.3	55.6	82.4	17.51
ID3, bagged	99.7	99.9	100.0	0.15	30.3	58.2	88.2	18.30
ID3, boosted	100.0	100.0	100.0	0.00	33.3	55.6	82.4	17.51
C5.0	90.7	91.7	93.2	0.75	38.7	58.7	81.8	14.30
C5.0, boosted	98.8	99.7	100.0	0.40	38.7	60.9	79.4	13.06
IBL	93.4	94.7	96.7	0.80	33.3	59.2	73.5	11.91
Discrete Naïve-Bayes	74.0	77.4	81.8	2.16	38.7	68.4	96.7	22.85
DNB, bagged	73.4	76.8	80.9	2.35	38.7	70.8	93.9	19.63
DNB, boosted	76.7	78.7	81.5	1.83	38.7	69.7	96.7	21.92
PEBLS	91.6	94.2	96.4	1.68	27.3	58.1	76.5	14.24
IR Expert	91.0	93.7	97.2	1.67	41.9	72.8	94.1	20.45
TDNN Expert	91.9	96.8	99.7	2.02	48.4	74.8	93.8	14.40
Pseudo-HME	98.2	98.9	100.0	0.54	52.9	79.0	96.9	14.99

difference between training and test set error (perfect purity is achieved in all five folds) and the larger number of attributes actually used compared to the wrappers. *Jenesis* and *FSS-ID3* perform comparably in terms of test set error, though *FSS-ID3* has less difference between training and test set error. and *Jenesis* is less likely to overprune the attribute subset. Note that *FSS-ID3* consistently selects the fewest attributes, but still overfits (*Jenesis* achieves lower test set error in three of five cross validation cases). The test set errors of *Jenesis* and *FSS-ID3* are not significantly different, so generalization quality is not conclusively distinguishable in this case. We note, however, that excessively shrinking the subset indicates a significant tradeoff regarding generalization quality. The classification model was used to audit an existing rule-based classification system over the same instance space, and to calibrate an underwriting model (to guide pricing decisions for policies) for an experimental market.

We have observed that the aggregation method scales well across lines of business (the indemnity and non-indemnity companies) and states. This was demonstrated using many of our decision tree experiments and visualizations using *ALLVAR-2* samples and subsamples by state.

ACKNOWLEDGMENTS

Support for this research was provided in part by the Army Research Lab under grant ARL-PET-IMT-KSU-07, by the Office of Naval Research under grant N00014-01-1-0519, and by the Naval Research Laboratory under grant N00014-97-C-2061. The author thanks Nathan D. Gettings for helpful discussions on data fusion and time series analysis and an anonymous reviewer for comments on background material. Thanks also to David Clutter, Matt A. Durst, Nathan D. Gettings, James A. Louis, Yuching Ni, Yu Pan, Mike Perry, James W. Plummer, Victoria E. Lease, Tom Redman, Cecil P. Schmidt, and Kris Wuollett for implementations of software components of the system described in this chapter.

Table 4: Results from Jenesis *for One Company (5-way cross validation), representative data sets*

		Cross Validation Segment						
		0	1	2	3	4	Mean	Stdev
Training Set Accuracy (%)	ID3	*100.0*	*100.0*	*100.0*	*100.0*	*100.0*	*100.0*	0.00
	FSS-ID3	55.00	54.29	67.86	50.36	60.71	57.64	6.08
	Jenesis	65.71	67.14	71.43	71.43	55.71	66.29	5.76
Test Set Accuracy (%)	ID3	41.43	*42.86*	28.57	41.43	44.29	39.71	5.67
	FSS-ID3	*48.57*	35.71	*34.29*	47.14	54.29	44.00	7.74
	Jenesis	41.43	42.86	31.43	*52.86*	*55.71*	***44.86***	8.69
Attributes Selected	ID3	35	35	37	40	35	36.40	1.96
	FSS-ID3	7	8	7	13	18	10.60	4.32
	Jenesis	20	19	22	20	23	20.80	1.47

ENDNOTES

[1] S is a recurrence known as the Stirling Triangle of the Second Kind. It counts the number of partitions of an n-set into k classes (Bogart, 1990).

[2]   This idea is based upon suggestions by Michael I. Jordan.

REFERENCES

Benjamin, D. P. (ed.) (1990). *Change of representation and inductive bias*. Norwell, MA: Kluwer Academic Publishers.

Bogart, K. P. (1990). *Introductory combinatorics, 2nd Ed.* Orlando, FL: Harcourt.

Booker, L. B., Goldberg, D. E., & Holland, J. H. (1989). Classifier systems and genetic algorithms. *Artificial Intelligence, 40*, 235-282.

Box, G. E. P., Jenkins, G. M., & Reinsel, G. C. (1994). *Time series analysis, forecasting, and control (3rd ed.)*. San Francisco, CA: Holden-Day.

Breiman, L. (1996) Bagging predictors. *Machine Learning, 24*, 123-140.

Brooks, F. P. (1995). *The mythical-man month, Anniversary edition: Essays on software engineering*. Reading, MA: AddisonWesley.

Cantu-Paz, E. (1999). *Designing efficient and accurate parallel genetic algorithms*. Ph.D. thesis, University of Illinois at Urbana-Champaign. Technical report, Illinois Genetic Algorithms Laboratory (IlliGAL).

Cormen, T. H., Leiserson, C. E., Rivest, R. L., & Stern, C. (2001). *Introduction to algorithms, 2nd edition*. Cambridge, MA: MIT Press.

Cover, T. M. & Thomas, J. A. (1991). *Elements of iInformation theory*. New York: John Wiley & Sons.

DeJong, K. A., Spears, W. M., & Gordon, D. F. (1993). Using genetic algorithms for concept learning. *Machine Learning, 13*, 161-188.

Donoho, S. K. (1996). *Knowledge-guided constructive induction*. Ph.D. thesis, Department of Computer Science, University of Illinois at Urbana-Champaign.

Duda, R. O., Hart, P. E., & Stork, D. (2000). *Pattern classification, 2nd ed.* New York: John Wiley & Sons.

Engels, R., Verdenius, F., & Aha, D. (1998). *Proceedings of the 1998 Joint AAAI-ICML Workshop on the Methodology of Applying Machine Learning (Technical Report WS-98-16)*. Menlo Park, CA: AAAI Press.

Freund, Y. & Schapire, R. E. (1996). Experiments with a new boosting Algorithm. In *Proceedings of the 13th International Conference on Machine Learning*, pp. 148-156. San Mateo, CA: Morgan Kaufmann.

Fu, L.-M. & Buchanan, B. G. (1985). Learning intermediate concepts in constructing a hierarchical knowledge base. In *Proceedings of the International Joint Conference on Artificial Intelligence (IJCAI-85)*, pp. 659-666, Los Angeles, CA.

Gaba, D. M., Fish, K. J., & Howard, S. K. (1994). *Crisis management in anesthesiology*. New York: Churchill Livingstone.

Geman, S., Bienenstock, E., & Doursat, R. (1992). Neural networks and the bias/variance dilemna. *Neural Computation, 4*, 1-58.

Gershenfeld, N. A. & Weigend, A. S. (eds). (1994). The future of time series: Learning and understanding. In *Time Series Prediction: Forecasting the Future and Understanding the Past (Santa Fe Institute Studies in the Sciences of Complexity XV)*. Reading, MA: AddisonWesley.

Goldberg, D. E. (1989). *Genetic algorithms in search, optimization, and machine learning*. Reading, MA: AddisonWesley.

Goldberg, D. E. (1998). *The race, The hurdle, and The sweet spot: Lessons from genetic algorithms for the automation of design innovation and creativity*. Technical report, Illinois Genetic Algorithms Laboratory (IlliGAL).

Grois, E., Hsu, W. H., Voloshin, M., & Wilkins, D. C. (1998). Bayesian network models for generation of crisis management training scenarios. In *Proceedings of IAAI-98*. Menlo Park, CA: AAAI Press, pp. 1113-1120.

Harik, G. & Lobo, F. (1997). *A parameter-less genetic algorithm*. Technical report, Illinois Genetic Algorithms Laboratory (IlliGAL).

Hassoun, M. H. (1995). *Fundamentals of artificial neural networks*. Cambridge, MA: MIT Press.

Hayes-Roth, B., Larsson, J. E., Brownston, L., Gaba, D., & Flanagan, B. (1996). *Guardian Project home page*, URL: http://www-ksl.stanford.edu/projects/guardian/.

Haykin, S. (1999). *Neural networks: A comprehensive foundation, 2nd ed.* Englewood Cliffs, NJ: Prentice Hall.

Heckerman, D. A. (1991). *Probabilistic similarity networks*. Cambridge, MA: MIT Press.

Heckerman, D. A. (1996). *A tutorial on learning with Bayesian networks*. Microsoft Research Technical Report 95-06, revised June 1996.

Hjorth, J. S. U. (1994). *Computer intensive statistical methods: Validation, model selection and nootstrap*. London: Chapman and Hall.

Horn, J. (1997). *The nature of niching: Genetic algorithms and the evolution of optimal, cooperative populations*. Ph.D. thesis, University of Illinois at Urbana-Champaign. Technical report, Illinois Genetic Algorithms Laboratory (IlliGAL).

Horvitz, E. & Barry, M. (1995). Display of information for time-critical decision making. In *Proceedings of the 11th International Conference on Uncertainty in Artificial Intelligence (UAI-95)*. San Mateo, CA: Morgan-Kaufmann, pp. 296-305.

Hsu, W. H. (1998). *Time series learning with probabilistic network composites*. Ph.D. thesis, University of Illinois at Urbana-Champaign. Technical Report UIUC-DCS-R2063. URL: http://www.kddresearch.org/Publications/Theses/PhD/Hsu.

Hsu, W. H., Gettings, N. D., Lease, V. E., Pan, Y., & Wilkins, D. C. (1998). A new approach to multi-strategy learning from heterogeneous time series. In *Proceedings of the International Workshop on Multi-strategy Learning*, Milan, Italy, June.

Hsu, W. H., Ray, S. R., & Wilkins, D. C. (2000). A multi-strategy approach to classifier learning from time series. *Machine Learning, 38*, 213-236.

Hsu, W. H., Welge, M., Redman, T., & Clutter, D. (2002). Constructive induction wrappers in high-performance commercial data mining and decision support systems. *Data Mining and Knowledge Discovery, 6(4)*: 361-391, October.

Jordan, M. I., & Jacobs, R. A. (1994). Hierarchical mixtures of wxperts and the EM algorithm. *Neural Computation, 6*, 181-214.

Kohavi, R. & John, G. H. (1997). Wrappers for feature subset selection. *Artificial Intelligence, Special Issue on Relevance, 97(1-2)*, 273-324.

Kohavi, R., Sommerfield, D., & Dougherty, J. (1996). Data mining using *MLC++*: A machine learning library in C++. In *Tools with Artificial Intelligence*, p. 234-245. Rockville, MD: IEEE Computer Society PressURL: http://www.sgi.com/Technology/mlc.

Kohonen, T. (1990). The self-organizing map. In *Proceedings of the IEEE*, *78*:1464-1480.

Koza, J. R. (1992). *Genetic programming*. Cambridge, MA: MIT Press.

Lang, K. J., Waibel, A. H., & Hinton, G. E. (1990). A time-delay neural network architecture for isolated word recognition. *Neural Networks*, *3*, 23-43.

Lee, K.-F. (1989). *Automatic speech recognition: The development of the SPHINX system*. Norwell, MA: Kluwer Academic Publishers.

Li, T., Fang, L. & Li, K. Q-Q. (1993). Hierarchical classification and vector quantization with neural trees. *Neurocomputing*, *5*, 119-139.

Lowe, D. (1995). Radial basis function networks. In M. A. Arbib (Ed.), *The handbook of brain theory and neural networks*, 779-782. Cambridge, MA: MIT Press.

Mehrotra, K., Mohan, C. K., & Ranka, S. (1997). *Elements of artificial neural networks*. Cambridge, MA: MIT Press.

Michalski, R. S. (1993). A theory and methodology of inductive learning. *Artificial Intelligence*, *20(2)*, 111-161. Reprinted in B. G. Buchanan, & D. C. Wilkins (Eds.), *Readings in knowledge acquisition and learning*,. San Mateo, CA: MorganKaufmann.

Michalski, R. S., &Stepp, R. E. (1983). Learning from observation: Conceptual clustering. In R.S. Michalski, J.G. Carbonell, J& Mitchell, T. M. (Eds.), *Machine learning: An artificial intelligence approach*. San Mateo, CA: Morgan Kaufmann.

Mitchell, T. M. (1997). *Machine learning*. New York: McGraw-Hill.

Mozer, M. C. (1994). Neural net architectures for temporal sequence processing. In A.S.Weigend. & N.A.Gershenfeld. (eds.), *Time series prediction: Forecasting the future and understanding the past (Santa Fe Institute Studies in the Sciences of Complexity XV)*. Reading, MA: AddisonWesley.

Neal, R. M. (1996). *Bayesian learning for neural networks*. New York: Springer-Verlag.

Palmer, W. C. (1965). *Meteorological drought*. Research Paper Number 45, Office of Climatology, United States Weather Bureau.

Principé, J. & deVries, B. (1992). The Gamma model – A new neural net model for temporal processing. *Neural Networks*, *5*, 565-576.

Principé, J. & Lefebvre, C. (2001). *NeuroSolutions v4.0,* Gainesville, FL: NeuroDimension. URL: http://www.nd.com.

Ray, S. R. & Hsu, W. H. (1998). Self-organized-expert modular network for classification of spatiotemporal sequences. *Journal of Intelligent Data Analysis*, *2(4)*.

Resnick, P. & Varian, H. R. (1997). Recommender systems. *Communications of the ACM*, *40(3)*:56-58.

Russell, S. & Norvig, P. (1995). *Artificial intelligence: A modern approach*. Englewood Cliffs, NJ: Prentice Hall.

Sarle, W. S. (ed.) (2002). *Neural network FAQ*.Periodic posting to the Usenet newsgroup *comp.ai.neural-nets*, URL: ftp://ftp.sas.com/pub/neural/FAQ.html.

Schuurmans, D. (1997). A new metric-based approach to model selection. In *Proceedings of the Fourteenth National Conference on Artificial Intelligence (AAAI-97)*, Providence, RI, 552-558. Menlo Park, CA: AAAI Press.

Stein, B. & Meredith, M. A. (1993). *The merging of the senses*. Cambridge, MA: MIT Press.

Stone, M. (1997). An asymptotic equivalence of choice of models by cross-validation and Akaike's criterion. *Journal of the Royal Statistical Society, Series B, 39,* 44-47.

Watanabe, S. (1985). *Pattern recognition: Human and mechanical.* New York: John Wiley and Sons.

Witten, I. H. & Frank, E. (2000). *Data mining: Practical machine learning tools and techniques with Java implementations.* San Mateo, CA: MorganKaufmann.

Wolpert, D. H. (1992). Stacked generalization. *Neural Networks, 5,* 241-259.

Chapter III

Cooperative Learning and Virtual Reality-Based Visualization for Data Mining

Herna Viktor
University of Ottawa, Canada

Eric Paquet
National Research Council, Canada

Gys le Roux
University of Pretoria, South Africa

ABSTRACT

Data mining concerns the discovery and extraction of knowledge chunks from large data repositories. In a cooperative datamining environment, more than one data mining tool collaborates during the knowledge discovery process. This chapter describes a data mining approach used to visualize the cooperative data mining process. According to this approach, visual data mining consists of both data and knowledge visualization. First, the data are visualized during both data preprocessing and data mining. In this way, the quality of the data is assessed and improved throughout the knowledge discovery process. Second, the knowledge, as discovered by the individual learners, is assessed and modified through the interactive visualization of the cooperative data mining process and its results. The knowledge obtained from the human domain expert also forms part of the process. Finally, the use of virtual reality-based visualization is proposed as a new method to model both the data and its descriptors.

INTRODUCTION

The current explosion of data and information, mainly caused by the extensive use of the Internet and its related technologies, e-commerce and e-business, has increased the urgent need for the development of techniques for intelligent data analysis. Data mining, which concerns the discovery and extraction of knowledge chunks from large data repositories, is aimed at addressing this need.

However, there are a number of factors that militate against the widespread adoption and use of this existing new technology in business. First, individual data mining tools frequently fail to discover large portions of the knowledge embedded in large data repositories. This is mainly due to the choice of statistical measures used by the individual tools. A number of data mining researchers and practitioners are, therefore, currently investigating systems that combine two or more diverse data mining tools. In particular, the combination of techniques that share their individual knowledge with one another is being investigated, leading to the fusion of information representing different viewpoints.

Second, the results of many data mining techniques are often difficult to understand. For example, a data mining effort concerning the evaluation of a census data repository produced 270 pages of rules (Pretorius, 2001). The visual representation of the knowledge embedded in such rules will help to heighten the comprehensibility of the results. The visualization of the data itself, as well as the data mining process, should go a long way towards increasing the user's understanding of and faith in the data mining process. That is, data and information visualization provides users with the ability to obtain new insights into the knowledge, as discovered from large repositories. Human beings look for novel features, patterns, trends, outliers and relationships in data (Han & Kamber, 2001). Through visualizing the data and the concept descriptions obtained (e.g., in the form of rules), a qualitative overview of large and complex data sets can be obtained. In addition, data and rule visualization can assist in identifying regions of interest and appropriate parameters for more focused quantitative analysis (Thearling, Becker, DeCoste, Mawby, Pilote & Sommerfield,2002). The user can thus get a "rough feeling" of the quality of the data, in terms of its correctness, adequacy, completeness, relevance, etc. The use of data and rule visualization thus greatly expands the range of models that can be understood by the user, thereby easing the so-called "accuracy versus understandability" tradeoff (Thearling et al., 1998).

Visual data mining is currently an active area of research. Examples of related commercial data mining packages include the *DBMiner* data mining system, *See5* which forms part of the RuleQuest suite of data mining tools, *Clementine* developed by Integral Solutions Ltd (ISL), *Enterprise Miner* developed by SAS Institute, *Intelligent Miner* as produced by IBM, and various other tools (Han & Kamber, 2001). Neural network tools such as *NeuroSolutions* and *SNNS* and Bayesian network tools such as *Hugin, TETRAD*, and *Bayesware Discoverer*, also incorporate extensive visualization facilities. Examples of related research projects and visualization approaches include *MLC++, WEKA, AlgorithmMatrix, C4.5/See5* and *CN2*, amongst others (Clark & Niblett, 1989; Fayyad, Grinstein, & Wierse, 2001; Han & Kamber, 2001; Mitchell, 1997; Quinlan, 1994) Interested readers are referred to Fayyad, Grinstein, & Wierse (2001), which provides a detailed discussion of the current state of the art.

This paper describes the ViziMine data mining tool used to visualize the cooperative data mining process. The aim of the ViziMine tool is twofold: First, the knowledge, as discovered by the individual tools, is visualized throughout the data mining process and presented in the form of comprehensible rules; this aspect includes visualization of the results of data mining as well as the cooperative learning process. Second, the data are visualized prior to and during cooperative data mining. In this way, the quality of the data can be assessed throughout the *knowledge discovery process*, which includes data preprocessing, data mining, and reporting. During data mining, the visualization of data as covered by individual rules shows the portion of the data covered. The visual data mining process is interactive in that humans are able to adapt the results and data during mining. In addition, this chapter shows how virtual reality can be used to visualize the data and its descriptors.

The chapter is organized as follows: The next section introduces the cooperative inductive learning team (CILT) data mining system in which two or more data mining tools co-exist. An overview of current trends in visual data mining follows. The next section discusses the ViziMine system, which incorporates visual data mining components into the CILT system. Then we introduce the use of three-dimensional visualization, virtual reality-based visualization and multimedia data mining, which may be used to visualize the data used for data mining. Conclusions are presented in the last section of the chapter.

COOPERATIVE DATA MINING

Data mining concerns the automated discovery of hidden patterns and relationships that may not always be obvious. A number of data mining tools exist, including decision trees, rule induction programs and neural networks (Han & Kamber, 2001). Each of these tools applies a specific algorithm to the data in order to build a model based on the statistically significant relationships found in the data.

A number of data mining practitioners have found that, when supplied with the same data repository, different data mining tools produce diverse results. This fact is due to the so-called inductive bias that each algorithm uses when constructing the model (Mitchell, 1997). That is, each data mining tool uses a different learning style (based on one of a variety of different statistical measures) and criteria when building its model. The purpose of combining the results of diverse data mining tools, through the fusion thereof, is to produce high quality results. Therefore, the development of a hybrid multi-strategy learning system that incorporates more than one learning style is currently an active area of research (Honavar, 1995; Lin & Hendler, 1995; Sun, 1995). In this multi-strategy learning approach, the strengths of each technique are amplified, and the weaknesses are ameliorated.

In the CILT system, two or more diverse data mining techniques are combined into a multi-strategy learning system (Viktor, 1999). The system currently includes three different data mining tools with different knowledge representations. The C4.5 tool constructs a decision tree using the information gain ratio criteria (Quinlan, 1994). This tree is pruned to produce a set of rules. The CN2 method induces rules from examples using the Laplace error estimate (Clark & Niblett, 1989). Third, the ANNSER learner creates rules from a trained neural network (Viktor, Engelbrecht, & Cloete, 1998). In addition, the rules of the domain expert are included through a personal assistant (PA) learner, which contains a knowledge base constructed after interviews with one or more domain experts (Viktor, 1999). That is, the user plays an active role in the data mining process, and is able to make and implement decisions that will affect its outcome (Hinke & Newman, 2001).

In the CILT system, the individual results are fused into one through a three-phase process, as follows (Viktor, 1999; Viktor, le Roux, & Paquet, 2001):

Phase 1: Individual learning. First, each individual data mining tool (or learner) uses a training set to form an initial representation of the problem at hand. In addition, the results of the user, a domain expert, are modeled as part of the system (Viktor, 1999). Each individual component's knowledge is stored in a separate knowledge base, in the form of disjunctive normal form (DNF) rules.

Phase 2: Cooperative learning. During phase 2, the individual data mining tools share their knowledge with one another. A rule accuracy threshold is used to distinguish between low- and high-quality rules. Cooperative learning proceeds in four steps as follows (Viktor, le Roux, & Paquet, 2001):

1)   each data mining tool queries the knowledge bases of the others to obtain the high-quality rules that it may have missed. These rules are compared with the rules contained in its rule set. In this way, a NewRule list of relevant rules is produced.

2)   the NewRule list is compiled by identifying the following relationships between the rules, where R1 denotes a high-quality rule contained in the tool's rule set and R2 denotes a high-quality rule created by another data mining tool.

   •   *Similarities.* Two rules, R1 and R2, are similar if two conditions hold: the training examples covered by rule R1 are a subset of those covered by R2; andthe rules contain the same attributes with similar values. For example, the attribute-value test (petal-width > 49.0) is similar to the test (petal-width >49.5). If R1 and R2 are similar, it implies that the learner has already acquired the knowledge as contained in rule R2 and that R2 should not be added to the NewRule list.

   •   *Overlapping rules.* Two rules overlap when they contain one or more attribute-value tests that are the same. For example, rule R1 with attribute-value tests (petal-length > 7.5) and (petal-width < 47.5) and rule R2 with attribute-value tests (petal-length > 7.5) and (sepal-length < 35.5) overlap. Rule R2 is placed on the tool's NewRule list. Note that, for the example, a new rule R3 with form (petal-length > 7.5) and petal-width < 47.5) and (sepal-length < 35.5)} may be formed. This rule represents a specialization that will usually be less accurate than the original general rules and will cover fewer cases. Such a specialization should be avoided, since it leads to overfitting.

   •   *Subsumption.* A rule R2 subsumes another R1 if and only if they describe the same concept and the attribute-value tests of R2 form a subset of that of rule R1. In other words, rule R2 is more general than R1. If R2 subsumes rule R1, it is placed on the NewRule list.

3)   the rule combination procedure is executed. Here, the rules as contained in the NewRule list are used to form new rules, as follows. The attribute-value tests of the rules as contained in the NewRule list are combined with the attribute-value tests of the rules in the tools rule set to form a new set of rules. Each of these new rules is evaluated against the test set. The new high-quality rules, which are dissimilar to, do not overlap with, and are not subsumed by existing rules, are retained on the NewRule list. These rules act as input to the data generation step.

4)   the data generator uses each of the rules in the NewRule list to generate a new set of training instances. The newly generated training instances are added to the original training set, and the learner reiterates the individual learning phase. In this way, a new training set that is biased towards the particular rule is generated. This process is constrained by ensuring that distribution of the data as contained in the original training set is maintained. Interested readers are referred to Viktor (1999) for a detailed description of this process.

Steps 1 to 4 are reiterated until no new rules can be generated. Lastly, redundant rules are pruned using a reduced error pruning algorithm.

Phase 3: Knowledge fusion. Finally, the resulting knowledge, as contained in the individual knowledge bases, is fused into one. Again, redundant rules are pruned and a fused knowledge base that reflects the results of multi-strategy learning is created.

Note that a detailed description of the cooperative learning approach falls beyond the scope of this paper. Interested readers are referred to Viktor (1999) for a description thereof. This chapter concerns the visual representation of the cooperative data mining process and results, as well as the data itself, using visual data mining techniques, as discussed next.

VISUAL DATA MINING

Data mining techniques, as discussed above, construct a model of the data through repetitive calculation to find statistically significant relationships within the data. However, the human visual perception system can detect patterns within the data that are unknown to a data mining tool (Johnson-Laird, 1993). The combination of the various strengths of the human visual system and data mining tools may subsequently lead to the discovery of novel insights and the improvement of the human's perspective of the problem at hand.

Data mining extracts information from a data repository of which the user may be unaware. Useful relationships between variables that are non-intuitive are the jewels that data mining hopes to locate. The aim of visual data mining techniques is thus to discover and extract implicit, useful knowledge from large data sets using data and/or knowledge visualization techniques. Visual data mining harnesses the power of the human vision system, making it an effective tool to comprehend data distribution, patterns, clusters, and outliers in data (Han & Kamber, 2001).

Visual data mining integrates data visualization and data mining and is thus closely related to computer graphics, multimedia systems, human computer interfaces, pattern recognition, and high performance computing. Since there are usually many ways to graphically represent a model, the type of visualizations used should be chosen to maximize their value to the user (Johnson-Laird, 1993). This requirement implies that we understand the user's needs and design the visualization with the end user in mind.

Note that, in order to ensure the success of visualization, the visual data mining process should be interactive. In interactive visual data mining, visualization tools can be used to help users make smart data mining decisions (Docherty & Beck, 2001; Han & Kamber, 2001). Here, the data distribution in a set of attributes is displayed using color sectors or columns, giving the user the ability to visually understand the data and therefore allowing him or her to be interactively part of the mining process. In the CILT environment, the user participates (through the PA learner) in the cooperative process and is therefore able to validate the knowledge, as well as add his personal knowledge to the process.

The following observation is noteworthy. Visual data mining concerns both visualizing the data, and visualizing the results of data mining and the data mining process itself. In a cooperative data mining environment, as introduced in the last section, result visualization includes the interactive visualization of the results of multiple data mining techniques and the cooperation processes. Data visualization is important not only during data mining, but also during data preprocessing, as discussed next.

Data Visualization During Data Preprocessing

Data preprocessing is one of the most important aspects of any data mining exercise. According to Adriaans and Zantinge (1996), data preprocessing consumes 80% of the time of a typical, real-world data mining effort. Here, the "garbage-in, garbage-out" rule applies. According to a survey conducted by Redman (1996), a typical operational data repository contains 1% to 5% incorrect values. It follows that the poor quality of data may lead to nonsensical data mining results, which will subsequently have to be discarded. In addition, the implicit assumption that the data do in fact relate to the case study from which they were drawn and thus reflect the real world is often not tested (Pyle, 1999).

Figure 1 shows the different components of the knowledge discovery process, which includes the selection of appropriate tools, the interpretation of the results, and the actual data mining itself. Data preprocessing concerns the selection, evaluation, cleaning, enrichment, and transformation of the data (Adriaans & Zantinge, 1996; Han & Kamber, 2001; Pyle, 1999). Data preprocessing involves the following aspects:

- *Data cleaning* is used to ensure that the data are of a high quality and contain no duplicate values. If the data set is large, random samples are obtained and analyzed. The data-cleaning process involves the detection and possible elimination of incorrect and missing values. Such values may have one of a number of causes. These causes include data capturing errors due to missing information, deliberate typing errors, and negligence. Moreover, end users may fraudulently supply misleading information.

Figure 1: Data preprocessing and data mining tasks [Adapted from Docherty & Beck, 2001].

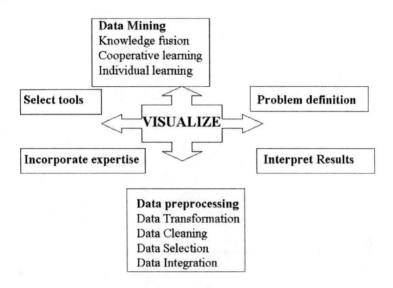

- *Data integration*. When integrating data, historic data and data referring to day-to-day operations are merged into a uniform format. For example, data from source A may include a "date of recording" field, whereas the data from source B implicitly refer to current operations.
- *Data selection* involves the collection and selection of appropriate data. High-quality data collection requires care to minimize ambiguity, errors, and randomness in data. The data are collected to cover the widest range of the problem domain.
- *Data transformation* involves transforming the original data set to the data representations of the individual data mining tools. Neural networks, for example, use numeric-valued attributes, while decision trees usually combine numeric and symbolic representations. Care should be taken to ensure that no information is lost during this coding process.

Data visualization provides a powerful mechanism to aid the user during the important data preprocessing steps (Foong, 2001). Through the visualization of the original data, the user can browse to get a "feel" for the properties of that data. For example, large samples can be visualized and analyzed (Thearling et al., 2001). In particular, visualization can the used for outlier detection, which highlights surprises in the data, that is, data instances that do not comply with the general behavior or model of the data (Han & Kamber, 2001; Pyle, 1999). In addition, the user is aided in selecting the appropriate data through a visual interface. During data transformation, visualizing the data can help the user to ensure the correctness of the transformation. That is, the user may determine whether the two views (original versus transformed) of the data are equivalent. Visualization may also be used to assist users when integrating data sources, assisting them to see relationships within the different formats.

Data mining relies heavily on the training data, and it is important to understand the limitations of the original data repository. Visualizing the data preprocessing steps thus helps the user to place the appropriate amount of trust in the final model (Thearling et al., 2001).

The next section discusses data visualization techniques.

Data Visualization

According to Grinstein and Ward (2002), data visualization techniques are classified in respect of three aspects: their focus, i.e., symbolic versus geometric; their stimulus (2D versus 3D); and whether the display is static or dynamic. In addition, data in a data repository can be viewed as different levels of granularity or abstraction, or as different combinations of attributes or dimensions. The data can be presented in various visual formats, including box plots, scatter plots, 3D-cubes, data distribution charts, curves, volume visualization, surfaces, or link graphs, among others (Thearling et al., 2001).

Scatter plots refer to the visualization of data items according to two axes, namely X and Y values. The data are shown as points on this 2-D coordinated plane, with possible extra information on each point, such as a name or a number, or even a color. 3D-cubes are used in relationship diagrams, where the data are compared as totals of different categories. According to Hoffman and Grinstein (2002), the scatter plot is probably the most popular visualization tool, since it can help find clusters, outliers, trends, and correlations. In surface charts, the data points are visualized by drawing a line between them. The area defined by the line, together with the lower portion of the chart, is subsequently filled. Link or line graphs display the relationships between data points through fitting a line connecting them (CAESAR™Project, http://www.sae.org/technicalcommittees/caesumm.htm; NRC Cleopatra Anthropometric Search Engine, http://www.cleopatra.nrc.ca; Paquet, Robinette & Rioux, 2000). They are normally used for 2D data where the X value is not repeated (Hoffman & Grinstein, 2001).

Note that advanced visualization techniques greatly expand the range of models that can be understood by domain experts, thereby easing the so-called accuracy versus understandability tradeoff (Singhal & Zyda, 1999). However, due to the so-called "curse of dimensionality," highly accurate models are usually less understandable, and vice versa. In a data mining system, the aim of data visualization is to obtain an initial understanding of the data and the quality thereof. The actual accurate assessment of the data and the discovery of new knowledge are the tasks of the data mining tools. Therefore, the visual display should preferably be highly understandable, possibly at the cost of accuracy.

Three components are essential for understanding a visual model of the data, namely representation, interaction and integration (Singhal et al., 1999):

- *Representation* refers to the visual form in which the model appears. A high-quality representation displays the model in terms of visual components that are already familiar to the user.
- *Interaction* refers to the ability to view the model "in action" in real time, which allows the user to play with the model. Examples are "what-if" analysis and forecasting based on the data and the business scenario.

- *Integration* concerns the ability to display relationships between the model and alternative views of the data, thus providing the user with a holistic view of the data mining process.

A number of "rule of thumb" guidelines have to be kept in mind when developing and evaluating the data visualization techniques, including the following (Tufte, 1990): color should be used with care, and context-sensitive expectations and perceptual limitations should be kept in mind; intuitive mappings should be used as far as possible, keeping in mind non-intuitive mappings may reveal interesting features; the representation should be appealing to the eye, and there should be a balance between simplicity and pleasing color combinations while avoiding excessive texture variations and distracting flashes; and data distortion should be avoided and data should be scaled with care.

The use of one or more of the above-mentioned data visualization techniques thus helps the user to obtain an initial model of the data, in order to detect possible outliers and to obtain an intuitive assessment of the quality of the data used for data mining. The visualization of the data mining process and results is discussed next.

Processes and Result Visualization

According to Foster and Gee (2002), it is crucial to be aware of what users require for exploring data sets, small and large. The driving force behind visualizing data mining models can be broken down into two key areas, namely, understanding and trust (Singhal et al., 1999; Thearling et al., 2001). Understanding is undoubtedly the most fundamental motivation behind visualization. Understanding means more than just comprehension; it also involves context. If the user can understand what has been discovered in the context of the business issue, he will trust the data and the underlying model and thus put it to use. Visualizing a model also allows a user to discuss and explain the logic behind the model to others. In this way, the overall trust in the model increases and subsequent actions taken as a result are justifiable (Thearling et al., 2001).

According to Gershon and Eick (1995), the art of information visualization can be seen as the combination of three well-defined and understood disciplines, namely, cognitive science, graphic art, and information graphics. A number of important factors have to be kept in mind during process and result visualization, including the following: the visualization approach should provide an easy understanding of the domain knowledge, explore visual parameters, and produce useful outputs; salient features should be encoded graphically; and the interactive process should prove useful to the user.

As stated in a previous section, the CILT learning strategy involves the cooperation of two or more data mining tools. During the cooperative data mining effort, the data mining processes of both the individual and the cooperative learning process are visualized. This type of visualization presents the various processes of data mining. In this way, the user can determine how the data are extracted, from which data repository the data are extracted, as well as how the selected data are cleaned, integrated, preprocessed, and mined. Moreover, it is also indicated which method is selected for data mining, where the results are stored, and how they may be viewed.

The format of knowledge extracted during the mining process depends on the type of data mining task and its complexity. Examples include classification rules, association rules, temporal sequences and casual graphs (Singhal et al., 1999). Visualization of these data mining results involves the presentation of the results or knowledge obtained from data mining in visual forms, such as decision trees, association rules, clusters, outliers, and generalized rules. An example is the Visual Query-Language-Based Control Interface, where the user is allowed to make queries based on visual inputs and to manipulate the visual representations, i.e., the system provides a visual query capability (Multiple Authors,2000). The Silicon Graphics (SGI) MineSet 3.0 toolset, on the other hand, uses connectivity diagrams to visualize decision trees, and simple Bayesian and decision table classifiers (Carter & Hamilton, 1997; Han & Kamber, 2001; Thearling et al., 2001). Other examples include the Evidence Visualizer, which is used to visualize Bayesian classifiers (Becker, Kohavi, & Sommerfield, 2002); the DB-Discover system that uses multi-attribute generalization to summarize data (Carter & Hamilton, 1997; Hilderman, Li, & Hamilton, 2002); and the NASD Regulation Advanced Detection System, which employs decision trees and association rule visualization for surveillance of the NASDAQ stock market (Senator, Goldberg, & Shyr, 2002).

In addition, the model-building process may be visualized. For example, the Angoss decision tree builder gives the user full control over the decision tree building process (http//www.angoss.com). That is, the user is able to suggest splits, prune the tree or add his knowledge through the manual construction of the tree.

Alternatively, visualization of the constructs created by a data mining tool (e.g., rules, decision tree branches, etc.) and the data covered by them may be accomplished through the use of scatter plots and box plots. For example, scatter plots may be used to indicate the points of data covered by a rule in one color and the points *not* covered by another color.   This visualization method allows users to ask simple, intuitive questions interactively (Thearling et al., 2001). That is, the user is able to complete some form of "what-if" analysis. For example, consider a rule *IF Temp > 70 THEN Thunder* used on a Weather Prediction data repository. The user is subsequently able to see the effect when the rule's conditions are changed slightly, to *IF Temp > 72 THEN Thunder,* for instance.

This section provides an overview of current techniques used to visualize the data mining process and its results. The next section discusses the implementation of the ViziMine tool.

Visual Data Mining with ViziMine

As stated in the previous section, the driving forces behind visual data mining are understanding and trust. ViziMine addresses the comprehensibility and trust issues in two ways: first, by visualizing the data, the cooperative data mining process, and the results of data mining in a meaningful way, and second, by allowing the user to participate in the cooperative data mining process, through manipulation of the data and the rules. In this way, the user is able to interact and participate in the data mining process. Because of the user's active participation and understanding of and trust in the data, the data mining process and its underlying model should improve. Therefore, the main aim of the ViziMine tool is to illustrate the cooperative data mining process and to provide a tool that can be used by the domain expert to incorporate his knowledge into the system. This type of visualization attempts to provide a greater understanding of the data and the cooperative data mining process (Docherty & Beck, 2001).

Data Visualization

Interaction is an essential part of a data exploration effort. The user should be able to interact with data to discover information hidden in it (Cruz-Neira, Sandin & Defanti, 1993). Manipulation of the data dynamically allows the user to "get a feel" for the dynamics and test whether the data accurately reflect the business environment.

The current implementation of ViziMine provides an option to visualize the data by means of scatter diagrams. This graphical representation is simple enough to be easily understood, while being complete enough to reveal all the information present in the model. Experience shows that, in order to illustrate simple relational data, the problem is to navigate through these visualizationsand to stay focused on the object of interest. As indicated in the previous section, this technique is popular due to its strength when attempting to locate clusters, outliers, trends, and correlations. Scatter plots work well for small data sets that contain a small amount of input features and a few classes. With larger data sets, the use of colors allows the user to gain a good understanding of the data and to detect possible tendencies in the data.

For example, consider the well-known Iris benchmarking data set. The problem concerns the classification of Irises into one of three classes, i.e.,Setosa, Virginica, and

Figure 2: Graphical representation of rules.

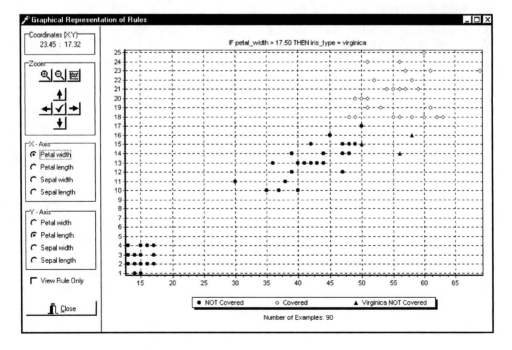

Versicolor. The flowers are classified in terms of four inputs, namely, the sepal-width, sepal-length, petal-width, and petal-length. Figure 2 shows how two input values, namely petal-width and petal-length, are plotted in a Cartesian space. The figure illustrates the usefulness of scatter plots for identifying possible clusters of data points. This tool can convey enormous amounts of information in a compact representation. The user is able to view a data set by making a projection along any two input dimensions. The user uses this tool to obtain a general idea of the contents and quality of the data set.

However, from a cooperative learning perspective, the main objective of the data visualization component is to visualize the portion of the data set covered by a particular rule, as described next. For example, Figure 2 depicts how the rule (henceforth referred to as Rule 1)

IF petal-width > 17.50 THEN Iris = Virginica

is visualized by means of a scatter diagram. The diagram depicts the petal-width and petal-length input dimensions. The scatter diagram shows the Virginica examples covered by the rule (in yellow), together with those examples that were not covered (in black or red). The diagram indicates that the petal-lengths of most Virginica Irises are larger than 46.50. Note that any two of the inputs can be depicted on the X-axis or Y-axis. This may lead to the identification of new clusters that are not described in the rule. For example, a new cluster identifying a relationship between the sepal-widths and petal-widths of Virginicas may be identified, merely by changing the two inputs displayed. This information may then subsequently be used to form a new rule to be used for further training (Viktor, le Roux, & Paquet, 2001).

Visual Cooperative Learning

As stated previously, the CILT system currently incorporates the results of a number of data mining tools that are used for classification. The ViziMine tool imports the rules (or initial knowledge) produced by each tool as an ASCII file and subsequently represents the rules visually as part of the team. This allows the user to easily understand the rule, and provides an interface between the user and the data mining tool.

The ViziMine tool thus provides the user with a detailed description of the current state of each data mining tool. This interface also allows the user to incorporate his knowledge into the system by participating as a learning team member.

The visualization of, for example, a C4.5 decision tree, provides a user with an initial understanding of the knowledge discovered. However, the ability to drag-and-drop the rules onto the data and see the impact immediately allows the user first to understand the rules, and then to play with various "what-if" analysis techniques. ViziMine allows the user to achieve this by illustrating the rules visually on selected data axes by means of a scatter plot of 2D data graphs. This is made possible by the easily comprehensible interface, where the user can select a rule, either directly from one of the learners, or from the manipulated rules of the domain expert, and then drop it onto the data visualization. The portion of the data covered by the rule is subsequently shown on the data, as illustrated in Figure 2.

The data-items (inputs) of the class that is covered by the rule are displayed in color, while the data points of the complementary classes are displayed using round black dots. For example, in Figure 2, the data-items of Iris types Setosa and Versicolor are shown as round black dots. For the Virginica Irises, the data-items covered by Rule 1 are displayed as diamond-shaped yellow dots. The data-items of Virginicas that are not covered by Rule 1 are indicated through the use of red triangles. This information is used to assess the individual rule's accuracy and coverage. By interacting in this way, the user can understand the data that underlies a particular rule constructed by the data mining tool. That is, a clearer understanding of the knowledge discovered by the various mining toolsthat coexist in the cooperative learning environment is obtained.

The user is also able to participate in the learning process by manually combining parts of the rules. The Rule Builder models an individual data mining tool's participation during the cooperative learning phase, as discussed in earlier in the chapter. Note that the learning team operates in one of two modes:

1.   In automatic mode, the cooperative learning phase is dynamically reiterated until no new rules can be created. That is, the rule combining, data generation, and rule pruning steps are completed without any feedback from the user. Here, the user acts as a spectator, viewing the data mining tools' cooperation. This is especially useful when the user wishes to trace the learning process.

2.   In manual mode, the user actively participates in the learning process. He monitors and guides the reiteration of new rules and the data generation process. Importantly, the user can promote the cooperation process by removing or adapting rules. In this way, the user guides the learning process by incorporating his domain knowledge into the system.

The Rule Builder interface is shown in Figure 3. The top part of the interface displays the rules as generated by the active learner. The current rule accuracy threshold, which

Figure 3: Rule Builder interface.

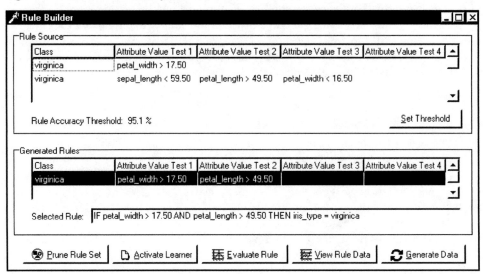

is equal to the average rule accuracy, is displayed next. Here one will recall that this value is used to distinguish between high- and low-quality rules. The window also displays the newly generated rules. These rules are generated using the rule combination algorithm described earlier. In this way, the visualization helps the user to easily understand the various rules. For an expert user, the tool also provides an additional function allowing the user to add his own rules to the combined knowledge.

As has been indicated, the three components essential for understanding a visual model are high-quality representation, real-time interaction, and model and data integration. The current implementation of the ViziMine system thus addresses these three requirements through the real-time integration of both data visualization and data mining result visualization into one.

The next section discusses the use of three-dimensional visualization and virtual reality as a powerful tool for visualizing the data during the data preprocessing and mining processes.

THREE-DIMENSIONAL VISUALIZATION, VIRTUAL REALITY AND DATA MINING

Three-dimensional visualization has the potential to show far more information than two-dimensional visualization, while retaining its simplicity. Current and future research efforts will include the ability to model relationships between data in a three-dimensional rule grid. This visualization technique quickly reveals the quantity and relative strength of relationships between elements, helping to focus attention on important data entities and rules. It therefore aids both the data preprocessing and data mining processes.

Note that, although the data set and the data context determine the visualization technique, the size also plays a very important role. Unfortunately, the more data items on the visual graph, the more complex the graph becomes, and thus the user is faced with information overload or the so-called "curse of dimensionality."

The next section contains general considerations on Virtual Reality (VR) and data mining, but most of the conclusions can be applied to the ViziMine tool as well. The ViziMine tool relies on bidimensional visualization, but the importance of each rule can be better visualized if three-dimensional visualization is utilized.

Dimensionality Reduction

The curse of dimensionality is not restricted to data mining. This problem can arise in information retrieval, and Bayesian and multivariate analysis, to mention just a few. Many solutions have been designed, including the principal component analysis (or PCA). Under certain conditions, defined formally in Reinsel and Velu (1998), it is possible to drastically reduce the number of dimensions, while keeping most of the knowledge by performing a PCA on the data. The approach can be summarized as follows. The covariance matrix of the data is first computed, and then the corresponding Eigen values and vectors are evaluated. Because the covariance matrix is symmetric, the Eigen values and vectors can be easily calculated with a deterministic algorithm like the Jacobi method.

The amplitude of the Eigen values is representative of the importance of a particular dimension: the greater the value, the higher the importance. The corresponding Eigen vectors provide the basis that spans the subspace. It can be shown that the dimensions corresponding to the smallest Eigen values can be neglected. It can also be proved that the truncated Eigen decomposition is the decomposition that minimizes the quadratic error between the truncated decomposition and the real one.

The algorithm can be better understood by considering a bidimensional data distribution. Let us suppose that the data are distributed along a regression line. The Eigen vectors corresponding to this distribution are respectively oriented parallel and perpendicularly to the regression line; the biggest Eigen value corresponds to the Eigen vector oriented parallel to the regression line while the smallest Eigen value corresponds to the Eigen vector normal to the regression line. This particular case shows a fundamental limitation of the PCA method; i.e., in order to reduce the number of dimensions, the data must be correlated in the sense that a linear relationship must exist between them. Even if such a correlation is common in practice, that constraint constitutes an important limitation.

Many researchers have tried to overcome the limitation inherent in the linear relation by working on a generalization of the previous algorithm. A case of particular interest is the piecewise linear relation, which is an immediate generalization of the previous case. Instead of assuming a global linear relation, it is assumed that the domain can be divided into small domains to which a linear relationship applies. That means that the dimensions reduction is performed on a local basis and not on a global basis as in the previous case. More details about this method can be found in Chakrabarti and Menrotra (2000).

In addition to PCA, other methods like neural networks, clustorization, and latent semantic indexing can be utilized for dimension reduction. Clustorization allows representation of the data by a few archetypes corresponding to representative or typical data within the clusters. Neural networks reduce the data set to a limited number of classes. The classes can be determined in advance, as it is the case for a multilayer perceptron and radial basis neural networks, or determined by the network itself, as in the self-organizing Kohonen map.

Three-Dimensional Representation and Visualization of Data

Even if the number of dimensions can be reduced, it is well known that the number of remaining dimensions is much higher than three. Under these circumstances, it is legitimate to ask whether or not there is a clear advantage to increasing the number of dimensions from two to three. Doing so has many advantages. It is well known that complicated data sets are very difficult to visualize in two dimensions. There are many reasons for that. Let us look at three of them: the amount of information that can be displayed, the navigation through the data set, and the way data can be represented.

Let us suppose that N information elements can be displayed in each dimension. If the data are displayed in two dimensions with a volumetric display, it is theoretically possible to display up to N^2 information elements. If three dimensions are utilized, it is then possible to display up to N^3 information elements simultaneously. In practice, the number of displayed information elements is much lower, but this simple example illustrates the fact that an increase in the number of dimensions dramatically increases the bandwidth of the display system.

In visual data mining (Fayyad, Grinstein, & Wierse, 2001), the way data are looked at or the point of view from which they are considered is very important. A pattern that can be evident from a certain point of view might be very difficult to see from a different point of view. Consequently, it is very important that the analyst is able to navigate through the data in order to determine the best localization for his analysis. It is well known that bidimensional representations cannot take into account more that one point of view. Of course, it is always possible to reprocess the data in order to show them from a different point of view, but in practice that is not convenient. First, it can take a lot of time to reprocess the data. Such delays can greatly hamper the analysis process. Second, it is very difficult to determine the right point of view if one cannot navigate through the data in a non-stepwise manner.

The above-mentioned problems can be overcome by using an additional dimension. Three-dimensional data can be viewed from any point of view just by navigating through them. If the system is properly designed, the navigation can be done in realtime. The determination of the right point of view is much easier because the user can walk or fly though the data and look at them from any suitable direction. These systems can be implemented using a VRML browser, a virtual reality environment, or any suitable graphical system.

Multimedia Standards

In order to represent the data, new multimedia alternatives are becoming available, including the X3D and MPEG-4 standards. X3D allows the analyst to define a graphical library adapted to the class of problem he is trying to solve. Not only is it possible to create templates, but also to define a grammar for a specific class of problems. Once the grammar has been defined, it can be reused transparently with various data sets. More details about X3D can be found at the Web3D Consortium web site (http://www.web3d.com).

MPEG-4 is the first, if not the only, real multimedia format. It can transparently handle sound, images, videos, and 3-D objects, as well as events, synchronization, and scripting languages. MPEG-4 is specially adapted to represent very complex multimedia data sets and to facilitate the interaction between those data sets and the analysts. The data mining task could be further simplified by using MPEG-7. MPEG-7 is a multimedia description standard that can describe the content of any multimedia object. That means that MPEG-7 can provide the analyst with additional information. For a video, this information could be the duration, the title, and a trailer. Even if the MPEG-4 and MPEG-7 standards look very promising, it is too early to draw a conclusion about their usefulness in data mining. More details about MPEG-4 and MPEG-7 can be found at http://mpeg.telecomitalialab.com.

Three-Dimensional Visualization Techniques

In two dimensions, data representation is limited to bidimensional graphical elements. In three dimensions, both two- and three-dimensional graphical elements can be utilized. These elements are much more numerous and diversified in three dimensions than in two. Furthermore, three-dimensional representations can be either volumetric or surface-based depending on whether the internal structure is of interest or not. A surface-based representation only takes into account the outer appearance or the shell of the object, while a volumetric approach assigns a value to each volume element. The latter approach is quite common in biomedical imagery like CAT scanning.

Many techniques are available to visualize data in three dimensions (Harris, 2000). Let us review a few of them. It is very common to represent data by glyphs (Hoffman & Grinstein, 2001; Fayyad, Grinstein, & Wierse, 2001). A glyph can be defined as a three-dimensional object suitable for representing data or subsets of data. The object is chosen in order to facilitate both the visualization and the data mining process. The glyph must be self-explanatory and unambiguous. Glyphs can have various attributes like their color and scale. Even if most glyphs are rigid objects, non-rigid and articulated objects can be used as well. It is then possible to use the deformation and the pose of the glyph to represent some specific behavior of the data set. Furthermore, glyphs can be animated in order to model some dynamic process. A scene is defined as the set of all glyphs and their surroundings, as explained by the following example.

Furniture Store Example

Assume that the original data come from a furniture store. The data concern a data mining effort initiated by the Orders Department. The aim of data mining is to determine the purchase patterns of customers indicating the popularity of items, e.g., of sofas. In this example, each sold category is represented by a glyph in the virtual scene. The color of the glyph represents the warehouse stock status: a warm color means that the item is a back order, a cold color means that the item is being overproduced, and a gray color corresponds to a normal inventory. The relative sizes indicate the current sales status. For example, a small sofa would indicate that the sales are too low, while a big sofa would indicate that the sofas are selling well on the market. If the sofa is much bigger than anything else, it means that the sales are unbalanced. The position of the glyphs in the virtual scene is related to the localization of the corresponding items in the store. From an analysis of the localization, it is possible to determine the disposition that maximizes the sales. In addition to the geometrical content, aural attributes can be added to the scene as well (Begault, 1994). These attributes can be utilized to attract the analyst's attention to some particular characteristics of the data or to bias the data mining process in a certain way. The sounds can signal points of interest or can be voice recordings of a previous analysis. When used in a moderate way, aural attributes do not interfere with the visual content and can provide additional information about the data. The overall efficiency of aural attributes can be enhanced if they are spatialized, i.e., they can only be heard at certain locations and within a certain spatial range. The scene can be illuminated in various ways. Depending on the angle of incidence, the number of luminaires, and their nature, it is possible to enhance or hide various aspects of the data. If many analysts are simultaneously working on the data set, the lighting can be used to help them to better visualize their mutual understanding of the data by enhancing features or patterns related to their respective understanding of the situation. The lighting does not need to be static; the dynamic nature of the data can be taken into account as well. A time-dependent lighting can facilitate understanding the evolution of data over time. The interaction of the lighting with the scene can be used to model the interaction of the data with an external agent.

Glyphs can be shown at various levels of detail (LOD). The LOD can be adjusted to provide the analyst with the right amount of information for the task he has to perform. The LOD can be related to the number of triangles used to represent the glyph in a surface-based representation or by the resolution of the basic volumetric element in a volumetric representation. A low LOD glyph can be seen as a sketch of the situation while a high LOD glyph corresponds to a more detail representation. It is important to point out that each glyph can have a different LOD in the scene.

The LOD can be increased by either adding more details to the structure of the glyph or by repeating the structure of the glyph when a scaling operation is performed; this is equivalent to using a fractal representation for the glyph. A fractal is an object that can repeat itself at different scales or LOD. The object does not necessarily repeat itself in an identical fashion at each scale; random variations are allowed. The fractal behavior is usually valid only on a certain range of scales. Fractal structures are very useful for representing data that have a high degree of auto-similarity at various levels, like organizational data. By varying the number of levels on which the symmetry is valid, it is possible to determine whether or not it is suitable to repeat a structure or a behavior within an organization.

Not only can three-dimensional representations be used to model data efficiently, but they can also be utilized to model interrelations. The fractal structure described above is an interesting example. It is also possible to utilize complicated graphs like the octree and the cone diagram, to mention but a few. Although these graphs can be very useful, they must be utilized with great care because they can rapidly become difficult to visualize. A possible solution to this problem is to transpose the data into another context. The basic idea is to map the data space, which can be very abstract, to a well-known problem that can be easily visualized and understood. That kind of paradigm is called a metaphor. The metaphor maps the problem space into a space familiar to the analyst called the "metaphoric space." There must be a one-to-one correspondence between the real space and the metaphoric space. The reason for this is that if a pattern is found in the metaphoric space, the transformation must be invertible in order to find the corresponding pattern in the real space.

Attempts have been made to use more than three geometric dimensions at once by continuously showing subsets of the higher dimension space; dimensions are sampled at random and displayed to the analyst at regular time intervals. Even though these systems are of great interest from a research point of view, they have proved to be very difficult to use, because the computing load is very high and can only be handled by high-end computers, and because it is very difficult for the analyst to make sense of all the subsets that are shown to him. It is clear that classical visualization paradigms are not suited to those systems. However, computers that are more powerful and new visualization paradigms should open the door to multidimensional data mining.

Virtual Reality and Data Mining

Three-dimensional visualization can be made more efficient by the use of virtual reality (VR) (Hoffman & Grinstein, 2001). It is commonly admitted that a virtual environment (VE) is a three-dimensional environment characterized by the fact that it is immersive, interactive, illustrative, and intuitive.

The fact that the environment is immersive is of great importance in data mining. In an image, one looks at the data from outside, while in a VR environment the user is part of the data world. This means that the user can utilize all his senses in order to navigate and understand the data. This also implies that the representation is more intuitive. VR is particularly well adapted to representing the scale and the topology of various sets of data. That becomes even more evident when stereo visualization is utilized. Stereo vision allows the analyst to have real depth perception. This depth perception is important to estimate the relative distances and scales between the glyphs. Such estimation can be difficult without stereo vision if the scene does not correspond to the paradigms our brain is used to processing. In certain cases, the depth perception can be enhanced by the use of metaphors.

If more than three dimensions are required, more dimensions can be added locally by inserting an image or a graph at a specific position in the VR world. Dimensions can also be added by modifying the lighting conditions. It is also possible to add more dimensions by using feedback or haptic devices (Burdea, 1996). These devices can be very useful if the user interacts with the data. The force applied by the haptic device to the user simulates the difficulty of performing a given operation on the data. Color and texture can be used as well to represent additional dimensions or to enhance specific features within the VR world.

Collaborative Virtual Environments (CVEs) (Churchill, Snowdon & Munro, 2001; Singhal et al., 1999) can be considered as a major breakthrough in data mining. By analogy, they can be considered the equivalent of collaborative agents in visualization. Traditionally, one or more analysts perform visualization at a unique site. This operational model does not reflect the fact that many enterprises are distributed worldwide and so are their operations, data, and specialists. It is consequently impossible for those enterprises to centralize all their data mining operations in a single center. Not only must they collaborate on the data mining process, which can be carried out automatically to a certain extent by distributed and collaborative agents, but they must also collaborate on visualization and on the visual data mining aspect.

CVE allows these enterprises to work on data originating from various sources and to analyze them simultaneously from various physical locations. Each location has its own VE. For most CVEs, the VEs do not need to be of the same type; one VE could be a workstation, another a tiled wall display (Cruz-Neira, Sandin & Defanti, 2000), and the third one could be a surround screen environment like a CAVE™(Cruz-Neira et al., 1993). The VEs can exchange data, video, and sound. All data can be accessed and manipulated from all VEs simultaneously. If needed, a monitor can ensure that the VEs do not apply conflicting manipulations to the data.

Note that it is important to choose the VE that is best adapted to the data and their analysis. Graphical workstations are perfect for simple data sets analyzed by a few specialists. Tiled wall displays are made up of a set of flat panels with liquid crystal displays (LCDs) that are carefully aligned on a flat or a curved surface. They usually cover a very large area and consequently allow many specialists to work on the same data simultaneously. Surround screen environments are usually made up of many surfaces. Each surface is either a titled wall display or a projection surface. Surround screen environments are used to achieve an optimum level of immersion. For many technical reasons, the projector is based on digital micromirror device technology or DMD (Digital Light Processing, http://www.dlp.com). Stereo vision can be achieved by alternatively projecting the left-eye and right-eye views and by synchronizing the rendering with shutter glasses. Stereo vision can also be achieved by simultaneously projecting polarized right-eye and left-eye views on the screen. In that case, passive polarized glasses replace the active synchronized glasses. It should be noted that a metallic screen must be utilized to preserve the polarization. The polarization system has a refreshing rate that is twice the refreshing rate of the corresponding shutter system. A high refreshing rate is suitable in order to avoid tiredness and VR-sickness. Since data mining usually involves long sessions, the polarization-based system is the most suitable.

Multimedia Data Mining and VR

Over the past decades, data mining has mostly been applied to alphanumerical data. Data mining is also applied to multimedia data, but most of the time the data mining process is restricted to the associated metadata and to the surrounding text. Multimedia objects contain a huge amount of information. Their description is directly related to their content and for that reason they are called "content-based." Most of the time, the descriptor is a feature vector that contains a set of abstract data representing the characteristics of interest.

Multimedia data mining is currently in its infancy. For that reason, the discussion will be limited to the description of the data mining of three-dimensional objects in the context of the CAESAR™Project and of the National Research Council of Canada's – (NRC) Cleopatra multimedia data mining system.

The CAESAR™Project is an international project that involves the USA, Canada, Italy, and the Netherlands. The purpose of the project is to collect statistical and anthropometrical data about the worldwide population. The anthropometrical data are made up of various measurements performed on thousands of individuals, as well as of three-dimensional scans of their bodies. The statistical data contain information about their perceptions, consumer habits, and lifestyle. The CAESAR™database is intended for utilization mainly by the apparel and the transportation industries. The apparel industry needs body archetypes to design clothes that fit the population, and the transportation industry needs archetypes to design car interiors and seats in planes that are suitable for its clients.

In this project, clustering and filtering is used as a method to group individuals within the population into clusters (Han & Kamber, 2001). That is, we use the clustering data mining technique to find similar individuals within the population, based on an archetype. An archetype is defined as a typical individual within a cluster. It should be noted that an archetype is usually not the center of the cluster; it is an individual that is statistically representative of the behavior of the population within the cluster. Note that the archetype must be a real individual belonging to the database. Average and median individuals usually lead to archetypes that do not exist at all in the general population.

The clustering method is based on the description of the individuals as contained in the Cleopatra system designed by the NRC. Cleopatra analyzes the body scans as contained in the CAESAR™database and subsequently generates a shape descriptor for each one of them. The descriptor is an abstract and compact representation of the human body. Cleopatra then loads the shape descriptors, and the anthropometrical and statistical data into an Oracle8i™database. An object-oriented-relational representation has been adopted for the data. The Cleopatra Search Engine can query the database by human shape, anthropometrical data, and statistical data.

Given a subject and some of his characteristics, like weight, the Cleopatra Search Engine retrieves similar bodies from the database. The alphanumerical data act as a filter; bodies that meet the filter requirements are accepted, while bodies that do not meet the requirements are rejected. Once the filtering process is completed, the search engine retrieves similar bodies based on their 3-D shape. The outcome of the retrieval operation is a cluster corresponding to the proposed subject. By reiterating the process, it is possible to validate the cluster and to find the right archetype. More details can be found in Paquet, Robinette, and Rioux (2000) and The Caesar™Project (http://www.sae.org/technicalcommittees/caesumm.htm), and a demonstration of the system can be found at the NRC's web site(http://www.cleopatra.nrc.ca). Once the cluster has been characterized, it can be visualized by using a VE; the archetype occupies the center of the visual field while the various individuals belonging to the cluster are distributed around the archetypes according to their similarity. In order not to bias the visualization process, the individuals can be subjected to a random motion on spherical trajectory of constant radius, the radius being related to the degree of similarity.

CONCLUSIONS

The ViziMine tool provides a comprehensive visualization tool to support the cooperative data mining process. This tool gives the user the ability to visualize the data and the data covered by the rules in various ways in order to understand it, and to gain new insight into the data mining process. The ability to visualize the results of the data mining effort, both during individual and cooperative learning, helps the user to understand and trust the knowledge embedded in it. The tool thus gives the user the ability to get an intuitive "feel" for the data and the rules created. This ability can be fruitfully used in many business areas, for example, for fraud detection, diagnosis in medical domains, and credit screening, among others.

Recall that the user is modeled as one of the participants in the CILT cooperative data mining environment, as visualized by the ViziMine tool. The visualization process is chronological, following the data mining life cycle, and is thus intuitive, easy to use, and understandable (Multiple Authors, 2000). ViziMine provides a mechanism to enable the user to monitor the data mining process, its inputs, and results, and to interact with the cooperative data mining process and influence the decisions being made. In this way, the powerful human visual system is used to increase the user's understanding of and trust in the data mining effort.

Future development of the ViziMine tool will include the study of a suitable visualization technique for a variety of data set sizes and types, as well as an investigation into the scalability of our approach. This will allow the tool to be compatible with additional real-world data mining problems. The use of our approach for Web mining, with the subsequent application thereof for e-commerce and e-business, should be further investigated. Recall that current implementation of the ViziMine tool incorporates the C4.5, CN2, and ANNSER data mining tools. Other data mining tools may be incorporated through the transformation of their outputs to DNF rule format. This aspect will be further investigated.

Virtual reality and virtual collaborative environments are opening up challenging new avenues for data mining. There is a wealth of multimedia information waiting to be data mined. In the past, due to a lack of proper content-based description, this information was neglected. With the recent advent of a wide variety of content-based descriptors and the MPEG-7 standard to handle them, the fundamental framework is now in place to undertake this task. Virtual reality is perfectly adapted to manipulate and visualize both data and descriptors. VR is also perfectly adapted to analyze alphanumerical data and to map them to a virtually infinite number of representations.

VEs are intuitive and, as such, can help specialists to efficiently transfer their analysis to upper management. Data are distributed worldwide and enterprises operate from various remote locations. These enterprises have a huge amount of data but they lack the right framework to convert them into a valuable asset. Collaborative virtual environments provide a framework for collaborative and distributed data mining by making an immersive and synergic analysis of data and related patterns possible.

REFERENCES

Adriaans, P. & Zantinge, D. (1996). *Data mining.* Harlowi, UK: Addison Wesley.

Agrawal, R., Imielinski, T., & Swami, A. (1993). Database mining: A performance perspective. *IEEE Transactions on Knowledge and Data Engineering,* 5(6): 914-25, December.

Angel, E. (1997). Interactive computer graphics, a top down approach with OpenGL. New York: Addison Wesley.

Becker, B., Kohavi, R., & Sommerfield, S. (2001). Visualizing the simple Bayesian classifier. In U. Fayyad, G.G.Grinstein & A. Wierse (eds.), *Information visualization in data mining and knowledge discovery*, pp.237-250. San Francisco: Morgan Kaufmann.

Begault, D.R. (1994). *3D sound for virtual reality and multimedia.* New York: Academic Press.

Burdea, G.C. (1996). *Force and touch feedback for virtual reality.* New York: Wiley Interscience.

Carter, C.L. & Hamilton, H.J. (1997). Efficient attribute-oriented algorithms for knowledge discovery from large databases. *IEEE Transactions on Knowledge and Data Engineering* 10(2), pp. 193-208.

Chakrabarti, K. & Mehrotra, S. (2000). Local dimensionality reduction: A new approach to indexing high dimensional spaces. In *Proceedings of Very Large Data Bases - VLDB '00*, Cairo, Egypt, pp. 89-100, September.

Churchill, E.F., Snowdon, D. N. & Munro, A. J. (2001). *Collaborative virtual environments.* Berlin: Springer- Verlag.

Clark, P. & Niblett, T. (1989). The CN2 induction algorithm. *Machine Learning*, 3: 261-283.

Cruz-Neira, C., Sandin, D. & Defanti, T. (1993). Surround-screen projection-based virtual reality.   In *Proceedings of The Design and Implementation of the CAVE, SIGGRAPH '93*, Anaheim, California, pp.135-142. August.

Docherty, P. & Beck, A. (2001). A visual metaphor for knowledge discovery: An integrated approach to visualizing the task, data and results. In U. Fayyad, G. G. Grinstein & A. Wierse (eds.), *Information vizualization in data mining and knowledge discovery*, pp.191-204. San Francisco: Morgan Kaufmann.

Fayyad, U., Grinstein, G. G., & Wierse, A. (2001). *Information visualization in data mining and knowledge discovery.* San Francisco: Morgan Kaufmannn.

Fischer, M., Scholten, H.J., & Unwin, D. (1996). Spatial analytical perspectives on GIS. GISDATA 4, London:Taylor & Francis.

Foong, D.L.W. (2001). A visualization-driven approach to strategic knowledge discovery. In U. Fayyad, G.G. Grinstein & A. Wierse (eds.), *Information visualization in data mining and knowledge discovery*, pp.181-190.   San Francisco: Morgan Kaufmann.

Foster, M. & Gee, A.G. (2002). The data visualization environment. In U. Fayyad, G.G. Grinstein & A. Wierse (eds.), *Information visualization in data mining and knowledge discovery*, pp.83-94. San Francisco: Morgan Kaufmann.

Ganesh, M., Han, E.H., Kumar, V., Shekar, S., & Srivastava, J. (1996). *Visual data mining: Framework and algorithm development.* Working Paper. Twin Cities, MN: University of Minnesota, Twin Cities Campus.

Gershon, N. & Eick, S.G. (1995). Visualization's new tack: Making science of Information. *IEEE Spectrum*, November, pp.38-56.

Grinstein, G.G. & Ward, M.O. (2001). Introduction to data visualization. In U. Rayyad, G.G. Grinstein, & A. Wierse (eds.). *Information visualization in data mining and knowledge discovery*, pp.21-26. San Francisco: Morgan Kaufmann.

Han, J. & Kamber, M. (2001). *Data mining concepts and techniques.* San Francisco: Morgan Kaufmann.

Harris, R.L. (2000). Information graphics : A comprehensive illustrated reference. Oxford, UK: Oxford University Press.

Hilderman, R.J., Li, L., & Hamilton, H.J. (2001). Visualizing data mining results with domain generalization graphs. In U. Fayyad, G. Grinstein & A. Wierse (eds.), *Information visualization in data mining and knowledge discovery*, pp.251-269. San Francisco: Morgan Kaufmann.

Hinke, T.H. & Newman, T.S. (2001). A taxonomy for integrating data mining and data visualization. In U. Fayyad, G. Grinstein & A. Wierse (eds.), *Information visualization in data mining and knowledge discovery*, pp. 291-298. San Francisco: Morgan Kaufmann.

Hoffman, P.E. & Grinstein, G.G. (2001). A survey of visualization for high-dimensional data mining. In U. Fayyad, G.G. Grinstein, & A. Wierse (eds.), *Information visualization in data mining and knowledge discovery*, pp.47-82. San Francisco: Morgan Kaufmann.

Honavar, V. (1995). Symbolic artificial intelligence and numeric artificial neural networks: Towards a resolution of dichotomy, computational architectures integrating neural and symbolic processes. Boston, MA: Kluwer Academic Publishers.

Johnson-Laird, P. (1993). *The computer and the mind: An introduction to cognitive science (2nd ed.).* London: Fontana Masterguides.

Keim, D.A. & Kriegel, H.P. (1995). Issues in visualizing large databases. In *Visual Information Management, Proceedings of the 3rd IFIP 2.6 Working Conference on Visual Database Systems.* London, UK: Chapman and Hall, pp. 203-14.Keim, D.A., Lee, J.P., Thuraisinghaman, B., & Wittenbrink, C. (1998). Database issues for data visualization: Supporting interactive database exploration. *IEEE Visualization '95 Workshop, Proceedings.* Berlin, Germany: Springer-Verlag, pp. 12-25.

Lin, L. & Hendler, S. (1995). Examining a hybrid connectionist/symbolic system for the analysis of ballistic signals. In R. Sun (ed.), *Computational Architectures Integrating Neural and Symbolic Processes,* pp.113-130. Boston, MA: Kluwer Academic Press.

Mitchell, T. (1997). *Machine learning.* New York: McGraw-Hill.

Multiple Authors (2000). Special issue on large wall displays. *IEEE Computer Graphics and Applications,* 20 (4).

O'Rourke (1998). *Principles of three-dimensional computer animation – Modeling, rendering & animating with 3D computer graphics* (Revised Ed.). New York: W. W. Norton & Company, ISBN: 0393730247.

Paquet, E, Robinette, K.M., &. Rioux, M. (2000). Management of three-dimensional and anthropometric databases: Alexandria and Cleopatra. *Journal of Electronic Imaging,* 9, 421-431.

Pretorius, J. (2001). *Using geographic information systems for data mining.* Working paper. University of Pretoria, South Africa.

Pyle, D. (1999). *Data preparation for data mining.* San Francisco:Morgan Kaufmann.

Quinlan, R. (1994). *C4.5: Programs for machine learning.* San Francisco:Morgan Kaufmann.

Redman, T.C. (1996). *Data quality for the information age.* Norwood, MA: Artech House.

Reinsel, G.C. & Velu, R.P. (1998). *Multivariate reduced rank regression: Theory and applications.* Berlin: Springer-Verlag.

Ruhle, R.,Land, U., & Wierse, A. (1993). Cooperative visualization and simulation in a supercomputer environment. In *Proceedings of the Joint International Conference on Mathematical Methods and Supercomputing in Nuclear Applications* 2, April 19-23, pp.530-541.

Senator, T.E., Goldberg, H.G., & Shyr, P. (2001). The NASD regulation advanced detection system . In U. Fayyad, G.G. Grinstein, & A. Wierse (eds.), *Information visualization in data mining and knowledge discovery,* pp.363-371. San Francisco: Morgan Kaufmann.

Singhal, S. & Zyda, M. (1999). *Networked virtual environments: Design and implementation.* Reading, MA: Addison Wesley.

Sun, R. (1995). *Computational architectures iIntegrating neural and symbolic pro-*

cesses. An introduction: On symbolic processing in neural networks, pp. 1-21. Boston, MA: Kluwer Academic Press.

Thearling, K., Becker, B., DeCoste, D., Mawby, W. D., Pilote, M. & Sommerfield, D. (2001). Visualizing data mining models. In U. Fayyad, G.G. Grinstein, & A. Wierse (eds.), *Information visualization in data mining and knowledge discovery*, pp.205-222. San Francisco: Morgan Kaufmann.

Tufte, E. (1990). *The visual display of quantitative information.* Cheshire, CT: Graphics Press.

Viktor, H.L. (1999). The CILT multi-agent learning system. *South African Computer Journal (SACJ)*, 24,171-181.

Viktor, H.L., Engelbrecht, A.P., & Cloete, I. (1998). Incorporating rule extraction from artificial neural networks into a computational network. In *Proceedings of the International Conference on Neural Networks and Their Applications (NEURAP'98)*, March 11-13, Marseille: France, pp.421-429.

Viktor, H.L., le Roux, J.G., & Paquet, E. (2001). The ViziMine visual data mining tool. In *Proceedings of International Conference on Advances in Infrastructure for Electronic Business, Science, and Education on the Internet (SSGRR'2001)*, L'Aquila: Italy, August 6-11, CD-ROM.

Chapter IV

Feature Selection in Data Mining

YongSeog Kim
University of Iowa, USA

W. Nick Street
University of Iowa, USA

Filippo Menczer
University of Iowa, USA

ABSTRACT

Feature subset selection is an important problem in knowledge discovery, not only for the insight gained from determining relevant modeling variables, but also for the improved understandability, scalability, and, possibly, accuracy of the resulting models. The purpose of this chapter is to provide a comprehensive analysis of feature selection via evolutionary search in supervised and unsupervised learning. To achieve this purpose, we first discuss a general framework for feature selection based on a new search algorithm, Evolutionary Local Selection Algorithm (ELSA). The search is formulated as a multi-objective optimization problem to examine the trade-off between the complexity of the generated solutions against their quality. ELSA considers multiple objectives efficiently while avoiding computationally expensive global comparison. We combine ELSA with Artificial Neural Networks (ANNs) and Expectation-Maximization (EM) algorithms for feature selection in supervised and unsupervised learning respectively. Further, we provide a new two-level evolutionary algorithm, Meta-Evolutionary Ensembles (MEE), where feature selection is used to promote the diversity among classifiers in the same ensemble.

INTRODUCTION

Feature selection has been an active research area in pattern recognition, statistics, and data mining communities. The main idea of feature selection is to choose a subset of input variables by eliminating features with little or no predictive information. Feature selection can significantly improve the comprehensibility of the resulting classifier models and often builds a model that generalizes better to unseen points. Further, it is often the case that finding the correct subset of predictive features is an important problem in its own right. For example, based on the selected features, a physician may decide whether a risky surgical procedure is necessary for treatment or not.

Feature selection in supervised learning where the main goal is to find a feature subset that produces higher classification accuracy has been well studied. Recently, several researchers (Agrawal, Gehrke, Gunopulos, & Raghavan, 1998; Devaney & Ram, 1997; Dy &Brodley, 2000b) have studied feature selection and clustering together with a single or unified criterion. For feature selection in unsupervised learning, learning algorithms are designed to find natural grouping of the examples in the feature space. Thus, feature selection in unsupervised learning aims to find a good subset of features that forms high quality clusters for a given number of clusters.

However, the traditional approaches to feature selection with a single evaluation criterion have shown limited capability in terms of knowledge discovery and decision support. This is because decision-makers should take into account multiple, conflicted objectives simultaneously. No single criterion for unsupervised feature selection is best for every application (Dy & Brodley, 2000a), and only the decision-maker can determine the relative weights of criteria for her application. In order to provide a clear picture of the possibly nonlinear trade-offs among the various objectives, feature selection has been formulated as a *multi-objective* or *Pareto* optimization problem.

In this framework, we evaluate each feature subset in terms of multiple objectives. Each solution s_i is associated with an evaluation vector $F = F_1(s_i),...,F_C(s_i)$ where C is the number of quality criteria. One solution s_1 is said to *dominate* another solution s_2 if $\forall c: F_C(s_1) \geq F_C(s_2)$ and $\exists c: F_C(s_1) > F_C(s_2)$, where F_C is the c-th criterion, $c \in \{1,...,C\}$. Neither solution dominates the other if $\exists c_1, c2: F_{C1}(s_1) > F_{C2}(s_2), F_{C2}(s_2) > F_{C2}(s_1)$. We define the *Pareto front* as the set of nondominated solutions. In feature selection such as a Pareto optimization, the goal is to approximate the *Pareto front* as best as possible, presenting the decision-maker with a set of high-quality solutions from which to choose.

We use Evolutionary Algorithms (EAs) to intelligently search the space of possible feature subsets. A number of multi-objective extensions of EAs have been proposed (VanVeldhuizen, 1999) to consider multiple fitness criteria effectively. However, most of them employ computationally expensive selection mechanisms to favor dominating solutions and to maintain diversity, such as Pareto domination tournaments (Horn, 1997) and fitness sharing (Goldberg & Richardson, 1987). We propose a new algorithm, Evolutionary Local Selection Algorithms (ELSA), where an individual solution is allocated to a local environment based on its criteria values and competes with others to consume shared resources only if they are located in the same environment.

The remainder of the chapter is organized as follows. We first introduce our search algorithm, ELSA. Then we discuss the feature selection in supervised and unsupervised learning, respectively. Finally, we present a new two-level evolutionary environment, Meta-Evolutionary Ensembles (MEE), that uses feature selection as the mechanism for boosting diversity of a classifier in an ensemble.

EVOLUTIONARY LOCAL SELECTION ALGORITHMS (ELSA)

Agents, Mutation, and Selection

ELSA springs from artificial life models of adaptive agents in ecological environments (Menczer & Belew, 1996). In ELSA, an agent may die, reproduce, or neither, based on an endogenous energy level that fluctuates via interactions with the environment. Figure 1 outlines the ELSA algorithm at a high level of abstraction.

The representation of an agent consists of the D bits, and each of the D bits is an indicator as to whether the corresponding feature is selected or not (1 if a feature is selected, 0 otherwise). Each agent is first initialized with some random solution and an initial reservoir of *energy*, and competes for a scarce resource, energy, based on multidimensional fitness and the proximity of other agents in solution space. The mutation operator randomly selects one bit of the agent and flips it. Our commonality-based crossover operator (Chen, Guerra-Salcedo, & Smith, 1999) makes the offspring inherit all the common features of the parents.

In the selection part of the algorithm, each agent compares its current energy level with a constant reproduction threshold θ. If its energy is higher than θ, the agent reproduces: the agent and its mutated clone that was just evaluated become part of the new population, each with half of the parent's energy. If the energy level of an agent is positive but lower than θ, only the agent itself joins the new population. If an agent runs out of energy, it is killed. The population size is maintained dynamically over iterations and is determined by the carrying capacity of the environment, depending on the costs incurred by any action, and the replenishment of resources (Menczer, Street, & Degeratu, 2000).

Figure 1: ELSA pseudo-code.

```
initialize population of agents, each with energy θ/2
    while there are live agents and for T iterations
        for each energy source c
            for each v (0 .. 1)
                E_envt^c(v) ← 2 v E_tot^c;
        for each agent a
            a' ← mutate(crossover(a, random mate));
            for each energy source c
                v ← Fitness(a',c);  ΔE ← min(v,E_envt^c(v));
                E_envt^c(v) ← E_envt^c(v) - ΔE;  E_a ← E_a + ΔE;
            E_a ← E_a - E_cost;
            if (E_a > θ)
                insert a' into population;
                E_a' ← E_a / 2;  E_a ← E_a - E_a';
            else if (E_a < 0)
                remove a' from population;
    endwhile
```

Energy Allocation and Replenishment

In each iteration of the algorithm, an agent explores a candidate solution similar to itself. The agent collects ΔE from the environment and is taxed with E_{cost} for this action. The net energy intake of an agent is determined by its offspring's fitness and the state of the environment that corresponds to the set of possible values for each of the criteria being optimized.[1] We have an energy source for each criterion, divided into bins corresponding to its values. So, for criterion fitness F_c and bin value v, the environment keeps track of the energy $E_{envt}{}^c(v)$ corresponding to the value $F_c = v$. Further, the environment keeps a count of the number of agents $P_c(v)$ having $F_c = v$. The energy corresponding to an action (alternative solution) a for criterion F_c is given by

$$Fitness(a,c) = F_c(a) / P_c(F_c(a)). \qquad (1)$$

Agents receive energy only inasmuch as the environment has sufficient resources; if these are depleted, no benefits are available until the environmental resources are replenished. Thus, an agent is rewarded with energy for its high fitness values, but also has an interest in finding unpopulated niches in objective space, where more energy is available. E_{cost} for any action is a constant ($E_{cost} < \theta$). When the environment is replenished with energy, each criterion c is allocated an equal share of energy as follows:

$$E_{tot}{}^c = p_{max}E_{cost} / C \qquad (2)$$

where C is the number of criteria considered. This energy is apportioned in linear proportion to the values of each fitness criterion, so as to bias the population toward more promising areas in objective space.

Advantages and Disadvantages

One of the major advantages of ELSA is its minimal centralized control over agents. By relying on *local* selection, ELSA minimizes the communication among agents, which makes the algorithm efficient in terms of computational time and scalability (Menczer, Degaratu, & Street, 2000). Further, the local selection naturally enforces the diversity of the population by evaluating agents based on both their quality measurements and the number of similar individuals in the neighborhood in objective space. Note also that ELSA can be easily combined with any predictive and clustering models.

In particular, there is no upper limit of number of objective functions that ELSA can accommodate. Noting that no single criterion is best for every application, we consider all (or at least some) of them simultaneously in order to provide a clear picture of the (possibly nonlinear) trade-offs among the various objectives. The decision-maker can select a final model after determining her relative weights of criteria for application.

ELSA can be useful for various tasks in which the maintenance of diversity within the population is more important than a speedy convergence to the optimum. Feature selection is one such promising application. Based on the well-covered range of feature vector complexities, ELSA is able to locate most of the Pareto front (Menczer, Degeratu, & Street, 2000). However, for problems requiring effective selection pressure, local selection may not be ideal because of its weak selection scheme.

FEATURE SELECTION IN SUPERVISED LEARNING

In this section, we propose a new approach for the customer targeting that combines evolutionary algorithms (EAs) and artificial neural networks (ANNs). In particular, we want to address the multi-objective nature of the customer targeting applications — maximizing hit rate and minimizing complexity of the model through feature selection. We use ELSA to search the possible combinations of features, and ANNs to score the probability of buying new services or products using only the feature selected by ELSA.

Problem Specification and Data Sets

Direct mailings to potential customers have been one of the most common approaches to market a new product or service. With a better understanding of who its potential customers were, the company would know more accurately who to target, and it could reduce expenses and the waste of time and effort. In particular, we are interested in predicting potential customers who would be interested in buying a recreational vehicle (RV) insurance policy[2] while reducing feature dimensionality.

Suppose that one insurance company wants to advertise a new insurance policy based on socio-demographic data over a certain geographic area. From its first direct mailing to 5822 prospects, 348 purchased RV insurance, resulting in a hit rate of 348/5822 = 5.97%. Could the company attain a higher response rate from another carefully chosen direct mailing from the top $x\%$ of a new set of 4000 potential prospects?

In our experiment, we use two separate data sets— a training (5822 records) and an evaluation set (4000 records). Originally, each data set had 85 attributes, containing socio-demographic information (attributes 1-43) and contribution to and ownership of various insurance policies (attributes 44-85). The socio-demographic data was derived using zip codes, and thus all customers living in areas with the same zip code were assumed to have the same socio-demographic attributes. We omitted the first feature (customer subtype) mainly because it would expand search space dramatically with little information gain if we represented it as a 41-bit variable. Further, we can still exploit the information of customer type by recording the fifth feature (customer main type) as a 10-bit variable. The other features are considered continuous and scaled to a common range (0-9).

ELSA/ANN Model Specification

Structure of the ELSA/ANN Model

Our predictive model is a hybrid model of the ELSA and ANN procedures, as shown in Figure 2. ELSA searches for a set of feature subsets and passes it to an ANN. The ANN extracts predictive information from each subset and learns the patterns using a randomly selected two-thirds of the training data. The trained ANN is then evaluated on the remaining one-third of the training data, and returns two evaluation metrics, $F_{accuracy}$ and $F_{complexity}$ (described below), to ELSA. Note that in both the learning and evaluation procedures, the ANN uses only the selected features. Based on the returned metric values, ELSA biases its search to maximize the two objectives until the maximum number of iterations is attained.

Among all evaluated solutions over the generations, we choose for further evaluation the set of candidates that satisfies a minimum hit-rate threshold. With chosen candidates, we start a 10-fold cross validation. In this procedure, the training data is divided into 10 non-overlapping groups. We train an ANN using the first nine groups of training data and evaluate the trained ANN on the remaining group. We repeat this procedure until each of the 10 groups has been used as a test set once. We take the average of the accuracy measurements over the 10 evaluations and call it an *intermediate* accuracy. We repeat the 10-fold cross validation procedure five times and call the average of the five intermediate accuracy estimates *estimated* accuracy.

We maintain a superset of the Pareto front containing those solutions with the highest accuracy at every $F_{complexity}$ level covered by ELSA. For evaluation purposes, we subjectively decided to pick a "best" solution with the minimal number of features at the marginal accuracy level.[3] Then we train the ANN using all the training data with the selected features only, and the trained model is used to select the top $x\%$ of the potential customers in the evaluation set, based on the estimated probability of buying RV insurance. We finally calculate the *actual* accuracy of our model.

Evaluation Metrics

We use two heuristic evaluation criteria, $F_{accuracy}$ and $F_{complexity}$, to evaluate selected feature subsets. Each objective, after being normalized into 25 intervals to allocate energy, is to be maximized by ELSA.

$F_{accuracy}$: The purpose of this objective is to favor feature sets with a higher hit rate. We define two different measures, $F_{accuracy}{}^1$ and $F_{accuracy}{}^2$ for two different experiments.

In Experiment 1, we select the top 20% of potential customers in descending order of the probability of purchasing the product and compute the ratio of the number of actual customers, AC, out of the chosen prospects, TC. We calculate $F_{accuracy}{}^1$ as follows:

Figure 2: The ELSA/ANN model.

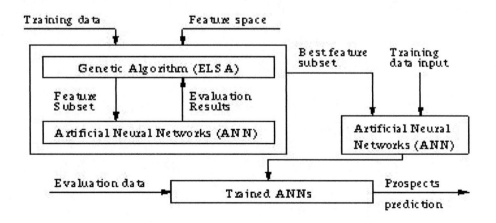

$$F_{accuracy}{}^1 = (1 \,/\, Z_{accuracy}{}^1)\,(AC\,/\,TC) \tag{3}$$

where $F_{accuracy}{}^1$ is a normalization constant.

In Experiment 2, we measure accuracy at the first m intervals[4] after dividing the range of customer selection percentages into 50 intervals with equal width (2%). At each interval $i \le m$, we select the top $(2 \times i)\%$ of potential customers in descending order of the probability of purchasing the product and compute the ratio of the number of actual customers, AC_i, out of the total number of actual customers in the evaluation data, Tot. We multiply the width of interval and sum those values to get the area under the lift curve over m intervals. Finally, we divide it by m to get our final metric, $F_{accuracy}{}^2$. We formulate it as follows:

$$F_{accuracy}{}^2 = \frac{1}{Z_{accuracy}{}^2} \frac{1}{m} \sum_{i=1}^{m} \frac{AC_i}{Tot} \cdot 2 \tag{4}$$

where $Tot = 238$, $m = 25$ and $Z_{accuracy}{}^2$ is an empirically derived normalization constant.

$F_{complexity}$: This objective is aimed at finding parsimonious solutions by minimizing the number of selected features as follows:

$$F_{complexity} = 1 - (d-1)/(D-1). \tag{5}$$

Note that at least one feature must be used. Other things being equal, we expect that lower complexity will lead to easier interpretability of solutions and better generalization.

Experimental Results

Experiment 1

In this experiment, we select the top 20% of customers to measure the hit rate of each solution as in Kim and Street (2000). For comparison purpose, we implement the PCA/logit model by first applying PCA on the training set. We select 22 PCs — the minimum required to explain more than 90% of the variance in the data set — and use them to reduce the dimensionality of the training set and the evaluation set.

We set the values for the ELSA parameters in the ELSA/ANN and ELSA/logit models as follows: $Pr(mutation) = 1.0$, $p_{max} = 1,000$, $E_{cost} = 0.2$, $\theta = 0.3$, and $T = 2,000$. In both models, we select the single solution with the highest expected hit rate among those solutions with fewer than 10 features selected. We evaluated each model on the evaluation set and summarized our results in Table 1.

The column marked "# Correct" shows the number of actual customers who are included in the chosen top 20%. The number in parenthesis represents the number of selected features, except for the PCA/logit model, where it represents the number of PCs selected.

Table 1: Results of Experiment 1

Model (# Features)	Training set Hit Rate ± s.d	Evaluation set # Correct	Evaluation set Hit Rate
PCA/logit (22)	12.83 ± 0.498	109	13.63
ELSA/logit (6)	15.73 ± 0.203	115	14.38
ELSA/ANN (7)	15.92 ± 0.146	120	15.00

In terms of the actual hit rate, ELSA/ANN returns the highest actual hit rate. Feature selection (the difference in actual hit rate between PCA/logit and ELSA/logit) and non-linear approximation (the difference in actual hit rate between ELSA/logit and ELSA/ANN) contribute about half of the total accuracy gain respectively. The improvement of the ELSA/ANN model in actual hit rate could make a meaningful difference in profit as the number of targeted prospects increases.

The resulting model of ELSA/ANN is also easier to interpret than that of PCA/logit. This is because, in the PCA/logit model, it is difficult to interpret the meaning of each of PC in high-dimensional feature spaces. Further, the ELSA/ANN model makes it possible to evaluate the predictive importance of each features. The chosen seven features by the ELSA/ANN model are: customer main type (average family), contribution to third-party policy, car policy, moped policy, fire policy, number of third-party policies, and social security policies. Among those features, we expected at least one of the car insurance-related features to be selected. Moped policy ownership is justified by the fact that many people carry their mopeds or bicycles on the back of RVs. Those two features are selected again by the ELSA/logit model.[5] Using this type of information, we were able to build a potentially valuable profile of likely customers (Kim & Street, 2000).

The fact that the ELSA/ANN model used only seven features for customer prediction makes it possible to save a great amount of money through reduced storage requirements (86/93 ≈ 92.5%) and through the reduced labor and communication costs for data collection, transfer, and analysis. By contrast, the PCA/logit model needs the whole feature set to extract PCs. We also compare the lift curves of the three models. Figure 3 shows the cumulative hit rate over the top $x\%$ of prospects ($2 \leq x \leq 100$).

As expected, our ELSA/ANN model followed by ELSA/logit is the best when marketing around the top 20% of prospects. However, the performance of ELSA/ANN and ELSA/logit over all other target percentages was worse than that of PCA/logit. This is understandable because our solution is specifically designed to optimize at the top 20% of prospects, while PCA/logit is not designed for specific selection points. This observation leads us to do the second experiment in order to improve the performance of the ELSA/ANN model over all selection points.

Experiment 2

In this experiment, we search for the best solution that maximizes the overall accuracy up to the top 50% of potential customers. ELSA/ANN and ELSA/logit models are adjusted to maximize the overall area under the lift curve over the same intervals. In practice, we optimize over the first 25 intervals that have the same width, 2%, to approximate the area under the lift curve. Because this new experiment is computationally

Figure 3: Lift curves of three models that maximize the hit rate when targeting the top 20% of prospects.

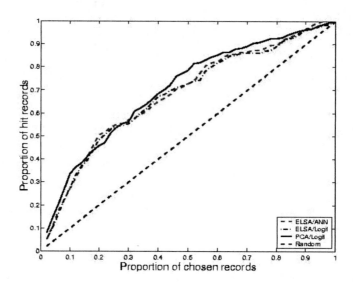

expensive, we use two-fold cross validation estimates of all solutions. We, however, set the values of the ELSA parameters with the same as in the previous experiment except $p_{max} = 200$ and $T = 500$. Based on the accuracy estimates, we choose a solution that has the highest estimated accuracy with less than half of the original features in both models. We evaluate the three models on the evaluation set and summarize the results in Table 2 and in Figure 4.

The ELSA/ANN model works better than PCA/logit and ELSA/logit over the targeting range between 15% and 50%. In particular, ELSA/ANN is best at 15%, 20%, 25%, and 50% of targeted customers, and approximately equal to the best at 30-45%. The overall performance of ELSA/logit is better than that of PCA/logit. We attribute this to the fact that solutions from both ELSA models exclude many irrelevant features. PCA/logit, however, is competitive for targeting more than 50% of the customers, since ELSA/ANN and ELSA/logit do not optimize over these ranges. Though the well-established parsimony of the ELSA/ANN models in Experiment 1 is largely lost in Experiment 2, the ELSA/ANN model is still superior to PCA/logit model in terms of the parsimony of selected features since the PCA/logit model needs the whole feature set to construct PCs.

Table 2: Summary of Experiment 2. The hit rates of three different models are shown over the top 50% of prospects

Model(# Features)	% of selected									
	5	10	15	20	25	30	35	40	45	50
PCA/logit (22)	20.06	20.06	16.04	13.63	12.44	11.20	10.81	10.22	9.87	9.38
ELSA/logit (46)	23.04	18.09	15.56	13.79	12.13	12.04	10.97	10.54	10.03	9.53
ELSA/ANN(44)	19.58	17.55	16.40	14.42	13.13	11.96	10.97	10.40	9.98	9.64

Figure 4: Lift curves of three models that maximize the area under lift curve when targeting up to top 50% of prospects.

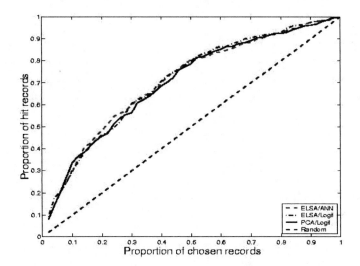

Conclusions

In this section, we presented a novel application of the multi-objective evolutionary algorithms for customer targeting. We used ELSA to search for possible combinations of features and an ANN to score customers based on the probability that they will buy the new service or product. The overall performance of ELSA/ANN in terms of accuracy was superior to the traditional method, PCA/logit, and an intermediate model, ELSA/logit. Further, the final output of the ELSA/ANN model was much easier to interpret because only a small number of features are used.

In future work, we want to investigate how more general objectives affect the parsimony of selected features. We also would like to consider a marketing campaign in a more realistic environment where various types of costs and net revenue for additional customers are considered. We could also consider budget constraints and minimum/maximum campaign sizes. This way, the number of targeted customers would be determined inside an optimization routine to maximize the expected profit.

FEATURE SELECTION IN UNSUPERVISED LEARNING

In this section, we propose a new approach to feature selection in *clustering* or unsupervised learning. This can be very useful for enhancing customer relationship management (CRM), because standard application of cluster analysis uses the complete set of features or a pre-selected subset of features based on the prior knowledge of market managers. Thus, it cannot provide new marketing models that could be effective but have not been considered. Our data-driven approach searches a much broader space of models and provides a compact summary of solutions over possible feature subset sizes and numbers of clusters. Among such high-quality solutions, the manager can select a specific model after considering the model's complexity and accuracy.

Our model is also different from other approaches (Agrawal et al., 1998; Devaney & Ram, 1997; Dy & Brodley 2000b) in two aspects: the evaluation of candidate solutions along multiple criteria, and the use of a local evolutionary algorithm to cover the space of feature subsets and of cluster numbers. Further, by identifying newly discovered feature subsets that form well-differentiated clusters, our model can affect the way new marketing campaigns should be implemented.

EM Algorithm for Finite Mixture Models

The expectation maximization algorithm (Dempster, Laird, & Rubin, 1977) is one of the most often used statistical modeling algorithms (Cheeseman & Stutz, 1996). The EM algorithm often significantly outperforms other clustering methods (Meila & Heckerman, 1998) and is superior to the distance-based algorithms (e.g., K-means) in the sense that it can handle categorical data. The EM algorithm starts with an initial estimate of the parameters and iteratively recomputes the likelihood that each pattern is drawn from a particular density function, and then updates the parameter estimates. For Gaussian distributions, the parameters are the mean μ_k and covariance matrix Σ_k. Readers who are interested in algorithm detail refer to Buhmann (1995) and Bradley, Fayyad, and Reina (1998).

In order to evaluate the quality of the clusters formed by the EM algorithm, we use three heuristic fitness criteria, described below. Each objective is normalized into the unit interval and maximized by the EA.

$F_{accuracy}$: This objective is meant to favor cluster models with parameters whose corresponding likelihood of the data given the model is higher. With estimated distribution parameters μ_k and Σ_k, $F_{accuracy}$ is computed as follows:

$$F_{accuracy} = \frac{1}{Z_{accuracy}} \sum_{n=1}^{N} \log \left(\sum_{k=1}^{K} p_k \cdot c_k (x_n \mid \mu_k, \Sigma_k) \right) \tag{6}$$

where $Z_{accuracy}$ is an empirically derived, data-dependent normalization constant meant to achieve $F_{accuracy}$ values spanning the unit interval.

$F_{clusters}$: The purpose of this objective is to favor clustering models with fewer clusters, if other things being equal.

$$F_{clusters} = 1 - (K - K_{min}) / (K_{max} - K_{min}) \tag{7}$$

where $K_{max} (K_{min})$ is the maximum (minimum) number of clusters that can be encoded into a candidate solution's representation.

$F_{complexity}$: The final objective is aimed at finding parsimonious solutions by minimizing the number of selected features:

$$F_{complexity} = 1 - (d - 1)/(D - 1). \tag{8}$$

Note that at least one feature must be used. Other things being equal, we expect that lower complexity will lead to easier interpretability and scalability of the solutions as well as better generalization.

The Wrapper Model of ELSA/EM

We first outline the model of ELSA/EM in Figure 5. In ELSA, each agent (candidate solution) in the population is first initialized with some random solution and an initial reservoir of energy. The representation of an agent consists of $(D + K_{max} - 2)$ bits. D bits correspond to the selected features (1 if a feature is selected, 0 otherwise). The remaining bits are a unary representation of the number of clusters.[6] This representation is motivated by the desire to preserve the regularity of the number of clusters under the genetic operators; changing any one bit will change K by one.

Mutation and crossover operators are used to explore the search space and are defined in the same way as in previous section. In order to assign energy to a solution, ELSA must be informed of clustering quality. In the experiments described here, the clusters to be evaluated are constructed based on the selected features using the EM algorithm. Each time a new candidate solution is evaluated, the corresponding bit string is parsed to get a feature subset J and a cluster number K. The clustering algorithm is

Figure 5: The pseudo-code of ELSA/EM.

```
initialize p_max agents, each with energy η/2;
while there are alive agents in Pop^g and t < T
       Replenishment();
       for each agent a in Pop^g
              Search & Evaluation();  Selection();  t = t+1;
       g = g+1;
endwhile

Replenishment(){
       for each energy source c ∈ {1, ..., C}
              for each v ∈ (1/B, 2/B, ..., 1)  where B is number of bins
                     E_envt^c(v) ← 2vE_tot^c;  }

Search & Evaluation() {
       a' ← mutate(crossover(a, random mate));
       for each energy source c ∈ {1, ..., C}
              v ← Fitness(a');  ΔE ← min(v,E_envt^c(v));
              E_envt^c(v) ← E_envt^c(v) - ΔE;  E_a ← E_a + ΔE;  E_a ← E_a - E_cost;  }

Selection(){
       if (E_a > η)
              insert a,a' into Pop^{g+1};  E_a' ← E_a / 2;  E_a ← E_a - E_a';
       else if (E_a > 0)
              insert a into Pop^{g+1};  }
```

given the projection of the data set onto J, uses it to form K clusters, and returns the fitness values.

Experiments on the Synthetic Data

Data set and baseline algorithm

In order to evaluate our approach, we construct a moderate-dimensional synthetic data set, in which the distributions of the points and the significant features are known, while the appropriate clusters in any given feature subspace are not known. The data set has $N = 500$ points and $D = 30$ features. It is constructed so that the first 10 features are significant, with five "true" normal clusters consistent across these features. The next 10 features are Gaussian noise, with points randomly and independently assigned to two normal clusters along each of these dimensions. The remaining 10 features are white noise. We evaluate the evolved solutions by their ability to discover five pre-constructed clusters in a 10-dimensional subspace.

We present some two-dimensional projections of the synthetic data set in Figure 6. In our experiments, individuals are represented by 36 bits— 30 for the features and 6 for K ($K_{max} = 8$). There are 15 energy bins for all energy sources, $F_{clusters}$, $F_{complexity}$, and $F_{accuracy}$. The values for the various ELSA parameters are: $\Pr(mutation) = 1.0$, $\Pr(crossover)$ $= 0.8$, $p_{max} = 100$, $E_{cost} = 0.2$, $E_{total} = 40$, $h = 0.3$, and $T = 30,000$.

Experimental results

We show the candidate fronts found by the ELSA/EM algorithm for each different number of clusters K in Figure 7.

We omit the candidate front for $K = 8$ because of its inferiority in terms of clustering quality and incomplete coverage of the search space. Composition of selected features is shown for $F_{complexity}$ corresponding to 10 features (see text).

Figure 6: A few two-dimensional projections of the synthetic data set.

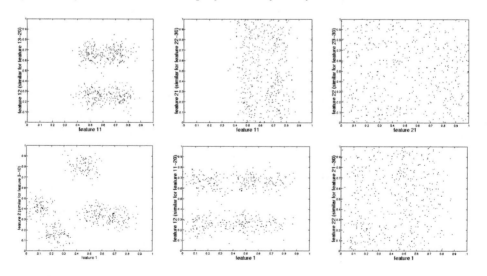

We analyze whether our ELSA/EM model is able to identify the correct number of clusters based on the shape of the candidate fronts across different values of K and $F_{accuracy}$. The shape of the Pareto fronts observed in ELSA/EM is as follows: an ascent in the range of higher values of $F_{complexity}$ (lower complexity), and a descent for lower values of $F_{complexity}$ (higher complexity). This is reasonable because adding additional significant features will have a good effect on the clustering quality with few previously selected features. However, adding noise features will have a negative effect on clustering quality in the probabilistic model, which, unlike Euclidean distance, is not affected by dimensionality. The coverage of the ELSA/EM model shown in Figure 7 is defined as:

$$\text{cov} erage_{EM} = \sum_{i \in F_{complexity}} F_{accuracy}^{i} \tag{9}$$

We note that the clustering quality and the search space coverage improve as the evolved number of clusters approaches the "true" number of clusters, $K = 5$. The candidate front for $K = 5$ not only shows the typical shape we expect, but also an overall improvement in clustering quality. The other fronts do not cover comparable ranges of the feature space either because of the agents' low $F_{clusters}$ ($K = 7$) or because of the agents' low $F_{accuracy}$ and $F_{complexity}$ ($K = 2$ and $K = 3$). A decision-maker again would conclude the right number of clusters to be five or six.

We note that the first 10 selected features, $0.69 \le F_{complexity} \le 1$, are not all significant. This notion $_{coverage}$ is again quantified through the number of significant / Gaussian noise / white noise features selected at $F_{complexity} = 0.69$ (10 features) in Figure 7.[7] None of the "white noise" features is selected. We also show snapshots of the ELSA/EM fronts for $K = 5$ at every 3,000 solution evaluations in Figure 8. ELSA/EM explores a broad subset of the search space, and thus identifies better solutions across $F_{complexity}$ as more solutions are evaluated. We observed similar results for different number of clusters K.

Figure 7: The candidate fronts of ELSA/EM model.

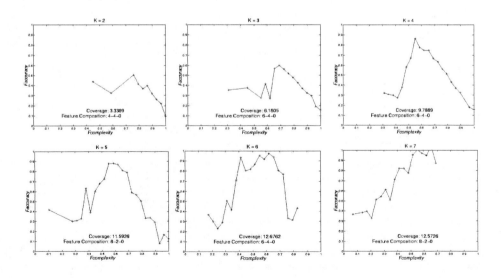

Table 3 shows classification accuracy of models formed by both ELSA/EM and the greedy search. We compute accuracy by assigning a class label to each cluster based on the majority class of the points contained in the cluster, and then computing correctness *on only those classes*, e.g., models with only two clusters are graded on their ability to find two classes. ELSA results represent individuals selected from candidate fronts with less than eight features. ELSA/EM consistently outperforms the greedy search on models with few features and few clusters. For more complex models with more than 10 selected features, the greedy method often shows higher classification accuracy.

Figure 8: Candidate fronts for K = 5 *based on* $F_{accuracy}$ *evolved in ELSA/EM. It is captured at every 3,000 solution evaluations and two fronts (t = 18,000 and t = 24,000) are omitted because they have the same shape as the ones at t = 15,000 and t = 21,000, respectively.*

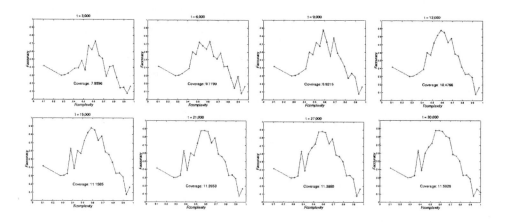

Table 3: The average classification accuracy (%) with standard error of five runs of ELSA/EM and greedy search. The "-" entry indicates that no solution is found by ELSA/ EM. The last row and column show the number of win-loss-tie (W-L-T) cases of ELSA/ EM compared with greedy search

K		Number of selected features						
		2	3	4	5	6	7	W-L-T
2	ELSA/EM	52.6±0.3	56.6±0.6	92.8±5.2	100±0.0	100±0.0	100±0.0	5-0-1
	Greedy	51.8±1.3	52.8±0.8	55.4±1.1	56.6±0.4	62.8±3.2	80.2±8.5	
3	ELSA/EM	83.2±4.8	52.0±6.6	91.6±5.7	93.8±6.2	99.0±1.0	100±0.0	4-0-2
	Greedy	40.6±0.3	40.8±0.2	40.2±0.2	63.6±3.8	100±0.0	100±0.0	
4	ELSA/EM	46.2±2.2	-	50.6±0.6	89.6±5.9	52.0±1.0	60.6±5.1	4-2-0
	Greedy	27.8±0.8	27.8±0.4	29.0±0.4	29.6±0.9	38.0±4.4	74.2±3.5	
5	ELSA/EM	44.6±2.0	32.6±3.8	72.0±3.8	62.4±1.9	66.4±3.7	88.0±4.9	5-0-1
	Greedy	23.0±0.4	22.2±0.8	24.2±0.9	23.8±0.5	29.6±1.7	81.2±3.0	
	W-L-T	3-0-1	3-1-0	4-0-0	4-0-0	3-0-1	1-1-2	18-2-4

Experiments on WPBC Data

We also tested our algorithm on a real data set, the Wisconsin Prognostic Breast Cancer (WPBC) data (Mangasarian, Street, & Wolberg, 1995). This data set records 30 numeric features quantifying the nuclear grade of breast cancer patients at the University of Wisconsin Hospital, along with two traditional prognostic variables — tumor size and number of positive lymph nodes. This results in a total of 32 features for each of 198 cases. For the experiment, individuals are represented by 38 bits— 32 for the features and 6 for K (K_{max} = 8). Other ELSA parameters are the same as those used in the previous experiments.

We analyzed performance on this data set by looking for clinical relevance in the resulting clusters. Specifically, we observe the actual outcome (time to recurrence, or known disease-free time) of the cases in the three clusters. Figure 9 shows the survival characteristics of three prognostic groups found by ELSA/EM. The three groups showed well-separated survival characteristics. Out of 198 patients, 59, 54, and 85 patients belong to the good, intermediate, and poor prognostic groups, respectively. The good prognostic group was welldifferentiated from the intermediate group (p < 0.076), and the intermediate group was significantly different from the poor group (p < 0.036). Five-year recurrence rates were 12.61%, 21.26%, and 39.85% for the patients in the three groups. The chosen dimensions by ELSA/EM included a mix of nuclear morphometric features, such as the mean and the standard error of the radius, perimeter, and area, and the largest value of the area and symmetry along three other features.

We note that neither of the traditional medical prognostic factors— tumor size and lymph node status— is chosen. This finding is potentially important because the lymph node status can be determined only after lymph nodes are surgically removed from the patient's armpit (Street, Mangasarian, & Wolberg, 1995). We further investigate whether other solutions with lymph node information can form three prognostic groups as good as our EM solution.

Figure 9: Estimated survival curves for the three groups found by ELSA/EM.

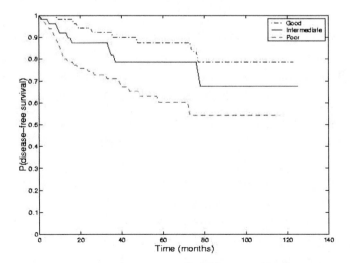

For this purpose, we selected Pareto solutions across all different K values that have fewer than 10 features including lymph node information, and formed three clusters using these selected features, disregarding the evolved value of K. The survival characteristics of the three prognostic groups found by the best of these solutions were very competitive with our chosen solution. The good prognostic group was welldifferentiated from the intermediate group ($p < 0.10$), and the difference between the intermediate group and the poor group was significant ($p < 0.026$). This suggests that lymph node status may indeed have strong prognostic effects, even though it is excluded from the best models evolved by our algorithms.

Conclusions

In this section, we presented a new ELSA/EM algorithm for unsupervised feature selection. Our ELSA/EM model outperforms a greedy algorithm in terms of classification accuracy while considering a number of possibly conflicting heuristic metrics. Most importantly, our model can reliably select an appropriate clustering model, including significant features and the number of clusters.

In future work, we would like to compare the performance of ELSA on the unsupervised feature selection task with other multi-objective EAs, using each in conjunction with clustering algorithms. Another promising future direction will be a direct comparison of different clustering algorithms in terms of the composition of selected features and prediction accuracy.

FEATURE SELECTION FOR ENSEMBLES

In this section, we propose a new meta-ensembles algorithm to directly optimize ensembles by creating a two-level evolutionary environment. In particular, we employ feature selection not only to increase the prediction accuracy of an individual classifier, but also to promote diversity among component classifiers in an ensemble (Opitz, 1999).

Feature Selection and Ensembles

Recently, many researchers have combined the predictions of multiple classifiers to produce a better classifier, an ensemble, and often have reported improved performance (Bauer & Kohavi, 1999; Breiman, 1996b). Bagging (Breiman, 1996a) and Boosting (Freund & Schapire, 1996) are the most popular methods for creating accurate ensembles. The effectiveness of Bagging and Boosting comes primarily from the diversity caused by resampling training examples while using the complete set of features to train component classifiers.

Recently, several attempts have been made to incorporate the diversity in feature dimension into ensemble methods. The Random Subspace Method (RSM) in Ho (1998a & 1998b) was one early algorithm that constructed an ensemble by varying the feature subset. RSM used C4.5 as a base classifier and randomly chose half of the original features to build each classifier. In Guerra-Salcedo and Whitley(1999), four different ensemble methods were paired with each of three different feature selection algorithms: complete, random, and genetic search. Using two table-based classification methods, ensembles constructed using features selected by the GA showed the best performance. In Cunningham and Carney (2000), a new entropy measure of the outputs of the component classifiers was used to explicitly measure the ensemble diversity and to produce good feature subsets for ensemble using hill-climbing search.

Genetic Ensemble Feature Selection (GEFS) (Opitz, 1999) used a GA to search for possible feature subsets. GEFS starts with an initial population of classifiers built using up to $2D$ features, where D is the complete feature dimension. It is possible for some features to be selected more than once in GEFS, and crossover and mutation operators are used to search for new feature subsets. Using 100 most-fit members with majority voting scheme, GEFS reported better estimated generalization than Bagging and AdaBoost on about two-thirds of 21 data sets tested. Longer chromosomes, however, make GEFS computationally expensive in terms of memory usage (Guerra-Salcedo & Whitley, 1999). Further, GEFS evaluates each classifier after combining two objectives in a subjective manner using *fitness* = *accuracy* + λ *diversity*, where *diversity* is the average difference between the prediction of component classifiers and the ensemble.

However, all these methods consider only one ensemble. We propose a new algorithm for ensemble feature selection, Meta-Evolutionary Ensembles (MEE), that considers multiple ensembles simultaneously and allows each component classifier to move into the best-fit ensemble. We evaluate and reward each classifier based on two different criteria, accuracy and diversity. A classifier that correctly predicts data examples that other classifiers in the same ensemble misclassify contributes more to the accuracy of the ensemble to which it belongs. We imagine that some limited "energy" is evenly distributed among the examples in the data set. Each classifier is rewarded with some portion of the energy if it correctly predicts an example. The more classifiers that correctly classify a specific example, the less energy is rewarded to each, encouraging them to correctly predict the more difficult examples. The predictive accuracy of each ensemble determines the total amount of energy to be replenished at each generation. Finally, we select the ensemble with the highest accuracy as our final model.

Meta-Evolutionary Ensembles

Pseudocode for the Meta-Evolutionary Ensembles (MEE) algorithm is shown in Figure 10, and a graphical depiction of the energy allocation scheme is shown in Figure 11.

Each agent (candidate solution) in the population is first initialized with randomly selected features, a random ensemble assignment, and an initial reservoir of energy. The representation of an agent consists of $D + log_2(G)$ bits. D bits correspond to the selected features (1 if a feature is selected, 0 otherwise). The remaining bits are a binary representation of the ensemble index, where G is the maximum number of ensembles. Mutation and crossover operators are used to explore the search space and are defined in the same way as in previous section.

In each iteration of the algorithm, an agent explores a candidate solution (classifier) similar to itself, obtained via crossover and mutation. The agent's bit string is parsed to get a feature subset J. An ANN is then trained on the projection of the data set onto J, and returns

Figure 10: Pseudo-code of Meta-Evolutionary Ensembles (MEE) algorithm.

```
initialize population of agents, each with energy θ/2
while there are alive agents in Pop^i and i < T
    for each ensemble g
        for each record r in Data_test
            prevCount_{g,r} = count_{g,r};  count_{g,r} = 0;
        for each agent a in Pop^i
            a' = mutate(crossover(a, randomMate));
            g = group(a);
            train(a);
            for each record r in Data_test
                if (class(r) == prediction(r,a))
                    count_{g,r}++;  ΔE = E_envt^{g,r} / min(5, prevCount_{g,r});
                    E_envt^{g,r} = E_envt^{g,r} - ΔE;  E_a = E_a + ΔE;
            E_a = E_a - E_cost;
            if (E_a > θ)
                insert a, a' into Pop^{i+1};  E_{a'} = E_a / 2;  E_a = E_a - E_{a'};
            else if (E_a > 0)
                insert a into Pop^{i+1};
    for each ensemble g
        replenish energy based on predictive accuracy;
    i = i+1;
endwhile
```

Figure 11: Graphical depiction of energy allocation in the MEE. Individual classifiers (small boxes in the environment) receive energy by correctly classifying test points. Energy for each ensemble is replenished between generations based on the accuracy of the ensemble. Ensembles with higher accuracy have their energy bins replenished with more energy per classifier, as indicated by the varying widths of the bins.

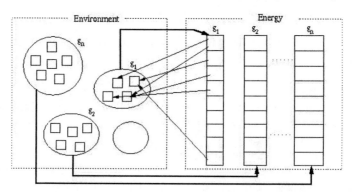

the predicted class labels for the test examples. The agent collects ΔE from each example it correctly classifies, and is taxed once with E_{cost}. The net energy intake of an agent is determined by its classification accuracy. But the energy also depends on the state of the environment. We have an energy source for each ensemble, divided into bins corresponding to each data point. For ensemble g and record index r in the test data, the environment keeps track of energy $E_{envt}^{g,r}$ and the number of agents in ensemble g, $count_{g,r}$ that correctly predict record r. The energy received by an agent for each correctly classified record r is given by

$$\Delta E = E_{envt}^{g,r} / min(5, prevCount_{g,r}). \tag{10}$$

An agent receives greater reward for correctly predicting an example that most in its ensemble get wrong. The *min* function ensures that for a given point there is enough energy to reward at least five agents in the new generation. Candidate solutions receive energy only inasmuch as the environment has sufficient resources; if these are depleted, no benefits are available until the environmental resources are replenished. Thus, an agent is rewarded with energy for its high fitness values, but also has an interest in finding unpopulated niches, where more energy is available. The result is a natural bias toward diverse solutions in the population. E_{cost} for any action is a constant ($E_{cost} < \theta$).

In the selection part of the algorithm, an agent compares its current energy level with a constant reproduction threshold θ. If its energy is higher than θ, the agent reproduces; the agent and its mutated clone become part of the new population, with the offspring receiving half of its parent's energy. If the energy level of an agent is positive but lower than θ, only that agent joins the new population.

The environment for each ensemble is replenished with energy based on its predictive accuracy, as determined by majority voting with equal weight among base classifiers. We sort the ensembles in ascending order of estimated accuracy and apportion energy in linear proportion to that accuracy, so that the most accurate ensemble is replenished with the greatest amount of energy per base classifier. Since the total amount of energy replenished also depends on the number of agents in each ensemble, it is possible that an ensemble with lower accuracy can be replenished with more energy in total than an ensemble with higher accuracy.

Experimental Results

Experimental results of MEE/ANN

We tested the performance of MEE combined with neural networks on several data sets that were used in Opitz(1999). In our experiments, the weights and biases of the neural networks are initialized randomly between 0.5 and -0.5, and the number of hidden nodes is determined heuristically as the square root of *inputs*. The other parameters for the neural networks include a learning rate of 0.1 and a momentum rate of 0.9. The number of training epochs was kept small for computational reasons. The values for the various parameters are: Pr(*mutation*) = 1.0, Pr(*crossover*) = 0.8, E_{cost} = 0.2, q = 0.3, and T = 30. The value of E_{envt}^{tot} = 30 is chosen to maintain a population size around 100 classifier agents.

Experimental results are shown in Table 4. All computational results for MEE are based on the performance of the best ensemble and are averaged over five standard 10-

Table 4: Experimental results of MEE/ANN

Data sets	Single net		Bagging	AdaBoost	GEFS	MEE		
	Avg.	S.D.				Avg.	S.D.	Epochs
Credita	84.3	0.30	86.2	84.3	86.8	86.4	0.52	40
Creditg	71.7	0.43	75.8	74.7	75.2	75.6	0.78	50
Diabetes	76.4	0.93	77.2	76.7	77.0	76.8	0.42	50
Glass	57.1	2.69	66.9	68.9	69.6	61.1	1.73	100
Cleveland	80.7	1.83	83.0	78.9	83.9	83.3	1.54	50
Hepatitis	81.5	0.21	82.2	80.3	83.3	84.9	0.65	40
Votes-84	95.9	0.41	95.9	94.7	95.6	96.1	0.44	40
Hypo	93.8	0.09	93.8	93.8	94.1	93.9	0.06	50
Ionosphere	89.3	0.85	90.8	91.7	94.6	93.5	0.81	100
Iris	95.9	1.10	96.0	96.1	96.7	96.5	0.73	100
Krvskp	98.8	0.63	99.2	99.7	99.3	99.3	0.10	50
Labor	91.6	2.29	95.8	96.8	96.5	94.4	0.78	50
Segment	92.3	0.97	94.6	96.7	96.4	93.2	0.28	50
Sick	95.2	0.47	94.3	95.5	96.5	99.3	0.03	50
Sonar	80.5	2.03	83.2	87.0	82.2	85.2	1.57	100
Soybean	92.0	0.92	93.1	93.7	94.1	93.8	0.19	50
Vehicle	74.7	0.48	79.3	80.3	81.0	76.4	1.12	50
Win-loss-tie	15-0-2		7-4-6	9-6-2	4-7-6			

fold cross-validation experiments. Within the training algorithm, each ANN is trained on two-thirds of the training set and tested on the remaining third for energy allocation purposes. We present the performance of a single neural network using the complete set of features as a baseline algorithm. In the win-loss-tie results shown at the bottom of Table 4, a comparison is considered a tie if the intervals defined by one standard error[8] of the mean overlap. Of the data sets tested, MEE shows consistent improvement over a single neural network.

We also include the results of Bagging, AdaBoost, and GEFS from Opitz (1999) for indirect comparison. In these comparisons, we did not have access to the accuracy results of the individual runs. Therefore, a tie is conservatively defined as a test in which the one standard-deviation interval of our test contained the point estimate of accuracy from Opitz(1999). In terms of predictive accuracy, our algorithm demonstrates better or equal performance compared to single neural networks, Bagging and Boosting. However, MEE shows slightly worse performance compared to GEFS, possibly due to the methodological differences. For example, it is possible that the more complex structure of neural networks used in GEFS can learn more difficult patterns in data sets such as Glass and Labor data.

From the perspective of computational complexity, our algorithm can be very slow compared to Bagging and Boosting. However, MEE can be very fast compared to GEFS, because GEFS uses twice as many as input features as MEE. Further, the larger number of hidden nodes and longer training epochs can make GEFS extremely slow.

Guidelines toward optimized ensemble construction

In this section, we use MEE to examine ensemble characteristics and provide some guidelines for building optimal ensembles. We expect that by optimizing the ensemble construction process, MEE will in general achieve comparable accuracy to other methods using fewer individuals. We use data collected from the first fold of the first cross-validation routine for the following analyses.

We first investigate whether the ensemble size is positively related with the predictive accuracy. It has been well established that, to a certain degree, the predictive accuracy of an ensemble improves as the number of classifiers in the ensemble increases. For example, our result in Figure 12 indicates that accuracy improvements flatten out at an ensemble size of approximately 15-25. We also investigate whether the diversity among classifiers is positively related with the ensemble's classification performance. In our experiments, we measured the diversity based on the difference of predicted class between each classifier and the ensemble. We first define a new operator $\oplus$ as follows: $\alpha \oplus \beta = 0$ if $\alpha = \beta$, 1 otherwise. When an ensemble e consists of g classifiers, the diversity of ensemble e, $diversity^e$, is defined as follows:

$$diversity^e = \frac{\sum_{i=1}^{g}\sum_{j=1}^{N}(pred_j^i \oplus pred_j^e)}{g \cdot N} \qquad (11)$$

where N is the number of records in the test data and $pred_j^i$ and $pred_j^e$ represent the predicted class label for record j by classifier i and ensemble e respectively. The larger the value of $diversity^e$, the more diverse the ensemble is.

We show the relationship between the predictive accuracy and ensemble diversity in Figure 12. This shows the expected positive relationship between accuracy and diversity. However, our results show that too much diversity among classifiers can deteriorate ensemble performance, as the final decision made by ensemble becomes a random guess.

Figure 12: The relationship between the predictive accuracy and ensemble size (left), and between the predictive accuracy and ensemble diversity (right) with 95% confidence interval on the Soybean data. We observed similar patterns on other data sets.

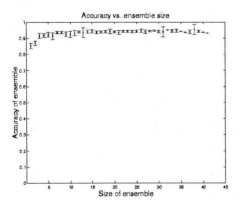 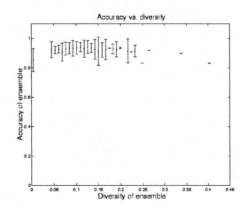

Conclusions

In this section, we propose a new two-level ensemble construction algorithm, Meta-Evolutionary Ensembles (MEE), that uses feature selection as the diversity mechanism. At the first level, individual classifiers compete against each other to correctly predict held-out examples. Classifiers are rewarded for predicting difficult points, relative to the other members of their respective ensembles. At the top level, the ensembles compete directly based on classification accuracy.

Our model shows consistently improved classification performance compared to a single classifier at the cost of computational complexity. Compared to the traditional ensembles (Bagging and Boosting) and GEFS, our resulting ensemble shows comparable performance while maintaining a smaller ensemble. Further, our two-level evolutionary framework confirms that more diversity among classifiers can improve predictive accuracy. Up to a certain level, the ensemble size also has a positive effect on the ensemble performance.

The next step is to compare this algorithm more rigorously to others on a larger collection of data sets, and perform any necessary performance tweaks on the EA energy allocation scheme. This new experiment is to test the claim that there is relatively little room for other ensembles algorithm to obtain further improvement over decision forest method (Breiman, 1999). Along the way, we will examine the role of various characteristics of ensembles (size, diversity, etc.) and classifiers (type, number of dimensions/data points, etc.). By giving the system as many degrees of freedom as possible and observing the characteristics that lead to successful ensembles, we can directly optimize these characteristics and translate the results to a more scalable architecture (Street & Kim, 2001) for large-scale predictive tasks.

CONCLUSIONS

In this chapter, we proposed a new framework for feature selection in supervised and unsupervised learning. In particular, we note that each feature subset should be evaluated in terms of multiple objectives. In supervised learning, ELSA with neural networks model (ELSA/ANN) was used to search for possible combinations of features and to score customers based on the probability of buying new insurance product respectively. The ELSA/ANN model showed promising results in two different experiments, when market managers have clear decision scenario or when they don't. ELSA was also used for unsupervised feature selection. Our algorithm, ELSA/EM, outperforms a greedy algorithm in terms of classification accuracy. Most importantly, in the proposed framework we can reliably select an appropriate clustering model, including significant features and the number of clusters.

We also proposed a new ensemble construction algorithm, Meta-Evolutionary Ensembles (MEE), where feature selection is used as the diversity mechanism among classifiers in the ensemble. In MEE, classifiers are rewarded for predicting difficult points, relative to the other members of their respective ensembles. Our experimental results indicate that this method shows consistently improved performance compared to a single classifier and the traditional ensembles.

One major direction of future research on the feature selection with ELSA is to find a way to boost the weak selection pressure of ELSA while keeping its local selection mechanism. For problems requiring effective selection pressure, local selection may be too weak because the only selection pressure that ELSA can apply comes from the sharing of resources. Dynamically adjusting the local environmental structure based on the certain ranges of the observed fitness values over a fixed number of generations could be a promising solution. In this way, we could avoid the case in which the solution with the worst performance can survive into the next generation because there are no other solutions in its local environment.

Another major direction of future research is related with the scalability issue. By minimizing the communication among agents, our local selection mechanism makes ELSA efficient and scalable. However, our models suffer the inherent weakness of the wrapper model, the computational complexity. Further by combining EAs with ANN to take the advantages of both algorithms, it is possible that the combined model can be so slow that it cannot provide solutions in a timely manner. With the rapid growth of records and variables in database, this failure can be critical. Combining ELSA with faster learning algorithms such as decision tree algorithms and Support Vector Machine (SVM) will be worth pursuing.

ENDNOTES

[1]   Continuous objective functions are discretized.

[2]   This is one of main tasks in the 2000 CoIL challenge (Kim & Street, 2000). For more information about CoIL challenges and the data sets, please refer to *http:// www.dcs.napier.ac.uk/coil/challenge/*.

[3]   If other objective values are equal, we prefer to choose a solution with small variance.

[4]   This is reasonable because as we select more prospects, the expected accuracy gain will go down. If the marginal revenue from an additional prospect is much greater than the marginal cost, however, we could sacrifice the expected accuracy gain. Information on mailing cost and customer value was not available in this study.

[5]   The other four features selected by the ELSA/logit model are: contribution to bicycle policy, fire policy, number of trailer, and lorry policies.

[6]   The cases of zero or one cluster are meaningless, therefore we count the number of clusters as $K = \kappa + 2$ where κ is the number of ones and $K_{min} = 2 \leq K \leq K_{max}$.

[7]   For $K = 2$, we use $F_{complexity} = 0.76$, which is the closest value to 0.69 represented in the front.

[8]   In our experiments, standard error is computed as standard deviation / $iter^{0.5}$ where $iter = 5$.

REFERENCES

Agrawal, R., Gehrke, J., Gunopulos, D., & Raghavan, P. (1998). Automatic subspace clustering of high dimensional data for data mining applications. In *Proceedings of the ACM SIGMOD Int'l Conference on Management of Data*, pp. 94-105, Seattle, WA.

Bauer, E. & Kohavi, R. (1999). An empirical comparison of voting classification algorithms: Bagging, boosting, and variants. *Machine Learning*, 36:105-139.

Bradley, P. S., Fayyad, U. M., & Reina, C. (1998). Scaling EM (expectation-maximization) clustering to large databases. Technical Report MSR-TR-98-35, Microsoft, Redmond, WA.

Breiman, L. (1996a). Bagging predictors. *Machine Learning*, 24(2):123-140.

Breiman, L. (1996b). Bias, variance, and arching classifiers. Technical Report 460, University of California, Department of Statistics, Berkeley, CA.

Breiman, L. (1999). Random forests-Random features. Technical Report 567, University of California, Department of Statistics, Berkeley, CA.

Buhmann, J. (1995). Data clustering and learning. In Arbib, M. (ed.), *Handbook of Brain Theory and Neural Networks*. Cambridge, MA: Bradfort Books/MIT Press.

Cheeseman, P. & Stutz, J. (1996). Bayesian classification system (AutoClass): Theory and results. In U. Fayyad, G. Piatetsky-Shapiro, P. Smyth, & R. Uthurusamy (eds.), *Advances in Knowledge Discovery and Data Mining*, pp. 153-180, San Francisco: AAAI/MIT Press.

Chen, S., Guerra-Salcedo, C., & Smith, S. (1999). Non-standard crossover for a standard representation - Commonality-based feature subset selection. In *Proceedings of the Genetic and Evolutionary Computation Conference*, pp. 129-134. San Francisco: Morgan Kaufmann.

Cunningham, P. & Carney, J. (2000). Diversity versus quality in classification ensembles based on feature selection. Technical Report TCD-CS-2000-02, Trinity College, Department of Computer Science, Dublin, Ireland.

Dempster, A. P., Laird, N. M., & Rubin, D. B. (1977). Maximum likelihood from incomplete data via the EM algorithm. *Journal of the Royal Statistical Society, Series B*, 39(1):1-38.

Devaney, M. & Ram, A. (1997). Efficient feature selection in conceptual clustering. In *Proceedings of the 14th Int'l Conference on Machine Learning*, pp. 92-97. San Francisco: Morgan Kaufmann.

Dy, J. G. & Brodley, C. E. (2000a). Feature subset selection and order identification for unsupervised learning. In *Proceedings of the 17th Int'l Conference on Machine Learning*, pp. 247-254. San Francisco: Morgan Kaufmann.

Dy, J. G. & Brodley, C. E. (2000b). Visualization and interactive feature selection for unsupervised data. In *Proceedings of the 6th ACM SIGKDD Int'l Conference on Knowledge Discovery & Data Mining (KDD-00)*, pp. 360-364, ACM Press.

Freund, Y. & Schapire, R. (1996). Experiments with a new boosting algorithm. In *Proceedings of the 13th Int'l Conference on Machine Learning*, pp. 148-156, Bari, Italy, Morgan Kaufmann.

Goldberg, D. E. & Richardson, J. (1987). Genetic algorithms with sharing for multimodal function optimization. In *Proceedings of the 2nd International Conference on Genetic Algorithms*, pp. 41-49. Hillsdale, NJ: Lawrence Erlbaum.

Guerra-Salcedo, C. & Whitley, D. (1999). Genetic approach to feature selection for ensemble creation. In *GECCO-99: Proceedings of the Genetic and Evolutionary Computation Conference*, pp. 236-243. San Francisco: Morgan Kaufmann.

Ho, T. K. (1998a). C4.5 decision forests. In *Proceedings of the 14th International Conference on Pattern Recognition*, IEEE Computer Society, pp. 545-549.

Ho, T. K. (1998b). The random subspace method for constructing decision forests. *IEEE Transactions on Pattern Analysis and Machine Intelligence*, 20(8):832-844.

Horn, J. (1997). Multi-criteria decision making and evolutionary computation. In T. Back, D. B. Fogel & Z. Michaelevicz (Eds.), *Handbook of Evolutionary Computation*. London: Institute of Physics Publishing.

Kim, Y. & Street, W. N. (2000). CoIL challenge 2000: Choosing and explaining likely caravan insurance customers. Technical Report 2000-09, Sentient Machine Research and Leiden Institute of Advanced Computer Science. *http://www.wi.leidenuniv.nl/~putten/library/cc2000/*.

Mangasarian, O. L., Street, W. N., & Wolberg, W. H. (1995). Breast cancer diagnosis and prognosis via linear programming. *Operations Research*, 43(4):570-577.

Meila, M. & Heckerman, D. (1998). An experimental comparison of several clustering methods. Technical Report MSR-TR-98-06, Microsoft, Redmond, WA.

Menczer, F. & Belew, R. K. (1996). From complex environments to complex behaviors. *Adaptive Behavior*, 4:317-363.

Menczer, F., Degeratu, M., & Street, W. N. (2000). Efficient and scalable Pareto optimization by evolutionary local selection algorithms. *Evolutionary Computation*, 8(2):223-247.

Menczer, F., Street, W. N., & Degeratu, M. (2000). Evolving heterogeneous neural agents by local selection. In V. Honavar, M. Patel & K. Balakrishnan(eds.), *Advances in the Evolutionary Synthesis of Intelligent Agents*. Cambridge, MA: MIT Press.

Opitz, D. (1999). Feature selection for ensembles. In *Proceedings of the 16th National Conference on Artificial Intelligence (AAAI)*, pp. 379-384, Orlando, FL, AAAI.

Street, W. N. & Kim, Y. (2001). A streaming ensemble algorithm (SEA) for large-scale classification. In *Proceedings of the 7th ACM SIGKDD International Conference on Knowledge Discovery & Data Mining (KDD-01)*, pp.377-382, ACM Press.

Street, W. N., Mangasarian, O. L., & Wolberg, W. H. (1995). An inductive learning approach to prognostic prediction. In A. Prieditis & S. Russell(eds.), *Proceedings of the 12th International Conference on Machine Learning*, pp. 522-530, San Francisco: Morgan Kaufmann.

Van Veldhuizen, D. A. (1999). *Multiobjective evolutionary algorithms: Classifications, analyses, and new innovations*. PhD thesis, Air Force Institute of Technology.

Chapter V

Parallel and Distributed Data Mining through Parallel Skeletons and Distributed Objects

Massimo Coppola
University of Pisa, Italy

Marco Vanneschi
University of Pisa, Italy

ABSTRACT

We consider the application of parallel programming environments to develop portable and efficient high performance data mining (DM) tools. We first assess the need of parallel and distributed DM applications, by pointing out the problems of scalability of some mining techniques and the need to mine large, eventually geographically distributed databases. We discuss the main issues of exploiting parallel and distributed computation for DM algorithms. A high-level programming language enhances the software engineering aspects of parallel DM, and it simplifies the problems of integration with existing sequential and parallel data management systems, thus leading to programming-efficient and high-performance implementations of applications. We describe a programming environment we have implemented that is based on the parallel skeleton model, and we examine the addition of object-like interfaces toward external libraries and system software layers. This kind of abstractions will be included in the forthcoming programming environment ASSIST. In the main part of the chapter, as a proof-of-concept we describe three well-known DM algorithms, Apriori, C4.5, and DBSCAN. For each problem, we explain the sequential algorithm and a structured parallel version, which is discussed and compared to parallel solutions found in the literature. We also discuss the potential gain in performance and expressiveness from the addition of external objects on the basis of the experiments we performed so far. We evaluate the approach with respect to performance results, design, and implementation considerations.

INTRODUCTION

The field of knowledge discovery in databases, or *Data Mining* (DM), has evolved in the recent past to address the problem of automatic analysis and interpretation of larger and larger amounts of data. Different methods from fields such as machine learning, statistics, and databases, just to name a few, have been applied to extract knowledge from databases of unprecedented size, resulting in severe performance and scalability issues. As a consequence, a whole new branch of research is developing that aims to exploit parallel and distributed computation in the computationally hard part of the mining task. The parallelization of DM algorithms, in order to find patterns in terabyte datasets in real-time, has to confront many combined problems and constraints, e.g., the irregular, speculative nature of most DM algorithms, data physical management, and issues typical of parallel and distributed programming, like load balancing and algorithm decomposition. Fast DM of large or distributed data sets is needed for practical applications, so the quest is not simply for parallel algorithms of theoretical interest. To efficiently support the whole knowledge discovery process, we need high-performance applications that are easy to develop, easy to migrate to different architectures, and easy to integrate with other software. We foster the use of high-level parallel programming environments to develop portable and efficient high-performance DM tools. An essential aspect of our work is the use of structured parallelism, which requires the definition of the parallel aspects of programs by means of a fixed, formal definition language. High-level parallel languages of this kind shelter the application programmer from the low-level details of parallelism exploitation, in the same way that structured sequential programming separates the complexity of hardware and firmware programming models from sequential algorithm design. Structured parallel languages are a tool to simplify and streamline the design and implementation of parallel programs.

A common issue in DM and in high-performance computing is the need to efficiently deal with a huge amount of data in complex memory hierarchies. Managing huge input data and intermediate results in the former case, and avoiding excessive amounts of communications in the latter case, highly complicate the algorithms and their implementation. Even if current research trends aim at pushing more and more of the mining task into the database management support (DBMS), and at developing massively parallel DBMS support, the problem of scaling up such support beyond the limits of shared-memory multiprocessors is yet to be solved. In our view, high-level programming environments can also provide a higher degree of encapsulation for complex data management routines, which at run-time exploit the best in-core and out-of-core techniques, or interface to existing, specialized software support for the task. The enhanced interoperability with existing software is definitely a great advantage in developing high-performance, integrated DM applications. We will sustain our perspective by showing how to apply a structured parallel programming methodology based on skeletons to DM problems, also reporting test results about commonly used DM techniques, namely association rules, decision tree induction, and spatial clustering.

In the first part of the chapter, we provide a background about parallel DM and parallel programming. The following section analyzes the general problems of DM algorithms, discussing why parallel and distributed computation are needed, and what are the advantages and issues they bring us. The integration issues with other applications and with DBMS supports are especially important. Two sections recall the structured parallel programming approach and its application within the skeleton language of the SkIE environment. One more section is devoted to the problems coming from explicit management of the memory hierarchy. The first part of the chapter ends with the proposal of a common interface from parallel applications to external services, based on the object abstraction. We discuss the advantages that this new feature brings in terms of enhanced modularity of code, and the ability to interface with different data management software layers. The experiences made with the development of SkIE and of this kind of language extensions will be used in the design of the second-generation structured parallel language called ASSIST.

In the second part of the chapter, we show three well-known DM algorithms and their skeleton implementation. We discuss association rule mining, classification ,and clustering in three sections, according to a common presentation outline. We define each one of the DM problems, and we present a sequential algorithm that solves it. They are respectively Apriori, C4.5, and DBSCAN. We explain how the algorithm can be made parallel and its expected performance, discussing related approaches in the literature. We present skeleton structures that implement the parallel algorithm and describe its characteristics. The structured parallel C4.5 also uses a first prototype of external object library. A final section reports test results performed with real applications implemented with SkIE over a range of parallel architectures. To assess the performance and portability aspects of the methodology, we discuss the development costs of the prototypes. We conclude by pointing out future developments and open research issues.

PARALLEL AND DISTRIBUTED DATA MINING

The need for high-performance DM techniques grows as the size of electronic archives becomes larger. Some databases are also naturally distributed over several different sites, and cannot always be centralized to perform the DM tasks for cost reasons or because of practical and legal restrictions to data communication. *Parallel data mining* (PDM) and *distributed data mining* (DDM) are two closely related research fields aiming at the solution of scale and performance problems. We summarize the advantages they offer, looking at similarities and differences between the two approaches.

PDM essentially deals with parallel systems that are tightly coupled. Among the architectures in this class, we find *shared memory multiprocessors* (SMP), distributed memory architectures, clusters of SMP machines, or large clusters with high-speed interconnection networks. DDM, on the contrary, concentrates on loosely coupled systems such as clusters of workstations connected by a slow LAN, geographically distributed sites over a wide area network, or even computational grid resources. The common advantages that parallel and distributed DM offer come from the removal of sequential architecture bottlenecks. We get higher I/O bandwidth, larger memory, and computational power than the limits of existing sequential systems, all these factors leading to lower response times and improved scalability to larger data sets. The common drawback is that algorithm and application design becomes more complex in order to enjoy higher performance. We need to devise algorithms and techniques that distribute the I/O and the computation in parallel, minimizing communication and data transfers to avoid wasting resources. There is of course a part of the theory and of the techniques that is common to the distributed and parallel fields.

In this view, PDM has its central target in the exploitation of massive and possibly fine-grained parallelism, paying closer attention to work synchronization and load balancing, and exploiting high-performance I/O subsystems where available. PDM applications deal with large and hard problems, and they are typically designed for intensive mining of centralized archives.

By contrast, DDM techniques use a coarser computation grain and loose hypotheses on interconnection networks. DDM techniques are often targeted at distributed databases, where data transfers are minimized or replaced by moving results in the form of intermediate or final knowledge models. A widespread approach is independent learning integrated with summarization and meta-learning techniques. The two fields of PDM and DDM are not rigidly separated, however. Often the distinction between fine-grained, highly synchronized parallelism, and coarse-grained parallelism gets blurred, depending on problem characteristics, because massively parallel architectures and large, loosely coupled clusters of sequential machines can be seen as extremes of a range of architectures that have progressively changing nature. Actually, high-performance computer architectures become more and more parallel, and it is definitely realistic to study geographically distributed DDM algorithms where the local task is performed by a PDM algorithm on a parallel machine.

Integration of Parallel Tools into Data Mining Environments

It is now recognized that a crucial issue in the effectiveness of DM tools is the degree of interoperability with conventional databases, data warehouses and OLAP services. Maniatty and Zaki (2000) state several requirements for parallel DM systems, and the issues related to the integration are clearly underlined. They call *System Transparency* the ability to easily exploit file-system access as well as databases and data warehouses. This feature is not only a requirement of tool interoperability, but also an option to exploit the best software support available in different situations. Most mining algorithms, especially the parallel ones, are designed for *flat-file mining*. While this simplification eases initial code development, it imposes an overhead when working with higher-level data management supports (e.g., data dumping to flat files and view materialization from DBMS). Industry standards are being developed to address this issue in the sequential setting, and research is ongoing about the parallel case (see for instance the book by Freitas and Lavington, 1998). We can distinguish three main approaches:

- Development of DM algorithms based on existing standard interfaces (e.g., SQL). Many algorithms have been rewritten or designed to work by means of DBMS primitives. DBSCAN is designed assuming the use of a spatial database system.

- Development of a few new database-mining primitives within the frame of standard DBMS languages (a crucial issue is the expressive power that we may gain or lose).
- Design of dedicated, possibly parallel mining interfaces to allow tight integration of the mining process with the data management.

Pushing more of the computational effort into the data management support means exploiting the internal parallelism of modern database servers. On the other hand, scalability of such servers to massive parallelism is still a matter of research. While integration solutions are now emerging for sequential DM, this is not yet the case for parallel algorithms.

The bandwidth of I/O subsystems in parallel architectures is theoretically much higher than that of sequential ones, but a conventional file system or DBMS interface cannot easily exploit it. We need to use new software supports that are still far from being standards, and sometimes are architecture-specific. Parallel file systems, high-performance interfaces to parallel database servers are important resources to exploit for PDM. DDM must also take into account remote data servers, data transport layers, computational grid resources, and all the issues about security, availability, and fault tolerance that are commonplace for large distributed systems. Our approach is to develop a parallel programming environment that addresses the problem of parallelism exploitation within algorithms, while offering uniform interfacing characteristics with respect to different software and hardware resources for data management. Structured parallelism will be used to express the algorithmic parallelism, while an object-like interface will allow access to a number of useful services in a portable way, including other applications and CORBA-operated software.

STRUCTURED PARALLEL PROGRAMMING

Parallel programming exploits multiple computational resources in a coordinated effort to solve large and hard problems. In all but the really trivial cases, the classical problems of algorithm decomposition, load distribution, load balancing, and communication minimization have to be solved. Dealing directly with the degree of complexity given by communication management, concurrent behavior and architecture characteristics lead to programs that are error prone, difficult to debug and understand, and usually need complex performance tuning when ported to different architectures. The *restricted* approach to parallel programming takes into account these software engineering issues (Skillicorn & Talia, 1998). Restricted languages impose expressive constraints to the parallelism allowed in programs, which has to be defined using a given formalism. Requiring the explicit description of the parallel structure of programs leads to enhanced programmability, to higher semantics clearness, and to easier correctness verification. Compilation tools can take advantage of the explicit structure, resulting in more efficient compilation and automatic optimization of code. Porting sequential applications to parallel can proceed by progressive characterization of independent blocks of operations in the algorithm. They are moved to separate modules or code sections, which become the basic components of a high-level description. Prototype development and refinement is thus much faster than it is with low-level programming languages.

The SkIE programming environment (Vanneschi, 1998b) belongs to this line of research. There is, of course, not enough space here to describe in full detail all the characteristics of the programming environment, which builds on a research track about structured parallel programming, so we will only outline its essential aspects and the development path that we are following. SkIE aims at easing parallel software engineering and sequential software reuse by facilitating code integration from several different host languages.

The parallel aspects of programs are specified using a skeleton-based high-level language, which is the subject of the next section. The key point is that parallelism is essentially expressed in a declarative way, while the sequential operations are coded using standard sequential languages. This approach preserves useful sequential software tools and eases sequential software conversion and reuse, while keeping all the advantages of a structured parallel approach.

Parallel compilation is performed in a two-phase fashion, with global optimizations and performance tuning at the application level performed by the parallel environment, and local optimizations introduced by sequential compilers. The low-level support of parallel computation is based on industry standards like MPI, to ensure the best portability across different architectures.

The Skeleton Model in SkIE

SkIE-CL, the programming language of the SkIE environment, is a coordination language based on parallel skeletons. The parallel skeleton model, originally conceived by Cole (1989), uses a set of compositional building blocks to express the structure of parallel code. Skeleton models have been subsequently exploited in the design of structured parallel programming environment; see for instance the work of Au et al. (1996), or that of Serot, Ginhac, Chapuis and Derutin (2001). A coordination language allows the integration of separately developed software fragments and applications to create bigger ones. In SkIE-CL, this approach is applied to the sequential portion of algorithms, and it is combined with the structured description of parallelism given by skeletons. As shown in Danelutto (2001), skeletons are close to parallel *design patterns*, as both provide solutions to common problems in term of architectural schemes. Some of the main differences are that skeletons are more rigidly defined and paired with specific implementation solutions (usually called templates), while design patterns are more like recipes of solutions to be detailed. As a result, skeleton programming languages are more declarative in style, while existing languages based on design patterns provide a number of generic classes and objects to be instantiated and completed, thus requiring at least partial knowledge of the underlying software architecture.

A program written in SkIE-CL integrates blocks of sequential code written in several conventional languages (C and C++, various Fortran dialects, and Java) to form parallel programs. The skeletons are defined as language constructs that provide the parallel patterns to compose the sequential blocks. The basic parallel patterns are quite simple because skeletons, and SkIE skeletons in particular, can be nested inside each other to build structures of higher complexity. The interfaces between different modules are given by two *in* and *out* lists of data structures for each module. These defined interfaces are the only mean of interaction among different modules. Each parallel module specifies the actual data that are passed to the contained modules, and the language support handles all the details of communication, synchronization and concurrency management. This is especially important in the general case, when modules receive a stream of data structures and have to perform their computation over all the data. The general intended semantics of the SkIE skeletons is that the overall computation is performed in a data-flow style, each module beginning its work as soon as its input is available, and starting a new computation as soon as new input data arrives.

SkIE skeletons are represented in Figure 1, both as basic parallel communication schemes and as simple code fragments in the SkIE syntax. The in/out interfaces of some of the examples are instantiated to basic type definitions to show how the various skeletons use their parameters. Lists of parameters of C-like, user-defined types are allowed in the general case. The simplest skeleton is the *seq*, whose purpose is to contain the definition and the interfaces of a fragment of serial code. Almost obviously, the *seq* is the only skeleton that cannot contain other skeletons. In Figure 1, we identify a *seq* module with a sequential process communicating with other ones by means of channels. We explicitly note that the graphical representation abstracts from the actual implementation of the skeleton on a particular hardware. Viewing sequential blocks and interfaces as processes and channels is a useful concept to intuitively understand the behavior of the parallel program, but doesn't constrain the program implementation devised by the compiler.

SkIE provides with skeletons that model the two basic classes of parallel computations, namely, task parallel computations and data parallel computations. We talk about task parallelism and *streams* of tasks when a series of input elements or independent computation results flow from one module to a different one. The data-parallel skeletons rely instead on explicit decomposition and composition rules to split the computation of a large data structure into an organized set of sub-computations, and to compose the results back into a new structure. We call computational grain the size of the tasks we distribute to other processors for parallel computation. A small grain can lead to excessive overhead. In the case of the farm and other stream-parallel skeletons, packing a number of tasks together for communication optimizes the grain, enhancing the computation/communication ratio.

The *pipe* skeleton defines the basic pattern of pipeline functional evaluation over a stream of tasks. Given a set of modules (of arbitrary internal complexity), their pipeline composition evaluates a functional composition $f(g(h...(input_i)))$. The $f,g,h...$ functions over different elements of the input are evaluated in parallel in an assembly-line fashion. A nested module defines each function. A stage of the pipe sends its results to the next one as soon as it finishes its computation. The general syntax of the pipe construct is shown in Figure 1. This general form obeys the constraint that the output of a stage (the out parameters of the module for that stage of the pipe) is the input of the following stage. The *farm* skeleton expresses a load-balanced replication of a functional module W, each copy separately performing the same computation over different tasks of the input stream. The type of the in and out parameters of the contained worker module must be the same farm ones. The execution order is assumed to be irrelevant; incoming tasks are accepted as soon as a worker module is free of computation. The implementation of the *farm* skeleton in SkIE can also exploit other compile and run-time optimizations, like buffered communications and computation grain tuning. The *loop* skeleton defines

Figure 1: Some of the parallel skeletons available in SkIE, their graphical representation and concrete syntax. Examples of simple data types inside interface definitions, in place of full parameter lists.

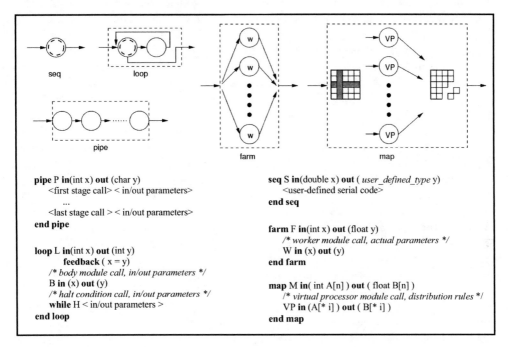

```
pipe P in(int x) out (char y)
    <first stage call> < in/out parameters>
    ...
    <last stage call > < in/out parameters>
end pipe


loop L in(int x) out (int y)
    feedback ( x = y)
    /* body module call, in/out parameters */
    B in (x) out (y)
    /* halt condition call, in/out parameters */
    while H < in/out parameters >
end loop
```

```
seq S in(double x) out ( user_defined_type y)
    <user-defined serial code>
end seq


farm F in(int x) out (float y)
    /* worker module call, actual parameters */
    W in (x) out (y)
end farm


map M in( int A[n] ) out ( float B[n] )
    /* virtual processor module call, distribution rules */
    VP in (A[* i] ) out ( B[* i] )
end map
```

cyclic, eventually interleaved dataflow computations. The nested *body* module repeatedly computes all the tasks that enter the *loop*. A feedback declaration defines the mapping among the in and out parameters when tasks are sent to the loop entry point. Interleaving of different computation is supported and is dealt with by the language support. Tasks leave the *loop* as soon as they satisfy the condition evaluated by the sequential module *halt*. In Figure 1 ,we show the *while*-like variant of *loop*, the *do-until* and *for* versions differing only in the way the halt condition is evaluated.

The *map* skeleton performs data parallel computations over multidimensional arrays. SkIE defines a specific syntax (which we don't describe here) to express a set of useful decomposition rules for the input structure, also including several kinds of stencils. The data structure is thus decomposed and distributed to a set of virtual processors (VP) modules, in a way that allows them to compute independently. The output of the VPs is then recomposed to a new structure, which is the output of the *map*. In the example, we show the syntax for distributing an array of integers one element per VP, and then collecting back an array of the same size. For the sake of conciseness, we skip the formal description of the other data-parallel skeletons (*reduce* and *comp*).

Memory Hierarchies

All modern computers employ a memory hierarchy to optimize the average memory access time. Programming models usually hide all the details of memory hierarchy, and intuitive understanding of program complexity relies on a uniform memory access cost. Real experience and theoretical results show that several common computational tasks have very different costs if we take into account external memory references, and very large constant terms suddenly creep in as soon as the data size exceeds the size of a memory level. When data structures do not fit in main memory, the oblivious resort to virtual memory can cause severe latency and bandwidth degradation, especially for random access patterns, because of the huge speed gap among main and mass memory. External memory-aware computation models, algorithms, and data structures have been designed to overcome the problem, appropriately exploiting core memory and the I/O blocking factor to amortize the secondary memory accesses. A deep survey of the topic can be found in Vitter (2001).

The issue is clearly relevant for database and DM applications, which manage both input and working data structures of huge size. On the other hand, computational models and algorithms for parallel I/O exploitation have been developed too, in the effort to solve larger and larger problems. All these solutions can be quite complex, having to match the algorithm structure to the constraints of efficient utilization of different levels of memory. In some cases, there is already a data management layer that can integrate these results in a black-box fashion, as it happens with relational DBMS and GIS databases (Freitas & Lavington, 1998). In the general case, new interfaces have been studied also to simplify the implementation of external memory algorithms, and to exploit parallel I/O resources. Both the black-box approach and the generic one can be useful for high-performance DM. Efficient, tight integration with database, data warehouse, and data transport management services highly enhances flexibility and efficiency of the DM tools, because they can easily benefit from any improvements of the underlying software levels. On the other hand, new (parallel) DM applications often need to directly manage huge data structures, and we want to exploit the same advanced techniques with the minimum programming effort.

Skeletons and External Objects

In this section, we outline the reasons that led us to the addition of an external objects (EO) abstraction to a high-level parallel language. The skeleton programming approach allows us to express parallel programs in a simple, portable way. Parallel applications need, however, to interface to hardware and software resources, and ideally, we want this part of the program to enjoy the same degree of portability. But usually access to databases, file systems, and other kinds of software services from within sequential code is done differently, depending on the sequential language and the operating system.

We explore the option of developing an object-like interface used from within parallel applications to access generalized external services. With external services, we denote a wide range of different resources, and software layers, like shared memory and out-of-core data structures, sequential and parallel file systems, DBMS and data warehouse systems with SQL interface, and CORBA software components. These can be usefully exploited regardless of the configuration details of the parallel program.

Support for object-oriented external libraries is already available or easily added to different sequential languages. The parallel language recognizes parallel *external objects* as fully qualified types. The support of the language can accomplish set-up and management tasks, such as locating or setting up servers and communication channels. The sequential host languages can interact with the object support code as external libraries with a fixed interface, and, of course, object-oriented languages like C++ and Java can develop more complex functionalities by encapsulating the SkIE external objects into user-defined ones.

The definition of internally parallel objects is a responsibility that remains in the hands of the language developer. It is a complex task, and it is subject to the constraints that the implementation is portable and does not conflict with the parallel language support. More complex objects with an explicitly parallel behavior can be defined in terms of the basic ones, to ease parallel programming design. A first experiment in adding external objects to the pre-existing SkIE language has looked at distributed data structures in virtually shared memory (Carletti & Coppola, 2002). The results were evaluated with the application to the parallel C4.5 classifier described in this chapter. The long-term goal of the design is to develop objects that manage huge distributed data structures by exploiting available shared memory or parallel file systems, and using the best in-core and out-of-core methods according to problem size and memory space. The management algorithms for this kind of task can become quite involved, having to deal with multiple levels of external memories and problems of caching, prefetching, and concurrent semantics. It is, of course, a complex and not yet portable design; however, expressing parallel DM algorithms in such a level of detail makes them complex and non-portable as well, and the effort made is not easily reused. On the other hand, we want to exploit this way the well-established standards we already mentioned, like CORBA components and SQL databases, in order to enhance the integration of the high-performance core of DM application with existing software and data support layers. As portability is needed with respect to both the hardware architecture and the software layer that manages the data, we can profitably use object-oriented interfaces to hide the complexity of data retrieval.

STRUCTURED PARALLEL DATA MINING ALGORITHMS

This second part of the chapter is devoted to the analysis of three parallel DM applications developed using the SkIE environment, also including a distributed-tree external object library in the case of C4.5. The descriptions of the problems are self-contained, but we also suggest looking for more results and literature references in the papers of Carletti and Coppola (2002) and Coppola and Vanneschi (2002). We will use the symbol $\mathcal{D}$ to denote the input database. $\mathcal{D}$ is viewed as a square table of N records, which are the rows, and where the number of fields in a record is a. By horizontal representation (or partitioning), we mean that the input is represented (or partitioned) using a row-wise database layout, keeping each record as a whole unit. In vertical representation, the input is instead represented in terms of columns of data, each containing the values of corresponding fields from different input records. An example of the two data representations is given in the next section about association rules.

Association Rule Mining: Partitioned Apriori

The problem of association rule mining (ARM) was proposed back in 1993, and its classical application is *market basket analysis*. From a sell database, we want to detect rules of the form $AB \Rightarrow C$, meaning that a customer who buys both objects A and B also buys C with some minimum probability. We refer the reader to the complete description of the problem given in Agrawal, Mannila, Ramakrishnan, Toivonen, and Verkamo (1996), while we concentrate on the computationally hard subproblem of finding *frequent sets*. In the ARM terminology the database $\mathcal{D}$ is made up of transactions (the rows), each one consisting of a unique identifier and a number of boolean attributes from a set I. The attributes are called *items*, and a *k-itemset* contained in a transaction r is a set of k items that are true in r. The support $\sigma(X)$ of an itemset X is the proportion of transactions that contain X. Given $\mathcal{D}$, the set of items I, and a fixed real number $0 < s < 1$, called *minimum support*, the solution of the frequent set problem is the collection $\{X \mid X \subseteq I, \sigma(X) \geq s\}$ of all itemsets that have at least that minimum support. The support information of the frequent sets can be used to infer all the valid association rules in the input. The power set $\mathcal{P}(I)$ of the set of items has a lattice structure, which is naturally defined by the set inclusion relation. In Figure 2, we see a simple representation of a lattice of all subsets of {A,B,C,D}, with the itemset ABD and its subsets evidenced. A level in this lattice is a set of all itemsets with equal number of elements. The minimum support property is anti-monotonic in this lattice, i.e., it is preserved over decreasing chains:

$$(\sigma(X) \geq s) \wedge (Y \subseteq X) \Rightarrow \sigma(Y) \geq s.$$

To put the frequent set problem in the right perspective, we must remember that the support is taken to be the probability of itemsets. Two interestingness measures for association rules (in the form $A \Rightarrow B$, where A and B are generic itemsets) are defined from itemset support, the *confidence* of a rule, which is the conditional probability of B given A, and the *support* of a rule. It is easy to use the information about frequent sets to compute all association rules that satisfy minimum significance requirements.

Figure 2: Different representations for boolean transaction data. The lattice of itemsets, with the subsets of frequent set ABD put in evidence.

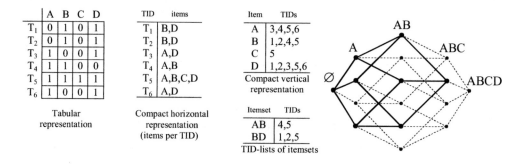

	A	B	C	D
T_1	0	1	0	1
T_2	0	1	0	1
T_3	1	0	0	1
T_4	1	1	0	0
T_5	1	1	1	1
T_6	1	0	0	1

Tabular representation

TID	items
T_1	B,D
T_2	B,D
T_3	A,D
T_4	A,B
T_5	A,B,C,D
T_6	A,D

Compact horizontal representation (items per TID)

Item	TIDs
A	3,4,5,6
B	1,2,4,5
C	5
D	1,2,3,5,6

Compact vertical representation

Itemset	TIDs
AB	4,5
BD	1,2,5

TID-lists of itemsets

Sequential Apriori

Computing the support count for a single itemset requires a linear scan of $\mathcal{D}$. The database is often in the order of gigabytes, and the number of potentially frequent itemsets is $2^{|I|}$, which easily exceeds the available memory. To efficiently compute the frequent sets, their structure and properties have to be exploited. We classify algorithms for ARM according to their lattice exploration strategy. Sequential and parallel solutions differ in the way they arrange the exploration, in the fraction of the itemset lattice that they actually have to explore, and in how they distribute the data structures to minimize computation, I/O, and memory requirements. In the following we will essentially restrict the attention to the Apriori algorithm and its direct evolutions.

Apriori (see Figure 3) builds the lattice level-wise and bottom-up, starting from the 1-itemsets and using the fact that non-frequent itemsets cannot have frequent supersets as a pruning heuristic. From each level L_k of frequent itemsets, a set of candidates C_{k+1} is derived. For the sake of conciseness we give a declarative definition of the *generate* and *computesupport* procedures in Figure 3, but clearly the actual algorithm implementation is critical for performance. The candidates are all the itemsets that satisfy the anti-monotonic property, used as a filtering heuristic. The support for all the current candidates is verified in a single scan of the input, extracting the next level of frequent itemsets L_{k+1} from the set of candidates. The Apriori algorithm is a breakthrough with respect to a naive approach (the amount of work done for support computation is greatly reduced), but some issues arise when applying it to huge databases. A linear scan of $\mathcal{D}$

Figure 3: Apriori pseudo-code for frequent itemsets.

```
FrequentItemsets(𝒟, MinSup)
   L(1) = computesupport (I)
           //  computes the L(1) frequent itemsets
   k = 2
   while( L(k-1) is not empty )
      generate C(k) from L(k-1)
      L(k) = computesupport for sets in C(k)
           //  computes the freq.sets of length k
      k=k+1
   end while
```

$$generate\ (L(k-1),k)$$
$$C(k) = \left\{ \begin{array}{l} x : (|x| = k) \wedge \\ \forall y \subset x, |y| = k - 1 \Rightarrow y \in L(k-1) \end{array} \right\}$$

computesupport (C(k))
   compute $\sigma(x)$ for all x in C(k) by scanning $\mathcal{D}$ once
   return L(k) = $\left\{ \forall x \in C(k) : \sigma(x) > MinSup \right\}$

is required for each level of the solution. The computation can thus be slow, depending on the maximum length of frequent itemsets in the input data. Apriori is based on the assumption that itemsets in C_k are much fewer than all the possible k-itemsets, but this is often false for k=2,3, because the pruning heuristic is not yet fully effective. If C_k is large or doesn't even fit in memory, computing the support values for the candidates becomes quite hard.

Related Work

Some design choices mainly distinguish sequential and parallel algorithms for ARM. In the following, we mention the distinguishing features of the different algorithms.

- The way data and candidates are partitioned and distributed. The data and candidate distribution schemes obviously interact with and constrain parallel work decomposition.

- The lattice exploration approach. Most Apriori evolutions work level-wise, but the lattice structure of the frequent itemsets can be also exploited using random or deterministic sampling and graph properties to quickly gain knowledge of the solution structure.

- The horizontal or vertical approach to database representation. The transaction records may be the basic elements, or we may use TID lists (lists of all identifiers of transactions to which each item belongs). Different implementation solutions depend on this choice; see for instance Savasere, Omiecinski and Navathe (1995), and Zaki (2000).

In the following, we will analyze the main parallel techniques. A more comprehensive report about them can be found in Joshi, Han, Karypis and Kumar (2000).

Following Agrawal and Shafer (1996), we can classify the parallel implementations of Apriori into three main classes, *Count, Data,* and *Candidate Distribution*, according to the interplay of the partitioning schemes for the input and the C_k sets. *Count Distribution* solutions horizontally partition the input among the processors, distributing the database scan for support computation. In order to compute global candidate support counts for each new level of the solution, all the processors have to synchronize and exchange support information with each other. *Data Distribution* solutions keep the C_k set distributed, allowing the management of huge amounts of candidates. The downside of this approach is the need to send local data to most of the processors, if not to fully replicate the database, to let each processor compute the correct support of its own candidates. The *Candidate Distribution* strategy tries to coordinately partition the candidate sets and the input in order to minimize data communication and balance the workload. The approximate information needed to choose a good distribution is gathered in the first steps of the algorithm, or by analyzing a sample of the data.

The three previous solutions share the level-by-level approach of Apriori. This usually involves keeping in memory a set of candidate itemsets with their support counts, using data structures like the hash tree to encode part of the itemset lattice. Each node of the hash tree is labeled with an item, and the path to a node at level k corresponds to a k-itemset. Frequent itemsets are kept in the tree, exploiting the lexicographic order of items and using hash tables at the nodes and additional pointers to reach an average access time proportional to the depth of the tree.

When switching to a vertical data representation, the Apriori internal operations can be rewritten into *TID-lists* intersections (see the example in Figure 2). The TID-list for an itemset is the intersection of the lists of its items, and the support count is the length of the list. List intersections can be computed efficiently, and also offer the advantage of easily changing the lattice exploration strategy from breadth-first to a more general one. Information on support counts of a few long itemsets can be exploited, in the first part of the algorithm, to quickly compute an approximation of the frontier of the set of frequent sets. Zaki (2000) applied similar techniques to the partitioning of 2-itemset TID lists in order to enhance the locality of data access in parallel ARM computation.

Parallel Partitioned Apriori

We studied the partitioned algorithm for ARM introduced in Savasere et al. (1995), which is a two-phase algorithm. The data are horizontally partitioned into blocks that fit inside the available memory, and frequent sets are identified separately in each block, with the same relative value of s. It is easy to show that a frequent itemset in $\mathcal{D}$ must be *locally* frequent in at least one of the partitions (the converse is not true, not all the itemsets that are locally frequent are also frequent in the original dataset $\mathcal{D}$).

The algorithm, shown in Figure 4, is divided in two phases, the first one being to solve the frequent set problem working in memory, separately for each block. Here parallelism is exploited from all the independent computations. The union of the frequent sets for all the blocks is a superset of the globally frequent sets. In a general case, the information gathered so far is partial. It contains a certain amount of *false positives* (itemsets that are only locally frequent in some of the blocks) and contains incomplete support information for those frequent itemsets that are not locally frequent in every partition (they are local *false negatives* in some blocks).

Figure 4: Pseudo-code of partitioned ARM with mapping to parallel modules.

$$
\begin{aligned}
&\textbf{\textit{PartitionedFrequentItemsets}}\ (\mathcal{D},\ \text{MinSup},\ p)\\
&\text{partition } \mathcal{D} \text{ into } p \text{ blocks } B_1 \ldots B_p\\
&\qquad\qquad\qquad\qquad\qquad // \text{ Phase I}\\
&\text{for all } B_i \text{ do} \qquad\qquad\quad // \text{ farm skeleton}\\
&\qquad\qquad // \text{ the Apriori module}\\
&\qquad\qquad H_i = \textbf{FrequentItemsets}\ (B_i,\ \text{MinSup})\\
&H = \bigcup_i H_i \qquad\qquad\qquad // \text{ the ReduceHash module}\\
&\qquad\qquad\qquad\qquad\qquad // \text{ Phase II}\\
&\text{for all } B_i \text{ do} \qquad\qquad\quad // \text{ farm skeleton}\\
&\qquad\qquad // \text{ the SupportCount module}\\
&\qquad\qquad F_i = \text{compute } \sigma\ (x) \text{ for all } x \text{ in } H\\
&\qquad\qquad\qquad\qquad \text{by scanning } B_i \text{ once}\\
&F = \sum_i F_i \qquad\qquad\qquad\quad // \text{ the ReduceSum module}\\
&\text{return } F\ " = \left\{\forall x \in F : \sigma(x) > MinSup\right\}
\end{aligned}
$$

The second phase is a linear scan of $\mathcal{D}$ to compute the correct support counts for all the elements in the approximate solution, and to discard false positives. Here parallelism on different blocks can be exploited too, if we sum support information once at the end of Phase II. As in the work of Savasere et al., we obtain the frequent sets with only two I/O scans. Phase II is efficient, and so the whole algorithm, if the approximation built in Phase I is not too coarse, i.e., the amount of false positives is not overwhelming. The degenerate behavior happens if the data distribution is too skewed, which we can often avoid by a preliminary step of random data permutation. On the other hand, data skew cannot generally be avoided if the input partitions are too small with respect to $\mathcal{D}$.

We have applied the two-phase partitioned scheme without the vertical representation described in the original work. This sacrificed some advantages of the vertical representation, but allowed us to reuse an existing sequential implementation of Apriori as the core of the first phase. This parallel-partitioned scheme is more asynchronous and efficient than parallel Count Distribution, because it avoids both I/O and global communication before each new level of the solution. Nevertheless, our implementation asymptotically behaves like Count Distribution with respect to the parameters of the algorithm. It is quite scalable with the size of $\mathcal{D}$, but cannot deal with huge candidate or frequent sets, i.e., it is not scalable with lower and lower values of the s support parameter. Its essential limits are that both the intermediate solution and a block of data have to fit in memory, and that too small a block size causes data skew. The clear advantages are that almost all work is done independently on each partition, with two I/O passes, and that the scheme can also exploit parallel I/O. We will now show that the algorithm structure can be easily mapped to a skeleton composition, producing an efficient implementation.

Skeleton Implementation

The structure of the Partitioned algorithm is clearly reflected in the skeleton composition we have used, which is shown in Figure 5 and Figure 6. The two phases are connected within a *pipe* skeleton. Since there is no parallel activity between them, they are in fact mapped on the same set of processors. Phase II, if $\mathcal{D}$ is huge, can be easily and usefully parallelized over separate partitions, too. The common internal scheme of the two phases is a three-stage pipeline. The first module within the inner *pipe* reads the input and controls the computation, generating a stream of tasks that are actually partitions of the input data. The second module is a *farm* containing *p seq* modules running the Apriori code. The internal results of Phase I are hash-tree structures containing all the locally frequent sets. The third module contains sequential code to perform a stream reduction over these results. They are summed up to produce a hash tree containing the union of the local solutions. Phase II broadcasts the approximate solution to all the workers at the beginning. The worker modules contain a simpler code that only gathers support counts for the elements in the approximate solution. The results are arrays of support values that are added together by a second stream reduction to compute the global support for all the frequent itemsets.

The skeleton structure described so far allows the application of two different I/O schemes, from which we choose depending on the underlying architecture and on the kind of database interface we want to exploit. It is important to note that the two phases have the same structure and that the second begins after the completion of the first one.

Figure 5: SkIE code for the parallel APriori.

```
pipe main in() out(HashTree support)
   PhaseI  in() out(HashTree hsum)
   PhaseII in(hsum) out(support)
end pipe

pipe PhaseI in() out(HashTree hsum)
   LoaderI    in()
              out(stream of partition p)
   Apriori    in(p) out(HashTree h)
   ReduceHash in(stream of h) out(hsum)
end pipe

pipe PhaseII in(HashTree h) out(HashTree s)
   LoaderII   in(hsum)
              out(stream of partition p)
   Count      in(p) out(HashTree h)
   ReduceSum  in(stream of h) out(s)
end pipe

farm Apriori in(partition p) out(HashTree h)
   AprioriSeq in(p) out(h)
end farm

farm Count    in(candidate p) out(neighb n)
   SupportCount in(p) out(n)
end farm
```

Figure 6: Parallel structure of Partitioned Apriori.

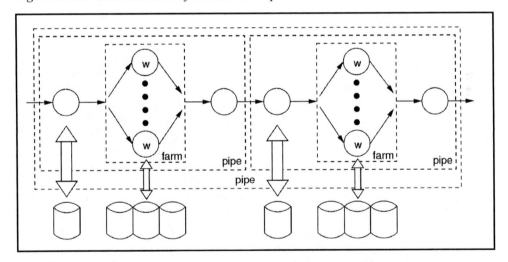

We can thus map them on the same set of processors to use the same I/O approach and resources twice. If we cannot assume the availability of parallel, independent access to disk-resident data, we use the sequential modules in the beginning of each phase to read the data partitions and to distribute them to the following modules. This is the case if the interprocess transfer bandwidth is higher than the I/O one (as in some SMP and parallel architectures), or if we have no other choice than a file system or a database server that provides single-point access to the data for architectural or performance reasons. This approach is scalable as long as the single point of I/O is not a bottleneck.

The case is different if we can afford to replicate the data, exploiting massively parallel I/O to local disks, or if we can access the data from multiple points with no heavy performance penalty, by means of a parallel file system, for instance. Data replication may be needed if the network performance is inadequate to that of the processors and local disks, e.g., on a cluster of workstation. We can implement distributed I/O directly in the *farm* workers, using the first sequential module only as supervisor. We still profit from the load balancing properties of the *farm* skeleton, which takes care of work distribution and synchronization, but we avoid the physical data transfer among distinct modules. This second approach relies on distributed I/O capabilities, but it is much more scalable.

Classification: C4.5 and Tree Induction-Based Classifiers

Classification is one of the most important tasks in DM. The input database $\mathcal{D}$ is a set of records called *cases*, each one having a fixed set of attributes. All the cases have an assigned class label. A classification model is a knowledge model that describes membership of cases to a class in terms of other attribute values. Each attribute, i.e., a column in the data, is either continuous (a numeric value) or categorical (a label). The class attribute is assumed to be categorical. Most classification models are both descriptive and predictive, thus they can classify unlabelled data. We use an inductive process to look for the model. It is a common practice to exploit part of the data, the *training set*, to generate a model, and use the remaining data, the *test set*, to evaluate the model by comparing the predicted class with the real one.

Many widely used classifiers are based on *decision trees*, among them the C4.5 algorithm by Quinlan (1993). A decision tree (see Figure 7) recursively partitions the input set until the partitions consist mostly of data from a same class. The root of the tree corresponds to all the input, and each *decision node* splits the cases according to some test on their attributes. The leaves are class-homogeneous, disjoint subsets of the input.

A path from the root to any given leaf thus defines a series of tests. All cases in the leaf satisfy these tests, and they belong to a certain class (there are only two classes in the example, Yes and Not). The tree describes the structure of the classes, and it is easy to use to predict the class of new, unseen data.

Apart from some implementation issues, the general form of the tree induction process is mainly a divide-and-conquer (D&C) computation, proceeding from the root and recursively classifying smaller and smaller partitions of the input. However, tree induction-based classifiers differ in significant details, like the kind of tests that are used, how they are chosen, what is the stopping criterion of the recursion (the homogeneity condition), and how the data is actually partitioned. The C4.5 algorithm will be the reference for our discussion.

Sequential C4.5

C4.5 is made up of two phases, the building one, which is the actual tree induction process, and the pruning and evaluation phase. We will focus on the former as it is the

Figure 7: Example of decision tree.

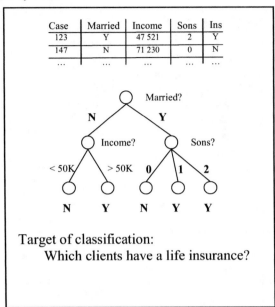

Target of classification:
Which clients have a life insurance?

actual model search, and because its sequential and parallel implementation for huge databases is challenging.

Following the general scheme of tree induction, the building phase proceeds from the root by choosing a new test at each node (step Div1 in Figure 8). C4.5 decision nodes employ tests over a single attribute. Boolean tests of the form *x< threshold* are used for continuous attributes, while multiple-choice tests create a son node for each different value of a categorical attribute. Each decision node thus splits its data into two or more son nodes (steps Div3 or Div2, respectively). The test for a node is selected by evaluating the Information Gain (IG) cost function over all the possible attributes. The IG is essentially a measure of diversity of a set of values, used to recognize which attribute best separates cases of current node into class-homogeneous subsets.

Tree construction is recursive (steps Conq1, Conq3), and branch expansion stops at nearly homogeneous, possibly empty partitions (step Conq2). The model search is locally exhaustive, but globally greedy; no backtracking happens in the building phase.

Each node split requires several operations on all the data contained in the local partition, some of them to evaluate the IG, and other ones to split the data according to the selected attribute. The tree itself is a compact knowledge model, but the data partitions for a node can be as large as the whole input. Ensuring efficiency and locality of data accesses is the main issue in building the decision tree. Assuming that the data fit in memory, to evaluate the IG for a categorical attribute A, histograms of the couples (class, A) in the current partition are computed. This operation requires $O(n)$ operations per column, where n is the size of current partition. IG computation for continuous attributes needs the class column to be sorted according to the attribute. The cost of repeated sorting (operations) at each node expansion accounts for most of the running

Figure 8: Pseudocode of C4.5, tree-building phase.

C4.5_Build_Tree($\mathcal{N}$)

Div1   evaluate **IG** over all the attributes $A_1 \ldots A_a$
        select best splitting attribute B
Div2   if B is categorical with b values
        partition $\mathcal{N}$ into b distinct nodes according to B
Div3   if B is numerical
        partition $\mathcal{N}$ into $\mathcal{N}_1$, $\mathcal{N}_2$ according to B
        compute the exact threshold value T from $\mathcal{D}$
Conq1 for all nodes $\mathcal{N}_i$
Conq2   If $\mathcal{N}$ satisfies the **homogeneity criterion**
        $\mathcal{N}$ is a leaf; assign it a class label
Conq3   else
        C4.5_Build_Tree($\mathcal{N}_i$)

---

time of the algorithm. Once the split test has been selected, a further step $O(n)$ is required to partition the data accordingly.

The serial algorithm as described is not practically scalable. For out-of-core partitions, the complexity given above is in terms of I/O operations and virtual memory page faults. The in-core algorithm quickly becomes unusable, and explicit external-memory solutions are needed to overcome the limitation. Sequential and parallel classifiers address the problem by using clever techniques to evaluate the IG, by turning to less costly, possibly approximate cost functions, or by decomposing the computation to reduce the amount of useless data transfers. In the original formulation of C4.5, the selection of a continuous attribute for the split in step Div3 also requires a linear search for a global threshold T, which is done over all the input data. This $O(N)$ search clearly breaks the D&C paradigm, both with respect to locality of data accesses and with respect to the expected computation time of subproblems. However, the exact threshold value T is not needed to split a node, because it is used only later, during the evaluation phase. All the thresholds in the generated tree can be computed in an amortized manner at the end of the building phase. As a consequence, locality of data access is enhanced, and the computational cost of split operations lowers from to $O\left(\max\left(N, n \log n\right)\right)$ to $O(n \log n)$.

Related Work

Several different parallel strategies for classification have been explored in the literature. Three of them can be considered as basic paradigms, which are combined and specialized in real algorithms. *Attribute* parallelism vertically partitions the data and distributes to different processors the IG calculation over different columns. *Data* parallelism employs horizontal partitioning of the data and coordinates computation of all processors to build each node. *Task* parallelism is the independent classification of separate nodes and subtrees. These fundamental approaches may use replicated or partitioned data structures, do static or dynamic load balancing and computation grain optimization.

We have seen that the computation of IG accounts for much of the complexity of C4.5. Some alternative split evaluation functions have been proposed that do not require the data to be sorted and to be memory-resident, but in the following, we will concentrate on the works based on the same definition of information gain used in C4.5. Much of the research effort has been made to avoid sorting the partitions to evaluate the IG and to split the data using a reasonable number of I/O operations or communications. A common variation is to use a vertical representation, each attribute stored in a separate data structure, keeping the columns of data in sorted order. The drawback is that horizontal partitioning is done at each node split, so most of the algorithm design is devoted to split the data according to one column, while maintaining order information in the other ones. Many parallel algorithms expand the classification tree breadth-first and employ a binary tree classification model. Binary splits require some extra processing to form two groups of values from each categorical attribute, but simplify dealing with the data and make the tree structure more regular. The algorithms SLIQ and SPRINT use these two solutions (Shafer, Agrawal & Mehta, 1996). ScalParC (Joshi, Karypis & Kumar, 1998) also builds a binary tree breadth-first, but with a level-synchronous approach. It employs a custom parallel hashing and communication scheme, reducing the memory requirements and the amount of data transfers. ScalParC is memory-scalable and has a better average split communication cost than the former algorithms, even if its worst-case communication cost is $O(N)$ for a whole level of the tree.

Skeleton Parallel C4.5

Our research has focused on developing a structured parallel classifier based on a D&C formulation. Instead of balancing the computation and communications for a whole level, we aim at a better exploitation of the locality properties of the algorithm. A similar approach is the one reported in Sreenivas, AlSabti and Ranka (2001) for the parallel CLOUDS algorithm. The sequential classifier CLOUDS uses a different and computationally more efficient way of evaluating the split gain on numeric attributes, which results in lower I/O requirements than other classifiers. Sreenivas et al. (2001) propose, as a general technique for parallel solution of D&C problems, a mixed approach of data-parallel and task-parallel computation. Substantially, in pCLOUDS, all the nodes above a certain size are computed in a data-parallel fashion by all the processors. The smaller nodes are then classified using a simple task parallelization.

The problem of locality exploitation has also been addressed in Srivastava, Han, Kumar and Singh (1999) with a *Hybrid Parallelization*. A level-synchronous approach is used here, but as the amount of communications exceeds the estimated cost of data reorganization, the available processors are split in two groups that operate on separate sets of subtrees.

We started from a task parallelization approach instead. Each node classification operation is a task, which generates as subtasks the input partitions for the child nodes. Each processor receives a task and executes one or more recursive calls to the classifying procedure. The resulting partitions that are not homogeneous become new tasks to compute. We used a skeleton composition that allows tasks to loop back through a classifier module (see Figure 9 and Figure 10), which is internally parallel. Each task requires a certain amount of data to be communicated, which in a first implementation is proportional to the size of the node.

Figure 9: SkIE code for parallel C4.5.

```
loop C45 in(ST_Ref Tin)
        out(ST_Ref Tout, bool f)
    feedback(Tin=Tout)
    DivAndConq in(Tin) out(Tout, f)
    while test in(f) out(bool cont)
end loop

pipe DivAndConq in(ST_Ref Tin)
                out(ST_Ref Tout, bool f)
    TaskExpand in(Tin) out(f, ST_Ref Task)
    Conquer in(Task) out(Tout)
end pipe

farm TaskExpand in(ST_Ref Task)
                out(ST_Ref Tout)
    Divide in(Task) out(Tout)
end farm
```

Figure 10: Block Structure of parallel C4.5.

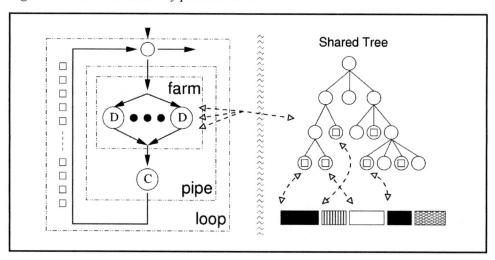

To throttle the computation grain size (i.e., to balance the amount of communications with enough local computation), we vary the amount of computation done. A single task computation may execute a single classification recursive call and return the set of sons of the given node. We can also expand a node to a subtree of more than one level, and return as subtasks all the nodes in the frontier of the subtree. Very small nodes are completely classified locally. To control how deep a subtree is generated for each task (how many recursive calls are executed), we use a task *expansion policy*, balancing the communication and computation times of the workers. We made a choice similar to that of Sreenivas et al. (2000) in distinguishing the nodes according to their size. In our case, we balance the task communication and computation times, which influence dynamic load balancing, by using three different classes of tasks. The base heuristic is that *large* tasks are expanded to one level only to increase available parallelism, while *small* ones are fully computed sequentially. Intermediate size tasks are expanded to incomplete subtrees up to a given number of nodes and within computation time bounds. The actual size and time limits were tuned following the same experimental approach described in our previous work (Carletti & Coppola, 2002).

We verified that if threshold calculation for continuous attributes is delayed until the pruning phase, the distribution of computation load for different tasks in the D&C becomes more regular and can be better exploited by means of application-level parallel policies. In our case, the task *selection policy* that is most effective is to schedule the tasks in size order, first expanding large tasks that generate more parallelism, then the smaller ones. Note that this overall scheme does not relieve us from the task of resorting data at each node, which has not been addressed yet.

Test Implementations with Skeletons and External Objects

The skeleton structure in Figure 9 implements the recursive expansion of nodes by letting tasks circulate inside a *loop* skeleton. The anonymous workers in the *farm* skeleton expand each incoming node to a separate subtree. The template underlying the *farm* skeleton takes care of load balancing. Its efficiency depends on the available parallelism and the computation to communication ratio, and the sequential code in the workers apply the task expansion policy we described before. The second stage in the *pipe* is a sequential *Conquer* process coordinating the computation. C4.5 is a D&C algorithm with a very simple conquer step that simply consists of merging subtrees back into the classification tree. In our implementations, the conquer module takes care of the task selection policy by ordering waiting tasks according to their size.

The structure described so far has been implemented in two variants. In a pure skeleton based version, all the input data were replicated in the workers, while the decision tree structure was local to the Conquer module. Each task consists of index structures that allow the workers to select the data for the node. Similar information has to flow through the Conquer module to allow decision tree building and task scheduling. Regardless of the good exploitation of task parallelism, the scalability of such a simple approach is limited by memory requirements, by communications issues, and by the bottleneck due to tree management.

The situation is different if we employ external objects inside the skeleton program. We have designed a Shared Tree (ST) library, an implementation of a general tree object in shared memory. We have added it to the previous prototype, using it to represent the decision tree, and we have performed some experiments. The ST is a shared, distributed object whose nodes and leaves can contain arbitrary data. Since data locality follows the evolution of the decision tree, in our solution the whole input is held inside the ST, distributed over the frontier of the expanding tree, and is immediately accessible from each process in the application. All the operations required by the algorithm are done in the sequential workers of the farm. They access the shared structure to fetch their input data, then create the resulting subtree and store back the data partitions on the frontier of the tree.

The Conquer module no longer manages the tree structure and the contained data. It only applies the task *selection policy*, resulting in a clear separation in the code between the sequential computation and the details of parallelism exploitation. A simple priority queue is used to give precedence to larger tasks, leading to a data-driven expansion scheme of the tree, in contrast to the depth-first scheme of sequential C4.5 and to the level-synchronous approach of ScalParC.

The external object Shared Tree lets parallel modules operate on out-of-core data in a virtual shared memory. Following the approach we have described in the first part of the chapter, the next steps are to extend the ST support with methods that implement the most common elementary operations of C4.5 (sort, scan, summarization), using external memory algorithms when needed. Once this is accomplished, the external object will have the option to choose at run-time the best available sharing support (shared/virtually shared memory, parallel file systems, memory mapped I/O, database servers). Such a technique, which is to be supported in the new ASSIST project, can enhance the scalability of parallel applications to out-of-core datasets, exploiting globally available memory resources, without losing the advantages of structured high-level programming.

Clustering: DBSCAN Density-Based Approach

Clustering is the problem of grouping input data into sets in such a way that a similarity measure is high for objects in the same cluster, and low elsewhere. Many different clustering models and similarity measures have been defined to work on various kinds of input data. For the sake of *Spatial Clustering,* the input data are seen as points in a suitable space R^a, and discovered clusters should describe their spatial distribution. Many kinds of data can be represented this way, and their similarity in the feature space can be mapped to a concrete meaning, e.g., for spectral data to the similarity of two real-world signals. A high dimension a of the data space is quite common and can lead to performance problems (Beyer, Goldstein, Ramakrishnan & Shaft, 1999). Usually, the spatial structure of the data has to be exploited by means of appropriate index structures to enhance the locality of data accesses. Clustering methods based on distances and cluster representatives have the basic limit that the shape of clusters is geometrically biased by the distance measure being used, so clusters whose shape is not convex are easily missed. On the other hand, relying solely on point-to-point distance means using cluster evaluation functions that require computing a quadratic number of distances, making the algorithm unpractical. Density-based clustering identifies clusters from the density of objects in the feature space. Compared to other spatial clustering methods, density-based ones still make use of the concept of distance, but only in a local sense, so that the global shape of clusters is less influenced by the chosen distance measure. One of the advantages of density-based methods is the ability to discover clusters of almost any shape.

Sequential DBSCAN

DBSCAN is a density-based spatial clustering technique introduced in Ester, Kriegel, Sander and Xu (1996), whose parallel form we recently studied. DBSCAN measures densities in R^a by counting the points inside a given region of the space. The key concept of the algorithm is that of *core point,* a point belonging to a locally dense part of the input set. Having fixed two user parameters ε and MinPts, a core point must have at least MinPts other data points within a neighborhood of radius ε. A suitable relation can be defined among the core points, which allows us to identify dense clusters made up of core points. The points that fail the density test are either assigned to the boundary of a neighboring cluster, or labeled as noise.

To assign cluster labels to all the points, DBSCAN repeatedly applies a simple strategy—it searches for a core point, and then it explores the whole cluster it belongs to (Figure 11). The process of cluster expansion performed by the *ExpandCluster* procedure is quite similar to a graph visit where connected points are those closer than ε, and the visit recursively explores all reached core points. When a point in the cluster is considered as a *candidate*, we first check if it is a core point; if it has enough neighbors, it is labeled with the current cluster identifier, and its neighbors are also placed in the candidate queue. DBSCAN holds the whole input set inside the R*-tree spatial index structure. The R*-tree is a secondary memory tree, with an ad hoc directory organization and algorithms for building, updating, and searching designed to efficiently access spatial data. The data are kept in the leaves, while interior nodes contain bounding boxes for the son subtrees, used by the management algorithms. Holding some conditions, the R*-tree can answer to spatial queries (which are the points in a given region) with time and I/O complexity proportional to the depth of the tree, $O(\log N)$. Since for each point in the input there is exactly one neighborhood retrieval operation, the expected complexity of DBSCAN is $O(N \log N)$.

Figure 11: Pseudo-code of DBSCAN.

```
DBSCAN (Input_Set, ε, MinPts)
foreach p in the Input_Set
    if (p is not in any cluster)
        if (p is a core point)
            generate a new ClusterID
            label p with ClusterID
            ExpandCluster (p, Input_Set, ε, MinPts,
                           ClusterID)
        else
            label(p, NOISE)


ExpandCluster (p, Input_Set, ε, MinPts, ClusterID)
put p in a seed queue
while the queue is not empty
    extract c from the queue
    retrieve the ε-neighborhood of c
    if there are at least MinPts neighbours
        for each neighbour n
            if n is labeled NOISE
                label n with ClusterID
            if n is not labeled
                label n with ClusterID
                put n in the queue
```

We need the hypothesis that almost all regions involved in the queries are small with respect to the dataset, so that the search algorithm needs to examine only a small number of leaves of the R*-tree. We can assume that the ε parameter is not set to a neighborhood radius comparable to that of the whole dataset. But we have no guarantee that a suitable value for ε exists. It is well known that all spatial data structures lose efficiency as the dimension a of the space grows, in some cases already for $a > 10$. The R*-tree can be easily replaced with any improved spatial index that supports neighborhood queries, but for a high value of a this could not lead to an efficient implementation anyway. It has been argued in Beyer et al. (1999) and is still a matter of debate, that for higher and higher dimensional data the concept of neighborhood of fixed radius progressively loses its meaning for the sake of spatial organization of the data. As a consequence, for some distributions of the input, the worst-case performance of *good* spatial index structures is that of a linear scan of the data (Bertchold, Keim & Kriegel, 1996).

Skeleton Parallel DBSCAN

We develop a parallel implementation of DBSCAN that is a practical way to make it scalable with N, when the $O(N \log N)$ sequential cost is too high. This can be due to large constant terms in the real running time, or because of the spatial access overhead for a large value of the spatial dimensionality a. Our parallel implementation does not presently aim at being fully scalable with respect to a. We have to modify the sequential algorithms to turn it into a parallel one, but a simple and efficient solution is obtained by applying standard forms of parallelism.

When looking at DBSCAN performance, it is clear from previous analysis that we have to exploit parallelism in the spatial queries. A very simple way to enhance the service time of a large number of operations is to perform them in parallel. In the original formulation of the algorithm, the candidate points, which are the centers of the following spatial queries, are queued as they are generated. We decouple the tasks of checking results, assigning labels and selecting new candidates, from the computation of neighborhoods, which relies on the R*-tree.

The resulting decomposition in a pair of modules is shown in Figure 12. A *Master* module executes the sequential algorithm, demanding all spatial tree operations to a *retrieve* module which is internally parallel. This decoupled scheme exposes two kinds of parallelism. There is pipeline parallelism between the Master and the Slave modules, because the Slave can start processing the stream of queries that in the sequential algorithm would have been queued. Moreover, we are able to exploit farm parallelism over this stream of independent tasks (the retrieve module hosts several *Slave* modules). Since DBSCAN cluster definition is insensitive to the order of cluster expansion, out-of order answers can be immediately used, and we take advantage of the load-balancing properties of the farm template. Two factors make the overall structure effective:

1. The sequential operations in the Master are not hard and do not actually need to use a spatial access structure. Cluster labels are integers; even if we use a spatial structure for storing them, it doesn't need to be the R*-tree used to store the whole database.

2. A lot of independent queries are generated when a cluster starts growing in all directions, and the Slaves need no information about cluster labeling to process these queries (we will come back to this assumption). On the other hand, we have

Figure 12: Parallel decomposition of DBSCAN.

```
Master :
while (there are pending results)
    get { p, s, Setn } from the result stream
    if (s > MinPts )
        foreach point n in Setn
            if n is labeled NOISE
                label n with ClusterID
            if n is not labeled
                label n with ClusterID
                put n in the candidate stream

Slave :
forever
    get point c from the candidate stream
    Setn = ε-neighborhood ( c )
    put { c, | Setn |, Setn } in the result stream

FilteringSlave :
forever
    get point c from the candidate stream
    mark c as sent
    Setn = ε-neighborhood ( c )
    if ( | Setn | < MinPts)
        put { c, | Setn |, Ø} in the result stream
    else
        Setf = filter ( Setn )
        mark points in Setf as sent
        put { c, | Setn |, Setf } in the result stream
```

made the non-trivial hypothesis that all the Slaves can access the R*-tree structure to perform their task.

The computation is clearly data-flow like, with queries and answers being the elementary tasks that flow across the modules. The structure described is plainly mapped to a set of skeleton reported in Figure 13 and Figure 14, where we find a *pipe* of the Master and Slave modules, with a set of Slave-independent modules contained in a *farm*. A *loop* skeleton is used to let the answers return to the Master until all clusters have been explored. The amount of computation in the Master module depends on the amount of points returned by the spatial queries, and we have modified their behavior by moving them to separate modules. The process of oblivious expansion of different parts of a cluster exploits parallelism in the Slave module, but may repeatedly generate the same candidates. While in sequential DBSCAN neighbor points are counted, and only *unlabeled* ones are selected as new candidates, now there is no label information to allow this kind of immediate pruning. But if we send all neighborhood sets for each query each time, we end up in receiving exponentially many results in the Master.

A simple filtering heuristics allows the Slaves to send each result once at most. The heuristic is reported in Figure 12 as a modified pseudo-code for a *FilteringSlave* module.

Figure 13: The SkIE code of parallel DBSCAN.

```
farm retrieve in(candidate p) out(neighb n)
  Slave in(p) out(n)
end farm

pipe body in(neighb a) out(neighb b)
  Master in(a) out(candidate p)
  retrieve in(p) out(b)
end pipe

loop dbscan in(neighb i) out(neighb o)
  feedback(i=o)
  body in(i) out(o)
  while test in(o) out(bool cont)
end loop
```

Figure 14: Block structure of parallel DBSCAN.

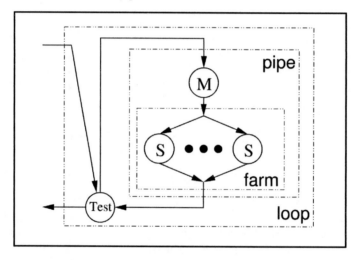

Each sub-Slave can detect a sufficient condition for not resending points already queued as candidates, while still providing the Master with the exact number of neighbors discovered in each query ($| \text{Set}_n |$ is this number), which is needed by the clustering algorithm. The effect of this distributed filtering is reported in Figure 15, where we can see that the ratio of duplicates to results is bounded by the degree of parallelism.

Like its sequential counterpart, the parallel structure we have described for DBSCAN is general with respect to the spatial index, and can be applied to different spatial data structures. It is thus easy to exploit any improvement or customization of the data management that may speed up the computation. Further investigation is needed to evaluate the practical scalability limits of our heuristics at higher degrees of parallelism, and possibly to devise better ones. To improve the filtering ratio, more informed heuristics could exploit non-local information gained by communications among the

Figure 15: Average number of points per query answer, versus parallelism and epsilon.

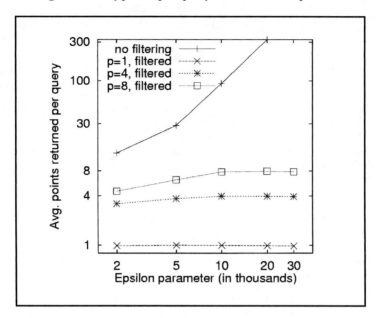

slaves, or between the Master and the Slave module. Another solution is to use a separate, parallel module to apply global filtering to the results returning to the Master.

A final comment must be made about the availability of the R*-tree to all the components of the Slave module. In our tests, the data structure was actually replicated, which is a consistent waste of disk space. This could be a limit for practical scalability, but the parallel algorithm does not actually need replication. Since the R*-tree is used as a read-only index structure, it can be shared among all the Slaves by means of a networked/parallel file system. The R*-tree is a secondary memory structure, so its access time is not subject to a sharp degradation. A single copy on a networked sequential file system would become a bottleneck if shared among a large number of Slaves. Sharing a single copy across a bounded number of processors could help reduce the amount of replication, and may be the only choice in a DDM setting. Using instead a parallel file system to store the data is not subject to the same limitations, and may actually increase the performance of the accesses, thanks to the fact that the size of parallel file system caches increases with the size of the employed parallel architecture.

Related Work

We compare our approach with the PDBSCAN one described in Xu, Jager and Kriegel (1999). That work also addressed the issue of speeding up the region queries by means of parallel computation. They develop a Master-Slave scheme in which the Slaves independently run a slightly modified version of sequential DBSCAN on separate partitions of the multi-dimensional input space. The data are held in a distributed version of the R*-Tree, which partitions the data pages of the R*-Tree (the leaves) among available processors and fully replicates the index structure (the interior part of the tree). This approach relies on the same constraint we exploited, i.e., that the spatial structure is essentially read-only. Slaves have to communicate with each other to answer spatial queries near partition boundaries, so the distribution of data pages among processors is performed following a Hilbert space-filling curve, a commonplace tool to enhance locality for huge spatial data structures and problems. The Master module is idle during the parallel clustering phase, but the cluster identifiers assigned in distinct partitions are completely unrelated. A merging phase is run after the clustering to map local cluster IDs to global ones. Information collected at run time by the Slaves is used to match the different parts of clusters that span partition boundaries.

In the Master-Slave decomposition of PDBSCAN, the Master has little control on the first part of the computation, and there is no bottleneck, so the application shows a good speed up for a small number of processors. On the other hand, when increasing the degree of parallelism, the amount of communications among the Slaves raises quickly, and it is not clear how high could be the cost of the merging phase—an entirely sequential task of the Master processor.

PDBSCAN required the definition of an ad hoc distributed data structure, the dR*-Tree, and its implementation using a low-level approach (C++ and PVM). The dataset is carefully partitioned among the processors, and this is a strong assumption in a distributed computing environment. On the contrary, our solution does not rely on an exact partitioning of the data and is implemented in a high-level fashion reusing the code of the sequential application; it assumes that the data is accessible from every processor, at least in secondary memory. Both solutions seem to perform well on small clusters, with datasets larger than one hundred-thousand points. The distinction between the two approaches is partly apparent, anyway. As we have shown with parallel C4.5, special purpose distributed data structures can be easily integrated into high-level applications by encapsulating them into external objects, and this opportunity is certainly available also for the structured parallel DBSCAN. In our view this is the best way to make the most of the effort put in developing complex solutions.

Test Results

We have actually implemented the described parallel structures using SkIE, and several prototypes have been run on a range of different parallel architectures. We present some test results and we analyze them in terms of speed-up and efficiency. Results over different machines show the characteristics of performance portability of structured parallel applications. We used

- Clusters of LINUX workstations on a LAN network;
- Beowulf clusters with dedicated Fast Ethernet;
- Small SMP workstations; and
- Parallel, distributed-memory machines, like the Meiko CS-2 and the Cray T3E.

This is a quite heterogeneous set of parallel architectures. The different number of processors, their technology, the bandwidth and latency of the interconnection network result in variable communication/computation ratios for the same problem on different

*Figure 16: Apriori efficiency versus parallelism (* = centralized I/O).*

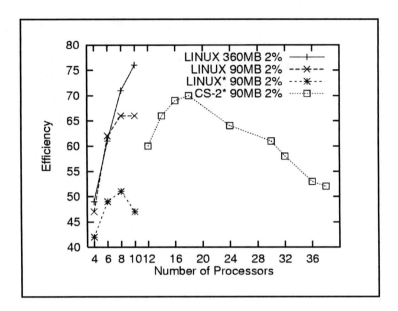

hardware platforms. The T3E and recent LINUX workstations offer the highest raw CPU speed, but from the point of view of communication versus computation speed, the SMP and the distributed memory multiprocessors offer the highest figures. I/O bandwidth and scalability are crucial to DM applications, and the test platforms offer quite different performances, with the CS-2 and the cluster platforms exploiting a higher degree of I/O parallelism. We note that the T3E platform of our tests had a single RAID disk server, which is a bottleneck at high degree of parallelism. Moreover, slower processor architectures are less sensitive to the I/O speed gap.

The Partitioned Apriori has been tested on the full range of hardware platforms. Test results are reported and discussed in full in previous works. Now we just point out that the application exhibits high efficiency and it is scalable with the size of data. In Figure 16, we see the efficiency on the CS-2 and a Beowulf cluster. The dataset is obtained with the most commonly used test set generator (see Agrawal et al., 1996), and tests with centralized (*) and distributed I/O are reported, with the latter ensuring higher performance. Figure 17 shows speed-up figures for a LINUX cluster at a higher computational load. The completion time on a T3E (Figure 18) evidences the bottleneck of a single disk server at higher degrees of parallelism. Here the I/O time dominates execution time, unless the computational load of the sequential algorithm is very high.

We obtained comparable results from the DBSCAN prototype. A common behavior of these two programs is a performance loss when the input is too small. We can explain this behavior in terms of the startup phase that the *farm* parallelism has to go through, when computing a stream of tasks, before reaching the steady state. For the Apriori prototype, small data files mean few partitions (we cannot make them small because of

Figure 17: Apriori speedup versus parallelism.

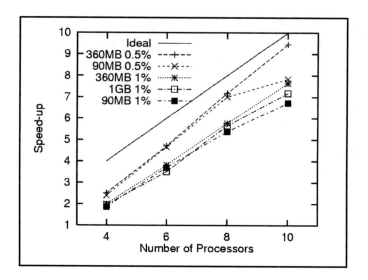

Figure 18: Parallel Apriori, T3E completion time.

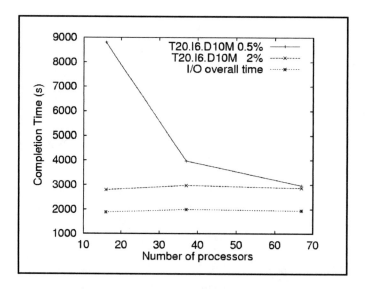

data skew), so the steady state of the computation is too short to balance the length of the startup phase. In the case of DBSCAN, the startup phase occurs in the beginning and at the end of the expansion of each cluster, when not enough candidate points are produced to exploit the degree of parallelism in the Slave. Of course, small datasets and small clusters prevent the *farm* module from ever reaching the steady state.

The skeleton implementation of C4.5 performs well with respect to other task parallel schemes, but it is limited precisely by the task parallel approach. The first target of this design was to experiment with the option of exploiting the aggregate memory, by means of the Shared Tree external object. The addition of the shared structure enhances the performance of the program, whose sequential code still works in main memory. The implementation of out-of-core and low-level parallel functionalities in the external objects is the following step in our research about parallel languages. Merging the task-parallel approach and the data-parallel one within the same program will clearly enhance the performance of this kind of D&C applications.

ADVANTAGES OF STRUCTURE PARALLELISM

Table 1 reports some software cost measures from our experiments, which we review to underline the qualities of the structured approach: fast code development, code portability, and performance portability.

Development Costs and Code Expressiveness

When restructuring the existing sequential code to parallel, most of the work is devoted to making the code modular. The amount of sequential code needed to develop the building blocks for structured parallel applications is reported in Table 1 as *modularization*, separate from the true parallel code. Once modularization has been accomplished, several prototypes for different parallel structures are usually developed and evaluated. The skeleton description of a parallel structure is shorter, quicker to write and far more readable than its equivalent written in MPI. As a test, starting from the same

Table 1: Software development costs for Apriori, DBSCAN and C4.5: Number of lines and kind of code, development times, best speedup on different target machines

		APRIORI	DBSCAN
Sequential code		2900 lines, C++	10138 lines, C++
Kind of parallelization		SkIE	SkIE
Modularization, l. of code		630, C++	493, C++
Parallel structure, l. of code		350, SkIE-CL, C++	793, SkIE-CL, C++
Effort (man-months)		3	2,5
Best speed-up and (parallelism)	CS2	20 (40)	-
	COW	9.4 (10)	6 (9)
	SMP	3.73 (4)	-

	C4.5		
Sequential code	8179 lines, non-ANSI C, uses global variables		
Kind of parallelization	SkIE	SkIE + Shared Tree	MPI
Modularization, l. of code	977, C, C++	977, C, C++	1087, C, C++
Parallel structure, l. of code	303, SkIE-CL	380, SkIE-CL, C++	431, MPI, C++
Effort (man-months)	4	5	5
Best speed-up and (parallelism) CS2	2.5 (7)	5 (14)	-
COW	2.45 (10)	-	2.77 (9)

sequential modules, we developed an MPI version of C4.5. Though it exploits simpler solutions (Master-Slave, no pipelined communications) than the skeleton program, the MPI code is longer, more complex and error-prone than the structured version. On the contrary, the speed-up results showed no significant gain from the additional programming effort.

Performance

The speed-up and scale-up results of the applications we have shown are not all breakthrough, but comparable to those of similar solutions performed with unstructured parallel programming (e.g., MPI). The Partitioned Apriori is fully scalable with respect to database size, like count-distribution implementations. The C4.5 prototype behaves better than other pure task-parallel implementations. It suffers the limits of this parallelization scheme, due to the support of external objects being incomplete. We know of no other results about spatial clustering using our approach to the parallelization of cluster expansion.

Code and Performance Portability

Skeleton code is by definition portable over all the architectures that support the programming environment. Since the SkIE two-level parallel compiler uses standard compilation tools to build the final application, the intermediate code and the run-time support of the language can exploit all the advantages of parallel communication libraries. We can enhance the parallel support by using architecture-specific facilities when the performance gain is valuable, but as long as the intermediate code complies with industry standards the applications are portable to a broad set of architectures. The SMP and T3E tests of the ARM prototype were performed this way, with no extra development time, by compiling on the target machine the MPI and C++ code produced by SkIE. These results also show a good degree of performance portability.

CONCLUSIONS

We have shown how a structured parallel approach can reduce the complexity of parallel application design, and that the approach can be usefully applied to commonly used DM algorithms. The ease of sequential to parallel conversion and the good qualities of code reuse are valuable in the DM field, because of the need for fast prototyping applications and implementation solutions. Performance is achieved by means of careful design of the application parallel structure, with low-level details left to the compiler and the parallel language support.

Within the structured parallelism framework, the proposal of external objects aims at unifying the interfaces to different data management services: in-core memory, shared memory, local/parallel file systems, DBMS, and data transport layers. By decoupling the algorithm structure from the details of data access, we increase the architecture independence, and we allow the language support to implement the accesses in the best way, according to the size of the data and the underlying software and hardware layers. These are very important features in the perspective of merging high-performance algorithms into DM environments for large-scale databases. Such a vision is strongly called for in the literature; nevertheless, only sequential DM tools currently address integration issues. On the grounds of the experiments described here with the SkIE environment, we are designing a full support for external objects in the new structured programming environment, ASSIST.

Several of the points we have mentioned are still open research problems. Which levels of the implementation will exploit parallelism is one of the questions. The development of massively parallel DBMS systems, and the progressive adoption of parallel file system servers, will both have a profound impact on high performance DM, with results that are not easy to foresee. We believe that high-level parallel languages can also play an important role in the organization and coordination of Grid computational resources into complex applications. Executing collective DM tasks over distributed systems requires finding the right balance between result accuracy, reduction of data movement, and balancing of the computational workload. To prevent us from having to deal with more and more complex management details at the same time, ASSIST will actively support Grid protocols and communication libraries.

REFERENCES

Agrawal, R., Mannila, H., Ramakrishnan, S., Toivonen, H., & Verkamo, A.I. (1996). Fast discovery of association rules. In U.M. Fayyad, G. Piatetsky-Shapiro, P. Smyth, & R. Uthurusamy (eds.), *Advances in knowledge discovery and data mining,* pp. 307-328. Cambridge, MA: AAAI Press / MIT Press.

Agrawal, R., & Shafer, J. (1996). Parallel mining of association rules, *IEEE Transactions on Knowledge and Data Engineering* 8 (6) 962-969.

Au, P., Darlington, J., Ghanem, M., Guo, Y., To, H.W., & Yang, J. (1996). Coordinating heterogeneous parallel computation. In L. Bouge, P.Fraigniaud, A. Mignotte & Y.Roberts (eds.), *Europar '96*, Vol. 1124 of *Lecture Notes in Computer Science,* Berlin: Springer-Verlag.

Bertchold, S., Keim, D. A., & Kriegel, H.-P. (1996). The X-Tree: An index structure for high-dimensional data. In *Proceedings of the 22nd International Conference on Very Large Data Bases*, Morgan Kaufmann Publishers, pp. 28-39.

Beyer, K., Goldstein, J., Ramakrishnan, R., & Shaft, U. (1999). When is "nearest neighbor" meaningful? In C. Beeri, & P. Buneman (eds.), *Database Theory - ICDT'99 7th International Conference*, Vol. 1540 of *Lecture Notes in Computer Science*, pp. 217-235. Berlin: Springer-Verlag.

Carletti, G. & Coppola, M. (2002). Structured parallel programming and shared projects: Experiences in data mining classifiers. In G.R. Joubert, A. Murli, F.J. Peters, & M. Vanneschi (Ed.), *Parallel Computing, Advances and Current Issues, Proceedings of the ParCo 2001International Conference*. London: Imperial College Press.

Cole, M. (1989). Algorithmic skeletons: Structured management of parallel computations. *Research Monographs in Parallel and Distributed Computing*. London: Pitman.

Coppola, M. & Vanneschi, M. (2002). High-performance data mining with Skeleton-based structured parallel programming. In *Parallel Computing*, special issue on Parallel Data Intensive Computing, 28(5), 793-813.

Danelutto, M. (2001). On Skeletons and design patterns. To appear in *Parallel Computing, Advances and Current Issues, Proceedings of ParCo 2001 International Conference*. London: Imperial College Press.

Ester, M., Kriegel, H.-P., Sander, J., & Xu, X. (1996). A density-based algorithm for discovering clusters in large spatial databases with noise. In E. Simoudis, J. Han & U. Fayyad (Eds.), *Proceedings of KDD '96*, AAAI Press, pp.226-231.

Fayyad, U. M., Piatetsky-Shapiro, G., Smyth, P., & Uthurusamy, R. (eds.) (1996). *Advances in knowledge discovery and data mining*. Cambridge, MA: AAAI Press / MIT Press.

Freitas, A. A. & Lavington, S.H. (1998). *Mining very large databases with parallel processing*. Boston, MA: Kluwer Academic Publisher.

Joshi, M. V., Han, E.-H., Karypis, G., & Kumar, V. (2000). Efficient parallel algorithms for mining associations. In M. J. Zaki & C.-T. Ho (eds.), Large-scale parallel data mining. Vol. 1759 of *Lecture Notes in Artificial Intelligence*. New York: Springer.

Joshi, M. V., Karypis, G. & Kumar, V (1998). ScalParC: A new scalable and efficient parallel classification algorithm for mining large datasets. In *Proceedings of 1998 International Parallel Processing Symposium*, IEEE CS Press, pp. 573-579.

Maniatty, W. A. & Zaki, M. J. (2000). A requirement analysis for parallel KDD Systems. In J. Rolim et al. (eds.) Parallel and distributed processing, Volume 1800 of *Lecture Notes in Computer Science*. Berlin: Springer-Verlag.

Quinlan, J. (1993). *C4.5: Programs for machine learning*. San Mateo, CA: Morgan Kaufmann.

Savasere, A., Omiecinski, E., & Navathe, S. (1995). An efficient algorithm for mining association rules in large databases. In U. Dayal, P. Gray, and S. Nishio (eds.), Proceedings of 21st International Conference on Very Large Data Bases -VLDB '95 Zurich, pp. 432-444. San Francisco: Morgan Kaufmann.

Serot, J., Ginhac, D., Chapuis, R., & Derutin, J. (2001). Fast prototyping of parallel vision applications using functional skeletons. *Machine Vision and Applications*, 12, 217-290.

Shafer, J., Agrawal, R., & Mehta, M. (1996). SPRINT: A scalable parallel classifier for data mining. In *Proceedings of the 22nd International Conference on Very Large Data Bases - VLDB '96.*, Morgan Kaufmann, pp. 544-555.

Skillicorn, D. B., & Talia, D. (1998). Models and languages for parallel computation. *ACM Computing Surveys*. 30 (2) 123-169.

Sreenivas, M.K., AlSabti, K., & Ranka, S. (2000). Parallel out-of-core decision tree classifiers. In H. Kargupta & P. Chan (eds.), *Advances in distributed and parallel knowledge discovery*. Cambridge, MA: AAAI/MIT Press.

Srivastava, A., Han, E.-H., Kumar, V., & Singh, V. (1999). Parallel formulations of decision-tree classification algorithms. *Data Mining and Knowledge Discovery: An International Journal*, 3(3) 237-261.

Vanneschi, M. (1998a). PQE2000: HPC tools for industrial applications. *IEEE Concurrency: Parallel, Distributed & Mobile Computing*, 6 (4) 68-73.

Vanneschi, M. (1998b). Heterogeneous HPC environments. In D. Pritchard & J. Reeve (eds.), *Euro-Par '98 Parallel Processing*, Vol. 1470 of Lecture Notes in Computer Science. Berlin: Springer-Verlag.

Vanneschi, M. (2002). ASSIST: A programming environment for parallel and distributed portable applications. Internal Report, ASI-PQE2000 Project, January. Submitted for publication.

Vitter, J. S, (2001). External memory algorithms and data structures: Dealing with MASSIVE DATA. ACM Computing Surveys, 33 (2) 209-271.

Xu, X., Jager, J., & Kriegel, H.-P. (1999). A fast parallel clustering algorithm for large spatial databases. *Data Mining and Knowledge Discovery: An International Journal*, 3(3) 263-290.

Zaki, M. J. (2000). Scalable algorithms for association Mining. *IEEE Transactions on Knowledge and Data Engineering*, 12, 372-390.

Zaki, M. J. & Ho, C.-T. (2000). *Large scale parallel data mining.* Vol. 1759 of *Lecture Notes in Artificial Intelligence.* Berlin: Springer-Verlag.

Chapter VI

Data Mining Based on Rough Sets

Jerzy W. Grzymala-Busse
University of Kansas, USA

Wojciech Ziarko
University of Regina, Canada

ABSTRACT

The chapter is focused on the data mining aspect of the applications of rough set theory. Consequently, the theoretical part is minimized to emphasize the practical application side of the rough set approach in the context of data analysis and model-building applications. Initially, the original rough set approach is presented and illustrated with detailed examples showing how data can be analyzed with this approach. The next section illustrates the Variable Precision Rough Set Model (VPRSM) to expose similarities and differences between these two approaches. Then, the data mining system LERS, based on a different generalization of the original rough set theory than VPRSM, is presented. Brief descriptions of algorithms are also cited. Finally, some applications of the LERS data mining system are listed.

INTRODUCTION

Discovering useful models capturing regularities of natural phenomena or complex systems was, until recently, almost entirely limited to finding formulas fitting empirical data. This worked relatively well in physics, theoretical mechanics, and other classical and fundamental areas of Science and Engineering. However, in social sciences, market research, medical area, pharmacy, molecular biology, learning and perception in biology, and in many other areas, the complexities of the natural processes and their common lack of analytical "smoothness" almost totally exclude the possibility of using standard mathematical tools for the purpose of data-based modeling. To serve the modeling needs of all these areas, a fundamentally different approach is needed. The availability of fast data processors creates new possibilities in that respect. To take advantage of the possibilities, new mathematical theories oriented towards creating and manipulating empirical functions and relations need to be developed. In fact, this need for alternative approaches to modeling from data was recognized some time ago by researchers working in the areas of neural nets, inductive learning, rough sets, and, more recently, in the area of data mining. The models, in the form of data-based structures of decision tables or rules, play a similar role to formulas in classical analytical modeling. Such theories can be analyzed, interpreted, and optimized using the methods of rough set theory.

In this chapter, we are assuming that the reader is familiar with basic concepts of set theory and probability theory.

General Overview of Rough Set Theory

The theory of rough sets (RST) was originated by Pawlak in 1982 as a formal mathematical theory, modeling knowledge about the domain of interest in terms of a collection of equivalence relations (Pawlak, 1982). Its main application area is in acquisition, analysis, and optimization of computer-processible models from data. The models can represent functional, partial functional, and probabilistic relations existing in data in the extended rough set approaches (Katzberg & Ziarko, 1996; Ziarko, 1993, 1999). The main advantage of rough set theory is that it does not need any preliminary or additional information about data (like probability in probability theory, grade of membership in fuzzy set theory, etc.) (Grzymala-Busse, 1988).

The Original Rough Set Model

The original rough set model is concerned with investigating the properties and the limitations of knowledge with respect to being able to form discriminative descriptions of subsets of the domain. The model is also used to investigate and prove numerous useful algebraic and logical properties of the knowledge and approximately defined sets, called rough sets. The inclusion of the approximately defined sets in the rough set model is a consequence of the knowledge imperfections in practical situations. In general, only an approximate description of a set can be formed. The approximate description consists of definitions of lower approximation and upper approximation. The approximations are definable sets, that is, having a discriminative description. The upper approximation is the smallest definable set containing the target set. The lower approximation is the largest definable set included in the target set. This ability to create approximations of non-definable, or rough, sets allows for development of approximate classification algorithms for prediction, machine learning, pattern recognition, data mining, etc. In these algorithms, the problem of classifying an observation into an indefinable category, which is not tractable in the sense that the discriminating description of the category does not exist, is replaced by the problem of classifying the observation into a definable approximation of the category that is tractable. If the approximations are "tight" enough, then the likelihood of an error of decisionmaking or prediction based on such an approximate classifier is minimal.

Variable Precision Rough Set Model (VPRSM)

The original rough set theory has been applied with success to a number of classification-related problems in control, medicine, machine learning, data mining, etc. (see, for example, Polkowski & Skowron, 1998). However, developing practical applications also revealed the limitations of this approach. The most serious one was related to the observation that often, when dealing with empirical data such as market survey data, it was not possible to identify non-empty lower approximation of the target category, for example, of the category of buyers of a service or product. Similarly, it was often not possible to identify non-trivial upper approximation of the target category, which do not extend over the whole domain. These limitations are the natural consequence of the fact that the classification problems are often inherently non-deterministic. This means that the available information does not permit for error-free, deterministic classification, even on a subset of the domain. For example, one can never 100% correctly predict the buying behavior of a customer based on typical market survey results.

Consequently, the desire to make rough set model applicable to larger class of practical problems leads to the development of a generalized model of rough sets referred to as variable precision rough set model (VPRSM) (Ziarko, 1993). As in the original rough set model, set approximations are also formed in VPRSM. However, the criteria for forming the lower and upper approximations are relaxed, in particular allowing a controlled degree of misclassification in the lower approximation. The resulting lower approximation represents an area of the domain where the correct classification can be made with the desired probability of success, rather than deterministically. In this way, the VPRSM approach can handle large class of problems that require developing non-deterministic predictive models from data. VPRSM preserves all basic properties and algorithms of the original rough sets. In particular, the basic algorithms for decision table analysis, optimization, and decision rules acquisition are directly inherited by VPRSM from the original rough set model (Pawlak, 1991). In VPRSM, they are additionally enhanced with the frequency distribution or probabilistic information acquired from data (Katzberg & Ziarko, 1996; Ziarko, 1999). As a result, the classifier systems developed within the framework of VPRSM have probabilistic confidence factors associated with them to reflect the degree of uncertainty in classificatory decisionmaking. The main goal of such classifiers is to *improve* the probability of success rather than hopelessly trying to guarantee 100% correct classification.

Decision Tables Acquired From Data

When deriving predictive models from data within rough set framework, one of the primary constructs is a decision table (Pawlak, 1991). The decision table represents knowledge about the domain of interest and the relation between the knowledge and the prediction target. Some columns of the table correspond to descriptive attributes used to classify objects of the domain of interest; other columns represent prediction targets. The rows of the table represent the classes of the classification of the domain in terms of the descriptive attributes. If the decision table contains representatives of all or almost all classes of the domain, and if the relation with the prediction targets is completely or almost completely specified, then the table can be treated as a model of the domain. Such a model represents descriptions of all or almost all objects of the domain and their relationship to the prediction target.

The specification of the relationship may include empirical assessments of conditional probabilities, if the VPRSM approach is used in model derivation. The model is called a probabilistic decision table. If the model is complete enough, and if the estimates of conditional probabilities are relatively close to real values, then the decision table can be used as a basis of approximate classifier system. To ensure relative completeness and generality of the decision table model, the values of the attributes used to construct the classification of the domain need to be sufficiently general. For example, in many practical problems, rather than using precise numeric measurements, value ranges are often used after preliminary discretization of original precise values (Nguyen, 1998). This conversion of original data values into secondary, less precise representation is one of the major pre-processing steps in rough set-based methodology of decision table acquisition from data. Once the decision table has been acquired, it can be further analyzed and optimized using classical algorithms for inter-attribute dependency computation and minimal non-redundant subset of attributes (attribute reduct) identification (Pawlak, 1991).

Rule Generation Based on a Generalization of the Rough Set Theory (LERS)

The data mining system, Learning from Examples using Rough Sets (LERS), was developed at the University of Kansas. The first implementation of LERS was done in Franz Lisp in 1988. The current version of LERS, implemented in C++, is a family of data mining systems. The LERS system is universal—it may compute rules from any kind of data. Computed rule sets may be used for classification of new cases or for interpretation of knowledge. One potential application of rule sets is rule-based expert systems.

The LERS system may compute rules from imperfect data (Grzymala-Busse, 1988, 1991, 1992), e.g., data with missing attribute values or inconsistent cases. LERS is also equipped with a set of discretization schemes to deal with numerical attributes. Similarly, a variety of LERS methods may help to handle missing attribute values. But, most importantly, LERS accepts inconsistent input data. Two cases are inconsistent when they are characterized by the same values of all attributes, but they belong to two different concepts. LERS handles inconsistencies using rough set theory. For inconsistent data, LERS computes *lower* and *upper approximations* of all concepts. The ideas of lower and upper approximations are fundamental for rough set theory. LERS uses a different generalization of the original rough set theory than VPRSM. Rules formed by LERS are equipped with numbers characterizing rule quality (uncertainty). Also, LERS is assisted with tools for rule validation: leaving-one-out, ten-fold cross validation, and hold-out.

LERS has proven its applicability, having been used for two years by NASA Johnson Space Center (Automation and Robotics Division), as a tool to develop expert systems of the type most likely to be used in medical decisionmaking on board the International Space Station. LERS was also used to enhance facility compliance under Sections 311, 312, and 313 of Title III of the Emergency Planning and Community Right to Know (Grzymala-Busse, 1993). That project was funded by the U. S. Environmental Protection Agency. The LERS system was used in other areas as well, e.g., in the medical field to compare the effects of warming devices for postoperative patients, to assess preterm birth (Woolery & Grzymala-Busse, 1994), and for diagnosis of melanoma (Grzymala-Busse, Grzymala-Busse, & Hippe, 2001).

LERS Classification System

For classification of unseen cases, the LERS system uses a "bucket brigade algorithm" (Booker, Goldberg, & Holland, 1990; Holland, Holyoak, & Nisbett, 1986), extended to use partial matching of rules and cases. The decision to which class a case belongs is made on the basis of two parameters: strength and support. They are defined as follows: *Strength* is the total number of cases correctly classified by the rule during training. The second parameter, *support*, is defined as the sum of scores of all matching rules from the class. As follows from experiments, partial matching is a valuable mechanism when complete matching fails (Grzymala-Busse, 1994). In the LERS classification system, the user may use 16 strategies for classification. However, as a result of experiments, again, it can be shown that the most successful strategy is based on strength, support, and partial matching while ignoring specificity (number of conditions in a rule) (Grzymala-Busse & Zou, 1998).

LERS equips rules with numbers characterizing quality of rules. Thus, like VPRSM, LERS goes beyond the original rough set theory. The generalizations of the original rough set theory represented by VPRSM and LERS are different. The prime concern of VPRSM is forming decision tables, while LERS was designed to form rule sets. However, all numbers related with rules and defined on the basis of VPRSM may be computed from numbers allocated by LERS to each rule. On the other hand, the LERS classification system uses ideas that are foreign to VPRSM, such as specificity, support, and partial matching. Thus, the two generalizations are independent and neither can be reduced to the other.

Related Work

The basics of the theory are summarized in Pawlak's book (Pawlak, 1991). He also introduced novel theories of rough functions and rough relations, which directly apply to the creation of approximate functional and relational models from data (Pawlak, 1996). Since the introduction of the original RST, several extensions of the original model were proposed (Greco, Matarazzo, Slowinski, & Stephanowski, 2000; Ziarko, 1993). In particular, VPRSM was first published in Ziarko (1993) and was further investigated by Beynon (2000), Kryszkiewicz (1994), and others, and served as a basis of a new approach to inductive logic programming (Mahesvari, Siromoney, Mehata, & Inoue, 2001). The initial notion of a data-acquired decision table, also called an information system, is credited to Pawlak (1991). The probabilistic decision tables were introduced by Ziarko (1998b). The LERS system was first described in Grzymala-Busse, 1992). Its most important algorithm, LEM2, was also presented in Chan and Grzymala-Busse(1994). Initial versions of LERS were presented by Budihardjo, Grzymala-Busse , and Woolery (1991), and Grzymala-Busse (1997, 1998).

There exists an extensive body of literature on rough set theory applications to knowledge discovery and data mining. A comprehensive review of the state art is available in Polkowski and Skowron (1998). A number of sources reported experiments with using rough set theory for pattern recognition, including speech recognition, handwriting recognition, and music fragment classification (Kostek, 1998; Plonka & Mrozek, 1995; Zhao, 1993). The rough set theory was first applied to trainable control by Mrozek (1986) when modeling control behavior of cement mill operators. Important applications of LERS were published in Freeman, Grzymala-Busse, Riffel, and Schroeder (2001), Grzymala-Busse *et al.* (2001), Grzymala-Busse and Gunn (1995), Grzymala-Busse and Woolery (1994), Gunn and Grzymala-Busse (1994), Loupe, Freeman, Grzymala-Busse, and Schroeder (2001), Moradi, Grzymala-Busse, and Roberts (1995), and Woolery, Grzymala-Busse, Summers, and Budihardjio(1991). Some other rough set theory-based control applications are reported in Peters, Skowron and Suraj (1999).

ROUGH SET THEORY

Rough set theory was created as a tool to handle inconsistent data. This section presents the fundamentals of the original rough set theory. The complete description of the theory may be found in Pawlak (1991) (see also Grzymala-Busse, 1995).

Global Coverings

We are assuming that the input data set is in a form of a table. Rows of the table are called *cases* (or *examples*). Columns are labeled by *attributes* and a *decision*. An example of such a table is presented in Table 1.

Table 1 depicts a simplified data base showing eight homeowners (cases) applying to a bank for a loan to buy a car. Any such table defines an information function ρ that maps the set of all ordered pairs (case, attribute) into the set of attribute values. For example, ρ ($c1$, *Home*) is equal to *expensive*.

Table 1: Consistent data set

	Attributes				Decision
	Home	Boat	Credit_Card	Age	Loan_Application
c1	expensive	no	yes	old	approved
c2	middle	yes	no	old	rejected
c3	expensive	yes	no	old	approved
c4	cheap	yes	yes	young	rejected
c5	middle	yes	yes	middle	approved
c6	middle	no	no	old	rejected
c7	middle	no	yes	young	approved
c8	expensive	no	no	young	rejected

One of the fundamental ideas of rough set theory is the relation of the set of all cases implied by a subset P of the set A of all attributes, called an *indiscernibility* relation, and denoted by IND(P). For any two cases c and c', the relation indiscernibility is defined as follows:

$$(c, c') \in \text{IND}(P) \text{ if and only if } \rho(c, a) = \rho(c', a) \text{ for all } a \in P.$$

Obviously, IND(P) is an equivalence relation, so it may be represented by the partition on U induced by IND(P). This partition will be denoted by U/IND(P). Two cases c and c' belong to the same set of the partition U/IND(P) if and only if $(c, c') \in$ IND(P). For example,

$$U/\text{IND}(\{Home\}) = \{\{c1, c3, c8\}, \{c2, c5, c6, c7\}, \{c4\}\}$$

and

$$U/\text{IND}(\{Home, Boat\}) = \{\{c1, c8\}, \{c2, c5\}, \{c3\}, \{c4\}, \{c6, c7\}\}.$$

Sets belonging to the partition U/IND(P) are called *P-elementary sets* or *blocks*. Elements $c1$ and $c3$ belong to the same {*Home*}-elementary set (or block) of U/ND({*Home*}) because the value of variable *Home* is the same for both $c1$ and c3.

In a special case where set P contains only one variable, the decision, usually denoted by d, the corresponding sets that constitute U/IND(P) are called *concepts*. In Table 1, we distinguish two concepts: $\{c1, c3, c5, c7\}$, and $\{c2, c4, c6, c8\}$. The former concept consists of all accepted applicants, the latter concept consists of all rejected.

The basic problem is how to determine a subset P of the set A describes all concepts. In different words, our problem is whether a subset P of A is sufficient to distinguish all concepts. For example, the single attribute {*Home*} is not sufficient, since *Home* has the same value *expensive* for $c1$ and $c8$, yet $c1$ and $c2$ belong to two different concepts. Moreover, a subset {*Home, Boat*} is not sufficient either, since both have the same values for $c1$ and $c8$ (*expensive, no*), and $c1$ and $c2$, as observed before, belong to two different concepts. On the other hand, the set of all attributes: {*Home, Boat, Credit_Card, Age*} is sufficient, since values of all four attributes are unique for corresponding concepts. The value vector (*expensive, no, yes, old*) of attribute vector (*Home, Boat, Credit_Card, Age*) characterize only one case, $c1$, that belongs to the concept approved loan applications. We say that {d} *depends* on the subset $P = \{Home, Boat, Credit\_Card, Age\}$. The necessary and sufficient condition for {d} to depend on P is

$$U/\text{IND}(P) \leq U/\text{IND}(\{d\})$$

The sign "$\leq$" in the above expression concerns partitions. For partitions π and τ on U, $\pi \leq \tau$ if and only if for each block B of π there exists a block B' of τ such that $B \subseteq B'$. In other words, {d} depends on P if and only if every concept defined by {d} is the union of some P-elementary sets (or blocks of U/IND(P)).

In our example,

$U/\text{IND}(\{Loan\_Application\}) = \{\{c1, c3, c5, c7\}, \{c2, c4, c6, c8\}\}$,
$U/\text{IND}(\{Home, Age\}) = \{\{c1, c3\}, \{c2, c6\}, \{c4\}, \{c5\}, \{c7\}, \{c8\}\}$,

so

$$U/\text{IND}(\{Home, Age\} \leq U/\text{IND}(\{Loan\_Application\}$$

or, {*Loan_Application* depends on {*Home, Age*}. It is not difficult to check that *U*/IND({*Home, Age*} ≤ *U*/IND({*Loan_Application*}: every block of *U*/IND({*Home, Age*}) is a subset of corresponding block from *U*/IND({*Loan_Application*}).

The minimal subset *P* such that {*d*} depends on *P* is called a *global covering of* {*d*}. The global covering is also called *relative reduct* (Pawlak, 1991). In the example in Table 1, there exist precisely two global coverings of *Loan_Application*: {*Home, Age*} and {*Home, Credit_Card, Boat*}. Algorithms for finding the set of all global coverings was published in Grzymala-Busse (1991).

Algorithm for Finding the Set of All Global Coverings

The aim of the algorithm is to find the set *C* of all global coverings of {*d*}. The cardinality of the set *X* is denoted |*X*|. Let *k* be a positive integer. The set of all subsets of the same cardinality *k* of the set *A* is denoted P_k, i.e., $P_k = \{\{xi1, xi2, ..., xik\} \mid xi1, xi2, ..., xik \in A\}$.

```
Algorithm Find_the_set_of_all_global_coverings;
      begin
            C := Ø;
            for each attribute x in A do
                    compute partition U/IND({x});
            compute partition U/IND({d});
            k := 1;
            while k ≤ |A| do
                    begin
                          for each set P in Pk do
                                if (P is not a superset of any member of C) and
                                (∏  U/IND({x}) ≤ U/IND({d}))
                                 x∈P

                                then add P to C;
                          k := k+1
                    end {while}
      end {procedure}.
```

Time complexity of the algorithm for finding the set of all coverings of *R* in *S* is exponential.

Local Coverings

In the definition of global covering, all involved attributes and decision are considered globally, i.e., for all cases. Here we will introduce a local covering, defined by variable-value pairs. Let x be a variable (an attribute or a decision), and let v be a value of x. The *block* of a variable-value pair (x, v), denoted $[(x, v)]$, is the set of all elements of the universe U that for variable x have value v. Thus, the concept is a block of $[(d, w)]$ for some value w of decision d. For example, in Table 1, the block of $(Home, expensive)$ is $\{c1, c3, c8\}$.

Let B be a subset of the universe U. Let T be a non-empty set of attribute-value pairs, where all involved attributes are different. The block of T, denoted $[T]$, is defined as

$$\bigcap_{(x, v) \in T} [(x, v)].$$

Let B be the set $\{c1, c3, c5, c7\}$, that is, B is the block of $(Loan\_Application, approved)$. In the example from Table 1, let X be the set $\{(Home, expensive), (Boat, no)\}$. The block $[X]$ of X is equal to

$$[(Home, expensive)] \cap [(Boat, no)] = \{c1, c3, c8\} \cap \{c1, c6, c7, c8\} =$$
$$\{c1, c8\} \not\subseteq \{c1, c3, c5, c7\} = B.$$

Thus $B = \{c1, c3, c5, c7\}$ does not depend on X. On the other hand, for Y equal to $\{(Home, expensive), (Age, Old)\}$, the block $[Y]$ of Y is equal to

$$[(Home, expensive)] \cap [(Age, Old)] = \{c1, c3, c8\} \cap \{c1, c2, c3, c6\} =$$
$$\{c1, c3\} \subseteq \{c1, c3, c5, c7\} = B$$

so $B = \{c1, c3, c5, c7\}$ depends on $\{(Home, expensive), (Age, Old)\}$.

We say that B *depends* on a set T of attribute-value pairs if and only if $[T] \subseteq B$. Set T is a *minimal complex* of B if and only if B depends on T and no proper subset T' of T exists such that B depends on T'.

The set $Y = \{(Home, expensive), (Age, Old)\}$ is a minimal complex of $B = \{c1, c3, c5, c7\}$, since B does not depend on any subset of Y, because

$$[(Home, expensive)] \not\subseteq B$$

and

$$[(Age, Old)] \not\subseteq B.$$

However, there exist more minimal complexes of B. For example, $Z = \{(Home, Middle), (Credit\_Card, yes)\}$ is another minimal complex of B, because

$$[Y] = [\{(Home, Middle), (Credit\_Card, yes)\}] =$$
$$[(Home, Middle)] \cap [(Credit\_Card, yes)] = \{c2, c5, c6, c7\} \cap \{c1, c4, c5, c7\} =$$
$$\{c5, c7\} \subseteq B,$$
$$[\{(Home, Middle)\} \not\subseteq B, \text{ and } [(Credit\_Card, yes)\}] \not\subseteq B.$$

Let T be a non-empty family of non-empty sets of attribute-value pairs. Set T is called a *local covering* of B if and only if the following three conditions are satisfied

(1)   each member T of T is a minimal complex of B,

(2) $\bigcup_{T \in \text{T}} [T] = B$, and

(3)   T is minimal, i.e., no subset of T exists that satisfies conditions (1) and (2).

For the example in Table 1, the set $\{Y, Z\}$, where $Y = \{(Home, expensive), (Age, Old)\}$ and $Z = \{(Home, Middle), (Credit\_Card, yes)\}$ is a local covering of $B = \{c1, c3, c5, c7\}$. The local covering is also called *value reduct* (Pawlak, 1991).

Lower and Upper Approximations of a Set

Real-life data are frequently inconsistent, i.e., data that contain conflicting cases. Two cases are conflicting when they are characterized by the same values of all attributes, but they belong to two different concepts. For example, Table 2 presents inconsistent data. Cases $c8$ and $c9$ are conflicting.

Let $[x]_P$ denote the p-elementary set of $U/\text{IND}(P)$. Any finite union of elementary sets of P is called a definable set by P. Let B be a concept. For inconsistent data, in general, B is not a definable set in P. However, set B may be approximated by two definable sets in P; the first one is called a *lower approximation of B* in P, denoted by PB and defined as follows

$$\{x \in U \mid [x]_P \subseteq B\}.$$

Table 2: Inconsistent data set

	Attributes				Decision
	Home	Boat	Credit_Card	Age	Loan_Application
c1	expensive	no	yes	old	approved
c2	middle	yes	no	old	rejected
c3	expensive	yes	no	old	approved
c4	cheap	yes	yes	young	rejected
c5	middle	yes	yes	middle	approved
c6	middle	no	no	old	rejected
c7	middle	no	yes	young	approved
c8	expensive	no	no	young	rejected
c9	expensive	no	no	young	approved

The second set is called an *upper approximation of B in P*, denoted by $\overline{P}B$ and defined as follows

$$\{x \in U \mid [x]_P \cap B \neq \emptyset\}.$$

The lower approximation of B in P is the greatest definable set by P, contained in B. The upper approximation of B is the least definable set by P containing B. A *rough set* of B in P is the family of all subsets of U having the same lower and the same upper approximations of B in P.

For Table 2,

$$U/\text{IND}(\{Loan\_Application\}) = \{\{c1, c3, c5, c7, c9\}, \{c2, c4, c6, c8\}\}$$

the lower approximation of $B = \{c1, c3, c5, c7, c9\}$ in $A = \{Home, Boat, Credit\_Card, Age\}$ is the set $\{\{c1, c3, c5, c7\}$, the upper approximation of $B = \{c1, c3, c5, c7, c9\}$ in A is the set $\{c1, c3, c5, c7, c8, c9\}$, and the rough set of B in A is the set $\{\{B\}\}$.

For inconsistent data, lower and upper approximations of a set may be used for defining two different kinds of set membership: *certain* and *possible*. Say that the concept B is not definable by the subset P of the set A of all attributes. An element $x \in U$ is said to be *certainly* in B if and only if $x \in \underline{P}B$. An element $x \in U$ is said to be *possibly* in B if and only if $x \in \overline{P}B$. Both definitions have straightforward interpretation. We have to decide whether x is or is not in B on the basis of accessible information, i.e., attributes from P. This means that we may describe the membership of x in terms of members of $U/$IND(P). On the other hand, both sets, $\underline{P}B$ and $\overline{P}B$ are constructed from $U/$IND(P). Moreover,

$$\underline{P}B \subseteq B \subseteq \overline{P}B,$$

so if $x \in \underline{P}B$ then x is certainly in B. However, if $x \in \overline{P}B$, then x does not need to be in B. If B is not definable, $\overline{P}B - B \neq \emptyset$, and x may be a member of $\overline{P}B - B$ and not a member of B. Thus x is only possibly in B.

In our example, for $B = \{c1, c3, c5, c7, c9\}$ and $A = \{Home, Boat, Credit\_Card, Age\}$, $c1 \in \underline{A}B$, so $c1 \in B$. However, $c8 \in \overline{A}B$ and $c8 \notin B$.

A few numbers characterizing a degree of uncertainty may be associated with a rough set. These numbers, sometimes useful for evaluation, have limited value, because the most important tool of rough set theory are sets—lower and upper approximations of a given concept B, a subset of the universe U.

There are two universal measures of uncertainty for rough sets, introduced in Grzymala-Busse (1987) (see also Grzymala-Busse, 1991). We will assume that P is a subset of the set A of all attributes. The first measure is called a *quality of lower approximation* of B in P, denoted γB, and equal to

$$\frac{|\underline{P}B|}{|U|}.$$

In Pawlak (1984), γB was called simply quality of approximation of B in P. The quality of lower approximation of B in P is the ratio of the number of all certainly classified elements of U by attributes from P as being in B to the number of elements of U. It is a kind of relative frequency. There exists a nice interpretation of γB in terms of evidence theory, also called Dempster-Shafer theory (see Shafer, 1976). With this interpretation, γB becomes a belief function, as it was observed for the first time in Grzymala-Busse (1987).

The second measure of uncertainty for rough sets, a *quality of upper approxima-tion* of B in P, denoted γB, is equal to

$$\frac{|PB|}{|U|} .$$

The quality of upper approximation of B in P is the ratio of the number of all possibly classified elements of U by attribute from P as being in B to the number of elements of U. Like the quality of lower approximation, the quality of upper approximation is also a kind of relative frequency. It is a plausibility function of evidence theory (Grzymala-Busse, 1987).

VARIABLE PRECISION ROUGH SET MODEL (VPRSM)

One of the primary difficulties experienced when applying the rough set approach to practical problems is the lack of consistency in data. In other words, it is quite common that a given combination of observations is associated with two or more different outcomes. For example, a set of symptoms observed in a patient may be linked to two or more diseases. There exists a large body of medical knowledge on which medical professionals base their assessment of the likelihood of correct diagnoses in such uncertain situations. However, it is rare to be able to make conclusive diagnosis without any uncertainty. In terms of rough set-based data analysis, it means that the relation between symptoms and diseases is grossly non-deterministic, resulting in all or almost all rough boundary representation of the diseases.

In such representation, only upper approximation-based or *possible* rules could be computed from data. The possible rules associate a number of possible outcomes with a combination of observations without providing any hints regarding the probability of each outcome. This is not sufficient in many practical situations where the differentiation must be made between less likely versus more likely outcomes. To deal with this problem, the possibility of using the variable precision extension of the rough set approach was introduced Ziarko (1993). VPRSM includes the frequency distribution information in its basic definitions of rough set approximations, thus making the model applicable to a large class of "inconsistent" or non-deterministic data analysis problems.

Classification Table

As in the original rough set model, VPRSM is based on the prior knowledge of indiscernibility relation IND(C), as defined previously. The indiscernibility relation represents pre-existing knowledge about the universe of interest. It is expressed in terms of identity of values of the set C of all attributes. The *C-elementary sets* or just *elementary sets* for simplicity, of the classification so defined are the basic building blocks from which the definable sets are constructed. They are also used to build lower and upper approximations of any arbitrary subset X of the universe, as described previously. In VPRSM, each *C-elementary* set E is additionally associated with two measures:

1. The probability $P(E)$ of the elementary set, which is normally estimated based on available data by

$$P(E) = \frac{|E|}{|U|}.$$

2. The conditional probability $P(X|E)$, which represents the likelihood of such an event that an object belonging to the *C*-elementary set E would also belong to the set X. The conditional probability $P(X|E)$ is typically estimated by calculating the relative degree of overlap between sets X and E, based on available data, that is $P(X|E) = \frac{|X \cap E|}{|E|}$.

For example, Table 3 illustrates the classification of a domain U in terms of the attributes *Home, Boat, Credit, Age,* along with the specification of the conditional probabilities with respect to a subset X, which is defined here as collection of low income earners. The decision *Income* specifies the target set X characterized by *Income = low*. The set X is specified by providing the estimate of the conditional probability $P(X|E_i)$ for each elementary set E_i, ($i = 1, 2,..., 8$).

In the above example, the classification represented in the table might have been obtained from the analysis of millions of data records drawn from very large domain. To

Table 3: Classification table

Elementary Sets	Attribute Set C				Conditional Probability $P(Income = low \mid E_i)$	$P(E_i)$
	Home	Boat	Credit	Age		
E_1	expensive	no	yes	old	0.10	0.15
E_2	middle	yes	no	old	0.85	0.05
E_3	expensive	yes	no	old	0.01	0.10
E_4	cheap	yes	yes	young	1.00	0.01
E_5	middle	yes	yes	middle	0.82	0.24
E_6	middle	no	no	old	0.12	0.05
E_7	middle	no	yes	young	0.92	0.15
E_8	expensive	no	no	young	0.91	0.15

conduct rough set-based analysis of such a domain in the framework of VPRSM, it is essential to:

1.   Identify all feasible combinations of attributes occurring in the domain, that is, to know identifying descriptions of all elementary sets appearing in the domain;

2.   Compute close estimate of the probability $P(E)$ for each elementary set E_i; and

3.   Compute close estimates of conditional probabilities $P(X|E_i)$ associated with elementary sets E_i for the given target set X.

The table summarizing all this information is referred to as a *classification table*. It should be noted that, in the likely absence of all feasible combinations of attributes occurring in the domain in the classification table, all conclusions derived from the table will only apply to a sub-domain of the domain. This sub-domain equals the union of all known elementary sets. For example, the results of the analysis of the information contained in Table 3 apply exclusively to the sub-domain $U_8 = \cup \{E_i : i = 1, 2, ..., 8\}$ of the whole domain (universe) U. In what follows, for the sake of simplicity, we will assume that the descriptions and the associated probability distributions are known for all elementary sets of the domain U. The reader should be aware, however, that in practice that assumption may not be satisfied.

Approximation Regions

The information contained in the classification table can be used to construct generalized, rough approximations of the subset $X \subseteq U$. Similar to the original rough set model definitions, the approximations are defined in terms of unions of some elementary sets. The defining criteria are expressed here in terms of conditional probabilities rather than in terms of relations of set inclusion and overlap. Two criteria parameters are used. The first parameter referred to as the *lower limit l* represents the highest acceptable degree of the conditional probability $P(X|E_i)$ to include the elementary set E_i in the negative region of the set X. In other words, the *l-negative region* of the set X, $NEG_l(X)$ is defined as

$$NEG_l(X) = \cup \{E_i : P(X|E_i) \leq l\}.$$

The *l-negative region* of the set X is a collection of objects which, based on the available information, cannot be classified as included in the set with the probability higher than *l*. Alternatively, the *l-negative region* is a collection of objects about which it can be said— with certainty greater or equal to *STET*— that they do not belong to the set *X*.

The positive region of the set *X* is defined using *upper limit* parameter *u* as the criterion. The upper limit reflects the least acceptable degree of the conditional probability $P(X|E_i)$ to include the elementary set E_i in the positive region, or *u-lower approximation* of the set *X*. In other words, the *u-positive region* of the set *X*, $POSu(X)$ is defined as

$$POS_u(X) = \cup \{E_i : P(X|E_i) \geq u\}.$$

Table 4: Probabilistic decision table

Elementary Sets	Attribute Set C				Rough Region for Income = low	$P(E_i)$
	Home	Boat	Credit	Age		
E_1	expensive	no	yes	old	NEG	0.15
E_2	middle	yes	no	old	POS	0.05
E_3	expensive	yes	no	old	NEG	0.10
E_4	cheap	yes	yes	young	POS	0.01
E_5	middle	yes	yes	middle	POS	0.24
E_6	middle	no	no	old	BND	0.05
E_7	middle	no	yes	young	POS	0.15
E_8	expensive	no	no	young	POS	0.15

The *u-positive region* of the set X is a collection of objects which, based on the available information, can be classified as included in the set with the probability not less than *u*. Alternatively, the *u-positive region* is a collection of objects about which it can be said—with certainty greater or equal to *u*— that they do belong to the set *X*.

When defining the approximations, it is assumed that $0 \leq l < u \leq 1$. Intuitively, *l* specifies those objects in the universe *U* that are *unlikely* to belong to the set *X*, whereas *u* specifies objects that are *likely* to belong to the set *X*. The parameters *l* and *u* associate concrete meaning with these verbal subjective notions of probability.

The objects that are not classified as being in the *u-positive region* nor in the *l-negative region* belong to the *(l, u)-boundary region* of the set *X*, denoted as $BNR_{l,u}(X) = \cup \{E_i : l < P(X|E_i) < u\}$. This is the specification of objects about which it is known that they are not sufficiently likely to belong to set *X* and also not sufficiently unlikely to not belong to the set *X*. In other words, the boundary area objects cannot be classified with sufficient certainty, as both members of the set *X* and members of the complement of the set *X*, the set ¬*X*.

In Table 4, referred to as a *probabilistic decision table,* each elementary set E_i is assigned a unique designation of its *rough region* with respect to set *X* of low-income individuals by using $l = 0.1$ *and* $u = 0.8$ as the criteria. This table is derived from the previous classification presented in Table 3.

After assigning respective rough region to each elementary set, the resulting decision table becomes fully deterministic with respect to the new decision *Rough Region*. Consequently, the techniques of the original model of rough sets, as described in previous sections, can be applied from now on to conduct analysis of the decision table. In particular, they can be used to analyze dependency between attributes, to eliminate redundant attributes, and to compute optimized rules by eliminating some redundant values of the attributes.

Analysis of Probabilistic Decision Tables

The analysis of the probabilistic decision tables involves inter-attribute dependency analysis, identification and elimination of redundant attributes, and attribute significance analysis (Ziarko, 1999).

Attribute Dependency Analysis

The original rough sets model-based analysis involves detection of functional, or partial functional dependencies, and subsequent dependency-preserving reduction of attributes. In VPRSM, (l, u)-*probabilistic dependency* is a subject of analysis. The (l, u)-probabilistic dependency is a generalization of partial-functional dependency.

The (l, u)-probabilistic dependency $\gamma_{l,u}(C, d, v)$ between attributes C and the decision d specifying the target set X of objects with the value v of the attribute d is defined as the total probability of (l, u)-positive and (l, u)-negative approximation regions of the set X. In other words,

$$\gamma_{l,u}(C, d, v) = P(POS_u(X) \cup NEG_l(X)).$$

The dependency degree can be interpreted as a measure of the probability that a randomly occurring object will be represented by such a combination of attribute values that the prediction of the corresponding value of the decision, or of its complement, could be done with the acceptable confidence. That is, the prediction that the object is a member of set X could be made with probability not less than u, and the prediction that the object is not the member of X could be made with probability not less than $1 - l$. The lower and upper limits define acceptable probability bounds for predicting whether an object is or is not the member of the target set X. If (l, u)-dependency is less than one, it means that the information contained in the table is not sufficient to make either positive or negative prediction in some cases.

For example, the $(0.1, 0.8)$-dependency between $C = \{Home, Boat, Credit, Age\}$ and *Income = low* is 0.95. It means that in 95% of new cases, we will be able to make the determination with confidence of at least 0.8 that an object is member of the set X or of its complement $U - X$. In cases when the complement is decided, the decision confidence would be at least 0.9.

Reduction of Attributes

One of the important aspects in the analysis of decision tables extracted from data is the elimination of redundant attributes and identification of the most important attributes. By redundant attributes, we mean any attributes that could be eliminated without negatively affecting the dependency degree between remaining attributes and the decision. The minimum subset of attributes preserving the dependency degree is termed *reduct*. In the context of VPRSM, the original notion of reduct is generalized to accommodate the (l, u)-probabilistic dependency among attributes. The generalized (l, u)-*reduct* of attributes, $RED_{l,u}(C, d, v) \subseteq C$ is defined as follows:

1. $\gamma_{l,u}(RED_{l,u}(C, d, v), d, v) \geq \gamma_{l,u}(C, d, v)$;
2.   For every attribute a belonging to the reduct $RED_{l,u}(C, d, v)$ the following relation holds: $\gamma_{l,u}(RED_{l,u}(C, d, v), d, v) > \gamma_{l,u}(RED_{l,u}(C, d, v) - \{a\}, d, v)$

The first condition imposes the dependency preservation requirement according to which the dependency between target set X and the reduct attributes should not be less than the dependency between the target set C of all attributes.

The second condition imposes the minimum size requirement according to which no attribute can be eliminated from the reduct without reducing the degree of dependency.

For example, one (l, u)-reduct of attributes in Table 4 is {*Home, Boat, Credit*}. The decision table reduced to these three attributes will have the same predictive accuracy as the original Table 4. In general, a number of possible reducts can be computed, leading to alternative minimal representations of the relationship between attributes and the decision.

Analysis of Significance of Condition Attributes

Determination of the most important factors in a relationship between groups of attributes is one of the objectives of factor analysis in statistics. The factor analysis is based on strong assumptions regarding the form of probability distributions, and therefore is not applicable to many practical problems. The theory of rough sets has introduced a set of techniques that help in identifying the most important attributes without any additional assumptions. These techniques are based on the concepts of attribute significance factor and of a core set of attributes. The *significance factor* of an attribute a is defined as the relative decrease of dependency between attributes and the decision caused by the elimination of the attribute a. The *core set of attributes* is the intersection of all reducts; that is, it is the set of attributes that would never be eliminated in the process of reduct computation. Both of these definitions cannot be applied if the nature of the practical problem excludes the presence of functional or partial functional dependencies. However, as with other basic notions of rough set theory, they can be generalized in the context of VPRSM to make them applicable to non-deterministic data analysis problems. In what follows, the generalized notions of attribute significance factor and core are defined and illustrated with examples.

The (l, u)-*significance*, $SIG_{l,u}(a)$ of an attribute a belonging to a reduct of the collection of attributes C can be obtained by calculating the relative degree of dependency decrease caused by the elimination of the attribute a from the reduct:

$$SIG_{l,u}(a) = \frac{\gamma_{l,u}(RED_{l,u}(C, d, v), d, v) - \gamma_{l,u}(RED_{l,u}(C, d, v) - \{a\}, d, v)}{\gamma_{l,u}(RED_{l,u}(C, d, v), \{a,\} v)}$$

For instance, the $(0.1, 0.8)$-dependency between reduct {*Home, Boat, Credit*} and *Income = low* is 0.95. It can be verified that after elimination of the attribute *Credit* the dependency decreases to 0.4. Consequently, the $(0.1, 0.8)$-significance of the attribute *Credit* in the reduct {*Home, Boat, Credit*} is

$$\frac{0.95 - 0.4}{0.95}$$

Similarly, the $(0.1, 0.8)$-significance can be computed for other reduct attributes.

The set of the most important attributes, that is, those that would be included in every reduct, is called *core set of attributes* (Pawlak, 1982). In VPRSM, the generalized notion of (l, u)-core has been introduced. It is defined exactly the same way as in the original rough set model, except that the definition requires that the (l, u)-core set of attributes be included in every (l, u)-reduct. It can be proven that the core set of attributes $CORE_{l,u}(C, d, v)$, the intersection of all CLOSE UP THIS SPACE (l, u)-reducts, satisfies the following property:

$$CORE_{l,u}(C, d, v) = \{a \in C : \gamma_{l,u}(C, d, v) - \gamma_{l,u}(C - \{a\}, d, v) > 0 \}.$$

The above property leads to a simple method for calculating the core attributes. To test whether an attribute belongs to core, the method involves temporarily eliminating the attribute from the set of attributes and checking if dependency decreased. If dependency did not decrease, the attribute is not in the core; otherwise, it is one of the core attributes.

For example, it can be verified by using the above testing procedure that the core attributes of the decision table given in Table 4 are *Home* and *Boat*. These attributes will be included in all (0.1, 0.8)-reducts of the Table 4, which means that they are essential for preservation of the prediction accuracy.

Identification of Minimal Rules

During the course of rough set-related research, considerable effort was put into development of algorithms for computing minimal rules from decision tables. From a data mining perspective, the rules reflect persistent data patterns representing potentially interesting relations existing between data items. Initially, the focus of the rule acquisition algorithms was on identification of deterministic rules, that is, rules with unique conclusion, and possibilistic rules, that is, rules with an alternative of possible conclusions. More recently, computation of uncertain rules with associated probabilistic certainty factors became of interest, mostly inspired by practical problems existing in the area of data mining where deterministic data relations are rare. In particular, VPRSM is directly applicable to computation of uncertain rules with probabilistic confidence factors. The computation of uncertain rules in VPRSM is essentially using standard rough-set methodology and algorithms involving computation of global coverings, local coverings, or *decision matrices* (Ziarko & Shan, 1996). The major difference is in the earlier steps of bringing the set of data to the probabilistic decision table form, as described earlier in this chapter. The probabilistic decision table provides an input to the rule computation algorithm. It also provides necessary probabilistic information to associate conditional probability estimates and rule probability estimates with the computed rules.

For example, based on the probabilistic decision table given in Table 4, one can identify the deterministic rules by using standard rough-set techniques (see Figure 1).

Based on the probabilistic information contained in Table 4, one can associate probabilities and conditional probabilities with the rules. Also, the rough region designations can be translated to reflect the real meaning of the decision, in this case *Income = low*. The resulting uncertain rules are presented in Figure 2.

Figure 1: Rule set.

> (Home, cheap) -> (Rough Region, POS),
> (Home, expensive) & (Age, old) -> (Rough Region, NEG),
> (Home, expensive) & (Age, young) -> (Rough Region, POS),
> (Home, middle) & (Age, young) -> (Rough Region, POS).

Figure 2: Rule set.

> (Home, cheap) -> (Income, low) with conditional probability = 1.0 and strength = 0.01,
> (Home, expensive) & (Age, old) -> (Income, not low) with conditional probability = 0.9 and probability = 0.15,
> (Home, expensive) & (Age, young) -> (Income, low) with conditional probability = 0.91 and probability = 0.15,
> (Home, middle) & (Age, young) -> (Income, low) with conditional probability = 0.92 and probability = 0.15.

All of the above rules have their conditional probabilities within the acceptability limits, as expressed by the parameters $l = 0.1$ and $u = 0.8$. The rules for the boundary area are not shown here since they do not meet the acceptability criteria.

Some algorithms for rule acquisition within the framework of VPRSM have been implemented in the commercial system DataLogic and in the system KDD-R (Ziarko, 1998b). A comprehensive new system incorporating the newest developments in the rough set area is currently being implemented.

DATA MINING SYSTEM LERS

The rule induction system, called Learning from Examples using Rough Sets (LERS), was developed at the University of Kansas. The first implementation of LERS was done in Franz Lisp in 1988.

The current version of LERS, implemented in C and C++, contains a variety of data-mining tools. LERS is equipped with the set of discretization algorithms to deal with numerical attributes. Discretization is an art rather than a science, so many methods should be tried for a specific data set. Similarly, a variety of methods may help to handle missing attribute values. On the other hand, LERS has a unique way to work with inconsistent data, following rough set theory. If a data set is inconsistent, LERS will always compute lower and upper approximations for every concept, and then will compute certain and possible rules, respectively.

The user of the LERS system may use four main methods of rule induction: two methods of machine learning from examples (called LEM1 and LEM2; LEM stands for Learning from Examples Module) and two methods of knowledge acquisition (called All

Table 5: Input data for LERS

```
< a a a a d >
```

[Home	Boat	Credit_Card	Age	Loan_Application]
expensive	no	yes	old	approved
middle	yes	no	old	rejected
expensive	yes	no	old	approved
cheap	yes	yes	young	rejected
middle	yes	yes	middle	approved
middle	no	no	old	rejected
middle	no	yes	young	approved
expensive	no	no	young	rejected
expensive	no	no	young	approved

Global Coverings and All Rules). Two of these methods are global (LEM1 and All Global Coverings); the remaining two are local (LEM2 and All Rules).

Input data file is presented to LERS in the form illustrated in Table 5. In this table, the first line (any *line* does not need to be one physical line—it may contain a few physical lines) contains declaration of variables: *a* stands for an attribute, *d* for decision, *x* means "ignore this variable." The list of these symbols starts with "<" and ends with ">". The second line contains declaration of the names of all variables, attributes, and decisions, surrounded by brackets. The following lines contain values of all variables.

LEM1—Single Global Covering

In this option, LERS may or may not take into account priorities associated with attributes and provided by the user. For example, in a medical domain, some tests (attributes) may be dangerous for a patient. Also, some tests may be very expensive, while—at the same time—the same decision may be made using less expensive tests. LERS computes a single global covering using the following algorithm:

Algorithm SINGLE GLOBAL COVERING
Input: A decision table with set A of all attributes and decision d;
Output: a single global covering R;
begin
     compute partition U/IND(A);
     P : = A;
     R := Ø;

```
if U/IND(A) ≤ U/IND({d})
    then
        begin
            for each attribute a in A do
                begin
                    Q := P – {a};
                    compute partition U/IND(Q);
                    if U/IND(Q) ≤ U/IND({d}) then P := Q
                end {for}
            R := P
        end {then}
end {algorithm}.
```

The above algorithm is heuristic, and there is no guarantee that the computed global covering is the simplest. However, the problem of looking for all global coverings—in order to select the best one—is of exponential complexity in the worst case. LERS computes all global coverings in another option, described below. The option of computing of all global coverings is feasible for small input data files and when it is required to compute as many rules as possible. After computing a single global covering, LEM1 computes rules directly from the covering using a technique called *dropping conditions* (i.e., simplifying rules).

For data from Table 1 (this table is consistent), the rule set computed by LEM1 is presented in Figure 3. CLOSE UP THIS SPACE.Note that rules computed by LERS are preceded by three numbers: specificity, strength, and the total number of training cases matching the left-hand side of the rule. These parameters are defined previously.

The LEM1 applied to data from Table 2 (this table is inconsistent) computed the rule set presented in Figure 4.

Figure 3: Rule set computed by LEM1 from consistent data.

```
2, 2, 2
(Home, expensive) & (Age, old) -> (Loan_Application, approved)
1, 1, 1
(Age, middle) -> (Loan_Application, approved)
2, 1, 1
(Home, middle) & (Age, young) -> (Loan_Application, approved)
2, 2, 2
(Home, middle) & (Age, old) -> (Loan_Application, rejected)
1, 1, 1
(Home, cheap) -> (Loan_Application, rejected)
2, 1, 1
(Home, expensive) & (Age, old) -> (Loan_Application, rejected)
```

Figure 4: Rule set computed by LEM1 from inconsistent data.

Certain rules:
2, 2, 2
(Home, expensive) & (Age, old) -> (Loan_Application, approved)
1, 1, 1
(Age, middle) -> (Loan_Application, approved)
2, 1, 1
(Home, middle) & (Age, young) -> (Loan_Application), approved)
2, 2, 2
(Home, middle) & (Age, old) -> (Loan_Application), rejected)
1, 1, 1
(Home, cheap) -> (Loan_Application, rejected)

Possible rules:
1, 3, 4
(Home, expensive) -> (Loan_Application, approved)
1, 1, 1
(Age, middle) -> (Loan_Application, approved)
2, 1, 1
(Home, middle) & (Age, young) -> (Loan_Application, approved)
2, 2, 2
(Home, middle) & (Age, old) -> (Loan_Application, rejected)
1, 1, 1
(Home, cheap) -> (Loan_Application, rejected)
2, 1, 2
(Home, expensive) & (Age, young) -> (Loan_Application, rejected)

LEM2—Single Local Covering

Like in LEM1 (single global covering option of LERS), in the option LEM2 (single local covering), the user may take into account attribute priorities. In LEM2 option, LERS uses the following algorithm for computing a single local covering:

Algorithm SINGLE LOCAL COVERING
Input: A decision table with a set A of all attributes and concept B;
Output: A single local covering **T** of concept B;
begin
    G := B;
    T := ∅;
    while G " ∅
        begin
        T := ∅;
        T(G) := {(a, v) | a ∈   A, v is a value of a, [(a, v)] ∩ G ≠ ∅};
        while T = ∅ **or** [T] ⊄ B

begin

    select a pair $(a, v) \in$ T(G) with the highest attribute priority, if a tie occurs, select a pair $(a, v) \in$ T(G) such that $|[(a, v)] \cap G|$ is maximum; if another tie occurs, select a pair $(a, v) \in$ T(G) with the smallest cardinality of $[(a, v)]$; if a further tie occurs, select first pair;

    $T := T \cup \{(a, v)\};$

    $G := [(a, v)] \cap G;$

    $T(G) := \{(a, v) \mid [(a, v)] \cap G \neq \emptyset\};$

    $T(G) := T(G) - T;$

end {while}

for each (a, v) in T **do**

    if $[T - \{(a, v)\}] \subseteq B$ **then** $T := T - \{(a, v)\};$

    $\mathbf{T} := \mathbf{T} \cup \{T\};$

    $G := B - \underset{T \in \mathbf{T}}{\cup} [T];$

end {while};

for each T in **T do**

    if $\underset{S \in \mathbf{T} - \{T\}}{\cup} [S] = B$ **then** $\mathbf{T} := \mathbf{T} - \{T\};$

end {algorithm}.

    Like the LEM1 option, the above algorithm is heuristic. The choice of used criteria was found as a result of many experiments (Grzymala-Busse & Werbrouck, 1998). Rules are eventually computed directly from the local covering, no further simplification (as in LEM1) is required. For Table 1, LEM2 computed the rule set presented in Figure 5.

All Global Coverings

    The All Global Coverings option of LERS represents a knowledge acquisition approach to rule induction. LERS attempts to compute all global coverings, and then all minimal rules are computed by dropping conditions. The following algorithm is used:

Figure 5: Rule set computed by LEM 2.2, 2, 2.

(Credit_Card, yes) & (Home, middle) -> (Loan_Application, approved)
2, 2, 2
(Home, expensive) & (Age, old) -> (Loan_Application, approved)
2, 2, 2
(Credit_Card, no) & (Home, middle) -> (Loan_Application, rejected)
1, 1, 1
(Home, cheap) -> (Loan_Application, rejected)
2, 1, 1
(Home, expensive) & (Age, young) -> (Loan_Application, rejected)

Algorithm ALL GLOBAL COVERINGS
Input: A decision table with set A of all attributes and decision d;
Output: the set R of all global coverings of {d};
begin
    R := ∅;
    for each attribute a in A **do**
        compute partition U/IND({a});
    k := 1;
    while $k \leq |A|$ **do**
        begin
            for each subset P of the set A with $|P| = k$ **do**
                if (P is not a superset of any member of R)
$$\textbf{and} \left(\prod_{a \in P} U/IND(\{a\}) \right) \leq U/IND(\{d\})$$
                then add P to R,
        k := k+1
        end {while}
    end {algorithm}.

Figure 6: Rule set computed by All Global Coverings option of LERS.

1, 1, 1
(Age, middle) -> (Loan_Application, approved)
2, 2, 2
(Home, expensive) & (Age, old) -> (Loan_Application, approved)
2, 1, 1
(Home, middle) & (Age, young) -> (Loan_Application, approved)
2, 1, 1
(Home, expensive) & (Credit_Card, yes) -> (Loan_Application, approved)
2, 2, 2
(Home, middle) & (Credit_Card, yes) -> (Loan_Application, approved)
2, 1, 1
(Home, expensive) & (Boat, yes) -> (Loan_Application, approved)
2, 2, 2
(Credit_Card, yes) & (Boat, no) -> (Loan_Application, approved)
1, 1, 1
(Home, cheap) -> (Loan_Application, rejected)
2, 2, 2
(Home, middle) & (Age, old) -> (Loan_Application, rejected)
2, 1, 1
(Home, expensive) & (Age, young) -> (Loan_Application, rejected)
2, 2, 2
(Home, middle) & (Credit_Card, no) -> (Loan_Application, rejected)
2, 2, 2
(Credit_Card, no) & (Boat, no) -> (Loan_Application, rejected)

As we observed before, the time complexity for the problem of determining all global coverings (in the worst case) is exponential. However, there are cases when it is necessary to compute rules from all global coverings (Grzymala-Busse & Grzymala-Busse, 1994). Hence, the user has an option to fix the value of a LERS parameter, reducing in this fashion the size of global coverings (due to this restriction, only global coverings of the size not exceeding this number are computed).

For example, from Table 1, the rule set computed by All Global Coverings option of LERS is presented in Figure 6.

All Rules

Yet another knowledge acquisition option of LERS is called All Rules. It is the oldest component of LERS, introduced at the very beginning in 1988. The name is justified by

Figure 7: Rule set computed by All Rules option of LERS.

```
1, 1, 1
(Age, middle) -> (Loan_Application, approved)
2, 1, 1
(Home, expensive) & (Credit_Card, yes) -> (Loan_Application, approved)
2, 2, 2
(Home, middle) & (Credit_Card, yes) -> (Loan_Application, approved)
2, 2, 2
(Home, expensive) & (Age, old) -> (Loan_Application, approved)
2, 1, 1
(Home, middle) & (Age, young) -> (Loan_Application, approved)
2, 1, 1
(Home, expensive) & (Boat, yes) -> (Loan_Application, approved)
2, 1, 1
(Credit_Card, yes) & (Age, old) -> (Loan_Application, approved)
2, 2, 2
(Credit_Card, yes) & (Boat, no) -> (Loan_Application, approved)
1, 1, 1
(Home, cheap) -> (Loan_Application, rejected)
2, 2, 2
(Home, middle) & (Credit_Card, no) -> (Loan_Application, rejected)
2, 2, 2
(Home, middle) & (Age, old) -> (Loan_Application, rejected)
2, 1, 1
(Home, expensive) & (Age, young) -> (Loan_Application, rejected)
2, 1, 1
(Credit_Card, no) & (Age, young) -> (Loan_Application, rejected)
2, 2, 2
(Credit_Card, no) & (Boat, no) -> (Loan_Application, rejected)
2, 1, 1
(Age, young) & (Boat, yes) -> (Loan_Application, rejected)
```

the way LERS works when this option is invoked: all rules that can be computed from the decision table are computed, all in their simplest form. The algorithm takes each example from the decision table and computes all potential rules (in their simplest form) that will cover the example and not cover any example from other concepts. Duplicate rules are deleted. For Table 1, this option computed the rule et presented in Figure 7.

Classification

In LERS, the first classification system to classify unseen cases using a rule set computed from training cases was used in the system, Expert System for Environmental Protection (ESEP). This classification system was much improved in 1994 by using a modified version of the bucket brigade algorithm (Booker *et al.*, 1990; Holland *et al.*, 1986). In this approach, the decision to which concept an example belongs is made using three factors: *strength*, *specificity*, and *support*. They are defined as follows: *Strength factor* is a measure of how well the rule has performed during training. *Specificity* is the total number of attribute-value pairs on the left-hand side of the rule. The third factor, *support*, is related to a concept and is defined as the sum of scores of all matching rules from the concept. The concept getting the largest support wins the contest.

In LERS, the strength factor is adjusted to be the *strength* of a rule, i.e., the total number of examples correctly classified by the rule during training. The concept *C* for which support, i.e., the following expression

$$\sum_{\text{matching rules } R \text{ describing } C} \text{Strength factor}(R) * \text{Specificity}(R)$$

is the largest is a winner, and the example is classified as being a member of *C*.

If an example is not completely matched by any rule, some classification systems use *partial matching*. System AQ15, during partial matching, uses a probabilistic sum of all measures of fit for rules (Michalski *et al.*, 1986).

In the original bucket brigade algorithm, partial matching is not considered a viable alternative of complete matching. Bucket brigade algorithm depends instead on default hierarchy (Holland *et al.*, 1986).

In LERS, partial matching does not rely on the user's input. If complete matching is impossible, all partially matching rules are identified. These are rules with at least one attribute-value pair matching the corresponding attribute-value pair of an example.

For any partially matching rule *R*, the additional factor, called *Matching factor* (*R*), is computed. Matching factor(*R*) is defined as the ratio of the number of matched attribute-value pairs of a rule *R* with the case to the total number of attribute-value pairs of the rule *R*. In partial matching, the concept *C* for which the following expression is the largest

$$\sum_{\text{partially matching rules } R \text{ describing } C} \text{Matching factor}(R) * \text{Strength factor}(R) * \text{Specificity}(R)$$

is the winner, and the example is classified as being a member of *C*.

LERS assigns three numbers to each rule: specificity, strength, and the total number of training cases matching the left-hand side of the rule. These numbers, used during classification, are essential for the LERS generalization of the original rough set theory. Note that both rule parameters used in VPRSM, probability and conditional probability, may be computed from the three numbers supplied by LERS to each rule. The probability, used in VPRSM, is the ratio of the third number (the total number of training cases matching the left-hand side of the rule) to the total number of cases in the data set. The conditional probability from VPRSM is the ratio of the second number (strength) to the third number (the total number of training cases matching the left-hand side of the rule).

APPLICATIONS

LERS has been used in the medical field, nursing, global warming, environmental protection, natural language, and data transmission. LERS may process big datasets and frequently outperforms not only other rule induction systems but also human experts.

Medical Field

In the medical field, LERS was used for prediction of preterm birth, for diagnosis of melanoma, for prediction of behavior under mental retardation, and for analysis of animal models for prediction of self-injurious behavior.

Predicting which pregnant woman is at risk for giving birth prematurely is a difficult problem in health care. Medical science and research has not offered viable solutions for the prematurity problem. In one of our projects, completed in 1992-93, three large prenatal databases were acquired. Each database was divided in two halves—50% for training data and 50% for testing data. Each data set was then analyzed using statistical and data-mining programs. The best predictive accuracy was accomplished using LERS. Manual methods of assessing preterm birth have a positive predictive value of 17-38%. The data-mining methods based on LERS reached a positive predictive value of 59-92%.

Another project was associated with melanoma diagnosis based on the well-known ABCD formula. Our main objective was to check whether the original ABCD formula is optimal. As a result of more than 20,000 experiments, the optimal ABCD formula was found, reducing thus the error rate from 10.21% (original ABCD formula) to 6.04% (optimal ABCD formula).

In yet another project, data on heart rate were linked to environmental and behavioral data coded from videotapes of one adult subject diagnosed with severe mental retardation who engaged in problem behavior. The results of the analysis suggest that using the LERS system will be a valuable strategy for exploring large data sets that include heart rate, environmental, and behavioral measures.

Similarly, LERS was used for prediction of animal models based on their behavioral responsiveness to a dopamine agonist, GBR12909. The three animal groups received five injections of GBR12909 and were observed for stereotyped and self-injurious behaviors immediately following the injections and six hours after injections. Differences in the rule sets computed for each group enabled the prediction of the stereotyped behaviors that may occur prior to occurrence of self-injurious behavior.

Also, LERS has been used by the NASA Johnson Space Center as a tool to develop an expert system that may be used in medical decisionmaking on board the International Space Station.

Natural Language

One of our projects was to derive data associated with the word *concept* from the Oxford English Dictionary and then place additional terms in Roget's Thesaurus. Two rule sets were computed from training data, using algorithms LEM2 and All-Rules of LERS, respectively. Both rule sets were validated by testing data. The rule set computed by the All-Rules algorithm was much better than the rule set computed by LEM2 algorithm. This conclusion is yet another endorsement of the claim that the knowledge acquisition approach is better for rule induction than the machine-learning approach.

Another project in this area was a data-mining experiment for determining parts of speech from a file containing the last three characters of words from the entire Roget's Thesaurus. Every entry was classified as belonging to one of five parts of speech: nouns, verbs, adjectives, adverbs, and prepositions. The file had 129,797 entries. Only a small portion of the file (4.82%) was consistent. LEM2 algorithm of LERS computed 836 certain rules and 2,294 possible rules. Since the file was created from the entire Roget's Thesaurus, the same file was used for training and testing. The final error rate was equal to 26.71%, with the following partial error rates: 11.75% for nouns, 73.58% for verbs, 11.99% for adverbs, 33.50% for adjectives, and 85.76% for prepositions.

CONCLUSIONS

This chapter presents two approaches to data mining based on rough sets. In both cases generalizations of the original rough set theory are used. The first one, called VPRSM, may be used, for example, to acquire decision tables. The second approach, exemplified by LERS, is used for rule generation. Formed rules may be used for classification of new, unseen cases or for interpretation of regularities hidden in the input data.

When VPRSM is used for the generation of decision tables, global computations are involved, i.e., all attributes are taken into account in operations such as reducing the attribute set or analysis of significance of attributes. On the other hand, LERS usually uses a local approach. Computations in LERS involve attribute-value pairs rather than entire attributes, since the main task is to form rules containing attribute-value pairs.

Data mining based on rough set theory or, more exactly, on generalizations of rough set theory, were successfully used for more than a decade. A number of real-life projects, listed in this chapter, confirmed viability of data mining based on rough set theory.

REFERENCES

Beynon, M. (2000). An investigation of beta-reduct selection within variable precision rough sets model. *2nd International Conference on Rough Sets and Current Trends in Computing*, Banff, 2000, LNAI 2005, pp. 82-90. Berlin: Springer-Verlag.

Booker, L. B., Goldberg, D. E., & Holland, J. F. (1990). Classifier systems and genetic algorithms, In J.G. Carbonell (ed.), *Machine Learning. Paradigms and Methods*, pp. 235-282. Cambridge, MA: MIT Press.

Budihardjo, A., Grzymala-Busse J., & Woolery, L. K. (1991). Program LERS_LB 2.5 as a tool for knowledge acquisition in nursing. *4th International Conference on Industrial and Engineering Applications of Artificial Intelligence and Expert Systems*, Koloa, Kauai, Hawaii, pp. 735-740, June 2-5, 1991, The University of Tennessee Space Institute Press.

Chan, C. C. & Grzymala-Busse, J. W. (1994). On the two local inductive algorithms: PRISM and LEM2. *Foundations of Computing and Decision Sciences*, 19, 185–203.

Freeman, R. L., Grzymala-Busse, J. W., Riffel, L. A., & Schroeder, S. R. (2001). Analysis of self-injurious behavior by the LERS data mining system. In the *Proceedings of the Japanese Society for Artificial Intelligence International Workshop on Rough Set Theory and Granular Computing, RSTGC-2001*, May 20–22, pp. 195-200, Matsue, Shimane, Japan, Bulletin Internet, *Rough Set Society*, 5(1/2).

Goodwin, L. K. & Grzymala-Busse, J. W. (2001). Preterm birth prediction/System LERS. In W. Klösgen and J. Zytkow (eds.), *Handbook of Data Mining and Knowledge Discovery*. Oxford, UK: Oxford University Press.

Greco, S., Matarazzo, B., Slowinski, R., & Stefanowski, J. (2000). Variable consistency model of dominance-based rough sets approach. *2nd International Conference on Rough Sets*, Banff, 2000, LNAI 2005, pp. 138-148. Berlin: Springer-Verlag.

Grzymala-Busse, D. M. & Grzymala-Busse, J. W. (1994). Evaluation of machine learning approach to knowledge acquisition. *14th International Avignon Conference*, Paris, May 30-June 3, pp. 183–192, EC2 Press.

Grzymala-Busse, J. P., Grzymala-Busse, J. W., & Hippe, Z. S. (2001). Melanoma prediction using data mining system LERS. *Proceedings of the 25th Anniversary Annual International Computer Software and Applications Conference COMPSAC 2001*, Chicago, IL, October 8–12, pp. 615–620, IEEE Press.

Grzymala-Busse, J. W. (1987). Rough-set and Dempster-Shafer approaches to knowledge acquisition under uncertainty—A comparison. Manuscript.

Grzymala-Busse, J. W. (1988). Knowledge acquisition under uncertainty—a rough set approach. *Journal of Intelligent & Robotic Systems* 1, 1, 3–16.

Grzymala-Busse, J. W. (1991). *Managing Uncertainty in Expert Systems*. Boston, MA: Kluwer Academic Publishers.

Grzymala-Busse, J. W. (1992). LERS—A system for learning from examples based on rough sets. In R. Slowinski (ed.), *Intelligent decision support. Handbook of applications and advances of the rough set theory*. pp.3-18. Dordrecht, Boston, London: Kluwer Academic Publishers.

Grzymala-Busse, J. W. (1993). ESEP: An expert system for environmental protection. RSKD–93, *International Workshop on Rough Sets and Knowledge Discovery*, Banff, Alberta, Canada, October 12-15, pp. 499–508.

Grzymala-Busse, J. W. (1994). Managing uncertainty in machine learning from examples. *Third Intelligent Information Systems Workshop*, Wigry, Poland, pp. 70–84, IPI PAN Press.

Grzymala-Busse, J. W. (1995). Rough Sets. *Advances in Imaging and Electron Physics* 94, 151–195.

Grzymala-Busse, J. W. (1997). A new version of the rule induction system LERS. *Fundamenta Informaticae* 31, 27–39.

Grzymala-Busse, J. W. (1998a). Applications of the rule induction system LERS. In L. Polkowski and A. Skowron (eds.), *Rough Sets in Knowledge Discovery* 1, *Methodology and Applications*, pp. 366-375. Heidelberg-New York: Physica-Verlag.

Grzymala-Busse, J. W. (1998b). LERS—A knowledge discovery system. In L. Polkowski and A. Skowron (eds.), *Rough Sets in Knowledge Discovery* 2, *Applications, Case Studies and Software Systems*. pp.562-565. Heidelberg-New York: Physica-Verlag.

Grzymala-Busse, J. W. & Gunn, J. D. (1995). Global temperature analysis based on the rule induction system LERS. *4th Workshop on Intelligent Information Systems* WIS'95, Augustow, Poland, pp.148–158, IPI PAN Press.

Grzymala-Busse, J. W. & Old, L. J. (1997). A machine learning experiment to determine part of speech from word-endings. *10th International Symposium on Methodologies for Intelligent Systems* ISMIS'97, Charlotte, NC, October 15-18—, In Z. W. Ras and A. Skowron (eds.), *Foundations of Intelligent Systems Lecture Notes in AI* 1325, pp. 497-506. Berlin: Springer-Verlag.

Grzymala-Busse, J. W. & Wang, C. P. B. (1986). Classification and rule induction based on rough sets. *5th IEEE International Conference on Fuzzy Systems* FUZZ-IEEE'96, New Orleans, Louisiana, September 8-11, pp. 744–747, IEEE Press.

Grzymala-Busse, J. W. & Werbrouck, P. (1998). On the best search method in the LEM1 and LEM2 algorithms. In E. Orlowska (ed.), *Incomplete Information: Rough Set Analysis*, pp. 75-91. Heidelberg-New York: Physica-Verlag.

Grzymala-Busse, J. W. & Woolery, L. K. (1994). Improving prediction of preterm birth using a new classification scheme and rule induction. *18th Annual Symposium on Computer Applications in Medical Care*, SCAMC, Washington, DC, pp.730–734, Hanley & Belfus, Inc. Publishers.

Grzymala-Busse, J. W. & Zou X. (1998). Classification strategies using certain and possible rules. *1st International Conference on Rough Sets and Current Trends in Computing*, Warsaw, Poland, June 22-26. *Lecture Notes in Artificial Intelligence*, No. 1424, 37–44 Berlin: Springer-Verlag.

Grzymala-Busse, J. W., Grzymala-Busse, W. J., & Goodwin, L. K. (1999). A closest fit approach to missing attribute values in preterm birth data. *7th International Workshop on Rough Sets, Fuzzy Sets, Data Mining and Granular-Soft Computing*, RSFDGrC'99, Ube, Yamaguchi, Japan. *Lecture Notes in Artificial Intelligence*, No. 1711, 405–413, Berlin: Springer-Verlag.

Gunn, J. D. & Grzymala-Busse, J. W. (1994). Global temperature stability by rule induction: An interdisciplinary bridge. *Human Ecology* 22, 59–81.

Holland, J. H., Holyoak K. J., & Nisbett, R. E. (1986). *Induction. Processes of inference, learning, and discovery*. Cambridge, MA: MIT Press.

Katzberg, J. & Ziarko, W. (1996). Variable precision extension of rough sets. *Fundamenta Informaticae*, Special Issue on Rough Sets, 27, 155-168.

Kostek, B. (1998). Computer-based recognition of musical phrases using the rough set approach. *Journal of Information Science*, 104, 15-30.

Kryszkiewicz, M. (1994). Knowledge reduction algorithms in information systems. Ph.D. thesis, Faculty of Electronics, Warsaw University of Technology, Poland.

Loupe, P. S., Freeman, R. L., Grzymala-Busse, J. W., & Schroeder, S. R. (2001). Using rule induction for prediction of self-injuring behavior in animal models of development disabilities. *14th IEEE Symposium on Computer-Based Medical Systems*, CBMS 2001, July 26-27-, pp. 171–176, Bethesda, MD, IEEE Press.

Maheswari, U., Siromoney, A., Mehata, K., & Inoue, K. (2001). The variable precision rough set inductive logic programming model and strings. *Computational Intelligence*, 17, 460-471.

Michalski, R. S. (1983). A theory and methodology of inductive learning. In R.S. Michalski, J.G. Carbonell, & T.M. Mitchell (eds.): *Machine Learning. An Artificial Intelligence Approach*, pp.83-134. San Francisco, CA: Morgan Kauffman.

Michalski, R.S., Carbonell J.G., & Mitchell, T.M. (1983). *Machine learning. An artificial intelligence approach.* San Francisco, CA: Morgan Kauffman.

Michalski, R. S., Mozetic, I., Hong, J. & Lavrac, N. (1986). The AQ15 inductive learning system: An overview and experiments. Report UIUCDCD-R-86-1260, Department of Computer Science, University of Illinois.Moradi, H., Grzymala-Busse, J. W., &Roberts, J. A. (1995). Entropy of English text: Experiments with humans and a machine learning system based on rough sets. *2nd Annual Joint Conference on Information Sciences*, JCIS'95, Wrightsville Beach, North Carolina, pp. 87–88, Paul R. Wang Press.

Mrozek, A. (1986). Use of rough sets and decision tables for implementing rule-based control of industrial processes. *Bulletin of the Polish Academy of Sciences*, 34, 332-356.

Nguyen, H. S. (1998). Discretization problems for rough set methods. *1st International Conference on Rough Sets and Current Trends in Computing*, Warsaw, Poland. *Lecture Notes in AI* 1424, pp.545-552. Berlin: Springer-Verlag.

Pawlak, Z. (1982). Rough Sets. *International Journal of Computer and Information Sciences*, 11, 341-356.

Pawlak, Z. (1984). Rough Sets. *International Journal of Man-Machine Studies* 20, 469.

Pawlak, Z. (1991). *Rough Sets. Theoretical Aspects of Reasoning about Data.* Kluwer Academic Publishers, Dordrecht, Boston, London.

Pawlak, Z. (1996). Rough sets, rough relations and rough functions. *Fundamenta Informaticae*, 27, 103-108.

Pawlak, Z., Grzymala-Busse, J. W., Slowinski, R., & Ziarko, W. (1995). Rough sets. *Communications of the ACM* 38, 89-95.

Peters, J. Skowron, A. & Suraj, Z. (1999). An application of rough set methods in control design. *Workshop on Concurrency*, Warsaw, pp. 214-235.

Plonka, L. & Mrozek, A. (1995). Rule-based stabilization of the inverted pendulum. *Computational Intelligence*, 11, 348-356.

Polkowski, L. & Skowron, A. (1998). *Rough sets in knowledge discovery*, 2, *Applications, case studies and software systems*, Appendix 2: Software Systems. pp. 551–601. Heidelberg-New York: Physica Verlag.

Shafer, G. (1976). *A mathematical theory of evidence.* Princeton, NJ: Princeton University Press.

Stefanowski, J. (1998). On rough set based approaches to induction of decision rules. In L. Polkowski & A. Skowron (eds.), *Rough sets in data mining and knowledge discovery*, pp. 500-529. Heidelberg-New York: Physica-Verlag.

Woolery, L., Grzymala-Busse, J., Summers, S., & Budihardjo, A. (1991). The use of machine learning program LERS_LB 2.5 in knowledge acquisition for expert system development in nursing. *Computers in Nursing* 9, 227-234.

Zhao, Z. (1993). Rough set approach to speech recognition. M.Sc. thesis, Computer Science Department University of Regina, Canada.

Ziarko, W. (1993). Variable precision rough sets model. *Journal of Computer and Systems Sciences*, 46, 39-59.

Ziarko, W. (1998a). Approximation region-based decision tables. *International Conference on Rough Sets and Current Trends in Computing*, Warsaw, Lecture Notes in AI 1424, pp.178-185. Berlin: Springer-Verlag.

Ziarko, W. (1998b). KDD-R: Rough sets-based data mining system. In L. Polkowski & A. Skowron (eds.), *Rough sets in knowledge discovery*, Part II. *Studies in Fuzziness and Soft Computing*, pp. 598-601. Berlin: Springer-Verlag.

Ziarko, W. (1999). Decision making with probabilistic decision tables. *7th International. Workshop on Rough Sets, Fuzzy Sets, Data Mining and Granular Computing*, RSFDGrC'99, Yamaguchi, Japan, *Lecture Notes in AI* 1711, pp. 463-471. Berlin: Springer-Verlag.

Ziarko, W. & Shan, N. (1996). A method for computing all maximally general rules in attribute-value systems. *Computational Intelligence: an International Journal*, 12, 223-234.

Chapter VII

The Impact of Missing Data on Data Mining

Marvin L. Brown
Hawaii Pacific University, USA

John F. Kros
East Carolina University, USA

ABSTRACT

Data mining is based upon searching the concatenation of multiple databases that usually contain some amount of missing data along with a variable percentage of inaccurate data, pollution, outliers, and noise. The actual data-mining process deals significantly with prediction, estimation, classification, pattern recognition, and the development of association rules. Therefore, the significance of the analysis depends heavily on the accuracy of the database and on the chosen sample data to be used for model training and testing. The issue of missing data must be addressed since ignoring this problem can introduce bias into the models being evaluated and lead to inaccurate data mining conclusions.

THE IMPACT OF MISSING DATA

Missing or inconsistent data has been a pervasive problem in data analysis since the origin of data collection. More historical data is being collected today due to the proliferation of computer software and the high capacity of storage media. In turn, the issue of missing data becomes an even more pervasive dilemma. An added complication is that the more data that is collected, the higher the likelihood of missing data. This will require one to address the problem of missing data in order to be effective.

During the last four decades, statisticians have attempted to address the impact of missing data on information technology.

This chapter's objectives are to address the impact of missing data and its impact on data mining. The chapter commences with a background analysis, including a review of both seminal and current literature. Reasons for data inconsistency along with definitions of various types of missing data are addressed. The main thrust of the chapter focuses on methods of addressing missing data and the impact that missing data has on the knowledge discovery process. Finally, trends regarding missing data and data mining are discussed in addition to future research opportunities and concluding remarks.

Background

The analysis of missing data is a comparatively recent discipline. With the advent of the mainframe computer in the 1960s, businesses were capable of collecting large amounts of data on their customer databases. As large amounts of data were collected, the issue of missing data began to appear. A number of works provide perspective on missing data and data mining.

Afifi and Elashoff (1966) provide a review of the literature regarding missing data and data mining. Their paper contains many seminal concepts, however, the work may be dated for today's use. Hartley and Hocking (1971), in their paper entitled "The Analysis of Incomplete Data," presented one of the first discussions on dealing with skewed and categorical data, especially maximum likelihood (ML) algorithms such as those used in Amos. Orchard and Woodbury (1972) provide early reasoning for approaching missing data in data mining by using what is commonly referred to as an expectation maximization (EM) algorithm to produce unbiased estimates when the data are missing at random (MAR). Dempster, Laird, and Rubin's (1977) paper provided another method for obtaining ML estimates and using EM algorithms. The main difference between Dempster, Laird, and Rubin's (1977) EM approach and that of Hartley and Hocking is the Full Information Maximum Likelihood (FIML) algorithm used by Amos. In general, the FIML algorithm employs both first- and second-order derivatives whereas the EM algorithm uses only first-order derivatives.

Little (1982) discussed models for nonresponse, while Little and Rubin (1987) considered statistical analysis with missing data. Specifically, Little and Rubin (1987) defined three unique types of missing data mechanisms and provided parametric methods for handling these types of missing data. These papers sparked numerous works in the area of missing data. Diggle and Kenward (1994) addressed issues regarding data missing completely at random, data missing at random, and likelihood-based inference. Graham, Hofer, Donaldson, MacKinnon, and Schafer (1997) discussed using the EM algorithm to estimate means and covariance matrices from incomplete data. Papers from Little (1995) and Little and Rubin (1989) extended the concept of ML estimation in data mining, but they also tended to concentrate on data that have a few distinct patterns of missing data. Howell (1998) provided a good overview and examples of basic statistical calculations to handle missing data.

The problem of missing data is a complex one. Little and Rubin (1987) and Schafer (1997) provided conventional statistical methods for analyzing missing data and discussed the negative implications of naïve imputation methods. However, the statistical literature on missing data deals almost exclusively with the training of models rather than prediction (Little, 1992). Training is described as follows: when dealing with a small proportion of cases containing missing data, you can simply eliminate the missing cases for purposes of training. Cases cannot be eliminated if any portion of the case is needed in any segment of the overall discovery process.

In theory, Bayesian methods can be used to ameliorate this issue. However, Bayesian methods have strong assumptions associated with them. Imputation methods are valuable alternatives to introduce here, as they can be interpreted as an approximate Bayesian inference for quantities of interest based on observed data.

A number of articles have been published since the early 1990s regarding imputation methodology. Schafer and Olsen (1998) and Schafer (1999) provided an excellent starting point for multiple imputation. Rubin (1996) provided a detailed discussion on the interrelationship between the model used for imputation and the model used for analysis. Schafer's (1997) text has been considered a follow up to Rubin's 1987 text. A number of conceptual issues associated with imputation methods are clarified in Little (1992). In addition, a number of case studies have been published regarding the use of imputation in medicine (Barnard & Meng, 1999; van Buuren, Boshuizen, & Knook, 1999) and in survey research (Clogg, Rubin, Schenker, Schultz, & Weidman, 1991). A number of researchers have begun to discuss specific imputation methods. Hot deck imputation and nearest neighbor methods are very popular in practice, despite receiving little overall coverage with regard to Data Mining (see Ernst, 1980; Kalton & Kish, 1981; Ford, 1983; and David, Little, Samuhel, & Triest, 1986).

Breiman, Friedman, Olshen, and Stone (1984) developed a method known as CART®, or classification and regression trees. Classification trees are used to predict membership of cases or objects in the classes of categorical dependent variables from their measurements on one or more predictor variables. Loh and Shih (1997) expanded on classification trees with their paper regarding split selection methods. Some popular classification tree programs include FACT (Loh & Vanichestakul, 1988), THAID (Morgan & Messenger, 1973), as well as the related programs AID, for Automatic Interaction Detection (Morgan & Sonquist, 1963), and CHAID, for Chi-Square Automatic Interaction Detection (Kass, 1980). Classification trees are useful data-mining techniques as they are easily understood by business practitioners and are easy to perceive visually. Also, the basic tree induction algorithm is considered to be a "greedy" approach to classification, using a recursive divide-and-conquer approach (Han & Kamber, 2001). This allows for raw data to be analyzed quickly without a great deal of preprocessing. No data is lost, and outliers can be identified and dealt with immediately (Berson, Smith and Thearling, 2000).

Agrawal, Imielinski, and Swami (1993) introduced association rules for the first time in their paper, "Mining Association Rules between Sets of Items in Large." A second paper by Agrawal and Srikant (1994) introduced the Apriori algorithm. This is the reference algorithm for the problem of finding Association Rules in a database. Valuable "general purpose" chapters regarding the discovery of Association Rules are included in the texts: *Fast Discovery of Association Rules* by R. Agrawal, H. Mannila, R. Srikant, H. Toivonen and A. I. Verkamo, and *Advances in Knowledge Discovery and Data Mining*. Association rules in data-mining applications search for interesting relationships among a given set of attributes. Rule generation is based on the "interestingness" of a proposed rule, measured by satisfaction of thresholds for minimum support and minimum confidence. Another method for determining interestingness is the use of correlation analysis to determine correlation rules between itemsets (Han & Kamber, 2001).

In addition to the aforementioned data-mining techniques, neural networks are used to build explanatory models by exploring datasets in search of relevant variables or groups of variables. Haykin (1994), Masters (1995), and Ripley (1996) provided information on neural networks. For a good discussion of neural networks used as statistical tools, see Warner and Misra (1996). More recent neural net literature also contains good papers covering prediction with missing data (Ghahramani & Jordan, 1997; Tresp, Neuneier, & Ahmad, 1995). Neural networks are useful in data-mining software packages in their ability to be readily applied to prediction, classification, and clustering problems, and can be trained to generalize and learn (Berson, Smith, & Thearling, 2000). When prediction is the main goal of the neural network, it is most applicable for use when both the inputs to, and outputs from, the network are well-understood by the knowledge worker. The answers obtained from neural networks are often correct and contain a considerable amount of business value (Barry & Linoff, 1997).

Finally, genetic algorithms are also learning-based data mining techniques. Holland (1975) introduced genetic algorithms as a learning-based method for search and optimization problems. Michalewicz (1994) provided a good overview of genetic algorithms, data structures, and evolution programs. A number of interesting articles discussing genetic algorithms have appeared. These include Flockhart and Radcliffe (1996), Szpiro (1997), and Sharpe and Glover (1999). While neural networks employ the calculation of internal link weights to determine the best output, genetic algorithms are also used in data mining to find the best possible link weights. Simulating natural evolution, genetic algorithms generate many different genetic estimates of link weights, creating a population of various neural networks. Survival-of-the-fittest techniques are then used to weed out networks that are performing poorly (Berson, Smith & Thearling, 2000).

In summation, the literature to date has addressed various approaches to data mining through the application of historically proven methods. The base theories of nearest neighbor, classification trees, association rules, neural networks and genetic algorithms have been researched and proven to be viable methodologies to be used as the foundation of commercial data mining software packages. The impact of incomplete or missing data on the knowledge discovery (data mining) process has more recently been approached in association with these individual methodologies. Prior research in this area has resulted in updates to commercial software in order to address issues concerning the quality and preprocessing of both training and new data sets, as well as the nature and origin of various problematic data issues.

In the future, many hybrid methods utilizing the proven algorithms currently used for successful data mining will be developed to compete both in the realms of research and private industry. In addition to these algorithmic hybrids, new methodologies for dealing with incomplete and missing data will also be developed, also through the merging of proven and newly developed approaches to these issues. Other research gaps to pursue will include the warehousing of all "dirty data," warehousing of pattern recognition results, and the development of new techniques to search these patterns for the very nature of the problem and its solution. In areas that are found to have unavailable practical solutions, methods for handling individual "special interest" situations must be investigated.

DATA MINING WITH
INCONSISTENT DATA/MISSING DATA

The main thrust of the chapter focuses on methods of addressing missing data and the impact that missing data has on the knowledge discovery process (depending on the data-mining algorithm being utilized). Finally, trends regarding missing data and data mining are discussed along with future research opportunities and concluding remarks.

Reasons For Data Inconsistency

Data inconsistency may arise for a number of reasons, including:

- Procedural Factors;
- Refusal of Response; or
- Inapplicable Responses.

Procedural Factors

Errors in databases are a fact of life; however, their impact on knowledge discovery and data mining can generate serious problems. Data entry errors are common. Dillman (1999) provided an excellent text for designing and collecting data. He also promoted discussion for the reduction of survey error including coverage, sampling, measurement, and nonresponse.

Whenever invalid codes are allowed to slip into a database, inaccurate classifications of new data occur resulting in classification error or omission. Erroneous estimates, predictions, and invalid pattern-recognition conclusions may also take place. Correlation between attributes can also become skewed which will result in erroneous association rules.

Data from questionnaires that are left blank by the respondent further complicate the data-mining process. If a large number of similar respondents fail to complete similar questions, the deletion or misclassification of these observations can take the researcher down the wrong path of investigation or lead to inaccurate decision making by end-users. Methods for prevention of procedural data inconsistency are presented in Jenkins and Dillman (1997). Included are topics such as how to design a questionnaire with regard to typography and layout in order to avoid data inconsistency. Another excellent paper is Brick and Kalton (1996) which discusses the handling of missing data in survey research.

Refusal of Response

Some respondents may find certain survey questions offensive, or they may be personally sensitive to certain questions. For example, questions that refer to one's education level, income, age, or weight may be deemed too personal by some respondents. In addition, some respondents may have no opinion regarding certain questions, such as political or religious affiliation.

Furthermore, respondents may simply have insufficient knowledge to accurately answer particular questions (Hair, 1998). Students, in particular, may have insufficient knowledge to answer certain questions. For example, when polled for data concerning future goals and/or career choices, they may not have had the time to investigate certain aspects of their career choice (such as salaries in various regions of the country, retirement options, insurance choices, etc.).

Inapplicable Responses

Sometimes questions are left blank simply because the questions apply to a more general population than to an individual respondent. In addition, if a subset of questions on a questionnaire does not apply to the individual respondent, data may be missing for a particular expected group within a data set. For example, adults who have never been married or who are widowed or divorced are not likely to answer a question regarding years of marriage. Likewise, graduate students may choose to leave questions blank that concern social activities for which they simply do not have time.

Types of Missing Data

It is important for an analyst to understand the different types of missing data before he or she can address the issue. The following is a list of the standard types of missing data:

- Data Missing At Random;
- Data Missing Completely At Random;
- Non-Ignorable Missing Data; and
- Outliers Treated As Missing Data

[Data] Missing At Random (MAR)

Cases containing incomplete data must be treated differently than cases with complete data. The pattern of the missing data may be traceable or predictable from other variables in the database, rather than being attributable to the specific variable on which the data are missing (Stat. Serv. Texas, 2000). Rubin (1976) defined missing data as Missing At Random (MAR) "when given the variables X and Y, the probability of response depends on X but not on Y." For example, if the likelihood that a respondent will provide his or her weight depends on the probability that the respondent will not provide his or her age, then the missing data is considered to be MAR (Kim, 2001).

Consider the situation of reading comprehension. Investigators may administer a reading comprehension test at the beginning of a survey administration session in order to find participants with lower reading comprehension scores. These individuals may be less likely to complete questions that are located at the end of the survey.

[Data] Missing Completely At Random (MCAR)

Missing Completely At Random (MCAR) data exhibits a higher level of randomness than does MAR. Rubin (1976) and Kim (2001) classified data as MCAR when "the probability of response [shows that] independence exists between X and Y." In other words, the observed values of Y are truly a random sample for all values of Y, and no other factors included in the study may bias the observed values of Y.

Consider the case of a laboratory providing the results of a decomposition test of a chemical compound in which a significant level of iron is being sought. If certain levels of iron are met or missing entirely and no other elements in the compound are identified to correlate with iron at that level, then it can be determined that the identified or missing data for iron is MCAR.

Non-Ignorable Missing Data

Given two variables, X and Y, data is deemed Non-Ignorable when the probability of response depends on variable X and possibly on variable Y. For example, if the likelihood of an individual providing his or her weight varied within various age categories, the missing data is non-ignorable (Kim, 2001). Thus, the pattern of missing data is non-random and possibly predictable from other variables in the database.

In contrast to the MAR situation where data missingness is explained by other measured variables in a study, non-ignorable missing data arise due to the data missingness pattern being explainable —and only explainable —by the very variable(s) on which the data are missing (Stat. Serv. Texas, 2000).

In practice, the MCAR assumption is seldom met. Most missing data methods are applied on the assumption of MAR, although that is not always tenable. And in correspondence to Kim (2001), "Non-Ignorable missing data is the hardest condition to deal with, but, unfortunately, the most likely to occur as well."

Outliers Treated As Missing Data

Data whose values fall outside of predefined ranges may skew test results. Many times, it is necessary to classify these outliers as missing data. Pre-testing and calculating threshold boundaries are necessary in the pre-processing of data in order to identify those values that are to be classified as missing. Reconsider the case of a laboratory providing the results of a decomposition test of a chemical compound. If it has been predetermined that the maximum amount of iron that can be contained in a particular compound is 500 parts/million, then the value for the variable "iron" should never exceed that amount. If, for some reason, the value does exceed 500 parts/million, then some visualization technique should be implemented to identify that value. Those offending cases are then presented to the end-users.

For even greater precision, various levels of a specific attribute can be calculated according to its volume, magnitude, percentage, and overall impact on other attributes and subsequently used to help determine their impact on overall data-mining performance.

Suppose that the amount of silicon in our previous chemical compound example had an impact on the level of iron in that same compound. A percentile threshold for the level of silicon that is permissible in a compound before it has a significant impact on the content of iron can be calculated in order to identify the threshold at which silicon significantly alters both the iron content and, therefore, the overall compound. This "trigger" should be defined somewhere in the data-mining procedure in order to identify which test samples of a compound may be polluted with an overabundance of silicon, thus skewing the iron sample taken from the compound.

METHODS OF ADDRESSING MISSING DATA

Methods for dealing with missing data can be broken down into the following categories:

- Use Of Complete Data Only;
- Deleting Selected Cases Or Variables;
- Data Imputation; and
- Model-Based Approaches.

These categories are based on the randomness of the missing data and how the missing data is estimated and used for replacement. The next section describes each of these categories.

Use of Complete Data Only

One of the most direct and simple methods of addressing missing data is to include only those values with complete data. This method is generally referred to as the "complete case approach" and is readily available in all statistical analysis packages. This method can only be used successfully if the missing data are classified as MCAR. If missing data are not classified as MCAR, bias will be introduced and make the results non-generalizable to the overall population. This method is best suited to situations where the amount of missing data is small. When the relationships within a data set are strong enough to not be significantly affected by missing data, large sample sizes may allow for the deletion of a predetermined percentage of cases.

Delete Selected Cases or Variables

The simple deletion of data that contains missing values may be utilized when a non-random pattern of missing data is present. Even though Nie, Hull, Jenkins, Steinbrenner, and Bent (1975) examined this strategy, no firm guidelines exist for the deletion of offending cases. Overall, if the deletion of a particular subset (cluster) significantly detracts from the usefulness of the data, case deletion may not be effective. Further, it may simply not be cost effective to delete cases from a sample. Assume that new automobiles costing $20,000 each have been selected and used to test new oil additives. During a 100,000-mile test procedure, the drivers of the automobiles found it necessary to add an oil-additive to the engine while driving. If the chemicals in the oil-additive significantly polluted the oil samples taken throughout the 100,000-mile test, it would be ill-advised to eliminate ALL of the samples taken from a $20,000 test automobile. The researchers may determine other methods to gain new knowledge from the test without dropping all sample cases from the test.

Also, if the deletion of an attribute (containing missing data) that is to be used as an independent variable in a statistical regression procedure has a significant impact on the dependent variable, various imputation methods may be applied to replace the missing data (rather than altering the significance of the independent variable on the dependent variable).

Imputation Methods for Missing Data

The definition of imputation is "the process of estimating missing data of an observation based on valid values of other variables" (Hair, Anderson, Tatham, & Black, 1998). Imputation methods are literally methods of filling in missing values by attributing them to other available data. As Dempster and Rubin (1983) commented, "Imputation is a general and flexible method for handling missing-data problems, but is not without its pitfalls. Imputation methods can be dangerous as they can generate substantial biases between real and imputed data." Nonetheless, imputation methods tend to be a popular method for addressing missing data.

Commonly used imputation methods include:

- Case Substitution
- Mean Substitution
- Hot Deck Substitution
- Cold Deck Substitution
- Regression Imputation
- Multiple Imputation

Case Substitution

The method most widely used to replace observations with completely missing data. Cases are simply replaced by non-sampled observations. Only a researcher with complete knowledge of the data (and its history) should have the authority to replace missing data with values from previous research. For example, if the records were lost for an automobile test sample, an authorized researcher could review similar previous test results and determine if they could be substituted for the lost sample values. If it were found that all automobiles had nearly identical sample results for the first 10,000 miles of the test, then these results could easily be used in place of the lost sample values.

Mean Substitution

Accomplished by estimating missing values by using the mean of the recorded or available values. This is a popular imputation method for replacing missing data. However, it is important to calculate the mean only from responses that been proven to be valid and are chosen from a population that has been verified to have a normal distribution. If the data is proven to be skewed, it is usually better to use the median of the available data as the substitute. For example, suppose that respondents to a survey are asked to provide their income levels and choose not to respond. If the mean income from an availably normal and verified distribution is determined to be $48,250, then any missing income values are assigned that value. Otherwise, the use of the median is considered as an alternative replacement value.

The rationale for using the mean for missing data is that, without any additional knowledge, the mean provides the best estimate. There are three main disadvantages to mean substitution:

1. Variance estimates derived using this new mean are invalid by the understatement of the true variance.
2. The actual distribution of values is distorted. It would appear that more observations fall into the category containing the calculated mean than may actually exist.

3.   Observed correlations are depressed due to the repetition of a single constant value.

Mean imputation is a widely used method for dealing with missing data. The main advantage is its ease of implementation and ability to provide all cases with complete information. A researcher must weigh the advantages against the disadvantages. These are dependent upon the application being considered.

Cold Deck Imputation

Cold Deck Imputation methods select values or use relationships obtained from sources other than the current database (Kalton & Kasprzyk, 1982,1986; Sande, 1982, 1983). With this method, the end-user substitutes a constant value derived from external sources or from previous research for the missing values. It must be ascertained by the end-user that the replacement value used is more valid than any internally derived value. Unfortunately, feasible values are not always provided using cold deck imputation methods. Many of the same disadvantages that apply to the mean substitution method apply to cold deck imputation. Cold deck imputation methods are rarely used as the sole method of imputation and instead are generally used to provide starting values for hot deck imputation methods. Pennell (1993) contains a good example of using cold deck imputation to provide values for an ensuing hot deck imputation application. Hot deck imputation is discussed next.

Hot Deck Imputation

The implementation of this imputation method results in the replacement of a missing value with a value selected from an estimated distribution of similar responding units for each missing value. In most instances, the empirical distribution consists of values from responding units. Generally speaking, hot deck imputation replaces missing values with values drawn from the next most similar case. This method is very common in practice, but has received little attention in the missing data literature (although one paper utilizing SAS to perform hot deck imputation was written by Iannacchione (1982)). For example, Table 1 displays the following data set.

From Table 1, it is noted that case three is missing data for item four. Using hot deck imputation, each of the other cases with complete data is examined and the value for the most similar case is substituted for the missing data value. In this example, case one, two, and four are examined. Case four is easily eliminated, as it has nothing in common with

Table 1: Illustration of Hot Deck Imputation: Incomplete data set

Case	Item 1	Item 2	Item 3	Item 4
1	10	2	3	5
2	13	10	3	13
3	5	10	3	???
4	2	5	10	2

Table 2: Illustration of Hot Deck Imputation: Imputed data set

Case	Item 1	Item 2	Item 3	Item 4
1	10	2	3	5
2	13	10	3	13
3	5	10	3	13
4	2	5	10	2

case three. Case one and two both have similarities with case three. Case one has one item in common whereas case two has two items in common. Therefore, case two is the most similar to case three.

Once the most similar case has been identified, hot deck imputation substitutes the most similar complete case's value for the missing value. Since case two contains the value of 13 for item four, a value of 13 replaces the missing data point for case three.

Table 2 provides the following revised data set displays the hot deck imputation results.

The advantages of hot deck imputation include conceptual simplicity, maintenance and proper measurement level of variables, and the availability of a complete set of data at the end of the imputation process that can be analyzed like any complete set of data. One of hot deck's disadvantages is the difficulty in defining what is "similar". Hence, many different schemes for deciding on what is "similar" may evolve.

Regression Imputation

Single and multiple regression can be used to impute missing values. Regression Analysis is used to predict missing values based on the variable's relationship to other variables in the data set. The first step consists of identifying the independent variables and the dependent variables. In turn, the dependent variable is regressed on the independent variables. The resulting regression equation is then used to predict the missing values. Table 3 displays an example of regression imputation.

From the table, twenty cases with three variables (income, age, and years of college education) are listed. Income contains missing data and is identified as the dependent variable while age and years of college education are identified as the independent variables.

The following regression equation is produced for the example:

$$\hat{y} = 33912.14 + 300.87(\text{age}) + 1554.25(\text{years of college education})$$

Predictions of income can be made using the regression equation. The right-most column of the table displays these predictions. Therefore, for cases eighteen, nineteen, and twenty, income is predicted to be $59,785.56, $50,659.64, and $53,417.37, respectfully. An advantage to regression imputation is that it preserves the variance and covariance structures of variables with missing data.

Table 3: Illustration of Regression Imputation

Case	Income	Age	Years of College Education	Regression Prediction
1	$ 45,251.25	26	4	$ 47,951.79
2	$ 62,498.27	45	6	$ 56,776.85
3	$ 49,350.32	28	5	$ 50,107.78
4	$ 46,424.92	28	4	$ 48,553.54
5	$ 56,077.27	46	4	$ 53,969.22
6	$ 51,776.24	38	4	$ 51,562.25
7	$ 51,410.97	35	4	$ 50,659.64
8	$ 64,102.33	50	6	$ 58,281.20
9	$ 45,953.96	45	3	$ 52,114.10
10	$ 50,818.87	52	5	$ 57,328.70
11	$ 49,078.98	30	0	$ 42,938.29
12	$ 61,657.42	50	6	$ 58,281.20
13	$ 54,479.90	46	6	$ 57,077.72
14	$ 64,035.71	48	6	$ 57,679.46
15	$ 51,651.50	50	6	$ 58,281.20
16	$ 46,326.93	31	3	$ 47,901.90
17	$ 53,742.71	50	4	$ 55,172.71
18	???	55	6	$ 59,785.56
19	???	35	4	$ 50,659.64
20	???	39	5	$ 53,417.37

Although regression imputation is useful for simple estimates, it has several inherent disadvantages:

1. This method reinforces relationships that already exist within the data. As this method is utilized more often, the resulting data becomes more reflective of the sample and becomes less generalizable to the universe it represents.
2. The variance of the distribution is understated.
3. The assumption is implied that the variable being estimated has a substantial correlation to other attributes within the data set.
4. The estimated value is not constrained and therefore may fall outside predetermined boundaries for the given variable. An additional adjustment may necessary.

In addition to these points, there is also the problem of over-prediction. Regression imputation may lead to over-prediction of the model's explanatory power. For example, if the regression R^2 is too strong, multicollinearity most likely exists. Otherwise, if the

R^2 value is modest, errors in the regression prediction equation will be substantial (see Graham et al., 1994).

Mean imputation can be regarded as a special type of regression imputation. For data where the relationships between variables is sufficiently established, regression imputation is a very good method of imputing values for missing data.

Overall, regression imputation not only estimates the missing values but also derives inferences for the population (see discussion of variance and covariance above). For discussions on regression imputation see Royall and Herson (1973), Hansen, Madow, and Tepping (1982).

Multiple Imputation

Rubin (1978) was the first to propose multiple imputation as a method for dealing with missing data. Multiple imputation combines a number of imputation methods into a single procedure. In most cases, expectation maximization (see Little & Rubin, 1987) is combined with maximum likelihood estimates and hot deck imputation to provide data for analysis. The method works by generating a maximum likelihood covariance matrix and a mean vector. Statistical uncertainty is introduced into the model and is used to emulate the natural variability of the complete database. Hot deck imputation is then used to fill in missing data points to complete the data set. Multiple imputation differs from hot deck imputation in the number of imputed data sets generated. Whereas hot deck imputation generates one imputed data set to draw values from, multiple imputation creates multiple imputed data sets.

Multiple imputation creates a summary data set for imputing missing values from these multiple imputed data sets. Multiple imputation has a distinct advantage in that it is robust to the normalcy conditions of the variables used in the analysis and it outputs complete data matrices. The method is time intensive as the researcher must create the multiple data sets, test the models for each data set separately, and then combine the data sets into one summary set. The process is simplified if the researcher is using basic regression analysis as the modeling technique. It is much more complex when models such as factor analysis, structural equation modeling, or high order regression analysis are used.

A comprehensive handling of multiple imputation is given in Rubin (1987) and Schafer (1997). Other seminal works include Rubin (1986), Herzog and Rubin (1983), Li (1985), and Rubin and Schenker (1986).

Model-Based Procedures

Model-based procedures incorporate missing data into the analysis. These procedures are characterized in one of two ways: maximum likelihood estimation or missing data inclusion.

Dempster, Little, and Rubin (1977) give a general approach for computing maximum likelihood estimates from missing data. They call their technique the EM approach. The approach consists of two steps, "E" for the conditional expectation step and "M" for the maximum likelihood step. The EM approach is an interactive method. The first step makes the best possible estimates of the missing data, and the second step then makes estimates of the parameters (e.g., means, variances, or correlations) assuming the missing data are replaced. Each of the stages is repeated until the change in the estimated values is negligible. The missing data is then replaced with these estimated values. This approach has become extremely popular and is included in commercial software packages such as SPSS. Starting with SPSS 7.5, a missing value module employing the EM procedure for treating missing data is included.

Cohen and Cohen (1983) prescribe inclusion of missing data into the analysis. In general, the missing data is grouped as a subset of the entire data set. This subset of missing data is then analyzed using any standard statistical test. If the missing data occurs on a non-metric variable, statistical methods such as ANOVA, MANOVA, or discriminant analysis can be used. If the missing data occurs on a metric variable in a dependence relationship, regression can be used as the analysis method.

THE IMPACT OF MISSING DATA ON DATA-MINING ALGORITHMS

Missing data impacts the Knowledge Discovery Process in various ways depending on which data-mining algorithm is being utilized. We will now address the impact of missing data on various types of data mining algorithms.

The Impact on the *k*-Nearest Neighbor Algorithm

The very nature of the k-Nearest Neighbor algorithm is based on the accuracy of the data. Missing and inaccurate data have a severe impact on the performance of this type of algorithm. If data is missing entirely, misrepresented clusters (data distributions) can occur depending upon the frequency and categorization of the cases containing the missing data. One method to help solve this problem is to use the k-Nearest Neighbor data-mining algorithm itself to approach the missing data problem. The imputed values obtained can be used to enhance the performance of the Nearest Neighbor algorithm itself.

First, the k-Nearest Neighbors (those containing *no* missing data) to the observation that does contain missing data are identified. The *k* stands for a predetermined constant representing the number of neighbors containing *no* missing data to be considered in the analysis. According to Witten and Frank (2000), it is advised to keep the value for *k* small, say five, so that the impact of any noise present will be kept to a minimum.

Hence, this algorithm is not recommended for large data sets (Adriaans & Zantinge, 1996). Once these "neighbors" have been identified, the majority class for the attribute in question can be assigned to the case containing the missing value. Berson, Smith and Thearling (2000) maintained that an historical database containing attributes containing similar predictor values to those in the offending case can also be utilized to aid in the classification of unclassified records.

Of course, the three main disadvantages mentioned in the imputation section (variance understatement, distribution distortion, and correlation depression) should be addressed whenever a constant value is used to replace missing data. The proportion of values replaced should be calculated and compared to all clusters and category identification that existed prior to the replacement of the missing data.

Further, inaccurate data and outliers must be identified. Predetermined "impossible" and "improbable" values are determined, along with minimum and maximum boundary thresholds, to act as identifiers for inaccurate data and outliers. The "closeness" of values to these boundaries can be determined using the Euclidean distance between the two points (Han & Kamber, 2001). These values are then visualized to the end-user and treated as though the data were actually missing. An imputation method is then selected and implemented as previously described to replace offending values.

The Impact on Decision Trees

If missing data is a frequent occurrence in the data mining application in question, decision trees are a good methodology for dealing with them (Berry & Linoff, 1997).

They also scale up very well for large data sets (Adriaans & Zantinge, 1997).

A popular method utilized when using decision trees is to treat the missing values as if they were an actual data type for a given attribute. In fact, an entire coding scheme may be developed for any number of types of missing data that may be identified in a given system. A separate branch for missing data may be implemented into a tree for a given attribute and various limbs developed for each of the missing data code types.

For instance, data that is known but "not yet" entered could be coded as "NYE," while data that does not apply to particular case may be entered as "DNA."

When missing data is to be replaced, a popular solution is to record the number of elements in the training set that follows each branch for a that particular attribute and then use the most popular branch as the default replacement value for the missing data. However, any of the aforementioned imputation methods could be utilized to replace the missing data.

It is sometimes useful to prune the tree whenever there is an overabundance of missing data in certain branches (Berry & Linoff, 1997). Eliminating particular paths may be necessary to ensure that the overall success of the decision-making process is not inhibited by the inclusion of cases containing missing data. Witten and Frank (2000) advise the use of prepruning during the tree-building process to determine when to stop developing subtrees. Postpruning can be utilized after a tree is completely built. If one chooses postpruning, decisions for pruning rules can then be made after the tree has been built and analyzed.

The Impact on Association Rules

Association Rules help to identify how various attribute values are related within a data set. They are developed to predict the value of an attribute (or sets of attributes) in the same data set (Darling, 1997). Since Association Rules are often developed to help identify various regularities (patterns) within a data set, algorithms that utilize association rules have been found to work best with large data sets. Attributes containing missing or corrupted data values may easily result in the creation of invalid rule sets or in the failure of identifying valid patterns that normally exist within the data. Since the main focus of association rule discovery is to identify rules that apply to large numbers of cases to which the rules can directly relate, missing data may overstate both the support and the confidence of any newly discovered rules sets (Witten & Frank, 2000).

However, if the data set used to train the algorithm contains only "pristine" data, overfitting the model based on the patterns included in the training set typically results.

Therefore, rules need to be developed for the "exceptions-to-rule" sets that have been developed in violation of correct or "clean" data. It is then necessary to populate the training set for algorithms that utilize Association Rules with a sufficient percentage of "noisy data," representing all possible types of exceptions to existing rules. In this way, exception rules can be developed to handle all patterns of noise that may be associated with a given data set, rather than redesigning rule sets that deal with "clean" data or attempting to force cases that do not belong to existing rule sets into those sets.

Default outcomes should normally be defined for exception rules as well as for "normal" data. The most frequently occurring outcome (type of missing data or noise) is chosen as the default outcome.

As exceptions are discovered for initial exceptions, a type of tree structure is created, forming a decision list for the treatment of missing and noisy data for the data set. It becomes necessary to utilize both propositional rules and relational rules in the rule set for the treatment of missing or noisy data.

Propositional rules test an attribute's value against a constant value, thereby developing very concise limits to delineate between "clean" and "noisy" data. In extreme instances, the constants, breakpoints, and values from associated attributes are used to grow a regression tree in order to estimate missing data values under various conditions.

As these regression trees become larger they can also be utilized as a model tree for a missing data rule set. Relational rules are used to test the relationships between attributes. For nominal attributes, tests are made for equality and inequality. Numeric attributes, on the other hand, test the conditions of less than, greater than, less than or equal to, and greater than or equal to.

Incorporating an additional rule or rule set to deal with exceptions (such as missing data) can easily be accomplished since some rules may be developed to predict multiple outcomes. Failure to allow for the missing data exception may easily misrepresent some of the associations between attributes.

Although a rule may have both high support and confidence, a subjective evaluation by the end-user may determine how interesting a newly discovered rule is (Groth, 2000). Some association rule software packages may be trained to automatically prune "uninteresting rules." Therefore, minimum values (breakpoints) must be established for both the confidence and support of newly discovered rules. In some instances, a hierarchy of rules can be developed so that some rules may imply other rules. In some cases, only the strongest rule is presented as a newly discovered rule and rules of "lesser strength" (support and confidence) are linked to the stronger rule for use at a later time (Han & Kamber, 2001). These resulting item sets may also be stored as metadata for further investigation as the process of final evaluation and pruning takes place by the end-user.

The Impact on Neural Networks

Since neural networks have been found to be both reliable and effective when applied to applications involving prediction, classification, and clustering (Adriaans & Zantinge, 1997), it can be seen that the issue of missing data has a similar impact on neural networks as it does on other types of classification algorithms, such as k-Nearest Neighbor. These similarities include variance understatement, distribution distortion, and correlation depression.

Since the internal weights used to calculate outputs are created and distributed within the network without providing the insight as to how a solution is developed, missing or dirty data can distort the weights that are assigned as the associations between nodes in a manner unknown to the research analyst.

Further, numeric outliers containing extremely large values tend to "swamp" attributes of lesser value, which can impact the correlations between both these and other attributes. These distorted weights can throw off the performance of the entire network while also falsely identifying some attributes as being "more important" than others (Han & Kamber, 2001).

Categorical attributes containing missing data may also be impacted negatively. Since data used as input to a neural network is usually massaged to values between 0 and 1, a categorical attribute containing five values (say, 0.0, 0.25, 0.50, 0.75, and 1.0) can be grossly misrepresented whenever missing data is heavy for that attribute (Berson, Smith, & Thearling, 2000). For instance, if our chemical breakdown analysis were to contain a categorical attribute that rated the breakdown as:

0.0=Rejected   0.25=Poor   0.50=Fair   0.75=Good   1.0=Excellent,

and that attribute contained a high degree of missing data, an overall rating value for multiple tests can easily be misclassified (when unmassaged) as "Good" or "Poor" rather than perhaps a more accurate rating of "Fair."

Another point regarding the issue of missing data and neural networks is that it may be necessary to "train" the initial network with missing data if the data to be tested and evaluated later is itself going to contain missing data. By training the network with only "clean" data, the internal weights developed using the training set cannot be accurately applied to the test set later.

In conjunction with the issue of training the model with a representative amount of missing data, it must also be remembered to refresh the model with a certain amount of missing data. This is done so that, as the model ages, it does not become insensitive to the fact that the application does, in fact, face missing data as input when the network is actually being utilized with fresh data.

These issues may be regarded as simply "housekeeping" functions when using neural networks. If an application involves the use of missing data as input, it only makes sense to both train and refresh the training set with a similar percentage of missing data.

How does missing data actually impact the internal execution of the neural network? While the hidden layer is where the actual weights are developed for the network, the activation function combines the inputs to the network into a single output (Westphal & Blaxton, 1998). The output remains low until the combined inputs reach a predetermined threshold, and small changes to the input can have a dramatic effect on the output (Groth, 2000). The activation function can be very sensitive to missing data.

Let's take this a step further. The activation function of the basic unit of a neural network has two sub-functions: the combination function and the transfer function.

The combination function commonly uses the "standard weighted sum" (the summation of the input attribute values multiplied by the weights that have been assigned to those attributes) to calculate a value to be passed on to the transfer function.

The transfer function applies either a linear or non-linear function to the value passed to it by the combination function. Even though a linear function used in a feed-forward neural network is simply performing a linear regression, missing values can distort the coefficients in the regression equation and therefore pass on invalid values as output (Berry & Linoff, 1997).

Between the linear and non-linear function types is the most commonly used transfer function: the S-Shaped Sigmoid Function. This function represents a gradual change from a linear model to a non-linear model and is the transfer function most commonly used in "off the shelf" neural network packages. Since the result of the combination function is usually between −1 and 1, the function is deemed "near-linear" and satisfies most linear and non-linear applications. However, the impact of missing data on the sigmoid function goes back to how the combination function derives its value for the sigmoid function to act upon (Skapura, 1995).

FUTURE TRENDS

Poor data quality has plagued the knowledge discovery process and all associated data-mining techniques. Future data-mining systems should be sensitive to noise and have the ability to deal with all types of pollution, both internally and in conjunction with end-users. As data gathers noise, the system should only reduce the level of confidence associated with the results provided and not "suddenly alter" the direction of discovery. We cannot dismiss the dangers of blind data mining that can deteriorate into a data-dredging process. Systems should still produce the most significant findings from the data set possible, even if noise is present. Systems will be robust against uncertainty and missing data issues (Fayyad & Piatetsky-Shapiro, 1996).

As software products evolve and new data-mining algorithms are developed, alternative methods for the identification and deletion/replacement of missing data will also be developed. New hybrid methodologies for dealing with noisy data will continue to evolve as end-users uncover previously undiscovered patterns of missing data within their applications. Commonality of patterns discovered within a particular industry should result in the sharing of new methodologies for dealing with these discoveries. Warehousing missing data patterns and allowing end-users the capability of selecting and testing a variety of patterns and imputation methods will become commonplace, in-house and in the public domain.

Software from other applications in the software industry will also prove to positively impact the area of data cleansing and preparation for proper data mining. For instance, simulation software using various approaches for prediction and projection will be interwoven with current techniques to form new hybrids for the estimation of missing values. Software for sensitivity analysis and noise tolerance will also be utilized to determine a measurement of volatility for a data set prior to the deletion/replacement of cases (Chung & Gray, 1999). Maintaining stability without altering original data is an issue that end-users may wish to address, instead of dealing with case deletion or data imputation methods.

As data mining continues to evolve and mature as a viable business tool, it will be monitored to address its role in the technological life cycle. While data mining is currently regarded as being at the third stage of a six-stage maturity process in technological evolution, it will soon gain momentum and grow into the area of Early Majority. The maturity stages include:

- Innovators;
- Early Adopters;
- Chasm;
- Early Majority;
- Late Majority; and
- Laggards.

The "chasm" stage is characterized by various hurdles and challenges that must be met before the technology can become widely accepted as mainstream. As tools for the preprocessing and cleansing of noisy data continue to be proven to be effective, advancement toward a level of "early majority" (where the technology becomes mature and is generally accepted and used) will be accomplished.

Tools for dealing with missing data will also grow from being used as a horizontal solution (not designed to provide business-specific end solutions) into a type of vertical solution (integration of domain-specific logic into data mining solutions). As the gigabyte-, terabyte-, and petabyte-size data sets become more prevalent in data warehousing applications, the issue of dealing with missing data will itself become an integral solution for the use of such data rather than simply existing as a component of the knowledge discovery and data mining processes (Han & Kamber, 2001).

As in other maturing applications, missing or incomplete data will be looked upon as a global issue. Finding clues to terrorist activities will be uncovered by utilizing textual data-mining techniques for incomplete and unstructured data (Sullivan, 2001). For instance, monitoring links and searching for trends between news reports from commercial news services may be used to glean clues from items in cross-cultural environments that might not otherwise be available.

Although the issue of statistical analysis with missing data has been addressed since the early 1970s (Little & Rubin, 1987), the advent of data warehousing, knowledge discovery, data mining, and data cleansing has brought the concept of dealing with missing data into the limelight. Costs associated with the deletion of data will make the imputation of data a focal point for independent data-sleuthing entities. For example, an independent firm involved in the restructuring of incomplete data sets will be able to obtain or purchase fragmented data that has been deemed unusable by mainstream corporations and produce complete data with a level of support worthy of use in actual production environments.

An extended topic in this arena will be the ownership of such newly created data sets and/or algorithms and imputation methods that are discovered within an application or industry. What if an independent firm discovers new knowledge based on findings from data sets that were originally incomplete and made available by outside firms? Are the discoveries partially owned by both firms? It is up to the legal system and the parties involved to sort out these issues.

It can be seen that future generations of data miners will be faced with many challenges concerning the issues of missing data. As the industry as a whole continues to evolve and mature, so will end-user expectations of having various, readily available methods of dealing with missing data .

CONCLUSIONS

The issues concerning the impact of inconsistent data and missing data are a fact of life in the world of knowledge discovery and data mining. They must be faced with rigor by developers of new data-mining applications before viable decisions can be developed by the end-users of these systems.

Following a background analysis and literature review of missing data concepts, the authors addressed reasons for data inconsistency. Included in the discussion were procedural factors, refusal of response, and inapplicable questions. Following was the classification of missing data types into the areas of (data) missing at random (MAR), (data) missing completely at random (MCAR), non-ignorable missing data ,and outliers treated as missing data. Next, a review of existing methods for addressing the problem of missing data was conducted for the deletion of cases or variables and various imputation methods. Imputation methods included were case substitution, mean substitution, cold deck imputation, hot deck imputation, regression imputation, and multiple imputation.

The impact of missing data on various data mining algorithms was then addressed. The algorithms reviewed included k-Nearest Neighbor, Decision Trees, Association Rules, and Neural Networks.

Finally, the authors offered their opinions on future developments and trends that developers of knowledge discovery software can expect to face, and the needs of end-users when confronted with the issues of data inconsistency and missing data.

It is the goal of the authors that the issues of inconsistent data and missing data be exposed to individuals new to the venues of knowledge discovery and data mining. It is a topic worthy of research and investigation by developers of fresh data-mining applications, as well as a method of review for systems that have already been developed or that are currently under construction.

This concludes the chapter concerning the impact of missing data on data mining. It is our sincere hope that readers of this topic have gained a fresh perspective for the necessity of data consistency and an exposure to alternatives for dealing with the issues of missing data.

REFERENCES

Adriaans, P. & Zantinge, D. (1997). *Data mining*. New York: Addison-Wesley.

Afifi, A. & Elashoff, R. (1966). Missing observations in multivariate statistics, I: Review of the literature. *Journal of the American Statistical Association*, 61:595-604.

Agrawal, R., Imielinski, T., & Swami, A. (1993). Mining associations between sets of items in massive databases. *Proceedings of the ACM SIGMOD International Conference on Management of Data*, Washington, DC, 207-216.

Agrawal, R., Mannila, H., Srikant, R., Toivonen, H., & Verkamo, A. (1995). Fast discovery of association rules. *Advances in Knowledge Discovery and Data Mining*, Chapter 12. Cambridge, MA: AAAI/MIT Press.

Agrawal, R. & Srikant, R. (1994). Fast algorithms for mining association rules. *Proceedings of the 20th International Conference on Very Large Databases*, Santiago de Chile, Chile: Morgan Kaufmann.

Barnard, J., & Meng, X. (1999). Applications of multiple imputation in medical studies: From AIDS to NHANES. *Statistical Methods in Medical Research*, 8, 17-36.

Berry, M. & Linoff, G. (1997). *Data mining techniques*. New York: Wiley.

Berson, A., Smith, S., & Thearling, K. (2000). *Building data mining applications for CRM*. New York: McGraw-Hill.

Breiman, L., Friedman, J., Olshen, R., & Stone, C. (1984). *Classification and regression trees*. Monterey, CA: Wadsworth & Brooks/Cole Advanced Books & Software.

Brick, J. M. & Kalton, G. (1996). Handling missing data in survey research. *Statistical Methods in Medical Research*, 5, 215-238.

Chung, H. M. & Gray, P. (1999). Special section: Data mining. *Journal of Management Information Systems, 16*(1): 11-17.

Clogg, C., Rubin, D., Schenker, N., Schultz, B., & Weidman, L. (1991). Multiple imputation of industry and occupation codes in census public-use samples using Bayesian logistic regression. *Journal of the American Statistical Association*, 86, 413, 68-78.

Cohen, J., and Cohen, P. (1983). *Applied multiple regression/correlation analysis for the behavioral sciences, 2nd ed.* Hillsdale, NJ: Lawrence Erlbaum Associates.

Darling, C. B. (1997). Data mining for the masses, *Datamation*, 52(5).

David, M., Little, R., Samuhel, M., & Triest, R. (1986). Alternative methods for CPS income imputation. *Journal of the American Statistical Association*, 81, 29-41.

Dempster, A., Laird, N., & Rubin, D. (1977). Maximum likelihood from incomplete data via the EM algorithm (with discussion). *Journal of the Royal Statistical Society*, B39, 1-38.

Dempster, A. & Rubin, D. (1983). Overview. In W. G. Madow, I. Olkin, & D. Rubin (eds.), *Incomplete data in sample surveys, Vol. II: Theory and annotated bibliography*. pp.3-10. New York: Academic Press.

Diggle, P. & Kenward, M. (1994). Informative dropout in longitudinal data analysis (with discussion). *Applied Statistics*, 43, 49-94.

Dillman, D. A. (1999). *Mail and Internet surveys: The tailored design method*. New York, NY: John Wiley & Sons.

Ernst, L. (1980). Variance of the estimated mean for several imputation procedures. In the *Proceedings of the Survey Research Methods Section*, Alexandria, VA: American Statistical Association, 716-720.

Fayyad, U., Piatetsky-Shapiro, G. & Smyth, P. (1996). The KDD process for extracting useful knowledge from volumes of data, *Communications of the ACM, 39*(11): 27-34, November.

Flockhart, I. & Radcliffe, N. (1996). A genetic algorithm-based approach to data mining., *Proceedings of the ACM SIGMOD International Conference on Management of Data,* 299-302.

Ford, B. (1981). An overview of hot deck procedures. In W. G. Madow, I. Olkin, & D. Rubin (eds.), *Incomplete data in sample surveys, Vol. II: Theory and annotated bibliography* New York: Academic Press.

Ghahramani, Z. & Jordan, M. (1997). Mixture models for learning form incomplete data. In J. Cowan, G. Tesauro, & J. Alspector (eds.), *Advances in Neural information processing systems 6.* pp.120-127. San Mateo, CA: Morgan Kaufmann. 120-127.

Graham, J., Hofer, S., Donaldson, S., MacKinnon, D., & Schafer, J. (1997). Analysis with missing data in prevention research. In K. Bryant, W. Windle, & S. West (eds.), *New methodological approaches to alcohol prevention research.* Washington, DC: American Psychological Association.

Graham, J., Hofer, S., & Piccinin, A. (1994). Analysis with missing data in drug prevention research. In L. M. Collins & L. Seitz (eds.), *Advances in data analysis for prevention intervention research.* NIDA Research Monograph, Series (#142). Washington, DC: National Institute on Drug Abuse.

Groth, R. (2000*). Data mining: Building competitive advantage.* Upper Saddle River, NJ: PrenticeHall.

Hair, J., Anderson, R., Tatham, R., & Black, W. (1998), *Multivariate data analysis.* Upper Saddle River, NJ: PrenticeHall.

Han, J. & Kamber, M. (2001). *Data mining: Concepts and techniques.* San Francisco: Academic Press.

Hansen, M., Madow, W., & Tepping, J. (1983). An evaluation of model-dependent and probability-sampling inferences in sample surveys. *Journal of the American Statistical Association,* 78, 776-807.

Hartley, H. & Hocking, R. (1971). The analysis of incomplete data. *Biometrics,* 27, 783-808.

Haykin, S. (1994). *Neural networks: A comprehensive foundation.* New York: Macmillan Publishing.

Heitjan, D.F. (1997). Annotation: What can be done about missing data? Approaches to imputation. *American Journal of Public Health,* 87(4), 548-550.

Herzog, T., & Rubin, D. (1983). Using multiple imputations to handle nonresponse in sample surveys. In G. Madow, I. Olkin, & D. Rubin (eds.), *Incomplete data in sample surveys, Volume 2: Theory and bibliography.* pp. 209-245. New York: Academic Press.

Holland, J. (1975). *Adaptation in natural and artificial systems.* Ann Arbor, MI: University of Michigan Press.

Howell, D.C. (1998). Treatment of missing data [Online]. Available http://www.uvm.edu/~dhowell/StatPages/More_Stuff/Missing_Data/Missing.html [2001, September 1].

Iannacchione, V. (1982). Weighted sequential hot deck imputation macros. In the *Proceedings of the SAS Users Group International Conference, San Francisco, CA,* 7, 759-763.

Jenkins, C. R., and Dillman, D. A. (1997). Towards a theory of self-administered question-
naire design. In E. Lyberg, P. Bierner, M. Collins, D. Leeuw, C. Dippo, N. Schwartz
& D. Trewin (Eds.), *Survey measurement and process quality*. New York: John
Wiley & Sons.

Kalton, G. & Kasprzyk, D. (1982). Imputing for missing survey responses. In the
Proceedings of the Section on Survey Research Methods, Alexandria, VA: American Statistical Association, pp.22-31.

Kalton, G. & Kasprzyk, D. (1986). The treatment of missing survey data *Survey
Methodology, 12*: 1-16.

Kalton, G. & Kish, L. (1981). Two efficient random imputation procedures. In the
Proceedings of the Survey Research Methods Section, Alexandria, VA: American
Statistical Association, pp.146-151.

Kass, G. (1980). An exploratory technique for investigating large quantities of categorical data, *Applied Statistics*, 29, 119-127.

Kim, Y. (2001). The curse of the missing data [Online]. Available http://209.68.240.11:8080/
2ndMoment/978476655/addPostingForm [2001, September 1].

Li, K. (1985). Hypothesis testing in multiple imputation - With emphasis on mixed-up
frequencies in contingency tables, Ph.D. Thesis, The University of Chicago,
Chicago, IL.

Little, R. (1982). Models for nonresponse in sample surveys. *Journal of the American
Statistical Association*, 77, 237-250.

Little, R. (1992). Regression with missing X's: A review. *Journal of the American
Statistical Association*, 87, 1227-1237.

Little, R. (1995). Modeling the drop-out mechanism in repeated-measures studies.
Journal of the American Statistical Association, 90, 1112-1121.

Little, R. & Rubin, D. (1987). *Statistical analysis with missing data*. New York: Wiley.

Little, R. & Rubin, D. (1989). The analysis of social science data with missing values.
Sociological Methods and Research, 18, 292-326.

Loh, W. & Shih, Y. (1997). Split selection methods for classification trees. *Statistica
Sinica*, 7, 815-840.

Loh, W. & Vanichestakul, N. (1988). Tree-structured classification via generalized
discriminant analysis (with discussion). *Journal of the American Statistical
Association* 83, 715-728.

Masters, T. (1995). *Neural, novel, and hybrid algorithms for time series predictions*.
New York: Wiley.

Michalewicz, Z. (1994). *Genetic algorithms + data structures = evolution programs*.
New York: Springer-Verlag.

Morgan, J. & Messenger, R. (1973). THAID: A sequential analysis program for the
analysis of nominal scale dependent variables. Technical report, Institute of Social
Research, University of Michigan, Ann Arbor, MI.

Morgan, J. & Sonquist, J. (1973). Problems in the analysis of survey data and a proposal.
Journal of the American Statistical Association, 58, 415-434.

Nie, N., Hull, C., Jenkins, J., Steinbrenner, K., & Bent, D. (1975). *SPSS, 2nd ed*. New York:
McGraw-Hill.

Orchard, T. & Woodbury, M. (1972). A missing information principle: Theory and
applications. In the *Proceedings of the 6th Berkeley Symposium on Mathematical
Statistics and Probability, University of California, Berkeley, CA*, 1, 697-715.

Pennell, S. (1993). Cross-sectional imputation and longitudinal editing procedures in the survey of income and program participation. Technical report, Institute of Social Research, University of Michigan, Ann Arbor, MI.

Ripley, B. (1996*). Pattern recognition and neural networks*. Cambridge, UK: Cambridge University Press.

Roth, P. (1994). Missing data: A conceptual review for applied psychologists. *Personnel Psychology*, 47, 537-560.

Royall, R. & Herson, J. (1973). Robust estimation from finite populations. *Journal of the American Statistical Association*. 68, 883-889.

Rubin, D. (1978). Multiple imputations in sample surveys - A phenomenological Bayesian approach to nonresponse, *Imputation and Editing of Faulty or Missing Survey Data*, U.S. Department of Commerce, 1-23.

Rubin, D. (1986). Statistical matching using file concatenation with adjusted weights and multiple imputations. *Journal of Business and Economic Statistics*, 4, 87-94.

Rubin, D. (1996). Multiple imputation after 18+ years (with discussion. *Journal of the American Statistical Association*, 91, 473-489.

Rubin, D. & Schenker, N. (1986). Multiple imputation for interval estimation from simple random sample with ignorable nonresponse, *Journal of the American Statistical Association*, 81, 366-374.

Sande, L. (1982). Imputation in surveys: Coping with reality. *The American Statistician*, Vol. 36, 145-152.

Sande, L. (1983). Hot-deck imputation procedures. In W.G. Madow & I. Olkin (eds.), *Incomplete data in sample surveys, Vol. 3, Proceedings of the Symposium on Incomplete Data: Panel on Incomplete Data, Committee of National Statistics, Commission on Behavioral and Social Sciences and Education, National Research Council, Washington, D. C., 1979, August 10-11*, pp. 339-349. New York: Academic Press.

Schafer, J. (1997). *Analysis of incomplete multivariate data*. London: Chapman and Hall.

Schafer, J. (1999). Multiple imputation: A primer. *Statistical Methods in Medical Research*, 8, 3-15.

Schafer, J. & Olsen, M. (1998). Multiple imputation for multivariate missing-data problems: A data analyst's perspective. *Multivariate Behavioral Research*, 33, 545-571.

Sharpe, P. & Glover, R. (1999). Efficient GA based techniques for classification, *Applied Intelligence*, 11, 3, 277-284.

Skapura, D. (1995). *Building neural networks*. New York: Addison Wesley.

Statistical Services of University of Texas (2000). General FAQ #25: Handling missing or incomplete data [Online]. Available http://www.utexas.edu/cc/faqs/stat/general/gen25.html. [2001, September 1].

Sullivan, D. (2001). *Document warehousing and text mining*. New York: John Wiley & Sons.

Szpiro, G. (1997). A search for hidden relationships: Data mining with genetic algorithms, *Computational Economics*, 10, 3, 267-277.

Tresp, V., Neuneier, R., & Ahmad, S. (1995). Efficient methods for dealing with missing data in supervised learning. In G. Tesauro, D. Touretzky, and T. Keen (eds.), *Advances in neural information processing systems 7*. pp. 689-696. Cambridge, MA: The MIT Press.

van Buren, S., Boshuizen, H., & Knook, D. (1999). Multiple imputation of missing blood pressure covariates in survival analysis. *Statistics in Medicine*, 18, 681-694.

Warner, B., & Misra, M. (1996). Understanding neural networks as statistical tools. *The American Statistician*, 50, 284-293.

Westphal, C. & Blaxton, T. (1998). *Data mining solutions*. New York: Wiley.

Witten, I. & Frank, E. (2000). *Data mining*. San Francisco: Academic Press.

Wothke, W. (1998). Longitudinal and multi-group modeling with missing data. In T.D. Little, K.U. Schnabel, & J. Baumert (eds.), *Modelling longitudinal and multiple group data: Practical issues, applied approaches and specific examples*. Mahwah, NJ: Lawrence Erlbaum Associates.

Chapter VIII

Mining Text Documents for Thematic Hierarchies Using Self-Organizing Maps

Hsin-Chang Yang
Chang Jung University, Taiwan

Chung-Hong Lee
Chang Jung University, Taiwan

ABSTRACT

Recently, many approaches have been devised for mining various kinds of knowledge from texts. One important application of text mining is to identify themes and the semantic relations among these themes for text categorization. Traditionally, these themes were arranged in a hierarchical manner to achieve effective searching and indexing as well as easy comprehension for human beings. The determination of category themes and their hierarchical structures was mostly done by human experts. In this work, we developed an approach to automatically generate category themes and reveal the hierarchical structure among them. We also used the generated structure to categorize text documents. The document collection was trained by a self-organizing map to form two feature maps. We then analyzed these maps and obtained the category themes and their structure. Although the test corpus contains documents written in Chinese, the proposed approach can be applied to documents written in any language, and such documents can be transformed into a list of separated terms.

INTRODUCTION

In text categorization, we try to assign a text document to some predefined category. When a set of documents is well categorized, both storage and retrieval of these documents can be effectively achieved. A primary characteristic of text categorization is that a category reveals the common theme of those documents under this category; that is, these documents form a natural cluster of similar context. Thus, text categorization provides some knowledge about the document collection. An interesting argument about text categorization is that before we can acquire knowledge through text categorization, we need some kinds of knowledge to correctly categorize documents. For example, two kinds of key knowledge we need to perform text categorization are 1) the categories that we can use, and 2) the relationships among the categories. The first kind of knowledge provides a set of themes that we can use to categorize documents. Similar documents will be categorized under the same category if they have the same theme. These categories form the basis of text categorization. The second kind of knowledge reveals the structure among categories according to their semantic similarities. Ideally, similar categories, i.e., categories with similar themes, will be arranged "closely" within the structure in some manner. Such arrangement provides us with an effective way to store and retrieve documents. Moreover, such structure may make the categorization result more comprehensible by humans.

Traditionally, human experts or some semi-automatic mechanisms that incorporate human knowledge and computing techniques such as natural language processing provided these kinds of knowledge. For example, the MEDLINE corpus required considerable human effort to carry out categorization using a set of Medical Subject Headings (MeSH) categories (Mehnert, 1997). However, fully automatic generation of categories and their structure are difficult for two reasons. First, we need to select some important words as category terms (or *category themes*). We use these words to represent the themes of categories and to provide indexing information for the categorized documents. Generally, a category term contains only a single word or a phrase. The selection of the terms will affect the categorization result as well as the effectiveness of the categorization. A proper selection of a category term should be able to represent the general idea of the documents under the corresponding category. Such selections were always done by human linguistic experts because we need an insight of the underlying semantic structure of a language to make the selections. Unfortunately, such insight is hard to automate. Certain techniques such as word frequency counts may help, but it is the human experts who finally decide what terms are most discriminative and representative. Second, for the ease of human comprehension, the categories were always arranged in a tree-like hierarchical structure. This hierarchy reveals the relationships among categories. A category associated with higher-level nodes of the hierarchy represents a more general theme than those associated with lower level nodes. Also, a parent category in the hierarchy should represent the common theme of its child categories. The retrieval of documents of a particular interest can be effectively achieved through such hierarchy. Although the hierarchical structure is ideal for revealing the similarities among categories, the hierarchy must be constructed carefully such that irrelevant categories may not be the children of the same parent category. A thorough investigation of the semantic relations among category terms must be conducted to establish a well-organized hierarchy. This process is also hard to automate. Therefore, most of text categorization systems focus on developing methodologies to categorize documents according to some human-specified category terms and hierarchy, rather than on generating category terms and hierarchy automatically.

In this work, we provide a method that can automatically generate category themes and establish the hierarchical structure among categories. Traditionally, category themes were selected according to the popularity of words in the majority of documents, which can be done by human engineering, statistical training, or a combination of the two. In this work, we reversed the text categorization process to obtain the category themes. First, we should cluster the documents. The document collection was trained by the self-organizing maps (SOM) (Kohonen, 1997) algorithm to generate two feature maps, namely the *document cluster map* (DCM) and the *word cluster map* (WCM). A neuron in these two maps represents a document cluster and a word cluster, respectively. Through the self-organizing process, the distribution of neurons in the maps reveals the similarities among clusters. We selected category themes according to such similarities. To generate the category themes, dominating neurons in the DCM were first found as centroids of some *super-clusters* that each represent a general category. The words associated with the corresponding neurons in WCM were then used to select category themes. Examining the correlations among neurons in the two maps may also reveal the structure of categories.

The corpus that was used to train the maps consists of documents that are written in Chinese. We decided to use a Chinese corpus for two reasons. First, over a quarter of the earth's population use Chinese as their native language. However, experiments on techniques for mining Chinese documents were relatively less than those for documents written in other languages. Second, demands for Chinese-based, bilingual, or multi-lingual text-mining techniques arise rapidly nowadays. We feel that such demands could not be easily met if experiments were only conducted in English corpora. On the other hand, a difficult problem in developing Chinese-based text-mining techniques is that research on the lexical analysis of Chinese documents is still in its infancy. Therefore, methodologies developed for English documents play an inevitable role in developing a model for knowledge discovery in Chinese documents. In spite of the differences in grammar and syntax between Chinese and English, we can always separate the documents, whether written in English or Chinese, into a list of terms that may be words or phrases. Thus, methodologies developed based on word frequency count may provide an unified way in processing documents written in any language that can be separated into a list of terms. In this work, a traditional term-based representation scheme in information retrieval field is adopted for document encoding. The same method developed in our work can naturally extend to English or multi-lingual documents because these documents can always be represented by a list of terms.

RELATED WORK

Text categorization or classification systems usually categorized documents according to some predefined category hierarchy. An example is the work by the CMU text-learning group (Grobelnik & Mladenic, 1998) that used the Yahoo! hierarchy to categorize documents. Most text categorization research focused on developing methods for categorization. Examples are Bayesian independent classifier (Lewis, 1992), decision trees (Apte, Damerau, & Weiss, 1994), linear classifiers (Lewis,, Schapire, Callan, & Papka, 1996), context-sensitive learning (Cohen & Singer, 1996), learning by combining classifier (Larkey & Croft, 1996), and instance-based learning (Lam, Ruiz, & Srinivasan, 1999). Another usage of category hierarchy is browsing and searching the retrieval results. An example is the Cat-a-Cone system developed by Hearst and Karadi (1997). Feldman, Dargan, and Hirsh (1998) combined keyword distribution and keyword hierarchy to perform a range of data-mining operations in documents. Approaches on automatically generating the category themes are similar in context with research on topic identification or theme generation of text documents. Salton and Singhal (1994) generated a text relationship map among text excerpts and recognized all groups of three mutually related text excerpts. A merging process is applied iteratively to these groups to finally obtain the theme (or a set of themes) of all text excerpts. Another approach by Salton (1971) and Salton and Lesk (1971) clusters the document set and constructs a thesaurus-like structure. For example, Salton and Lesk divide the whole dataset into clusters where no overlap is allowed and construct a dictionary. The approach is *nonhierarchy* in this sense. Clifton and Cooley (1999) used traditional data-mining techniques to identify topics in a text corpus. They used a hypergraph partitioning scheme to cluster frequent item sets. The topic is represented as a set of named entities of the corresponding cluster. Ponte and Croft (1997) applied dynamic programming techniques to segment text into relatively small segments. These segments can then be used for topic identification. Lin (1995) used a knowledge-based concept counting paradigm to identify topics through the WordNet hierarchy. Hearst and Plaunt (1993) argued that the advent of full-length documents should be accompanied by the need for subtopic identification. They developed techniques for detecting subtopics and performed experiments using sequences of locally concentrated discussions rather than full-length documents. All these works, to some extent, may identify topics of documents that can be used as category themes for text categorization. However, they either rely on predefined category hierarchy (e.g., Lin, 1995) or do not reveal the hierarchy at all.

Recently, researchers have proposed methods for automatically developing category hierarchy. McCallum and Nigam (1999) used a bootstrapping process to generate new terms from a set of human-provided keywords. Human intervention is still required in their work. Probabilistic methods were widely used in exploiting hierarchy. Weigend, Wiener, and Pedersen (1999) proposed a two-level architecture for text categorization. The first level of the architecture predicts the probabilities of the meta-topic groups, which are groups of topics. This allows the individual models for each topic on the second level to focus on finer discrimination within the group. They used a supervised neural network to learn the hierarchy where topic classes were provided and already assigned. A different probabilistic approach by Hofmann (1999) used an unsupervised learning architecture called Cluster-Abstraction Model to organize groups of documents in a hierarchy.

Research on Chinese text processing focused on the tasks of retrieval and segmentation. Some work can be found in Chen, He, Xu, Gey, and Meggs (1997); Dai, Loh, and Khoo (1999); Huang & Robertson (1997a); Nie, Brisebois, and Ren (1996); Rajaraman, Lai, and Changwen (1997); and Wu and Tseng (1993, 1995). To our knowledge, there is still no work on knowledge discovery in Chinese text documents. The self-organizing maps model used in this work has been adopted by several other researchers for document clustering (for example, Kaski, Honkela, Lagus & Kohonen, 1998; Rauber & Merkl, 1999; and Rizzo, Allegra, & Fulantelli, 1999). However, we found no work similar to our research.

GENERATING CLUSTERS

To obtain the category hierarchy, we first perform a clustering process on the corpus. We then apply a category hierarchy generation process to the clustering result and obtain the category hierarchy. This section describes the clustering process. We will start with the preprocessing steps, follow by the clustering process by the SOM learning algorithm. Two labeling processes are then applied to the trained result. After the labeling processes, we obtain two feature maps that characterize the relationship between documents and words, respectively. Two maps are obtained after the labeling processes. The category hierarchy generation process, which will be described in the next section, is then applied to these two maps to develop the category hierarchy.

Preprocessing and Encoding Documents

Our approach begins with a standard practice in information retrieval (Salton & McGill, 1983), i.e., the vector space model, to encode documents with vectors, in which each element of a document vector corresponds to a different indexed term. In this work the corpus contains a set of Chinese news documents from the Central News Agency (CNA). First, we extract index terms from the documents. Traditionally, there are two schemes for extracting terms from Chinese texts. One is a character-based scheme and the other is a word-based scheme (Huang & Robertson, 1997b). We adopted the second scheme because individual Chinese characters generally carry no context-specific meaning. Two or more Chinese characters compose a word in Chinese. After extracting words, they are used as index terms to encode the documents. We use a binary vector to represent a document. A value of 1 for an element in a vector indicates the presence of the corresponding word in the document; otherwise, a value of 0 indicates the absence of the word.

A problem with this encoding method is that if the vocabulary is very large, the dimensionality of the vector is also high. In practice, the resulting dimensionality of the space is often tremendously huge, since the number of dimensions is determined by the number of distinct index terms in the corpus. In general, feature spaces on the order of 1,000 to 100,000 are very common for even reasonably small collections of documents. As a result, techniques for controlling the dimensionality of the vector space are required. Such a problem could be solved, for example, by eliminating some of the most common and some of the most rare indexed terms in the preprocessing stage. Several other techniques may also be used to tackle the problem; e.g., multidimensional scaling (Cox & Cox, 1994), principal component analysis (Jolliffe, 1986), and latent semantic indexing (Deerwester, Dumais, Furnas, & Landauer, 1990).

In information retrieval, several techniques are widely used to reduce the number of index terms. Unfortunately, these techniques are not fully applicable to Chinese documents. For example, stemming is generally not necessary for Chinese texts. On the other hand, we can use stop words and a thesaurus to reduce the number of index terms.

In this work, we manually constructed a stop list to filter out the meaningless words in the texts. We did not use a thesaurus simply because it was not available. Actually, the self-organizing process will cluster similar words together (Lee & Yang, 1999) and automatically generate a thesaurus. We have initiated a project for this part of research. We believe that the dimensionality of the document vectors can be dramatically reduced if we successfully applied such a thesaurus.

A document in the corpus contains about 100-200 characters. We discarded over-lengthy (more than 250 words) and duplicate documents for a better result. This step is not necessary because it affects less than 2% of documents in the corpus. Keeping these documents may only slightly increase the number of index terms and the processing time. However, if the corpus contains many duplicate or over-lengthy documents, the clustering result may be deteriorated.

We used the binary vector scheme to encode the documents and ignore any kind of term weighting schemes. We decided to use the binary vector scheme due to the following reasons. First, we clustered documents according to the co-occurrence of the words, which is irrelevant to the weights of the individual words. Second, our experiments showed no advantage in the clustering result to using term weighting schemes (classical *tf* and *tf·idf* schemes were used), but an additional amount of computation time was wasted on computing the weights. As a result, we believe the binary scheme is adequate to our needs.

Generating the Word Cluster Map and Document Cluster Map

The documents in the corpus were first encoded into a set of vectors by the terms that appeared in the documents, as in a vector space model. We intended to organize these documents into a set of clusters such that similar documents would fall into the same cluster. Moreover, similar clusters should be "close" in some regard. That is, we should be able to organize the clusters such that clusters that contain similar documents should be close in some measurement space. The unsupervised learning algorithm of SOM networks (Kohonen, 1997) meets our needs. The SOM algorithm organizes a set of high-dimensional vectors into a two-dimensional map of neurons according to the similarities among the vectors. Similar vectors, i.e., vectors with small distance, will map to the same or nearby neurons after the training (or learning) process. That is, the similarity between vectors in the original space is preserved in the mapped space. Applying the SOM algorithm to the document vectors, we actually perform a clustering process about the corpus. A neuron in the map can be considered as a cluster. Similar documents will fall into the same or neighboring neurons (clusters). In addition, the similarity of two clusters can be measured by the geometrical distance between their corresponding neurons. To decide the cluster to which a document or a word belongs, we apply a labeling process to the documents and the words respectively. After the labeling process, each document associates with a neuron in the map. We record such associations and form the document cluster map (DCM). In the same manner, we label each word to the map and form the word cluster map (WCM). We then use these two maps to generate the category themes and hierarchy.

We define some denotations and describe the training process here. Let $\mathbf{x}_i=\{x_{in}|1\leq n\leq N\}$, $1\leq i\leq M$, be the encoded vector of the ith document in the corpus, where N is the number of indexed terms and M is the number of the documents. We used these vectors as the training inputs to the SOM network. The network consists of a regular grid of neurons. Each neuron in the network has N synapses. Let $\mathbf{w}_j=\{w_{jn}|1\leq n\leq N\}$, $1\leq j\leq J$, be the synaptic weight vector of the jth neuron in the network, where J is the number of neurons in the network. Figure 1 depicts the formation of the map. We trained the network by the SOM algorithm:

Step 1. Randomly select a training vector $\mathbf{x}_i$ from the corpus.

Step 2. Find the neuron j with synaptic weights $\mathbf{w}_j$ that is closest to $\mathbf{x}_i$, i.e.,

$$\left\|\mathbf{x}_i-\mathbf{w}_j\right\|=\min_{1\leq k\leq J}\left\|\mathbf{x}_i-\mathbf{w}_k\right\| \tag{1}$$

Step 3. For every neuron l in the neighborhood of neuron j, update its synaptic weights by

$$\mathbf{w}_l^{new}=\mathbf{w}_l^{old}+\alpha(t)\left(\mathbf{x}_i-\mathbf{w}_l^{old}\right), \tag{2}$$

where $\alpha(t)$ is the training gain at time stamp t.

Step 4. Increase time stamp t. If t reaches the preset maximum training time T, halt the training process; otherwise decrease $\alpha(t)$ and the neighborhood size, go to Step 1.

The training process stops after time T is sufficiently large so that every vector may be selected as training input for certain times. The training gain and neighborhood size both decrease when t increases.

After training, we perform a labeling process to establish the association between each document and one of the neurons. The labeling process is described as follows. Each document feature vector $\mathbf{x}_i, 1\leq i\leq M$ is compared to every neuron in the map. We *label* the

Figure 1: The formation of neurons in the map.

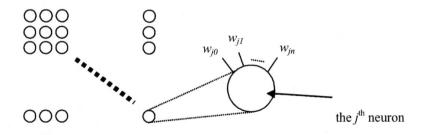

the jth neuron

*i*th document to the *j*th neuron if they satisfy Eq. 1. After the labeling process, each document is labeled to some neuron or, from a different viewpoint, each neuron is labeled with a set of documents. We record the labeling result and obtain the DCM. In the DCM, each neuron is labeled with a list of documents that are considered similar and are in the same cluster.

We explain why the SOM algorithm performs a clustering process here. In the labeling process, those documents that contain similar words will map to the same or neighboring neurons. Since the number of the neurons is usually much smaller than the number of the documents in the corpus, multiple documents may label to the same neuron. Thus, a neuron forms a document cluster. In addition, neighboring neurons represent document clusters of similar meaning, i.e., high word co-occurrence frequency in our context. On the other hand, it is possible that some neurons may not be labeled by any document. We call these neurons the *unlabeled neurons*. Unlabeled neurons exist when one of two situations occur: 1) when the number of documents is considerably small compared to the number of neurons; or 2) when the corpus contains too many conceptually similar documents such that a great part of documents will fall into a small set of neurons. However, unlabeled neurons will not diminish the result of the clustering since they do not affect the similarity measurement between any pair of clusters.

The map forms the WCM by labeling each neuron with certain words. This is achieved by examining the neurons' synaptic weight vectors. The labeling process is based on the following observations. Since we use binary representation for the document feature vectors, ideally the trained map should consist of synaptic weight vectors with component values near either 0 or 1. Since a value of 1 in a document vector represents the presence of a corresponding word in that document, a component with value near 1 in a synaptic weight vector also shows that such neuron has recognized the importance of the word and tried to "learn" the word. According to such interpretation, we design the following word labeling process. For the weight vector of the *j*th neuron $\mathbf{w}_j$, if its *n*th component exceeds a predetermined threshold, the corresponding word of that component is labeled to this neuron. To achieve a better result, the threshold is a real value near 1. By virtue of the SOM algorithm, a neuron may be labeled by several words that often co-occurred in a set of documents. Thus, a neuron forms a word cluster. The labeling method may not completely label every word in the corpus. We call these words the *unlabeled words*. Unlabeled words happen when several neurons compete for a word during the training process. The competition often results in imperfect convergence of weights, As a result, some words may not be learned well; i.e., their corresponding components may not have values near 1 in any neuron's weight vectors. We solve this problem by examining all the neurons in the map and labeling each unlabeled word to the neuron with the largest value of the corresponding component for that word. That is, the *n*th word is labeled to the *j*th neuron if

$$\mathbf{w}_{j_n} = \max_{1 \leq k \leq J} \mathbf{w}_{k_n}.$$ (3)

Note that we ignore the unlabeled neurons in Eq. 3.

The WCM autonomously clusters words according to their similarity of co-occurrence. Words that tend to occur simultaneously in the same document will be mapped to neighboring neurons in the map. For example, the translated Chinese words for "neural" and "network" often occur simultaneously in a document. They will map to the same neuron, or neighboring neurons, in the map because their corresponding components in the encoded document vector are both set to 1. Thus, a neuron will try to learn these two words simultaneously. Conversely, words that do not co-occur in the same document will map to distant neurons in the map. Thus, we can reveal the relationship between two words according to their corresponding neurons in the WCM.

DEVELOPING THEMATIC HIERARCHIES FOR TEXT DOCUMENTS

After the clustering process, each neuron in the DCM and the WCM actually represents a document cluster and a word cluster, respectively. Such clusters can be considered as categories in text categorization of the underlying corpus. In this section, we will describe two aspects of finding implicit structures of these categories. First, we will present a method for revealing the hierarchical structure among categories. Second, a category theme identification method is developed to find the labels of each category for easy human interpretation. The implicit structures of a text corpus can then be discovered and represented in a humanly comprehensible way through our methods.

Automatic Category Hierarchy Generation

To obtain a category hierarchy, we first cluster documents by the SOM using the method described in last section to generate the DCM and the WCM. As we mentioned before, a neuron in the document cluster map represents a cluster of documents. A cluster here also represents a category in text categorization terminology. Documents labeled to the same neuron, or neighboring neurons, usually contain words that often co-occur in these documents. By virtue of the SOM algorithm, the synaptic weight vectors of neighboring neurons have the least difference compared to those of distant neurons. That is, similar document clusters will correspond to neighboring neurons in the DCM. Thus, we may generate a cluster of similar clusters—or a *super-cluster*— by assembling neighboring neurons. This will essentially create a two-level hierarchy. In this hierarchy, the parent node is the constructed super-cluster and the child nodes are the clusters that compose the super-cluster. The hierarchy generation process can be further applied to each child node to establish the next level of this hierarchy. The overall hierarchy of the categories can then be established iteratively using such top-down approach until a stop criterion is satisfied.

To form a super-cluster, we first define distance between two clusters:

$$D(i,j) = \| \mathbf{G}_i - \mathbf{G}_j \|, \tag{4}$$

where i and j are the neuron indices of the two clusters, and $\mathbf{G}_i$ is the two-dimensional grid location of neuron i. For a square formation of neurons, $\mathbf{G}_i = (i \bmod J^{1/2}, i \operatorname{div} J^{1/2})$. $D(i,j)$ measures the Euclidean distance between the two coordinates $\mathbf{G}_i$ and $\mathbf{G}_j$. We also define the dissimilarity between two clusters:

$$\Delta(i,j) = \| \mathbf{w}_i - \mathbf{w}_j \|, \tag{5}$$

where $\mathbf{w}_i$ is the weight vector of neuron i. We may compute the supporting cluster similarity $\mathfrak{I}_i$ for a neuron i from its neighboring neurons by

$$S(i,j) = \frac{\text{doc}(i)\text{doc}(j)}{F(D(i,j)\Delta(i,j))}$$

$$\mathfrak{I}_i = \sum_{j \in B_i} S(i,j) \qquad (6)$$

where $\text{doc}(i)$ is the number of documents associated to neuron i in the document cluster map, and B_i is the set of neuron index in the neighborhood of neuron i. The function F: $\mathbf{R}^+ \rightarrow \mathbf{R}^+$ is a monotonically increasing function that takes $D(i,j)$ and $\Delta(i,j)$ as arguments. The super-clusters are developed from a set of *dominating neurons* in the map. A dominating neuron is a neuron that has locally maximal supporting cluster similarity. We may select all dominating neurons in the map by the following algorithm:

1. Find the neuron with the largest supporting cluster similarity. Select this neuron as dominating neuron.
2. Eliminate its neighbor neurons so that they will not be considered as dominating neurons.
3. If there is no neuron left or the number of dominating neurons exceeds a predetermined value, stop. Otherwise go to Step 1.

The algorithm finds dominating neurons from all neurons under consideration and creates a level of the hierarchy. The overall process is depicted in Figure 2. As shown in that figure, we may develop a two-level hierarchy by using a super-cluster (or dominating neuron) as the parent node and the clusters (or neurons) that are similar to the super-cluster as the child nodes. In Figure 2, super-cluster k corresponds to the dominating neuron k. The clusters associated with those neurons in the neighborhood of neuron k are used as the child nodes of the hierarchy.

A dominating neuron is the centroid of a super-cluster, which contains several child clusters. We will use the neuron index of a neuron as the index of the cluster associated with it. For consistency, the neuron index of a dominating neuron is used as the index of its corresponding super-cluster. The child clusters of a super-cluster can be found by the following rule: The ith cluster (neuron) belongs to the kth super-cluster if

$$\Delta(i,k) = \min_l \Delta(i,l), \quad l \text{ is a super - cluster.} \qquad (7)$$

The above process creates a two-level hierarchy of categories. In the following, we will show how to obtain the overall hierarchy. A super-cluster may be thought of as a category that contains several sub-categories. In the first application of the super-cluster generation process (denoted by STAGE-1), we obtain a set of super-clusters. Each super-cluster is used as the root node of a hierarchy. Thus the number of generated hierarchies is the same as the number of super-clusters obtained in STAGE-1. Note that we can put these super-clusters under one root node and obtain one single hierarchy by

Figure 2: (a) A two-level hierarchy comprises a super-cluster as root node and several clusters as child nodes. (b) The dominating neuron k is selected and used as a super-cluster. Its neighboring neurons compose the super-cluster. We only show a possible construction of the hierarchy here.

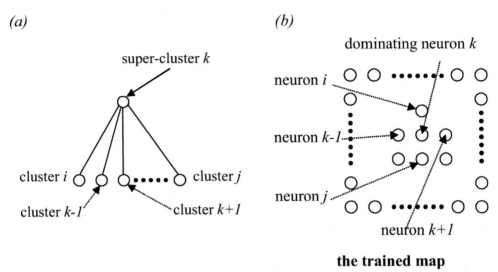

the trained map

setting a large neighborhood in Step 2 of the hierarchy generation algorithm. However, we see no advantage to doing this because the corpus generally contains documents of a wide variety of themes. Trying to put all different themes under a single general theme should be considered meaningless.

To find the children of the root nodes obtained in STAGE-1, we may apply the super-cluster generation process to each super-cluster (STAGE-2). Notice that in STAGE-2, we only consider neurons that belong to the same super-cluster. A set of sub-categories will be obtained for each hierarchy. These sub-categories will be used as the third level of the hierarchy. The overall category hierarchy can then be revealed by recursively applying the same process to each newfound super-cluster (STAGE-n). We decrease the size of neighborhood in selecting dominating neurons when the super-cluster generation process proceeds. This will produce a reasonable number of levels for the hierarchies, as we will discuss later.

Each neuron in the trained map will associate with a leaf node in one of the generated hierarchies after the hierarchy generation process. Since a neuron corresponds to a document cluster in the DCM, the developed hierarchies naturally perform a categorization of the documents in the training corpus. We may categorize new documents as follows. An incoming document A with document vector $\mathbf{x}_A$ is compared to all neurons in the trained map to find the document cluster to which it belongs. The neuron with synaptic weight vector that is the closest to $\mathbf{x}_A$ will be selected. The incoming document is categorized into the category where the neuron has been associated with a leaf node in one of the category hierarchies. This is depicted in Figure 3. In the figure, document A is the closest to neuron i, which is in the third level of the first hierarchy. Therefore, A will be categorized in the category that neuron

Figure 3: The text categorization process.

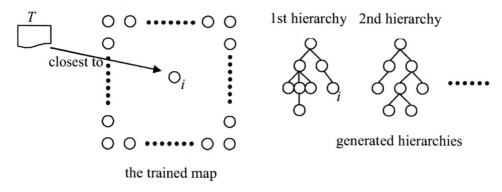

the trained map

generated hierarchies

i represents. Its parent categories as well aschild categories, if any, can be easily obtained. Through this approach, the task of text categorization has been done naturally by the category hierarchy generation process.

The neighborhood B_i in calculating supporting cluster similarity of a neuron *i* may be arbitrarily selected. Two common selections are circular neighborhood and square neighborhood. In our experiments, the shapes of the neighborhood are not crucial. It is the sizes of the neighborhood, denoted by N_{c1}, that matter. Different sizes of neighborhoods may result in different selections of dominating neurons. Small neighborhoods may not capture the necessary support from similar neurons. On the other hand, without proper weighting, a large N_{c1} will incorporate the support from distant neurons that may not be similar to the neuron under consideration. In addition, large neighborhoods have the disadvantage of costing much computation time.

Neighborhoods are also used to eliminate similar clusters in the super-cluster generation process. In each stage of the process, the neighborhood size, denoted by N_{c2}, has a direct influence on the number of dominating neurons. Large neighborhoods will eliminate many neurons and result in less dominating neurons. Conversely, a small neighborhood produces a large number of dominating neurons. We must decrease the neighborhood size when the process proceeds because the number of neurons under consideration is also decreased.

In Step 3 of the super-cluster generation process algorithm, we set three stop criterions. The first criterion stops finding super-clusters if there is no neuron left for selection. This is a basic criterion, but we need the second criterion—which limits the number of dominating neurons—to constrain the breadth of hierarchies. The lack of the second criterion may result in shallow hierarchies with too many categories in each level if the neighborhood size is considerably small. An extreme case happens when the neighborhood size is 0. In such a case, Step 2 of the algorithm will not eliminate any neuron. As a result, every neuron will be selected as dominating neurons, and we will obtain *J* single level hierarchies. Determining an adequate neighborhood size and a proper number of dominating neurons is crucial to obtaining an acceptable result. The third criterion constrains the depth of a hierarchy. If we allow a hierarchy having large depth, then we will obtain a set of "slimy" hierarchies. Note that setting large depths may cause no effect because the neighborhood size and the number of dominating neurons may already satisfy the stop criterion. An ad hoc heuristic rule used in our experiments is to determine the maximum depth *d* if it satisfies the following rule:

Find the first d such that $\dfrac{J}{K^{2d}} \leq 1.0$ for $d = 1,2,\ldots$ (8)

where K is the dimension of the neighborhood and is defined as a ratio to the map's dimension. For example, if the map contains an 8×8 grid of neurons, $K=4$ means that the dimension of the neighborhood is one-fourth of the map's dimension, which is 2 in this case. The depth d that satisfies Eq. 8 is then 2.

Notice that there some "spare" neurons may exist that are not used in any hierarchy after the hierarchy generation process. These neurons represent document clusters that are not significant enough to be a dominating neuron of a super-cluster in any stage of the process. Although we can extend the depths in the hierarchy generation process to enclose all neurons into the hierarchies, sometimes we may decide not to do so because we want a higher document-cluster ratio, that is, a cluster that contains a significant amount of documents. For example, if all clusters contain very few documents, it is not wise to use all clusters in the hierarchies because we may have a set of hierarchies that each contains many nodes without much information. To avoid producing such over-sized hierarchies, we may adopt a different approach. When the hierarchies have been created and there still exist some spare neurons, we simply assign each spare neuron to its nearest neighbor. This in effect merges the document clusters associated with these spare neurons into the hierarchies. The merging process is necessary to achieve a reasonable document-cluster ratio.

Automatic Category Theme Identification

In last section we showed how to obtain the category hierarchies from the DCM. In each category hierarchy, a leaf node represents an individual neuron as well as a category. In this subsection, we will show a method to assign each node in a hierarchy to a label and create a human-interpretable hierarchy. These labels reflect the themes of their associated nodes, that is, categories. Moreover, the label of a parent category in a hierarchy should represent the common theme of its child categories. Thus, the label of the root node of a hierarchy should represent the common theme of all categories under this hierarchy. Traditionally, a label usually contains only a word or a simple phrase to allow easy comprehension for humans. In this work, we try to identify category themes, i.e., category labels, by examining the WCM. As we mentioned before, any neuron i in the DCM represents a category and includes a set of similar documents. The same neuron in the WCM contains a set of words that often co-occur in such set of documents. Since neighboring neurons in the DCM contain similar documents, some significant words should occur often in these documents. The word that many neighboring neurons try to learn most should be the most important word and, as a result, the theme of a category. Thus, we may find the most significant word of a category by examining the synaptic weight vectors of its corresponding neuron and neighboring neurons. In the following, we will show how to find the category themes. Let C_k denote the set of neurons that belong to the kth super-cluster, or category. The category terms are selected from those words that are associated with these neurons in word cluster map. For all neurons $j \in C_k$, we select the n^*th word as the category term if

$$\sum_{j \in C_k} w_{j_{n^*}} = \max_{1 \leq n \leq N} \sum_{j \in C_k} w_{j_n} \qquad (9)$$

where G: $\mathbf{R}^+ + \{0\} \rightarrow \mathbf{R}^+$ is a monotonically non-decreasing weighting function. $G(j,k)$ will increase when the distance between neuron j and neuron k increases. The above equation selects the word that is most important to a super-cluster since the weight vector of a synaptic in a neuron reflects the willingness of that neuron to learn the corresponding input data, i.e., word. We apply Eq. 9 in each stage of the super-cluster generation process so when a new super-cluster is found, its theme is also determined. In STAGE-1, the selected themes label the root nodes of every category hierarchy. Likewise, the selected themes in STAGE-n are used as labels of the nth level nodes in each hierarchy. If a word has been selected in previous stages, it will not be a candidate of the themes in the following stages.

The terms selected by Eq. 9 form the top layer of the category structure. To find the descendants of these terms in the category hierarchy, we may apply the above process to each super-cluster. A set of sub-categories will be obtained. These sub-categories form the new super-clusters that are on the second layer of the hierarchy. The category structure can then be revealed by recursively applying the same category generation process to each newfound super-cluster. We decrease the size of neighborhoods in selecting dominating neurons when we try to find the sub-categories.

EXPERIMENTAL RESULTS

We applied our method to the Chinese news articles posted daily on the Web by the CNA (Central News Agency). Two corpora were constructed in our experiments. The first corpus (CORPUS-1) contains 100 news articles posted on August 1, 2, and 3, 1996. The second corpus (CORPUS-2) contains 3,268 documents posted between October 1 and October 9, 1996. A word extraction process was applied to the corpora to extract Chinese words. A total of 1,475 and 10,937 words were extracted from CORPUS-1 and CORPUS-2, respectively. To reduce the dimensionality of the feature vectors, we discarded those words that occurred only once in a document. We also discarded the words that appeared in a manually constructed stoplist. This reduced the number of words to 563 and 1,976 for CORPUS-1 and CORPUS-2, respectively. A reduction rate of 62% and 82% was achieved for the two corpora respectively.

To train CORPUS-1, we constructed a self-organizing map that contains 64 neurons in an 8×8 grid format. The number of neurons was determined experimentally so that a better clustering could be achieved. Each neuron in the map contains 563 synapses. The initial training gain was set to 0.4, and the maximal training time was set to 100. These settings were also determined experimentally. We tried different gain values ranging from 0.1 to 1.0 and various training time setting ranging from 50 to 200. We simply adopted the setting that achieved the most satisfying result. After training, we labeled the map by documents and words respectively, and obtained the DCM and the WCM for CORPUS-1. The above process was also applied to CORPUS-2 and obtained the DCM and the WCM for CORPUS-2 using a 20×20 map.

After the clustering process, we then applied the category generation process to the DCM to obtain the category hierarchies. In our experiments, we limited the number of dominating neurons to 10. We limited the depths of hierarchy to 2 and 3 for CORPUS-1 and CORPUS-2, respectively. In Figures 4 and 5, we show the overall category hierarchies developed from CORPUS-1. Each tree depicts a category hierarchy where the number on the root node depicts the super-cluster found. The number of hierarchies is the same as the number of super-clusters found at the first iteration of the hierarchy generation process (STAGE-1). Each leaf node in a tree represents a cluster in the DCM. The parent node of some child nodes in level n of a tree represents a super-cluster found in STAGE-$(n-1)$. For example, the root node of the largest tree in Figure 4 has a number 35, specifying that neuron 35 is one of the 10 dominating neurons found in STAGE-1. This node has 10 children, which are the 10 dominating neurons obtained in STAGE-2. These child nodes comprise the second level of the hierarchy. The third level nodes are obtained after STAGE-3. The number enclosed in a leaf node is the neuron index of its associated cluster in the DCM. The identified category themes are used to label every node in the hierarchies. In Figure 6, we only show the largest hierarchy developed from CORPUS-2 due to space limitation.

We examined the feasibility of our hierarchy generation process by measuring the intra-hierarchy and extra-hierarchy distances. Since text categorization performs a kind of clustering process, measuring these two kinds of distance reveals the effectiveness of the hierarchies. A hierarchy can be considered as a cluster of neurons that represent similar document clusters. These neurons share a common theme because they belong to the same hierarchy. We expect that they will produce a small intra-hierarchy distance that is defined by:

$$S_{int\,ra}^{h} = \frac{1}{|L_h|} \sum_{i \in L_h} \|\mathbf{w}_i - \mathbf{w}_h\|, \tag{10}$$

Figure 4: The category hierarchies of CORPUS-1.

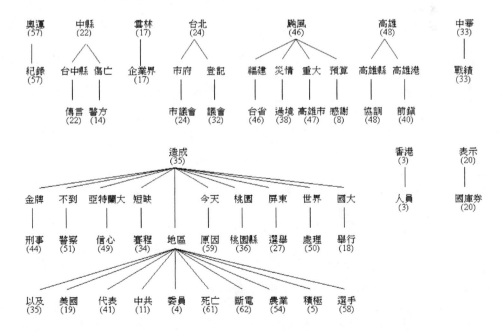

Figure 5: English translation of Figure 4.

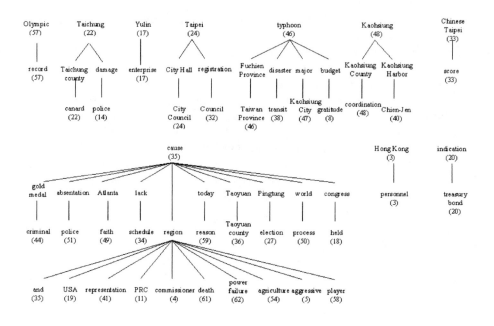

Figure 6: One of the category hierarchies developed from CORPUS-2.

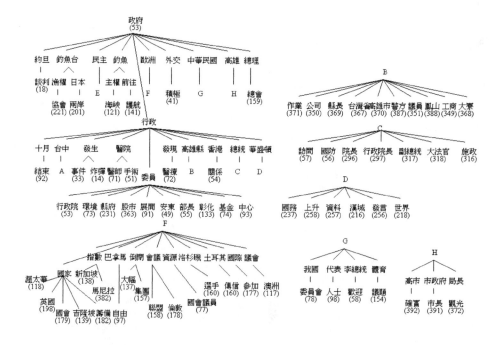

Table 1: The intra- and extra-hierarchy distances of every hierarchy developed from CORPUS-1 and CORPUS-2. The root node columns show the neuron indices of the root node of each hierarchy

CORPUS-1			
Hierarchy	**Root node**	**Intra-hierarchy distance**	**Extra-hierarchy distance**
1	57	0	2.62
2	22	0.97	2.59
3	17	0	2.71
4	24	1.23	2.57
5	46	2.77	2.45
6	48	1.13	2.54
7	35	1.82	2.20
8	3	0	3.10
9	33	0	2.71
10	20	0	2.63

CORPUS-2			
Hierarchy	**Root node**	**Intra-hierarchy distance**	**Extra-hierarchy distance**
1	53	2.18	2.39
2	5	2.01	2.64
3	2	1.37	3.08
4	119	1.90	2.87
5	81	1.95	2.88
6	200	2.17	2.77
7	40	1.73	3.48
8	310	2.41	2.60
9	36	1.86	2.92
10	259	1.60	2.90z

where h is the neuron index of the root node of the hierarchy, and L_h is the set of neuron indices of its leaf nodes. On the other hand, neurons in different hierarchies should be less similar. Thus, we may expect that a large extra-hierarchy distance will be produced. The extra-hierarchy distance of hierarchy h is defined as follow:

$$S^h_{inter} = \frac{1}{J - |L_h|} \sum_{k \notin L_h} \|\mathbf{w}_k - \mathbf{w}_h\|. \tag{11}$$

Table 1 lists the intra- and extra-hierarchy distances for each hierarchy. We can observe that only one of twenty hierarchies has an intra-hierarchy distance greater than its extra-hierarchy distance. Therefore, we may consider that the generated hierarchies successfully divide the document clusters into their appropriate hierarchies.

We also examined the feasibility of the theme identification process by comparing the overall importance of an identified theme to the rest of the terms associated with the same category. For any category k, we calculated the average synaptic weight of every terms over

Table 2: The ranks of all themes over all terms for all hierarchies

Hierarchy	CORPUS-1 (563 terms)	CORPUS-2 (1,976 terms)
1	1	3
2	1	1
3	1	2
4	1	1
5	1	1
6	1	1
7	1	1
8	1	1
9	1	1
10	1	1

C_k. Let t_n be the term corresponding to the nth component of a neuron's synaptic weight vector. We calculate the average synaptic weight of t_n over category k by

$$\overline{w_n} = \frac{1}{N} \sum_{j \in C_k} w_j \qquad (12)$$

Table 2 lists the ranks of the identified themes over all terms for all hierarchies. It is obvious that the identified themes are generally the most important term among all terms and therefore should be the themes of these hierarchies.

FUTURE WORK

Our approach evaluates the performance using a mathematical metric. However, it is the human who finally judges the goodness of the generated hierarchy. Therefore, subjective evaluations that are conducted on human subjects are necessary for constructing a human-readable hierarchy. The result of this work will be shown to several human subjects to evaluate the result in the near future. In addition, the constructed hierarchies are to be used for text categorization. Both subjective and objective evaluations of the performance of text categorization will also be conducted. Finally, we will compare the effectiveness of using our hierarchies for text categorization with the hierarchies constructed by some other methods.

CONCLUSIONS

In this chapter, we presented a method to automatically generate category hierarchies and identify category themes. The documents were first transformed to a set of feature vectors. The vectors were used as input to train the self-organizing map. Two maps—the word cluster map and the document cluster map—were obtained by labeling the neurons in the map with words and documents, respectively. An automatic category generation process was applied to the document cluster map to find some dominating neurons that are centroids of some super-clusters. The category terms of super-clusters were also determined. The same processes were applied recursively to each super-clusters to reveal the structure of the categories. Our method used neither human-provided terms nor predefined category structure. Text categorization can easily be achieved in our method.

REFERENCES

Apte, C., Damerau, F., & Weiss, S. M. (1994). Automated learning of decision rules for text categorization. *ACM Trans. Information Systems, 12*(3), 233-251.

Chen, A., He, J. Z., Xu, L. J., Gey, F. C., & Meggs, J. (1997). Chinese text retrieval without using a dictionary. *20th International ACM SIGIR Conference on Research and Development in Information Retrieval*, pp. 42-49, ACM.

Clifton, C., & Cooley, R. (1999). TopCat: Data mining for topic identification in a text corpus. *European Conference on Principles of Data Mining and Knowledge Discovery*, PKDD'99. pp. 174-183. Springer, Lecture Notes in Computer Science, Vol. 1704.

Cohen, W. W., & Singer, Y. (1996). Context-sensitive learning methods for text categorization. *19th International ACM SIGIR Conference on Research and Development in Information Retrieval*, pp. 307-315, ACM.

Cox, T. F., & Cox, M. A. A. (1994). *Multidimensional scaling*. London: Chapman & Hall.

Dai, Y., Loh, T. E., & Khoo, C. (1999). A new statistical formula for Chinese text segmentation incorporating contextual information. *22nd International ACM SIGIR Conference on Research and Development in Information Retrieval*, pp. 82-89, ACM.

Deerwester, S., Dumais, S., Furnas, G., & Landauer, K. (1990). Indexing by latent semantic analysis. *Journal of the American Society for Information Science, 40*(6), 391-407.

Feldman, R., Dagan, I., & Hirsh, H. (1998). Mining text using keyword distributions. *Journal of Intelligent Information Systems, 10*, 281-300.

Grobelnik, M., & Mladenic, D. (1998). Efficient text categorization. *Text Mining Workshop on ECML-98*. Chemnitz, Germany: Springer, Lecture Notes in Computer Science, Vol. 1398.

Hearst, M. A., & Karadi, C. (1997). Cat-a-Cone: An interactive interface for specifying searches and viewing retrieval results using a large category hierarchy. *20th International ACM SIGIR Conference on Research and Development in Information Retrieval*, pp. 246-255, ACM.

Hearst, M. A., & Plaunt, C. (1993). Subtopic structuring for full-length document access.

16th International ACM SIGIR Conference on Research and Development in Information Retrieval, pp. 59-68, ACM.

Hofmann, T. (1999). The cluster-abstraction model: Unsupervised learning of topic hierarchies from text data. *International Joint Conference on Artificial Intelligence, IJCAI'99*, pp. 682-687, Morgan Kaufmann.

Huang, X., & Robertson, S. E. (1997a). Experiments on large test collections with probabilistic approaches to Chinese text retrieval. *2nd International Workshop on Information Retrieval With Asian Languages*. Tsukuba, Japan, pp. 129-140, Taiwan: Academia Sinica.

Huang, X., & Robertson, S. E. (1997b). Okapi Chinese text retrieval experiments at TREC-6. *6th Text REtrieval Conference, TREC-6.* pp. 137-142, National Institute of Standards and Technology (NIST), special publication 500-240.

Jolliffe, I. T. (1986). *Principal component analysis.* Berlin: Springer-Verlag.

Kaski, S., Honkela, T., Lagus, K., & Kohonen, T. (1998). WEBSOM-Self-organizing maps of document collections. *Neurocomputing, 21*, 101-117.

Kohonen, T. (1997). *Self-Organizing Maps.* Berlin: Springer-Verlag.

Lam, W., Ruiz, M., & Srinivasan, P. (1999). Automatic text categorization and its application to text retrieval. *IEEE Trans. Knowledge and Data Engineering, 11*(8), 865-879.

Larkey, L. S., & Croft, W. B. (1996). Combining classifiers in text categorization. *19th International ACM SIGIR Conference on Research and Development in Information Retrieval*, pp. 289-297, ACM.

Lee, C. H., & Yang, H. C. (1999). A Web text-mining approach based on self-organizing map. *ACM CIKM'99 2nd Workshop on Web Information and Data Management.* Kansas City, MI, pp. 59-62, Taiwan: Academia Sinica.

Lewis, D. D. (1992). Feature selection and feature extraction for text categorization. *Speech and Natural Language Workshop.* Arden House, 212-217.

Lewis, D. D., Schapire, R. E., Callan, J. P., & Papka, R. (1996). Training algorithms for linear text classifiers. *19th International ACM SIGIR Conference on Research and Development in Information Retrieval*, pp. 298-306, Morgan Kaufmann.

Lin, C. Y. (1995). Knowledge-based automatic topic identification. *Meeting of the Association for Computational Linguistics, ACL 95*, pp. 308-310, Morgan Kaufmann.

McCallum, A., & Nigam, K. (1999). Text classification by bootstrapping with keywords, EM and shrinkage. *ACL '99 Workshop for Unsupervised Learning in Natural Language Processing*, pp. 52-58, Morgan Kaufmann.

Mehnert, R. (1997). *Federal agency and federal library reports.* Providence, NJ: National Library of Medicine.

Nie, J. Y., Brisebois, M., & Ren, X. (1996). On Chinese text retrieval. *19th International ACM SIGIR Conference on Research and Development in Information Retrieval*, pp. 225-233, ACM.

Ponte, J. M., & Croft, W. B. (1997). Text segmentation by topic. *European Conference on Digital Libraries, ECDL '97.* Lecture Notes in Computer Science, Vol. 1324, Springer, pp.113-125.

Rajaraman, K., Lai, K. F., & Changwen, Y. (1997). Experiments on proximity based Chinese text retrieval in TREC 6. *6th Text REtrieval Conference, TREC-6*, National Institute of Standards and Technology (NIST), special publication 500-240, pp. 559-576.

Rauber, A., & Merkl, D. (1999). Using self-organizing maps to organize document archives and to characterize subject matter: How to make a map tell the news of the world. *10th International Conference on Database and Expert Systems Applications*, Lecture Notes in Computer Science, Vol. 1677, Springer, pp. 302-311.

Rizzo, R., Allegra, M., & Fulantelli, G. (1999). Hypertext-like structures through a SOM network. *HYPERTEXT '99, Proceedings of the 10th ACM Conference on Hypertext and Hypermedia: Returning to Our Diverse Roots, February 21-25, 1999, Darmstadt, Germany*, ACM, pp. 71-72.

Rocchio, J. J. (1966). Document retrieval systems – optimization and evaluation, Ph.D. Thesis, Harvard University, Cambridge. MA.

Salton, G. (1971). Cluster search strategies and the optimization of retrieval effectiveness. In G. Salton (eds.), *The SMART retrieval system - experiment in automatic document processing*. Englewood Cliffs, NJ: Prentice-Hall.

Salton, G. & Lesk, M. (1971). Information analysis and dictionary construction. In G. Salton (ed.), The SMART retrieval system - experiments in automatic document processing. Englewood Cliffs, NJ: Prentice-Hall.

Salton, G. & McGill, M. J. (1983). *Introduction to modern information retrieval*. New York: McGraw-Hill.

Salton, G. & Singhal, A. (1994). Automatic text theme generation and the analysis of text structure. *Technical Report TR 94-1438*, Dept. Computer Science, Cornell University, Ithaca, NY.

Weigend, A. S., Wiener, E. D., & Pedersen, J. O. (1999). Exploiting hierarchy in text categorization. *Information Retrieval, 1*(3), 193-216.

Wu, Z. M., & Tseng, G. (1993). Chinese text segmentation for text retrieval: achievements and problems. *Journal of the American Society for Information Science, 44*(9), 532-542.

Wu, Z. M., & Tseng, G. (1995). An automatic Chinese text segmentation system for full text retrieval. *Journal of the American Society for Information Science, 46*(2), 83-96.

Chapter IX

The Pitfalls of Knowledge Discovery in Databases and Data Mining

John Wang
Montclair State University, USA

Alan Oppenheim
Montclair State University, USA

ABSTRACT

Although Data Mining (DM) may often seem a highly effective tool for companies to be using in their business endeavors, there are a number of pitfalls and/or barriers that may impede these firms from properly budgeting for DM projects in the short term. This chapter indicates that the pitfalls of DM can be categorized into several distinct categories. We explore the issues of accessibility and usability, affordability and efficiency, scalability and adaptability, systematic patterns vs. sample-specific patterns, explanatory factors vs. random variables, segmentation vs. sampling, accuracy and cohesiveness, and standardization and verification. Finally, we present the technical challenges regarding the pitfalls of DM.

INTRODUCTION

"Knowledge discovery in databases (KDD) is a new, multidisciplinary field that focuses on the overall process of information discovery in large volumes of warehoused data" (Abramowicz & Zurada, 2001). Data mining (DM) involves searching through databases (DBs) for correlations and/or other non-random patterns. DM has been used by statisticians, data analysts, and the management information systems community, while KDD has been mostly used by artificial intelligence and machine learning researchers. The practice of DM is becoming more common in many industries, especially in the light of recent trends toward globalization. This is particularly the case for major corporations who are realizing the importance of DM and how it can provide help with the rapid growth and change they are experiencing. Despite the large amount of data already in existence, much information has not been compiled and analyzed. With DM, existing data can be sorted and information utilized for maximum potential.

Although we fully recognize the importance of DM, another side of the same coin deserves our attention. There is a dark side of DM that many of us fail to recognize and without recognition of the pitfalls of DM, the data miner is prone to fall deep into traps. Peter Coy (1997) noted four pitfalls in DM. The first pitfall is that DM can produce "bogus correlations" and generate expensive misinterpretations if performed incorrectly. The second pitfall is allowing the computer to work long enough to find "evidence to support any preconception." The third pitfall is called "story-telling" and says "a finding makes more sense if there's a plausible theory for it. But a beguiling story can disguise weaknesses in the data." Coy's fourth pitfall is "using too many variables."

Other scholars have mentioned three disadvantages of mining a DB: the high knowledge requirement of the user; the choice of the DB; and the usage of too many variables during the process (Chen & Sakaguchi, 2000; Chung, 1999). "The more factors the computer considers, the more likely the program will find relationships, valid or not." (Sethi, 2001, p.69).

Our research indicated that the pitfalls of DM might be categorized into several groups. This chapter will first describe the potential roadblocks in an organization itself. Next, we explore the theoretical issues in contrast with statistical inference. Following that, we consider the data related issues that are the most serious concern. Here we find different problems related to the information used for conducting DM research. Then, we present the technical challenges regarding the pitfalls of DM. Finally, there are some social, ethical, and legal issues related to the use of DM— the most important of which is the privacy issue, a topic that is covered in Chapter 18.

ORGANIZATIONAL ISSUES

DM in an organization has both benefits and drawbacks. Naturally, the manner in which we interpret data will determine its ultimate benefit. Gathering data is generally not the issue here; there is much data already stored in data warehouses. We need to remember that DM, when misinterpreted, may lead to costly errors. There are a number of organizational factors and issues that also may be drawbacks and limit DM's implementation and effectiveness. These factors will be discussed in this section.

A recent survey of retail IT indicated that of the companies using DM, 53% attribute no direct benefit to their bottom line from DM. About 20% of respondents indicated that DM has contributed very little, while only 8.4% of the respondents indicated that DM has contributed substantially to profitability. Additionally, 64% of all companies responding indicated that they do not plan to use dedicated technology to manage their customer relationships (Anonymous, 2001).

The lack of bottom line results can be partially attributed to a number of organizational factors. First, start-up costs for implementing DM projects are very high and can create barriers that many corporations choose not to overcome. There are also short-term and long-term administrative costs associated with DM. The information and output provided by DM systems must be delivered to end-users within the organization in a meaningful form, otherwise the information may not be useable, or worse, may be used inappropriately. This can actually lead to a reduction in the return on investment (ROI).

Finally, organizations implementing DM systems must view the project as an enterprise-wide endeavor, rather than a departmental endeavor. Failure to address these problems will limit a firm's ability to successfully implement DM initiatives and recognize the benefits to its profitability.

Qualifications of Information Technology (IT) Staff

The move by corporations to DM has added to the administrative burdens of already overworked IT staffs. Often, DM requires that data be accessible 24 hours a day, 7 days a week, and that it is adequately protected at all times. This is a very difficult task given the shortage of personnel available for around-the-clock management. Before the project even begins, it is vital that IT staffs qualify the current network hardware and software, particularly in terms of how much data will be held on the servers.

Additionally, they must qualify the amount of data that will be handled on a daily basis, the devices that are already in place to perform data backup and recovery, and the software running those devices. Careful analysis must be given to the current network configuration, the number of servers, their location, where those servers are administered, and where and how the data are backed up. Administrators must also analyze future needs for the corporation, such as employees, functions, and business processes.

Successful DM projects require two components: appropriate technical expertise, and an appropriate technical infrastructure for accessing the Web. Many problems can be traced back to these two issues. Other pitfalls include inadequate technical expertise, inadequate planning, inadequate integration, and inadequate security (Griffin, 2000).

Requirements of Information Technology Infrastructure (ITIS)

In general, for most corporations that are involved in the process of DM, ITIS is not a major issue because they will already have an ITIS and sufficient hardware/software in place to handle DM algorithms. Please note that the IT structure meant here is not limited to hardware and software but also includes personnel. Another simple point to keep in mind here is that the more data being mined, the more powerful the ITIS required.

An ITIS does become an issue for companies that do not have one in place. Establishing one will usually involve rather large capital expenditures, and this cost would not be limited to a one-time event. Instead, as software and hardware modifications are made, it will be necessary for capital expenditures to continue to be made for maintenance and future upgrades of the existing ITIS. Total cost of ownership (TCO) will be very high. This might become even more of an issue for smaller to medium-sized firms that might not have sufficient resources for such measures.

Accessibility and Usability

Many organizations have experienced serious problems implementing a standard DM project. Most problems can do not lie with the technology, but rather with the people using it. To have a successful impact on an organization, a DM system must be speedy, accessible, and user friendly. In today's highly technological society, many of these systems employ very sophisticated tools running against data stored on high-end systems, but it is important that management can interpret the end results. The information desired must be accessible quickly through a PC or Web browser. If the end-users have difficulty using a system or cannot deliver needed information in a short time and be able to resolve their needs, they may abandon the application altogether, and hence the benefits will not be realized.

Affordability and Efficiency

A simple pitfall that must be viewed by potential DM users is its cost, which can range from a just a few thousand to millions of dollars for both hardware and software. Implementing an effective DM system can be a very complicated and expensive endeavor for a firm. META Group (2001) estimates that within the next two years, "the top 2000 global firms will spend $250 million each on Customer Relationship Management (CRM) and DM solutions." On the average, data warehouse users spent an average of $6 million on their data warehouse in 1998. This cost has been rising at an annual rate of 35% since 1996 (Groth, 2001).

Given these costs, corporate executives who may be seeking to cut expenses and contain losses may not want to invest the resources needed to develop such a system. Add to this that this development may take a few years to implement and may not have an immediate, observable impact on the firm's profitability, and corporate reluctance is even clearer. Furthermore, even with all of the money being spent on DM projects, many companies have not been able to calculate the resulting ROI for these systems. As a result, all too often corporate executives do not view DM projects in the appropriate manner, i.e., as long-term strategic investments.

It becomes apparent that expenditures towards maintaining DM through faster hardware and more powerful DM applications will become a constant cash outflow for many companies. As the DB increases in size over time, more capital will be needed for hardware and software upgrades. While this might not represent a large commitment for companies of substantial size, small to medium-sized firms may not be able to afford an ITIS or a DM application and the support it needs over the long term.

Efficiency may be defined as a measure of the ability to do a task within certain time and space constraints and should include the bottlenecks that might arise in a system when doing certain tasks (Wasserman, 1999). As a dataset becomes larger, most IT managers will want to reduce bottlenecks in the network to increase speed or supplement processing power through investment in new hardware.

The costs of implementing DM systems may include the costs of intellectual property, licensing, hardware, and software, and are especially burdensome to small firms because these represent a much larger percentage of small firm's revenues. This may place a greater burden on the small firm's ability to identify and realize measurable results quickly. Failure to do so may even jeopardize the company's very survival. This requires extreme patience, vision, and long-range planning to build a successful system.

Scalability and Adaptability

Scalability refers to how well a computer system's hardware or software can adapt to increased demands. Since DM tends to work with large amounts of data, scalability of the computer system often becomes a major issue. The network and computers on the network must be scalable or large enough to handle increased data flows, otherwise this may bring a network or individual computers on the network to a grinding halt. Also, system solutions need to be able to grow along with evolving user needs in such a way as to not lock the organization into a particular vendor's infrastructure as technology changes.

This is highlighted as an important issue as the volume of data has increased in recent years at a significant rate. One paper further points out, "that some companies already have data warehouses in the terabyte range (e.g., FedEx, UPS, Wal-Mart). Similarly, scientific data is reaching gigantic proportions (e.g., NASA space missions, Human Genome Project)" (Two Crows Corporation, 2001).

Most recent research notes scalability as a possible pitfall of DM. Even in the cases of very simple forms of data analysis, speed and memory become issues. Since hard drive access speed or network speed is not as fast as resident memory, many older DM applications prefer to be loaded into memory. As the datasets become larger or more variables are added, it follows that the amount of memory needed increases. Without this hardware, virtual memory may have to be used. In general terms, virtual memory is a process of using space on the hard drive to serve as actual memory. The problem with virtual memory is that it is slower, which in turn makes DM slower.

An Enterprise View

Another organizational factor that can be a problem to DM is not viewing the project as an enterprise-wide endeavor. In many failed DM projects, companies viewed DM as an IT project that was relegated to a specific department, rather than an enterprise-wide initiative. Most DM initiatives have been fragmented, implemented within departments without a cross-organizational perspective.

Given the cost and scope of DM projects, it is essential that all facets of the business have representation in the design of the system. Customer information is vital to the overall success of sales, marketing, and customer service, and this information must be shared across the organization. If one or more departments are excluded from this design process, there will be an inclination to not accept the finished product, or departments will lack the required knowledge to operate the system successfully.

Final Thoughts on Organizational Implications

There are many organizational factors that can serve as drawbacks to successful utilization of DM. Initially, organizations may balk at the high price tag that is associated with DM, and choose to not invest in items such as computer hardware, software, etc. The decision to do so may only come with plausible estimations of ROI, something, as was said above, that is often very difficult to measure. The output provided by DM must be usable information that can be quickly acted upon; otherwise, end-users will not rely on or effectively use the information.

Finally, DM must be viewed as a company-wide initiative. That way all employees will feel that they have a stake in the systems outcome. Failure to take this route may result in failure of the DM project. Remember that failure rates are often as high as 70%. Companies embarking on such projects must take these issues into account when making decisions.

STATISTICAL ISSUES
Systematic Patterns vs. Sample-Specific

There are two main goals of time series analysis: (a) identifying the nature of the phenomenon represented by the sequence of observations, and (b) forecasting (predicting future values of the time series variable). Both of these goals require that the pattern of observed time series data is identified and more or less formally described. Once the pattern is established, we can interpret and integrate it with other data. Regardless of the depth of our understanding and the validity of our interpretation of the phenomenon, we can extrapolate (ceteris paribus) the identified pattern to predict future events. Pyle (1999) argued that series data had many of the problems non-series data had. Series data also had a number of own special problems.

Temporal DM pertains to trying to forecast events that may occur in the future. Trends usually are regarded with the incline or decline of something. There could also be seasonal patterns that could be tracked over the years that will allow future outcomes to be predicted. There is also an irregular pattern that has erratic outcomes and follows no true pattern. The shortcoming of temporal DM is when something follows the irregular pattern. For the most part, events that follow a pattern continue to follow that course, but occasionally an outcome will occur that will be unexpected. These outcomes could be a result of something that the decision maker could not foresee happening in the near future, and may make the outcome of any analysis worthless. Temporal DM would not be able to foresee this happening because its user would not be able to predict this occurrence.

As DM is used more extensively, caution must be exercised while searching through DBs for correlations and patterns. The practice of using DM is not inherently bad, but the context in how it is used must be observed with a keen and practiced eye. Possibly the most notorious group of data miners are stock market researchers who seek to predict future stock price movement. Basically, past performance is used to predict future results. There are a number of potential problems in making the leap from a back-tested strategy to successfully investing in future real-world conditions. The first problem is determining the probability that the relationships occurred at random or whether the anomaly may be unique to the specific sample that was tested. Statisticians are fond of pointing out that if you torture the data long enough, it will confess to anything (McQueen & Thorley, 1999).

In describing the pitfalls of DM, Leinweber "sifted through a United Nations CD-ROM and discovered that, historically, the single-best predictor of the Standard & Poor's 500-stock index was butter production in Bangladesh." The lesson to learn here is that a "formula that happens to fit the data of the past won't necessarily have any predictive value" (Investor Home, 1999). The "random walk theory" of stock prices suggests that securities prices cannot be forecasted. Successful investment strategies—even those that have been successful for many years—may turn out to be fool's gold rather than a golden chalice.

Given a finite amount of historical data and an infinite number of complex models, uninformed investors may be lured into "overfitting" the data. Patterns that are assumed to be systematic may actually be sample-specific and therefore of no value (Montana, 2001). When people search through enough data, the data can be tailored to back any theory. The vast majority of the things that people discover by taking standard mathematical tools and sifting through a vast amount of data are statistical artifacts.

Explanatory Factors vs. Random Variables

The variables used in DM need to be more than variables; they need to be explanatory factors. If the factors are fundamentally sound, there is a greater chance the DM will prove to be more fruitful. We might review the relationship in several, distinct time periods. A common mistake made by those inexperienced in DM is to do "data dredging," that is, simply attempting to find associations, patterns, and trends in the data by using various DM tools without any prior analysis and preparation of the data. Using *multiple comparison procedures* indicates that data can be twisted to indicate a trend if the user feels so inclined (Jensen, 1999). Those who do "data dredging" are likely to find patterns that are common in the data, but are less likely to find patterns that are rare events, such as fraud.

An old saw that may fit in the analysis of DM is "garbage in, garbage out." One of the quirks of statistical analysis is that one may be able to find a factor that seems very highly correlated with the dependent variable during a specific time period, but such a relationship turns out to be spurious when tested in other time periods. Such spurious correlations produce the iron pyrite ("fool's gold") of DM. However, even when adjustments are made for excessive collinearity by removing less explanatory, co-linear variables from the model, many such models have trouble withstanding the test of time (Dietterich, 1999). Just as gold is difficult to detect in the ground because it is a rare and precious metal, so too are low-incidence occurrences such as fraud. The person mining has to know where to search and what signs to look for to discover fraudulent practice, which is where data analysis comes in.

Statistical inference "has a great deal to offer in evaluating hypotheses in the search, in evaluating the results of the search and in applying the results" (Numerical Machine Learning, 1997). Any correlation found through statistical inference might be considered completely random and therefore not meaningful. Even worse, "variables not included in a dataset may obscure relationships enough to make the effect of a variable appear the opposite from the truth" (Numerical Machine Learning, 1997). Furthermore, other research indicates that on large datasets with multiple variables, results using statistics can become overwhelming and therefore be the cause of difficulty in interpreting results.

Hypothesis testing is a respectable and sometimes valuable tool to assess the results of experiments. However, it too has difficulties. For example, there may be a problem with the asymmetry in the treatment of the null and alternative hypotheses, which will control the probability of Type I errors, but the probability of Type II errors may have to be largely guessed (Berger & Berry, 1988). In practice, the approach is not followed literally—common sense prevails. Rather than setting an α in advance and then acting accordingly, most researchers tend to treat the p-value obtained for their data as a kind of standardized descriptive statistic. They report these p-values, and then let others draw their own conclusions; such conclusions will often be that further experiments are needed. The problem then is that there is no standard approach to arriving at a final conclusion. Perhaps this is how it should be, but this means that statistical tests are used as a component in a slightly ill-defined mechanism for accumulating evidence, rather than in the tidy cut-and-dried way that their inventors were trying to establish. The rejection/acceptance paradigm also leads to the problem of biased reporting. Usually, positive results are much more exciting than negative ones, and so it is tempting to use low p-values as a criterion for publications of results. Despite these difficulties, those who seek rigorous analysis of experimental results will often want to see p-values, and provided its limitations are borne in mind, the hypothesis testing methodology can be applied in useful and effective ways.

Segmentation vs. Sampling

Segmentation is an inherently different task from sampling. As a segment, we deliberately focus on a subset of data, sharpening the focus of the analysis. But when we sample data, we lose information because we throw away data not knowing what to keep and what to ignore. Sampling will almost always result in a loss of information, in particular with respect to data fields with a large number of non-numeric values.

Most of the time it does not make sense to analyze all of variables from a large dataset because patterns are lost through dilution. To find useful patterns in a large data warehouse, we usually have to select a segment (and not a sample) of data that fits a business objective, prepare it for analysis, and then perform DM. Looking at all of the data at once often hides the patterns, because the factors that apply to distinct business objectives often dilute each other.

While sampling may seem to offer a short cut to faster data analysis, the end results are often less than desirable. Sampling was used within statistics because it was so difficult to have access to an entire population. Sampling methods were developed to allow for some rough calculations about some of the characteristics of the population without access to the entire population. This contradicts having a large DB. We build DBs of a huge customer's behavior exactly for the purpose of having access to the entire population. Sampling a large warehouse for analysis almost defeats the purpose of having all the data in the first place (Data Mines for Data Warehouses, 2001).

In discussing some pitfalls of DM, the issue of how to avoid them deserves mention. There are unique statistical challenges produced by searching a space of models and evaluating model quality based on a single data sample. Work in statistics on *specification searches* and *multiple comparisons* has long explored the implications of DM, and statisticians have also developed several adjustments to account for the effects of search. Work in machine learning and knowledge discovery related to *overfilling* and *oversearching* has also explored similar themes, and researchers in these fields have also developed techniques such as *pruning* and *minimum description length encoding* to adjust for the effects of the search (Jensen, 1999). However, this "dark side" of DM is still largely unknown to some practitioners, and problems such as *overfilling* and *overestimation* of accuracy still arise in knowledge discovery applications with surprising regularity. In addition, the statistical effects of the search can be quite subtle, and they can trip up even experienced researchers and practitioners.

A very common approach is to obtain new data or to divide an existing sample into two or more subsamples, using one subsample to select a small number of models and other subsamples to obtain unbiased scores. *Cross-validation* is a related approach that can be used when the process for identifying a "best" model is algorithmic. Sometimes, *incremental induction* is efficient (Hand, Mannila, & Smyth, 2001). A model is developed on a small data sample and, while suggestive of an interesting relationship, it does not exceed a prespecified critical value. Another small sample of data becomes available later, but it is also too small to confer statistical significance to the model. However, the relationship would be significant if considered in the context of both data samples together. This indicates the importance of maintaining both tentative models and links to the original data (Jensen, 2001).

Several relatively simple mathematical adjustments can be made to statistical significance tests to correct for the effects of multiple comparisons. These have been explored in detail within the statistical literature on experimental design. Unfortunately, the assumptions of these adjustments are often restrictive. Many of the most successful approaches are based on computationally intensive techniques such as *randomization* and *resampling* (Saarenvirta, 1999). *Randomization* tests have been employed in several knowledge discovery algorithms. Serious statistical problems are introduced by searching large model spaces, and unwary analysts and researchers can still fall prey to these pitfalls.

DATA ACCURACY AND STANDARDIZATION

Another important aspect of DM is the accuracy of the data itself. It follows that poor data are a leading contributor to the failure of DM. This factor is a major business challenge. The emergence of electronic data processing and collection methods has lead some to call recent times as the "information age." However, it may be more accurately termed as "analysis paralysis." Most businesses either posses a large DB or have access to one. These DBs contain so much data that it may be quite difficult to understand what that data are telling us. Just about all transactions in the market will generate a computer record somewhere. All those data have meaning with respect to making better business decisions or understanding customer needs and preferences. But discovering those needs and preferences in a DB that contains terabits of seemingly incomprehensible numbers and facts is a big challenge (Abbot, 2001).

Accuracy and Cohesiveness

A model is only as good as the variables and data used to create it. Many dimensions of this issue apply to DM, the first being the quality and the sources of the data. We repeatedly can find that data accuracy is imperative to very crucial functions. Administrative data are not without problems, however. Of primary concern is that, unlike a purposeful data collection effort, the coding of data is often not carefully quality controlled. Likewise, data objects may not necessarily be defined commonly across DBs or in the way a researcher would want. One of the most serious concerns is matching records across different DBs in order to build a more detailed individual record. In addition, administrative records may not accurately represent the population of interest, leading to issues similar to sampling and non-response bias. Transaction records and other administrative data are volatile, that is, rapidly changing over time, so that a snapshot of information taken at one time may not indicate the same relationships that an equivalent snapshot taken at a later time (or using a different set of tables) would reveal. Finally, programs and regulations themselves may introduce bias into administrative records, thus making them unreliable over time (Judson, 2000).

No matter how huge a company's datasets may be, freshness and accuracy of the data are imperative for successful DM. Many companies have stores of outdated and duplicate data, as anyone who has ever received multiple copies of the same catalog can attest. Before a company can even consider what DM can do for business, the data must be clean and fresh, up-to-date, and error- and duplication-free. Unfortunately, this is easier said than done. Computer systems at many large companies have grown rather complicated over the years by encompassing a wide variety of incompatible DBs and systems as each division or department bought and installed what they thought was best for their needs without any thought of the overall enterprise. This may have been further complicated through mergers and acquisitions that may have brought together even more varied systems. "Bad data, duplicate data, and inaccurate and incomplete data are a stumbling block for many companies" (E-commag, 2001).

The first step to achieve proper DM results is to start with the correct raw data. For companies to mine their customer transaction data (which sometimes has additional demographic information), they can figure out an "ad infinitum" value of revenue for each customer. It is clear here that it is very important for companies to get proper data accuracy for forecasting functions. Poor data accuracy can lead to the risk of poor pro forma financial statements.

With accurate data, one should be able to achieve a single customer view. This will eliminate multiple counts of the same individual or household within and across an enterprise or within a marketing target. Additionally, this will normalize business information and data. With an information quality solution, one will be able to build and analyze relationships, manage a universal source of information, and make more informed business decisions. By implementing an information quality solution across an organization, one can maximize the ROI from CRM, business intelligence, and enterprise applications.

If dirty, incomplete, and poorly structured data are employed in the mining, the task of finding significant patterns in the data will be much harder. The elimination of errors, removal of redundancies, and filling of gaps in data (although tedious and time-consuming tasks), are integral to successful DM (Business Lounge, 2001).

Standardization and Verification

Data in a DB or data store are typically inconsistent and lacking conformity. In some cases, there are probably small variations in the way that even the subscriber's name or address appear in a DB. This will lead to the allocation of organizational resources based on inaccurate information. This can be a very costly problem for any organization that routinely mails against a large customer DB. An added difficulty of getting these correct data sources for data accuracy is the large amount of the sources themselves. The number of enterprise data sources is growing rapidly, with new types of sources emerging every year. The newest source is, of course, enterprise e-business operations. Enterprises want to integrate clickstream data from their Web sites with other internal data in order to get a complete picture of their customers and integrate internal processes. Other sources of valuable data include Enterprise Resource Planning (ERP) programs, operational data stores, packaged and home-grown analytic applications, and existing data marts. The process of integrating these sources into one dataset can be complicated and is made even more difficult when an enterprise merges with or acquires another enterprise.

Enterprises also look to a growing number of external sources to supplement their internal data. These might include prospect lists, demographic and psychographic data, and business profiles purchased from third-party providers (Hoss, 2001). Enterprises might also want to use an external provider for help with address verification, where internal company sources are compared with a master list to ensure data accuracy. Additionally, some industries have their own specific sources of external data. For example, the retail industry uses data from store scanners, and the pharmaceutical industry uses prescription data that are totaled by an outsourced company.

Although data quality issues vary greatly from organization to organization, we can discuss these issues more effectively by referring to four basic types of data quality categories that affect IT professionals and business analysts on a daily basis. These categories —standardization, matching, verification, and enhancement — make up the general data quality landscape (Moss, 2000).

Verification is the process of verifying any other type of data against a known correct source. For example, if a company decided to import some data from an outside vendor, the U.S. Postal Service DB might be used to make sure that the ZIP codes match the addresses and that the addresses were deliverable. If not, the organization could potentially wind up with a great deal of undeliverable mail. The same principle would apply to verifying any other type of data. Using verification techniques, a company ensures that data are correct based on an internal or external data source that has been verified and validated as correct.

Enhancement of data involves the addition of data to an existing data set or actually changing the data in some way to make it more useful in the long run. Enhancement technology allows a company to get more from its data by enriching the data with additional information.

Data Sampling and Variable Selection

Data accuracy can also fall victim to the potential of corruption by means of data sampling. This is not to say that the information is necessarily wrong per se, but in fact the sample of information that is taken may not be wholly representative of what is being mined.

Apart from sampling, *summarization* may be used to reduce data sizes (Parsaye, 1995). But summarization can cause problems too. In fact, the summarization of the same dataset with two sampling or summarization methods may yield the same result, and the summarization of the same dataset with two methods may produce two different results.

Outliers and Noise

Outliers are variables that have a value that is far away from the rest of the values for that variable. One needs to investigate if there is a mistake due to some external or internal factor, such as a failing sensor or a human error. If it can be established that the outlier is due to a mistake, Pyle (1999) suggests that it should be corrected by a *filtering* process or by treating it like a missing value.

Noise is simply a distortion to the signal and is something integral to the nature of the world, not the result of a bad recording of values. The problem with noise is that it does not follow any pattern that is easily detected. As a consequence of this, there are no easy ways to eliminate noise but there are ways to minimize the impact of noise.

Missing Values or Null Values

Companies rely on data for a variety of different reasons —from identifying opportunities with customers to ensuring a smooth manufacturing process — and it is impossible to make effective business decisions if the data are not good. In order to be able to fully assess these solutions, it is helpful to have a thorough understanding of the basic types of data quality problems. As companies look to address the issue of data quality, there are five basic requirements to consider when looking for a total data quality management solution: ease of use, flexibility, performance, platform independence, and affordability (Atkins, 2000).

Because DBs often are constructed for other tasks than DM, attributes important for a DM task could be missing. Data that could have facilitated the DM process might not even be stored in the DB. Missing values can cause big problems in series data and series modeling techniques. There are many different methods for "repairing" series data with missing values such as multiple regression and autocorrelation. Chapter 7 addresses this problem in detail.

Therefore, data quality control is a serious problem. Data inconsistency and data redundancy might mire any data-mining effort. Data quality is a company-wide problem that requires company-wide support. A total data quality solution must be able to address the needs of every individual within an organization, from the business analysts to the IT personnel. To meet the needs of these diverse groups, a solution must integrate with current IT tools and still be easy to use. For companies to truly thrive and achieve successful business intelligence, data quality must be an issue that is elevated to top priority.

TECHNICAL ISSUES

There are many technical challenges regarding DM. These technical issues can cover a whole spectrum of possibilities. However, in this discussion, technical issues will be limited to the pitfalls regarding certain DM methods and other general technical issues affecting a standard IT department. The selected technical methods reviewed for pitfalls that are used by DM are neural networks, decision trees, genetic algorithms, fuzzy logic, and data visualization. General technical issues covered relate to requirements of disaster planning.

When reviewing DM for technical issues, an obvious point that might be initially missed by new users is that DM does not automatically happen by just loading software onto a computer. Many issues must be painstakingly thought out prior to moving forward with DM. There is no single superior DM method that exists among the more than 25 different types of methods currently available. If there were one specific method that was best and without any disadvantages, then there would be no need for all of these different types of methods. One company even noted, with regards to DM, that there "is no predictive method that is best for all applications" (International Knowledge Discovery Institute, 1999). Therefore, when a company begins dealings with prospective clients, after having already gained a thorough understanding of the client's problem, it will use 8 to 10 different DM methods in an effort to find the best application for the client. Listed below are a few examples of some DM methods generally used.

The Problems with Neural Networks (NNs)

Neural networks (or neural nets) are computer functions that are programmed to imitate the decision-making process of the human brain. NNs are one of the oldest and most frequently used techniques in DM. This program is able to choose the best solution for a problem that contains many different outcomes. Even though the knowledge of how human memory works is not known, the way people learn through constant repetition is not a mystery. One of the most important abilities that humans possess is the capability to infer knowledge. NNs are very useful, not because the computer is coming up with a solution that a human would not come up with, but rather that they are able to arrive at that solution much faster. "In terms of application, NNs are found in systems performing image and signal processing, pattern recognition, robotics, automatic navigation, prediction and forecasting, and a variety of simulations" (Jones, 2001).

There are several possible pitfalls regarding NNs. One issue is related to learning. A drawback of this process is that learning or training can take a large amount of time and resources to complete. Since results or the data being mined are time critical, this can pose a large problem for the end-user. Therefore, most articles point out that NNs are better suited to learning on small to medium-sized datasets as it becomes too time inefficient on large-sized datasets (Hand, Mannila, & Smyth, 2001).

Also, NNs lack explicitness. As several researchers have pointed out, the process it goes through is considered by most to be hidden and therefore left unexplained. One article summarized, "It is almost as if the pattern-discovery process is handled within a black box procedure" (Electronic Textbook Statsoft.com, 2001). This lack of explicitness may lead to less confidence in the results and a lack of willingness to apply those results from DM, since there is no understanding of how the results came about. It becomes obvious as the datasets variables increase in size, that it will become more difficult to understand how the NN came to its conclusions.

Another possible weakness is that the program's capability to solve problems could never exceed that of the user's. This means that the computer will never able to produce a solution that a human could not produce if given enough time. As a result, the user has to program problems and solutions into the computer so that it can decide what are the best solutions. If the user has no answer(s), chances are neither will the computer.

A final drawback of NNs noted in one paper is that "there is a very limited tradition of experience on which to draw when choosing between the nets that are on offer" (Australian National University, 2001). This lack of knowledge or general review on which type of NNs is best might result in the purchase of an application that will not make the best predictions or in general will just work poorly.

The Problems with Decision Trees (DTs)

The Decision Tree (DT) is a method that uses a hierarchy of simple if-then statements in classifying data. This tends to be one of the most inexpensive methods to use. However, it is faster to use, easier to generate understandable rules, and simpler to explain since any decision that is made can be understood by viewing the path of decisions. DTs provide an effective structure in which alternative decisions and the implications of taking those decisions can be laid down and evaluated. They also help to form an accurate, balanced picture of the risks and rewards that can result from a particular choice. However, for all its advantages, there are also some disadvantages or possible pitfalls of which users should be aware.

The problems with DTs can be divided into two categories: algorithmic problems that complicate the algorithm's goal of finding a small tree, and inherent problems with the representation. The conventional DT is useful for small problems but quickly becomes cumbersome and hard to read for intermediate-sized problems. In addition, special software is required to draw the tree. Representing all the information on the tree requires writing probability numbers and payoff numbers under the branches or at the ends of the nodes of the tree (KDNuggets, 2001).

In DTs learning, the goal is to arrive at a classification while minimizing the depth of the final tree. Choosing attributes that divide the positive examples from the negative examples does this. Thus, if there is noise in the training set, DTs will fail to find a valid tree.

A big headache is that the data used must be interval or categorical. Therefore, any data not received in this format will have to be recoded to this format in order to be used.

This recoding could possibly hide relationships that other DM methods would find. Also, *overfitting* can occur whenever there is a large set of possible hypotheses. A technique to deal with this problem is to use DT *pruning*. Pruning prevents recursive splitting if the relevance of the attribute is low.

Another possible drawback is that the DTs generally represent a finite number of classes or possibilities. It becomes difficult for decision makers to quantify a finite amount of variables. Due to this limitation, the accuracy of the output will be limited to the number of classes selected that may result in a misleading answer. Even worse, if the user does try to cover an acceptable number of variables, as the list of variables increase, the if-then statements created can become more complex.

Finally, there are two other separate drawbacks due to variable systematic risk. First, DTs are not appropriate for estimation. This is based on the fact that complicated, but understandable, rules must be adhered to. Therefore, estimation would not be appropriate. Second, this method is not useful for all types of DM. It is "hard to use DTs for problems involving time series data unless a lot of effort is put into presenting the data in such a way that trends are made visible" (Knowledge Acquisition Discovery Management, 1997).

The Problems with Genetic Algorithms (GAs)

Genetic Algorithms (GAs) relate to evolutionary computing that solves problems through application of natural selection and evolution. Evolutionary computing is a component of machine learning, "a sub-discipline of artificial intelligence" (Sethi, 2001, p. 33). It is a "general-purpose search algorithm" (Chen, 2001, p. 257) that utilizes rules mimicking a population's natural genetic evolution to solving problems. Fundamentally, they are free of derivatives (or outgrowths) and are best utilized in optimization problems with allegories founded in evolutionary operations such as selection, crossover, and mutation.

A chromosome in computer language is a string of binary bits in which the possible solution is encoded. The term "fitness function" is designated to mean the quality of the solution. Beginning with a random accumulation of potential solutions, the search creates what is termed the "gene pool or population" (Sethi, 2001, p. 37). Upon each completion of a search, a new pool is constructed by the GA, and the pool has evolved with improved "fitness values." The most desirable solution is chosen from resulting generations of GAs.

Despite these advantages, these algorithms have not yet been applied to very large-scale problems. One possible reason is that GAs require a significant computational effort with respect to other methods, when parallel processing is not employed (Sethi, 2001, p. 39).

The Problems With Fuzzy Logic (FL)

Fuzzy Logic (FL), first developed by Lotfi Zadeh, uses fuzzy set theory. FL is a multi-valued (as opposed to binary) logic developed to deal with imprecise or vague data.

Although there are some limitations to using FL, the main reason that it is not used very widely is that many people are misinformed about it. The difficulties of using FL are different than those of using conventional logic. In addition to technical difficulties, lack of knowledge about this rather new field also causes many problems.

How to define membership functions is a common problem. The rules will be based on trial and error, rather than the designer's intuition and knowledge. Critics argue that this process—in contrast to the rigid mathematical design process of conventional devices— could lead to undesired outcomes under abnormal circumstances (Pagallo & Haussler, 1990).

Lack of knowledge and/or misinformation about FL are the main reasons it is still a relatively small field. Many critics argue that FL is a fad. They feel it will not be useful since there is no known way to guarantee that it will work under all circumstances. Also, many argue that conventional methods work just or nearly as well, so it is not worthwhile to develop new methods (Chen, 2001).

Another concern seems to be the language barrier. Japanese engineers have pursued FL even though the University of California was its birthplace. It seems as if many American researchers have shunned it. Although technical terms often have a neutral connotation, the Japanese term for FL clearly has a positive tone *(clever)*. Unlike the trendy Japanese term, Americans assign a negative connotation to *fuzzy*. Despite Japanese and worldwide successes, this technology is still somewhat underdeveloped in the United States.

The Problems with Data Visualization

This is a method that allows the user to gain a more intuitive understanding of the data. Generally, graphics tools used better illustrate relationships among data. Data visualization further allows the user to more easily focus and see the patterns and trends amongst the data. However, the major pitfall in this case is that as the volume of data increases, it can become increasingly difficult to discern accurate patterns from the data sets.

Disaster Planning

Finally, disaster recovery plans must be analyzed. This may result in the need to redesign data backup management techniques to accommodate business growth. Once a coherent plan to accommodate the current and future business needs of the corporation has been developed, it must be implemented quickly. Administrators must know that the backup systems that are in place will work each time and that the data are properly protected. These systems must be reviewed once or twice per year to ensure that they are delivering the protection that the business needs in the most cost-effective manner.

In conclusion, there are high administrative and maintenance costs to the firm for DM in terms of both time and money. Failure to recognize the investment necessary to maintain the system can lead to data corruption and system failure.

CONCLUSION

DM helps deliver tremendous insights for businesses into the problems they face and aids in identifying new opportunities. It further helps businesses to solve more complex problems and make smarter decisions. DM is a potentially powerful tool for companies; however, more research is needed to measure the benefits of DM. If managers are better able to quantify the benefits of DM, they will be in a better position to justify its relatively high costs. In concert with better justification and acceptance will come the treatment of DM as a more legitimate and serous tool in organizational development.

With DM, the same process should be applied as with any other organizational development tool. Once a DM process has been implemented, a company should take the steps needed to monitor the process and obtain feedback from all elements of the process. Monitoring and feedback will give a company the information necessary to determine if it is encountering any of the potential pitfalls and develop corrective strategies to take through the implementation → monitoring → feedback loop. For example, if a company sees lowered costs as a result of the use of information obtained through DM but loses revenues as a result of a loss of customers having concerns about privacy issues, then no real grain is made. Through the process of monitoring and feedback, firms can better maximize opportunities to increase revenues and lower costs while minimizing the risks posed by any of the pitfalls to DM.

Regardless of the many pitfalls that were found and discussed by this chapter, DM should still be considered as a valuable tool to many corporations. DM is only a beginning. DM does not make decisions, people do —knowledge and experience are the most important factors.

REFERENCES

Abbot, D. (November 2001). Data mining accuracy. Available online at: <http://www.the_modeling agency.com>.

Abramowicz, W., & Zurada, J. (2001). *Knowledge discovery for business information systems*. Boston, MA: Kluwer Academic Publishers.

Anonymous (October 2001). Data mining/CRM: Searching for an ROI. *Chain Store Age, Retail IT 2001*, 24-26.

Atkins, M.E. (2000). A jump start in winning: understanding enterprise data quality management. Available online at: <http://www.datawarehouse.com/iknowledge/articles/article.efm?ContentID=278>.

Australian National University. (2001). Data mining from a statistical perspective. Available online at: <http://wwwmaths.anu.edu.au/~johnm/dm/dmpaper.html>.

Berger, J.O. & Berry, D.A. (1988). The relevance of stopping rules in statistical inference. In S. Gupta & J.O. Berger (eds.) *Statistical decision theory and related topics*. Springer-Verlag.

Berry, M. & Linoff, G. (2000). *Mastering data mining: The art and science of customer relationship management.* New York: Wiley Computer Publishing.

Business Lounge (2001). Data mining: A new branch of knowledge discovery. Available online at: <http://www.bl.com.au/pages/articles/data-mining.htm>.

Chen, L. & Sakaguchi, T. (2000). Disadvantages of data mining. *Information Systems Management*, 17(1), 65.

Chen, Z. (2001). *Data mining and uncertain reasoning, An integrated approach*. New York: John Wiley & Sons, Inc.

Chung, H. M. (1999). Data mining. *Journal of Management Information Systems,* 16(1), 11-17.

Cline, K. (1997). Data mining's promise & pitfalls, *Banking Strategies LXXIII*, 40-46.

Coy, P. (1997). He who mines data may strike fool's gold. *Business Week, #3531, 40.*

DataMines for Data Warehouses (2001). Available online at: <http://www.ite.poly.edu/ mg/mg693/e0025984/projects/WrightBro/DforD.htm>

Dietterich, T.G. (1999). Machine learning. In R. Wilson and F. Keil (eds.) *The MIT encyclopedia of the cognitive sciences. Cambridge, MA:* MIT Press.

E-commag (2001). Solutions to data inaccuracies. Available online at: <http://www. E-commag.com>.

Electronic Textbook Statsoft.com (2001). Data mining techniques. Available online at: <http://www.statsoft.com/textbook/stdatmin.html>.

Griffin, J. (2000), Fundamental pitfalls to avoid in your data warehouse. Available online at: <http://www.datawarehouse.com/iknowledge/article/>.

Griffin, J. (2001). Four big pitfalls to avoid when Web-enabling your data warehouse - and how to avoid them. Available online at: <http://www.datawarehouse.com / iknowledge/articles/article.cfm?contentID=1214>.

Groth, R. (2001). *Data mining: Building competitive advantage.* New York: Prentice Hall.

Gunter, B. (1996). Data mining: Mother lode or fool's gold? *Quality Progress*, 29 (4), 113-118.

Hand, D., Mannila, H., & Smyth, P. (2001). *Principles of data mining.* Cambridge, MA: MIT Press.

Hoss, D. (2001). Data mining: Pitfalls. Available online at: <http:// www.datawarehouse.com>.

International Knowledge Discovery Institute (1999). What is data mining? Available online at: <http://www.ikdi.net/data-mining.html>.

Investor Home (1999). Data mining. Available online at: <http://www.investorhome.com/ mining.htm>.

Jensen, D. (1999). Data snooping, dredging and fishing: the dark side of data mining. *A SIGKDD99 Panel Report.* 1 (2), 52, ACM, Inc.

Jensen, H. (2001) Using data mining with statistics. Available online at: <http://ww w/ isi.edu>.

Jones, L. (2001). Neural networks. Available online at: <http://ei.cs.vt.edu/~NEURALNET/ html>.

Judson, H. (2000). Make data mining work for you. Available online at: <http:// wwwksi.cpsc.ucalgary.ca>.

KDNuggets (2001). Data mining frequently asked questions. Available online at: <http:/ /www.kdnuggcts.com/publications/index.html#Definitions>.

Knowledge Acquisition Discovery Management (1997). Introduction to data mining and knowledge discovery. Available online at: <http://scanner-group.mit.edu /htdocs/ thesis/angeclagethesis.html>.

McQueen, G. & Thorley, S. (1999). Mining fool's gold. *Financial Analysts Journal*, Available online at: <http://www.indexfunds.com/articles/19990315_mining-iss_gen RS.htm>.

META Group (2001). META Group research summary. The Internet <http://www.metagroup.com/>.

Montana, J.C. (2001). Data mining: A slippery slope, *Information Management Journal*, 35 (Oct), 50-54.

Moss, L. (2000). Data warehouse goals and objectives: Part 3: Long-term objectives. Available online at: <http://www.datawarehouse.com/iknowledge/articles/topic_sub.cfm>.

Numerical Machine Learning (1997). What is data mining? Available online at: <http://www.cc.gatech.edu/~kingd/datamine/datamine.html>.

Pagallo, G. & Haussler D. (1990). Boolean feature discovery in empirical learning. *Machine Learning, 5*(1), pp. 71-99, March.

Parsaye, K. (1995). Using correct data. Available online at: <http://www.datamining.com>.

Pyle, D. (1999). *Data preparation for data mining.* San Francisco, CA: Morgan Kaufmann.

Saarenvirta, G. (February). Slice and dice. *CMA Management*, 73(1), 26-30.

Sauter, V. (1999). Intuitive decision-making. *Communications of the ACM*, 42(6), 109-115.

Sethi, I. K. (2001). *Data mining: An introduction.* Available online at: <http://www.cs.ubc.ca/nest/temporal.html>.

Teo, T.S.H. & Ang, J.S.K. (2000). Building a data warehouse at the housing and development board. *Database for Advances in Information Systems*, V31, 35-45.

Two Crows Corporation (2001). Two Crows White Paper: Scalable data mining. Available online at: <http://www.twocrows.com/whilep.htm>.

Wasserman, M. (1999). Efficiency as an issue in cognitive architectures, trust your data? Available online at: <http://www.bos.frb.org>.

Wu, J. (2000). A framework for information quality in a data warehouse. *NCR: Data warehousing report,* 3(4).

Chapter X

Maximum Performance Efficiency Approaches for Estimating Best Practice Costs

Marvin D. Troutt
Kent State University, USA

Donald W. Gribbin
Southern Illinois University at Carbondale, USA

Murali S. Shanker
Kent State University, USA

Aimao Zhang
Georgia Southern University, USA

ABSTRACT

Data mining is increasingly being used to gain competitive advantage. In this chapter, we propose a principle of maximum performance efficiency (MPE) as a contribution to the data-mining toolkit. This principle seeks to estimate optimal or boundary behavior, in contrast to techniques like regression analysis that predict average behavior. This MPE principle is explained in the context of activity-based costing situation. Specifically, we consider the activity-based costing situation in which multiple activities generate a common cost pool. Individual cost drivers are assigned to the respective activities, but allocation of the cost pool to the individual activities is regarded as impractical or expensive. Our study focuses on published data from a set of property tax collection offices, called Rates Departments, for the London metropolitan area. We define what may be called benchmark or most efficient average costs per unit of driver. The MPE principle is then used to estimate the best practice cost rates. A validation approach for this estimation method is developed in terms of what we call normal-like-or-better performance effectiveness. Extensions to time-series data on a single unit, and marginal cost-oriented basic cost models are also briefly described. In conclusion, we discuss potential data-mining applications and considerations.

INTRODUCTION

In recent years, companies have started to realize the potential of using data-mining techniques as a form of competitive advantage. For example, in the finance industry, in the decade from 1980 to 1990, the number of credit cards issued doubled to about 260 million. But, in the next ten years, there was not another doubling of this number. Given that there are now about 280 million people in the United States, it is widely believed that the credit card market is saturated (Berson, Smith, & Thearling, 2000). In such situations, any gains by one company leads to a loss for another — a zero-sum game. To gain competitive advantage, credit card companies are now resorting to data-mining techniques to retain and identify good customers at minimal cost.

The cell phone industry is also expected to go the way of the credit card market. Soon, the cellular industry will be saturated; everybody who needs cells phone will have one. Companies who are able to predict and understand customer needs better, will probably be the ones who will survive. The cellular industry, like the credit card industry, is likewise resorting to data-mining techniques to identify traits for retaining good customers.

Research in data mining has so far focused on either developing new techniques or on identifying applications. Being a multidisciplinary field, data-mining techniques have originated from areas of artificial intelligence, database theory, visualization, mathematics, operations research, and statistics, among others. Many of the well-known statistical techniques like nearest neighbor, clustering, and regression analysis are now part of the data-mining toolkit.

In this chapter, we present a new technique based on the principal of *maximum performance efficiency* (MPE). While techniques like linear regression analysis are used to predict average behavior, MPE seeks to predict boundary or optimal behavior. In many cases, such models are actually more desirable. For example, in a saturated credit card or cellular phone market, a company may seek to predict characteristics of its best customers. In essence, choosing to concentrate on customers who are low risk/cost to maximize profit. Such models, usually called ceiling/floor models, can also be used as part of data-mining techniques for benchmarking. For example, a company may be interested in comparing the quality of its products over different product lines. The MPE criterion seeks to identify the characteristics of the best performing unit, thus allowing the company to implement these measures in other units to improve their quality, and hence the competitive advantage of the company across product lines.

We propose the MPE principle and show how it can be used to estimate the best practice costs in an activity-based costing situation. The rest of the chapter is organized as follows. In the next section, we present our initial motivation for developing the MPE principle. As an example, we consider an activity-based costing situation where multiple activities generate a common cost pool. Our objective is to estimate the best practice cost rates. The following section then distinguishes between basic cost models and the models used to estimate the parameters of the basic cost models. The maximum performance efficiency (MPE) principle is developed using an aggregate efficiency measure that is the sum or average of performance efficiencies. Then the MPE principle is used to derive the linear programming estimation model. The next section describes the data for the study. The MPE criterion is applied to this data, and the results are compared with a previous analysis to assess face validity for the proposed new method. The following section proposes a model aptness theory based on the gamma distribution and a technique called vertical density representation. The fitted performance efficiency scores are required to satisfy a benchmark for validity of the goal assumption called normal-like-or-better performance effectiveness. This is followed by limitations and some extensions to other basic cost models. The next section discusses potential data-mining applications and considerations, and is followed by the Conclusions section.

Remarks on notation: In summation notations using Σ, the lower limit is omitted when it is clear from the context. Omission of upper limits indicates summation over all values of the index.

MOTIVATION

Managerial accountants are often called upon to provide measures of performance efficiency. Such a task is essentially trivial if there is a single input measure and a single output measure. One could simply divide the output measure by the input measure and use the resulting performance efficiency measure to either: (1) compare the unit's performance over time, or (2) compare the unit's performance with other comparable units.

While there are numerous purposes for performance efficiency measures (i.e., performance evaluation, managerial compensation, benchmarking, and cost control, to name a few), the specific purpose of this research is to explain and illustrate how a proposed estimation principle can be used with activity-based costing for determining performance efficiency measures for the purpose of cost control. Activity-based costing is one approach that could be used to develop a performance measure for such purposes. Activity-based costing consists of disaggregating costs into specific cost pools that can be linked causally with their respective activities. Cooper and Kaplan (1992) illustrate how such an approach can be used with purchase order data. The approach consists of dividing the monthly cost of processing purchase orders by the number of purchase orders processed per month. This purchase order cost can then be used as a benchmark for comparison purposes. This approach is very simple and easy to use if there is only one cost pool and one activity with a single cost driver. But there are many realistic scenarios in which there are multiple cost drivers for a single cost pool. For example, faculty salaries for an academic unit (department or college) appear to be driven by at least two cost drivers. Both student credit hours generated and the level of academic degrees offered (bachelor's, master's, and doctorate) appears to drive the amount of faculty salaries for an academic unit. The dilemma is that faculty salaries are in a single cost pool, and there is no simple and objective method for disaggregating faculty salaries. The task of attributing the faculty salary pool to separate activities and cost drivers is essentially impossible. There is no easy way for determining how much of the faculty salary pool is due to: (1) the generation of student credit hours, and (2) the level of academic degrees offered by academic unit.

The methodology explained and illustrated in this chapter allows for the inclusion of multiple cost drivers in determining performance efficiency measures. The allocation of the combined cost pool to individual activities might be regarded as not objectively possible, impractical, expensive, or of insufficient additional value for the costing system. We first consider the problem of estimating average costs per unit of cost driver in such situations when cross-sectional data are available for a set of what we call *comparable* business units. We also consider application of the same techniques to basic cost models having marginal cost assessment capability, and briefly discuss the setting in which a single business unit is observed over several time periods.

We define benchmark or best practice average costs per unit of cost driver as the average cost rates associated with the most efficient unit(s). A principle of *maximum performance efficiency* (MPE) is proposed and estimation criteria based on efficiency measures are derived from this principle. This is a generalization of the maximum decisional efficiency (MDE) principle introduced in Troutt (1995) and also discussed in Troutt (1997) and Troutt, Zhang, Tadisina, and Rai (1997). The efficiency measure used may be considered analogous to the cost of unused capacity concept proposed by Cooper and Kaplan (1992). These models also provide a different view on the lack of proportionality of costs to driver levels documented in Noreen and Soderstrom (1994).

A basic assumption underlying the estimation principle employed here is that all business units under comparison seek to maximize their efficiencies in performing their services. The data we study are from public service entities that are presumed to have this goal on behalf of the public interest. However, this assumption needs verification as a kind of model aptness or validation issue similar to the requirement of normally distributed errors in OLS regression. As an estimation model aptness test, we propose what may be called a *normal-like-or-better* performance effectiveness measure. The estimation models proposed here are linear programming (LP) models. Use of such models in cost accounting is not new. See for example, Demski (1967), Itami and Kaplan (1980), Kaplan and Thompson (1971), and Onsi (1970). These previous works have generally utilized *LP* models assuming that data are known. That is, they assume that technological coefficients and resource levels are given. Then the dual optimal solution (especially the shadow prices) of these fully specified LP models has been employed for (1) overhead allocation (Kaplan & Thompson, 1971), (2) transfer pricing (Onsi, 1970), and (3) reallocation of costs to multiple products (Itami & Kaplan, 1980). However, the use of LP models enters in a different way in this chapter. Namely, the estimation models are themselves LP problems in which the decision variables are the unknown best practice cost rates. The next section distinguishes between basic cost models and the models used to estimate the parameters of the basic cost models. The MPE principle is also presented here.

BASIC COST MODELS AND ESTIMATION MODELS

There are two uses of the word "model" in this chapter. By the basic cost model, we mean the assumed relationship between the cost driver of an activity and its contribution to the total cost pool. The simplest case is that of proportional variation. Let y_r be the amount of the r-th cost driver. Under the basic cost model, the contribution to the total cost pool will be $a_r y_r$, where a_r may be called the average cost per unit of y_r or simply the cost rate. This chapter focuses on this basic cost model. Some other models such as for estimating marginal costs are discussed briefly. The other use of the word "model" refers to the method used to solve for estimates of the basic cost model parameters — the a^*_r. The estimation models used here are LP models. As noted above, this usage of LP does not appear to be similar to previous uses in the accounting literature, but is a consequence of the estimation principle used.

Suppose there are $r=1\ldots R$, activities with associated cost driver quantities of y_r, respectively. Then, as in Cooper and Kaplan (1992), the cost of *resources consumed* is given by $\sum a_r y_r$. If x is the actual total cost pool associated with these activities, the cost of resources *supplied*, then there may be a difference, $s \geq 0$, such that

$$\sum a_r y_r + s = x. \tag{2.1}$$

Cooper and Kaplan (1992) call s the *cost of unused capacity*. In their analysis, the x value was a budget figure and the y_r could vary due to decreased demands. We start from the same construct but regard variations of the y_r and x as due to more or less efficiency. By defining what may be called best practice a_r values, we therefore associate the s value with possible inefficiency of a business unit, a cost of inefficiency.

Thus suppose we have $j = 1\ldots N$ *comparable* business units, achieving y_{rj} units of driver r, respectively, and with associated cost pools, x_j. In addition to having the same activities and cost drivers, we further require that comparable units be similar in the sense that the practices, policies, technologies, employee competence levels, and managerial actions of any one should be transferable, in principle, to any other. Define a_r^* as the vector of cost rates associated with the most efficient unit or units under comparison. Then in the equation

$$\sum_{r=1}^{R} a_r^* y_{rj} + s_j = x_j \quad \text{for all } j, \tag{2.2}$$

the cost of unused capacity, s_j, may be interpreted as an inefficiency suffered by a failure to achieve larger y_{rj} values, smaller x_j value, or some combination of these. The ratio $v_j = \sum a_r^* y_{rj} / x_j$, is an efficiency measure for the j-th unit when the a_r^* are the true benchmark cost rates and $\sum a_r^* y_{rj} \leq x_j$ holds for all units. A technique for estimating parameters in efficiency ratios of the above form was proposed in Troutt (1995). In that paper, the primary data were specific decisions. Here a more general form of that approach called *maximum performance efficiency* (MPE) is proposed and applied to estimate the benchmark a_r^* values. Assume that each unit $j = 1\ldots N$, seeks to achieve maximum (1.0) efficiency. Then the whole set of units may be regarded as attempting to maximize the sum of these efficiency ratios, namely, $\sum\sum a_r^* y_{rj}/x_j$. The maximum performance efficiency estimation principle proposes estimates of the a_r^* as those which render the total, or equivalently the average, of these efficiencies a maximum.

Maximum Performance Efficiency (MPE) Estimation Principle: *In a performance model depending on an unknown parameter vector, select as the estimate of the parameter vector that value for which the total performance is greatest.*

Use of the word performance is stressed in the MPE name to emphasize the more general utility of the approach than was indicated by the earlier MDE term. Managerial performance, such as in the units under study here, involves many kinds, levels, and horizons of decisions.

Define the data elements Y_{rj} by $Y_{rj} = y_{rj}/x_j$. Then the MPE estimation criterion for the benchmark a_r^* values is given by

$$\text{MPE:} \qquad \max \sum_{j=1}^{N} \sum_{r=1}^{R} a_r Y_{rj} \qquad (2.3)$$

$$\text{s.t.} \qquad \sum_{r=1}^{R} a_r Y_{rj} \leq 1 \ \text{ for all j} \qquad (2.4)$$

$$a_r \geq 0 \ \text{ for all r} \qquad (2.5)$$

Problem MPE is a linear programming problem. Its unknown variables are the best practice cost rates, the a_r^* values. Solution of this model provides values for the a_r^* as well as the unit efficiencies, v_j. A model adequacy or validation approach for this estimation procedure is proposed in a later section. As a linear programming problem, the MPE model is readily solved by a wide variety of commonly available software products. MPE may be seen here to be an estimation criterion analogous to the ordinary least squares error criterion in regression. The cost model, $\sum a_r Y_{rj}$ is analogous to the regression model.

APPLICATION TO THE DATA

In this section, we describe the data and apply the MPE estimation criterion. In the initial application of the MPE criterion one cost rate was estimated to be zero. Here we concentrate on the case in which all estimated cost rates must be positive and show how the MPE criterion is modified for that case.

The data for this study are from Dyson and Thanassoulis (1988) and are reproduced here in Table 1, first six columns. These data were collected for a set of property tax collection offices, called Rates Departments, in the London Boroughs and Metropolitan Districts. A more complete description of the data is given in Thanassoulis, Dyson, and Foster (1987). Total annual costs, measured in units of £100,000 for these offices (units), were collected along with activity driver levels for four activities. The first three activities—collection of

Table 1: British rates departments data based on Dyson and Thanassoulis (1988). Efficiency rating based on model MDE-2 with preemptive positive weights modification

Rates Department	Total Costs	Non-cnl Heredita- ments	Rate rebts grtd	Summons & d'ress wrnts	NPV of non-cnl rates	Efficiency Rating
Lewisham	9.13	7.53	34.11	21.96	3.84	0.7881
Brent	13.60	8.30	23.27	35.97	8.63	0.6920
Stockport	5.76	10.91	13.39	11.53	4.93	1.0000
Bradford	11.24	16.62	36.82	27.55	9.52	1.0000
Leeds	15.57	22.81	95.78	23.61	12.27	1.0000
City of London	5.65	1.78	0.16	1.31	39.01	0.9641
Liverpool	21.60	15.11	70.96	54.22	10.81	0.7577
Walsall	8.57	7.92	48.69	14.03	5.92	0.8361
Rotherham	6.01	7.07	36.30	5.45	2.94	0.7926
Wakefield	8.02	8.86	43.61	13.77	4.27	0.8631
Lambeth	9.93	9.00	36.85	20.66	8.15	0.8122
Sunderland	7.90	8.28	45.22	6.19	5.33	0.7492
Solihull	5.15	6.76	18.70	10.62	3.54	0.8958
Redbridge	6.42	8.98	13.60	12.32	3.75	0.8110
Calderdale	5.94	7.69	25.91	8.24	2.48	0.7994
Haringey	8.68	7.23	16.97	17.58	6.27	0.6864
Barking &Dagenham	4.86	3.36	23.67	4.30	2.48	0.6076
Newcastle-upon-Tyne	10.33	8.56	30.54	17.77	8.01	0.6985
Manchester	21.97	12.23	92.02	29.53	14.76	0.6230
Wolverhampton	9.70	7.67	41.16	13.27	4.50	0.6649
Trafford	6.34	8.17	16.61	8.26	5.05	0.7466
Tameside	7.70	7.88	15.75	14.50	3.03	0.6808
St Helens	5.99	5.67	27.55	5.24	3.41	0.5188
Sutton	5.20	6.92	12.61	4.30	3.04	0.6556
Rochdale	6.36	7.35	23.51	5.74	4.21	0.8471
Barnsley	8.87	6.46	38.10	9.65	3.09	0.5974
Kirklees	10.71	13.64	23.86	14.63	4.63	0.6876
Oldham	6.49	7.68	17.97	8.27	2.76	0.6766
Sheffield	15.32	15.34	55.42	16.36	12.53	0.6905
Havering	7.00	8.37	14.92	9.88	4.33	0.6915
Dudley	10.50	9.61	37.91	13.49	5.04	0.6563
Sefton	10.88	10.65	36.96	14.25	4.84	0.6617
Bexley	8.52	8.97	24.67	11.84	3.75	0.6669
Gateshead	7.61	6.11	31.73	7.66	2.87	0.6031
Wigan	10.91	9.78	42.73	12.17	4.66	0.6363
Kensington & Chelsea	9.72	7.71	5.90	14.60	9.25	0.5646
Coventry	12.63	11.08	41.59	16.42	5.65	0.6289
Sandwell	11.51	9.07	28.49	16.28	5.96	0.5898
Bury	6.22	6.63	14.67	7.70	3.08	0.6294
South Tyneside	5.29	3.96	20.42	1.96	1.84	0.4808

*Table 1: British rates departments data based on Dyson and Thanassoulis (1988).
Efficiency rating based on model MDE-2 with preemptive positive weights modification
(continued)*

Salford	8.78	6.56	31.72	8.60	4.83	0.5783
Hackney	13.50	4.77	26.47	20.88	4.17	0.4434
Camden	12.60	6.68	30.28	9.09	19.45	0.5478
Hillingdon	8.10	8.10	9.71	8.53	7.50	0.5821
Tower Hamlets	9.67	6.00	19.46	10.71	8.03	0.5187
Barnet	12.37	11.25	28.50	12.53	6.74	0.5604
Bolton	9.50	8.67	23.54	8.99	3.66	0.5411
Ealing	11.47	10.30	15.58	13.74	6.46	0.5388
Bromley	11.78	12.22	14.33	10.10	5.02	0.5039
Wandsworth	12.57	10.43	18.31	16.39	3.92	0.5098
Birmingham	50.26	32.33	150.00	45.10	19.58	0.3565
Enfield	12.70	9.50	22.39	14.90	5.80	0.5030
Southwark	13.30	7.53	21.99	14.66	8.32	0.4608
Knowsley	5.60	3.73	12.21	5.39	2.84	0.4786
Islington	11.75	5.20	13.28	13.62	7.10	0.4079
North Tyneside	8.47	6.15	19.45	6.51	3.30	0.4587
Kingston-upon-Thames	8.36	5.96	17.11	4.66	3.08	0.4107
Hounslow	11.07	7.25	16.34	8.69	6.62	0.4274
Richmond-upon-Thames	10.38	7.76	16.44	6.01	3.31	0.3941
Hammersmith & Fulham	11.83	5.35	12.41	12.24	4.57	0.3622
Newham	12.71	6.32	13.63	8.53	5.16	0.3268
Merton	11.19	6.58	10.90	3.52	3.46	0.2839
Mean	10.45	8.81	29.41	13.33	6.41	0.6314
Standard Deviation	6.21	4.50	23.54	9.38	5.57	0.1699

non-council hereditaments, rate rebates generated, and summonses issued and distress warrants obtained—were measured in units of 10,000, 1,000, and 1,000, respectively. The fourth—net present value of non-council rates collected, was measured in units of £10,000. This last one was included as a cost driver (called an output by Dyson and Thanassoulis, and Thanassoulis et al.) to reflect the additional administrative effort exerted to ensure the timely payment of large revenue producing cases.

Thanassoulis et al. (1987) briefly discussed the possible disaggregation of the cost pools. They indicate that this would have been possible to some extent but decided against this for several reasons. First, these costs represented the cost of real resources used and available for management deployment. Next, they felt that the increased number of variables that would result might tend to decrease the discrimination power of the data envelopment analysis (DEA) method they were studying. Next, and importantly, it was felt that the disaggregated data were less reliable. This concern is well founded, particularly in the present context. Datar and Gupta (1994) have shown that disaggregation can actually increase errors.

The method used in both Dyson and Thanassoulis (1988) and Thanassoulis et al (1987) was a modification of data envelopment analysis (DEA), another efficiency estimation technique. It is worthwhile to briefly discuss DEA in regard to the above and other relevant points. An introduction to DEA is contained in Charnes, Cooper, Lewin, and Seiford. (1994). There are several DEA models, but we limit our coverage to that used in Dyson and Thanassoulis. If we use the a_r notation for output weights in the DEA model M1 of Dyson and Thanassoulis (page 564), we obtain the model(s):

$$M1(j_o) \qquad \max \quad h_o = \sum_r a_r Y_{rjo} \qquad\qquad (3.1)$$

$$\text{s.t.} \quad \sum_{r=1}^{R} a_r Y_{rj} \leq 1, \text{ for all } j \qquad\qquad (3.2)$$

$$a_r \geq 0, \text{ for all } r \qquad\qquad (3.3)$$

Unlike the one-pass solution of model MPE, Model $M1(j_o)$ is solved for each unit, (j_o), in turn. The solutions a_{rjo} therefore depend on which unit is being featured in the objective function. Typically, some of the a_{rjo} values will be zero for various units. In the present cost rates context, the following interpretation can be given to the $M1(j_o)$ DEA model. If unit j_o were allowed to choose the activities and drivers to become applicable for the entire group of units, then the $M1(j_o)$ model solution obtains these in such a way as to give that unit the most favorable efficiency score. The principal difficulty here is that no consensus is being achieved on the most efficient cost rates. With the $M1(j_o)$ DEA model, each unit can select cost rates that make it look most favorable. Dyson and Thanassoulis (1988) call this phenomenon *weights flexibility*. Their work was motivated, in part, to modify the $M1(j_o)$ DEA technique to limit this flexibility, and provides a more extensive discussion of this DEA limitation.

Except in unusual circumstances, activity cost rates, a_r, can only be positive. In this section, we consider this requirement as a preemptive priority. For the solution values, a_r^*, to be strictly positive, it is necessary that they be basic variables in an optimal solution. This may occur gratuitously. Otherwise one or more may be non-basic, and therefore have value zero. The standard LP solution report provides reduced costs. For a variable with optimal value of zero, the reduced cost may be interpreted as follows. It indicates the smallest amount by which the objective function coefficient for the variable must be increased in order that the variable becomes positive in an optimal solution.

The last column of Table 1 gives the efficiency scores obtained by model MPE with preemptive positive costs. Descriptive statistics have been added as supplemental information. The MPE model was solved using SAS/IML software (1995), which includes a linear programming call function. The initial solution assigned a zero optimal value only to a_1^*. (The full solution for this case was $a_1^*=0, a_2^*=0.0882, a_3^*=0.2671, a_4^*=0.0664$.) Thus, it was deemed necessary to implement the preemptive positive weights modification. The reduced cost for variable a_1 was given as -1.220440. The objective coefficient was 55.52898. Therefore, the modified procedure required increasing the coefficient of a_1 to 56.747. The resulting estimates were as follows:

$$a_1^*=0.2618, a_2^*=0.0494, a_3^*=0.1398, a_4^*=0.1280 \qquad\qquad (3.4)$$

Table 2: Descriptive statistics for the derived data, Y_r

Variable	Y_1	Y_2	Y_3	Y_4
Mean	0.8948	2.8492	1.2622	0.6665
Standard Deviation	0.3013	1.3959	0.5290	0.8320

The corresponding efficiency scores of the units are shown in the last column of Table 1. Table 2 gives descriptive statistics for the Y_r data.

While not true for the example presented here, it is possible that more than one cost rate is initially estimated as zero or the reduced cost is also zero when strict positivity is required. Then, it is necessary to proceed as follows. Suppose an auxiliary variable m, and n_r new constraints $a_r \geq m$ are joined to the MPE model. If the optimal value of m is positive, then so it must be also for all the cost rates. Let λ be a non-negative parameter chosen by the analyst and consider the modified objective function given by

$$\max \sum_j \sum_r a_r y_{rj} + \lambda m \qquad (3.5)$$

When the value of λ is zero, the objective function is the same as the original one with m* = 0. We have the following theorem whose proof is given the Appendix.

Theorem 1: Let $z^*(\lambda)$, $a_r^*(\lambda)$, and $m^*(\lambda)$ be the solution of the MPE (λ) model:

$$\text{MPE:} \qquad \max z(\lambda) = \sum_j \sum_r a_r y_{rj} + \lambda m \qquad (3.6)$$

$$\text{s.t.} \quad \sum a_r y_{rj} \leq 1, \text{ for all } j \qquad (3.7)$$

$$a_r \geq m, \text{ for all } r \qquad (3.8)$$

$$a_r \geq 0, \text{ for all } r, \text{ m unrestricted} \qquad (3.9)$$

Then (1): $z^*(\lambda)$ is monotone non-decreasing in λ and $z^*(\lambda) \to \infty$ as $\lambda \to 0$; and (2): $\sum a_r^*(\lambda) Y_{rj}$ is monotone non-increasing in λ.

We propose the solution for positive weights to be that corresponding to the greatest lower bound of λ values for which $m^*(\lambda) > 0$. This may be estimated by trial and error. We develop a rationale for such positive weights procedures by writing the MPE model objective function in the form $\sum a_r (\sum Y_{rj})$. If maximization of this objective function yields $a_1^* = 0$, then evidently the coefficient, $\sum Y_{1j}$ is too small in some sense relative to the other coefficients. It may be noted that the $Y_{rj} = y_{rj}/x_j$ data are in the nature of reciprocal costs. When the sum of these is too small, the implication is that their own reciprocals, the x_j/y_{rj}, are on average too large. This is suggestive of inefficiency with respect to the r-th activity. In such a case, assignment of a zero optimal cost estimate would mask this kind of inefficiency. By using the reduced cost adjustment, or adding the λm term to the objective function, a compensation is made for coefficients that are apparently too small in that sense.

Some comparisons with the results of Dyson and Thanassoulis (1988) can now be discussed. As part of their study, a regression through the origin was obtained. The coefficients of that regression model can be interpreted as average cost rates for these activities. The results were as follows:

$$\bar{a}_1 = 0.5042, \bar{a}_2 = 0.0785, \bar{a}_3 = 0.1765, \bar{a}_4 = 0.1940 \tag{3.10}$$

It will be noted that these average rates are uniformly higher than the presently estimated rates in (3.4), giving a measure of face validity. That is, it is necessary that the cost rates of the most efficient units be lower than the average cost rates for all the units. Also, the four departments rated as most efficient by the present method are the same as those indicated by the Dyson and Thanassoulis (1988) approach.

It may be observed that the preliminary regression step also gives information on the question of positivity of the cost rates. The positivity of $\bar{a}_1$ gives further evidence on that for $a_1{}^*$. Here $\bar{a}_1$ is positive and significant. (The significance level was not specified in Dyson and Thanassoulis). Since the units are assumed to be comparable, it appears unlikely that one or a few could perform activity one with no cost while the typical unit does incur cost for the activity. If a particular unit could produce an activity with zero cost ($a_r{}^* = 0$) while the average unit does incur cost for the activity, then it must have a radically superior process not actually comparable with the others. Similarly, this regression model also validates activity four as influential on costs. The next section discusses model aptness.

ESTIMATION CRITERION QUALITY ISSUES

A basic assumption underlying the MPE estimation principle's applicability is that the sample of units under analysis does, in fact, have the goal of achieving maximum (1.0) efficiency. This is a model aptness issue that parallels the requirement of $N(0,\sigma^2)$ residuals in OLS regression theory. In the present MPE case, the corresponding issue is to specify a measured characteristic of the v_j that indicates consistency with a goal or target of unity (1.0) efficiency. In this section, we propose what may be called the *normal-like-or-better* effectiveness criterion for these fitted efficiency scores.

As a model for appropriate concentration on a target, we begin with an interpretation of the multivariate normal distribution, $N(\mu,\Sigma)$, on $\mathfrak{R}^n$. If a distribution of attempts has the $N(\mu,\Sigma)$ or even higher concentration of density at the mode μ, then we propose this as evidence that μ is indeed a plausible target of the attempts. This is exemplified by considering a distribution model for the results of throwing darts at a bull's-eye target. Common experience suggests that a bivariate normal density represents such data reasonably well. Steeper or flatter densities would still be indicative of effective attempts, but densities whose modes do not coincide with the target would cause doubts about whether the attempts have been effective or whether another target better explains the data. We call this normal-like-or-better (NLOB) performance effectiveness. It is next necessary to obtain the analog of this criterion for the efficiency performance data Y_{rj} relevant to the present context.

If x is distributed as $N(\mu,\Sigma)$ on $\Re^n$, then it well known that the quadratic form, $w(x)=(x-\mu)'\Sigma^{-1}(x-\mu)$ is gamma(α,β), where $\alpha=n/2$ and $\beta=2$. This distribution is also called the Chi-square distribution with n degrees of freedom (see Law & Kelton, 1982). We may note that for this case $w(x)$ is in the nature of a squared distance from the target set $\{\mu\}$. It is useful to derive this result by a different technique. Vertical density representation (VDR) is a technique for representing a multivariate density by way of a univariate density called the ordinate or vertical density, and uniform distributions over the equidensity contours of the original multivariate density. VDR was introduced in Troutt (1993). (See also Kotz, Fang & Liang, 1997; Kotz & Troutt, 1996; Troutt, 1991; and Troutt & Pang, 1996.) The version of VDR needed for the present purpose can be derived as follows. Let $w(x)$ be a continuous convex function on $\Re^n$ with range $[0,\infty)$; and let $g(w)$ be a density on $[0,\infty)$. Suppose that for each value of $u \geq 0$, x is uniformly distributed on the set $\{x:w(x)=u\}$. Consider the process of sampling a value of u according to the $g(w)$ density, and then sampling a vector, x, according to the uniform distribution on the set $\{x:w(x)=u\}$. Next let $f(x)$ be the density of the resulting x variates on $\Re^n$. Finally, let $A(u)$ be the volume (Lebesgue measure) of the set $\{x:w(x) \leq u\}$. Then we have the following VDR theorem that relates $g(w)$ and $f(x)$ in $\Re^n$. The proof is given in the Appendix.

Theorem 2: If $A(u)$ is differentiable on $[0,\infty)$ with $A'(u)$ strictly positive, then x is distributed according to the density $f(x)$ where

$$f(x) = \phi(w(x)) \text{ and } g(w) = \phi(w)/A'(w).$$

Theorem 2 can be applied to derive a very general density class for performance related to squared distance type error measures. The set $\{x:(x-\mu)'\Sigma^{-1}(x-\mu) \leq u\}$ has volume, $A(u)$, given by $A(u) = \alpha_n|\Sigma|^{1/2}u^{n/2}$ where $\alpha_n = \pi^{n/2}/{}_2\Gamma({}^n/_2)$, (Fleming, 1977), so that $A'(u) = {}^n/_2\alpha_n|\Sigma|^{1/2}u^{n/2-1}$. The gamma$(\alpha,\beta)$ density is given by

$$g(u) = (\Gamma(\alpha)\beta^\alpha)^{-1}u^{\alpha-1}exp\{-u^2/\beta\}.$$

Therefore Theorem 2 implies that if $w(x) = (x-\mu)'\Sigma^{-1}(x-\mu)$ and $g(u) = gamma(\alpha,\beta)$, then the corresponding $f(x)$, which we now rename as $\psi(x) = \psi(x;n,a,\beta)$, is given by

$$\psi(x)=\Gamma({}^n/_2)(\pi^{n/2}\Gamma(\alpha)\beta^\alpha)^{-1}\left[(x-\mu)'\Sigma^{-1}(x-\mu)\right]^{\alpha-n/2}exp\{-{}^1/_\beta(x-\mu)'\Sigma^{-1}(x-\mu)\} \qquad (4.1)$$

For this density class we have the following observations:
(1)   If $\alpha = n/2$ and $\beta=2$, then $\psi(x)$ is the multivariate normal density, $N(\mu,\Sigma)$.
(2)   If $\alpha = n/2$ and $\beta \neq 2$, then $\psi(x)$ is steeper or flatter than $N(\mu,\Sigma)$ according to whether $\beta < 2$ or $\beta > 2$, respectively. We call these densities the normal-like densities.

(3) If $\alpha < n/2$, then $\psi(x)$ is unbounded at its mode, μ, but may be more or less steep according to the value of β. We call this class the better-than-normal-like density class.

(4) If $\alpha > n/2$, then $\psi(x)$ has zero density at the target, μ, and low values throughout neighborhoods of μ. This suggests that attempts at the target are not effective. The data may have arisen in pursuit of a different target or simply not be effective for any target.

For densities in Category (3), the unbounded mode concentrates more probability near the target and suggests a higher level of expertise than that evidenced by the finite-at-mode $N(\mu,\Sigma)$ class. It seems reasonable to refer to α in this context as the expertise, mode, or target effectiveness parameter, while β is a scale or precision parameter. Thus, if $\alpha \leq n/2$, we call $\psi(x)$ the normal-like-or-better performance density. To summarize, if attempts at a target set in $\mathfrak{R}^n$ have a basic squared distance error measure and this measure is distributed with the gamma(α,β) density with $\alpha \leq {}^n/_2$, then the performance with respect to this target set is normal-like-or-better (NLOB).

We extend this target effectiveness criterion to the present context as follows. The target set is $\{Y \in \mathfrak{R}^4 : \Sigma a_r Y_r = 1, Y_r \geq 0 \text{ for all } r\}$. If $\Sigma a_r Y_{rj} = v_j$, then the distance of Y_{rj} from the target set is $(1-v) Q\%aQ\%^{-1}$. Since $0 \leq v \leq 1$, we employ the transformation $w = (-ln\, v)^2 = (ln\, v)^2$. This transformation has the properties that $w \cong (1-v)^2$ near $v=1$ and $w \in [0,\infty)$. Therefore, $w/Q\%aQ\%^2 = (ln\, v)^2/Q\%aQ\%^2$ is an approximate squared distance measure near the target set. Since the $Q\%aQ\%^2$ term is a scale factor, it can be absorbed into the β parameter of gamma(α,β). We therefore consider the NLOB effectiveness criterion to hold if w has the gamma(α,β) density with $\alpha \leq {}^4/_2 = 2$. That is, such performance is analogous to that of unbiased normal-like-or-better distributed attempts at a target in $\mathfrak{R}^n$. There is one additional consideration before applying this effectiveness criterion to the present data. In the LP estimation model MPE, at least one efficiency, v_j, must be unity (and hence $w_j = 0$). This is because at least one constraint (2.6) must be active in an optimal solution of the MPE model. We therefore consider the model for the w_j to be

$$p\,\delta(0) + (1-p)\,\text{gamma}(\alpha,\beta), \tag{4.2}$$

where p is the frequency of zero values (here $p = 3/62 = 0.048$ from Table 1), and $\delta(0)$ is the degenerate density concentrated at $w = 0$. We call this the *gamma-plus-zero* density, gamma$(\alpha,\beta)+0$. For this data, we regard the NLOB criterion to hold if it holds for the gamma density in (4.2). When the gamma(α,β) density is fitted to the strictly positive w values, then NLOB requires that $\alpha \leq 2$. For the data of $w_j = (ln\, v_j)^2$ based on Table 1, Column 7, the parameter value estimates obtained by the Method of Moments (see, for example, Bickell & Doksum, 1977) are $\alpha = 1.07$ and $\beta = 0.32$. This method was chosen because the BESTFIT™ software experienced difficulty in convergence using its default Maximum Likelihood Estimation procedure. The Method of Moments estimates parameters by setting theoretical moments equal to sample moments. For the gamma(α,β) density, $\mu = \alpha\beta$, and $\sigma^2 = \alpha\beta^2$. If $\overline{w}$ and s^2 are the sample mean and variance of the positive w_j values, then the α and β estimates are given by

$$\hat{\alpha} = \overline{w}^2/s^2 \text{ and } \hat{\beta} = s^2/\overline{w}.$$

Tests of fit of the w_j data to the gamma ($\alpha = 1.07$, $\beta = 0.32$) density were carried out using the software BestFit™ (1995). All three tests provided in BestFit™—the Chi-square, Kolmogorov-Smirnov, and the Anderson-Darling— indicated acceptance of the gamma model with confidence levels greater than 0.95. In addition, for each of these tests, the gamma model was judged best fitting (rank one) among the densities in the library of BestFit™. We therefore conclude that the NLOB condition is met. Use of the NLOB criterion in this way may be regarded as somewhat stringent in that the zero data are only used to define the target and are not used to assess NLOB target effectiveness.

The NLOB criterion is important in establishing whether the estimated cost model is a plausible goal of the units being studied. The MPE model will produce estimates for any arbitrary set of Y_{rj} data. However, if the resulting v_j data were, for example, uniformly distributed on $[0,1]$, there would be little confidence in the estimated model.

LIMITATIONS

Limitations may be discussed for both the new estimation technique itself and for its application to the present context and data. In order to more fully parallel existing OLS theory for model aptness testing, attention should be given to potential outliers, independence of the v_j, and constancy of the distribution of the v_j from trial to trial (analogous to homoscedasticity in OLS theory; see, for example, Madansky, 1988, and Neter, Wasserman & Kutner, 1985). Theory developments for these issues are not yet available for the MPE model.

Hypothesis tests and confidence intervals for the estimates do not appear to be readily derivable from the proposed approach. However, information on their variances can be obtained by simulation using additional specific assumptions. As an illustration, 100 data sets of 62 observations each were simulated as follows. A value of v_j was generated using the density model (4.2) and the estimates of p, α, and β. Then a vector, Y_{rj}, was generated

according to the uniform distribution on the convex polytope $\{Y: \sum_r a_r^* Y_r = v_j, Y_r \geq 0\}$ where

a_r^* is given by (3.4). Then the MPE model, (2.3)—(2.5) was solved for each data set and descriptive statistics for the estimates were obtained. Additional details on the simulation steps are given in the Appendix. The results are shown in Table 3.

Table 3: Descriptive statistics estimated from 100 simulated data sets

Estimate	a_1^*	a_2^*	a_3^*	a_4^*
Mean	0.2687	0.0510	0.1446	0.1412
Standard Deviation	0.0625	0.0131	0.0314	0.0297

The proposed NLOB criterion is a strong standard for performance effectiveness. It requires that squared distance performance with respect to the target set be as good or better than that of unbiased multivariate normal-like performance with respect of a point target in $\mathfrak{R}^n$. A still weaker class of target effectiveness densities might be developed in further research by inclusion of a vector parameter corresponding to possible bias in the multivariate normal-like model.

With regard to limitations of the methodology for the application setting and data used here, we discuss first the cost of unused capacity connection again. A cost of unused capacity in the Cooper and Kaplan (1992) sense, which can be denoted as s_j^{ck}, might coexist along with a cost of inefficiency, s_j^I, as used in the present chapter; so that $s_j = s_j^{ck} + s_j^I$. The effect of such unused capacities, as distinct from costs of inefficiencies, on the present results would be to understate the true efficiencies. The approach taken with the MPE model is worst-case in the sense that when the s_j^{ck} are identifiable, the appropriate data adjustment would be $x_j' = x_j - s_j^{ck}$ and the average performance efficiency would be expected to be larger. Thanassoulis et al. (1987) also discuss what we have called comparability of these units. A concern was noted relative to activity four whose monetary driver level might have been affected by the prosperity of the community being served. That is, offices with above average community prosperity and corresponding activity four levels might be considered as being unfairly compared to the others. Other things being equal, units with an inappropriately inflated value of a driver level would be expected to exert heavy downward pressure on the corresponding estimate in model MPE. We believe this kind of incomparability should ideally be removed by some kind of normalization process such as division by a socio-economic index. For the sake of concentrating on essential features of the present technique and maintaining comparability with the results of Dyson and Thanassoulis (1988), we leave this level of detailed analysis beyond the scope of the chapter.

In the use of the NLOB criterion for this data, the α parameter was compared to n/2 when n=4 was chosen. This assumes that the Y_r data are truly four-dimensional. The discussion of the data in Thanassoulis et al. (1987) suggested to us that units were free to emphasize or vary all four drivers with the possible exception of the fourth one. If this driver is regarded as not available for improvement by the units, then the data should be considered as three-dimensional. In this case, the intended α would be compared with 1.5. Since $\hat{\alpha} = 1.07$, the NLOB criterion is still met by the data under this assumption.

EXTENSIONS TO OTHER BASIC COST MODELS

This section discusses extensions to the three cases: (1) time-series data, (2) marginal cost-oriented basic cost models, and (3) single driver-single cost pool data.

Time-Series Data

Suppose the data Y_{rt} are given over time periods indexed by t for a single business unit. Then the MPE model with index j replaced by t can be applied. First, it would be necessary to adjust all the x_t cost-pool figures and resulting Y_{rt} data to reflect current dollars using a cost index. This assumes that the estimated a_r^* cost rates are in terms of current dollars. Next, these rates would be interpretable as follows. The estimated a_r^* in the current dollar time-series case may be interpreted to be the cost rate vector achieved by the unit during its most efficient observation period or periods. The resulting v_t suggest periods of more or less efficiency, and would be a useful source for self-study aimed at productivity and process improvements.

The comparability issue for the units under comparison should be easier to accept in this case. However, process or technology changes during the data time span could be problematical. A more complete discussion of limitations for this case is left for specific future applications.

In addition to the NLOB effectiveness test, additional considerations can be brought to bear with respect to an improvement over time dimension. Effectiveness in this respect would be supported by establishing a significant fit of the v_t data to a monotone increasing function of time, for example, the reciprocal of a learning curve. Over longer periods of times, learning curve patterns for the estimated gamma parameters could serve similarly. That is, decreasing α indicates improving target effectiveness, while decreasing β would indicate improving precision.

Marginal Cost-Oriented Basic Cost Models

Both the time-series and cross-sectional versions of the MPE model can be adapted to nonlinear basic cost models with marginal cost features. For example, consider the original cross-sectional case, but using the basic cost model

$$\sum_r a_r y_{rj} + \sum_r b_r y_{rj}^2 + s_j = x_j \tag{6.1}$$

Again s is interpreted as a possible inefficiency due to experiencing higher than benchmark a_r and/or b_r values. The cost of service provided by activity r is $a_r^* y_r + b_r^* y_r^2$ for efficient units. By differentiation, the marginal cost by this model for activity r becomes $a_r^* + 2b_r^* y_r$ at the observed driver level. Defining new data elements $Y_{rj}^{(2)} = y_{rj}^2 / x_j$, the modified MPE model becomes

MMPE: $\max \sum\sum \ a_r Y_{rj} + b_r Y_{rj}^{(2)}$ \hfill (6.2)

s.t. $\sum a_r Y_{rj} + b_r Y_{rj}^{(2)} \leq 1$ for all j \hfill (6.3)

$\sum a_r Y_r + b_r Y_{rj}^{(2)} \geq 0$ for all j \hfill (6.4)

$a_r \geq 0$, for all j ,and b_r unrestricted \hfill (6.5)

The constraints (6.4) ensure that cost contributions can only be non-negative, even if some b_r is negative. In that case, the marginal rate is decreasing; if these coefficients are positive, the corresponding marginal rates are increasing. Here a quadratic basic cost model was used. More generally, other models with different marginal cost structures could be employed (e.g., Cobb-Douglas as in Noreen and Soderstrom, 1994).

Implications for the Single Driver Single Cost Pool Case

The MPE model for this case simplifies to max $\sum a Y_j$, s.t. $a Y_j \leq 1$, for all j, and $a \geq 0$. The solution of this model is clearly $a^* = \min Y_j^{-1} = \min x_j/y_j$. The NLOB criterion requires $\alpha^* \leq$ ½ in this case. If this condition fails to hold, then this minimum value may be unreasonably low, perhaps due to an outlier. Deletion of one or a few such tentative outliers would be well supported if the remaining data do, in fact, pass the NLOB test. Otherwise no credible a_r estimate is forthcoming from the present method. It should be noted that the simulation method could also be employed for this case, provided the NLOB criterion is met.

DATA-MINING APPLICATIONS AND CONSIDERATIONS

Benchmark estimation models, such as those considered here, may also be called frontier regression models. The general application of these in data mining has been discussed in Troutt, Hu, Shanker, and Acar (2001). They are formed to explain boundary, frontier or optimal behavior rather than average behavior as, for example, in ordinary regression models. Such a model may also be called a ceiling model if it lays above all the observations or a floor model in the opposite case. The cost-estimation model of this chapter is a floor model since it predicts the best, i.e., lowest, cost units.

The model considered here is a cross-sectional one. Although data mining is ordinarily thought of from the perspective of mining data from within a single organization, benchmarking type studies must often involve comparisons of data across organizations. Benchmarking partnerships have been formed for this purpose as discussed in Troutt, Gribbin, Shanker, and Zhang (2000). Such benchmarking-oriented data mining might be extended in a number of directions. Potential applications include comparisons of quality and other costs, processing and set-up times, and employee turnover. More generally, benchmarking comparisons could extend to virtually any measure of common interest across firms or other entities, such as universities, states, and municipalities. In the example in this chapter, a simple cost model was used to explain best practice performance. More generally, best practice performance may depend on other explanatory variables or categories of interest to the firm. Discovery of such models, variables, and categories might be regarded as the essence of data mining. With techniques discussed here, the difference is the prediction of frontier rather than average performance. For example, interest often centers on best instances such as customers most responsive to mailings, safest drivers, etc.

However, cross-sectional applications of benchmark performance models do not necessarily depend on the multiple firm situations. Mining across all a firm's customers can also be of interest. Consider a planned mail solicitation of a sales firm. For mailings of a given type, it is desirable to predict the set of most responsive customers so that it can be targeted. Similarly, a charitable organization may be interested in discovering how to characterize its best or worst supporters according to a model.

As noted above, under the topic of time-series data, such frontier models can be used within a single organization where the benchmarking is done across time periods. Models of this type might be used to mine for explanatory variables or conditions that account for best or worst performance periods. Some of the same subjects as noted above for cross-sectional studies may be worthwhile targets. For example, it would be of interest for quality assurance to determine the correlates of best and worst defect production rates.

Ordinary regression is one of the most important tools for data mining. Frontier models, such as considered here, may be desirable alternatives in connection with data-mining applications. This is especially the case when it is desired to characterize and model the best and/or worst cases in the data. Such data are typically of the managed kind. In general, such managed data or data from purposeful or goal-directed behavior will be amenable to frontier modeling.

CONCLUSIONS

This chapter proposes a method for estimating what may be called benchmark, or best practice unit and marginal cost rates. These rates provide plausible operational goals for the management of the units being compared. This method also provides efficiency measures and suggests which organizational units or time periods are more or less efficient, as well as an estimate of the degree of such inefficiency. Efficient units or time periods provide benchmarks for imitation by other units or can be studied for continuous improvement possibilities. As far as the authors can determine, the proposed methodology is the first technique with the capability to suggest plausible benchmark cost rates.

A principle of maximum performance efficiency (MPE) was proposed as a generalization of the maximum decisional efficiency estimation principle in Troutt (1995). This principle is more broadly applicable than the MDE principle. Also, a gamma distribution-based validation criterion was proposed for the new MPE principle. The earlier MDE principle appealed to the maximum likelihood estimation principle for model aptness validation, but required relatively inflexible density models for the fitted efficiency scores.

The estimation models derived here reduce to straightforward linear programming models and are therefore widely accessible. A case was made that an optimal cost rate estimate of zero for some activity may be indicative of generally poor efficiency across the units with respect to one or more activities. Modifications based on reduced costs and augmented objective functions were proposed to compensate in that case.

In these models, the unknown cost rate parameters resemble the coefficients of linear regression models. However, the maximum performance efficiency estimation principle is employed rather than a criterion such as ordinary least squares. This principle assumes that for each organizational unit and time period, the unit intends to minimize these costs. Model adequacy with respect to this assumption was judged by a test of normal-like-or-better performance effectiveness for the estimated efficiency scores.

These results are also consistent with Noreen and Soderstrom (1994) who found that costs were not generally proportional to activity levels in a cross-sectional study of hospital accounts. The results of this chapter suggest that one source of such non-proportionality, in addition to the possibly non-linear form of the basic cost model, is what we call performance inefficiency.

The proposed estimation criterion was applied to a published data set previously analyzed by a modified data envelopment analysis method. The resulting estimates were compared with the average costs obtained by the previous method. The estimated benchmark cost rates were uniformly and strictly lower than their average rate counterparts, consistent with their definitions and providing a strong measure of face validity.

Benchmarking estimation models, such as discussed here, provide a new tool for data mining when the emphasis is on modeling the best performers.

REFERENCES

Berson, A., Smith, S., & Thearling, K (2000). *Building data mining applications for CRM.* New York: McGraw-Hill.

BestFit™(1995). *User's guide.* Palisade Corporation, Newfield, NY.

Bickell, P.J. & Doksum, K.A. (1977). *Mathematical statistics: Basic ideas and selected topics.* San Francisco: Holden Day, Inc.

Charnes, A., Cooper, W.W., Lewin, A., & Seiford, L.M. (1994). *Data envelopment analysis: Theory, methodology, and applications.* Boston, MA: Kluwer Academic Publishers.

Cooper, R. & Kaplan, R.S. (1992). Activity-based systems: Measuring the costs of resource usage. *Accounting Horizons*, September, 1-13.

Datar, S. & Gupta, M. (1994). Aggregation, specification and measurement errors in product costing. *The Accounting Review*, 69(4), 567-591.

Demski, J. (1967). An accounting system structured on a linear programming model. *The Accounting Review*, 42(4), 701-712.

Devroye, L. (1986). *Non-uniform random variate generation.* New York: Springer-Verlag.

Dyson, R.G. & Thanassoulis, E. (1988). Reducing weight flexibility in data envelopment analysis. *Journal of the Operational Research Society,* 39(6), 563-576.

Fleming, W. (1997). *Functions of several variables,* 2nd ed. New York: Springer-Verlag.

Itami, H. & Kaplan, R. (1980). An activity analysis approach to unit costing with multiple interactive products. *Management Science,* 26(8), 826-839.

Kaplan, R. & Thompson, G. (1971). Overhead allocation via mathematical programming models. *The Accounting Review,* 46(2), 352-364.

Kotz, S., Fang, K.T., & Liang, J.T. (1997). On multivariate vertical density representation and its application to random number generation. *Statistics*, 30, 163-180.

Kotz, S. & Troutt, M.D. (1996). On vertical density representation and ordering of distributions. *Statistics,* 28, 241-247.

Law, A.M. & Kelton, W.D. (1982) *Simulation modeling and analysis.* New York: McGraw-Hill.

Madansky, A. (1988). *Prescriptions for working statisticians.,* New York: Springer-Verlag.

Neter, J., Wasserman, W., & Kutner, M.H. (1985). *Applied linear statistical models*, 2nd ed. Homewood, IL: Richard E. Irwin, Inc.

Noreen, E. & Soderstrom, N. (1994). Are overhead costs strictly proportional to activity? *Journal of Accounting and Economics*, 17, 255-278.

Onsi, M. (1970). Transfer pricing systems based on opportunity cost. *The Accounting Review,* 40(3), 535-543.

SAS/IML Software (1995). *Usage and reference.* Version 6, 1st ed., SAS Institute, Inc., Cary, N. C.

Schmeiser, B.W. & Lal, R. (1980). Squeeze methods for generating gamma variates. *Journal of the American Statistical Association,* 75, 679-682.

Thannassoulis, E., Dyson, R.G., & Foster, M.J. (1987). Relative efficiency assessments using data envelopment analysis: An application to data on rates departments. *Journal of the Operational Research Society,* 38(5), 397-411.

Troutt, M.D. (1991). A theorem on the density of the density ordinate and alternative derivation of the Box-Muller method. *Statistics,* 22, 436-466.

Troutt, M.D. (1993). Vertical density representation and a further remark on the Box-Muller method. *Statistics,* 24, 81-83.

Troutt, M.D. (1995). A maximum decisional efficiency estimation principle, *Management Science,* 41(1), 76-82.

Troutt, M.D. (1997). Derivation of the maximum efficiency ratio model from the maximum decisional efficiency principle. *Annals of Operations Research,* 73, 323-338.

Troutt, M.D., Gribbin, D.W., Shanker. M., & Zhang. A. (2000). Cost-efficiency benchmarking for operational units with multiple cost drivers. *Decision Sciences,* 31(4), 813-832.

Troutt, M.D., Hu, M., Shanker, M. & Acar, W. (2001). Frontier versus ordinary regression models for data mining. In Parag C. Pendharkar (ed.), Managing data mining technologies in organizations: Techniques and applications. Hershey, PA: Idea Group Publishing Co.

Troutt, M.D. & Pang, W.K. (1996). A further VDR-type density representation based on the Box-Muller method. *Statistics. 28, 1-8.*

Troutt, M.D., Zhang, A., Tadisina, S.K., & Rai, A. (1997). Total factor efficiency/productivity ratio fitting as an alternative to regression and canonical correlation models for performance data. *Annals of Operations Research,* 74, 289-304.

APPENDIX

Proof of Theorem 1:

(1)   Consider the potentially feasible solution $m^0 = k = a_r^0$ for all r. Then,

$$\sum_r a_r^0 Y_{rj} = k \sum_r (Y_{rj}) \le 1 \text{ if } k \le (\Sigma Y_{rj})^{-1} \text{ for all } j.$$

Thus the solution $m^0 = k = a_r^0$ is feasible for problem MPE (λ) for all $\lambda > 0$,

for $k^0 = \min (\Sigma y_{rj})^{-1}$ which is positive due to the positivity of the data. It follows that.

$$z(\lambda^*) \ge \sum_j \sum_r a_r^0 Y_{rj} + \lambda m^0 = k^0 \Sigma \Sigma Y_{rj} + \lambda k^0 \ge k^0 \lambda, \text{ for all } \lambda > 0.$$

(2)   Here we note that the $a_r^*(\lambda)$ for the MMPE model, while feasible, are not necessarily optimal for the original MPE model. Hence use of these values in the MPE objective function will generally give a lower objective function value.

Proof of Theorem 2:

This is a modification of a proof for a version of the theorem given in Troutt (1993). By the assumption that x is uniformly distributed on $\{x:w(x) = u\}$, $f(x)$ must be constant on these contours; so that $f(x) = \varphi(w(x))$ for some function, $\varphi(\cdot)$. Consider the probability $P(u \leq w(x) \leq u + \varepsilon)$ for a small positive number, ε. On the one hand, this probability is $\varepsilon\, g(u)$ to a first order approximation. On the other hand, it is also given by

$$\int \ldots \int_{\{x:u \leq w(x) \leq u+\varepsilon\}} f(x)\, \Pi\, dx_i \cong \varphi(u) \int \ldots \int_{\{w:u \leq w \leq u+\varepsilon\}} \Pi\, dx_i$$

$$\cong \qquad \varphi(u)\, \{\, A(u+\varepsilon) - A(u)\,\}$$

Therefore

$$\varepsilon\, g(u) \cong \varphi(u)\, \{\, A(u+\varepsilon) - A(u)\,\}$$

Division by ε and passage to the limit as $\varepsilon \to 0$ yields the result.

Further Details on the Simulation Experiment

To simulate observations within each data set, a uniform random number was used to choose between the degenerate and continuous portions in the density model

$$p\,\delta(0) + (1-p)\, \text{gamma}(\alpha, \beta)$$

where $p = 0.048$, $\alpha = 1.07$, and $\beta = 0.32$. With probability p, $\delta(0)$ was chosen and $w = 0$ was returned. With probability $1-p$, the gamma (α, β) density was chosen and a value, w, was returned using the procedure of Schmeiser and Lal (1980) in the IMSL routine RNGAM. The returned w was converted to an efficiency score, v, according to $v = exp\{-w^{0.5}\}$. For each v, a vector Y was generated on the convex polytope with extreme points $e_1 = (v/a_1^*,0,0,0)$, $e_2 = (0,v/a_2^*,0,0)$, $e_3 = (0,0,v/a_3^*,0)$ and $e_4 = (0,0,0,v/a_4^*)$ using the method given in Devroye (1986).

Chapter XI

Bayesian Data Mining and Knowledge Discovery

Eitel J. M. Lauria
State University of New York, Albany, USA
Universidad del Salvador, Argetina

Giri Kumar Tayi
State University of New York, Albany, USA

ABSTRACT

One of the major problems faced by data-mining technologies is how to deal with uncertainty. The prime characteristic of Bayesian methods is their explicit use of probability for quantifying uncertainty. Bayesian methods provide a practical method to make inferences from data using probability models for values we observe and about which we want to draw some hypotheses. Bayes' Theorem provides the means of calculating the probability of a hypothesis (posterior probability) based on its prior probability, the probability of the observations, and the likelihood that the observational data fits the hypothesis.

The purpose of this chapter is twofold: to provide an overview of the theoretical framework of Bayesian methods and its application to data mining, with special emphasis on statistical modeling and machine-learning techniques; and to illustrate each theoretical concept covered with practical examples. We will cover basic probability concepts, Bayes' Theorem and its implications, Bayesian classification, Bayesian belief networks, and an introduction to simulation techniques.

DATA MINING, CLASSIFICATION AND SUPERVISED LEARNING

There are different approaches to data mining, which can be grouped according to the kind of task pursued and the kind of data under analysis. A broad grouping of data-mining algorithms includes classification, prediction, clustering, association, and sequential pattern recognition.

Data Mining is closely related to machine learning. Imagine a process in which a computer algorithm learns from experience (the training data set) and builds a model that is then used to predict future behavior. Mitchell (1997) defines machine learning as follows: a computer program is said to learn from experience E with respect to some class of tasks T and performance measure P, if its performance at tasks in T, as measured by P, improves with experience E. For example, consider a handwriting recognition problem: the task T is to recognize and classify handwritten words and measures; the performance measure P is the percent of words correctly classified; and the experience E is a database of handwritten words with given class values. This is the case of classification: a learning algorithm (known as classifier) takes a set of classified examples from which it is expected to learn a way of classifying unseen examples. Classification is sometimes called supervised learning, because the learning algorithm operates under supervision by being provided with the actual outcome for each of the training examples.

Consider the following example data set based on the records of the passengers of the Titanic[1]. The Titanic dataset gives the values of four categorical attributes for each of the 2,201 people on board the Titanic when it struck an iceberg and sank. The attributes are social class (first class, second class, third class, crew member), age (adult or child), sex, and whether or not the person survived. Table 1 below lists the set of attributes and its values.

In this case, we know the outcome of the whole universe of passengers on the Titanic; therefore, this is good example to test the accuracy of the classification procedure. We can take a percentage of the 2,201 records at random (say, 90%) and use them as the input dataset with which we would train the classification model.

The trained model would then be used to predict whether the remaining 10% of the passengers survived or not, based on each passenger's set of attributes (social class, age, sex). A fragment of the total dataset (24 records) is depicted in Table 2.

The question that remains is how do we actually train the classifier so that it is able to predict with reasonable accuracy the class of each new instance it is fed? There are many different approaches to classification, including traditional multivariate statistical

Table 1: Titanic example data set

ATTRIBUTE	POSSIBLE VALUES
social class	crew, 1st, 2nd, 3rd
age	adult, child
sex	male, female
survived	yes, no

Table 2: Fragment of Titanic data set

Instance	Social class	Age	Sex	Survived		Instance	Social class	Age	Sex	Survived
1	2nd	adult	female	yes		13	3rd	adult	male	no
2	crew	adult	male	no		14	1st	adult	female	yes
3	crew	adult	male	yes		15	3rd	adult	male	no
4	2nd	adult	male	no		16	3rd	child	female	no
5	2nd	adult	female	yes		17	3rd	adult	male	no
6	crew	adult	male	yes		18	1st	adult	female	yes
7	crew	adult	male	no		19	crew	adult	male	no
8	1st	adult	male	no		20	3rd	adult	male	no
9	crew	adult	male	yes		21	3rd	adult	female	no
10	crew	adult	male	no		22	3rd	adult	female	no
11	3rd	child	male	no		23	3rd	child	female	yes
12	crew	adult	male	no		24	3rd	child	male	no

methods, where the goal is to predict or explain categorical dependent variables (logistic regression, for example), decision trees, neural networks, and Bayesian classifiers. In this chapter, we will focus on two methods: Naive Bayes and Bayesian Belief Networks.

THE BAYESIAN APPROACH TO PROBABILITY

The classical approach of probability ties probability to the physical nature of the world. This means that if we toss a coin, the probability of getting heads or tails is intrinsically linked to the physical properties of the coin. Under this interpretation, we could estimate the "probability of getting heads" as the frequency of heads after repeating the experiment a certain number of times. The (weak) Law of Large Numbers states that when the number of random observations of a certain event is very large, the relative frequency of the observations is a near exact estimate of the probability of the event. Since frequencies can be measured, this frequentist interpretation of probability seemed to be an objective measure for dealing with random phenomena.

There are many situations in which the frequency definition of probability exhibits its limited validity. Although the classical (frequentist) approach seems to be a good way of estimating probabilities, difficulties surface when facing situations in which experiments are not possible. For example, when trying to answer the question of "Who is going to be the next President of the United States of America?", the frequentist approach fails to provide an answer; the event has an associated probability, but there is no possible way of experimenting and measuring the relative frequencies because the event has a single occurrence. And there are many other cases in which a frequency approach is not applicable or is, at least, far-fetched. Why should we have to think of probability in terms of many repetitions of an experiment that never happened? As Sivia (1996) mentions, we are at liberty to think about a problem in any way that facilitates a solution or our understanding of it, but having to seek a frequentist interpretation for every data analysis problem seems rather perverse.

The Bayesian approach, instead, provides an elegant framework to deal with this kind of probability problems. To Bayesians, the probability of a certain event represents the degree of belief that such event will happen. We don't need to think of probabilities as frequency distributions— probability measures the degree of personal belief. Such belief is therefore governed by a probability distribution that can be updated by making use of the observed data. To do so, however, Bayesians address data analysis from a different perspective; i.e., the personal belief in the occurrence of a certain event starts with a given distribution, which stands before any data is considered and is therefore known as prior distribution. Observational data is incorporated into the data analysis process in order to obtain a posterior probability distribution by updating our prior belief. But how do we perform this update of our prior belief? And besides, where does the name Bayesian come from?

Bayesian thinking has its roots in the question of how to reason in situations in which it is not possible to argue with certainty, and in the difference between inductive and deductive logic. The problem of inductive reasoning has puzzled philosophers since the time of Aristotle, as a way of inferring universal laws from a finite number of cases, as opposed to deductive logic, the kind of reasoning typically used in mathematics. Deductive logic is based on deriving the conclusion from the implicit content of its premises, so that if the premises are true, then the conclusion is necessarily true. We can therefore derive results by applying a set of well-defined rules. Games of chance fall into this category as well. If we know that an unbiased die is rolled five times, we can calculate the chances of getting three ones, for example.

Inductive reasoning tackles a different problem, actually the reverse of the above situation; i.e., given that a finite number of effects can be observed, derive from them a general (causal) law capable of explaining each and all of the effects (premises) from which it was drawn. Going back to the previous example, inductive reasoning would try to explain whether the rolled die is biased or not after observing the outcome of five repeated throws.

Bayes' Theorem

Bayes' Theorem is derived from a simple reordering of terms in the product rule of probability:

$$P(B|A) = \frac{P(A \mid B) * P(A)}{P(B)}$$

If we replace B by H (a hypothesis under consideration) and A by D (the evidence, or set of observational data), we get:

$$P(H|D) = \frac{P(D \mid H) * P(H)}{P(D)}$$

Note that:

− P(H|D) is the probability of a certain hypothesis based on a set of observational data given a certain context (posterior probability of hypothesis H);

− P(D|H) is the likelihood of the observations given a certain hypothesis in a given context;

− P(H) is the intrinsic probability of hypothesis H, before considering the evidence D (prior probability);

− P(D) is the probability of the observations, independent of the hypothesis, that can be interpreted as a normalizing constant rendering P(H/D) to a value interval of [0,1].

Bayes' Theorem can then be reformulated in the following way: the probability of a certain hypothesis given a set of observations in a given context depends on its prior probability and on the likelihood that the observations will fit the hypothesis.

$$P(H|D) \propto P(H) * P(D|H)$$

This means that the probability of the hypothesis is being updated by the likelihood of the observed data. The result of the Bayesian data analysis process is the posterior probability distribution of the hypothesis that represents a revision of the prior distribution in the light of the evidence provided by the data.

Conjugate Prior Distributions

Let us first reformulate Bayes' Theorem in terms of probability distributions. As such, Bayes' formula can be rewritten as:

$$p(\theta|x) \propto p(x|\theta) * p(\theta)$$

where the prior $p(\theta)$ on the unknown parameter θ characterizes knowledge or beliefs about θ before seeing the data; the likelihood function $p(x|\theta)$ summarizes the sample information about θ.

In order to assess the prior distribution of θ, many Bayesian problems make use of the notion of conjugacy. For each of the most popular statistical families, there exists a family of distributions for the parameter such that, if the prior distribution is chosen to be a member of the family, then the posterior distribution will also be a member of that family. Such a family of distributions is called a conjugate family. Choosing a prior distribution from that family will typically simplify the computation of the posterior.

For example, suppose that X1, X2,..Xn form a random sample drawn from a Bernoulli distribution for which the parameter θ is unknown. Suppose that we choose a Beta distribution for prior, with parameters α and β, both > 0 Then the posterior distribution of θ given the sample observations is also a Beta, with parameters

$$\alpha + \sum x_i \text{ and } \beta + n - \sum x_i \; .$$

$$p(\theta \mid x) \propto \underbrace{\theta^{\sum x_i} \theta^{n-\sum x_i} * \theta^{\alpha-1} (1-\theta)^{\beta-1}}_{} = \text{Beta}(\alpha + \sum x_i, \ \beta + n - \sum x_i)$$

likelihood   prior

As can be seen in the previous expression, given that the likelihood is a binomial distribution, by choosing the prior as a Beta distribution, the posterior distribution can be obtained without the need of integrating a rather complex function. Although this is a very convenient approach, in many practical problems there is no way of approximating our prior beliefs by means of a "nice" (conjugate) prior distribution.

Critique of the Bayesian Framework

The Bayesian approach did not come without difficulties. The concerns regarding subjectivity of its treatment of probability is understandable. Under the belief interpretation, probability is not an objective property of some physical setting but is conditional to the prior assumptions and experience of the learning system. The prior probability distribution can arise from previously collected observations, but if the data is not available, it should be derived from the subjective assessment of some domain expert. According to this personal, or subjective, interpretation of probability, the probability that a person assigns to a possible outcome of some process represents his/her judgment of the likelihood that the outcome will be obtained. This subjective interpretation can be formalized, based on certain conditions of consistency. However, as DeGroot (1986) describes, the requirement that a person's judgment of the relative likelihood of a large number of events be completely consistent and free of inconsistencies is humanly unattainable. And besides, a subjective interpretation may not provide a common basis for an objective theory about a certain topic of interest. Two different persons may have two different interpretations and may not reach a common evaluation of the state of knowledge. Now, how much does this subjectivity issue affect the Bayesian framework? As Sivia (1996) points out, the Bayesian view is that a probability does indeed represent how much do we believe that a certain event is true, but this belief should be based on all the relevant information available. This is not the same as subjectivity; it simply means that probabilities are conditional on the prior assumptions and that these assumptions must be stated explicitly. Janes (1996) explains that objectivity only demands that two individuals who are given the same information and who reason according to the rules of probability theory should make the same probability assignment. Interestingly enough, Cox (1946) studied the quantitative rules necessary for logical and consistent reasoning and showed that plausible reasoning and calculus of beliefs map exactly into the axioms of probability theory. He found that the only rules that met the requirements for logical and consistent reasoning were those derived from probability theory.

The other source of criticism is based on scalability. Within the field of artificial intelligence, for example, the use of Bayesian methods in expert systems was criticized because the approach did not scale well for real-world problems. To visualize these scalability issues, let us consider the typical problems faced when trying to apply the Bayesian framework. The Bayes' formula can be expressed as:

$$p(\theta \mid x) = \frac{p(x \mid \theta) * p(\theta)}{p(x)} = \frac{p(x \mid \theta) * p(\theta)}{\int_{\Theta} p(x \mid \theta) * p(\theta) d\theta} \propto p(x \mid \theta) * p(\theta)$$

Note that the normalizing factor $p(x)$ is calculated by integrating over all the possible values of θ. But what happens when we deal with multidimensional parameters, that is that $\theta \in \Re^n$? In such case, the normalizing factor must be calculated as $\int_{\Re^n} p(x \mid \theta) * p(\theta) d\theta$, and the resulting expressions may not have a straightforward analytical solution and, in the worst case, may be computationally infeasible. Similar situations arise when trying to calculate marginal densities or expected values. In the case of expectation, the goal of the analysis may be to obtain the expected value of a function $g(\theta)$ for which we have:

$$E[g(\theta) \mid x] = \int_{\Re^n} g(\theta) * p(\theta \mid x) * d\theta$$

As can be observed, we encounter a similar kind of problem as before. For high-dimensional spaces, it is usually impossible to evaluate these expressions analytically, and traditional numerical integration methods are far too computationally expensive to be of any practical use.

Luckily, new developments in simulation during the last decade have mitigated much of the previous criticism. The inherent scalability problems of traditional Bayesian analysis, due to the complexity of integrating expressions over high-dimensional distributions, have met an elegant solution framework. The introduction of Markov Chain Monte Carlo methods (MCMC) in the last few years has provided enormous scope for realistic Bayesian modeling (more on this later in this chapter).

BAYESIAN CLASSIFICATION

In discussing Bayes' Theorem, the focus has been to find the most probable hypothesis given a set of observations. But in data-mining problems, one of the major tasks is to classify (predict the outcome of) a new observation based on a previous set of observations (the training data set). Suppose we have a classification problem where the class variable is denoted by **C** and can take values $c_1,..,c_k$. Consider a data set D represented by m attributes A1, A2, …, Am of which the observations $(a_1, a_2, …,a_m)$ have been taken for each instance of D. This implies that any given instance of D may be expressed as (A1=a_1, A2=a_2, .,Am=a_m). Suppose that each instance of the data set D is classified as $c_1,…,c_k$; the

Bayesian approach to classifying a new instance would be to assign the most probable target value (a class value of type c_i) by calculating the posterior probability for each class, given D, and selecting the one with the maximum a posteriori (MAP) probability. Following Mitchell's notation:

$$c_{MAP} = \arg P(c_{chosen} | D) = \text{argmax} [P(D|ci) * P(ci))], ci \in C$$

Any system that classifies new instances according to the above expression is known as an "optimal Bayesian classifier." It can be proven that an optimal Bayesian classifier renders the highest probability that the new instance is classified correctly using the same hypothesis space and the same prior knowledge (Mitchell, 1997).

Although the idea of applying full-blown Bayesian criteria to analyze a hypothesis space in search of the most feasible hypothesis is conceptually attractive, it usually fails to deliver in practical settings. This is because, although we can successfully estimate P(ci) from the training data, calculating the joint probability $P(D|ci) = P(A1=a_1, A2=a_2, .., An=a_n | Ci)$ is usually not possible because the number of possible combinations is equal to the number of possible instances times the number of class values. Unless the training data set is very large (which on the other hand might render the procedure computationally intractable), the resulting estimates would be representative of a small fraction of the instance space and hence would be unreliable.

The Naive Bayes Classifier

The Naive Bayes Classifier facilitates the estimation of the conditional probabilities by introducing two simplifying assumptions:

1) Assume conditional independence among attributes of the data sample. This means that the posterior probability of D, given c_i is equal to the product of the posterior probability of each attribute.

$$P(D|c_i) = P(A1=a1 | c_i) * .. * P(Am=a_m|c_i) = \prod_{j=1}^{n} P(Aj = a_j | c_i), c_i \in C$$

The conditional probabilities of each individual attribute can be estimated from the frequency distributions of the sample data set D. (Note that if attribute values are continuous, they need to be discretized first, making some assumptions regarding the probability density functions for each of them. For more information regarding discretization procedures, see Dougherty, Kohavi, & Sahami, 1995.)

2) If the prior probabilities P(Ci) are unknown, they can also be estimated assuming that classes Ci are equally likely and therefore computing the probabilities from the sample data set frequency distributions.

These assumptions lead to a substantial reduction of the number of distinct conditional probability factors that must be estimated from the training data. For example, in the sample of 24 records extracted from the Titanic dataset (see Table 2), we can estimate the class probabilities P(survived=yes) and P(survived=no), as follows:

P(survived=yes) = (# of instances were survived=yes) / (total # of instances) = 8/24
P(survived=no) = (# of instances were survived=no) / (total # of instances) = 16/24

Next, the conditional probabilities are computed as follows:

P(socialclass=crew | survived=yes) = # of instances where socialclass=crew and survived=yes = 3
                                     # of instances were survived=yes   8

P(socialclass=crew | survived=yes) = # of instances where socialclass=1st and survived=yes = 2
                                     # of instances were survived=yes   3

This procedure is repeated for every conditional probability of the form $P(A_j | c_i)$ until every element in the conditional probability table is computed. Note that with such a reduced sample, the probability estimate will be inaccurate; the example was chosen for illustrative purposes.

Although these assumptions may seem over-simplifying, the fact is that they work quite well in certain classification problems. To illustrate the practical importance of the Naive Bayes algorithm in classification tasks, the authors coded a simple version of the Naive Bayes Classifier[2] and tested it using the full Titanic dataset, with 90% of the original dataset used for training purposes and the remaining 10% to test the accuracy of the classifier. Given two possible class values (survived or not), we could expect a classification accuracy of approximately 50%, based on random guessing. In our case, the algorithm yielded an accuracy of 88%, impressive enough if we consider that the dataset contained a very small number of attributes.

Various empirical studies of the Naive Bayes Classifier have rendered comparable results to those obtained by using state of the art classifiers such as decision tree algorithms or neural network models. The studies have reported accuracy levels of 89% when using a Naive Bayesian model to classify Usenet news articles. For more details see Mitchell (1997) and Joachims (1996).

Coping with Zero-Frequency Attributes

An aspect that may drastically affect the outcome of a Naive Bayes Classifier is when a particular attribute does not occur in the training set for one or more class values. Suppose, for example ,that in the Titanic data set there are no first class passengers who died in the wreck. This would mean that the number of instances for which *socialclass = 1st* and *survived = no* would be equal to zero.

In such a case, the conditional probability *P(socialclass=1st|survived=no)* would be zero, and since *P(D|survived=no)* is equal to the product of the individual conditional probabilities, *P(D|survived=no)* would also be equal to zero, eliminating class *survived=no* from consideration. This "zero-frequency" attribute may bias the maximum a posteriori (MAP) criteria used for choosing the best class. This condition severely limits the practical use of the Naive Bayes Classifier; however, it can be easily remedied by applying minor adjustments to the method of calculating probabilities from frequencies. Two general approaches that are typically considered in the literature are the following (more details can be found in Kohavi, Becker, and Sommerfield, 1997):

- The no match approach, in which a zero frequency (no count) is replaced by a value that is inversely proportional to the number of instances.
- Use of Laplace estimator, where the strategy is to add 1 to the count for every attribute value-class value combination, so that, given an attribute A with d values $a_1, a_2, .., a_d$, a count of n_k for the class value $C=c_k$, and m_{jk} matches of attribute value $A=a_j$ and class value $C=c_k$, the "new" relative frequency is calculated as $(m_{jk} + 1) / (n_k + d)$.

Witten and Frank (2000) have suggested using a Bayesian approach to estimating probabilities using an estimator of the form $(m_{jk} + \pi_j * \omega) / (n_k + \omega)$, where ω is a small constant and π_j is the prior probability for each attribute value $A = a_j$ in our previous formulation. A typical way of estimating π_j in the absence of other information is to assume uniform priors; that is, if an attribute has d values, the probability of each attribute value is $1/d$.

BAYESIAN BELIEF NETWORKS

Bayesian belief networks (BBNs) follow a middle-of-the-road approach when compared to the computationally intensive optimal Bayesian classifier and the over-simplified Naive Bayesian approach. A BBN describes the probability distribution of a set of attributes by specifying a set of conditional independence assumptions together with a set of causal relationships among attributes and their related joint probabilities. When used in this way, BBNs result in a powerful knowledge representation formalism, based in probability theory that has the potential of providing much more information about a certain domain than visualizations based on correlations or distance measures.

Building a Graphical Model

Given a set of attributes A1, A2,...,Am, a directed acyclic graph[3] (DAG) is constructed in which each node of the graph represents each of the attributes (including the class attribute) and the arcs represent the causal relationship between the arcs. In this case, the joint probability distribution $P(A1 = a_1, A2 = a_2, .. Am = a_m)$ is no longer the product of the independent probabilities, as the model includes the causal relationship among attributes. Recalling the product probability rule, the joint probability distribution can be rewritten as:

$$P(A1 = a_1, A2 = a_2, .. Am = a_m) = \prod_{i=1}^{n} P(Ai = a_i \mid Parents(Ai))$$

Figure 1: Graph (causal) model of a BBN.

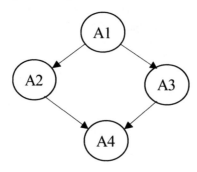

where parents (Ai) are the direct parents of Ai, linked to Ai through the causal arcs in the graph model. Note that the previous expression includes class C among the set of attributes Ai. For example, if we consider the graph model in Figure 1, the parents of A4 are A2 and A3. If there are no causal relationships among the nodes Ai, P(Ai= ai /Parents(Ai)) = P(Ai=ai); we therefore return to the expression of the joint probability. For the model depicted in Figure 1:

$$P(A1,A2,A3,A4) = \prod_{1}^{n} P(Ai = ai \mid Parents(Ai))_{) = P(A1)*P(A2|A1)*P(A3|A1)*P(A4|A2,A3)}$$

In addition to the graph structure, it is necessary to specify the parameters of the model. This means that we must specify the Conditional Probability Distribution (CPD) at each node, given the values of its parents. If the variables are discrete, this can be represented as a table, which lists the probability that the child node takes on each of its different values for each combination of values of its parents.

Inference in Bayesian Belief Networks

Once the belief network is formulated, it can be used for probabilistic inference, that is, to make probabilistic statements concerning the network attributes (nodes). Since a BBN uniquely defines a joint probability distribution, any probability can be computed from the network by specifying the joint probability distribution and applying basic rules of probability, such as conditioning and marginalization. Consider the example in Figure 2, extracted from Van der Gaag (1996). The BBN represents some fictitious medical knowledge concerning the diagnosis of acute cardiac disorders, and it comprises four binary nodes; i.e., each of them have two possible values, which we will denote by true and false. The listed nodes are S: smoking history of the patient; M: presence of heart attack; P: whether the patient was suffering chest pain or not; F: whether the patient had tingling fingers or not. The model assumes that the smoking history has direct influence on the occurrence of a heart attack. Besides, in such a condition, the patient will likely

Figure 2: Graphical model of a fictitious medical BBN.

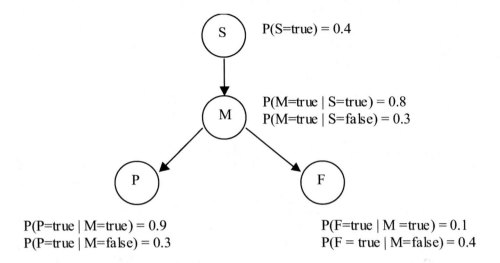

show signs of pain in the chest reflected by the high probability assigned to this case. On the other hand, given a heart attack, the patient is not likely to have tingling fingers; the low conditional probability value describes such a state. We see that the events P and F have a common cause (M) but do not depend on S. Applying the product rule to the graph above, we may decompose the joint probability of one case (P(S,M,P,F) = P(S=true, M=true, P=true, F=true)) into a set of independent parent-child contributions as P(S, M, P, F) = P(S) * P(M|S) * P(P|M) * P(F|M). Having specified the model we can calculate the prior probabilities of each node in the network. For example P(M=true) can be calculated as:

$$P(M=true) = P(M|S=true)*P(S=true) + P(M|S=false)*P(S=false) = 0.5$$

Then P(P=true) and P (F=true) are calculated as:

$$P(P=true) = P(P|M=true)*P(M=true) + P(P|M=false)*P(M=false) = 0.6$$
$$P(F=true) = P(F|M=true)*P(M=true) + P(F|M=false)*P(F=false) = 0.25$$

The previous probabilities corresponded to the beliefs that we had on each of the network attributes (nodes) without considering any additional evidence. As before, we may wish to find the most probable hypothesis given a set of observations. In this case, we might want to determine whether it is more likely that the patient has a heart attack or not, given the fact that he/she has signs of chest pain. For such purposes, we need to compare P(M=true|P=true) and P(M=false|P=true): if the first conditional probability is greater, we infer that the patient has a heart attack; if it is smaller we accept the hypothesis that the patient does not have a heart attack[4]. To calculate these posterior probabilities, we apply conditional probability in the following way:

$$P(M{=}true|P{=}true) = \frac{P(M{=}true, P{=}true)}{P(P = true)}$$

$$P(M{=}false|P{=}true) = \frac{P(M{=}false, P{=}true)}{P(P = true)}$$

The denominator is common to both expressions and can be eliminated for comparison purposes. The remaining criteria can be rewritten as:

Most probable Hypothesis = argmax [P(M= true, P= true), P(M= true, P= true)]

We can calculate both P(M= true, P= true) and P(M= true, P= true) from the conditional probability tables associated with each node:

P(M=true,P=true) = P(S=true, M=true, P=true, F=true) +
                     P(S=true, M=true, P=true, F=false) +
                     P(S=false, M=true, P=true, F=true) +
                     P(S=false, M=true, P=true, F=false)

P(M=false,P=true) = P(S=true, M=false, P=true, F=true) +
                      P(S=true, M=false, P=true, F=false) +
                      P(S=false, M=false, P=true, F=true) +
                      P(S=false, M=false, P=true, F=false)

It should be noted that each joint probability in the above expressions is calculated by applying the causal model depicted in Figure 2. For example, if we wish to calculate P(S=true, M=true, P=true, F=true) :

P(S=true, M=true, P=true, F=true) = P(S) * P(M|S) * P(P|M) * P(F|M)
                        = 0.4 * 0.8 * 0.9 * 0.1 = 0.0288

As indicated before, because a BBN determines a joint probability distribution for the set of attributes in the network, the Bayesian network can—in principle—be used to compute any probability of interest. For problems with many variables, however, this approach is not practical. Several researchers have developed probabilistic inference algorithms that apply variations of the conditional independence concept. Pearl (1988) and Lauritzen and Spieglelhalter (1988) developed the two most well known algorithms. Pearl's algorithm, for instance, is based on a message-passing concept. The new evidence is propagated over the network by sending messages to neighbor nodes. Through the arcs —acting as communication channels—the nodes send messages providing information about the joint probability distribution that is defined by the network and the evidence obtained so far.

Training Bayesian Belief Networks

Two questions arise in formulating BBNs: (1) how to determine the underlying causal model expressed as a graph, which includes the specification of the conditional independence assumptions among the attributes of the model? and (2) how to determine the conditional probability distributions that quantify the dependencies among the attributes in the model? In the following, we address these two questions, while noting that a detailed review of the topic is beyond the scope of this chapter.

As described by Ramoni and Sebastiani (1999), BBNs were originally supposed to rely on domain experts to supply information about the conditional independence graphical model and the subjective assessment of conditional probability distributions that quantify the dependencies among attributes. However, the statistical foundation of BBN soon led to the development of methods to extract both structure and conditional probability estimations from data, thus turning BBNs into powerful data analysis tools. Learning BBNs from data is a rapidly growing field of research that has seen a great deal of activity in recent years, including work by Lam and Bachus (1994), Friedman and Goldszmidt (1996), and Heckerman, Geiger and Chickering (1994).

There are a number of possible scenarios to consider when addressing the problem of training a BBN:

- When the structure of the BBN is known and all the attributes for all the instances are observable in the training examples, learning the conditional probabilities is quite straightforward. We simply estimate the conditional probabilities by maximizing the likelihood of the training data, as in the case of the Naive Bayes Classifier (estimating relative frequencies with zero-frequency corrections, for example).

- When the structure of the BBN is known but not all of the variables are observable (partially or totally) in the training data, we come across a more complicated problem. In such a case, we can resort to algorithms intended to deal with missing values, such as the Estimation Maximization (EM) algorithm. For a detailed explanation on the EM algorithm and its use in training BBNs, see Mitchell (1997). Another approach is assimilating the problem to the case of estimating the weights of the hidden nodes in a neural network. In that case, a gradient ascent approach can be used, where the algorithm searches through the space of hypotheses corresponding to the set of all possible entries in the conditional probability table.

- When the structure of the network is not known, we face a problem of model selection, typically a much more complicated problem than the two previously described cases. The goal is to find the network, or group of networks, that best describes the probability distribution over the training data. This optimization process is implemented in practice by using heuristic search techniques to find the best model over the space of possible BBNs. A scoring system is commonly used for choosing among alternative networks. Lam and Bachus (1994), for example, have used a score based on the minimum description principle (MDL), an information theoretic perspective of Occam's Razor principle according to which simple, sparse models should be preferred to complex overfitted models.[5]

MARKOV CHAIN MONTE CARLO TECHNIQUES

Markov Chain Monte Carlo (MCMC) techniques have been mainly responsible for the current momentum gained by Bayesian methods, since its application has enabled the use of A vast range of Bayesian models that had been previously deemed as intractable. With complicated models, it is rare that the posterior distribution can be computed directly. The simulation techniques described in the previous section are only adequate when dealing with low-dimensional problems but cannot be successfully applied in many real-world problems. This is where MCMC excels. MCMC is intrinsically a set of techniques for simulating from multivariate distributions. In order to introduce the topic, we need to provide some definitions regarding stochastic processes and Markov chains.

Markov Chains

A random or stochastic process is a family of random variables $\{X(t), t \in T\}$ defined over a given probability space and indexed by a parameter t that varies over an index set T. The values assumed by $X(t)$ are called states. If T is discrete then the process is called a discrete-time process and is denoted as $\{Xn, n=1,2,..,n\}$. X1 is the initial state of the process and Xn is the state of the process at time n.

A Markov chain is a special case of a discrete-time process in which the following rule applies: At any given time n, the probabilities of the future state n+1 depend only on the current state Xn. This is expressed as:

$$P(Xn+1 = x_{n+1} | X1 = x_1, X2 = x_2, .., Xn = x_n) = P(Xn+1 = x_{n+1} | Xn = x_n)$$

In other words, if we generate a sequence of random variables X1, X2, .., Xn, such that the next state Xn+1 is a sample from a distribution that depends only on the current state of the chain, Xn, and does not depend on the rest of the chain X1, X2,..Xn-1, this sequence is called a Markov chain.

The conditional probability $P(Xn+1 | Xn)$ is known as the transition kernel of the Markov chain. When the transition kernel is independent of n, then it is said to be stationary, and the process is referred to as a time-homogeneous Markov chain. A finite Markov chain is such that there are only a finite number k of possible states s1,s2,..,sk, and the process must be in one of these k states. If any of these states can be reached from any other state in a finite number of moves, the chain is said to be irreducible.

Markov Chain Simulation

The idea of Markov Chain simulation is to simulate a random walk in the parameter space that converges to a stationary distribution that is the target multivariate distribution $\pi(x)$ that we want to simulate (typically a joint posterior distribution). It is possible to construct a Markov chain such that this stationary distribution is the target distribution $\pi(x)$. Therefore, over time the draws Xn will look more and more like dependent samples from the target distribution. After hundreds of iterations, the chain will gradually forget the starting position X1, and it will gradually converge to the stationary distribution.

Several methods have been developed for constructing and sampling from transition distributions. Among them, the Metropolis algorithm and the Gibbs sampler are among the most powerful and popular methods currently in use. For a more complete description, see Gelman et al. (1995) and Neal (1993). Also, a complete set of lectures on this topic can be found in Rodriguez (1999).

The Metropolis Algorithm

The original algorithm was developed by Metropolis in 1953 with the purpose of simulating the evolution of a system in a heat bath towards thermal equilibrium. In its rather recent application to statistics, the Metropolis algorithm creates a sequence of points (X1, X2, ...) whose distributions converge to the target distribution $\pi(x)$. Let q(y| x) be the jumping (proposal) distribution. In the Metropolis algorithm, this jumping distribution must be symmetric, that is, q(x|y) = q(y|x) for all $X, Y,$ and n. The algorithm proceeds as follows:
1.   Given the current position Xn, the next candidate state is chosen by sampling a point Y from the proposal distribution q(y|x)

2.   The ratio of the densities is calculated as $r = \dfrac{\pi(y)}{\pi(x_n)}$

3.   Calculate $\alpha = \left\{ \begin{array}{l} \min(r,1) \\ 1 \end{array} \right.$

4.   With probability α accept the candidate value and set Xn+1 = Y; otherwise reject Y and set Xn+1= Xn
5.   Go to step 1

It can be proved that for a random walk on any proper distribution with positive probability of eventually jumping from a state to any other state, the Markov chain will have a unique stationary distribution. It can also be shown that the target distribution is the stationary distribution of the Markov chain generated by the Metropolis algorithm (see Gelman & Gelman, 1995).

CONCLUDING REMARKS

In this chapter, we have attempted to provide an overview on Bayesian methods as applied to the field of Data Mining. In doing so, we have deliberately focused on reviewing the most relevant concepts, techniques, and practical issues. Over the last few years, Bayesian data mining has emerged as a prominent modelling and data analysis approach from which both academicians and practitioners can benefit. We envisage that Bayesian Data Mining and Knowledge Discovery will continue to expand in the future, both from a theoretical and a practical applications perspective.

ENDNOTES

[1]   The complete dataset can be found at Delve, a machine learning repository and testing environment located at the University of Toronto, Department of Computer Science. The URL is http://www.cs.toronto.edu/~delve.

[2]   The algorithm was coded using S-Plus. The programs are available from the authors.

[3]   Recent research has established that the model is not limited to acyclic graphs. Direct or indirect cyclic causality may be included in BBNs.

[4]   Once again, the example has been created for illustrative purposes and should not be taken too seriously.

[5]   The philosophical debate regarding this approach has been going on for centuries. William of Occam (14th century) was one of the first thinkers to discuss the question of whether simpler hypotheses are better than complicated ones. For this reason, this approach goes by the name of *Occam's razor.*

REFERENCES

Cox, R. T. (1946). Probability, frequency and reasonable expectation. *American Journal of Physics*, 14:1-13.

DeGroot, M. (1986). *Probability and statistics.* Reading, MA: Addison Wesley.

Dougherty, J., Kohavi, R., & Sahami, M. (1995). Supervised and unsupervised discretization of continuous features, In A. Prieditis and S. Russell (eds.), *Proceedings of the Twelfth International Conference on Machine Learning*, pp. 194—202. San Francisco, CA: Morgan Kaufmann.

Friedman, N. & Goldzmidt, M. (1999). Learning Bayesian networks with local structure. In M.I. Jordan (ed.), *Learning in graphical models.* Cambridge, MA: MIT Press.

Friedman, N., Geiger, D.,& Goldszmidt, M. (1997). Bayesian network classifiers. *Machine Learning,* 29:131-163.

Gelman, A., Carlin, J., Stern, H., & Rubin, D. (1995). *Bayesian Data Analysis*, Chapman & Hall/CRC.

Heckerman, D., Geiger, D., & Chickering, D. (1994). Learning Bayesian networks: The combination of knowledge and statistical data. Technical Report MSR-TR-94-09, Microsoft Research.

Janes, E.T. (1996). *Probability theory: The logic of science*, Fragmentary Edition. Available online at: http://bayes.wustl.edu/etj/prob.html.

Joachims, T. (1996). A probabilistic analysis of the Rocchio algorithm with TFIDF for text categorization. Technical Report CMU-CS-96-118, School of Computer Science, Carnegie Mellon University, March.

Kohavi, R., Becker, B., & Sommerfield, D. (1997). Improving simple Bayes. *ECML-97: Proceedings of the Ninth European Conference on Machine Learning.*

Lam, W. & Bachus, F. (1994). Learning Bayesian networks: An approach based on the MDL principle *Computational Intelligence* 10(3), 269-293.

Lauritzen, S. L. & Spiegelhalter. D. J. (1988). Local computations with probabilities on graphical structures and their application to expert systems. Journal of the Royal Statistical Society, Series *B,* 50(2):157-224.

Mitchell. T. (1997). *Machine learning.* New York: McGraw-Hill.

Neal, R. M. (1993). *Probabilistic inference using Markov Chain Monte Carlo Methods.* Technical Report CRG-TR-93-1, Department of Computer Science, University of Toronto.

Pearl, J. (1988). *Probabilistic reasoning in intelligent systems: Networks of plausible inference.* San Mateo, CA: Morgan Kaufmann.

Ramoni, M. & Sebastiani, P. (1999). Bayesian methods for intelligent data analysis. In M. Berthold & D.J. Hand, (eds.), *Intelligent data analysis: An introduction.* New York: Springer-Verlag.

Rodriguez, C. (1999). *An introduction to Markov Chain Monte Carlo. Available online at:* http://omega.albany.edu:8008/cdocs/.

Sivia, D. (1996). *Data analysis: A Bayesian tutorial.* Oxford, UK: Oxford Science Publications.

Van der Gaag, L.C. (1996). Bayesian belief networks: Odds and ends. Technical Report UU-Cs-1996-14, Utretch University.

Witten, I. & Frank, E. (2000). *Data mining: Practical machine learning tools and techniques with Java implementations.* San Mateo, CA: Morgan Kaufmann.

Chapter XII

Mining Free Text for Structure

Vladimir A. Kulyukin
Utah State University, USA

Robin Burke
DePaul University, USA

ABSTRACT

Knowledge of the structural organization of information in documents can be of significant assistance to information systems that use documents as their knowledge bases. In particular, such knowledge is of use to information retrieval systems that retrieve documents in response to user queries. This chapter presents an approach to mining free-text documents for structure that is qualitative in nature. It complements the statistical and machine-learning approaches, insomuch as the structural organization of information in documents is discovered through mining free text for content markers left behind by document writers. The ultimate objective is to find scalable data mining (DM) solutions for free-text documents in exchange for modest knowledge-engineering requirements. The problem of mining free text for structure is addressed in the context of finding structural components of files of frequently asked questions (FAQs) associated with many USENET newsgroups. The chapter describes a system that mines FAQs for structural components. The chapter concludes with an outline of possible future trends in the structural mining of free text.

INTRODUCTION

When the manager of a mutual fund sits down to write an update of the fund's prospectus, he does not start his job from scratch. He knows what the fund's shareholders expect to see in the document and arranges the information accordingly. An inventor, ready to register his idea with the Patent and Trademark Office of the U.S. Department of Commerce, writes it up in accordance with the rules specifying the format of patent submissions. A researcher who wants to submit a paper to a scientific conference must be aware of the format specifications set up by the conference committee. Each of these examples suggests that domains of human activity that produce numerous documents are likely to have standards specifying how information must be presented in them.

Such standards, or presentation patterns, are a matter of economic necessity; documents whose visual structure reflects their logical organization are much easier to mine for information than unconstrained text. The ability to find the needed content in the document by taking advantage of its structural organization allows the readers to deal with large quantities of data efficiently. For example, when one needs to find out if a person's name is mentioned in a book, one does not have to read it from cover to cover; going to the index section is a more sensible solution.

Knowledge of the structural organization of information in documents[1] can be of significant assistance to information systems that use documents as their knowledge bases. In particular, such knowledge is of use to information retrieval systems (Salton & McGill, 1983) that retrieve documents in response to user queries. For example, an information retrieval system can match a query against the structural components of a document, e.g., sections of an article, and make a retrieval decision based on some combination of matches. More generally, knowledge of the structural organization of information in documents makes it easier to mine those documents for information.

The advent of the World Wide Web and the Internet have resulted in the creation of millions of documents containing unstructured, structured, and semi-structured data. Consequently, research on the automated discovery of structural organization of information in documents has come to the forefront of both information retrieval and natural language processing (Freitag, 1998; Hammer, Garcia-Molina, Cho, Aranha, & Crespo, 1997; Hsu & Chang, 1999; Jacquemin & Bush, 2000; Kushmerick, Weld, & Doorenbos, 1997). Most researchers adhere to numerical approaches of machine learning and information retrieval. Information retrieval approaches view texts as sets of terms, each of which exhibits some form of frequency distribution. By tracking the frequency distributions of terms, one can attempt to partition the document into smaller chunks, thus claiming to have discovered a structural organization of information in a given document. Machine-learning approaches view texts as objects with features whose combinations can be automatically learned by inductive methods.

Powerful as they are, these approaches to mining documents for structure have two major drawbacks. First, statistical computations are based on the idea of statistical significance (Moore & McCabe, 1993). Achieving statistical significance requires large quantities of data. The same is true for machine-learning approaches that require large training sets to reliably learn needed regularities. Since many documents are small in size, the reliable discovery of their structural components using numerical methods alone is problematic. Second, numerical approaches ignore the fact that document writers leave explicit markers of content structure in document texts. The presence of these markers in document texts helps the reader digest the information contained in the document. If these markers are ignored, document texts become much harder to navigate and under-stand.

This chapter presents an approach to mining free-text documents for structure that is qualitative in nature. It complements the statistical and machine-learning approaches insomuch as the structural organization of information in documents is discovered through mining free text for content markers left behind by document writers[2]. The ultimate objective is to find scalable data-mining solutions for free-text documents in exchange for modest knowledge-engineering requirements. The approach is based on the following assumptions:

- **Economic Necessity**. The higher the demand for a class of documents, the greater the chances that the presentation of information in those documents adheres to a small set of rigid standards. Mutual fund prospectuses, 10-Q forms, and USENET files of frequently asked questions (FAQs) are but a few examples of document classes that emerged due to economic necessity and whose formats were standardized by consumer demand.

- **Texts As Syntactic Objects**. As a source of information, text can be viewed as a syntactic object whose structural organization obeys certain constraints. It is often possible to find the needed content in a document by using the structural organization of its text.

- **Presentation Consistency**. Document writers are consistent in their presentation patterns. They do not change the chosen pattern within a single document. Many of them stick with the same pattern from document to document.

- **Presentation Similarity**. The logical components of a document that have the same semantic functionality are likely to be marked in the same or similar fashion within a presentation pattern. For example, many document writers tend to mark headers, tables, sections, bibliographies, etc., in the same or similar ways in document texts.

These assumptions form a theoretical basis of the approach. Collectively, they act as guidelines for researchers and developers who are interested in building free-text data-mining tools for individual domains. The rest of the chapter illustrates how these assumptions were applied to mine newsgroups' expertise.

The rest of the chapter is organized as follows. The next section provides the necessary background and a review of relevant literature. The following three sections constitute the main thrust of the chapter. First, we describe the problem of mining newsgroups' expertise for answers to frequently asked questions. Second, we state our solution to the problem of mining free text for structure. The problem is addressed in the context of finding structural components of FAQs associated with many USENET newsgroups. Third, we describe an evaluation of our mining approach. In the last two sections, we outline possible future trends in mining text for structure and present our conclusions.

RELATED WORK

In the context of data mining, structural mining of text is the task of partitioning text into components, each of which contains a specific kind of information. For example, if it is known that a given HTML text is a home page, one can design strategies to mine the text for the owner's name, address, e-mail, etc. The ever-increasing numbers of electronically available documents have intensified research on mining text for structure. Texts are typically divided into three broad categories: free, structured, and semi-structured.

If we view texts as islands of content, then free texts can be viewed as content islands without any road maps. To discover a road map in a free text requires a certain amount of data mining through parsing, statistical analysis, or machine learning. Many USENET FAQs and journal articles are good examples of free texts.

Structured texts are information islands whose content is organized according to a specific road map. Relational databases are a good example of structured texts where all of the relations between textual entities, i.e., records, are known and can be readily obtained through well-defined queries. In effect, in a structured text most of the structural data mining has been done.

Semi-structured texts cluster around the borderline between free and structured. Generally speaking, a semi-structured text offers more structure than a free text but less than a structured one. HTML pages are a good example of semi-structured texts. While they offer a standard set of tags that point to the structural organization of information in them, they do not specify the types of information that the tags can label. For example, an HTML list can contain names of people, phone numbers, top stories of the day, etc.

Current research efforts in structural text mining combine techniques of machine learning, natural language processing, and information retrieval. Many machine-learning approaches to text mining are based on the ideas of inductive learning (Mitchell, 1997). The problem of mining text for structure is cast in terms of taking a set of text instances representative of the general population of texts to be mined and extracting sets of rules from those instances. Approaches that use natural language processing (Allen, 1987) typically view texts as objects having a structure that can be discovered through parsing. The problem is stated in terms of a set of constraints that a given domain of texts exhibits and a means to use those constraints in finding text structure. Finally, information-retrieval approaches are based on the idea that texts are intellectual artifacts that consist of words related to each other semantically in a number of complex ways. The intellectual process of producing texts incidentally leaves behind simple statistical regularities (Hearst, 1997). Capturing those regularities through statistical analysis allows one to arrive at the structural organization of information in the texts.

Many authors are concerned with the problem of extracting database-like structures from Web pages, in effect reverse-engineering the process of database-backed Web page generation. Hammer et al. (1997) present a configurable tool for extracting semi-structured data from a set of HTML pages, given a declarative specification of where the data of interest is located. Creating such a specification can be a tedious process, however, and may require an extensive knowledge-engineering effort. The machine-learning approach to this problem has been labeled "wrapper induction" (Kushmerick et al., 1997). The extraction procedure, or wrapper, for a specific resource is learned from a set of representative pages from that resource. Several classes of wrappers have been identified that are both useful and efficiently learnable.

Hsu and Chang (1999) apply several aspects of automata theory to the problem of constructing information extractors for mining semi-structured documents. By semi-structured documents the authors mean HTML pages. The main argument of the proposed research framework rests on the idea that programming information extractors manually is not feasible due to the amount and degree of variation in information placed on the World Wide Web on a daily basis. The authors propose a machine-learning approach to the automated construction of such extractors. The approach is based on learning an extractor from a few examples of information extraction cases.

Hsu and Chang (1999) describe a formalism that represents extractors as Finite-State Transducers (FST). A finite-state transducer is a variation of a finite-state automaton (Hopcroft & Ullman, 1979). The input document is assumed to be tokenized before it is given to a finite-state transducer. The authors distinguish two types of transducers: single-pass and multi-pass. A single-pass transducer scans the text only once. A multi-pass transducer scans the text many times, each time focusing only on a specific type of object to extract. The ultimate goal of the approach proposed by Hsu and Chang (1999) is the automated construction of extractors from a set of training examples. However, the reported empirical evaluations assume that the space of possible graph structures, i.e., finite-state automata, is restricted or that the structure is given to the learner in advance.

Freitag (1998) also casts information extraction as a machine-learning problem. It is argued that one solution to that problem is relational learning. Relational learning represents hypotheses as sets of if-then rules. Because sets of if-then statements can be viewed as programs in a logic programming language, such as PROLOG, relational learning is often called Inductive Logic Programming (Mitchell, 1997). Freitag describes a general-purpose top-down relational learning algorithm for information extraction called "SRV." SRV takes as input a set of token-oriented features that encode most of the domain-specific information. For example, they may encode a standard set of questions that can be asked of someone's home page, such as the owner's name, affiliation, e-mail,

Figure 1: How FAQ Finder works.

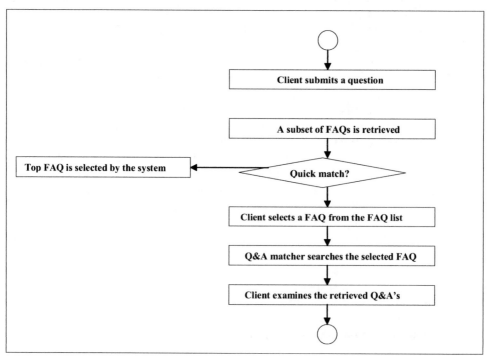

etc. An answer to each question is assumed to be a text fragment from that home page. Thus, the algorithm solves the problem of finding the best unbroken fragment of text that answers a question from a given set of questions. One of the definite advantages of the SRV algorithm is that it makes no assumption about document structure. Instead, structural information is supplied as input to the system. As a consequence, an argument is made that SRV may be better suited for new domains than other systems. The author reports a successful evaluation of an SRV-based tool in the domain of university course and research project pages. A way is suggested to make the tool Web-aware by extending it with HTML-specific features.

Jacquemin and Bush (2000) present a tool for the acquisition of named entities, e.g., names of companies, from textual sources. The authors' approach combines lexical indices with formatting instructions. Lexical indices are discourse markers, and formatting instructions are HTML tags. The system includes three shallow parsers for mining HTML texts for specific structures such as lists, enumerations, and anchors. The named entities are extracted from the found structures by analyzing discourse markers and HTML tags. While Jacquemin and Bush do not use any machine-learning techniques, their approach is similar in spirit to the approach advocated in Kushmerick et al. (1997) in that it advocates combining structural information about documents with linguistic patterns. The system described by Jacquemin and Bush focuses exclusively on HTML documents and does not tag anything. Its sole purpose is to build lists of named entities found in specified HTML pages.

Hearst (1997) and Hearst and Plaunt (1993) advocate a classic information-retrieval approach to mining documents for structure. The approach is called TextTiling. TextTiling is a method for partitioning full-length text documents into coherent multi-paragraph units. The units form a sequence of subtopical passages. The TextTiling algorithm assumes that a document moves from topic to topic. Each topic has its own vocabulary associated with it. When one topic changes to a different topic, the vocabulary changes, too. Consequently, sharp changes in the vocabulary signify boundaries between the elements of a document structure. The algorithm completely ignores all lexical markers provided by the document authors.

MINING NEWSGROUPS' EXPERTISE

Over the past several years, the Internet has seen a proliferation of newsgroups. A newsgroup is started by individuals interested in a topic, e.g., caffeine or cars. These individuals, who are experts on the topic, want to make their expertise publicly available, which they accomplish through the newsgroup's FAQ.

Looking for Answers to Transient Questions

Newsgroup-based expertise distribution works for people with a stable interest in the newsgroup's topic. However, many people have more transient interests. Typically, such transient interests are caused by questions whose answers are beyond an information seeker's area of expertise. There are three types of problems that information seekers with transient interests confront: insufficient knowledge, insufficient time, and privacy.

Let us illustrate these problems with an example. Consider a college student, who wants to write a report on the therapeutic effects of caffeine. The student may not know about the coffee newsgroup. This lack of knowledge may cause the student to spend much time searching for the newsgroup. Even if the student already knows about the newsgroup, his interest in finding an answer to his question does not necessarily mean that he is interested in subscribing to the newsgroup and subsequently reading a dozen messages a day, most of which have nothing to do with his question.

Even if the student knows about the newsgroup's FAQ, the student may not have the time to browse for an answer. This is because many newsgroups have FAQs containing hundreds and sometimes thousands of question-answer pairs (Q&A's) and provide no search or browsing tools to mine those Q&A's.

Finally, the student may be concerned about privacy. If he posts a question to the newsgroup, his name will be read by hundreds, possibly thousands, of subscribers. Some newsgroups are known for their inflammatory nature and are not friendly to novices or casual posters.

These problems signify a need for a system that provides Web and Internet users with a gateway to the newsgroups' expertise. Users who do not know a relevant newsgroup should not spend much time searching for it. Users with transient interests in the newsgroup's topic should not have to make unwanted commitments to obtain answers.

Outline of a Solution

FAQ Finder was developed to meet this need for a gateway to the newsgroups' expertise (Burke et al., 1997). The question-answering task is conceptualized as the retrieval of answers to similar questions answered previously. To answer a new question is to choose a suitable Q&A collection, i.e., a set of FAQs, and to retrieve from it the answer to a similar question. There is a substantial literature on FAQ Finder (Burke, Hammond, & Cooper, 1996; Burke, Hammond, & Young, 1996; Kulyukin, 1998a, 1998b). Here we only offer an outline of the system, because it grounds our free-text mining task in a proper context.

FAQ Finder answers natural language questions from a collection of 602 Usenet FAQs. Given a question, FAQ Finder:
- finds a small set of FAQs relevant to the question;
- displays short descriptions of those FAQs to the user; and,
- retrieves a small number of Q&A's relevant to the question from the chosen FAQ.

Figure 1 shows FAQ Finder's flowchart. The submitted question is mapped to a set of FAQs that are potentially relevant to the question (FAQ retrieval). A FAQ from the list is chosen either by the client or by the system. For example, if the client chooses the quick match option, the top FAQ is selected automatically by the system. The FAQ is searched for answers to the question. A list of relevant Q&A's, if such are found, is returned to the user (Q&A retrieval).

The FAQ retrieval is accomplished by the vector space retrieval model (Salton & McGill, 1983). Each FAQ is turned into a vector of term weights in a multidimensional vector space whose dimensions are the terms found in all of the FAQs in the collection.

Terms are computed from the free texts of FAQs. Common words, such as "and," "to," or "from," are removed. The remaining words become terms through *stemming*, a vocabulary normalization procedure that reduces word forms to their stems (Frakes & Baeza-Yates, 1992). For example, "information," "informed," "informant," and "inform-ing" are all reduced to "inform."

As a simple example, consider a collection of three FAQs, F_1, F_2, and F_3, where each FAQ contains three terms: T_1, T_2, and T_3. We have a three-dimensional vector space, in which each vector corresponds to a FAQ and consists of three term weights. A term's weight is a ratio of the term's frequency in the FAQ and the number of FAQs in which it occurs at least once. Each weight is a coordinate along the dimension of the corresponding term. A user's question is turned into a vector in the FAQ vector space. The similarity between the question vector and a FAQ vector is computed as the cosine of the angle between them. Thus, the smaller the angle, the more relevant the FAQ is to the question.

The Q&A retrieval begins when a FAQ is selected to be searched for answers. The Q&A Retriever computes the similarity score between the question and each Q&A in the FAQ. The score combines a statistical metric and a semantic metric.

To compute the statistical similarity, the question is turned into a term weight vector in the space of the selected FAQ. The cosine similarity score is computed between the question vector and each Q&A vector in the FAQ.

The semantic similarity is based on recognizing semantic relations among the words of the user's question and the words of a Q&A's question. Such relations are found through WordNet®, a semantic network of English words and phrases developed at Princeton University (Miller, 1995). For example, if the user's question contains "com-puter" and the Q&A's question contains "machine," the two questions are similar insomuch as "computer" is connected to "machine" via the *isa* link in WordNet's noun network (Kulyukin, 1998b). More details on the semantic and statistical similarities are provided in the Appendix.

MINING FAQS FOR STRUCTURE

The operation of FAQ Finder is based on the assumption that a FAQ is a sequence of Q&A's. In reality, however, the system must first find the Q&A's in the free text of the FAQ. Neither retrieval of answers nor their indexing is possible unless the system knows which text regions are answers and which are questions.

One may think that identifying Q&A's is not a serious problem. A typical argument runs as follows. Since questions end in a question mark, it should be possible to use a regular expression matcher that retrieves all of the sentences that end with question marks.

There are two flaws with this argument. First, it assumes that one knows how to segment free text into sentences. But, while the identification of sentence boundaries may be feasible in small domains with highly constrained texts, it remains a formidable challenge for free-text processors that go against large heterogeneous corpora (Charniak, 1997; Daniels & Rissland, 1995; Palmer & Hearst, 1994). Second, many questions in FAQs do not end in question marks, while many answers contain questions that do. Thus, even if it were possible to segment free text into sentences, simplistic regular expression approaches are too noisy to be useful (Kulyukin, Hammond, & Burke, 1996).

Exploiting Regularities in FAQ Structure

Finding Q&A's would be a serious obstacle, were it not for the fact that FAQs are structured free texts. Consider, for example, the following excerpt from the caffeine FAQ given in Figure 2.

The experts who wrote this FAQ used several lexical cues to mark each Q&A. Each question is marked with two Arabic numerals separated by a dot and followed by a right parenthesis, e.g., "1.2)." Each answer is separated from its question with another lexical cue, i.e., a line of hyphens. We refer to such cues as *lexical markers* or simply as *markers*. We have compiled the following list of the most frequent marker types found in FAQs:

- **Alpha Markers.** For example, "Q:", "A:", "Subject:", "Section:"
- **Alphanumeric Markers.** For example, "[1-0]", "1)", "10.2a", "VIII."
- **Symbolic Markers.** For example, "************", "===============".

Figure 2: A sample from a FAQ about caffeine.

> 1.1) Chemically speaking, what is caffeine?
> ---
>   Caffeine is an alkaloid. There are numerous compounds called
>   alkaloids...
> 1.2) Is it true that tea has no caffeine?
> ---
>   Caffeine is sometimes called "theine" when it's in tea...

Lexical markers are used to introduce structural regularity into FAQs. Structural regularities benefit the experts, i.e., FAQ writers, because they enable easy and fast maintenance of online expertise. They benefit the FAQ readers, because they help them find the needed content quickly.

Marker Sequences

Lexical markers arrange themselves into *marker sequences*. For example, "1.1), 1.2)'" is a sequence of two alphanumeric markers, i.e., markers that contain both numbers and characters. The last marker of a sequence is referred to as its *head marker*. An empty sequence has an empty head marker. When a new marker is added to a sequence, the sequence's head marker is said to be *extended* by the added marker. For example, the head marker of "1.1), 1.2)," which is "1.2)," can be extended on "1.3)."

The presence of these sequences suggests a way to build a FAQ parsing system to mine the free texts of FAQs for structural components, i.e., question-answer pairs, tables of contents, and bibliographies. The parser spots marker sequences that point to structural components and tracks the sequences in the FAQ's text, labeling the elements of the component along the way. The advantage of this approach is that mining for Q&A's requires no deep natural language processing (NLP), which is known to be a very hard task (Allen, 1987). All the parser needs to know is how the marker sequences behave in the FAQs.

Tracking Marker Sequences

An analysis of FAQs reveals that marker sequences obey a small number of constraints. The presence of such constraints is implied by the four assumptions stated in the introduction section. Since FAQ writers are interested in spreading their knowledge, they make sure that the knowledge is packaged in an easily digestible format. The constraints that we have found are as follows:

- **Lack of recursion**. Alphanumeric marker sequences do not recurse.

- **Fixed marker structure**. The structure of markers in a sequence remains the same.

- **Lack of criss-crossing**. A sequence does not cross another sequence if the latter has started before the former. This constraint applies only to symbolic sequences.

- **Proximity**. When two different sequences with the same marker structure can be extended on the same marker, only the sequence whose head marker is closer to the predicted marker is allowed to extend on it.

As an example of the non-recursiveness of marker sequences, consider the following pattern that occurs in numerous FAQs: "[1] ...[2] ...   [N]... [1] ..." The ellipses stand for pieces of free text. Since marker sequences do not recurse, the FAQ parser knows that a new sequence is started when it sees the second "[1]." This constraint enables the parser to determine when the FAQ's table of contents ends and the actual Q&A sequence begins.

As an example of the fixed marker structure constraint, consider "I) ... II) ... III) ... [4] ... IV) ..." When the parser detects "I)," it knows that the other markers of the sequence will have the same structure, i.e., a Roman numeral followed by a right parenthesis. Hence, it ignores "[4]" as belonging to another sequence or occurring as part of free text. The stability of marker structure allows the parser to track marker sequences in FAQs.

Another example of the fixed marker structure constraint is given in Figure 4, where the tab character is made visible. The parser ignores the first "<C>" marker, because it is not preceded by two tab characters, as are the other markers of the sequence. In other words, the two tabs that constitute the layout of the "<A> <B>" sequence allow us to ignore the first "<C>" marker as belonging to another sequence.

As an example of the criss-crossing constraint, consider the sequences in Figure 3. Here the crossing constraint forces the third "-" marker from above to start a new sequence, i.e., seq3. If it belonged to seq2, seq2 would have to cross seq1, which the constraint does not allow.

The proximity constraint simply says that the sequence always extends on the marker closest to its head marker.

Logical Map and Layout

FAQ writers frequently use markers in conjunction with layout. One way to compute the layout of a document is to digitize its text line by line according to a simple encoding scheme. The encoding scheme implemented in FAQ Minder treats each line of a document as a string. Each substring of the string is mapped into the integer denoting its length. The special layout characters like newline, tab, and space are mapped into the integers 1000, 2000, and 3000, respectively. This scheme works well, because all FAQs in our library have lines that are at most 100 characters long. Since the scheme uses only integers, it can be easily adjusted to other document formats with more characters per line.

The database of assertions about sequences detected in the text of a document is referred to as *the logical map of the document*. The presentation pattern of a document is determined by its logical map and its layout. As an example, consider the following chunk of text with the layout characters made visible given in Figure 5. The layout of the above text computed according to the above scheme is given in Figure 6. Part of the logical map of that text is offered in Figure 7. The symbols lsb, rsb and hphn stand for

Figure 3: Criss-crossing sequences.

```
< seq1 > **********************
< seq2 > - ..... text ......
< seq2 > - ..... text ......
< seq1 > **********************
< seq3 > - ..... text ......
< seq3 > - ..... text ......
< seq1 > **********************
```

Figure 4: Stable marker structure.

```
Tab Tab <A> ...
Tab Tab <B> ...
 <C> ...
Tab Tab <C> ...
Tab Tab <D>
Tab Tab <E>
Tab Tab <F>
```

Figure 5: Sample text.

```
<line 0> Tab Tab Space[1] first line.
<line 1> Newline
<line 2> Tab Tab Tab Space [1-0] second line.
<line 3> Newline
<line 4> Tab Tab Tab Space [1-1] third line.
<line 5> Newline
<line 6> Tab Tab Space [2] fourth line.
```

Figure 6: Layout of Figure 5.

```
2000 2000 3000 3 5 5
1000
2000 2000 2000 3000 5 6 5
1000
2000 2000 2000 3000 5 5 5
1000
2000 2000 3000 3 6 5.
```

Figure 7: Logical map of Figure 5.

```
(alphanum-sequence seq1)
(marker m1 seq1)
(marker m2 seq1)
(occurs-on-line m1 0)
(occurs-on-line m2 6)
(component m1 lsb 0)
(component m1 number 1)
(component m1 rsb 2)
```

left square bracket, right square bracket, and hyphen, respectively. The predicates used have the following semantics. The predicate *(alphanum-sequence s)* states that *s* is an alphanumeric sequence. The predicate *(marker m s)* states that *m* is a marker in a sequence *s*. The predicate *(occurs-on-line m n)* states that a marker *m* occurs on line number *n*. Finally, the predicate *(component m c n)* states that *c* is the *n*-th component of a marker *m*.

These databases are treated as sets of First-Order Predicate Calculus (FOPC) assertions. This format makes it straightforward to apply standard pattern matching and inference techniques well known in the Artificial Intelligence community (Norvig, 1992).

How FAQ Minder Works

FAQ Minder works in two modes: supervised and unsupervised. In the unsupervised mode, the system takes as input the text of a FAQ and mines it for structure on its own. The system deals with tables of contents, questions and answers, and bibliographies. Network headers and glossaries found at the beginning of many FAQs are not currently dealt with, because the current version of FAQ Finder does not utilize them during answer retrieval. In the supervised mode, FAQ Minder identifies the logical structure of a FAQ by interacting with the user through a set of simple interfaces.

Figure 8 shows FAQ Minder's architecture. The system consists of three modules: the sequence manager, the inference engine, and the tagger. The sequence manager reads the text of a document, builds its layout, and activates and deactivates marker sequences. The inference engine manages the logical map and the constraint satisfaction. The operation of the inference engine is based on a set of forward-chaining and backward-chaining rules (Norvig, 1992) about the logical structure of documents and

Figure 8: FAQ Minder's architecture.

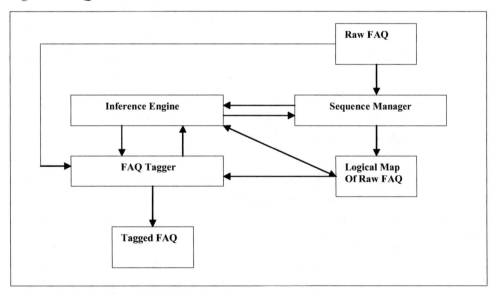

marker constraints. Old rules are adjusted and new rules are added as needed. Thus, documents from new domains can be processed by the system as long as the constraints are encoded as rules.

The tagger inserts tags into the text of the document given the document's layout and logical map. The current tag set consists of six tags: ":QUE," ":ANS," ":TOC," ":TOC-ITEM," ":BIB," ":BIB-ITEM." The ":QUE" tag is put at the beginning and the end of a question. The ":ANS" tag is put at the beginning and end of an answer. The ":TOC" tag is put at the beginning and end of a table of contents. The ":TOC-ITEM" is put at the beginning and end of an item in the table of contents. The ":BIB" and ":BIB-ITEM" tags are used in the same fashion for bibliographies. To prevent any possibility of symbol clashes, the tags are extended with randomly generated sequences of characters and numbers, e.g., ":QUE-a12b34." Once such a sequence is generated, it is appended at the end of each tag used in a given FAQ.

FAQs are read line by line. After a line is read, the sequence manager computes its layout, adds it to the document layout, and gives the currently active marker sequence a chance to examine the contents of the line. The manager distinguishes two types of marker sequences: *active* and *inactive*. An active sequence is started when a marker is recognized in the text. A sequence remains active as long as any markers found in the read line can extend it. When no found marker can extend the active sequence, it becomes inactive. Thus, there can be at most one active sequence, but potentially many inactive sequences.

The inference engine is used heavily by the sequence manager in deciding whether the currently active sequence can be extended on a marker found in the current line. To allow a marker to extend the active sequence, the marker and the sequence must satisfy at least one rule governing extension. For example, one of the backward-chaining sequence extension rules states that a marker extends a sequence if all of the following conditions are satisfied: the marker structure of the sequence's head marker is the same as the marker structure of the found marker; the layout of the sequence's head marker is the same as the layout of the found marker; and the found marker occurs on a line whose number is greater than the line number of the sequence's head marker. In other words, this backward-chaining rule is written as follows:

```
(<= (extends ?m ?s)
    (head-marker ?m1 ?s)
    (same-marker-structure ?m1 ?m)
    (same-layout ?m1 ?m)
    (occurs-on-line ?m ?ln)
    (occurs-on-line ?m1 ?ln1)
    (< ?ln1 ?ln))
```

The <= sign that starts the rule states that this is a backward-chaining rule. All backward-chaining rules have one consequent and at least one antecedent. Each backward-chaining rule has the following syntax: (<= <conseq> <ante1> ... <ante-n>). The semantics of a backward-chaining rule are that in order to show that the consequent is true, it must be shown that each antecedent is true. The forward-chaining rules are defined in a similar fashion, except that inference proceeds from antecedents to consequents. Each forward-chaining rule has at most one antecedent and at least one

Figure 9: Layout change.

```
<Tab> <Tab> [10] Where can I get APL software?
[11] Free Packages.
<Tab> <Tab> [12] APL software guidelines.
```

consequent, and has the following syntax: (=> <ante> <conseq1> ... <conseq-n>). The semantics of a forward-chaining rule are that if the antecedent is shown to be true, all of the consequents are asserted in the database. The question mark in front of a symbol states that that symbol is a variable that can have different bindings at run time, i.e., when the rule is applied. For example, in the above backward-chaining rule, the variables ?m and ?s are bound to the name of a marker and the name of a sequence, respectively.

At the beginning of the mining process, there are no active or inactive sequences. If a sequence recognizes a marker, it checks if the marker matches the layout of the previously recognized markers. The marker is ignored unless there is a layout match. When the sequence is finished with the line, it sends the sequence manager a message about its findings. If the sequence has recognized a marker and does not violate any constraints(which the inference engine checks against the logical map built thus far), the sequence is permitted to make the marker its current head marker and make the appropriate modifications in the logical map. If a constraint violation is inferred, the sequence manager puts the sequence on the list of inactive sequences.

After the active sequences have examined the line and failed, the sequence manager lets the inactive sequences, if there are any, do the same. This second chance heuristic has its empirical justification in the fact that some marker sequences start early in the document, become inactive because of other sequences, and resurface in the middle or at the end of the document.

After the layout and the logical map of the document have been computed, the tagger uses them to tag the text of the document. The tagger is allowed to interact with the inference engine, because it may need to do some additional inferences. The end result is the text of the FAQ whose logical components are tagged.

FAQ Minder functions as the front-end of FAQ Finder's indexing mechanism. Each FAQ is first mined for its structural components. Once the structural components of the FAQ are found and tagged, the FAQ is given to FAQ Finder for further indexing. The current implementation of FAQ Finder combines scalable, knowledge-intensive NLP techniques with numerical approaches of information retrieval. Thus, each question-answer pair in a tagged FAQ is indexed in terms of its question and its answer. The indexing of questions is done so that at run time FAQ Finder can compute the semantic similarity between the terms in a submitted question and the terms in every question in the FAQ. The statistical similarity is supported through indexing each found Q&A pair as a document in a vector space of Q&A's in a given FAQ.

EVALUATION

We have tested FAQ Minder on 100 FAQs. FAQ Minder's task was to identify tables of contents, question-answer pairs, and bibliographies. All in all, FAQ Minder had to identify 2,399 items. When FAQ Minder and a human judge were in agreement on an item, the item was said to be completely recognized. When FAQ Minder identified part of an item, the item was said to be partially recognized. When FAQ Minder wrongly tagged a chunk of text, that chunk of text was referred to as a false positive. The items identified by a human judge but missed by FAQ Minder were referred to as unrecognized.

Of 2,399 items, 1,943 items were completely recognized, 70 items were partially recognized, 81 were considered as false positives, and 305 items were unrecognized. In percentage terms, FAQ Minder completely recognized 81% of items, partially recognized 3%, wrongly tagged 3.4%, and failed to identify 12.6%.

We identified several causes of failure while analyzing the results of the experiments. The most prominent among them was what we call "sudden layout changes due to typos." In other words, the layout between two consecutive markers in a sequence was different due to a typo. As an example, consider the sequence in Figure 9 with the layout characters made visible. The markers "[10]," "[11]," and "[12]" clearly belong to the same sequence. Yet, because the layout of the "[11]" marker is different from the layout of the "[10]" marker, the sequence is prematurely terminated at "[10]."

We attributed the second cause of failure to typos in markers themselves. Consider the following example:

5) Perl books.
7) Perl software.

The current rules of marker extension do not allow the system to extend the "5)" marker on the "7)" marker.

Finally, we found markers for which the system had no rules of extension. For instance, we discovered that some FAQ writers use Roman numerals in conjunction with letters and Arabic numerals, e.g. "III.1.a)." FAQ Minder could not handle such cases.

These failures suggest several directions for future research. The first direction is to introduce some error recovery into the system. Since the typos are a norm rather than an exception, the system should have a coherent way to deal with them. The marker typo failures can be handled through a simulation mechanism. Sometimes a marker is found whose structure is consistent with the structure of the previous markers in the active sequence, but the sequence's head cannot be extended to the found marker. In such cases, the sequence manager can compute all of the possible extensions of the head marker and see if any of those extensions can be extended to the found marker. For example, if the head marker of the active sequence is "[5]" and the found marker is "[7]," the sequence manager can simulate the extension of "[5]" to "[6]" and then verify that "[6]" can be extended to "[7]."

The layout typo failures exemplified in Figure 9 can be handled by the same simulation mechanism, with one exception. After the sequence manager verifies that one of the possible extensions can be extended to the found marker, it then tries to find it in the text of the FAQ between the line with the current head marker and the line with the found marker. If the marker is found, possibly with a different layout, the sequence manager integrates it into the sequence. This strategy would allow the sequence manager to integrate the marker "[11]" into the sequence although the layout of "[11]" is different.

The second direction is to give FAQ Minder a limited ability to process natural language phrases. Many FAQ writers state explicitly that a table of contents, a glossary, or a bibliography is about to begin by using the following phrases: "Table of Contents," "List of Topics," "The following questions are answered below," etc. If FAQ Minder can recognize such phrases, it can assume that the sequence that follows marks the table of contents, the glossary, the topic list, etc. Toward this end, we have specified a number of the most common ways in which people can say that the table of contents is about to start. We have run our small program on 150 FAQs. The program correctly recognized such sentences in 111 FAQs.

The third research direction involves the supervised mode of FAQ Minder. In the supervised mode, FAQ Minder displays its progress through the text of a FAQ in a simple graphical user interface. As the system goes through the text of the FAQ, it highlights different FAQ components as soon as it detects them. For example, when the beginning of a table of contents is detected, the system informs the user that it has started tracking the table of contents. The user then has the opportunity to verify that the system has made a correct decision or tell the system that its decision is wrong.

The supervised mode requires little inference on the part of the system. However, it requires a large time commitment on the part of the user. Our conjecture here is that ultimately a system that recognizes its own limitations and overcomes them by asking the user intelligent questions saves the user more time than a completely independent system whose work requires laborious verification.

FUTURE TRENDS

We believe that text-based data mining will continue to evolve primarily in three directions: machine learning, natural language processing, and statistical analysis. A promising research direction seems to be a combination of natural language processing and machine learning. This is due to the fact that in many domains documents have a clearly recognizable structure that can be either learned from examples or encoded in a system of rules for parsing. Once that structure is found, its components can be mined for content with restricted natural language processing techniques.

Our work on FAQ Minder is a step in this research direction. Viewed abstractly, FAQ Minder is a rule-based document parser. The system presents a domain-dependent approach to free-text data mining. The rules that the system uses are domain-dependent and manually encoded. However, this need not be the case. These rules may well be learned automatically through a machine-learning approach. The trick here is how much manual knowledge engineering the machine-learning approach requires. Although many machine-learning approaches exhibit impressive learning rates and results, they require a domain theory that is either explicitly given to the learning algorithm or implicitly encoded in the way learning is done. Sometimes it is more practical to encode the rules manually than to first represent a domain theory and then wait for the learner to give you the rules automatically.

Statistical analysis is gaining prominence in text-based data mining due to the increasing availability of large text corpora. The corpora, due to their sheer volume, allow statistical techniques to achieve statistically significant results. In recent years, there has been a resurgence in research on statistical methods in natural language processing (Brill & Mooney, 1997). These methods employ techniques that aim to automatically extract linguistic knowledge from natural language corpora rather than require the system developer to do the knowledge engineering manually. While the initial results of the corpora-based text mining have been promising, most of the effort has been focused on very low-level tasks such as part-of-speech tagging, text segmentation, and syntactic parsing (Charniak, 1997), which suggests that some amount of domain-dependent knowledge engineering may well be mandatory. One exception to these low-level tasks is the research reported by Ng and Zelle (1997), who apply some corpus-based techniques to the problems of word-sense disambiguation and semantic parsing. But, while the reported results are encouraging, they are tentative.

Another prominent trend in textual data mining that relies heavily on statistical techniques is automatic thesaurus construction (Srinivasan, 1992). Thesauri are widely used in both indexing and retrieving textual documents. Indexers use thesauri to select the most appropriate terms to describe content; retrievers use thesauri to formulate better queries. For example, if a submitted query does not return acceptable results, the terms of the query can be extended with related terms from a thesaurus. Since manual thesaurus construction is extremely labor intensive, it is almost guaranteed that future research efforts will focus on completely or partially automating thesaurus construction. In automatic thesaurus construction, the domain is defined in terms of the available documents. The basic idea is to apply certain statistical procedures to identify important terms and, if possible, relationships among them. A promising direction of research in this area of text data mining is the identification of non-trivial semantic relationships. While statistical methods are good at detecting broad semantic relationships such as genus-species or association (Bookstein & Swanson, 1974), they alone are not sufficient for more subtle relationships such as part-whole, taxonomy, synonymy, and antonymy.

Question answering from large online collections is an area that uses many textual data-mining techniques. Given a collection of documents and a collection of questions, a question-answering system can be viewed as mining the document texts for answers to the questions. In contrast to standard information retrieval systems, e.g., search engines, question-answering systems are not allowed to return a full document or a set of documents in response to a question. The assumption here is that the user has no interest or time to sift through large texts looking for answers.

Question answering has recently achieved enough status and attracted enough research interest to be awarded a separate track at the annual Text Retrieval Conference (TREC) (Voorhees & Harman, 2000; Voorhees & Tice, 2000). A typical question-answering system requires short answers for short factual questions such as "Who is George Washington?" Most modern question-answering systems operate in two steps. Given a question, they first choose a small subset of the available documents that are likely to contain an answer to the submitted question and then mine each of those documents for a specific answer or a set of answers. Statistical means have been rather successful in narrowing questions to small collections of documents (Clarke, Cormack, & Lynam, 2001). However, they are not as successful at extracting the actual answers from the selected documents. As a system, FAQ Minder was built to address that very problem. More research into document structure and its interaction with document content is and will remain of great importance for question answering.

Information extraction is another emerging trend in textual data mining (Cardie, 1997). An information extraction system takes a free text as input and mines it for answers to a specified topic or domain of interest. The objective is to extract enough information about the topic of interest and encode that information in a format suitable for a database. Unlike in-depth NLP systems, information extractors do a cursory scan of the input text to identify potential areas of interest and then use more expensive text-processing techniques to mine those areas of interest for information. An example of an information extraction system is a system that constructs database records from news wires on mergers and acquisitions. Each news wire is turned into a set of slot-value pairs that specify who merged with whom, when, etc. One of the greatest challenges and research opportunities of information extraction is portability. Information extraction systems are very domain dependent. Currently, there are information extraction systems that analyze life insurance applications (Glasgow, Mandell, Binney, Ghemri, & Fisher, 1997) or summarize news wires on terrorist activities (MUC-3, 1991; MUC-4, 1992). These systems, however, use a lot of built-in knowledge from the domains in which they operate and are not easily portable to other domains. The main reason for using built-in knowledge lies in the nature of the task. The more domain-specific knowledge an information extractor has, the better it performs. The principal disadvantage is that the manual encoding of this knowledge is labor intensive and subject to errors. Thus, automating domain-specific knowledge acquisition is likely to be a promising direction of future research.

CONCLUSION

We examined the task of mining free-text electronic documents for structure. The task was examined in the context of the FAQ Minder system that does the structural mining of FAQs found in USENET newsgroups. The system finds the logical components of FAQs: tables of contents, questions, answers, and bibliographies. The found logical components of FAQs are used by FAQ Finder, a question-answering system.

The approach to mining free text for structure advocated in FAQ Minder is qualitative in nature. It is based on the assumption that documents in many domains adhere to a set of rigid structural standards. If those standards are known to a text-mining system, they can be successfully put to use for a variety of tasks, such as question answering or information extraction. This approach complements the numerical approaches insomuch as the structural organization of information in documents is discovered through mining free text for content markers left behind by document writers. The behavior of those markers is known to the system a priori.

We presented a number of alternative approaches to mining text for structure, of which the most prominent are the approaches based on machine-learning methods. What all of these approaches have in common is the assumption that there is some fixed structure, such as a set of database fields, whose contents are to be filled in with chunks of text derived from the text being processed. FAQs can be viewed as an example of this assumption, where there are slots for questions, answers, tables of contents, and bibliographies, and a minimal amount of surrounding context. However, FAQs are much closer to free text than HTML pages, which constitute the focus of most text-mining machine-learning systems.

The researchers who advocate machine-learning approaches to text mining often state that the manual encoding of rules is tedious and labor intensive. Consequently, machine-learning approaches are more promising, because they can learn the rules automatically. This argument has definite merits, but does not explain the full picture. In practice, all successful machine-learning approaches require a domain theory (Freitag, 1998), that must be encoded manually. Many machine-learning approaches also require that input data be represented in a specific way, effectively taking knowledge representation for granted. Thus, the promise of automation is never completely fulfilled.

Many text-oriented machine-learning techniques (Charniak, 1997; Ng & Zelle, 1997) are very powerful and promising. However, their main weakness is that they are created with no specific task in mind and do not easily yield to customization for specific domain-dependent problems. When this customization is feasible, it is effectively equivalent to manual knowledge engineering required in approaches similar to FAQ Minder's.

Numerical approaches in information retrieval offer yet another alternative to qualitative free-text mining. We presented one such approach called TextTiling (Hearst, 1997; Hearst & Plaunt, 1993). TextTiling was designed for large documents and large sections, containing enough word data for variances between topics to be statistically noticeable. This technique would probably not be effective in segmenting FAQ files or similar documents, since questions are one or two sentences and answers typically no more than 200 words.

Each approach presented in this chapter has its strengths and weaknesses. None of them solves the problem of free-text data-mining completely. Qualitative approaches, such as FAQ Minder's, produce good results but require manual knowledge engineering. Machine-learning methods can acquire complete data-mining models automatically but require domain theories and strict data formats. Information retrieval approaches do not require any knowledge engineering but cannot function without large text corpora. Hence, we believe that hybrid text-mining models are one of the most promising research directions in free-text data mining. A hybrid model is a model that requires a modest amount of knowledge engineering in exchange for scalable performance and acceptable results. The idea behind hybrid models is intuitively appealing: combine the relative strengths of the available alternatives, while minimizing their relative weaknesses.

ENDNOTES

[1]   We use the terms logical structure of documents and structural organization of information in documents interchangeably.

[2]   Since the approach presented in this chapter complements the existing approaches, it cannot be easily compared to them, because it is based on different assumptions. A comparison, by definition, is possible only among competing approaches.

ACKNOWLEDGMENTS

We would like to thank Kristian Hammond for his countless contributions to the FAQ Finder project. Kris was the founder of the FAQ Finder project, and deserves credit for putting together the original FAQ Finder team at the University of Chicago's Intelligent Information Laboratory. We would like to express our gratitude to Jay Budzik who contributed to the development of the FAQ Minder system. Steve Lytinen and Noriko Tomuro offered us many helpful comments.

REFERENCES

Allen, J. (1987). *Natural language understanding*. Menlo Park, CA: Benjamin/Cummings Publishing Company.

Bookstein, A. & Swanson, D. R. (1974). Probabilistic models for automatic indexing. *Journal of the American Society for Information Science*, 25(5), 312-318.

Brill, E. & Mooney, R. J. (1997). An overview of empirical natural language processing. *AI Magazine*, 18(4), 13-24.

Burke, R., Hammond, K., & Cooper, E. (1996). Knowledge-based information retrieval from semi-structured text. *Proceedings of the AAAI Workshop on Internet-Based Information Systems*. Madison, WI: AAAI Press, pp. 18-24.

Burke, R. D., Hammond, K. J., Kulyukin, V., Lytinen, S. L., Tomuro, N., & Schoenberg, S. (1997). Question answering from frequently asked question files: Experiences with the FAQ Finder System. *AI Magazine*, 18(2), 57-66.

Burke, R. D., Hammond, K. J., & Young, B. C. (1996). Knowledge-based navigation of complex information spaces. *Proceedings of the American Association for Artificial Intelligence Conference*. Madison, WI:AAAI Press, pp. 132-139.

Cardie, C. (1997). Empirical Methods in Information Extraction. *AI Magazine*, 18(4), 65-79.

Charniak, E. (1997). Statistical techniques for natural language parsing. *AI Magazine*, 18(4), 33-43.

Clarke, C., Cormack, G. V., & Lynam T. R. (2001-). Exploiting redundancy in question answering. *Proceedings of the Special Interest Group in Information Retrieval (ACM SIGIR) Conference*. New Orleans, USA, ACM Press, pp. 358-365.

Daniels, J. & Rissland, E. (1995). A case-based approach to intelligent information retrieval. *Proceedings of the Special Interest Group in Information Retrieval (ACM SIGIR) Conference, Seattle*, ACM Press, pp. 317-324.

Frakes, W. & Baeza-Yates, R. (Eds.). (1992). *Information retrieval: Data structures and algorithms*. Upper Saddle River, NJ: Prentice Hall.

Freitag, D. (1998). Information extraction from HTML: Application of a general machine learning approach. *Proceedings of the 15th Conference on Artificial Intelligence (AAAI-98)*. Menlo Park, CA: AAAI Press, pp. 517-523.

Glasgow, B., Mandell, A., Binney, D., Ghemri, L., & Fisher, D. (1997). MITA: An information-extraction approach to analysis of free-form text in life insurance applications. *Proceedings of the Ninth Conference on Innovative Applications of Artificial Intelligence*. Menlo Park, CA: AAAI Press, pp. 213-219.

Hammer, H., Garcia-Molina, J., Cho, R., Aranha, A., & Crespo. V. (1997). Extracting semistructured information from the Web. *Proceedings of the Workshop on Management of Semistructured Data (PODS/SIGMOD '97)*, Tucson, Arizona.

Hearst, M. (1997). TextTiling: Segmenting text into multi-paragraph subtopic passages. *Computational Linguistics*, 23(1), 33-64.

Hearst, M.A. & Plaunt C. (1993). Subtopic structuring for full-length document access. *Proceedings of the Special Interest Group in Information Retrieval (ACM SIGIR) Conference*. Pittsburgh, PA, pp. 59-68.

Hopcroft, J. E. & Ullman, J. D. (1979). *Introduction to automata theory, languages, and computation*. Reading, MA: AddisonWesley.

Hsu, C. N. & Chang, C. C. (1999). Finite-state transducers for semi-structured text mining. *Proceedings of International Joint Conference on Artificial Intelligence (IJCAI) Workshop on Text Mining*. IJCAI Press, pp. 76-82.

Jacquemin, C. & Bush, C. (2000). Combining lexical and formatting cues for named entity acquisition from the Web. *Proceedings of the Joint SIGDAT Conference on Empirical Methods in Natural Language Processing and Very Large Corpora*. Hong Kong University of Science and Technology, ACM Press, pp. 189-193.

Kulyukin, V. (1998a). FAQ Finder: A gateway to newsgroups' expertise. *Proceedings of the 40th Conference of Lisp Users, Association of Lisp Users*, pp. 19-26.

Kulyukin, V. (1998b). *Question-driven information retrieval systems*. Unpublished doctoral dissertation, The University of Chicago, Chicago, IL.

Kulyukin, V., Hammond, K., & Burke, R. (1996). Automated analysis of structured online documents. *Proceedings of the Workshop on Internet-Based Information Systems, Portland, Oregon*. Menlo Park, CA: AAAI Press, pp. 23-29.

Kushmerick, N., Weld, D., & Doorenbos, D. (1997). Wrapper induction for information extraction. *Proceedings of the International Joint Conference on Artificial Intelligence (IJCAI), Providence, Rhode Island*. IJCAI Press, pp. 25-34.

Miller, G. A. (1995). WordNet®: A lexical database for English. *Communications of the ACM*, 38(11), 39-41.

Mitchell, T. M. (1997). *Machine learning*. New York: McGraw-Hill.

Moore, D. S. & McCabe, G. P. (1993). *Introduction to the practice of statistics* (2nd ed.). New York: W.H. Freeman and Company.

MUC-3. (1991). *Proceedings of the Third Message-Understanding Conference (MUC-3)*. San Francisco, CA: Morgan Kaufmann.

MUC-4. (1992). *Proceedings of the Fourth Message-Understanding Conference (MUC-4)*. San Francisco, CA: Morgan Kaufmann.

Ng, H. T. & Zelle, J. (1997). Corpus-based approaches to semantic interpretation in NLP. *AI Magazine*, 18(4), 45-64.

Norvig, P. (1992). *Paradigms of artificial intelligence programming: Case studies in common lisp*. San Mateo, CA: Morgan Kaufmann.

Palmer, D. & Hearst, M. (1994). Adaptive sentence boundary disambiguation. *Proceedings of the 4th Conference on Applied Natural Language Processing*. Stuttgart, Germany, ACM Press, pp. 78-83.

Salton, G. & McGill, M. (1983). *Introduction to modern information retrieval*. New York: McGraw-Hill.

Srinivasan, P. (1992). Thesaurus construction. In W. Frakes & R. Baeza-Yates (eds.), *Information retrieval: Data structures and algorithms* (pp. 161-218). Upper Saddle River, NJ: Prentice Hall.

Voorhees, E. & Harman, D. (Eds.). (2000). *Proceedings of the Ninth Text Retrieval Conference (TREC)*, ACM Press.

Voorhees, E. & Tice, D. (2000). Building a question answering test collection. *Proceedings of the Special Interest Group in Information Retrieval (ACM SIGIR) Conference*. Athens, Greece, ACM Press, pp. 200-207.

APPENDIX

Spreading activation is used to account for lexical variation between the clients' questions and the FAQ answers. Spreading activation is based on WordNet, which consists of four subnets organized by the four parts of speech. Each subnet has its own relations: for example, nouns have *antonymy*, the *isa* relation, and three *part-of* relations. WordNet's basic unit is a *synset*, which contains words and phrases interchangeable in a context, e.g., "computer" and "data processor."

The activation procedure is depth-constrained. It takes a term and a depth integer specifying how many links away from the term the activation is to spread. Each term found during the spread is annotated with its part of speech and the depth at which it was found. Thus, "device 1 2" means that "device" is a noun found at depth 2. The origin term's depth is 0. If a word is found at several depths, only the smallest one is kept. Activation is spread only from terms found in the questions. Since questions in FAQs are shorter than answers, the number of non-relevant terms found during the spread is much smaller that it would be if the activation was spread from every nonstoplisted term in every answer.

The weight of a term combines its semantic and statistical properties. The semantic properties of a term constitute its intrinsic value. The statistical properties reflect its value in the collection of textual units. The semantic weight of a term t_i, $W_{wn}(t_i, r)$, is given by

$$W_{wn}(t_i, r) = \frac{W_{pos}(t_i) r^{d(t_i)}}{Poly(t_i)},$$

where $Poly(t_i)$ gives the term's polysemy, $d(t_i)$ gives the depth at which t_i was found, W_{pos} assigns a constant weight to each part of speech, i.e., 1 to nouns, .75 to verbs, and .5 to adjectives and adverbs, and the rate of decay, $r < 1$, indicates how much t_i's weight decreases with depth.

The statistical weight of a term combines several approaches. Let K be a collection of D documents. Let d_j be a document in K. If $f(t_i, d_j)$ denotes the frequency of occurrence of t_i in d_j, then $T_i = \sum_{j=1}^{D} f(t_i, d_j)$ denotes the number of occurrences of t_i in K. Let N_i be the number of documents containing at least one occurrence of t_i. N_i depends on the distribution of t_i among the documents of K. Let $\tilde{N}_i$ be the random variable that assumes

the values of N_i and let $E(\tilde{N}_i)$ be its expected value, assuming that each occurrence of t_i can fall into any of the D documents with equal probability.

The first statistical weight metric is the *inverse document frequency* (Salton & McGill, 1983). The inverse document frequency (IDF) of t_i in K, $W_{idf}(t_i, K)$, is given by $1 + \log(D/N_i)$. The *tfidf* weight of t_i in d_j, $W_{tfidf}(t_i, d_j)$, is given by $f(t_i, d_j) W_{idf}(t_i, K)$.

The second statistical weight metric is *condensation clustering* (Kulyukin, 1998b). A sequence of textual units proceeds from topic to topic. Terms pertinent to a topic exhibit a non-random tendency to condense in the units that cover the topic. One refers to such terms as *content-bearing*. Terms that do not bear content appear to be distributed randomly over the units. The condensation clustering (CC) weight of t_i, $W_{cc}(t_i, K)$, is a ratio of the actual number of documents containing at least one occurrence of t_i over the expected number of

such documents and is given by $A + \log(E(\tilde{N}_i)/N_i)$, where A is a constant.

The following lemma shows how to compute the expectation of N_i.

Lemma 1: Let T_i be the total number of occurrences of t_i in K. Then $E(\tilde{N}_i) = Dp_i$, where

$$p_i = 1 - (1 - 1/D)^{T_i}.$$

Proof: For each d_j, put $\tilde{n}_j = 1$ if $f(t_i, d_j) > 0$ and $\tilde{n}_j = 0$, otherwise. This random

variable assumes the values of 1 and 0 with corresponding probabilities of p_i and

$$1 - p_i. \text{ Hence, } E(\tilde{n}_i) = p_i. \text{ Since } \tilde{N}_i = \sum_{i=1}^{D} \tilde{n}_i, E(\tilde{N}_i) = Dp_i.$$

The CC weight of t_i captures its importance in K. To account for t_i's importance in d_j, its CC weight is multiplied by its frequency in d_j. Thus, we obtain another statistical weight metric $W_{tfcc}(t_i, d_j, K) = f(t_i, d_j) W_{cc}(t_i, K)$. The following lemma captures the relationship between IDF and CC.

Lemma 2: $W_{cc}(t_i) = W_{idf}(t_i) + \log(p_i)$

Proof: By lemma 1 and the definition of W_{idf}, $W_{cc}(t_i) = 1 + \log(E(\tilde{N}_i)/N_i)$. But,

$E(\tilde{N}_i) = Dp_i$. Hence, $W_{cc}(t_i) = W_{idf}(t_i) + \log(p_i)$, for $A = 1$.

Chapter XIII

Query-By-Structure
Approach for the Web

Michael Johnson
Madonna University, USA

Farshad Fotouhi
Wayne State University, USA

Sorin Draghici
Wayne State University, USA

ABSTRACT

This chapter presents three systems that incorporate document structure information into a search of the Web. These systems extend existing Web searches by allowing the user to request documents containing not only specific search words, but also to specify that documents be of a certain type. In addition to being able to search a local database (DB), all three systems are capable of dynamically querying the Web. Each system applies a query-by-structure *approach that captures and utilizes structure information as well as content during a query of the Web. Two of the systems also employ neural networks (NNs) to organize the information based on relevancy of both the content and structure. These systems utilize a supervised Hamming NN and an unsupervised competitive NN, respectively. Initial testing of these systems has shown promising results when compared to straight keyword searches.*

INTRODUCTION

The vast amount of information available to the users of the World Wide Web is overwhelming. However, what is even more overwhelming for users is trying to find the particular information they are looking for. Search engines have been created to assist in this process, but a typical keyword search using a search engine can still result in hundreds of thousands of different *relevant* Web documents. Savvy search engine users have learned to combine keywords and phrases with logical Boolean operators to pair down the number of *matched* Web pages. Unfortunately, results from these searches can still yield a significant number of pages that must then be viewed individually to determine whether they contain the content the user is interested in or not.

Search engines support keyword searches by utilizing *spiders* or *webots* to scan the textual content of Web documents, and then indexing and storing the content in a database for future user queries. The stored information typically consists of the document URL, various keywords or phrases, and possibly a brief description of the Web page. However, these search engines maintain very little, if any, information about the context in which the text of the Web page is presented. In other words, a search engine might be able to identify that a particular keyword was used in the title of the Web page or a phrase within the anchor tags. But, it would not distinguish between that same word or phrase being used in a paragraph, heading, or as alternate text for an image. However, the way in which text is *presented* in a Web page plays a significant role in the importance of that text. For example, a Web page designer will usually emphasize particularly important words, phrases, or names. By enabling a search engine to capture how text is presented, and subsequently, allowing the users of the search engine to query based on some presentation criteria, the performance of a search can be greatly enhanced. Since search engines that utilize spiders already scan the entire text of a Web page, it is a simple modification to incorporate a mechanism to identify the context in which the text is presented.

Motivation for this type of modification can best be described by illustration. Consider the following examples:

- A user wants to find Web pages containing images of Princess Diana. Using a typical keyword search, any Web page that mentions Princess Diana will be returned in the results of the request. However, by including presentation tags— namely, the HTML *img* tag—as part of the search, the user can specify that she is only interested in Web pages that contain "Princess Diana" and an image. Granted, this particular search would result in any page mentioning Diana that contains an image, regardless of whether the image was of Diana or not. However, many Web page designers include a brief textual description of an image using the *alt* attribute of the image tag. With this added knowledge, the user could specify that the content "Princess Diana" should appear as part of the *alt* attribute within the image tag.

- There are literally thousands of online publications available today on the Web. Most of these publications use a very rigid style for presenting their articles. For example, article authors are usually distinguished by having their name placed in a particular location within the document or highlighted with a specific font type, style, size, or color. If a user is interested in finding articles that were written by a particular author, a simple keyword search could yield many irrelevant Web pages, particularly if the author has a common name, is famous, or even has a famous namesake. However, a search that specifies that a particular name be presented in a particular way could greatly improve the results.

These two examples clearly illustrate how a user can significantly improve his or her search for particular Web document content by using presentation knowledge when performing a search.

This chapter will present three systems that have been designed to incorporate document structure into a search of the Web. Each of these systems applies a *query-by-structure* approach that captures and utilizes structure (presentation) information as well as content during a distributed query of the Web. In addition, two of the systems employ neural networks to organize the information based on relevancy of not only the content but the structure of the document as well. First, however, it would be worthwhile to provide a little background into various systems and approaches related to the query-by-structure systems presented in this chapter.

BACKGROUND

The following sections look into various systems and approaches used by others to study the areas of Web searching, Web querying, and the use of machine-learning techniques to perform Web searches. These systems and approaches are related in one way or another to various aspects of systems presented in the next section.

Web Search Engines

Searching the Web involves utilizing one of the many search engines publicly available to perform keyword searches for documents cataloged by the search engine's database. Popular World Wide Web search engines such as AltaVista (http://www.altavista.com) and Yahoo! (http://www.yahoo.com) allow users to search for Web pages by providing keywords. These keywords are then used to index the search engine's database for URLs of relevant Web pages. Some search engines also utilize some sort of *spider* or *webot* to index the pages on the Web. These programs scan currently indexed pages to identify new pages. The newly identified pages are then cataloged and indexed within the search engine's database. In addition, some search engines, such as HotBot (http://www.hotbot.com), allow the user to specify that the documents for which he is searching contain images, video, and/or Javascript code. One search engine that does utilize some structure information is the Google (http://www.google.com) search engine described below. However, most search engines utilize very little, if any, detailed structure information.

Until recently, the Google search engine was relatively unknown to the general public. However, many in computer science academia have known about Google for much longer. This was primarily due to the exceptional research paper, "The Anatomy of a Large-Scale Hypertextual Web Search Engine" (Brin & Page, 1998), published on the inner workings of the Google search engine. Additionally, the Google search engine has been available for public use since the publication of this paper. Today, the Google search engine actually *powers* several other mainstream search engines, including Yahoo!.

Google was initially constructed at Stanford University as a prototype large-scale search engine. According to the designers, the main goal of Google was to improve the quality of Web searches. The designers determined that it was necessary to provide tools that have a very high precision (number of relevant documents returned by the system), even at the expense of recall (number of relevant documents the system could return). Here, "relevant" was defined as only the very best documents, since there could be tens of thousands of slightly relevant documents. One thing that sets Google apart from other search engines is that, in addition to content, it makes use of the structure present in hypertext documents. In particular, two important features help the system to produce its high precision results. First, it makes use of the link structure of the Web to calculate a *PageRank*, or quality ranking, for each Web page. Second, Google utilizes anchor text to improve search results. These two features as well as a couple other features of note are discussed in greater detail in the following paragraphs.

In traditional documentation, authors provide references or citations when refer-ring to other individuals' work in their document. However, hypertext documents offer the unique ability of actually being able to link directly to the cited source. *PageRank* uses a citation or link graph to determine an objective measure of a Web document's importance. The idea is that when someone places a citation or link to another Web document within a page, he/she is indicating a level of importance to the linked document. Hence, pages can be ranked based on the number of pages that cite (link to) a given document, with the results being prioritized based on the number of pages that link to a given page. In addition, *PageRank* extends the results by not counting links from all pages equally and by normalizing by the number of links on a page. Formally, the authors defined *PageRank* as follows:

> *Assuming page A has pages $T_1...T_n$ that point to it (i.e. are citations), a parameter d which is a damping factor set between 0 and 1, and C(A) which is a count of the number of links going out of a page, the PageRank of page A is:*

$$PR(A) = (1-d) + d(PR(T_1)/C(T_1) + ... + PR(T_n)/C(T_n))$$

From the formula above, it can be seen that a page will have a higher *PageRank* if there are several pages that link to it. But, maybe even more significant is the fact that the *PageRank* of the document that is providing the link is factored into the equation as well. As a result, a page that may have only one link to it could have a higher page rank than a page that has several citations, because the one link page is being referenced by a very *important* page. Intuitively this makes sense, for if a document has a direct link from say the Yahoo! homepage, this should be an indication that this page likely carries some importance.

The second factor in ranking of pages is the use of the text within the anchor tags. *Google* not only associates the text of the link with the page containing the link, but also with the page to which the link points. The advantage to doing this is that it captures more detailed information about a given page, as the text within the anchor tags may provide an even more accurate description of a Web page than the page itself. Finally, in addition to *PageRank* and the use of anchor text, Google maintains location informa-tion for all hits and makes extensive use of proximity in search. Google also keeps track of some visual presentation details, such as font size of words where words in a larger or bolder font are weighted higher. Google's mainstream acceptance is a clear indication of the relevance of utilizing structure within a document search.

Web Query Systems

Most search engines dynamically search the Web. However, these searches are typically done in the *background*. In other words, these search engines do not allow the user to directly *query* the Web. Querying the Web requires a Web-query system that locates documents by dynamically retrieving and scanning the documents during the query process. Although there may not exist any mainstream search engine that can directly query the World Wide Web, there actually has been a significant amount of research done in this area. In this section, three such systems are compared.

The first system utilizes a query language called WebSQL (Mendelzon, Mihaila, & Milo, 1996) designed specifically to query the Web. The system navigates the Web starting from a known URL. In addition, it can traverse multiple child *links*. However, other than the text contained within the anchor tags, no other tag (structure) information is utilized in their queries. WebLog (Lakshmanan, Sadri & Subramanian1996) is another language designed to directly query the Web. WebLog allows the user to incorporate some forms of presentation knowledge into the query through a structures called *rel-infons*. However, utilizing rel-infons requires the user to have extensive knowledge of declarative logic concepts in order to write even the simplest of queries. In addition, the system does not use any type of catalog information, so every query requires a dynamic search of the appropriate Web documents. A third system that queries the Web is W3QS (Konopnicki & Shmueli, 1995). This system maintains the results of user queries in a database. In addition to the document content, specific node and link information relating to the document title and anchor tags is cataloged. Additionally, some presentation information such as HTML *form* elements is also maintained. Hence, this system does account for some types of document structure in its queries.

Machine-Learning Techniques

There has been a significant amount of research in an attempt to improve Web searches using machine-learning techniques. Since the content presented in the chapter incorporates neural networks to assist in the query-by-structure approach, it is worthwhile to study related approaches. The first system is *WebWatcher* (Armstrong, Freitag, Joachims, & Mitchell, 1995), which interactively assists users in locating desired information on a specific site. The system tracks a user's actions and utilizes machine-learning methods to acquire knowledge about the user's goals, Web pages the user visits, and success or failure of the search. Rankings are based on keywords. In a likely attempt to improve performance, the designers of the *WebWatcher* agent constructed another system called LASER (Boyan, Freitag, & Joachims, 1996). LASER, which stands for Learning Architecture for Search Engine Retrieval, utilized some of the methods applied to the *WebWatcher* system but eliminated the need for the user to provide feedback to the system. In addition, LASER incorporated document structure into the search process. Finally, a third system, called Syskill & Webert (Pazzani, Muramatsu, & Billsus, 1996), is studied. Syskill and Webert utilize six different machine-learning algorithms, including Perception and Backdrop neural networks. This system also requires user interaction by requesting that the user rate pages on a three-point scale. After analyzing information on each page, individual user profiles are then created. Based on the user profile, the system suggests other links that might be of interest to the user. These systems are discussed in further detail in the following paragraphs.

WebWatcher is a Web-based learning agent designed by graduate students and faculty at Carnegie Mellon University. The agent is described by its designers as an information-seeking assistant for the World Wide Web that interactively helps users locate desired information by employing learned knowledge about which hyperlinks are likely to lead to the target information. *WebWatcher* assists users by interactively advising them as they traverse Web links in search of information, and by searching autonomously on their behalf. In addition to suggesting to users which links they should follow next, it also learns about the users by monitoring their response to the suggestions. This monitoring involves not only analyzing which links the user followed but also any feedback the user provides as to whether the document retrieved by following the link was worthwhile or not. In a sense, *WebWatcher* is "backseat driving" as a user traverses the Web. Each time the user loads a new page, *WebWatcher* utilizes learned knowledge to suggest which links on that page might lead to the desired results. The user remains in full control as he or she has the option of either taking the advice or choosing his or her own path to follow. The search continues in this fashion, until the user terminates the search successfully by indicating "I found it" or unsuccessfully by indicating "I give up."

Clearly, the success of a *WebWatcher*-assisted search depends on the quality of the knowledge used in guiding the search. One form of knowledge considered by the designers was defined by a function called *UserChoice?*, which returns a probability value of between 0 and 1 based on the document the user is currently at (*Page*), the information being sought by the user (*Goal*), and link itself (*Link*). The *UserChoice?* function returns the probability that an arbitrary user will select *Link* given the current *Page* and *Goal*. In order to represent the *Page*, *Goal*, and *Link* information in a useable format, it was necessary—as it is with most machine-learning methods—to create a feature vector of the information. The challenge the designers had here was to convert the arbitrary-length text of a Web page into the fixed-length feature vector. Apparently, after significant experimentation, information about the current *Page*, the user's information search *Goal*, and a particular outgoing *Link* was represented by a vector of approximately 530 Boolean features, with each feature indicating the occurrence of a particular word within the text that originally defines these three attributes. According to the authors, the vector of 530 features is composed of the following four concatenated sub-vectors: u*nderlined words in the hyperlink, words in the sentence containing the hyperlink, words in the heading associated with the hyperlink, and words used to define the user goal.*

To explore possible learning approaches, determine the level of competence achievable by a learning agent, and to learn the general function that *UserChoice?*, given a sample of training data, logged from users, the designers applied the following four methods to training data collected by *WebWatcher* during 30 information sessions: Winnow (Littlestone, 1988), which learns a Boolean concept represented as a single linear threshold function of the instance features; Wordstat (Armstrong et al., 1995), which attempts to make a prediction whether a link is followed based directly on the statistics of individual words; TFIDF with cosine similarity measure (Salton & McGill, 1983), which is a method developed in information retrieval; and a Random method that simply selects a link on a page with uniform probability. The designers concluded that the Winnow method performed best and was a significant improvement over the Random method.

The *WebWatcher* agent showed promising results in being able to learn search-control knowledge in order to predict the links the user would select. However, it is unclear how much of the time *saved* is lost by the user because of the requirement to provide constant feedback. It is likely that, because of the continuous user input, some of the designers of the *WebWatcher* system modified their research and developed LASER. LASER utilizes some of the same machine-learning techniques as the *WebWatcher* system and does not really add anything new from this perspective. However, of significant importance to the research being presented in this chapter, the LASER system incorporates the use of document structure into the search process. According to the system designers, HTML documents consist of two forms of structure: internal and external. The general tags of an HTML document represent the *internal* structure, and the hyperlinks that point to the document (as well as the hyperlinks contained within the document) represent the *external* structure. The LASER system attempts to exploit both types of structure to index the Web.

From the perspective of a user, LASER functions much like the search engines discussed earlier. Like one of the approaches used in the *WebWatcher* system, LASER's machine-learning retrieval function is based on the TFIDF vector space retrieval model. However, unlike *WebWatcher,* LASER utilizes the structure of the HTML documents. Specifically, the system incorporates parameters for weighting words contained with the following HTML tags: title, heading (h1, h2, h3), bold (b), italics (i), blink, and anchor (a). The weight is based simply on the frequency in which the search words appear within the tags specified above.

From a machine-learning perspective, LASER's use of the external structure is the most interesting. To explain the use of external structure, the authors gave the following analogy to reinforcement learning: "Imagine that an agent searching for information on the Web can move from page to page only by following hyperlinks. Whenever the agent finds information relevant to its search goal, it gets a certain amount of reward." The LASER designers concluded that reinforcement learning could be used to have the agent learn how to maximize the reward it received, i.e., learn how to navigate to relevant information. More precisely, the goal was to have LASER rank pages higher if they serve as a good starting point for a search by the agent. Implementation of this aspect of the retrieval function was done using a complex formula that required 18 numerical parameters to allow for a wide variety of search engine behavior, from plain TFIDF to very complex ranking schemes.

LASER's designers chose not to request feedback from users on whether links returned by the system were good or bad (unlike *WebWatcher*). Instead, the system simply records the links the user selects. Unfortunately, for research purposes, without this feedback, the designers could provide no quantitative means to measure the system's performance. Although they did mention that they could collect information on the links the users select, it was indicated that the results would be skewed due to *presentation bias* (the user's choice of which link to follow is strongly biased toward documents appearing early in the search results, regardless of the quality of the search performed).

Syskill & Webert is another software agent that utilizes machine-learning techniques to rate pages on the World Wide Web. This system is different from the others previously discussed in that its primary function is to develop a *user profile* so it can suggest other Web sites that might be of interest to that specific user. The agent learns to rate Web pages by requiring the user to rank each page on a three-point scale and then analyzing information on each of those pages. The system uses the user profile in one of two ways. First, it can add annotations to each Web page a user visits to suggest that a particular link on that page might be of interest to the user. Secondly, it can annotate the results of a commercial search engine query to essentially re-rank the search results. In both cases, page rankings are represented as a real value between 0 and 1.

Although the authors defined it as a user profile, a more accurate name might be *user topic* profile. This is because the system actually can create multiple profiles for each user. Each profile for an individual user is focused on a specific topic. The authors contend that this makes sense, since most users will have multiple interests. In this way, users can create separate *index* pages for each topic, and then switch topics by changing to a different index page. Additionally, at each index page, users have the option of instructing Syskill & Webert to learn a user-profile for the current topic of that index page, make suggestions on links on that index page, or to consult a commercial search engine to search the Web. The agent learns a profile by first *capturing* the HTML source code of a Web page visited by the user. It then asks the user to rank the page with either two thumbs up (hot), two thumbs down (cold), or one thumb up/one thumb down (lukewarm).

In the next section, three query-by-structure systems are presented. As you will see, some of the concepts presented in this section, such as document feature vectors and querying the Web, are utilized by these systems. In particular, two of these systems utilize machine- learning techniques, namely neural networks, to analyze document structure. However, with the exception of the LASER system, the machine-learning systems studied in this section used very little, if any, document structure information.

QUERY-BY-STRUCTURE SYSTEMS

This section presents the CLaP (Fotouhi, Grosky, & Johnson, 1999) and the Neural Network Net Query-by-Structure systems (Johnson, Fotouhi, & Draghici, 2001). These systems have some features similar to those presented in the review in the previous section. In particular, all three systems are capable of dynamically querying the Web. In addition, each system can identify Web documents based on content. However, what sets these systems apart is there extensive use of document structure in the search process, hence the name query-by-structure.

CLaP

The CLaP system, which stands for Content, Link and Presentation, was designed in 1999 in an attempt to enhance Web searches by allowing the user to indicate that the desired documents contain not only specific keywords, but that those keywords be structured and presented in a specific way. This was achieved by allowing the user to request that the content information appear within particular presentation (HTML) tags. The CLaP system allowed the user to issue queries on a locally maintained database of Web documents. However, the system also allowed the user to directly query the Web. Hence, not only was the user able to search for Web documents already cataloged by the CLaP system, but he or she could also initiate a dynamic search of the Web by denoting a specific starting URL. Initial testing of the CLaP system showed promising results. Comparisons between straight keyword searches and searches that also utilize presentation information led to significant reductions in the number of documents selected.

CLaP System Overview

The query process began with the user selecting a *starting* URL and various characteristics of interest, such as "all documents containing images, forms, and/or tables." In addition, the user could select the content for which he or she was searching, and specifically request that it appear between a particular set of tags. The *request* was then transformed into a database query that was processed by the system. The user was able to specify that the request was to be processed locally, in which case the results (URLs of selected Web documents) were returned to the user. Additionally, the user could provide a starting URL and request that a dynamic query of the Web be performed to find the documents matching the user-specified criteria.

A dynamic query started by scanning the document specified by the starting URL. If that document contained the criteria requested by the user, it was included with the results. In addition, during the scanning process, any links to other HTML pages within the document were identified. These links were then traversed, and the documents they pointed to were scanned as well. In a sense, the system was capable of mining the Web to find other documents. This scanning process could potentially continue until no further links were found. Clearly, though, this type of a scan could take a considerable amount of time. Hence, the user was given the ability to limit the scanning by specifying a *depth* at which to stop the search. In addition, to allow the user to further refine his or her searches without having to query the Web, all relevant information obtained from the selected Web documents was then stored in the system database for any future query.

CLaP Architecture

The CLaP system architecture was divided into three layers: User, Database, and WWW, as shown in Figure 1. In addition, each layer was composed of specific *modules* that performed various functions within the system. The Visual Interface module is the user interface for the CLaP system that allowed the user to enter his or her query via an HTML form (Figure 2). This form enabled the user to query based on several different HTML presentation tags including title, anchor, image, table, etc. The user could also search on various attributes for these tags, as well as for content within the tags. When the form was *submitted*, a program within the database layer processed the information and converted the user selection into a SQL query.

Figure 1: CLaP system architecture.

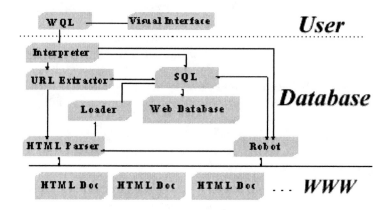

Figure 2: Visual Interface module.

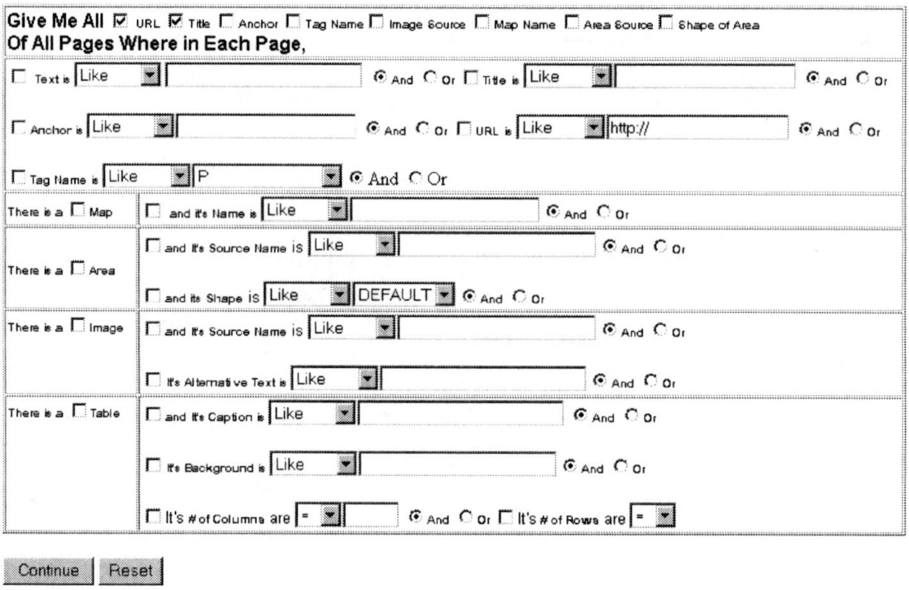

The Interpreter module is the program described above whose function is to convert the user query into a standard SQL query. The Interpreter module directly interfaced with the SQL module and the URL extractor module. When the SQL module received a SQL query from the Interpreter module, it initiated the query on the Database module, which will return the results to the user. In addition, the SQL module also interfaced with the

Figure 3: Example of an SQL query.

```
SELECT Document.url
FROM Document, element, dimension_element, TextDim, image_element
WHERE (Document.id=element.documentid)          AND
        (element.e_id=dimension_element.e_id)      AND
        (dimension_element.e_id=TextDim.E_id)    AND
        (substr(TextDim.InnerText ,'PRINCESS DIANA')<>NULL)  AND
        (dimension_element.e_id=Image_element.e_id)   AND
        (substr(Image_element.InnerText ,'DIANA' <>NULL) ;
```

URL Extractor module when a query needed to be initiated on the Web. Results from a query of the Web were loaded into the database, and the SQL module was initiated to issue the query on the Database module. Figure 3 shows the SQL query used by the system to find all pages mentioning "Princess Diana" that contain an image and contain the text "Diana" inside the image tags.

The URL Extractor module initiated the search of the World Wide Web. Initially, the module received the user-specified starting URL from the SQL module. The search was initiated by invoking the HTML Parser module that scanned the Web document at the starting URL. The URL Extractor module then captured *all* the links from the Web document scanned by the parser. These new links were then passed, one-by-one, to the HTML parser, and the scan/extract process repeated itself. Each time the URL extraction process was started, the URL extractor module was able to identify duplicate URLs. All duplicates were simply discarded by the Extractor module, thus eliminating redundant scans as well as cycles. In addition, URLs containing complex query strings were also discarded. However, the Extractor module was able to recognize relative, absolute, and local links, and properly structure them for the Parser module.

The HTML parser was responsible for retrieving documents on the Web. In addition, the HTML parser also scanned each retrieved document and determined whether the document satisfied the user's query. If a document did satisfy the user query, it was passed to the loader module. If it did not, then the document was *discarded* after its links had been extracted by the URL Extractor module. The Parser module utilizes the built-in parser provided with Microsoft Internet Explorer 4.0. The Loader module extracted the relevant content and presentation information from the Web document that it received from the HTML parser module. This information was then populated in the Web-Database module.

CLaP Performance Study

The query in Figure 3 was issued to the CLaP system for the following URL: http://www.mcs.drexel.edu/~gcmastra/diana.html. This URL was selected due to the relevancy to the query. Table 1 below shows the results of the query at search depths of 1, 2, and 3.

Table 1: Test results

Depth	Unique URLs Scanned	Pages with "Princess Diana" in Content	Pages Also Containing an Image	Pages also Containing "Diana" within IMG tags
1	35	15	13	4
2	187	25	22	8
3	595	145	142	26

Included in the results is the total number of unique URLs scanned and, from those URLs, the Web documents containing the text "Princess Diana." In addition, from this set of documents, the number of documents containing an image and the documents having the text pattern "Diana" within the image tags is also shown. Clearly, it can be seen from the results that a significant reduction in the number of Web pages selected can be observed.

The concept of querying the Web by content, link, and particularly structure was studied extensively with the CLaP system, and the system did provided promising results when comparing straight keyword searches and searches that utilized structure information. However, the query process was quite cumbersome to the users, as they were required to specify details about exactly where each search word in which they were interested would appear. Due primarily to this reason, as well as some other issues, another query-by-structure approach was needed.

A Neural Network Net Query-by-Structure Approach

Continuing the research into a query-by-structure approach, two new systems designed to capture and utilize structure information and content during a distributed query were developed. Both systems employ neural networks to organize the information based on relevancy of not only the content but the structure of the document as well. The primary goal of these systems was to test the feasibility of using neural networks to improve the query process. In addition, in order to become a viable querying system, the requirement of an extensive amount of information required of the user during the query process, such as in the CLaP system, needed to be resolved. Hence, another goal in the development of the neural network query-by-structure systems was to eliminate the need for the complex user queries.

The first issue that needed to be addressed was determining which type of neural network to utilize. For example, some types of neural networks, when provided a specific input, will identify which of a set of prototypes the input most closely matches. These types of neural networks are called supervised learning networks. Systems utilizing supervised learning neural networks could be useful in categorizing semi-structured documents based on how the structure of one document most closely matches the structure of other classified documents. Additionally, these types of neural network, when given a set of documents as input, can be utilized to identify document relevancy and quantify the results so that a ranking of documents can be obtained. However, to effectively perform the classification, it is necessary for systems utilizing supervised learning networks to create a set of prototype vectors corresponding to the predetermined set of prototypes.

When a predetermined set of prototypes is not available, a different type of neural network, namely unsupervised competitive networks, can be utilized. Unsupervised competitive neural networks utilize only the inputs and attempt to group together or cluster the inputs into related classes.   By performing the classification based on document structure, documents with similar structure will be clustered together.   Additionally, the results yielded from this approach can be used in different fashions. One approach could be to deem the largest cluster the most relevant cluster, with the notion being that several documents of similar structure are likely more useful.   Another approach could be to present the user with the groupings of clusters and allow him or her to select which documents to view, based on his or her opinion of the most relevant clusters. This approach provides the user with more flexibility, especially in light of the fact that ultimately it is the user who determines relevancy. But, it may not do as much in terms of reducing the number of relevant documents. So, it seems worthwhile to study both approaches, as it is likely that a hybrid of the two might serve best.

Neural Network Net Query-by-Structure Systems Overview

Although similar, the systems developed utilize different types of neural networks: a *supervised* Hamming Network and an *unsupervised* Competitive Network (Hagan, Demuth, & Beale, 1996).   The query process for both systems involves five steps (as shown in Figure 4).

Figure 4: Neural network query-by-structure process.

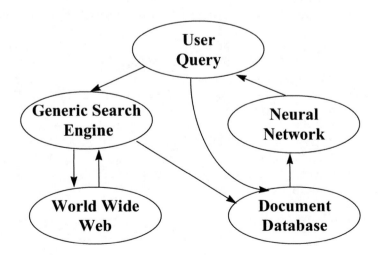

First, the user initiates a query to the User Query module by entering a standard generic search using keywords. In order to limit the number of Web documents that must be retrieved and parsed during a dynamic Web query, the user must also select a maximum number of URLs he or she wishes to receive in the results. Additionally, the supervised neural network system requires that the user select a document *type*. This type field is used by the system to categorize document structure. Upon issuance of a user query, the Generic Search engine module simply performs a standard Web search with the search words provided by the user using a commercial search engine. Any commercial search engine that produces results containing the URLs and descriptions of *relevant* documents can perform this operation.

Although these results are actual documents on the Web, the only Web query performed at this point was to contact the commercial search engine, which in turn simply performed a query on its local database. As a result, in order to capture document structure information, it was necessary to actually retrieve each of the Web documents specified in the results of the Generic Search Engine query. Hence, the Generic Search Engine module takes the list of URLs returned by the commercial search engine, and one at a time, retrieves the source code of each of the Web documents. These documents are then parsed in order to analyze the document structure.

For each Web document, document structure was quantified by creating a feature vector based on whether specific words appeared between specific HTML tags in the Web document's source code. The words selected are words deemed relevant to one of the document types specified in the initial user query. As an example, consider that a resume document, regardless of the creator's occupation, will likely contain several of the following words: business, education, experience, objective, title, and work. Potentially more significant is the fact that these words will likely be highlighted in the document by specific HTML tags, such as bold (<b>), heading (<h#>), font (<font>), and italics (<i>). Hence, the feature vector would contain an entry for each of the *resume* words, and if any of those words appeared at least once between *any* one of the specified HTML tags, a 1 would be placed in the feature vector for that word, and a 0 otherwise. It should be noted that most of the entries in the feature vector should be 0's because the feature vector will contain entries for several other words (recall that *WebWatcher* utilized a 530-element feature vector) for other document types that are not expected to appear in a resume document. This feature vector was then used as the input vector to the neural networks.

After construction, the document feature vectors are added to the Document Database module. This allows future user queries to be initiated directly to a database that already has captured document structure information, hence bypassing the time-consuming Web query. In addition, the feature vectors are then sent to the Neural Network module. Both systems then employ their respective neural network to organize the information based on relevancy of not only the content but the structure of the document as well. Lastly, the neural network outputs the results of the user query.

The following two sections describe in greater detail the supervised Hamming neural network and the unsupervised Competitive network. This book is not designed to be a text about neural networks, so the objective here is simply to provide a high-level description of the networks utilized by the query-by-structure process. Readers unfamiliar with neural networks should note that most neural networks are simply a series of mathematical manipulations performed on a set of vectors and matrices.

Hamming Neural Network

A Hamming neural network is a supervised learning network that consists of two layers (Hagan et al., 1996). The first layer (feedforward layer) performs a correlation between an input vector and a set of prototype vectors and produces the output $\mathbf{a}^1$ (the superscript indicates the network layer) as described by the following formula:

$$\mathbf{a}^1 = \mathbf{purelin}(\mathbf{W}^1\mathbf{p} + \mathbf{b}^1) \tag{3.1}$$

In formula (3.1), $\mathbf{W}^1$ is called the weight matrix. Each row in the weight matrix represents one of the prototype vectors. The weight matrix is multiplied by the vector $\mathbf{p}$, which represents an input vector. The resultant vector is then added to the bias vector $\mathbf{b}^1$ to produce the output vector $\mathbf{a}^1$. The **purelin** transfer function in the formula above is simply a linear function that produces the same output as its input.

The second layer (recurrent layer) performs a competition to determine which of the prototype vectors is closest to the input vector using the following formulas:

$$\mathbf{a}^2(0) = \mathbf{a}^1 \tag{3.2}$$

$$\mathbf{a}^2(t+1) = \mathbf{poslin}(\mathbf{W}^2\mathbf{a}^2(t)) \tag{3.3}$$

The initial input to the recurrent layer is show in (3.2), and is simply the output, $\mathbf{a}^1$, from layer 1. The recurrent layer also has a weight matrix $\mathbf{W}^2$. This matrix is constructed so that each element on its diagonal has a value of **1** and all remaining elements have a value of of -ε (where of -ε is some number less than $1 / (S - 1)$, and S is the number of rows in the weight matrix. Hence, the recurrent layer repeatedly multiplies the weight matrix by the $\mathbf{a}^2$ vector calculated in the previous iteration. Note that in this formula, the **poslin** linear transfer function is applied and produces linear results for positive values in the matrix and zero for negative values. The recurrent layer continually applies this function until every element but one in the resultant vector contains a zero. This nonzero $\mathbf{i}^{th}$ element represents that the initial input vector provided to the feedforward layer most closely matches the $\mathbf{i}^{th}$ prototype vector.

A Hamming neural network is considered supervised because the prototype vectors are determined in advance and are designed to resemble the expected input vectors. Hence, the first step in designing the Hamming network for the query-by-structure system was to initialize the prototype vectors. Each prototype vector was designed so that each element in the vector would contain a Boolean value indicating whether a given word appeared between a given HTML tag or not. Since each prototype vector represented a different document type, if a specific word was expected to appear within a given structure context inside that specific type of document, the value of that entry was set to one, and if not, the value was set to zero. For instance, using the example from the previous section, the *resume* prototype vector would be a vector that contained all 0's except for the entries that represented the *resume* words.

After initialization of the prototype vectors, the approach taken by the supervised neural network query-by-structure system was to slightly modify the Hamming neural network. First, the system performs the correlation between each of the input vectors and the prototype vectors, one at a time. Here, the number of input vectors (**n**) is equivalent to the number of URLs returned by the initial Web query. So, given **n** input vectors, the feedforward layer would need to be applied **n** times, once for each input vector. As a result, instead of a single valued vector a^1, the system produces a matrix of vectors A^1. Hence, the output of the feedforward layer is just the result of the matrix multiplication of the matrix of the input vectors P^1 with each of the prototype vectors in the matrix W^1. Assuming that the system has no bias vector, the feedforward layer can be described by the formula:

$$A^1 = purelin(W^1 P^1) \tag{3.4}$$

The recurrent layer performs the competition between each of the elements in the matrix A^1 produced as the output from feedforward layer. Hence, this layer can be described mathematically as:

$$A^2(0) = A^1 \tag{3.5}$$

$$A^2(t+1) = poslin(W^2 A^2(t)) \tag{3.6}$$

As a result, the output from the second layer of the neural network is a set of vectors representing which prototype vector most closely matches each input vector. Recall, though, that the objective of this system was to determine which of the Web documents (input vectors) most closely matches the selected document type (prototype vector). Fortunately, the output from the second layer works rather well in solving this problem. Consider that each of the columns represents one output vector. Each of these vectors contain elements containing all zeros but one. Additionally, since the document type is known, and the applicable corresponding prototype vector is known, all that needs be done is to extract each of the vectors from the output matrix A^2 that contain a nonzero value in the nonzero i^{th} element. This set of vectors now represents all the Web documents that most closely match the selected document type. In addition, the vector that has the largest value matches the prototype vector better than any other vector. Hence, sorting the values in each of the vectors, from highest to lowest, provides a new ranking of the Web documents. Finally, after sorting, the system simply outputs the URLs and descriptions captured in the initial search engine query, but in the order specified by the neural network.

Unsupervised Competitive Neural Network

The unsupervised competitive neural network replaces the recurrent layer in the Hamming network with a competition transfer function. Like the Hamming network, this competition layer still identifies the largest value in the vectors produced by the *feedforward* network. However, instead of applying the recurrence equation on the output vectors, the competition transfer function simply produces a vector of all 0's, except for the entry that contained the largest value in the vector produced by the feedforward network, which it sets to 1. In addition, the objective of the unsupervised network is significantly different than that of a supervised network. The goal of the supervised network is to match the input vectors to the predetermined prototype vectors.

However, in the unsupervised network, the prototype vectors are not known in advance. Instead, the input vectors are actually used to *train* the weight matrix. This was accomplished using the Kohonen learning rule (Hagan et al., 1996):

$$_i\mathbf{w(q)} =\ _i\mathbf{w(q\text{-}1)} + \alpha(\mathbf{p(q)} -\ _i\mathbf{w(q\text{-}1)}) \qquad \text{for } \mathbf{i = i^*} \qquad (3.7)$$

and

$$_i\mathbf{w(q)} =\ _i\mathbf{w(q\text{-}1)} \qquad\qquad \text{for } \mathbf{i\ != i^*} \qquad (3.8)$$

In equation (3.7) and (3.8), α represents a real value between 0 and 1 called the learning rate, $\mathbf{p(q)}$ represents the input vector, $_i\mathbf{w(q)}$ and $_i\mathbf{w(q\text{-}1)}$ represent the $\mathbf{i^{th}}$ row in the weight matrix at time $\mathbf{q}$ and $\mathbf{q\text{-}1}$, respectively, and $\mathbf{i^*}$ represents the row that had the largest value in the vector produced by the feedforward network, and hence the row that contained the 1 in the output vector. In general terms, all the vectors in the weight matrix at time $\mathbf{q}$ will remain the same as they were at time $\mathbf{q - 1}$ except for the row in the weight matrix that *won* the competition. The values in this row of the weight matrix will move from their current values at time $\mathbf{q - 1}$, toward the input vector at time $\mathbf{q}$. How quickly the row in the weight matrix moves towards the input vector is a factor of the learning rate α. For example, if α=1, then from (3.7) we can see that row $\mathbf{i}$ in the weight matrix would be set to the values of the input vector. However, if α=0, then no change would ever result. Clearly, the value of the learning rate is of utmost importance for this type of neural network.

The implementation of the unsupervised competitive neural network for the query-by-structure system was fairly straightforward. First, each Web document is transformed into an input vector. The only difference between this input vector and the input vector in the Hamming neural network is that each element contains a numeric value containing the number of occurrences of a specific word within the Web document (rather than a Boolean value), provided that the word was contained within the appropriate structure tags, as was described for the Hamming network. After being created, each input vector is then normalized. In order to initialize the network, a weight matrix for the prototype vectors was randomly generated. The values taken on by each entry was a real number between -1 to 1, inclusive.

Once the network was properly initialized, the process of training the weight matrix was simply a matter of randomly selecting an input vector from the set of input vectors of Web documents, applying the competitive layer in the neural network to find the largest value in the vectors produced by the feedforward layer, and updating the appropriate row in the weight matrix using the Kohonen rule. This process was repeated for a predetermined number of iterations, at which time the final weight vectors have been formed. Using these weight vectors, each input is classified and placed into one of $\mathbf{n}$ class vector sets. These class vector sets make up the final results of the neural network, where users are presented with the ordered results in each class instead of all the results ordered together in one list.

Experimental Performance and Results

Preliminary tests of the Hamming neural network system showed promising results.

Initially, four document types were selected: resumes, conference papers, news articles, and e-commerce Web documents. Obviously, there could be an infinite number of different document types, along with variations within those types, but the objective was not to classify as many different types of documents as possible, but rather to simply test the feasibility of using neural networks to improve query-by-structure performance. The following is the list of words used to construct the feature vectors for the initial testing of the system: abstract, activities, bibliography, business, by, buy, cart, conclusion, education, experience, introduction, mall, MasterCard, news, objective, price, purchase, related, references, resume, shop, sports, store, Visa, vitae, work. The HTML tags utilized by the system were: bold (<b>), strong (<strong>), emphasis (<emp>), underline (<u>), heading (<h#>), font (<font>), and italics (<i>). Hence, four prototype vectors were utilized, with each one representing a different document type. Each vector contained only Boolean values that represented whether or not one of the words specified above was expected to appear within a given structure context inside that specific type of document. According to the word ordering above, the four prototype vectors utilized are:

resume document   = (0,1,0,0,0,0,0,0,1,1,0,0,0,0,1,0,0,0,1,1,0,0,0,0,1,1)
research paper   = (1,0,1,0,0,0,0,1,0,0,1,0,0,0,1,0,0,1,1,0,0,0,0,0,0,1)
news article   = (0,0,0,1,1,0,0,0,0,0,0,0,0,1,0,0,0,0,0,0,0,1,0,0,0,0)
e-commerce document = (0,0,0,1,0,1,1,0,0,0,0,1,1,0,0,1,1,0,0,0,1,0,1,1,0,0)

As an example, consider a simple query that was applied to the system that retrieved only 10 URLs looking for a *resume* document type using the keywords: "Computer Science." The commercial search engine results for this query placed a career services Web site first and a Computer Science program's students resume *repository* second. After converting these results to input vectors and filtering them through the neural network, the career services Web site ended up ranked 7th, and the resume repository ended up dead last at 10th. In addition, in between these two documents were a very poorly structured resume and a Web page that simply contained a note stating that if you were interested in that individual's resume, you could contact him via e-mail. At the top of the rankings were Web documents containing actual resumes.

Other experiments were performed with different keywords, document types, and a varying numbers of URLs returned in the result with similar results to the example above. Table 2 compares the results of the system to the commercial search engine results for some of these tests. A brute force approach of viewing each document to determine if it actually was of the desired type was necessary.

The performance of the unsupervised competitive neural network was not as consistent as that of the supervised Hamming network. The hope for this network is that the input vectors will be clustered based on similar structure. However, much of the preliminary testing resulted in most documents being placed in only one or two classes (currently the system can only cluster to four classes). There are several contributing factors to these sporadic results. First, unlike the supervised neural network that creates the weight matrix based on the prototype vectors, this network randomly generates its weight matrix. As a result, each test yields different results. Secondly, the number of times the network iterates also plays a role in determining the results. This value can only be determined through extensive testing. Currently, the number of iterations performed

Table 2: Hamming network vs. commercial search engine result comparison

Keywords	Document Type	Pages Retrieved	Hamming Network	Commercial Search Engine
Biology	Resume	50	9 out of top 10 were resumes	5 out of top 10 were resumes
Secretary	Resume	30	4 out of top 6 were resumes	2 out of top 6 were resumes
Political Science	Research Paper	30	4 out of top 6 were research papers	0 out of top 6 were research papers
War	Research Paper	30	3 out of top 6 were research papers	1 out of top 6 were research papers
Microsoft	News Article	30	3 out of top 6 contained news articles	1 out of top 6 contained news articles
College Football	News Article	40	5 out of top 8 contained news articles	2 out of top 8 contained news articles
Textbooks	E-Commerce Site	40	7 out of top 8 are e-commerce sites	3 out of top 8 are e-commerce sites
Flowers	E-Commerce Site	30	5 out of top 6 are e-commerce sites	2 out of top 6 are e-commerce sites

is equal to three times the number of input vectors. Another variable factor in this network is the choice of the learning rate. This value ranges between 0 and 1, with higher values resulting in fast but unstable learning and lower values resulting in slow but stable learning. Once again, the optimal value for the learning rate can only be determined through extensive testing. Finally, a third issue is with the creation of the input vectors. As discussed earlier, these vectors are generated based on document structure. Hence, creating input vectors that properly distinguish between different types of documents is paramount to the performance of the network.

FUTURE TRENDS

A significant amount of research has already been done regarding the query-by-structure approach. The CLaP system was initially created to determine the feasibility of the query-by-structure approach. The system allowed the user to dynamically search the Web for documents based on an elaborate set of structure criteria. Even from the early testing with the CLaP system, it became clear that the results indicated that the use of document structure could improve query results. However, the queries, which required the user to specify exactly which tags the search words would appear between, were much too cumbersome for the user to make the system usable. So, although exhibiting promising results, the CLaP system was essentially abandoned in favor of systems using the neural network query-by-structure approach.

The results from the testing of the query-by-structure approach using neural networks has been promising enough to warrant further research, and development on a more enhanced version of the systems has already begun. The neural network systems did eliminate the need for extensive structure information during the query process. It does, however, require that the user select a document *type*. Consequently, the document structure criteria was predetermined by the system. However, the notion of how a specific type of document should look is something that should really be determined by the *user* of the system rather than the *designer* of the system. As a result, future enhancements to the system will allow the user to specify structure criteria, not by providing detailed structure information, but rather by providing examples of document types. Hence, the prototype vectors for the system will be constructed not by the designers of the system, but rather dynamically, based on the examples provided by the users. In simplistic terms, the user will be able to say, "Give me a document that looks like this but contains these words."

In addition to structure, another new trend to consider in the query process is *word semantics*. According to the online American Heritage® Dictionary (http://education.yahoo.com/reference/dictionary/), the definition of the word "semantics" is "the meaning or the interpretation of a word, sentence, or other language form." It should be noted that the meaning of a word and the interpretation of a word are two entirely different things altogether. For example, the word "screen" can have several different *meanings* depending upon to what it is referring. A computer has a screen; a window can have a screen; a movie theater has a screen; and, during the hiring process, it is standard practice to screen an applicant. Hence, the *interpretation* of the word "screen" is entirely dependent upon the context in which the word is used. Additionally, several different words could have the same meaning. For example, depending upon the context, the words auto, automobile, car, and vehicle could be interpreted as the same thing. Most search engines today, unless specifically designed to do so, cannot handle the semantics of the words. As a result, although a search issued on a commercial search engine will result in a significant number of purportedly relevant pages, in actuality, the results will likely contain several irrelevant pages as a result of one or more of the search words having different meanings. In addition, since there could be one or more words that has a meaning identical to one of the search words, several relevant pages will actually not be returned by the search engine.

Unfortunately, identifying word semantics is an extremely difficult task. However, a more feasible approach might be to instead identify *document semantics*. On a basic level, document semantics can be thought of as a document's *type*. In other words, almost every document typically has some sort of meaning. Some examples of this include resumes, research papers, news articles, etc., which are all specific types of documents. The general idea is that a document's type could provide information about the semantics of the words within the document. For example, if a document is classified as a resume, and the user specified "restaurant" as one of the search words, in this instance, the word "bar" would likely be synonymous with tavern. If, on the other hand, the user had specified "lawyer" as one of the search words, then the word "bar" would likely be referring to the legal bar. Hence, by allowing the user to specify semantic information in the form of a document type, and subsequently using this information during the query process, invaluable information about the semantics of the words within the document can potentially be captured.

Finally, it should be noted that there is currently a paradigm shift taking place towards a new Semantic Web (Berners-Lee, Hendler, & Lassila, 2001). The basic notion is that new Web documents are being created with specific semantic tags, primarily using XML. These new types of documents provide additional *meaning* to the text within the document. In other words, the HTML tags within a document are used to describe the structure or layout of the document, and the XML tags are used to provide a more detailed description of the content of the documents. New search tools are being created to identify documents containing these descriptive semantic tags that will potentially revolutionize the way Web searches are performed and immensely increase the quality of these searches.

CONCLUSION

The content of a document is clearly crucial in any type of query. However, based on the content presented in this chapter, it should be apparent that the query-by-structure has potential as well. The CLaP system demonstrated that utilizing structure as well as content could significantly improve query performance. The neural network systems resulted in an equally good performance and demonstrated that the burden of identifying structure within the document can become the responsibility of the system rather than the user. Since most data on the Web is in the form of HTML documents, this data can be thought of as at least semi-structured because the HTML tags within the document conform the data to some form of structure. Clearly, being able to take advantage of this structure could improve the query process.

At first glance, the new Semantic Web described earlier might lead one to think that the query-by-structure approach presented here could become obsolete rather shortly. However, there are at least two major implications that should lead one to conclude the exact opposite. First, what is to be done with the billions of already created or soon to be created Web pages containing only HTML with no semantic information whatsoever. Clearly, it would be unreasonable to think that all of these documents must be redesigned to adapt to this new Web. Secondly, if one thinks of these new semantic tags as simply another form of structure (i.e., semantic structure instead of presentation structure), the query-by-structure approach might, in fact, be extremely relevant to this new Semantic Web.

REFERENCES

Armstrong, R., Freitag, D., Joachims, T., & Mitchell, T. (1995). WebWatcher: A learning apprentice for the World Wide. *Workshop on Information Gathering for Heterogeneous Distributed Environments*, AAAI Spring Symposium Series, Stanford, CA, pp. 6-12. Menlo Park, CA: AAAI Press. http://www.cs.cmu.edu/afs/cs.cmu.edu/project/theo-6/Web-agent/www/ijcai97.ps.

Berners-Lee, T., Hendler, J. & Lassila, O. (2001). The semantic Web. *Scientific American*, May, pp. 35-43. *Available online at:* http://www.sciam.com/2001/0501issue/0501berners-lee.html.

Boyan, J., Freitag, D., & Joachims, T. (1996). A machine- learning architecture for optimizing Web search engines. *AAAI-96 Workshop on Internet-based Information Systems*, August, Portland, OR. pp. 334-335, Menlo Park, CA: AAAI Press.

Brin, S. & Page, L. (1998). The anatomy of a large-scale hypertextual Web search engine. *Proceedings of the 7th International World Wide Web Conference*, April, Brisbane, Australia, pp. 107-117, Elsevier Science. http://www7.scu.edu.au/programme/fullpapers/1921/com1921.htm.

Fotouhi, F., Grosky, G., & Johnson, M. (1999). CLaP: A system to query the Web using content, link, and presentation information. *Proceedings of the 14th International Symposium on Computer and Information Sciences*, October, Kusadasi, Turkey. pp.214-221, Springer-Verlag.

Hagan, M., Demuth, H., & Beale, M. (1996). *Neural network design*, 1st ed., Boston, MA: PWS Publishing Company.

Johnson, M., Fotouhi, F., & Draghici, S., (2001). A neural network net query-by-structure approach. *12th International Conference of the Information Resources Management Association, IRMA'01*, May, Toronto, Canada, pp. 108-111, Idea Group Publishing.

Konopnicki. D, & Shmueli, O. (1995). W3QS: A query system for the World Wide Web. *Proceedings of the 21st International Conference on Very Large Data Bases*. Zurich, Switzerland. pp. 11-15, Morgan Kaufmann.

Lakshmanan, L.V.S., Sadri, F., & Subramanian, I.N. (1996). A declarative language for querying and restructuring the Web. *Proceedings of the Sixth International Workshop on Research Issues in Data Engineering, New Orleans, LA, USA*, pp. 12-21, IEEE Computer Society Press.

Littlestone, N. (1988). Learning quickly when irrelevant attributes abound: A new linear-threshold algorithm. *Machine Learning* 2:285-318.

Mendelzon, A.O., Mihaila, G.A., & Milo, T. (1996). Querying the World Wide Web. *Proceedings of the International Conference on Parallel and Distributed Information Systems (PDIS'96)*. Miami, Florida. pp. 54-67, IEEE Computer Society Press.

Pazzani, M., Muramatsu, J., & Billsus D. (1996). Syskill & Webert: Identifying interesting Web sites. *Proceedings of the 13th National Conference on Artificial Intelligence, Menlo Park, CA, USA*, pp. 54-61, AAAI Press, <http://www.ics.uci.edu/~pazzani/RTF/AAAI.html>.

Salton, G., & McGill, M.J. (1983). *Introduction to modern information retrieval*. New York: *McGraw-Hill Inc.*

Chapter XIV

Financial Benchmarking Using Self-Organizing Maps – Studying the International Pulp and Paper Industry

Tomas Eklund
Turku Centre for Computer Science, Finland

Barbro Back
Åbo Akademi University, Finland

Hannu Vanharanta
Pori School of Technology and Economics, Finland

Ari Visa
Tampere University of Technology, Finland

ABSTRACT

Performing financial benchmarks in today's information-rich society can be a daunting task. With the evolution of the Internet, access to massive amounts of financial data, typically in the form of financial statements, is widespread. Managers and stakeholders are in need of a tool that allows them to quickly and accurately analyze these data. An emerging technique that may be suited for this application is the self-organizing map. The purpose of this study was to evaluate the performance of self-organizing maps for the purpose of financial benchmarking of international pulp and paper companies. For the study, financial data in the form of seven financial ratios were collected, using the Internet as the primary source of information. A total of 77 companies and six regional averages were included in the study. The time frame of the study was the period 1995-2000. A number of benchmarks were performed, and the results were analyzed based on information contained in the annual reports. The results of the study indicate that self-organizing maps can be feasible tools for the financial benchmarking of large amounts of financial data.

INTRODUCTION

There are many parties interested in the financial performance of a company. Investors want to find promising investments among the thousands of stocks available on the market today. Managers want to be able to compare the performance of their company to that of others in order to isolate areas in which the company could improve. Creditors want to analyze the company's long-term payment ability, and auditors want to assess the accuracy of a company's financial statements. Financial analysts want to compare the performance of a company to that of others in order to find financial trends on the markets. A tool commonly used by these parties is *financial competitor benchmarking* (Bendell, Boulter & Goodstadt, 1998).

The purpose of financial competitor benchmarking is to objectively compare the financial performance of a number of competing companies (Karlöf, 1997). This form of benchmarking involves using *quantitative* data, i.e., numerical data, usually in the form of a number of financial ratios calculated using publicly available financial information. The information required for these comparisons can commonly be found in companies' annual reports.

The problem with these comparisons is that the amount of data gathered quickly becomes unmanageable. Especially with the advent of the Internet, access to financial information is nearly infinite. This has led to a situation, faced by many managers and investors today, in which the amount of data available greatly exceeds the capacity to analyze it (Adriaans & Zantinge, 1996).

A possible solution to this problem is to use *data-mining tools*. Data-mining tools are applications used to find hidden relationships in data. One data-mining tool that could be particularly suitable for the problem in this case is the *self-organizing map*. Self-organizing maps are two-layer neural networks that use the *unsupervised learning* method. Self-organizing maps have been used in many applications. By 1998, over 3,300 studies on self-organizing maps had been published (Kaski, Kangas, & Kohonen, 1998). Today, this figure is over 4,300 (Neural Networks Research Centre, 2001). Most applications of self-organizing maps have dealt with speech recognition, engineering applications, mathematical problems, and data processing (Kaski et al., 1998). Some examples of more recent research papers include cloud classification (Ambroise, Seze, Badran, & Thiria, 2000), image object classification (Becanovic, 2000), breast cancer diagnosis (Chen, Chang, & Huang, 2000), industrial process monitoring and modeling (Alhoniemi et al., 1999), and extracting knowledge from text documents (Visa, Toivonen, Back, & Vanharanta, 2000).

Self-organizing maps group data according to patterns found in the dataset, making them ideal tools for data exploration. Kiang and Kumur (2001) compared the use of self-organizing maps to factor analysis and K-means clustering. The authors compared the tool's performances on simulated data, with known underlying factor and cluster structures. The results of the study indicate that self-organizing maps can be a robust alternative to traditional clustering methods. A similar comparison was made by Costea, Kloptchenko, and Back (2001), who used self-organizing maps and statistical cluster analysis (K-means) to compare the economic situations in a number of Central-East European countries, based on a number of economic variables. The authors found the self-organizing map "a good tool for the visualization and interpretation of clustering results."

However, although many papers on self-organizing maps have been published, very few studies have dealt with the use of self-organizing maps in financial benchmarking. An example of the application of neural networks for financial analysis is the study by Martín-del-Brío and Serrano-Cinca (1993). These authors used self-organizing neural networks to study the financial state of Spanish companies and to attempt to predict bankruptcies among Spanish banks during the 1977-85 banking crisis. Another example is the aforementioned study by Costea et al. (2001).

In our research group, we have conducted several studies on using self-organizing maps for benchmarking and data-mining purposes. Back, Sere, and Vanharanta (1998) compared 120 companies in the international pulp and paper industry. The study was based on standardized financial statements for the years 1985-89, found in the Green Gold Financial Reports database (Salonen & Vanharanta, 1990a, 1990b, 1991). The companies used in the experiment were all based in one of three regions: North America, Northern Europe or Central Europe. The companies were clustered according to nine different financial ratios: Operating profit, Profit after financial items, Return on Total Assets (ROTA), Return on Equity (ROE), Total Liabilities, Solidity, Current Ratio, Funds from Operations, and Investments. The ratios were chosen by interviewing a number of experts on which ratios they commonly used. The objective of the study was to investigate the potential of using self-organizing maps in the process of investigating large amounts financial data. Eklund (2000), Eklund, Back, Vanharanta, and Visa (2001), Karlsson (2001), Karlsson, Back, Vanharanta, and Visa (2001), and Öström (1999) continued assessing the feasibility of using self-organizing maps for financial benchmarking purposes.

Back, Sere and Vanharanta (1997) and Back, Öström, Sere, and Vanharanta (2000) are follow-up studies to the 1998 paper. The principle difference is that maps for the different years were trained separately in Back et al. (1998), while a single map was used in Back et al. (1997) and Back et al. (2000). Moreover, in Back et al. (2000), the data was from 1996-1997 and collected from Internet. The results showed that a single map makes it easier to follow the companies' movements over years. The results of the studies also gave further evidence that self-organizing maps could be feasible tools for processing vast amounts of financial data.

The purpose of this study is to continue to assess the feasibility of using self-organizing maps for financial benchmarking purposes. In particular, in analyzing the results, we will assess the discovered patterns by putting more emphasis on interpreting the results with existing domain knowledge. This chapter is based on the findings of Eklund (2000).

The rest of this chapter is organized as follows: the next section describes the methodology we have used, benchmarking, the self-organizing map, and choice of financial ratios. Following that, we present the companies included in the study, and then discuss the construction of the maps. The last two sections of the chapter present the analysis of the experiment and the conclusions of our study.

METHODOLOGY

Benchmarking

The Xerox Corporation, one of the pioneers in benchmarking, uses the following definition of benchmarking: "Benchmarking is the continuous process of measuring our products, services and practices against the toughest competitors recognized as industry leaders" (Gustafsson, 1992).

The purpose of benchmarking is to compare the activities of one company to those of another, using *quantitative* or *qualitative measures*, in order to discover ways in which effectiveness could be increased. Benchmarking using quantitative data is often referred to as financial benchmarking, since this usually involves using financial measures.

There are several methods of benchmarking. The type of benchmarking method applied depends upon the goals of the benchmarking process. Bendell et al. (1998) divide benchmarking methods into four groups: *internal, competitor, functional*, and *generic benchmarking*. This study is an example of financial competitor benchmarking. This implies that different companies that are competitors within the same industry are benchmarked against each other using various quantitative measures (i.e., financial ratios). The information used in the study is all taken from the companies' annual reports.

Self-Organizing Maps

Self-organizing maps (SOMs) are two-layer neural networks, consisting of an *input layer* and an *output layer*. SOMs are an example of neural networks that use the unsupervised learning method. This means that the network is presented with input data, but, as opposed to supervised learning, the network is not provided with desired outputs. The network is therefore allowed to freely organize itself according to similarities in the data, resulting in a map containing the input data. The SOM has turned out to be an excellent data-mining tool, suitable for exploratory data analysis problems, such as clustering, categorization, visualization, information compression, and hidden factor analysis.

Before the SOM algorithm is initiated, the map is randomly initialized. First, an array of nodes is created. This array can have one or more dimensions, but the most commonly used is the two-dimensional array. The two most common forms of lattice are rectangular and hexagonal, which are also the types used in the SOM_PAK software that was used to create the maps used in this experiment. These are illustrated in Figure 1. The figure represents *rectangular* and *hexagonal* lattices, i.e., 16 nodes. In the rectangular lattice, a node has four immediate neighbors with which it interacts; in the hexagonal lattice, it

Figure 1: (a) Rectangular lattice (size 4 x 4), and (b) Hexagonal lattice (size 4 x 4).

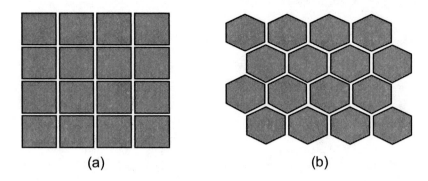

(a)   (b)

has six. The hexagonal lattice type is commonly considered better for visualization than the rectangular lattice type. The lattice can also be irregular, but this is less commonly used (Kohonen, 1997).

Each node i has an associated parametric reference vector m_i. The input data vectors, x, are mapped onto the array. Once this random initialization has been completed, the SOM algorithm is initiated.

The SOM algorithm operates in two steps, which are initiated for each sample in the data set (Kangas, 1994):

Step 1: The input data vector x is compared to the weight vectors m_i, and the best match m_c is located.

Step 2: The nodes within the neighborhood h_{ci} of c are "tuned" to the input data vector x.

These steps are repeated for the entire dataset, until a stopping criterion is reached, which can be either a predetermined amount of trials, or when the changes are small enough.

In Step 1, the best matching node to the input vector is found. The best matching node is determined using some form of distance function, for example, the smallest Euclidian distance function, defined as $\|x-m_i\|$. The best match, m_c, is found by using the formula in Equation 1 (Kohonen, 1997):

$$\|x - m_c\| = \min_i \left\{ \|x - m_i\| \right\}. \tag{1}$$

Once the best match, or winner, is found, Step 2 is initiated. This is the "learning step," in which the network surrounding node c is adjusted towards the input data vector. Nodes within a specified geometric distance, h_{ci}, will activate each other and learn something from the same input vector x. This will have a smoothing effect on the weight vectors in this neighborhood. The number of nodes affected depends upon the type of lattice and the neighborhood function. This learning process can be defined as (Kohonen, 1997):

$$m_i(t+1) = m_i(t) + h_{ci}(t)[x(t) - m_i(t)], \qquad (2)$$

where $t = 0,1,2,...$ is an integer, the discrete-time coordinate. The function $h_{ci}(t)$ is the neighborhood of the winning neuron c, and acts as the so-called *neighborhood function*, a smoothing kernel defined over the lattice points. The function $h_{ci}(t)$ can be defined in two ways. It can be defined as a neighborhood set of arrays around node c, denoted N_c, whereby $h_{ci}(t) = a(t)$ if $i \in N_c$, and $h_{ci}(t) = 0$ if $i \notin N_c$. Here $a(t)$ is defined as a learning rate factor (between 0 and 1). N_c can also be defined as a function of time, $N_c(t)$.

The function $h_{ci}(t)$ can also be defined as a *Gaussian* function, denoted:

$$h_{ci} = \alpha(t) \cdot \exp\left(-\frac{\|r_c - r_i\|^2}{2\sigma^2(t)}\right), \qquad (3)$$

where $\alpha(t)$ is again a learning rate factor, and the parameter $s(t)$ defines the width of the kernel, or radius of $N_c(t)$.

For small networks, the choice of process parameters is not very important, and the simpler neighborhood-set function for $h_{ci}(t)$ is therefore preferable (Kohonen, 1997). The training process is illustrated in Figure 2. The figure shows a part of a hexagonal SOM. First, the weight vectors are mapped randomly onto a two-dimensional, hexagonal lattice. This is illustrated in Figure 2 (a) by the weight vectors, illustrated by arrows in the nodes, pointing in random directions. In Figure 2 (a), the closest match to the input data vector x has been found in node c (Step 1). The nodes within the neighborhood h_{ci} learn from node c (Step 2). The size of the neighborhood h_{ci} is determined by the parameter $N_c(t)$, which is the neighborhood radius. The weight vectors within the neighborhood h_{ci} tune to, or learn from, the input data vector x. How much the vectors learn depends upon the learning rate factor $\alpha(t)$. In Figure 2 (b), the final, fully trained network is displayed. In a fully trained network, a number of groups should have emerged, with the weight vectors between the groups "flowing" smoothly into the different groups. If the neighborhood h_{ci} were to be too small, small groups of trained weight vectors would emerge, with largely untrained vectors in between, i.e., the arrows would not flow uniformly into each other. Figure 2 (b) is an example of a well-trained network.

The result of the SOM algorithm should be a map that displays the clusters of data, using dark shades to illustrate large distances and light shades to illustrate small distances (unified distance matrix, or U-matrix method) (Kohonen, 1997;Ultsch, 1993). On a finished map, lightly shaded borders indicate similar values, and dark borders indicate large differences. By observing the shades of the borders, it is possible to isolate clusters of similar data.

In order to identify the characteristics of the clusters on the U-matrix map, single vector-level maps, called feature planes, are also created. These maps display the distribution of individual columns of data— in this case, the values of individual financial

Figure 2: (a) A randomly initialized network after one learning step and (b) a fully trained network (Source: Kohonen, 1997).

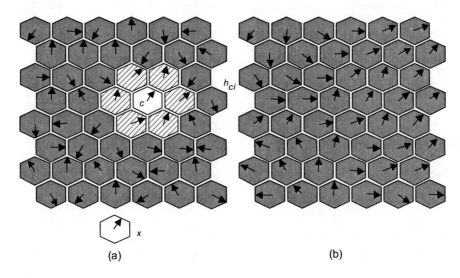

(a)   (b)

ratios. Three examples of feature planes are illustrated below in Figure 3 (a), (b), and (c). The feature planes display high values using lighter shades, and low values with dark shades. For example, in Figure 3 (a), companies located in the lower left corner of the map have the highest values in Operating Margin, while companies in the lower right corner have the lowest values. In Figure 3 (b), companies located in the upper left corner have the highest Return on Equity, while companies in the right corner again have the lowest values and so on.

Figure 3: (a) Operating Margin, (b) Return on Equity, and (c) Equity to Capital feature planes.

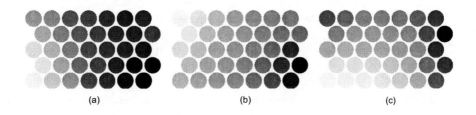

(a)   (b)   (c)

The quality of a map can be judged by calculating the average quantization error, E. The average quantization error represents the average distance between the best matching units and the sample data vectors. The average quantization error can be calculated using the formula:

$$E = \frac{1}{N} \sum_{i=1}^{N} \min_c \{ \| x_i - m_c \| \}, \tag{4}$$

where N is the total number of samples, xi is the input data vector, and mc is the best matching weight vector.

Often, the correct training of a SOM requires that the input data be standardized according to some method. Sarle (2001) suggests that the best alternative is one in which the data is centered on zero, instead of, for example, within the interval (0,1). This view is also advocated by Kohonen (1997). A common approach is to use the standard deviation when standardizing the data. Another option would be to use histogram equalization (Klimasauskas, 1991), used among others by Back et al. (1998, 2000).

Although the optimal parameters are different in each case, there are a number of recommendations for parameters used in the training process. These are actually more like starting points, from which to work out the optimal parameters for the experiment in particular. These recommendations will be discussed below.

The network topology refers to the shape of the lattice, i.e., rectangular or hexagonal. The topology should, in this case, be hexagonal, since hexagonal lattices are better for visualization purposes, as was previously mentioned.

Network size, or the dimensions of the map, is important for visualization purposes. If the map is too small, differences between units are hard to identify. Movements from map to map are also difficult to illustrate. However, a small map is best for cluster-identification purposes. On the other hand, if the map is too large, the clusters do not appear, and the map seems "flat." Another thing to remember is that the map dimensions should be rectangular instead of square. This is because the reference vectors must be oriented along with the x-axis in order for the network to stabilize during the learning process (Kohonen, Hynninen, Kangas, & Laaksonen, 1996). A commonly used principle is that the x-axis should be roughly 1.3 times the length of the y-axis.

The map is trained in two phases. The first phase is a rough training of the map, in which the network is allowed to learn a lot from each data vector. Therefore, learning rates and radiuses are high in the first phase, and there are less training steps (smaller training length). The second phase is a fine-tuning phase, in which the network learns less at a time, but data vectors are introduced to the network more times. Thus, learning rates and radiuses are lower than in the first phase, but the training length is much higher.

The training length in each phase refers to how many training steps are used, i.e., how many times data vectors are introduced to the network. The statistical accuracy of the mapping depends upon the number of steps in the final learning phase. This phase, therefore, has to be relatively large. A good rule of thumb is that, in order to achieve good statistical accuracy, the amount of steps in the final phase must be at least 500 times the amount of nodes in the network (Kohonen, 1997). It is common practice for the initial training phase to have at least 10% of the amount of steps used in the final phase.

The learning rate factor, or $\alpha(t)$, refers to how much a node learns from each data vector and should start out as fairly large in the first phase, but should be very low in the final phase. A commonly used starting point is 0.5 for the first phase, and 0.05 in the final phase.

The selection of the network neighborhood size, $N_c(t)$, is possibly the most important parameter. If the selected neighborhood size is too small, the network will not be ordered globally. This will result in various mosaic-like patterns, with unordered data in between. Therefore, the initial network radius should be rather large, preferably larger than half the network diameter (Kohonen, 1997). Generally, the final network radius should be about 10% of the radius used in the first part.

Financial Ratios

The performance of the companies included was rated according to seven different financial ratios. These were chosen based on an empirical study by Lehtinen (1996). Lehtinen rated different ratios according to two factors: their reliability in the international context, and the validity of the ratio. The reliability of a ratio implies how much the ratio is affected by international accounting differences, while validity measures how well the ratio measures the intended principle (Lehtinen, 1996). Since the comparison in this experiment is an international one, high reliability has been prioritized.

Financial ratios can be divided into four classes: profitability ratios, liquidity ratios, solvency ratios, and efficiency ratios (Lehtinen, 1996). The emphasis in this experiment has been on profitability, since this can be considered the most commonly used measure of a company's success. The chosen ratios are displayed below:

Profitability

1.   Operating Margin $\qquad \dfrac{Operating\ Profit}{Sales} \times 100$

2.   Return on Equity $\qquad \dfrac{Net\ Income}{Average\,(Share\,Capital + Retained\,Earnings)} \times 100$

3.   Return on Total Assets $\qquad \dfrac{Total\ Income + Interest\ Expense}{Average\,(Total\,Assets)} \times 100$

Liquidity

4.   Quick Ratio $\qquad \dfrac{Current\ Assets}{Current\ Liabilities}$

Solvency

5.   Equity to Capital $\dfrac{Share\ Capital + Retained\ Earnings}{Average\ (Total\ Assets)} \times 100$

6.   Interest Coverage $\dfrac{Interest\ Expense + Income\ Tax + Net\ Income}{Average\ (Accounts\ Receivable)}$

Efficiency

7.   Receivables Turnover $\dfrac{Net\ Sales}{Average\ (Accounts\ Receivable)}$

Profitability naturally measures how well a company is able to generate profit on the invested capital. Operating Margin was chosen as the first ratio for three reasons. First, it is a very commonly used ratio, and second, it is very simple and quick to calculate. Finally, and most importantly, it is a rather reliable measure in an international context. This is because it uses total income instead of net income, thus ignoring posts like extraordinary income/expenses, depreciation in excess of plan, and taxation. There is, however, a problem with Operating Margin. Since Operating Margin is an *income statement ratio*, implying that figures are only taken from the income statement, the ratio does not take capital into account. This makes the ratio less valid (Lehtinen, 1996).

In order to remedy this, Return on Equity (ROE) and Return on Total Assets (ROTA) were also included as profitability ratios. These ratios are called *mixed ratios*, since they take into account both the income statement and the balance sheet, thus providing us with ratios that take into account both profit and capital. This makes them very valid ratios for measuring profit. Of the two ratios, ROE is more sensitive to international accounting differences, thus making it slightly less reliable than Operating Margin or ROTA. This is because ROE uses net income, which is more heavily influenced by accounting differences than total income. Also, the denominator of ROE includes retained earnings, which contain differences retained from previous years. However, because of its very high validity, ROE was included in the experiment. ROTA, on the other hand, is both very valid and very reliable in an international context (Lehtinen, 1996).

Liquidity ratios measure the ability of a company to meet its short-term financial obligations, i.e., how much liquid assets (cash, sales receivables, inventories, etc.) a company has. Quick Ratio, like Operating Margin, was chosen because it is commonly used, is easy to calculate, and is very reliable. Quick ratio, unlike Current Ratio, does not include the value of inventories, since these are in many ways not as liquid as receivables or cash. However, Quick Ratio is less valid than ratios that include figures from both the income statement and balance sheet. However, such ratios are very complicated to calculate and are not as reliable as Quick Ratio and Current Ratio (Lehtinen, 1996).

Solvency ratios measure how indebted a company is, or how well a company is able to meet its long-term financial obligations. Equity to Capital is included because it is one of the most commonly used ratios in financial comparisons. However, it does suffer from much of the same problems as ROE and is not therefore as reliable as some other ratios. Therefore, Interest Coverage was included as a second solvency ratio, since it is much more reliable than Equity to Capital (Lehtinen, 1996).

Efficiency, as the name indicates, measures how efficiently a company uses its resources. In this experiment, Receivables Turnover was chosen since it is both valid and reliable (Lehtinen, 1996).

COMPANIES INCLUDED

Each year, in its September issue, *Pulp and Paper International* ranks the top 150 pulp and paper-producing companies in the world, according to net sales. The list for 1998 (Matussek, Janssens, Kenny, & Riannon, 1999) was used as the basis when choosing the companies in Eklund et al. (2001). Since then, an updated list has been reviewed (Rhiannon, Jewitt, Galasso, & Fortemps, 2001), and the changes were incorporated in the experiment. This experiment was limited to using data available through the companies' annual reports for the years 1995-2000. The primary source for these annual reports was the individual companies' homepages on the Internet, but any physical reports available were also used.

The principle problem in the choice of companies was getting annual reports for all five years. As it turns out, many companies did not provide enough information on their homepages, and we were forced to leave out many companies that were highly ranked on the Top 150 list. This problem was most common among European (excluding Scandinavian companies) and Asian countries, although some U.S. and Canadian companies also caused difficulties. However, through large online databases, we were able to obtain adequate financial information for most U.S., Canadian, and Japanese companies. Generally, the companies that provided the most financial information on their pages were Finnish or Swedish. The final selection of companies is illustrated in Table 1.

Some companies could not be included for other reasons. For example, on the list for 2000, Proctor & Gamble (P&G) was listed as the third largest producer in the world. However, as only 30% of P&G's turnover comes from pulp and paper, we decided not to include it. Also, number six on the list, Nippon Unipac holding, was formed by the merger of Nippon Paper Industries and Daishowa Paper in March 2001, and was, therefore, still included as two separate companies. Also, two companies (Stora Enso and UPM-Kymmene), were included as single companies, even though they emerged through the mergers of companies during the course of the experiment. However, using consolidated reports published by the companies after the merger, we included them as single companies, in order to simplify analysis.

Table 1: The included companies

Finland		
1	Average	
2	Ahlström	1995-00
3	M-Real Oy	1995-00
4	Stora Enso OY	1995-00
5	UPM-Kymmene OY	1995-00
Sweden		
6	Average	
7	AssiDomän	1995-00
8	Korsnäs	1995-00
9	MoDo AB	1995-00
10	Munksjö AB	1995-00
11	Rottneros AB	1995-00
12	SCA AB	1995-00
13	Södra AB	1995-00
Norway		
14	Average	
15	Norske Skog A.S.	1995-00
16	Peterson Group	1995-00
USA		
17	Average	
18	Boise Cascade	1995-00
19	Bowater	1995-00
20	Buckeye Techologies	1995-00
21	Caraustar Industries	1995-00
22	Champion International	1995-99
23	Consolidated Papers	1995-99
24	Crown Vantage	1995-99
25	Fort James	1995-99
26	Gaylord Container Corp	1995-00
27	Georgia-Pacific Corp	1995-00
28	International Paper	1995-00
29	Jefferson-Smurfit Corp.	1995-00
30	Kimberly-Clark	1995-00
31	Longview Fiber Corp.	1995-00
32	Mead	1995-00
33	P.H. Glatfelter	1995-00
34	Pope & Talbot	1995-00
35	Potlatch Corp.	1995-00
36	Rayonier	1995-00
37	Riverwood Holding	1995-00
38	Rock-Tenn Company	1995-00
39	Schweitzer-Mauduit Intl.	1995-00
40	Sonoco Products	1995-00
41	Stone Container	1995-97
42	Temple-Inland	1995-00
43	Union Camp.	1995-98

USA (Continued)		
44	Wausau-Mosinee Paper	1995-00
45	Westvaco	1995-00
46	Weyerhaeuser	1995-00
47	Willamette Industries	1995-00
Canada		
48	Average	
49	Abitibi Consolidated	1995-00
50	Alliance	1995-00
51	Canfor	1995-00
52	Cascades Inc.	1995-00
53	Crestbrook Forest Ind.Ltd.	1995-97
54	Doman Industries	1995-00
55	Domtar Inc.	1995-00
56	Donohue	1995-99
57	MacMillan Bloedel	1995-98
58	Nexfor	1995-00
59	Tembec Inc.	1995-00
60	West Fraser Timber	1995-00
Japan		
61	Average	
62	Daio Paper	1995-99
63	Daishowa Paper Manuf	1995-99
64	Chuetsu Paper	1995-99
65	Hokuetsu Paper Mills	1995-99
66	Japan Paperboard Industr	1995-99
67	Mitsubishi Paper	1995-99
68	Nippon Kakoh Seishi	1995-99
69	Nippon Paper Industries	1995-00
70	Oji Paper	1995-00
71	Pilot (Lintec)	1995-00
72	Rengo	1995-99
73	Settsu	1995-98
74	Tokai Pulp & Paper	1995-99
Europe		
75	Average	
76	ENCE Group (Spain)	1995-00
77	Frantschach (AUT)	1995-99
78	Industrieholding Cham (SUI)	1995-00
79	Inveresk (UK)	1995-00
80	Mayr-Melnhof (AUT)	1995-00
81	Reno de Medici (ITA)	1995-00
84	Cartiere Burgo (ITA)	1995-00
Australia & New Zealand		
82	Amcor (AUS)	1995-00
83	Fletcher Challenge Group (NZE)	1995-99

CONSTRUCTING THE MAPS

In order to improve the training process of the neural network, input data must often be preprocessed. In this case, we refer to preprocessing as the process of standardizing the data according to some method, although the term also includes the "cleaning" of data, i.e., the removal of errors, missing values, and inconsistencies. If data is not preprocessed, the neural network might expend its learning time on variables with large variances or values, and therefore ignore variables with smaller variances or values.

Preprocessing of data is a much-discussed method in literature concerning neural networks. Sarle (2001) suggests that the most suitable form of normalization centers the input values around zero, instead of, for example, within the interval [0,1]. This would imply the use of, for example, normalization by standard deviation. Kohonen (1997) suggests two methods for standardizing the data: normalization by standard deviation and heuristically justifiable rescaling. Another method, suggested by Klimasauskas (1991), and used, for example, by Back et al. (1998, 2000), is histogram equalization. Histogram equalization is a way of mapping rare events to a small part of the data range, and spreading out frequent events. This way the network is better able to discriminate between rare and frequent events.

Normally, the values should be scaled according to their relative importance. However, according to Kaski and Kohonen (1996), this is not necessary when no differences in importance can be assumed. As this is also the case in this experiment, we have not used any form of scaling according to importance. Instead, the relative importance of the different categories of ratios has been set through the balance of ratios (three in profitability, two in solvency, one in liquidity, and one in efficiency).

In this experiment, the data has been standardized according to the variance of the entire dataset (Equations 5 and 6), also the method used by Kaski and Kohonen (1996).

$$\sigma^2 = \frac{1}{MN-1} \sum_{n=1}^{M} \sum_{i=1}^{N} (x_{in} - \bar{x})^2, \tag{5}$$

$$\tilde{x}_{in} = \frac{(x_{in} - \bar{x}_i)}{\sigma^2}, \tag{6}$$

where M = number of ratios, N = number of observations, x = value of ratio, and $\bar{x}$ = the average of the financial ratios.

Normalizing the data according to the standard deviation was tried, but the maps obtained using this method were unsatisfactory for clustering purposes. Also, in order to achieve feasible results, a preliminary rescaling had to be done. This implied replacing extreme values with 50 (positive or negative). The reason for this is that a number of the ratios reached incredibly high values, which caused the SOM to illustrate one area with extreme values on the map, with the rest of the map being flat and uninterpretable. Therefore, such extreme values were replaced in this experiment.

The SOM_PAK 3.1 program package was used to train the maps in this experiment. SOM_PAK is a program package created by a team of researchers at the Neural Networks Research Centre (NNRC) at the Helsinki University of Technology (HUT). SOM_PAK can be downloaded from http://www.cis.hut.fi/research/som_pak/, and may be freely used for scientific purposes. Readers are referred to the program package for sample data. The maps were visualized using Nenet 1.1, another downloadable program. A limited demo version of Nenet is available at http://koti.mbnet.fi/~phodju/nenet/Nenet/Download.html. Nenet is actually a complete SOM training program, but the demo version is severely limited, and has been used for visualization, since the maps are illustrated in shades of green instead of black and white. In our opinion, this makes the maps easier to interpret.

Several hundred maps were trained during the course of the experiment. The first maps were trained using parameters selected according to the guidelines presented in the previous section. The best maps, rated according to quantization error and ease of readability, were then selected and used as a basis when training further maps. The final selected network size was 7×5. We felt that this map size offered the best balance between cluster identification and movement illustration. Clusters were easier to identify than on a 9×6 sized map, and movements within the clusters were easier to identify than on a 5×4 sized map. A smaller map could have been used if a separate map had been trained for each year, but our intention was to use the same map for the entire dataset. A 7×5 sized map seemed large enough to incorporate the data for each year included in the test. The 7×5 lattice also conforms to the recommendation that the x-axis be = $1.3 \times$ the y-axis. The simpler neighborhood-set function or *bubble*, referring to an array of nodes around the winning node, N_c (Kohonen et al., 1996) for $h_{ci}(t)$ is preferred over the Gaussian function in the training of smaller maps (Kohonen, 1997), and was therefore used in this experiment as well.

The number of steps used in the final phase was generated directly from the recommendations provided in the previous section. Therefore, the initial phase includes 1,750 steps and the final phase 17,500 steps. The learning rate factor was set to 0.5 in the first phase and 0.05 in the second, also as was recommended. The neighborhood radius was set to 12 for the first phase and 1.2 for the second. The initial radius was very large compared to the recommendations, but seemed to provide for the overall best maps. As the first phase is intended for rough training, the initial radius was allowed to be the entire map. In the fine-tuning phase, the radius was reduced considerably. Decreasing the radius in the first phase only resulted in poorer maps.

Kohonen (1997) noted that the selection of parameters appears to make little difference in the outcome when training small maps. This also appears to be the case in this experiment. As long as the initial selected parameters remained near the guidelines presented above, the changes in the quantization error were very small, usually as little as 0.001. Some examples of the parameters and outcomes are illustrated in Table 2. These are only a fraction of the entire training set, but illustrate well the small differences in results.

Table 2: Examples of trained 7x5 maps

7x5	1	2	3	4	5	6	7
X-Dimension	7	7	7	7	7	7	7
Y-Dimension	5	5	5	5	5	5	5
Training length 1	1,750	1,750	1,750	1,750	1,750	1,750	1,750
Training rate 1	0.5	0.5	0.6	0.5	0.3	0.4	0.4
Radius 1	12	12	12	12	12	13	12
Training length 2	17,500	20,000	17,500	17,500	17,500	17,500	17,500
Training rate 2	0.05	0.05	0.05	0.09	0.05	0.05	0.04
Radius 2	1.2	1.2	1.2	1.2	1.2	1.2	1.2
Error	0.048624	0.048626	0.049509	0.04877	0.049675	0.050086	0.048241

Table 2 shows that the changes in quantization errors are very small, irrespective of the parameters used. The map that was finally chosen was Map 1. It is notable that this map was trained using parameters generated directly from the recommendations above, with the exception of the network radius. Map 7 has a marginally better quantization error, but the difference is negligible, so the map closer to the original recommendations, Map 1, was selected. The appearance of the maps was monitored throughout the experiment, but very small differences in the resulting maps surfaced. Although the maps might look slightly different, the same clusters containing approximately the same companies, were found in the same positions relative to each other. While the "good" end of one map might have been found on the opposite side of another map, the same clusters could still be seen to emerge. This shows the random initialization process of the self-organizing map, but also proves that the results from one map to another are consistent.

A single map including all five years of data was trained. By studying the final U-matrix map (Figure 4a), and the underlying feature planes (Appendix) of the map, a number of clusters of companies, and the characteristics of these clusters, can be identified (Figure 4 b).

The groups and their characteristics are presented as the following:

Group A consists of the best performing companies. Group A is divided into two subgroups: A_1 and A_2. The companies in subgroup A_1 are the best performing of all companies, especially according to profitability ratios. These companies have very high profitability, solidity, and efficiency, and medium liquidity. Subgroup A_2 consists of well-performing companies with high profitability (especially in Return on Equity ratios), and average solidity and liquidity.

Figure 4: (a) The final U-matrix map, and (b) identified clusters on the map.

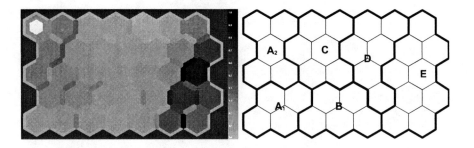

Table 3: Cluster descriptions

	A1	A2	B	C	D	E
Operating Margin	Very High	High	Low	Average	Low	Very Low
ROE	High	Very High	Average	High	Average	Low
ROTA	Very High	High	Average	Average	Low	Very Low
Equity to Capital	Very High	Low	Very High	Average	Average	Low
Quick Ratio	Average	High	Average	Very High	Low	Very Low
Interest Coverage	Very High	Average	Low	Low	Low	Very Low
Receivables Turnover	Very High	Average	High	Low	Very Low	Average

Group B is an average group, performing decently according to all ratios. The companies in Group B have low profitability but high solidity.

Group C can be classed as a slightly above-average group. Group C has lower Equity to Capital ratios than Group B. However, Group C has higher profitability, notably in Return on Equity ratios. In addition, Group C contains the companies that have the highest liquidity. Group C has average to high profitability, average solidity, and very high liquidity.

Group D is best classed as slightly below average. The group has average solidity, but low profitability and very low liquidity. This group also contains the companies with the lowest efficiency ratios.

Group E is the poorest performing group. The group contains companies that are performing poorly according to almost all ratios, especially profitability ratios.

The characteristics of the groups are summarized in Table 3.

RESULTS

Country Averages

The first benchmarking objects were the averages for each country or region included in the experiment. The regional averages consist of the average values of the ratios of all companies from that region. By benchmarking the national or regional averages first, it is possible to isolate differences due to accounting practices or other differences that affect all companies from a given country.

The results are presented in Figure 5. The arrows indicate movements from year to year, starting from 1995. The Finnish average's movements are shown using solid lines,

Figure 5: Country averages for the years 1995-2000.

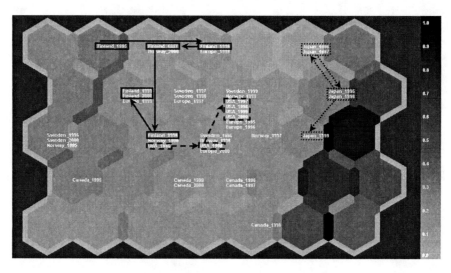

Figure 6: Market pulp prices 1985-99 (Source: Metsäteollisuus ry Internal report; Keaton, 1999).

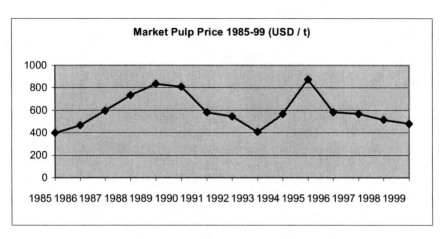

U.S. average's movements using dashed lines, and Japanese average's movements using dotted lines. The figure illustrates that the performance of Finnish companies, on average, has been slightly above average. The Finnish average has remained in Group C throughout the experiment, except for during 1995, when it was within Group A2. This implies that while Return on Equity has been high, other profitability ratios have been average. This is probably due to the common Finnish practice of heavy financing by debt. Where Return on Total Assets is considered, Finnish performance is merely average. Finnish Quick Ratios, on the other hand, are very good throughout, and excellent during 1998-2000.

The excellent performance of the Scandinavian countries during 1995 is very interesting. During 1995, Finnish, Swedish, and Norwegian companies, on average, outperformed all other companies, except for Canadian companies. However, the following years indicate drastically reduced profitability. A likely explanation for this trend is the fall in market pulp prices during the later half of the 1990s. In 1995, market pulp prices were very high (USD 871 / metric ton), but fell drastically during the following years to USD 480 / metric ton in mid 1999 (Keaton, 1999). Pulp prices are illustrated in Figure 6.

The poorest average is displayed by Japan. The Japanese average is consistently in one of the two poor groups, Group D or E. The drop during 1997 is likely due to the Asian financial crisis. Interestingly, the Asian financial crisis does not seem to affect other countries as badly as might be expected. The national averages of Sweden, Norway, and the U.S. do drop somewhat, but not nearly as dramatically or obviously as the Japanese average.

Another factor that might affect the Japanese average is prevailing accounting laws. Japanese accounting laws are very restrictive, compared to, for example, U.S. accounting laws. For example, Japanese companies value assets at historical costs, never at valuation. They are also forced to establish non-distributable legal reserves, and most costs must be capitalized directly. Also, with accounting statements being used to calculate taxation, there is an incentive to minimize profits. Overall, Japanese accounting principles can be seen as very conservative, and so might lead to understated asset and profit figures, especially when compared to U.S. or other Anglo-Saxon figures. These factors might partly explain the poor performance of the Japanese companies in this experiment (Nobes & Parker, 1991).

Sweden, Norway, Europe, and the U.S. exhibit rather similar behavior, only really differing during the year 1995, when Finnish, Swedish, and Norwegian performance was excellent (Group A_2). During most years, these countries show low to average profitability and average solvency. The companies in question are usually found in Groups C or D. Canadian companies consistently show better solvency than most companies from the other countries, being found in Group B during most years. Scandinavian accounting laws can also be seen as rather conservative, compared to Anglo-Saxon laws. Scandinavian companies also value assets at historical costs, but are, on the other hand, not forced to establish non-distributable legal reserves.

The widely differing results of the Finnish, Canadian, and Japanese companies indicate that national differences, such as financing practices or accounting differences, might have an effect on the overall positioning of companies on the map. On the other hand, the financial ratios have been chosen based on their reliability in international comparisons, in order to minimize differences relating to accounting practices.

The Five Largest Pulp and Paper Companies

In Figure 7, the Top Five pulp and paper manufacturing companies (Rhiannon et al., 2001) are benchmarked against each other. Again, the movements from year to year are illustrated with arrows: solid black lines for International Paper, dashed black lines for Georgia-Pacific, solid white lines for Stora Enso, dotted white lines for Oji Paper, and

Figure 7: Movements of the top five pulp and paper companies during the years 1995-2000.

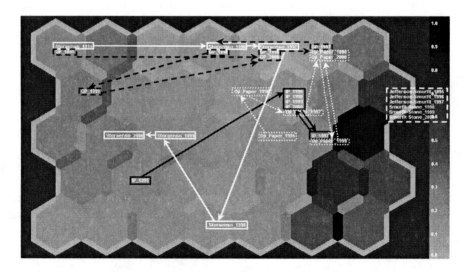

dashed white lines for Smurfit-Stone Container Corp. As was mentioned earlier, Proctor & Gamble and Nippon Unipac Holding could not be included in this study, and therefore, Smurfit-Stone Container Corp. rose into the Top Five instead.

An interesting note is that, with the exception of 1995, International Paper, the largest pulp and paper manufacturer in the world, is consistently found in one of the poorly performing groups, showing poor performance during most years, particularly according to profitability ratios.

Georgia-Pacific (GP), the second largest in the world, rose into the Top Five through its acquisition of Fort James in 2000. With exception of 1995 and 1999, GP's performance is not very convincing. Profitability is average to poor, and solidity is average. It is, however, interesting to note that the performance of Georgia-Pacific is very similar to that of Stora Enso during the years 1995-1997.

Stora Enso (fourth largest) moves from very good in 1995 to downright poor performance in 1997. The substantial change in position on the map in 1998 was due to a combination of two factors. The first was decreased profitability due to costs associated with the merger of Stora and Enso. The second factor was a strengthened capital structure, which of course further affected profitability ratios like ROE and ROTA. However, profitability improved again in 1999. Stora Enso was performing excellently in 1995, when pulp prices were high, but profitability fell as market pulp prices dropped. In 2000, however, Stora Enso was among the best performing companies.

As can be expected, the performance of Oji Paper (fifth largest) reflects the Japanese average and is very poor. This points to the effect of the Asian financial crisis, which is examined in the next section.

Smurfit-Stone Container Corp., the seventh largest in the world, is consistently a very poor performer. The company does not move at all during the experiment, being found in Group E during all years. The company consistently shows low profitability and liquidity, and very low solidity.

With the notable exception of Stora Enso, performance among the top companies is very poor, particularly in profitability ratios. In the Top 150 list from 1998 (Matusek et al., 1999), the Top Five still included Kimberly-Clark and UPM-Kymmene (currently eighth and ninth). These companies, in particular Kimberly-Clark, are very good performers, as will be shown in later in the chapter. The consolidation of the industry during the past few years has led to very large, but also largely inefficient companies.

The Impact of the Asian Financial Crisis

During the nineties, the Asian economy was hard hit by the financial crisis. This means that it will have affected many companies during a long period. However, the peak of the crisis was during 1997-98 (Corsetti, Pesenti, & Roubini, 1998), and should therefore show most dramatically during the years 1998 and 1999. As was mentioned in an earlier discussion, financial information for the year 2000 was very hard to find for Japanese companies. Therefore, only a few companies could be included for 2000.

Figure 8 illustrates the Japanese companies during the years 1997-99. Movements by the companies are illustrated using solid white arrows.

The effect of the crisis is obvious on the map. Although Japanese companies already appear to be performing worse than western companies (as discussed earlier), the trend towards even worse performance during the years 1998 and 1999 is obvious.

Figure 8: Japanese companies during the years 1997-2000.

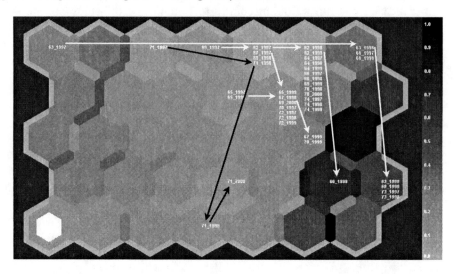

The most dramatic example of this is Daishowa Paper Manufacturing (Company No. 63), which moved from Group A$_2$ (excellent) to Group E (very poor) in three years. The same can be said, for example, of Nippon Paper Industries (No. 69), Daio Paper (No. 62), Mitsubishi Paper (No. 67), and Hokuetsu Paper Mills (No. 65), although the effect has not been as dramatic as for Daishowa Paper Manufacturing. Some companies appear unaffected and remain in the same node throughout the years 1997-99. Examples of such companies are Tokai Pulp & Paper (No. 74), Rengo (No. 72), and Chuetsu Paper (No. 64). The only example of the opposite behavior is Pilot (No. 71, illustrated using solid black arrows), which improves from Group D in 1998 to Group B in 1999-2000.

It is remarkable that, apart from Pilot, no Japanese company improved its positioning on the map during the years 1997-99. This is proof of the heavy effect that the crisis has had on the Japanese economy.

The Best Performers

In Figure 9, the best performing companies are shown. The criterion for being selected was that the company could be found in Group A during at least three years during the period 1995-99.

A number of interesting changes in companies' positions can be observed on the map in Figure 9. Some of the companies show a dramatic improvement in performance over the years. For example, Caraustar Industries (No. 21, solid white arrow) moves from being in Group E during 1995, to four straight years (1996-99) in Group A$_2$. Caraustar attributes this increase to completed acquisitions and lower raw material costs. However, in 2000, the company drops back into Group D. In its annual report, Caraustar states that this dramatic decrease in profitability is primarily due to restructuring and other nonrecurring costs, and also to a certain extent, higher energy costs and lower volumes. Kimberly-Clark exhibits a similar increase (No. 30, dashed white arrow), moving from the poor end of the

Figure 9: The best companies.

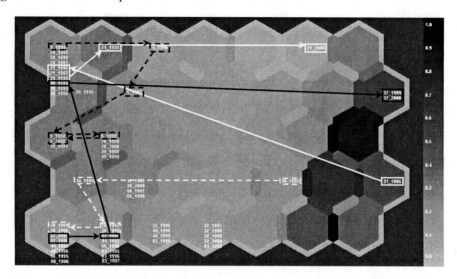

map in 1995, to Group A$_1$ during 1996-99. Kimberly-Clark explains the poor performance of 1995 with the merger between Kimberly-Clark and Scott Paper Company. The merger required the sale of several profitable businesses in order to satisfy U.S. and European competition authorities. The merger also caused a substantial one-time charge of 1,440 million USD, decreasing profitability further. However, profitability was back up again in 1996, and remained excellent through to 2000. On the other hand, Riverwood Holding (No. 37, solid black arrow) goes from Group A$_1$ in 1995-97, to Group A$_2$ in 1998, and Group E in 1999-00. This decrease in performance is rather dramatic, and can, according to Riverwood, be attributed to lower sales volumes in its international folding cartonboard markets. This was primarily due to weak demand in Asia, and to the effect of the canceling of a number of low-margin businesses in the U.K.

Some of the consistently best-performing companies include Wausau-Mosinee Paper (No. 44), Schweitzer-Mauduit Intl (No. 39), Buckeye Technologies (No. 20), UPM-Kymmene (No. 5, dashed black arrows), and Donohue (No. 56, which was acquired by Abitibi Consolidated in 2000).

The Poorest Performers

The poorest performing companies are illustrated in Figure 10. The criterion for being selected was that the company could be found in Group E (the poorest group) during at least three years.

This map also shows some dramatic movement. Crown Vantage (No. 24, solid black arrow) is perhaps the most dramatic example; in one year, the company fell from Group A$_2$ (1995) to Group E (1996-99). Crown Vantage states in its annual report that the reason for its poor performance in 1996 is the low price of coated ground-wood paper, and that when it spun off from James River Corporation (now Fort James) at the end of 1995, Crown

Figure 10: The poorest performing companies.

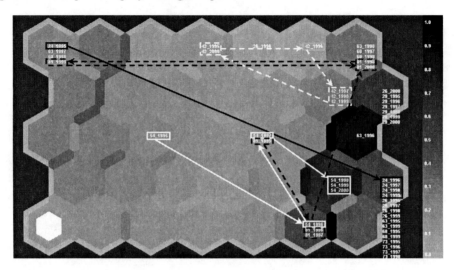

Vantage assumed a large amount of debt. Crown Vantage was unable to pay this debt, and applied for a Chapter 11 (bankruptcy) on March 15, 2000. Year 2000 data is therefore not available.

Doman Industries (No. 54, solid white arrows) exhibits similar, through not as dramatic, behavior. Doman falls from Group B (1995) to settle in Group D or E throughout the rest of the experiment. According to Doman, this was due to a poor pulp market. In 1997, the market for pulp improved, only to decline again in 1998. Doman cites the Asian financial crisis as the reason for the second drop, primarily the declining market in Japan. Temple-Inland (No. 42, dashed white arrow) falls from Group B in 1995 to Group E in 1997, from where it rises back to Group B in 2000. Temple-Inland states weak demand and lowered prices for corrugated packaging as the reason for this decline in 1997. An example of the opposite behavior is Reno de Medici (No. 81, dashed black arrows), which moves from Group D in 1995, through Group E in 1996, to Group A_2 in 1999. However, the company falls back into Group E in 2000.

A number of companies identified as very poor performers are also illustrated on the map. These are Crown Vantage (No. 24, solid black arrows), Gaylord Container Corp (No. 26), Jefferson-Smurfit Corp (No. 29), and Settsu (No. 73).

CONCLUSIONS

In this study, financial information for 77 companies in the international pulp and paper industry for the years 1995-2000 was collected using the Internet as a source of information, and a financial database was created. A number of financial ratios were selected and calculated based on the information in the database. Then, a data-mining tool, the self-organizing map, was used to perform a financial competitor benchmarking of these companies.

This tool offers a number of benefits over other alternatives. Using self-organizing maps, we can compare much larger amounts of data than by using spreadsheet programs. It is also useful for exploratory data analysis, where patterns are not known a priori. Unlike traditional clustering methods, like k-means clustering, the number or size of clusters does not have to be decided a priori, and visualization is much more graphic. A drawback with self-organizing maps is that the person who runs the analysis has to be an experienced user of neural networks. Also, like all neural networks, self-organizing maps are "black boxes," i.e., the user does not see how the network works or what it does, only the result. Finally, technical issues, such as standardizing the data, are very important for the final result.

The results of the study provide further evidence that the self-organizing map is a feasible and effective tool for financial benchmarking. The results are easy to visualize and interpret, and provide a very practical way to compare the financial performance of different companies. The discovered patterns were confirmed with existing domain knowledge.

FUTURE RESEARCH IN THIS AREA

With managers facing increasing amounts of information to process daily, the need for intelligent tools to perform these operations is likely to increase in the future. This situation is accentuated by the exponentially increasing amount of information available through the Internet. We simply cannot cope with this information overload any longer without using intelligent tools. Therefore, the use of data-mining tools, such as self-organizing maps, is likely to increase dramatically in the future.

In this study, the self-organizing map has been shown to be a feasible tool for financial benchmarking. The results are easy to visualize and interpret, provide a very practical way to compare the financial performance of different companies, and could be used as a complement to traditional net sales comparisons (Rhiannon, Jewitt, Galasso, & Fortemps, 2001).

Using this method, an interesting pattern emerges. It is interesting to note that most of the largest pulp and paper-producing companies in the world, with the exception of Kimberly-Clark, belong to below-average groups. The ranking shows that the largest companies according to net sales are not necessarily the best-performing companies. In fact, the smaller companies appear to utilize their resources much more effectively than their larger competitors.

As has been shown in several studies (Neural Networks Research Centre, 2001), the application range for self-organizing maps is virtually limitless, and is certainly not restricted to use in financial benchmarking. One potentially huge application for self-organizing maps in the future is within Web mining. Web mining is a data-mining technique for comparing the contents of Web pages in order to provide more accurate search engines. The possibility of applying neural network technology, called WEBSOM, to solve this problem is very interesting, and preliminary results are encouraging (Honkela, Kaski, Lagus, & Kohonen, 1997; Lagus, 2000).

ACKNOWLEDGMENTS

The financial support of TEKES (Grant Number 40943/99) and the Academy of Finland is gratefully acknowledged.

REFERENCES

Adriaans, P. & Zantinge, D. (1996). *Data mining.* Boston, MA: AddisonWesley Longman.

Alhoniemi, E., Hollmén, J., Simula, O., & Vesanto, J. (1999). Process monitoring and modeling using the self-organizing map. *Integrated Computer Aided Engineering,* 6(1), 3-14.

Ambroise, C., Seze, G., Badran, F., & Thiria, S. (2000). Hierarchical clustering of self-organizing maps for cloud classification. *Neurocomputing,* 30(1), 47-52.

Back, B., Sere, K., & Vanharanta, H. (1997). Analyzing financial performance with self-organizing maps. *Proceedings of the Workshop on Self-Organizing Maps WSOM'97,* June, Espoo, Finland: Helsinki University of Technology, 356-361.

Back, B., Sere, K., & Vanharanta, H. (1998). Managing complexity in large data bases using self-organizing maps. *Accounting Management and Information Technologies 8,* 191-210.

Back, B., Öström, K., Sere, K., & Vanharanta, H. (2000). Analyzing company performance using Internet data. *Proceedings of the 11th Meeting of the Euro Working Group on DSS,* June, Toulouse, France: IRIT, Université Paul Sabatier, 52-56.

Becanovic, V. G. M. U. (2000). Image object classification using saccadic search, spatio-temporal pattern encoding and self-organization. *Pattern Recognition Letters,* 21(3), 253-263.

Bendell, T., Boulter, L., & Goodstadt, P. (1998). *Benchmarking for competitive advantage.* London: Pitman Publishing.

Chen, D., Chang, R., & Huang, Y. (2000). Breast cancer diagnosis using self-organizing maps for sonography. *Ultrasound in Medicine and Biology,* 26, 405-411.

Corsetti, G., Pesenti, P., & Roubini, N. (1998). What caused the Asian currency and financial crisis? Part 1: A macroeconomic view. Available online at: < http://www.stern.nyu.edu/globalmacro/AsianCrisis.pdf >.

Costea, A., Kloptchenko, A., & Back, B. (2001). Analyzing economical performance of central-east-European countries Using neural networks and cluster analysis, *Proceedings of the Fifth International Symposium on Economic Informatics,* May, Bucharest, Rumania: Editura Inforec, pp. 1006-1011.

Eklund, T. (2000). *On the application of self-organizing maps in benchmarking – As applied to the pulp and paper industry.* Unpublished Masters Thesis. Department of Information Systems, Åbo Akademi University, Turku, Finland.

Eklund, T., Back, B., Vanharanta, H., & Visa, A. (2001). *Benchmarking international pulp and paper companies using self-organizing maps.* TUCS Technical Report No. 396, Turku Centre for Computer Science, Turku, Finland.

Gustafsson, L. (1992). *Bäst i klassen: Benchmarking för högre effektivitet.* Uppsala, Sweden: Sveriges Verkstadsindustrier.

Honkela, T., Kaski, S., Lagus, K., & Kohonen, T. (1997). WEBSOM – Self-organizing maps of document collections. *Proceedings of WSOM'97: Workshop on Self-Organizing Maps*, June, Espoo, Finland: Helsinki University of Technology, 310-315.

Kangas, J. (1994). *On the analysis of pattern sequences by self-organizing maps.* Espoo, Finland: Helsinki University of Technology.

Karlöf, B. (1997). *Benchmarking i verkligheten: De goda förebildernas inspiration till lärande och affärsutveckling.* Borgå: Werner Söderström.

Karlsson, J. (2001). *Financial benchmarking of telecommunications companies.* Unpublished Masters Thesis, Department of Information Systems, Åbo Akademi University, Turku, Finland.

Karlsson, J., Back, B., Vanharanta, H. & Visa, A. (2001). *Financial benchmarking of telecommunications companies.* TUCS Technical Report No. 395, Turku Centre for Computer Science, Turku, Finland.

Kaski, S., Kangas, J., & Kohonen, T. (1998). Bibliography of self-organizing map (SOM) papers: 1981-1997. *Neural Computing Surveys*, 1, 102-350

Kaski, S. & Kohonen, T. (1996). Exploratory data analysis by the self-organizing map: Structures of welfare and poverty in the world. *Proceedings of the Third International Conference on Neural Networks in the Capital Markets*, October, Singapore. London, England: World Scientific, 498-507.

Keaton, D. (1999), Grade profile. Market pulp: Prospects improving with increased demand, less new capacity. *Pulp and Paper International* August. Available online at: <http://www.paperloop.com/db_area/archive/p_p_mag/1999/9908/grade.htm>.

Kiang, M. & Kumar, A. (2001). An evaluation of self-organizing map networks as a robust alternative to factor analysis in data- mining applications. *Information Systems Research,* 12 (2), 177-194.

Klimasauskas, C. C. (1991). Applying neural networks, Part IV: Improving performance. *PC/AI Magazine*, 5 (4), 34-41.

Kohonen, T. (1997). *Self-organizing maps.* 2nd ed. Heidelberg: Springer-Verlag.

Kohonen, T., Hynninen, J., Kangas, J., & Laaksonen, J. (1996). *The self-organizing map program package.* Espoo, Finland: University of Technology.

Lagus, K. (2000). *Text mining with the WEBSOM.* Acta Polytechnica Scandinavica, Mathematics and Computing Series No. 110, Espoo, Finland: Helsinki University of Technology.

Lehtinen, J. (1996). *Financial ratios in an international comparison.* Vaasa: Universitas Wasaensis.

Martín-del-Brío, B. & Serrano-Cinca, C. (1993). Self-organizing neural networks for the analysis and representation of data: Some financial cases. *Neural Computing and Applications*, No. 1, 193-206.

Matussek, H., Janssens, I., Kenny, J., & Riannon, J. (1999). The Top 150: A tale of two halves. *Pulp and Paper International,* September, 27-39.

Neural Networks Research Centre (February, 2001), Bibliography of SOM Papers. Available online at: < http://www.cis.hut.fi/research/refs/ >.

Nobes, C. & Parker, R. (1991). *Comparative international accounting.* Cambridge, UK: Prentice Hall International.

Öström, K. (1999). *Addressing benchmarking complexity with data mining and neural networks.* Unpublished Masters Thesis, Department of Information Systems, Åbo Akademi University, Turku, Finland.

Raivio, O., Riihijärvi, J., & Mähönen, P. (2000). Classifying and clustering the Internet traffic by Kohonen network. *Proceedings of the ICSC Symposia on Neural Computation (NC'2000)*, May, Berlin, Germany. Reading, UK: ICSC Academic Press.

Rhiannon, J., Jewitt, C., Galasso, L., Fortemps, G. (2001). Consolidation changes the shape of the Top 150. *Pulp and Paper International, September,* 43 (9), 31-41.

Salonen, H. & Vanharanta, H. (1990a). Financial analysis world pulp and paper companies, 1985-1989, Nordic Countries. *Green Gold Financial Reports*, 1, Espoo, Finland: Ekono Oy.

Salonen, H. & Vanharanta, H. (1990b). Financial analysis world pulp and paper companies, 1985-1989, North America. *Green Gold Financial Reports*, 2, Espoo, Finland: Ekono Oy.

Salonen, H. & Vanharanta H. (1991). Financial analysis world pulp and paper companies, 1985-1989, Europe. *Green Gold Financial Reports*, 3, Espoo, Finland: Ekono Oy.

Sarle, W. S. (2001), Neural network FAQ, monthly posting to the Usenet newsgroup comp.ai.neural-nets. Available online at:ftp://ftp.sas.com/pub/neural/FAQ.html.

Ultsch, A. (1993). Self- organized feature maps for monitoring and knowledge of a chemical process. In *Proceedings of the International Conference on Artificial Neural Networks*, 864-867, London: Springer-Verlag.

Visa, A., Toivonen, J., Back, B., & Vanharanta, H. (2000). A New methodology for knowledge retrieval from text documents. *Proceedings of TOOLMET2000 Symposium – Tool Environments and Development Methods for Intelligent Systems*, Oulu, Finland: University of Oulu, 147-151.

APPENDIX:
THE FEATURE PLANES OF THE FINAL MAP

Lighter shades indicate high values, and darker shades indicate low values.

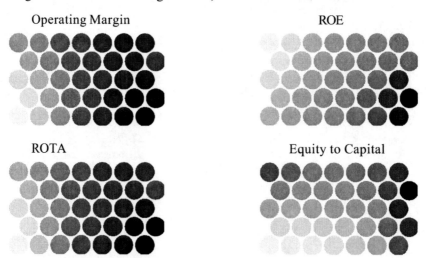

Operating Margin   ROE

ROTA   Equity to Capital

Quick Ratio

Interest Coverage

Receivables Turnover

Chapter XV

Data Mining in Health Care Applications[1]

Fay Cobb Payton
North Carolina State University, USA

ABSTRACT

Recent attention has turned to the healthcare industry and its use of voluntary community health information network (CHIN) models for e-health and care delivery. This chapter suggests that competition, economic dimensions, political issues, and a group of enablers are the primary determinants of implementation success. Most critical to these implementations is the issue of data management and utilization. Thus, health care organizations are finding value as well as strategic applications to mining patient data, in general, and community data, in particular. While significant gains can be obtained and have been noted at the organizational level of analysis, much attention has been given to the individual, where the focal points have centered on privacy and security of patient data. While the privacy debate is a salient issue, data mining (DM) offers broader community-based gains that enable and improve healthcare forecasting, analyses, and visualization.

INTRODUCTION

In this chapter, I provide general insight into data mining with emphasis on the health care industry. My discussion focuses on earlier electronic commerce health care initiatives, namely community health information networks (CHINs) in three regions of the United States. From my exploration of the implementation issues that impacted the success of each case, I offer Figure 1 to illustrate a cluster of factors that capture the dynamics of these live scenarios.

While my prior work (Payton & Ginzberg, 2001) focused on the information technology implementation process, here I provide insight regarding the mining of health data centered about new e-health models of care delivery. One such model for health care was the CHIN, which was a widely sought after model in the late 1990s, and continues to be widely debated by leading industry groups, such as The Healthy Cities Organization (http://www.healthycities.org) and the IEEE-USA Medical Technology and Policy Committee (http://www.ieeeusa.org/committees/MTPC).

While CHINs were said to enable multiple organizations to share health services data in order to meet common objective(s), ranging from profit maximization to improvement of public health conditions and wellness, health care organizations are now deploying e-health strategies to accomplish these goals while garnering data to address community and public health needs. Thus, health care organizations are finding value as well as strategic applications to mining patient data, in general, and community data, in particular. While significant gains can be obtained and have been noted at the organizational level of analysis, much attention has been given to the individual where the focal points have centered about privacy and security of patient data. While the privacy debate is a salient issue, data mining offers broader community-based gains that enable and improve health care forecasting, analyses, and visualization.

Thus, the objectives of this chapter are:
1)   To describe the uses of data-mining techniques in health care;
2)   To explore the intersection of data mining in the context of CHINs;
3)   To explain how the CHIN platform can be used for fraud detection, profitability analysis, patient profiling, and retention management;
4)   To discuss emerging and future trends; and
5)   To explore the technical and social issues that remain.

DATA MINING IN HEALTH CARE

Data mining has often been defined as a "process of extracting previously unknown, valid and actionable information from large databases and then using the information to make critical business decisions" (Cabena, Hadjinian, Stadler, Verhees, & Zanasi, 1998). This definition is based on the premise that an organization can link its myriad sources of data into a data warehouse (to potentially include data marts). Further, these data sources can evolve to a higher degree of analyses to include exploration using on-line analytical processing (OLAP), statistical analyses, and querying. One mechanism that can be used to migrate beyond exploration and permit organizations to engage in information discovery is the Sample, Explore, Modify, Model and Assess (SEMMA) Methodology, as developed by the SAS Corporation (http://www.sas.com). In sum, SEMMA enables its users to: 1) test a segment of data (test data) to be mined for preliminary outcomes; 2) assess this sample data for outliers, trends, etc.; 3) revise the sample data set for model testing, which can include neutral networks, linear regression, and decision trees; 4) evaluate the model for accuracy; and 5) validate the model using the complete data set (Groth, 1998).

In general, the rationale for mining data is a function of organizational needs and type of firm's role in the industry. Moreover, researchers (Hirji, 2001; Keim, 2001) have established that data-mining applications, when implemented effectively, can result in strategic planning and competitive advantage. In an effort to minimize the collection and storage of useless and vast amounts of data, mining can identify and monitor which data are most critical to an organization – thereby providing efficient collection, storage, and exploration of data (Keim, 2001). The efficiencies associated with mining of "most vital data" can result in improved business intelligence, heightened awareness of often overlooked relationships in data, and discovery of patterns and rules among data elements (Hirji, 2001). Others (http://www.sas.com; Groth, 1998) offer that data mining permits improved precision when executing:

- Fraud Detection and Abuse;
- Profitability Analysis;
- Customer (Patient) Profiling; and
- Retention Management.

In particular, data mining offers the health care industry the capabilities to tackle imminent challenges germane to its domain. Among them being:

- Fraud Detection and Abuse – identification of potential fraud and/or abuse; this is applicable to insurance claims processing, verification and payment
- Profitability Analysis – determination of categories of profit and loss levels; this can be practical for analyses of diagnosis related groups (DRGs) and managed care enrollments
- Patient Profiling – discovery of patients' health and lifestyle histories as they can impact medical coverage and service utilization
- Retention Management – identification of loyal patients and services they use; as well as those patients that depart from a particular insurance group, community and profile segment

COMMUNITY HEALTH INFORMATION NETWORKS (CHINS)

During the late 1990s and again more recently, CHINs were seen to offer the health care industry a platform to address and mine medical data to support public and rural health issues. CHINs have been defined as: "Interorganizational systems (IOSs) using information technology(ies) and telecommunications to store, transmit, and transform clinical and financial information. This information can be shared among cooperative and competitive participants, such as payors, hospitals, alternative delivery systems, clinics, physicians, and home health agencies" (Brennan, Schneider & Tornquist, 1996; Payton & Ginzberg, 2001). IOSs have emerged as a primary business model in a number of industries given the application of wireless, application-integration, Internet, and broadband technologies. Starting with reservation systems in the airline industry (e.g., the SABRE system), IOSs have been used to implement strategic and competitive advantage in the cotton, hospital supply, consumer goods retailing, and automotive industries, among others (Clemons & Row, 1993; Copeland & McKenney, 1988). Given their intended direction for extensive mining of medical data among health care providers, payors, employers, and research institutions, CHINs offer an immediate platform for patient profiling, fraud detection, profitability analysis, and retention management.

Based on a voluntary model of organizational participation, CHINs enable member organizations to share health services data in order to meet common objective(s), ranging from profit maximization to improvement of public health conditions and wellness. Further, CHINs can provide a myriad of services from electronic transaction processing to telephone-based referral information (Brennan et al., 1996). The deployment of CHINs is confronted with a tremendous number of implementation barriers, largely behavioral and political in nature. Among the numerous deterrents, as found in Payton and Ginzberg (2001), were loss of organizational autonomy and control; lack of vendor and patient support; and lack of understanding of customers' (patients) needs. Critical to e-health models, however, are the data quality issues that enable health care providers, researchers, payors, and consumers to make more informed medical decisions.

Cooper and Zmud (1990) adopted a diffusion process model of IT implementation that is based on stages and processes as outlined in Table 1. Cooper and Zmud suggest that the process model can be used as a framework for understanding how critical implementation factors evolve over time.

Cooper and Zmud (1990) identify five broad contextual factors that might impact the implementation process: user, organization, task, technology, and environment. Their description of the implementation process, however, suggests an alternative clustering of contextual variables. For instance, they state that, in the initiation stage, "pressure to change evolves from either organizational need (pull) technological innovation (push)

Table 1: IT Implementation process model from Cooper and Zmud (1990)

Stages	Process
Initiation	Active and/or passive scanning of organizational problems/opportunities and IT solutions are undertaken. Pressure to change evolves from either organizational need (pull), technological innovation (push), or both.
Adoption	Rational and political negotiations ensue to get organizational backing for implementation of IT applications.
Adaptation	The IT application is developed, installed, and maintained. Organizational procedures are revised and developed. Organizational members are trained both in the new procedures and in the IT application.
Acceptance	Organizational members are induced to commit to IT application usage.
Routinization	Usage of the IT application is encouraged as a normal activity.
Infusion	Increased organizational effectiveness is obtained by using the IT application in a more comprehensive and integrated manner to support higher level aspects of organizational work.

or both" (p. 124). In the adoption stage, they describe the processes of "rational and political" negotiations, and in subsequent stages, they suggest that "technology" impacts the system implementation. Following this, three factor classes are defined: *push/pull factors*, *behavioral factors* and *shared systems topologies*. That is, these sets of factors continue to be important as organizations are pressured to change, examine opportunities for IOS solutions, obtain organizational backing, develop the IOS applications, and continue to engage in cooperative IOS arrangements.

My proposed CHIN implementation model is shown in Figure 1. This implementation model is important to academicians and practitioners, alike – as it holds implications for data utilization, management, and mining.

Push or pull factors are contextual elements that can impact and influence an organization's willingness to participate in IOS initiatives and include perceived competitive advantage (Grover, 1993), competition (Johnston & Vitale, 1988; Copeland & McKenney, 1988; Grover, 1993), government actions and policies (Linder, 1992; Anderson, Aydin & Jay, 1994), and perceived economic benefits (Moritz, 1986).

Among the Push/Pull Factors, I expected both the *economic dimensions* and *government policies* to have a positive impact on the implementation effort. Health care organizations are currently being pressed toward greater cooperation by government decisions, policies, and practices (e.g., Medicare, Medicaid, Joint Commission on Accreditation of Healthcare Organizations, prospective payment system). Further, the need to reduce costs while maintaining or increasing quality is a key objective of numerous managed care models (Ferrat, Lederer, Hall, & Krella, 1996; Grover, 1993;

Figure 1: Cooperative CHIN implementation model.

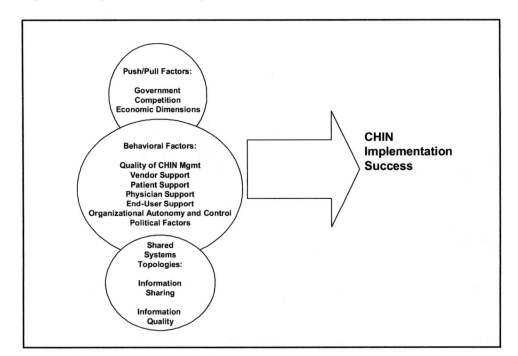

Kongstvedt, 1989; Little, 1994). *Competition* among institutions was expected to play a minor role, given the rise of community models of health care delivery (Brennan et al., 1996; Payton, Brennan, & Ginzberg, 1995), as health care players learn to cooperate and collaborate (Ferret et al., 1996) in an effort to overcome the limitations associated with previously noted economic dimensions.

Behavioral factors relate to attributes and actions of key system stakeholders. These include customer support (in this study, the customer is defined as the patient); end-user support (Anderson et al., 1994); organizational autonomy and control (Moritz, 1986); physician, application vendor, and top management support (Anderson et al., 1994; Grover, 1993; Lucas, Ginzberg, & Schultz, 1988). In the case of CHINs, application vendor support is vital for organizations to gain access to the needed products (Kim & Michelman, 1990). Another critical behavioral factor is the political dynamics of the implementation process, which often impacts system endorsement and resource commitment (Aydin & Rice, 1992; Kimberly & Evanisko, 1981).

Of the Behavioral Factors, *quality of CHIN management*, *vendor support*, *patient support*, *physician support*, and *end-user support* are all expected to have positive impact on implementation progress. Each of these factors has been shown to foster change in various intra- and inter-organizational domains (Anderson et al., 1994; Clemons & Row, 1993; Grover, 1993; Lucas et al., 1990; Whang, 1992), and the same result should obtain in the CHIN context. Strong *autonomy and control* of member organizations, however, will tend to inhibit successful CHIN implementation, as organizations struggle with the tradeoffs of losing some autonomy to the benefits of shared information (Brockhoff & Teichert, 1995). *Political factors,* arising from conflicting personal and organizational objectives among stakeholders, will tend to impede implementation progress (Beath, 1991; Linder, 1992).

Shared or integrated systems topologies represent certain aspects of the infrastructure needed for a CHIN. These factors include arrangements for cooperation and information sharing, as well as for assuring information quality (Clemons & Row, 1993; Kim & Michelman, 1990; Mason, 1991). These cooperative arrangements for CHINs may involve physicians, hospitals, third-party payors, laboratories, and pharmacies and will require an increased degree of electronic information sharing with anticipated improved information quality (Ernst & Young, 1994; Little, 1994).

Both elements of Shared System Topologies— *information sharing* and *information quality*—were predicted to have favorable impacts on implementation progress. The prior existence of shared systems would provide foundations for building more efficient and effective mechanisms for inter-organizational, community-based health care delivery. As the degree of information sharing among inter-organizational participants increased, the quality of information available was also expected to increase, thereby fostering successful implementation (Clemons & Row, 1993).

FINDINGS USING A CASE METHODOLOGY

Thus, using a case methodology to test the absence or presence of the factors listed in Figure 1, the results indicated in Table 2 emerged, based on data collected from 30 interviews, organizational documentation, participant observation and application demonstration.

In-depth case data was collected from three voluntary CHIN implementations: the Wisconsin Health Information Network (WHIN), Regional Health Information Network of Northeast Ohio (RHINNO) and Northeast Ohio Health Network (NEOHN). The parallels among these CHINs make them appropriate for investigation. Each CHIN is located in the Midwest USA; they cover the range from big city to rural areas, and share common initial objectives – i.e., sharing services among multiple health care players with the potential to increase profits. In addition, each of these CHINs is thought to have technology similarities with regard to data repositories, dedicated telecommunications media to enable interorganizational information sharing, and the IS expertise of a single vendor for technical, sales and marketing support. Thus, this sample of three CHINs is a starting point to uncover patterns in the CHIN/IOS implementation process which can later be studied in a broader sample.

The results demonstrate that WHIN, NEOHN, and RHINNO represent CHINs that have met with different degrees of success. Both NEOHN and RHINNO have experienced cycles of interest, investment, and development, but no sustained operation as CHINs.

Table 2: Summary of findings across cases

	WHIN	RHINNO	NEOHN	Expected Impact
Push/Pull Factors				
Government	No impact	Negative impact	No impact	+
Competition	No impact	Negative impact	Negative impact	None
Economic factors	Positive & negative impacts	Negative impact	Negative impact	+
Behavioral Factors				
Top management Support	Positive impact	Positive impact	Positive impact	+
Vendor support	Positive impact	Positive impact	Positive impact	+
Patient support	No impact	No impact	No impact	+
Physician support	Positive impact	Positive impact	Positive impact	+
End-user support	Positive impact	Positive impact	Positive impact	+
Organizational Autonomy & Control	No clear impact	Negative impact	Negative impact	-
Political issues	Negative impact	Negative impact	Negative impact	-
Shared System Topologies				
Information sharing	Positive impact	No impact	Potentially positive impact	+
Information quality	No evidence	Uncertain impact	Potentially positive impact	+
IOS Enablers Systems planning Needs assessment Organizational Readiness	No information – not assessed	Positive impact, if present	Positive impact, if present	Not in original model

On the other hand, WHIN serves as both an application (CHIN) vendor and an IOS venture electronically supporting its multiple health care participants. What differentiates these situations, and what implications can we draw from this for our model of IOS implementation?

Perhaps the biggest difference in the study results between WHIN on the one hand and RHINNO and NEOHN on the other, is the apparent impact of Push/Pull Factors. While these factors showed little impact in the WHIN case, they had a largely negative impact for both RHINNO and NEOHN implementation. These factors are, no doubt, related to the environment. The nature of the market, geographical location, and infrastructure supporting CHIN implementation differentiates WHIN from the other two cases. The Wisconsin market is characterized by a fairly large group of relatively small, non-competing health care providers. CHIN implementation in this environment is not a zero-sum game. CHIN participants stand to lose little by engaging in cooperative information exchange processes. WHIN participants, unlike those in RHINNO and NEOHN, do not appear to endorse the idea that one organization's gain is another's loss. Further, CHIN participation becomes particularly appealing as smaller organizations recognize their inability to fund such massive infrastructures on their own, and larger, free-standing hospitals and payors realize their limited ability to finance the expenditures associated with implementation. WHIN and its participants are located in a smaller urban environment (unlike CHIN initiatives in New York, Chicago, and Cleveland), where health care players tend to be geographically dispersed. This, in part, engenders the need to electronically share information and may explain the lack of concern for competitive forces in the WHIN case.

Figure 2 shows how the nature of the competitive environment might impact the desirability of shared IOS, including CHINs. In a large, urban market with many competing health care providers and/or payment plans, a highly competitive market develops (Box 1 of Figure 2). Institutions within this market are generally technologically sophisticated and often have their own, internal health care information systems and procedures in place to enable electronic data sharing. The nature of such markets could hinder CHIN implementations. Organizations in these competitive markets are likely to be unwilling to share information due to the perceived threat of competition. Consequently, there appears to be little justification for interorganizational cooperation or a voluntary CHIN in such markets. The Cleveland metropolitan market has these characteristics, and this may explain the failure of RHINNO to develop.

At the other extreme, small cities or rural areas with relatively few, geographically dispersed health care providers and payors present non-competitive markets (Box 4 of Figure 2). CHIN participation is most attractive in these cases, as organizations can engage in information sharing with little or no perceived threat of competition. The lack of service redundancy in the marketplace increases the likelihood that information sharing utilizing a shared infrastructure can add value. Markets in larger, less populous states are examples that fit this model. In such markets, push/pull factors like *competition* and *economics* as identified in the proposed CHIN implementation model (Figure 1) would likely favor implementation.

Boxes 2 and 3 represent moderately competitive markets, which can develop both in large and small metropolitan regions. These settings fall somewhere between the extremes of those markets characterized by Box 1 or 4. They are likely to be smaller markets, or markets with less "density" of medical providers and payors. These are likely

Figure 2: Market/location matrix.

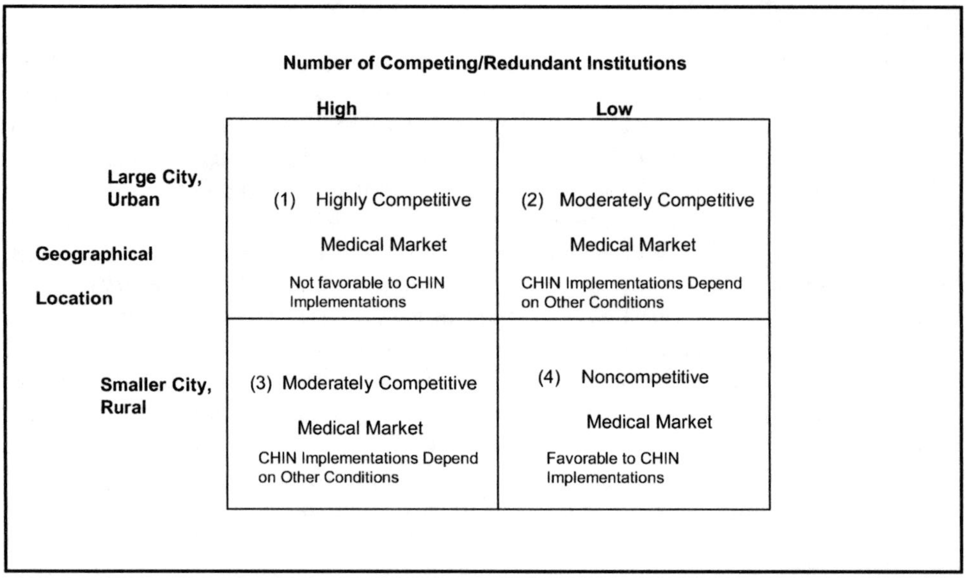

to be markets where the impact of competitive and economic factors on CHIN/IOS implementation is more difficult to predict. Markets like Milwaukee and Akron would seem to fall into this category. In Milwaukee, the lower degree of competition allowed WHIN to proceed successfully. In Akron, on the other hand, NEOHN was less successful, perhaps due to the proximity (and overlapping) of Cleveland (and RHINNO), a large, competitive (Box 1) market.

These different market situations suggest the need for alternative models, both for CHIN functioning and for CHIN implementation. Health care players in highly competitive environments may participate in IOS educational, general organizational information, and clinical services. Similar to trade associations, such health care cooperatives could pool resources to gain power through political lobbying, engage in knowledge transfer particularly in specialized domains, and seek purchase discounts for needed technologies and services. Widespread sharing of patient information, however, will not occur easily in such markets, as powerful players develop proprietary systems to serve their own needs and maximize their individual market shares. In less competitive markets, the true potential of CHIN functionality for sharing data among multiple providers is more likely to be realized.

As is evident from this study, the factors affecting CHIN implementation are likely to differ in different market situations. While Behavioral Factors seemed to play similar roles in each case, Push/Pull Factors and Shared System Topology (infrastructure) factors did not. The conditions for success depicted in the research model appear to be unattainable in certain environmental scenarios. This is particularly the case in environments characterized as a highly competitive. In these cases, the competitive forces, economic justification, political issues, and IOS enablers are most critical to determining implementation success – they emerged as the go/no-go factors in the research model. Thus, it appears that the market for cooperative CHINs may be limited.

HOW THE PLATFORM CAN BE USED

CHIN technology would enable health care constituents to electronically create, maintain, and transform medical data via internal organizational and network-wide databases. Medical information can be housed in several tables, such as patient info, employer info, dependent info, medical records, physician info, etc. Attributes describing each entity with appropriate relationships would be established. These databases can, then, feed into a data warehouse with data marts for each CHIN constituent. These data marts can be used to manage specialized processing by individual CHIN organization. Data from the CHIN overarching database is extractable to facilitate data-mining processes.

Data mining often follows one of several methods:

1) Predictive modeling — includes classification and regression techniques that are used to forecast unknown outcomes or variables;
2) Clustering – establishes clusters (based on an analogous statistic) in order to compare historical data to analyze new data;
3) Association – determines relationships between attributes in a database that often can be correlated as a result of causality; and
4) Summarization – generalizes task-specific data into a data cube that can create graphical representations.

While several organizations (IBM, Oracle, Silicon Graphics, Angoss, SAS, and SPSS) offer data-mining technologies, the SAS Enterprise model is provided, herein, to show the technology interface (Figure 3). The SAS system supports a myriad of mining models, including decision trees, regression, and neutral networks.

Once mined, the data offers its owners knowledge regarding fraud, profiling, retention, and profit analyses. In general, these methods provide organizations using on-line analytical processing (OLAP) with a multidimensional, logical view of critical data. Thus, strategic knowledge can be derived using forecasting, trend analyses, and statistical analyses. For health care organizations, in particular, data-mining solutions can provide payors, hospitals, alternative delivery systems, clinics, physicians, and home health agencies with more succinct, meaningful answers to issues, such as:

1) (In)effective methods of patient care;
2) Local and regional health statistics;
3) Cost analyses by segments of a population, provider plan, or demographic group;
4) Drug subscription, treatment, utilization, etc.;
5) Genetic treatment, medical research, and discovery; and
6) (In)effective methods for mining "text-based" clinical data.

As Figure 2 suggested, regional markets in Boxes 1 and 4 are best suited for these implementations. Moreover, Box 1 (Highly Competitive Medical Markets) is likely to

Figure 3: The SAS Enterprise data-mining technology (http://www.sas.com/products/ miner/index.html).

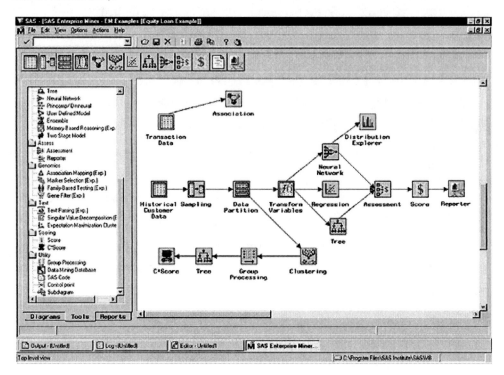

serve as an ideal environment given the presence of larger number of payor plans and enrollees – thereby resting on the notion that CHIN participants are in need of vital data analyses on cost effectiveness, profitability, treatment, resource utilization, etc. In noncompetitive environments (Box 4), the health information network fosters a coupling on dispersed groups where competition and economic dimensions are not the primary drivers of the implementation.

To this end, CHIN technologies offer the industry the ability to better mine larger sets of data to accomplish four critical analyses:

1) Fraud Detection – Of particular interest to health care providers, this application features provider and patient profiling along with behavior and resource utilization, charting tools, and detection functionality. Data mining via CHIN technologies permits continuous monitoring on the above, yet these analyses are performed on a broader scale (i.e., local, state, and regional levels).

Moreover, similar to fraud detection among credit card agencies, CHIN constituents, particularly government agencies, can mine data to discover (mis)uses of medical benefits, monetary losses, and legal infractions.

2) Profitability Analysis – Figure 1 and the material that follows clearly points out the criticality of the implementation process. As noted in Table 2, every CHIN

participant organization was significantly concerned about the economic dimensions associated with investing in the network technologies in question.

While the CHIN technology enables larger data sets to analyzed, its users can conduct additional regional analyses by metropolitan areas, counties, states, and districts. Effective health care plans, services, care delivery plans, and even those "profit generating" physicians - can be determined. Ineffective or non-profitable services can then be eliminated based on the more global analyses generated from data-mining technologies.

3) Patient Profiling – By using psychographic data, CHIN research members can gain amore extensive examination of patient behavior to uncover treatment and care service utilization patterns. For example, mined data could profile patients by physicians visited and medical tests ordered, drug treatment, gender, ethnicity, age, episode of illnesses, just to name a few.

4) Retention Management – Customer relationship management is linked to the notion of retention management. Ideally, health care payors would like to retain their existing customer bases while attracting and converting potential customers to enrollees. Data mining via the CHIN facilitates cross-selling and electronic marketing services. While the case can be made for preserving patient members, health care groups must also think in terms of "retaining" physician members as well. Thus, identifying services critical to participating physician groups can be just as fundamental.

DATA-MINING IMPLICATIONS: CONTROVERSIES AND ISSUES ASSOCIATED WITH CHINS

A close examination of Table 2 suggests the primary determinants in attaining a successful CHIN implementation are overcoming *Competition*, *Economic*, *Organizational Autonomy and Control* and *Political Issues* – thereby indicating that the technical or technology implementation is not the deterrent. Rather, the above issues relate to the broader social and political dynamics of the health care industry. Of the thirty interviews with members of these projects, there was consistent concern about two issues: 1) what is the purpose of warehousing community data?, and 2) how should the data be used?

To address the first question, numerous writings have offered rationale for warehousing health care data. For instance, the 2001 American Medical Informatics Association Conference (http://www.amia.org) hosted several panels and paper sessions to address the needs of warehousing medical data; these assessments included:

1) the critical integration of clinical and administrative data from a myriad of source systems;

2) determination of cost efficiency measures between the general population and individual patient; and

3) retrospective and prospective studies of medical history, prescriptions and laboratory results among patient medical records.

The warehousing of patient data, particularly in a CHIN domain, offers the industry the capability to more efficiency identify risk factors associated with disease episodes and prevention-focused public health requirements, and to electronically link the diverse players (e.g., providers and payors – insurance companies) along the health care continuum. Moreover, such applications lend themselves to intelligent data analysis that require accurate data quality technologies in the mining of health care data.

To determine how warehoused health care data can be best utilized, one can return to the outcomes of the CHIN cases. One recurring theme from each of the cases was the need to access data for resource utilization and determination of medical outcomes within a broader population, in general, and single patient, in particular. Other uses of these data include pattern identification by sample groups by statistically slicing the data by demographic, socio-economic and other characteristics. All of these uses of warehoused health care data stimulate more effective and efficient deployment resources and knowledge bases among communities - thereby influencing public policy implications.

While data-mining applications offer the industry these and other advantages, the social challenges abound. The erosion of personal privacy and the security of the data remain formidable issues. These are particularly of issue regarding existing health care Web sites (e.g., http://www.webmd.com, http://www.mayoclinic.com) that enable consumers to track data (e.g., on AIDS/HIV, diabetes, cancer, sickle cell anemia, etc.) and can provide marketing and medical leads for drug manufacturers and health care insurers. According to the Association of Computing Machinery (ACM) U.S. Public Policy Committee (http://www.acm.org/usacm) and other industry groups, horror stories about unauthorized disclosure of patient information are numerous; consumers continue to battle the losses and costs associated with privacy invasion. As pointed out by Barbara Simons, chair of the ACM Public Policy Committee, (http://www.acm.org/usacm/privacy/simons_medical.html) drafts from the National Information Infrastructure Task Force stated:

> "medical information is routinely shared with and viewed by third parties who are not involved in patient care. The American Medical Records Association has identified twelve categories of information seekers outside the health care industry who have access to health care files, including employers, government agencies, credit bureaus, insures, educational institutions and the media."

Further, and in the context of data mining and CHINs, several questions remain unanswered with regard to the warehousing and mining of health care information:
1) Who owns the data?
2) What are the costs associated with the "inability" to mine community data?
3) What security policies and procedures should be implemented in a CHIN (data-mining) application?
4) How do CHINs improve public health?
5) How should organizational practices be re-engineered to ensure that security policies and procedures are practiced within the organization?

CONCLUSION

The proposed IOS implementation model derived from Cooper and Zmud's (1990) single organization model is able to capture the some aspects of CHIN implementation. The model, however, seems best suited to less competitive market situations where there is recognition that competition does not necessarily preclude interorganizational cooperation. Further, my results suggest that competition is the overriding factor in the model, thereby implying that not all variables in the model are equally important. Health care organizations in some more competitive markets have yet to rationalize the web of players (e.g., physicians and production workers, payors, providers, patients, government, and larger external environment) that directly affect its (in)ability to form cooperative ventures. The case data indicate that large health care providers and payors in some markets are evolving toward less cooperative, more coercive IOS strategies. These organizations mandate IT direction, infrastructure support, and the degree to which competitors will form cooperatives. This is evident in emerging health care organizations, such as Healtheon/WebMD and CyberCare.

These results, while interesting, must be viewed as preliminary. This was an exploratory study and was limited to CHINs located in the Midwest. CHINs implemented in what the industry considers more advanced health care states, such as Oregon, Minnesota and California, are characterized by a high degree of managed care and competition, and potentially can be impacted by a different set of conditions. Thus, another implementation model or subset of the current model may be more appropriate, and these results may not be applicable in more mature health care markets. Moreover, these early CHIN efforts speak to the challenges the industry faces as we enter the age of customer (patient) relationship and supply chain models that stand to debunk archaic views of care delivery, patient as primary consumers, information privacy, and data management.

ENDNOTE

[1]   Reprinted/Adapted with Permission from *Health Care Management Review*, 26:2, 20-32, © 2001, Aspen Publishers, Gaithersburg, MD.

REFERENCES

Anderson, J. G., Aydin, C.E., & Jay, S.J. (Eds.) (1994*). Evaluating health information systems: Methods and applications.* Thousand Oaks, CA: Sage Publications.

Aydin, C. E. & Rice, R.E. (1992). Bringing social worlds together: Computers as catalysts for new interactions in health care organizations. *Journal of Health and Social Behavior*, 33:168-185.

Beath, C. M. (1991). Supporting the information technology champion. *MIS Quarterly,* 355-372.

Brennan, P. F., Schneider, S. J. & Tornquist, E. M. (1996). *Information Networks for Community Health.* New York, NY: Springer-Verlag Publications.

Brockhoff, K. & Teichert, T. (1995). Cooperative R&D and partners' measures of success. *International Journal of Technology Management*, 10:1, 111-123.

Cabena, P., Hadjinian, P., Stadler, R., Verhees, J., & Zanasi, A. (1998). *Discovering data mining: From conceptual to implementation*. Upper Saddle River, NJ: Prentice Hall PTR.

Clemons, E.K. & Row, M.C. (1993). Limits to Interfirm Coordination Through Information Technology: Results of a field study in consumer packaged goods distribution. *Journal of Management Information Systems*, 10:1, 73-95.

Cooper, R.B. & Zmud, R.W. (1990). Information technology implementation research: A technological diffusion approach. *Management Science*, 404-420.

Copeland, D.G. & McKenney, J.L. (1988). Airline reservations systems: Lessons from history. *MIS Quarterly*, 353-370.

Ernst & Young. 1994. Community Health Information Network Presentation Materials.

Ferratt, T.W., Lederer, A.L., Hall, S.R., & Krella, J.M. (1996). Swords and plowshares: Information technology for collaborative advantage. *Information and Management*, 30, 131-142.

Ginzberg, M.J. (1981). Key recurrent issues in the MIS implementation process. *MIS Quarterly*, 5:2, 47-59.

Glaser, P.F. (1988). Using technology for competitive advantage: The ATM experience at Citicorp. In B. Guile, & J. B. Quinn (eds.), *Managing innovation: Cases from the service industries*. Washington, DC: National Academy Press.

Groth, R. (1998). *Data mining: A hands-on approach for business professionals*. Upper Saddle River, NJ: Prentice Hall PTR.

Grover, V. (1993). Empirically derived model for the adoption of customer-based interorganizational systems. *Decision Sciences*, 603-640.

Hirji, K. 2001. Exploring data mining implementation. *Communications of the ACM*, 44:7, 87-93.

Johnston, H. R. & Vitale, M.R. (1988). Creating competitive advantage with interorganizational information systems. *MIS Quarterly*, 153-165.

Keim, D.A. (2001). Visual exploration of large data sets. *Communications of the ACM*, 44:8, 39-44.

Kim, K. K. & Michelman. J.E. (1990). An examination of factors for the strategic use of information systems in the healthcare industry. *MIS Quarterly*, 201-214.

Kimberly, J.R. & Evanisko, M.J. (1981). Organizational innovation: The influence of individual, organizational, and contextual factors on hospital adoption of technological and administrative innovations. *Academy of Management Journal*, 24:4, 689-713.

Kongstvedt, P.R. 1989. *The managed care handbook*. Gaithersburg, MD: Aspen Publications.

Kwon, T.H. & Zmud, R.W. (1987). Unifying the fragmented models of information systems implementation. In R. Boland & R. Hirchheim (eds.), *Critical issues in information systems research*. New York: John Wiley Publishing.

Linder, J.C. (1992). Outcomes measurement in hospitals: Can the system change the organization? *Hospital and Health Services Administration*, 37:2, 143-166.

Lindsey, D., Cheney, P.H., Kasper, G.M., & Ives, B. (1990). TELCOT: An application of information technology for competitive advantage in the cotton industry. *MIS Quarterly*, 347-357.

Little, A.D. (1994). Telecommunications: Can it solve America's health care problems?

Lucas, Jr., H.C., Ginzberg, M.J., & Schultz, R.(1990). Information systems implementation: Testing a structural model. Norwood, NJ: Ablex Corporation.

McGee, J.V. (1991). Implementing systems across boundaries: Dynamics of information technology and integration. Ph.D. Dissertation, Harvard University, Cambridge, MA.

Moritz, P.H. (1986). Interorganizational collaboration in multi-hospital systems: An analysis using the intriligator interorganizational relational (IOR Model). Ph.D. Dissertation, University of Maryland, College Park, MD.

Payton, F.C. (2000). Lessons learned from three interorganizational health care information systems. *Information and Management, 37*(6): 311-322.

Payton, F.C. & Ginzberg, M. (2001). Interorganizational health care systems implementations: An exploratory study of early electronic commerce initiatives. *Health Care Management Review*, 26:2, 20-32.

Payton, F. C., Brennan P.F., & Ginzberg, M.J. (1995). A community toward health care delivery. *International Journal of Technology Management - Special Issue Series on Technology in Health Care.*

Pemble, K. (1997). The Wisconsin health information network. In P. Brennan, S. Schenider & E. Tornquist (eds.), *Community Health Information Networks.*

SAS Institute White Paper (http://www.sas.com), (2001). Data mining in the insurance industry, and SAS Web site: http://www.sas.com/products/miner/index.html.

Whang, J. (1992). An empirical study of factors influencing interorganizational information systems implementation: A case of the real estate industry. Ph.D. Dissertation, University of Nebraska-Lincoln.

Yin, R.K. (1989). *Case study research: Design and methods.* Newbury Park, CA: Sage Publications.

Chapter XVI

Data Mining for Human Resource Information Systems

Lori K. Long
Kent State University, USA

Marvin D. Troutt
Kent State University, USA

ABSTRACT

This chapter focuses on the potential contributions that Data Mining (DM) could make within the Human Resource (HR) function in organizations. We first provide a basic introduction to DM techniques and processes and a survey of the literature on the steps involved in successfully mining this information. We also discuss the importance of data warehousing and datamart considerations. An examination of the contrast between DM and more routine statistical studies is given, and the value of HR information to support a firm's competitive position and organizational decision-making is considered. Examples of potential applications are outlined in terms of data that is ordinarily captured in HR information systems.

INTRODUCTION

The role of Human Resource (HR) professionals in organizations has evolved parallel to business-related technological advances. HR professionals are now able to dedicate more time to strategic business decisions as the development of technology has allowed for the automation of many transactional HR processes (Walker &Reif, 1999). While HR professionals may no longer need to manage the manual processing of data, they should not abandon their ties to data collected on and about the organization's employees. The human resources data that is available within organizations has the potential to help support their decision-making processes. The challenge is identifying useful information in vast human resources databases that are the result of the automation of HR-related transaction processing.

Data mining may be regarded as an evolving approach to data analysis in very large databases that could become a useful tool to HR professionals. Data mining involves extracting knowledge based on patterns of data in very large databases. Yet, data mining goes beyond simply performing data analysis on large data sets. Organizations that employ thousands of employees and track a multitude of employment-related information might find valuable information patterns contained within their databases to provide insights in such areas as employee retention and compensation planning. To develop an understanding of the potential of data mining HR information in a firm, this chapter will first discuss how HR-related information contributes to a firm's competitive advantage. Next, we will discuss the components of Human Resource Information Systems (HRIS) and gain an understanding of the steps in the data-mining process. Finally, we will identify opportunities as well as concerns in applying data-mining techniques to HR Information Systems.

BACKGROUND
Building a Competitive Advantage

The resource-based view of the firm posits that organizational resources and capabilities that are simultaneously rare, valuable, non-substitutable, and imperfectly imitable form the basis for a firm's sustainable competitive advantage (Barney, 1991). If a firm is able to uniquely manage its most valuable asset—its people— then it may be able to differentiate itself from the competition to create an advantage. Boxall (1993) suggests HR management can create a sustained competitive advantage by "hiring and developing talented staff and 'synergizing' their contributions within the resource bundle of the firm (p. 66)." Huselid, Jackson, and Schuler (1997) found investments in a firm's human resources are a potential source of competitive advantage in their examination of HR effectiveness. However, many organizations lack the management know-how or the information necessary to make strategic human resource decisions.

The competitive advantage is sustained if other firms are unable to imitate their resources. The management of a firm's human resources is often less susceptible to imitation because competitors rarely have access to a firm's HR management practices, as these practices are not transparent to those outside of the company (Pfeffer, 1994). For this reason, effective HR management provides a unique opportunity for firms to establish a sustainable competitive position. One step in the process of developing a firm's human resources involves planning. Human resource planning goes hand in hand with an organization's strategic planning. As a firm develops its business strategy, it must consider the abilities of its staff to meet its strategy. As a firm identifies its strategy, HR must then ensure the strategy's success by ensuring the right HR resources are in place. HR must collect, store, and analyze data to move forward in the planning process.

All organizations collect data about their employees. However, the actions taken with that data varies widely among organizations. Some organizations use the data only to perform required administrative tasks. Others transform the data into useful information for support in decision making (Kovach & Cathcart, 1999). Using HR data in decisionmaking provides a firm with the opportunity to make more informed strategic decisions. If a firm can extract useful or unique information on the behavior and potential of its people from HR data, it can contribute to the firm's strategic planning process. Another type of information a firm may seek is the evaluation of the effectiveness of its HR practices. Often a firm implements a recruiting source or training program, for example, without any clear method of evaluating the practice. Analyzing the data collected in the implementation and management of an HR practice can provide another resource for HR-related decisionmaking.

Human Resource Information Systems

Many organizations today have purchased or designed databases to collect, manage, and retrieve human resource-related data. As stated earlier, a HRIS serves two primary purposes. The first purpose is administrative in nature. In order to conduct basic human resource transactions such as payroll, benefits administration, and government reporting, organizations must collect basic personal and work-related data. The second purpose is to support organizational decisionmaking (Kovach & Cathcart., 1999) A HRIS is often an expensive investment for a firm, and the ability to use the data collected beyond only administrative issues can help justify that investment.

The HR information systems of most organizations today feature relational database systems that allow data to be stored in separate files that can be linked by common elements such as name or identification number. The relational database provides organizations with the ability to keep a virtually limitless amount of data on employees. It also allows organizations to access the data in a variety of ways. For example, a firm can retrieve data on a particular employee or it can retrieve data on a certain group of employees through conducting a search based on a specific parameter such as job classification. The development of relational databases in organizations along with advances in storage technology has resulted in organizations collecting a large amount of data on employees.

Table 1 outlines some examples of the type of data that can be captured and stored in an HRIS. Table 2 outlines some typical functional uses of the data. Every organization

Table 1: Data collected by an HRIS

Employee Data	Organization/Job Data
Name	Pre-employment test scores
Social security number	Job title
Date of birth	Job grade
Gender	Salary
Race	Benefit selections
Marital Status	Performance appraisal ratings
Address	Promotional history
Telephone Number	Corrective action records
Emergency Contact	Attendance history
Dependent Information	Training records
Education	

Table 2: Functional use of data collected by an HRIS

Functions Using Data	Regularly Generated and Ad Hoc Reports
Compensation and Benefits Health and Safety Performance Appraisal Training and Development EEO/AA Recruiting and Placement Labor Relations	Payroll runs Benefit costs Recruiting effectiveness Supply/demand forecasting Transaction histories Training completed Adverse impact analysis

Adapted from: Fisher, Schoenfeldt and Shaw (1999).

varies in the type of data it collects related to its employees. However, this outline will serve as an example of the kinds of data collected and typical uses of that data.

Organizations also use data stored in their HRIS to make calculations to evaluate the financial impact of their HR-related practices. HR functions use this type of information to support the continued development of HR programs and also demonstrate to managers how HR can help impact the bottom line. Some examples of these kinds of calculations are pay and benefits as a percent of operating expense, cost per hire, return on training, and turnover cost (Fitz-Enz, 1998).

While these calculations are helpful to quantify the value of some HR practices, the bottom-line impact of HR practices is not always so clear. One can evaluate the cost per hire, but does that information provide any reference to the value of that hire? Should a greater value be assessed to an employee who stays with the organization for an extended period of time? Most data analysis retrieved from HRIS does not provide an opportunity to seek out additional relationships beyond those that the system was originally designed to identify.

Data Mining

Traditional data analysis methods often involve manual work and interpretation of data that is slow, expensive, and highly subjective (Fayyad, Piatsky-Shapiro, & Smyth, 1996). For example, if an HR professional is interested in analyzing the cost of turnover, he or she might have to extract data from several different sources, such as accounting records, termination reports, and personnel hiring records. That data is then combined, reconciled, and evaluated. This process creates many opportunities for errors. As business databases have grown in size, the traditional approach has grown more impractical. Data mining is the process of extracting information from really large data sets through the use of algorithms and techniques drawn from the fields of statistics, machine learning, and database management (Feelders, Daniels, & Holsheimer, 2000). Data mining has been used successfully in many functional areas such as finance and marketing. HRIS applications in many organizations provide an as yet unexplored opportunity to apply data-mining techniques. These systems typically hold a large amount of data —a requirement for data mining. While most applications provide opportunities to generate adhoc or standardized reports from specific sets of data, the relationships between the data sets are rarely explored. It is this type of relationship that data mining seeks to discover.

Data Warehouses and Datamarts

Data-mining projects have been pursued, or at least attempted, for a long time. Several years ago, one of the authors worked in a university office of institutional research and studies. This office was charged with various queries, reporting, and decision-support assignments involving both students and personnel. Quite often, data was needed over a period of years for these projects. However, data files for previous years were difficult to locate and manipulate. Also, inconsistencies of various kinds tend to occur from year to year. For example, code systems and category definitions tend to mutate as time goes by. Similar problems have been experienced in most other organizations as well. Such projects were often practically impossible.

These problems led to the creation of special databases—typically relational databases that are integrated, consistent, and multidimensional, with time being the principal added dimension. When these special databases cover all of the data for an organization, they are called data warehouses. When they cover just one functional area, such as human resources, they are called datamarts. (See for example Agosta, 2000; Gray & Watson, 1998; and Mallach, 2000). A data warehouse is essentially a separate, customized repository of data for decision-support applications (Watson & Haley, 1998). They are kept separate from operational data. Data warehouses are widely regarded as a useful resource to consolidate corporate information and share it among organizational entities for the purpose of analysis and decision-making support (Subramanian, Smith, Nelson, Campbell, & Bird, 1997). This can be a costly endeavor, and the investment may not be worthwhile depending on the use an organization expects. The decision to enable data mining often necessitates at least the implementation of a datamart. Companies who have implemented enterprise resource planning (ERP) systems will often find this facility to be included with the ERP system, which itself can be quite expensive and time-consuming. However, without at least a datamart, if not a comprehensive data warehouse, data-mining projects would be doomed to laborious preliminary data collection, editing, and formatting.

Data Mining Versus Traditional Data Analysis

It is worth reviewing here the connections and differences between data mining and the more familiar activities of reports, queries, and routine statistical studies applied to a database. Queries and reports (reports are usually based on queries) are structured questions submitted to a database. For example, if an organization wanted to compare information on two different groups of employees, queries would be needed to extract the specific employees assigned to each group for further analysis. Thus, queries are typically an essential step in extracting data from the database. Data warehouses and datamarts greatly facilitate queries involving a time dimension. For example, trend analysis and forecasts require historical data that would be hard to obtain without such comprehensive databases. Such analysis might be applied to individual employee histories as part of performance analysis. Trends in statistics relating to Equal Employment Opportunity (EEO) could also be monitored in this way. In some respects, data mining can be regarded as a set of very sophisticated queries that involve sampling and statistical modeling. In any case, the additional query capabilities and uses should be factored into the decisions on implementation of a data warehouse or datamart for data-mining use.

Decision-support system applications may also be regarded as predecessors to data-mining applications. Decision-support system applications are tools that allow users to collect data from databases, analyze the data, and represent the analysis in many forms, such as graphs and reports. These systems may use statistical modeling packages to analyze data leading to information to support decisions in organizations. These systems can combine information from other functional areas within the firm, such as customer service and marketing, to help support human resource management decisions (Broderick & Boudreau, 1992). For example, a user might build a statistical model to analyze data such as time to fill service requests and time to delivery as they relate to customer satisfaction levels. Information obtained from this analysis may then be used to establish performance goals for employees. While decision-support system applications may provide useful information for decision-makers in organizations, very specific analysis plans must be established. Essentially, the user must know what relationships exist before analyzing the data. Further, several iterations of the model may have to be tested before useful information can be identified.

One of the authors of this chapter worked in a university office of institutional research and studies (OIRS). This office was responsible for certain decision-support and data-analysis studies that often involved university personnel. There was no datamart at the time. It was necessary to create special files from current databases and retain these year after year in order to do any kinds of longitudinal analyses. Special statistical studies were sometimes possible if the right data had been collected. An example was historical trends in Equal Opportunity Employment practices. Flexibility and usefulness depended on the foresight of office analysts. If they had collected the right data, then they would be able to respond to new requests from management, state and federal agencies, and so on. It that foresight had not been in effect, it was necessary to approximate or decline the information request, or to laboriously go through old files to reconstruct a usable database. While this permitted some statistical studies to be carried out, such limited access made data mining all but impossible. For specific statistical studies, one focuses on a specific set of variables and questions. For data mining, one essentially needs all the data to be accessible in a reasonably easy environment .and the specific questions may not always be known precisely.

Descriptive statistics were often reported, especially those based on the current state of the system. Thus, it was possible for the OIRS to readily answer such questions as the age distribution of current faculty, its ethnic distribution, and gender distribution. However, to answer questions about trends in these data would require retaining the corresponding data from year to year. Ordinarily, only a small number of such yearly data sets might be retained. However, to make reasonable forecasts, for instance, a much longer series of data is required. More importantly, data-mining questions aimed at explaining the relationship of such trends to other variables in the system were practically impossible. Thus, data mining seeks to go beyond the old days of ordinary statistical reports showing only *what is*. It aims to find out more of the *how* and *why*.

Size of Database

An important consideration in data mining is the size of the database. As we have stated, data mining is appropriate for very large databases. While an organization may collect a large volume of data on its employees, the size of the organization may affect the suitability of applying data-mining techniques to its HRIS. Smaller organizations may mine their HR data as part of a larger data-mining project. Some organizations may have an ERP system that holds data from several functional areas of the organization. For example, in 1996, the State of Mississippi launched a statewide data warehouse project called the Mississippi Executive Resource Library and Information Network (MERLIN) (Roberts, 1999). With an interest in mining HR data, this warehouse was designed to include other data in addition to employee data, such as data on finances, payroll, and capital projects. This $5 million investment created a need to go beyond the HR function in designing a data warehouse and satisfy organization-wide needs for data mining.

APPLYING DATA MINING TECHNIQUES TO HR INFORMATION SYSTEMS

Many organizations have hurriedly approached data mining as a solution to the problems presented by these large databases. However, caution must be exercised in using data mining. The blind application of data-mining techniques can easily lead to the discovery of meaningless and invalid patterns. If one searches long enough in any data set, it is possible to find patterns that appear to hold but are not necessarily statistically significant or useful (Fayyad, Piatsky-Shapiro, & Smyth, 1996). There has not been any specific exploration of applying these techniques to human resource applications; however, there are some guidelines in the process that are transferable to an HRIS. Feelders, Daniels and Holsheimer (2000) outline six important steps in the data-mining process: 1) problem definition, 2) acquisition of background knowledge, 3) selection of data, 4) pre-processing of data, 5) analysis and interpretation, and 6) reporting and use. At each of these steps, we will look at important considerations as they relate to data mining human resources databases. Further, we will examine some specific legal and ethical considerations of data mining in the HR context.

Problem Definition and Acquisition of Background Knowledge

The formulation of the questions to be explored is an important aspect of the data-mining process. As mentioned earlier, with enough searching or application of sufficiently many techniques, one might be able to find useless or ungeneralizable patterns in almost any set of data. Therefore, the effectiveness of a data-mining project is improved through establishing some general outlines of inquiry prior to starting the project. To this extent, data mining and the more traditional statistical studies are similar. Thus, careful attention to the scientific method and sound research methods are to be followed. A widely respected source of guidelines on research methods is the book by

Kerlinger and Lee (2000). A certain level of expertise is necessary to carefully evaluate questions. Obviously, a requirement is data-mining and statistical expertise, but one must also have some intimate understanding of the data that is available, along with its business context. Furthermore, some subject matter expertise is needed to determine useful questions, select relevant data, and interpret results (Feelders *et al.*, 2000). For example, a firm with interest in evaluating the success of an affirmative action program needs to understand the Equal Employment Opportunity (EEO) classification system to know what data is relevant.

Subject matter involvement is also necessary. A compensation specialist, for example, is needed to data mine a payroll system. Once again, the specialist in the area will tend to understand the coding and organization of information that will help in setting up the problem to be evaluated. Typically, when an organization has a database large enough to be mined, there is not necessarily one individual in the organization that is an expert in every area. By seeking out a specialist, the firm can ensure that the proper expertise is available.

Another important consideration in the process of developing a question to look at is the role of causality (Feelders *et al.*, 2000). A subject matter expert's involvement is important in interpreting the results of the data analysis. For example, a firm might find a pattern indicating a relationship between high compensation levels and extended length of service. The question then becomes, do employees stay with the company longer because they receive high compensation? Or do employees receive higher compensation if they stay longer with the company? An expert in the area can take the relationship discovered and build upon it with additional information available in the organization to help understand the cause and effect of the specific relationship identified.

Table 3: Examples of HR related questions

What are some characteristics of applicants that are eventually successful in the organization?

Is there a relationship between merit increases and improved performance?

Do benefit selections affect turnover?

Do certain educational degrees or programs make good matches with the firm?

Are there common career paths in the organization?

Is there a relationship between promotional history and length of service?

Are there any attributes that make an employee a productive telecommuter?

Is there a relationship between absenteeism and performance?

Is there a need for a company daycare facility and what would it cost?

How might an early retirement plan benefit the firm?

Once the proper expertise is available, the next step is to formulate a question for the data mining to explore. There are many questions for which HR professionals and company management would like to find answers. Table 3 provides some examples of questions organizations may consider important to their business operations. These are questions to which an HRIS and data mining could provide answers. These are just a few examples; the possibilities are plentiful.

Every organization has different data stored in its HRIS and different organizational-related information needs. The interest in relationships may depend upon the market in which a company is competing,, or its current growth cycle stage. A company that is still growing may focus on different aspects than would a mature company. For example, a growing company may focus on identifying effective recruiting techniques. A mature company that is looking to retain its already experienced staff may focus more on benefits and quality of life for its personnel. Following this discussion, we will walk through some specific examples of HR practices about which an organization may want to seek additional information.

Selection and Pre-processing of Data

Selecting and preparing the data is the next step in the data-mining process. Some organizations have independent Human Resource Information Systems that feature multiple databases that are not connected to each other. This type of system is sometimes selected to offer greater flexibility to remote organizational locations or sub-groups with unique information needs (Anthony, Perrewe, & Kacmar, 1996). The possible inconsistency of the design of the databases could make data mining difficult when multiple databases exist. Data warehousing can prevent this problem, and an organization may need to create a data warehouse before it begins a data-mining project. However, these kinds of editing can not be avoided altogether and similarly constitute a step in developing a data warehouse or datamart. The advantage gained in first developing the data warehouse or mart is that most of the data-editing work is done at the start.

Another challenge in mining data is dealing with the issues of missing or noisy data. Data quality may be insufficient if data is collected without any specific analysis in mind (Feelders *et al.*, 2000). This is especially true for human resource information. Typically when HR data is collected, the purpose is some kind of administrative need such as payroll processing. The need of data for the required transaction is the only consideration in the type of data to collect. Future analysis needs and the value in the data collected are not usually considered. Missing data may also be a problem, especially if the system administrator does not have control over data input. Many organizations have taken advantage of web-based technology to allow employees to input and update their own data (McElroy, 1991). Employees may choose not to enter certain types of data resulting in missing data. However, a data warehouse or datamart may help to prevent or systemized the handling of many of these problems.

If a data warehouse is not an economical solution for an organization, it still needs to properly prepare the data for analysis along the same lines. This step of data cleaning and pre-processing includes removing noise and deciding on strategies to handle missing data (Fayyad, Piatsky-Shapiro, & Smyth, 1996). Cleaning data may include steps such as ensuring that proper coding is used or making sure that employee identification numbers are correct. The type of data to be cleaned depends on the question being asked. Cleaning the data can be a big project, and, therefore, consideration of the end result is important.

Analysis and Interpretation

There are many types of algorithms in use in data mining. The choice of the algorithm depends on the intended use of the extracted knowledge (Brodley, Lane, & Stough, 1999). The goals of data mining can be broken down into two main categories. Some applications seek to verify the hypothesis formulated by the user. The other main goal is the discovery or uncovering of new patterns systematically (Fayyad, Piatsky-Shapiro, & Smyth, 1996). Within discovery, the data can be used to either predict future behavior or describe patterns in an understandable form. A complete discussion of data-mining techniques is beyond the scope of this chapter. However, what follows is a fairly extensive survey of some techniques that have so far been used or have the potential to be applicable for data mining of human resources information.

Clustering and classification is an example of a set of data-mining techniques borrowed from classical statistical methods that can help describe patterns in information. *Clustering* seeks to identify a small set of exhaustive and mutually exclusive categories to describe the data that is present (Fayyad, Piatsky-Shapiro, & Smyth, 1996). This might be a useful application to human resource data if an organization was trying to identify a certain set of employees with consistent attributes. For example, an employer may want to find out what are the main categories of top performers for its employees with an eye towards tailoring various programs to the groups or further study of such groups. One category may be more or less appropriate for one type of training program. Another category may be similarly targeted for various kinds of corporate communication modes, and so on. A difficulty with clustering techniques is that no normative techniques are known that specify the correct number of clusters that should be formed. In addition, there exist many different logics that may be followed in forming the clusters. Therefore, the art of the analyst is critical. Similarly, *classification* is a data-mining technique that maps a data item into one of several predefined classes (Fayyad, Piatsky-Shapiro, & Smyth, 1996). Classification may be useful in human resources to classify trends of movement through the organization for certain sets of successful employees. A company is at an advantage when recruiting if it can point out some realistic career paths for new employees. Being able to support those career paths with information reflecting employee success can make this a strong resource for those charged with hiring in an organization. Factor Analysis can also be mentioned here as it is sometimes described as clustering of variables (Kerlinger & Lee, 2000) instead of observations. If many measures exist for some desirable employee trait, factor analysis may help to reduce them to a few manageable factors.

Decision Tree Analysis, also called tree or hierarchical partitioning, is a somewhat related technique but follows a very different logic and can be rendered somewhat more automatic. Here, a variable is chosen first in such a way as to maximize the difference or contrast formed by splitting the data into two groups. One group consists of all observations having a value higher than a certain value of the variable, such as the mean. Then, the complement, namely those lower than that value, becomes the other group.

Then, each half can be subjected to successive further splits with possibly different variables becoming important to different halves. For example, employees might first be split into two groups–above and below average tenure with the firm. Then, the statistics of the two groups can be compared and contrasted to gain insights about employee turnover factors. A further split of the lower tenure group, say based on gender, may help prioritize those most likely to need special programs for retention. Thus, clusters or categories can be formed by binary cuts, a kind of divide and conquer approach. In addition, the order of variables can be chosen differently to make the technique more flexible. For each group formed, summary statistics can be presented and compared. This technique is a rather pure form of data mining and can be performed in the absence of specific questions or issues. It might be applied as a way of seeking interesting questions about a very large datamart. As another example, if applied to an HR datamart, one might notice that employees hired from a particular source have a higher average value on some desirable trait. Then, with a more careful random sampling and statistical hypothesis testing, the indicated advantage might be tested for validity. Also, the clusters or segments identified by either this approach or other clustering techniques can be further analyzed by another technique such as correlation and regression analysis.

Regression and related models, also borrowed from classical statistics, permits estimation of a linear function of independent variables that best explains or predicts a given dependent variable. Since this technique is generally well known, we will not dwell on the details here. However, data warehouses and datamarts may be so large that direct use of all available observations is impractical for regression and similar studies. Thus, random sampling may be necessary to use regression analysis. Various nonlinear regression techniques are also available in commercial statistical packages and can be used in a similar way for data mining. Recently, a new model-fitting technique was proposed in Troutt, Hu, Shanker, and Acar (2001). In this approach, the objective is to explain the highest or lowest performers, respectively, as a function of one or more independent variables.

Neural Networks may be regarded as a special type of nonlinear regression models. Special purpose data-mining software typically provides this option for model building. One may apply it in much the same way that regression would be used in the case of one dependent variable. However, neural networks have the additional flexibility to handle more than one dependent variable to be predicted from the same set of independent variables.

Virtually any statistical or data analysis technique may be potentially useful for data- mining studies. As noted above, however, it may be necessary to create a smaller sample by random sampling, rather than attempting to apply the technique directly to the entire set of available data.

Reporting and Use

The final step in the process emphasizes the value of the use of the information. The information extracted must be consolidated and resolved with previous information and then shared and acted upon (Fayyad, Piatsky-Shapiro, Smyth, & Uthurusamy, 1996). Too often, organizations go through the effort and expense of collecting and analyzing data without any idea of how to use the information retrieved. Applying data-mining techniques to an HRIS can help support the justification of the investment in the system. Therefore, the firm should have some expected use for the information retrieved in the process.

As mentioned earlier, one use of human resource related information is to support decisionmaking in the organization. The results obtained from data mining may be used for a full range of decision-making steps. It can be used to provide information to support a decision, or can be fully integrated into an end-user application (Feelders *et al.*, 2000). For example, a firm might be able to set up decision rules regarding employees based on the results of data mining. It might be able to determine when an employee is eligible for promotion or when a certain work group should be eligible for additional company benefits.

Legal and Privacy Issues

Organizational leaders must be aware of legislation concerning legal and privacy issues when making decisions about using personal data collected from individuals in organizations (Hubbard, Forcht, & Thomas, 1998). By their nature, systems that collect employee information run the risk of invading the privacy of employees by allowing access to the information to others within the organization. Although there is no explicit constitutional right to privacy, certain amendments and federal laws have relevance to this issue as they provide protection for employees from invasion of privacy and defamation (Fisher, Schoenfeldt, & Shaw, 1999). Organizations can protect themselves from these employee concerns by having solid business reasons for any data collection from employees.

There are also some potential legal issues if a firm uses inappropriate information extracted from data mining to make employment-related decisions. Even if a manager has an understanding of current laws, he or she could still face challenges as laws and regulations constantly change (Ledvinka & Scarpello, 1992). An extreme example that may violate equal opportunity laws is a decision to hire only females in a job classification because the data mining uncovered that females were consistently more successful.

One research study found that an employee's ability to authorize disclosure of personal information affected their perceptions of fairness and invasion of privacy (Eddy, Stone, & Stone-Romero, 1999). Therefore, it is recommended that firms notify employees upon hire that the information they provide may be used in data analyses. Another recommendation is to establish a committee or review board to monitor any activities relating to analysis of personal information (Osborn,1978). This committee can review any proposed research and ensure compliance with any relevant employment or privacy laws.

As noted in the above study (Eddy *et al.*, 1999), often the employee's reaction to the use of his or her information is based upon personal perceptions. If there is a perception that the company is analyzing the data to take negative actions against employees, employees are more apt to object to the use. However, if the employer takes the time to notify employees and obtain their permission—even if there may be no legal consequences— the perception of negativity may be removed. Employee confidence is something that employers need to maintain.

PRACTICAL APPLICATIONS OF DATA MINING HR INFORMATION

Only a few organizations have started data mining their HRIS. MERLIN, a data warehouse developed by the State of Mississippi, currently allows over 230 users to run and access aggregate reports on position vacancies, salary patterns, and other HR-related data (Roberts, 1999). In time, the State plans to use the data warehouse to help find trends to identify where it has retention problems, attrition rates and reasons, and average employee characteristics. *HR Vision,* an HR data warehouse product developed by SAS Institute, has helped Deere & Co. find a way to quickly make predictions and run reports from over 80,000 employee records (SAS Institute, 2001). For example, the company identified patterns in employee-benefit selections. Through this process, it was able to provide benefit options that were more attractive to workers, and, as a result, it was better able to manage the costs of the options provided.

The questions in Table 3 outline some areas of exploration for data mining an HRIS. As an organization comes to the realization that it has a vast amount of information stored that it isn't using, it will probably be able to identify many other questions to be explored. As mentioned earlier, it is important to formulate a question before jumping into data mining. Here we will look at forming questions in two specific areas—identifying effective sources of recruiting employees and estimating the value of training. These examples are fairly simple, but provide the reader with an idea of the how data-mining techniques can be used to support human resource decisions.

Employee Recruitment Support

Organizations are consistently looking for more effective recruiting methods to minimize recruiting costs and also to find employees that are more likely to stay with the organization for an extended period of time. High employee turnover can be very costly to companies. The cost of turnover goes beyond the fee for running an advertisement in a newspaper. Turnover costs include all replacement costs such as staff time in interviewing, the cost of lost productivity while the position remains open, and the cost of training the new employee (Cascio, 1991). Yet, very few employers evaluate the success of their recruiting sources.

There are many sources from which organizations fill open positions. An organization may place an advertisement in a newspaper or on the Internet, hold a job open house, collect employee referrals, use a third-party recruiter, or many other options. Recruiters may use a variety of approaches in very large companies without ever communicating to each other the success (or lack of success) of a particular source. Data mining offers a possible solution to this problem. If an organization tracks the recruitment source of new hires, it can search for patterns in recruitment source relating to successful employees. To do this, the organization must first identify the measure to identify successful employees. An organization might, for example, define a successful employee as an employee who received a top performance appraisal rating.

At least two different data-mining methods could be used for this question. First, a regression model or Neural Network model might be applied. In this approach, a success score would be assigned to employees in the data sample. Then the possible predictor variables would be decided. One or both of the above model types could be run on the data to obtain a formula that predicts the success score of an employee with the given predictor variable values. Secondly, a classification type of approach could be used. In this modeling approach, two samples—one of high performers and one of low performers—are obtained. Then, a statistical group score is developed. The data for a new potential hire can then be processed to predict in which group he or she will be.

Employee Training Evaluation

An important step in the instructional design process is the evaluation of training. Most training evaluation focuses on evaluating specific training programs and the specific change that has or has not occurred as a result of that program (Sackett & Nelson, 1993). This type of evaluation is helpful in determining the content of future training programs by understanding the components of specific training programs that were effective or ineffective. This type of evaluation is essential to organizations, but some organizations may want to look at the value of training in a different context.

Employee training and development activities in an organization are of significant strategic importance, and they are also very costly to organizations (Tannenbaum &Woods, 1992). Considering the high cost of training in an organization, company leaders may be interested in looking at training from the "big picture" perspective. If a company can identify its overall training budget, it may want to know what kind of impact this total figure is having on the company. One approach to identifying this effect would be to look at the success of employees who have participated in company training programs. Are they progressing through the organization? Are they receiving promotions and moving up the career ladder?

This type of information is not readily available to organizations. While they may be able to evaluate the results of a specific training effort, it is often difficult to evaluate training as a whole. Data mining might offer a solution to this evaluation question. Many organizations store training-related data in their HRIS. Some of the data stored includes the content of training programs and records of which courses an employee has taken (Herren, 1989). By setting up a data-mining program to search for patterns of training activities related to advancement in the organization, a company might uncover data to support further training investments.

CONCLUSIONS

All organizations collect data on employees to utilize in administrative tasks such as payroll processing and benefit enrollment. The use of the data beyond administrative purposes can provide the basis for a competitive advantage by allowing organizations to strategically analyze one of their most important assets— their employees. In order to use this data for strategic decision-making, organizations must be able to transform the data they have collected into useful information. When dealing with large sets of data, this transformation can be a challenge for organizations. Data mining provides an attractive opportunity that has not been thoroughly explored for human resource information systems. The application of data-mining techniques to human resource information systems requires organizational expertise and work to prepare the system for mining. In particular, a datamart for HR is a useful first step. Further, organizations must be aware of legal implications of decisionmaking based on personal employee information. With proper preparation and consideration, HR databases together with data mining create an opportunity for organizations to develop their competitive advantage through using that information for strategic decisionmaking.

REFERENCES

Agosta, L. (2000). *The essential guide to data warehousing.* Upper Saddle River. NJ: Prentice Hall PTR.

Anthony, W.P., Perrewe, P.L., & Kacmar, K.M. (1996). *Strategic human resource management.* Orlando, FL: Harcourt Brace & Company.

Barney, J. (1991). Firm resources and sustained competitive advantage. *Journal of Management,* 35 (1), 99-120.

Boxall, P. (1996). The strategic HRM debate and the resource-based view of the firm. *Human Resource Management Journal,* 6 (3), 59-75.

Broderick, R. & Boudreau, J.W. (1992) Human resource management, information technology, and the competitive edge. *Academy of Management Executive,* 6 (2), 7-17.

Brodley, C.E., Lane, T., & Stough, T.M. (1999). Knowledge discovery and data mining. *American Scientist,* 87, 54-61.

Cascio, W.F. (1991). *Costing human resources: The financial impact of behavior in organizations,* (3rd ed.), Boston, MA: PWS-Kent Publishing Co.

Eddy, E.R., Stone, D.L., & Stone-Romero, E.F. (1999). The effects of information management policies on reactions to human resource information systems: An integration of privacy and procedural justice perspectives. *Personnel Psychology,* 52 (2), 335-358.

Fayyad, U.M., Piatsky-Shapiro, G., & Smyth, P. (1996) From data mining to knowledge discovery in databases. *AI Magazine,* (7), 37-54.

Fayyad, U.M., Piatsky-Shapiro, G., Smyth, P., & Uthurusamy, R. (1996) *Advances in knowledge discovery and data mining. Menlo Park, CA:* AAAI Press. competitive

Feelders, A., Daniels, H., & Holsheimer, M. (2000). Methodological and practical aspects of data mining. *Information & Management,* (37), 271-281.

Fisher, C.D., Schoenfeldt, L.F., & Shaw, J.B. (1999). *Human resource management.* Boston, MA: Houghton Mifflin Company.

Fitz-Enz, J. (1998). Top 10 calculations for your HRIS. *HR Focus,* 75 (4), 53.

Gray, P. & Watson, H.J. (1998*). Decision support in the data warehouse.* Upper Saddle River, NJ: Prentice Hall PTR.

Herren, L.M. (1989). The right recruitment technology for the 1990s. *HR Magazine,* 34 (4), 48-52.

Hubbard, J.C., Forcht, K.A., & Thomas, D.S. (1998). Human resource information systems: An overview of current ethical and legal issues. *Journal of Business Ethics,* (17), 1319-1323.

Huselid, M.A., Jackson, S.E., & Schuler, R.S. (1997). Technical and strategic human resource management effectiveness as determinants of firm performance. *Academy of Management Journal*, 40 (1), 171-188.

Kovach, K.A. & Cathcart, Jr., C.E. (1999). Human resources information systems (HRIS): Providing business with rapid data access, information exchange and strategic advantage. *Public Personnel Management,* 28 (2), 275-282.

Kerlinger, F. N. & Lee, H. B. (2000). *Foundations of Behavioral Research*, (3rd ed.). Orlando, FL: Harcourt, Inc.

Ledvinka, J. & Scarpello, V.G. (1992). *Federal Regulation of Personnel and Human Resource Management*. Belmont, CA: Wadsworth Publishing Company.

Mallach, E.G. (2000). *Decision support and data warehouse systems*. Boston, MA: McGraw-Hill.

McElroy, J. (1991). The HRIS as an agent of change. *Personnel Journal*, 70 (5), 105-111.

Osborn, J.L. (1978). *Personal information: Privacy at the workplace*. New York: AMACOM.

Pfeffer, J. (1994). *Competitive advantage through people*. Cambridge, MA: Harvard Business School Press.

Roberts, B. (1999). HR's link to the corporate big picture. *HR Magazine*. 44 (4), 103-110.

Sackett, P.R. &.Nelson, A.C. (1993). Beyond formal experimental design: Towards an expanded view of the training evaluation process. *Personnel Psychology* (46), 613-627.

SAS Institute Inc. (2001). John Deere harvests HR records with SAS. Available online at: http://www.sas.com/news/success/johndeere.html.

Subramanian, A., Smith, L.D., Nelson, A.C., Campbell, J.F., & Bird, D.A. (1997) Strategic planning for data warehousing. *Information & Management*, (33), 99-113.

Tannenbaum, S.I. & Woods, S.B. (1992). Determining a strategy for evaluating training: Operating within organizational constraints. *Human Resource Planning*, 15 (2), 63-81.

Troutt, M.D., Hu, M., Shanker, M., &Acar, W. (2003). Frontier versus ordinary regression models for data mining. In P. C. Pendharkar (ed.), *Managing data mining technologies in organizations: Techniques and applications*. Hershey, PA: Idea Group Publishing Co.

Walker, J.W. & Reif, W.E. (1999) Human resource leaders: Capability, strengths and gaps. *Human Resource Planning*, 22 (4), 21-32.

Watson, H.J. & Haley, B.J. (1998). Managerial considerations. *Communications of the ACM,* 4 (9), 32-37.

Chapter XVII

Data Mining in Information Technology and Banking Performance

Yao Chen
University of Massachusetts at Lowell, USA

Joe Zhu
Worcester Polytechnic Institute, USA

ABSTRACT

Information technology (IT) has become the key enabler of business process expansion if an organization is to survive and continue to prosper in a rapidly changing business environment while facing competition in a global marketplace. In the banking industry, a large amount of IT budgets are spent with the expectation that the investment will result in higher productivity and improved financial performance. However, bank managers make decisions on how to spend large IT budgets without accurate performance measurement systems on the business value of IT. A survey on managing technology in the banking industry found that 55% of the 188 senior executives surveyed stated that the returns on their investments in IT were either good or excellent. However, 50% of the senior executives also stated that they did not have any formal systems in place to measure the return on investment. This illustrates a need for a proper data-mining technique that can examine the impact of IT investment on banking performance. It has been recognized that the link between IT investment and banking performance is indirect, due to the effect of mediating and moderating variables. This chapter presents a methodology that measures the efficiency of IT utilization and the impact of IT on banking performance when intermediate measures are present. A set of banks is used to illustrate how we (1) characterize the indirect impact of IT on banking performance, (2) identify the best practice of two principal value-added stages related to IT investment and profit generation, and (3) improve the financial performance of banking.

INTRODUCTION

In the financial services industry worldwide, the traditional face-to-face customer contacts are being replaced by electronic points of contact to reduce the time and cost of processing an application for various products and ultimately improve the financial performance. During this process, IT investment plays a critical role. Keen (1991) indicates that (1) IT costs have grown at an annualized rate of 15% in the last decade, and this is the only area of business in which investment has consistently increased faster than economic growth, and (2) annual IT investment may constitute up to one-half of a firm's annual capital expenditures. For example, a survey on managing technology in banking industry found that 55% of the 188 senior executives surveyed stated that the returns on their investments in IT were either good or excellent. However, 50% of the senior executives also stated that they did not have any formal systems in place to measure the return on investment. The increasing use of IT has resulted in a need for evaluating the impact of IT investment on firm performance. It is essential that we be able to extract valuable information from the IT investment and financial data in the banking industry.

It has been recognized that it is difficult to empirically link investment in IT with firm performance due to a number of measurement, model specification, and data availability problems. This is partly due to the fact that IT is indirectly linked with a firm's performance. In this regard, new data-mining methods are needed to evaluate the IT investment and the banking performance. Chen and Zhu (2001) developed a methodology using a two-stage model to explicitly incorporate the intermediate variables that link the IT investment with the firm performance. Their methodology (1) captures IT's impact on firm performance via intermediate variables; (2) views firm performance as a result of a series of value-added IT-related activities; and (3) identifies the best practice when intermediate measures are present.

Note that there are multiple financial and non-financial performance measures associated with banking performance. The current chapter uses data envelopment analysis (DEA) as the fundamental tool to extract performance patterns and to evaluate the banking performance. DEA has been proven successful in performance evaluation where multiple performance measures are present (Zhu, 2000). DEA does not require a priori information about the relationship among multiple performance measures, and estimates the empirical tradeoff curve (best practice) from the observations. A number of DEA softwares are available to perform the data-mining functions (see, e.g., Zhu, 2002).

DATA ENVELOPMENT ANALYSIS

DEA is a mathematical programming approach developed to evaluate the relative efficiency of a set of units that have multiple performance measures – inputs and outputs (Charnes, Cooper, & Rhodes, 1978). DEA is particularly useful when the relationship among the multiple performance measures are unknown. Through the optimization for each individual unit, DEA yields an efficient frontier or tradeoff curve that represents the relations among the multiple performance measures.

For example, consider the tradeoff between IT investment and the number of bank employees. Figure 1 illustrates the efficient frontier or tradeoff curve containing F1, F2, and F3 and the area dominated by the curve. A bank's performance (or IT investment strategy) on the efficient frontier is non-dominated (efficient) in the sense that there exists no performance that is strictly better in both IT investment and employee. Through performance evaluation, the efficient frontier that represents the best practice is identified, and any current inefficient performance (e.g., point F) can be improved onto the efficient frontier with suggested directions (to F1, F2, F3, or other points along the curve) (see Figure 1).

Suppose we have n observations on a set of banks; i.e., we have observed input and output values of x_{ij} ($i =1, \ldots, m$) and y_{rj} ($r =1, \ldots, s$) for bank j, respectively, where j = 1, ..., n. The (empirical) efficient frontier is formed by these n observations. The following two properties ensure that we have a piecewise linear approximation to the efficient frontier and the area dominated by the frontier (Banker, Charnes, & Cooper, 1984).

Figure 1: Efficient frontier.

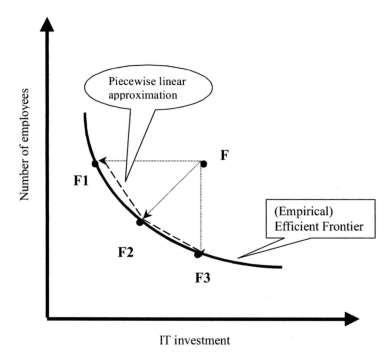

Property 1. Convexity. $\sum_{j=1}^{n} \pi_j \, x_{ij}$ $(i=1,\ldots,m)$ and $\sum_{j=1}^{n} \pi_j \, y_{rj}$ $(r=1,\ldots,s)$ are possible inputs

and outputs achievable by the banks, where π_j $(j=1,\ldots,n)$ are non-negative scalars

such that $\sum_{j=1}^{n} \pi_j = 1.$

Property 2. Inefficiency. The same y_{rj} can be obtained by using $\hat{x}_{ij}$, where $\hat{x}_{ij} > x_{ij}$ (i.e.,

the same outputs can be produced by using more inputs). The same x_{ij} can be used to

obtain $\hat{y}_{rj}$, where $\hat{y}_{rj} < y_{rj}$ (i.e., the same inputs can be used to produce less outputs).

Consider Figure 1 where the IT investment and the number of employees represent two inputs. Applying Property 1 to F1, F2, and F3 yields a piecewise linear approximation to the curve in Figure 1. Applying both properties expands the line segments F1F2 and F2F3 into the area dominated by the curve.

Applying the above two properties to specific inputs of x_i $(i=1,\ldots,m)$ and outputs of y_r $(r=1,\ldots,s)$ yields

$$
\begin{cases}
\sum_{j=1}^{n} \pi_j x_{ij} \leq x_i & i=1,\ldots,m \\[2mm]
\sum_{j=1}^{n} \pi_j y_{rj} \geq y_r & r=1,\ldots,s \\[2mm]
\sum_{j=1}^{n} \pi_j = 1
\end{cases}
\tag{1}
$$

The DEA efficient frontier is determined by the non-dominated observations satisfying (1). Based upon (1), we have the following DEA model:

$$
\theta^* = \min_{\pi_j, \theta} \theta
$$

subject to

$$
\sum_{j=1}^{n} \pi_j x_{ij} \leq \theta \, x_{ij_o} \qquad i=1,\ldots,m
$$

$$
\sum_{j=1}^{n} \pi_j y_{rj} \geq y_{rj_o} \qquad r=1,\ldots,s
\tag{2}
$$

$$
\sum_{j=1}^{n} \pi_j = 1
$$

$$
\pi_j \geq 0, \quad j=1,\ldots,n
$$

where x_{ij_o} is the ith input and y_{rj_o} is the rth output of the j_o th bank (observation) under evaluation.

If $\theta^* = 1$, then the j_o th bank is located on the frontier (or efficient). Otherwise if $\theta^* < 1$, then the j_o th bank is inefficient. Model (2) is called input-oriented DEA model where the goal is to minimize input usage while keeping the outputs at their current levels. Similarly, we can have an output-oriented DEA model where the goal is to maximize the output production while keeping the inputs at their current levels.

$$\phi^* = \max_{\pi_j,\phi} \phi$$

$subject \quad to$

$$\sum_{j=1}^{n} \pi_j x_{ij} \le x_{ij_o} \qquad i=1,2,...,m;$$

$$\sum_{j=1}^{n} \pi_j y_{rj} \ge \phi y_{rj_o} \qquad r=1,2,...,s;$$

$$\sum_{j=1}^{n} \pi_j = 1$$

$$\pi_j \ge 0 \qquad\qquad j=1,...,n. \tag{3}$$

Both models (2) and (3) identify the same efficient frontier, because $\theta^* = 1$ if and only if $\phi^* = 1$. To further illustrate the DEA methodology, we consider dual program of model (3)

$$\min \sum_{i=1}^{m} v_i x_{io} + v$$

$subject \quad to$

$$\sum_{i=1}^{m} v_i x_{ij} - \sum_{r=1}^{s} \mu_r y_{rj} + v \ge 0$$

$$\sum_{r=1}^{s} \mu_r y_{ro} = 1$$

$$\mu_r, v_i \ge 0 \quad \text{and} \quad v \quad \text{free}$$

The above model is equivalent to

$$h_o^* = \min_{\alpha,v_i,u_r} \frac{\alpha + \sum_{i=1}^{m} v_i x_{io}}{\sum_{r=1}^{s} u_r y_{ro}}$$

$subject \quad to$ $\tag{4}$

$$\frac{\alpha + \sum_{i=1}^{m} v_i x_{ij}}{\sum_{r=1}^{s} u_r y_{rj}} > 1, j = 1, \ldots, n$$

Let $h_j = \dfrac{\alpha + \sum_{i=1}^{m} v_i x_{ij}}{\sum_{r=1}^{s} u_r y_{rj}}$. Then the model (4) seeks to determine the relative efficiency

of each bank. It is clear from the model (4) that smaller value of h_o^* is preferred since we prefer larger values of y_{ro} and smaller values of x_{io} . Therefore, model (4) tries to find a set of weights v_i and u_r so that the ratio of aggregated x_{io} to aggregated y_{ro} reaches the minimum. Note that model (4) is solved for each bank. Therefore, model (4) does not seek the average best performance, but the efficient or best performance achievable by a proper set of optimized weights.

Note that when $h_o^* = 1$, we have

$$\sum_{r=1}^{s} u_r^* y_{ro} = \alpha^* + \sum_{i=1}^{m} v_i^* x_{io} \qquad (5)$$

where (*) represents the optimal values in model (4). It can be seen that (5) is similar to the regression model with α^* the intercept on the y-axis. The implicit difference between model (4) and the regression model lies in the fact that (i) model (4) deals with more than one dependent variables (y_{rj}) at the same time, and (ii) equation (5) is obtained for each bank with a score of one. Further, (5) represents the efficient frontier. Since different units with score of one in model (4) may not be on the same frontier, the resulting efficient frontier is a piecewise linear one, as shown in Figure 1.

From the above discussion, we can see that DEA can be an excellent data-mining approach with respect to extracting efficiency information from the performance data.

Consider three two-stage bank operations as presented in Table 1, where the first stage has two inputs (IT investment and labor) and one output (deposit), and the second stage has one input (deposit generated from the first stage) and one output (profit) (see, e.g., Figure 2).

Applying model (2) to the two stages indicates that the banks A and B in the first stage, and bank C in the second stage are efficient. Now, if we ignore the intermediate measure of deposit and apply model (2), the last column of Table 1 indicates that all banks are efficient.

This simple numerical example indicates that the conventional DEA fails to correctly characterize the performance of two-stage operations, since an overall DEA efficient performance does not necessarily indicate efficient performance in individual component. Consequently, improvement to the best practice can be distorted, i.e., the performance improvement of one stage affects the efficiency status of the other because of the presence

Table 1: Numerical example

Bank	IT Investment	Stage 1 Labor	Stage 2 Deposit	Profit	Efficiency Stage1	Stage2	Overall
A	7	9	4	16	1	0.75	1
B	9	4	6	14	1	0.5	1
C	11	6	3	23	0.791	1	1

of intermediate measures. In the next section, we present a DEA model that can directly evaluate the performance of two-stage operations, and set performance targets for intermediate measures.

THE MODEL

Consider the indirect impact of IT on banking performance where IT directly impacts certain intermediate measures which in turn are transformed to realize banking performance. Figure 2 describes the indirect impact of IT on banking performance where the first stage use inputs x_i ($i = 1, ..., m$) to produce outputs z_d ($d = 1, ..., D$), and then these z_d are used as inputs in the second stage to produce outputs y_r ($r = 1, ..., s$). It can be seen that z_d (intermediate measures) are outputs in stage 1 and inputs in stage 2. The first stage is viewed as an IT-related, value-added activity where deposit is generated and then used as the input to the second stage where revenue is generated.

Figure 2: IT impact on banking performance.

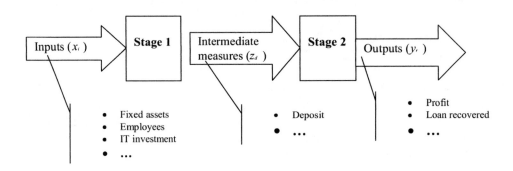

Based upon Chen and Zhu (2001), we have

$$\min w_1 \alpha + w_2 \beta$$

(stage 1)

$$\sum_{j=1}^{n} \lambda_j x_{ij} \leq \alpha x_{ij_o} \qquad i = 1, \dots, m$$

$$\sum_{j=1}^{n} \lambda_j z_{dj} \geq \tilde{z}_{dj_o} \qquad d = 1, \dots, D$$

$$\sum_{j=1}^{n} \lambda_j = 1$$

$$\lambda_j \geq 0, \quad j = 1, \dots, n$$

$$\alpha \leq 1$$

(stage 2) \hfill (6)

$$\sum_{j=1}^{n} \mu_j z_{dj} \leq \tilde{z}_{dj_o} \qquad d = 1, \dots, D$$

$$\sum_{j=1}^{n} \mu_j y_{rj} \geq \beta y_{rj_o} \qquad r = 1, \dots, s$$

$$\sum_{j=1}^{n} \mu_j = 1$$

$$\mu_j \geq 0, \quad j = 1, \dots, n$$

$$\beta \geq 1$$

where w_1 and w_2 are user-specified weights reflecting the preference over the two stages' performance, and symbol "~" represents unknown decision variables.

The rationale of model (6) is as follows: (i) when we evaluate the impact of IT investment on the intermediate measures, we want to minimize the input usage given the intermediate measures. For example, given the deposits generated, our objective is to examine whether a bank can reduce its input consumption (including IT investment) compared to the best practice, and (ii) when we evaluate bank performance as a result of the intermediate measures, we want to maximize the performance given the intermediate measures. For example, given the deposits it generated, our objective is to examine whether a bank can increase its profit. Model (6) characterizes the indirect impact of IT on banking performance in a single linear programming problem.

Theorem 1 If $\alpha^* = \beta^* = 1$, then there must exist an optimal solution such that $\lambda_{j_o}^* = \mu_{j_o}^* = 1$, where (*) represents optimal value in model (6).

[Proof]: Note that $\lambda_{j_o}^* = \mu_{j_o}^* = 1$, $\alpha^* = \beta^* = 1$, and $\tilde{z}_{d_{j_o}}^* = z_{d_{j_o}}$ are feasible solutions in model
(6). This completes the proof. ∎

Theorem 2 If $\alpha^* = \beta^* = 1$, then $\theta^* = 1$ and $\phi^* = 1$, where θ^* and ϕ^* are the optimal values
to models (2) and (3), respectively.

[Proof]: Suppose $\alpha^* = \beta^* = 1$ in model (6). By Theorem 1, we know that $\lambda_{j_o}^* = \mu_{j_o}^* = 1$, α^*

$= \beta^* = 1$, and $\tilde{z}_{d_{j_o}}^* = z_{d_{j_o}}$. Now, if $\theta^* < 1$ and $\phi^* > 1$, then this indicates that $\alpha^* =$

$\beta^* = 1$ is not optimal in model (6). A contradiction. ∎

Theorem 2 indicates if $\alpha^* = \beta^* = 1$, the value-chain achieves efficient performance
when the two-stage process is viewed as a whole.

If $\alpha^* = 1$ and $\beta^* > 1$ (or $\alpha^* < 1$ and $\beta^* = 1$), then model (6) indicates that one of the
stages can achieve 100% efficiency given a set of optimal intermediate measures. In this case,
the original DEA models (2) and (3) can be used to provide additional information.

From Theorem 2, we immediately have the following result:

Corollary A bank must be a frontier point in both stages with respect to $\alpha^* x_{ij_o}$ ($i = 1$,

..., m), $\tilde{z}_{d_{j_o}}^*$ ($d = 1, ..., D$), and $\beta^* y_{rj_o}$ ($r = 1, ..., s$), where (*) represents optimal value
in model (6).

Based upon the above Corollary, model (6) yields directions for achieving the best
practice of this two-stage process. Consequently, we can study the marginal impact of
IT investment on banking performance by using returns to scale estimation discussed
in Seiford and Zhu (1999) (see Chen & Zhu, 2001, for such a study).

In model (6), the intermediate measures for a specific bank under evaluation are set as

unknown decision variables, $\tilde{z}_{d_{j_o}}$. As a result, additional constraints can be imposed on the

intermediate measures. This can further help in correctly characterizing the indirect impact
of IT on banking performance.

APPLICATION

Consider a set of 15 banks obtained from the Functional Cost and Profit Analysis
data set collected by the Federal Reserve Bank under its Functional Cost Analysis (FCA)
program. The data for this study is based on the FCA Plus data set from 1997. Table 2
presents the data. In the first stage, we have three inputs: Transactional IT investment,
Strategic IT investment, and Labor expenses, and two outputs: number of Accounts and
number of Transactions. In the second stage, we have two outputs: Revenue and Equity.

The IT investment measures are constructed using data from the following FCA
defined expense categories: Vendor Data Processing (all expenses for data processing

Table 2:   Data for 15 banks

Bank	Tran IT	Strategic IT	Labor	Accounts	Transactions	Revenue	Equity
1	68,374,883	27,207,296	96,644,431	28,430.63	109,486,141	4,561,844,525	507,245,000
2	43,674,296	20,728,716	82,211,383	4,020.105	149,772,606	819,640,950	1,697,263,000
3	36,240,480	22,876,333	41,677,506	1,417,653	42,281,949	705,076,794	740,666,344
4	10,974,089	3,604,030	23,386,094	4,801.735	41,624,391	252,167,755	250,842,739
5	8,165,838	4,598,047	11,074,813	5,777.526	14,023,708	137,014,849	120,597,000
6	5,826,344	1,383,431	10,723,845	9,335	1,982,414	160,695,007	218,540,000
7	3,039,890	2,701,362	17,225,000	16,539.81	45,748,993	353,726,000	451,221,000
8	2,631,636	891,139.9	7,585,518	4,245.225	10,054,751	50,543,312	81,451,129
9	2,445,674	531,648.3	7,537,537	1,668.805	8,294,216	59,544,335	55,444,711
10	1,481,997	459,703.1	370,169	3,801	433,717	28,100,210	23,699,857
11	1,471,033	1,070,595	6,378,768	2,230.61	5,915,536	70,210,212	65,192,518
12	1,321,121	863,879.5	3,718,510	16,935.8	7,093,301	37,509,806	37,123,155
13	1,287,557	687,890.1	5,609,930	3,121.808	6,223,975	41,187,111	36,704,000
14	1,164,952	762,892.3	3,449,934	3,822.564	4,476,600	28,526,966	25,739,404
15	1,121,468	391,687.7	3,185,637	4,939.944	8,530,050	41,220,844	43,067,174

performed by outside banks, e.g., check processing centers); Telephone and Electronic Access (total expense for communications, including fees for telephone lines, online charges, software installation, and modification); Network Expense Fees (ATM) (all membership and participation fees charged by ATM networks); EFT/ACH Cost Center expense (all expenses related to electronic banking delivery systems other than ATMs; ATM Cost Center expenses (all expenses related to maintenance and support of all ATM transactions on ATMs either owned or leased by the bank); Proof & Transit Cost Center expense (all expenses related to check processing, such as encoding, check sorting, and generating account balances); and Data Processing Cost Center expense (all expenses related to internal data processing, i.e., services provided by the bank's own data processing staff, maintenance and support of institution's software, operating systems, PCs, mainframes, etc.).

Transactional IT refers to IT investment aimed at automation of routine and repetitive tasks to reduce processing costs. Thus, the Transactional IT measure is constructed by adding the total expenses for Vendor Data Processing, the Proof & Transit Cost Center, and the Data Processing Cost Center. On the other hand, Strategic IT refers to IT investment aimed at increasing market share or generating revenues. Thus, the Strategic IT measure is constructed by adding all expenses related to Electronic Access and Automation of customer interface, total expenses for Telephone and Electronic Access, ATM Network Fees, the EFT/ACH Cost Center, and the ATM Cost Center. The labor input is the sum of the salary plus benefits costs of full-time equivalent personnel.

Table 3 reports the efficiency based upon models (2) and (3) in the first and second stage, respectively. The last column reports the overall efficiency that is calculated using the model (2) with Transactional IT, Strategic IT, and Labor as the inputs and Revenue and Equity as the outputs. (i.e., we ignore the intermediate measures.) It can be seen that overall efficient banks do not necessarily indicate efficient performance in the two stages (see, e.g., banks 1, 7, 17, and 15). Also, if a bank is efficient in stages 1 and 2, this bank

Table 3: Banking performance

Bank	DEA θ^*	ϕ^*	Overall
1	0.59	1.00	1.00
2	1.00	1.00	1.00
3	1.00	1.00	0.88
4	0.68	1.83	0.52
5	0.47	1.82	0.44
6	0.33	1.00	1.00
7	1.00	1.40	1.00
8	0.55	2.04	0.68
9	0.74	1.00	0.97
10	1.00	1.00	1.00
11	0.76	1.00	0.88
12	1.00	6.89	0.85
13	0.87	2.40	0.87
14	0.96	3.23	0.96
15	1.00	3.68	1.00

may be identified as inefficient in overall efficiency. For example, bank 3. This indicates that we need to use model (6) to correctly characterize the banking performance.

Table 4 reports the results from model (6) with different weight combinations. When w_1 = w_2 = 1, we have, given the optimal intermediate measures of Accounts and Transactions, (i) two banks (2 and 10) that achieve 100% efficiency in both stage 1 and stage 2; (ii) 10 banks that achieve 100% efficiency in the IT-related activity (stage 1) without achieving 100% efficiency in stage 2; (iii) two banks (1 and 3) that do not achieve 100% efficiency in the IT-related activity while achieving 100% efficiency in stage 2; and (iv) two banks (4 and 6) that do not achieve 100% efficiency in both stages.

When w_1 = 5 and w_2 = 1, i.e., we are more interested in the potential saving on the IT investment. The efficiency of banks 1, 3, 10, 13, 14, and 15 stays the same. The efficiency of some other banks changes because of the tradeoff between the two stages. For example, bank 5 eliminates some inefficiency in its second stage in exchange of input savings in the first stage. If we use w_1 = 1 and w_2 = 5, (i.e., we are more interested in the potential improvement on the financial performance in the second stage), we obtain a set of different results as shown in the last two columns of the Table 4.

Table 4 only presents the efficiency scores. In fact, model (6) also yields benchmarks for the inefficient banks. For example, consider bank 3 with w_1 = w_2 = 1. In the first stage, we have $\lambda_2^* = 0.14$ (bank 2) and $\lambda_7^* = 0.86$ (bank 7), indicating that banks 2 and 7 are used as benchmarks. In the second stage, we have $\mu_1^* = 0.07$ (bank1), $\mu_2^* = 0.34$ (bank 2), and $\mu_6^* = 0.59$ (bank 3), indicating that banks 1, 2, and 6 are used as benchmarks.

Table 4: IT and banking performance

Bank	$w_1 = w_2 = 1$ α^*	β^*	$w_1 = 5, w_2 = 1$ α^*	β^*	$w_1 = 1, w_2 = 5$ α^*	β^*
1	0.59	1	0.59	1	0.59	1
2	1	1	1	1	1	1
3	0.62	1	0.62	1	1	1.31
4	0.75	2.42	0.13	1.05	1	2.61
5	1	3.72	0.18	1.89	1	3.72
6	0.86	1.84	0.33	1.29	1	1.98
7	1	1.4	0.68	1	1	1.4
8	1	4.43	0.51	3.5	1	4.43
9	1	4.98	0.88	4.8	1	4.98
10	1	1	1	1	1	1
11	1	4.82	0.82	3.99	1	4.82
12	1	7.51	0.96	7.41	1	7.51
13	1	7.5	1	7.5	1	7.5
14	1	8.17	1	8.17	1	8.17
15	1	3.68	1	3.68	1	3.68

Table 5: Optimal accounts and transactions

Bank	$w_1 = w_2 = 1$ Accounts	Transactions	$w_1 = 5, w_2 = 1$ Accounts	Transactions	$w_1 = 1, w_2 = 5$ Accounts	Transactions
1	28,431	109,486,141	28,431	109,486,141	28,431	109,486,141
2	4,020	149,772,606	4,020	149,772,606	4,020	149,772,606
3	14,845	59,830,119	14,845	59,830,119	11,829	84,890,085
4	16,540	45,748,993	9,571	7,936,096	15,913	50,957,680
5	11,458	29,444,588	9,745	4,664,650	11,458	2,9444,588
6	8,926	21,318,248	9,194	8,631,691	9,921	24,511,377
7	16,540	45,748,993	10,653	26,860,582	16,540	45,748,993
8	8,823	16,231,013	9,096	8,629,344	8,823	16,231,013
9	9,647	9,773,165	9,654	8,642,667	9,647	9,773,165
10	3,801	433,717	3,801	433,717	3,801	433,717
11	9,628	14,045,011	9,661	7,964,574	9,628	14,045,011
12	9,562	9,735,907	9,566	9,322,128	9,562	9,735,907
13	9,710	9,898,598	9,710	9,898,598	9,710	9,898,598
14	7,553	8,217,129	7,553	8,217,129	7,553	8,217,129
15	4,940	8,530,050	4,940	8,530,050	4,940	8,530,050

Model (6) provides optimized values on the intermediate measures of Accounts and Transactions. Table 5 reports optimal values of Accounts and Transactions. Consider bank 3 when $w_1 = w_2 = 1$. Model (6) indicates that bank 3 should increase its values on Accounts and Transactions. Such results are very important because they provide banks with valuable information in terms of how their business operations objectives should be.

CONCLUSIONS

This chapter applies DEA to evaluate IT investment efficiency and banking performance. The model is developed based upon DEA and a two-stage production process. It is important to continue to investigate our model with large-scale applications. Models are under development for the situations where more than two stages are present and each stage has its own inputs and outputs that are not intermediate measures.

REFERENCES

Banker, R.D., Charnes, A. & Cooper, W.W. (1984). Some models for the estimation of technical and scale inefficiencies in data envelopment analysis. *Management Science*, 30, 1078-1092.

Charnes, A., Cooper, W.W. & Rhodes, E. (1978). Measuring the efficiency of decision-making units. *European Journal of Operational Research*, 2, 429-444.

Chen, Y. & Zhu, J. (2001). Measuring information technology's indirect impact on firm performance. *Proceedings of the 6th INFORMS Conference on Information System & Technology*, Miami, FL.

Keen, P.G.W. (1991). *Shaping the future: Business design through information technology*. Cambridge, MA: Harvard Business School Press.

Seiford, L.M. & Zhu, J. (1999). An investigation of returns to scale in DEA. *OMEGA*, 27, 1-11.

Zhu, J. (2000). Multi-factor performance measure model with an application to Fortune 500 companies. *European J. of Operational Research*, 123 (1), 105-124.

Zhu, J. (2002). *Quantitative models for performance evaluation and benchmarking: Data envelopment analysis with spreadsheets and DEA Excel Solver*. Boston, MA: Kluwer Academic Publishers.

Chapter XVIII

Social, Ethical and Legal Issues of Data Mining

Jack S. Cook
Rochester Institute of Technology, USA

Laura L. Cook
State University of New York at Geneseo, USA

ABSTRACT

This chapter highlights both the positive and negative aspects of Data Mining (DM). Specifically, the social, ethical, and legal implications of DM are examined through recent case law, current public opinion, and small industry-specific examples. There are many issues concerning this topic. Therefore, the purpose of this chapter is to expose the reader to some of the more interesting ones and provide insight into how information systems (IS) professionals and businesses may protect themselves from the negative ramifications associated with improper use of data. The more experience with and exposure to social, ethical, and legal concerns with respect to DM, the better prepared you will be to prevent trouble down the road.

INTRODUCTION

What price are you willing to pay for convenience and personalization? Customers expect businesses to not only meet their needs but also anticipate them. Companies entice consumers to sing an elaborate song detailing their personal lives with offers of giveaways, discounts, and better service, while companies gladly listen and record the tune. With technological advances, companies regularly employ data-mining techniques to explore the contents of data warehouses looking for trends, relationships, and outcomes to enhance their overall operations and discover new patterns that theoretically allow companies to better serve their customers. The uses of data mining are numerous and implemented by many organizations including government agencies and not-for-profit organizations. However, with this great ability, concerns exist regarding social, ethical, and legal issues associated with data mining. Unfortunately, these issues are not fully defined, and the future of data mining is uncertain with the threat of regulation looming.

Data has been gathered and recorded for thousands of years and used to manage day-to-day operations. For a long time, financial and insurance companies have mined their data to detect patterns of fraudulent credit card usage, find hidden correlations between financial indicators, identify behavior patterns of risky customers, and analyze claims. Utility companies have used it for decades to predict when a generator might fail. Data mining is not new, but widespread interest in it is a recent phenomenon.

Until recently, data sets were small in size, typically containing fewer than ten variables (Fayyad, 2001). Data analysis traditionally revolved around graphs, charts, and tables. But the real-time collection of data, based on thousands of variables, is practically impossible for anyone to analyze today without the aid of information systems. With such aid however, the amount of information you can "mine" is astonishing. Organizations have only recently begun to examine how their vast collections of data can be mined strategically. Data mining extracts value from volume.

Numerous definitions of data mining exist. One definition is that it is the "mechanized process of identifying and discovering useful structures in data" (Fayyad, 2001, p. 62). In this context, "structure" refers to patterns, models, and relationships in the data. Data-mining techniques draw upon such diverse areas as probability theory, information theory, estimation, uncertainty, graph theory, and database techniques (Fayyad, 2001). In addition, artificial intelligence techniques such as neural networks, expert systems, and classification algorithms are used. Another definition states that data mining involves extracting hidden predictive information from databases to solve business problems (Brandel, 2001). Often the term is misused to describe new ways to present data. Data mining does more than just present existing data in new ways—it facilitates the discovery of previously unknown relationships among the data. To further illustrate the point, consider most standard database operations. These operations present results that users already intuitively knew existed in the database. Data mining extracts information from the database the user did not anticipate. Data mining creates information that can be leveraged by the organization to create a competitive advantage. However, it is just as likely to identify meaningless patterns or trends, wasting time and resources.

This chapter highlights both the positive and negative aspects of data mining. Specifically, the social, ethical, and legal implications of data mining are examined through recent case law, current public opinion, and small industry-specific examples. There are many issues concerning this topic. Therefore, the purpose of this chapter is to expose the reader to some of the more interesting ones and provide insight into how information systems (IS) professionals and businesses may protect themselves from the negative ramifications associated with improper use of data. The more experience with and exposure to social, ethical, and legal concerns with respect to data mining, the better prepared you will be to prevent trouble down the road. Before examining these issues, it is helpful to understand how data is gathered and what can be inferred from it.

WHAT CAN BE INFERRED FROM DATA?

Fear often accompanies progress. Historically, the threat of invading one's personal privacy was more of a potential than a reality. However, with the increased use of electronic communications and the World Wide Web (WWW), it has become quite easy and inexpensive to share information among trading partners. Prior to the mid-1990s, there were technical barriers as well as economic disincentives to the sharing of information. As these barriers have fallen, the potential for data-mining use and abuse has increased.

At one time, society was very concerned about "Big Brother" (the government) gathering data and determining what individuals were doing in their personal lives. Interestingly, as a new century begins, it appears as if the organizations most likely to invade your privacy are local businesses. When one considers the quantity of data collected about consumers, it is mind-boggling. Just consider the level of detail contained in the purchasing history of individuals who use VIP, shopper club cards, or credit cards to obtain store discounts. Through these membership cards, companies are able to track your purchases, possibly deducing your interests. In addition, data may be gathered about you in the most unlikely of places. For example, imagine working out at your local gym on a computerized stair stepper or stationary bike. A computer tracks your heartbeat or the number of steps taken per minute. Netpulse Communications Incorporated (www.netpulse.com) does just that. It links its exercise equipment to a national database of healthcare member profiles. "By surveying members, Netpulse plans to flesh out the profiles to include the person's age, weight, gender, birth date, address, and product-buying preferences" (Markoff, 1999, p. 96). Netpulse's intention is to provide online advertising based on individual profiles.

Data, information, and knowledge vary in their stability. For example, knowing a customer bought Scooby Doo fruit snacks is less important than the fact the customer has children. "The fact that a customer has diabetes is more stable than a particular pattern of food purchases that may allow inferring he or she has diabetes" (McCarthy, 2000, p. 75). More stable facts such as a person has children or diabetes are more predictive of future behaviors than simple observational facts such as diapers were purchased on the 12th of last month.

Needless to say, no matter how you categorize data, the quantity of data collected about an individual is substantial —demographic information, customer satisfaction, legal history, insurance records, purchase preferences, financial and banking information, as well as medical profiles. One thing that IS and business professionals must realize is that following ethical practices and respecting the privacy of individuals makes good business sense. Bad publicity associated with a single incident can taint a company's reputation for years, even when that company has followed the law and done everything that it perceives possible to ensure the privacy of those from whom the data was gathered. An example of a company that knows all too well the politics of the privacy debate is N2H2. Its Internet filtering software is used by 40% of U.S. schools. N2H2 decided last year to sell its aggregated data. It followed the rules set forth by the Children's Online Privacy Protection Act, and the data did not contain names or personal information (Wilder & Soat, 2001). However, it had so many people up in arms over the selling of this data that it scrapped the project. Thus, even though N2H2 was well within its legal rights to sell its aggregate data, the public viewed this as unethical. In the next section, we discuss ethics and their relevance to data mining.

ETHICAL ISSUES

You cannot separate technology and its uses and still be ethically and socially responsible. As a professional, you must explore how the technology you create will be used. Ethics are standards of conduct that are agreed upon by cultures and organizations. Supreme Court Justice Potter Stewart defines ethics as knowing the difference between what you have a right to do and what is right to do. It is important that IS professionals act according to the highest ethical standards or else face increased governmental intervention.

Often, when professionals in the data industry are asked what they think of their ethical obligation concerning databases and data mining, their response is that they are obligated to follow the letter of the law. Of course, they must adhere to the law. But ethics are oftentimes more restrictive than what is called for by the law. Sadly, there are a number of IS professionals who either lack an awareness of what their companies actually do with data, or purposely come to the conclusion that it is not their business. They are enablers in the sense that they solve management's problems. What management does with that data is not their concern.

Are there guidelines or an ethical code to help database experts as they grapple with ethical dilemmas? Should there be such guidelines? Many people in the IS arena say no. They argue it is not their place to decide how data is used, but rather up to others in the organization to make that determination. But what is the ethical obligation of an IS professional who, through whatever means, finds out that the data that he or she has been asked to gather or "mine" is going to be used in a manner that they believe is unethical. The answer to that question, of course, has to be addressed individually, based on one's own ethical standards. But as data mining becomes more commonplace and as companies push for even greater profits and marketshare, IS professionals will increasingly encounter ethical dilemmas.

Article 31 of *The Direct Marketing Association's Guidelines for Ethical Business Practice* states that "Marketers should be sensitive to the issue of consumer privacy and should only collect, combine, rent, sell, exchange, or use marketing data. Marketing data should be used only for marketing purposes" (DMA Ethical Guidelines, 2002). Essentially, what is of the utmost importance to consumers is that information collected for one purpose should not be analyzed for an unrelated secondary purpose unless it is clearly compatible with the original purpose. Michael Turner, executive director of the Information Services Executive Council, a New York-based affiliate of the Direct Marketing Association, states, "For instance, detailed consumer information lets apparel retailers market their products to consumers with more precision. But if privacy rules impose restrictions and barriers to data collection, those limitations could increase the prices consumers pay when they buy from catalog or online apparel retailers by 3.5% to 11%" (Thibodeau, 2001, p. 36). Obviously, if retailers cannot target their advertising, then their only option is to mass advertise, which drives up costs.

Technological advances make it possible to track in great detail what a person does in his or her personal life. With this profile of personal details comes a substantial ethical obligation to safeguard this data from disclosure to unauthorized individuals. Ignoring any legal ramifications, the ethical responsibility is firmly placed on IS professionals and businesses whether they like it or not. Otherwise, they risk lawsuits and harm individuals in the process.

> The data industry has come under harsh review. There is a raft of federal and local laws under consideration to control the collection, sale, and use of data. American companies have yet to match the tougher privacy regulations already in place in Europe, while personal and class-action litigation against businesses over data privacy issues is increasing. (Wilder & Soat, 2001, p. 38)

Figure 1 demonstrates the iterative nature of how business practices create ethical dilemmas that harm individuals who assert pressure on society to create laws and regulations that change business practices. In following the outer loop of the diagram starting at the top-left, what often happens is that organizations, through some unethical activity, ultimately harm one or more individuals. In addition to gathering data about purchases, businesses oftentimes share information with others who are required to process the order. For example, payment credit card clearinghouses and package delivery companies must be informed of the order, where to pick it up, who to deliver it to, and sometimes the contents of the shipment as well. These third party providers also must adhere to the highest ethical standards, but sometimes, based on this shared data, these third parties attempt to sell goods and services directly to individuals (consumers) or sell the data to others. Following the top-right-hand side of Figure 1, individuals who are negatively impacted by this experience create an awareness of the problem in society and help build pressure within society for lawmakers to address the issue. As illustrated by the bottom part of Figure 1, society creates pressure on the government and lawmakers to create laws and regulations; if enough pressure is placed upon the government and lawmakers, laws and regulations are created (illustrated at the left-hand side). These laws and regulations, in turn, place restrictions and penalties on organizations, and the cycle continues. Like all cycles, sometimes laws and regulations go too far in one direction or another, whether we are talking about being too restrictive for businesses or too lax in terms of protecting consumers. The situation where businesses are placed under too many restrictions ultimately harms consumers through, for example, inflated marketing costs.

The inner square deals with social and ethical implications that are presented. Organizations are concerned with the question of "How do we gather data?" without posing problems for individuals with respect to their right to privacy. Individuals are concerned with the question of "How do we protect our privacy?" while still maintaining national security and consuming customized goods and services? Sadly, many consumers have become accustomed or, more accurately, resigned to the fact that businesses gather personal information about them, often surreptitiously. With enough individuals concerned about privacy, society is concerned with the question of "How do we ensure data is used in a socially responsible manner?"

Lawmakers and the government must then be charged with the task of answering the question of "How do we enforce these laws and regulations?" Oftentimes, laws and

Figure 1: Ethical violations often fuel the creation of laws and regulations.

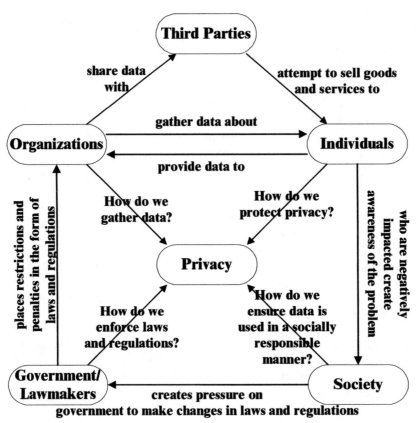
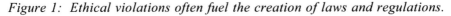

regulations are created by society – not to protect the individual, but rather to protect society itself. Consider what would happen if such laws and regulations did not exist. In that case, consumers might stop giving information (at least accurate information) if they were concerned about privacy. Then, information about purchasing behavior and all other aspects of society would become limited and unavailable to those who need to make decisions. So, although laws and regulations are often in response to abuses perpetrated by organizations on individuals, in reality, society is acting in its own self-interest. Those who make laws and regulations understand the importance, in this case, of information in our economy. Even privacy advocates concede there are benefits to society when personal data is shared. Privacy advocates do not argue that consumer information should not be shared, but rather that consumers themselves should be given the option of how much information is shared and with whom.

Businesses are correct when they complain that much of the regulatory initiatives are driven by unusual cases of misuse of information. However, society is predisposed to believe the worst. These stories of misuse only confirm its pre-existing fears. Therefore, businesses must be sensitive to how the public perceives their business practices, which include data mining. In an attempt to elevate data privacy to the level of importance that it should have within an organization, some organizations have created a management position known as the chief privacy officer, who attempts to limit liabilities or issues surrounding data collection, data storage, and data mining.

This cycle is best illustrated with an example. Suppose, based on your participation in a chat room or mailing list or your surfing behavior, someone deduces that either you or someone close to you has a terminal illness. First, what if you wanted this information to remain private? Second, how could such information be used in an unethical manner? Maybe you would start receiving solicitations for donation from organizations that are seeking cures for this illness. Even worse, what if you began to receive offers for cures that, at best, have questionable chances of success? Data-mining and profiling techniques that allow companies to identify their best customers could just as easily be used by unscrupulous businesses to zero in on vulnerable customers – the elderly, the poor, the sick, and the unsophisticated – offering them inferior or predatory deals ("Selling is getting personal," 2000). Luckily for the public, data-mining abuses have been rarely reported so far. "Canadian Banking Ombudsman Michael Lauber reports that of 175 formal complaints he has handled in 3 ½ years in office, not one has involved a breach of privacy associated with data warehousing or data mining" ("In praise of privacy," 2000, p. 18).

Social, legal, and ethical implications of data mining are very intertwined. Next, we examine data mining from a social perspective by using examples to highlight the benefits and drawbacks of data mining and their social implications.

SOCIAL IMPLICATIONS

After mounting complaints about excessive force, false arrests, and racial profiling, the Los Angeles Police Department (LAPD) is being forced under a federal consent decree to implement a computerized risk-management system that uses data mining to track officers' conduct and performance (Mearian & Rosencrance, 2001). In the year 2000, LAPD paid out more than $28 million as a result of civil lawsuits (Mearian & Rosencrance). The New Jersey State Police as well as the Pittsburgh Police Department have installed similar systems to track officers' use of force, search and seizure, citizen complaints, criminal charges, civil lawsuits, and commendations and awards earned. However, one cannot forget that these systems are only as good as the data entered. Here are some other examples of data-mining software used in well-known industries. "Advanced Scout" is a data-mining application developed by an IBM researcher. NBA coaches use it. It can provide information such as "Under what circumstances do the Chicago Bulls outscore the New York Knicks?" (Glode, 1997). This application can also be used by television announcers, fans at NBA Websites, and also used with other sports. In the automobile industry, manufacturers search huge databases of car repairs using pattern recognition algorithms to identify patterns of breakdowns (Waldrup, 2001). The University of California at Berkeley's LINDI system is "used to help geneticists search the biomedical literature and produce plausible hypotheses for the function of newly discovered genes" (Sheier, 2001). Carnegie Mellon University's Informedia II system produces a computer-searchable index of, for example, CNN news clips "by automatically dividing each clip into individual scenes accompanied by transcripts and headlines" (Sheier, 2001). Data mining is also used for national security and military applications – examples of which are provided in the next two paragraphs.

After the attack on the World Trade Center on September 11, 2001, the new antiterrorist law (The USA Patriot Act of 2001) allows wiretapping of the Net, among other things. However through this increased ability for surveillance comes the realization that we do not have enough personnel working for the FBI to analyze all this data. Therefore, data mining will play a part in providing national security. However, using data mining to search for suspicious keywords could be problematic.

> "As '60 Minutes' reported, the Canadian Security Agency identified a mother as a potential terrorist after she told a friend on the phone that her son had 'bombed' in his school play. Filtered or unfiltered information taken out of context is no substitute for the genuine knowledge about a person that can emerge only slowly over time." (Rosen, 2001, p. 19)

Advances in networking, medical remote sensing, and data mining will, in the future, be combined to detect the presence and origin of chemical weapons on the battlefield (Ceruti, 2000). This will be accomplished by:

> "Mining geographic patterns from networks of devices worn by troops in the field designed to record and transmit a soldier's or a marine's vital health data and environmental data. These geographic patterns will help to identify the origin of the attack. It will also affect the early response and treatment of wartime casualties with a result of more lives saved on the battlefield." (Ceruti, 2000, p. 1875)

Another military application of data mining revolves around intrusion detection systems for military networks. Unlike their commercial counterparts, military networks

> "often face unique constraints – operation over wireless media, unique message traffic, different perceived threats, limited bandwidth, mobile and dynamic environment, robustness in the face of direct attacks on infrastruc-ture – that lead to 'normal' operation that is different from civilian networks. This results in an unacceptably high false-alarm rate from Intrusion Detection systems." (Clifton & Gengo, 2000, p. 440)

Data mining can be used to identify patterns of false alarms created during battlefield conditions that are substantially different from commercial traffic.

What are the social implications of such systems? Next, we explore the benefits and drawbacks of data mining in terms of individuals, society, and businesses.

Data Mining and Consumers

Why pursue data mining? Simply satisfying customers is not enough. Relation-ships need to be built based on loyalty fostered by employee enthusiasm and customized product and service offerings that delight customers. Customers expect that businesses anticipate their needs. A number of studies have shown that it costs five to ten times as much money to attract a new customer as it does to sell to an existing customer. Data mining allows management to create and analyze customer profiles to appropriately customize marketing efforts. Companies are beginning to realize that they do not need to market to large masses of customers in order to maximize profits. Hence, data mining can be beneficial to both consumers and businesses. However, the benefits to a company, which may reduce costs for the consumer, may also be seen as an invasion of consumer privacy. Obviously, this has large-scale social implications. We will take a look at some examples of businesses mining data.

Insurance Rates: One insurer used data mining to help develop competitive rates for sports car owners. These owners are often charged higher rates because it is assumed these drivers are riskier than other drivers. One insurer found that a majority of sportscar owners are between 30 and 50 years old, married and own two cars. "Data mining uncovered the fact that those customers were not high-risk drivers, so the insurer reduced its premiums and provided a competitive edge" (Maciag, 2001, p. 35).

Manufacturing and Inventory: How can suppliers increase their ability to deliver the right products to the right place at the right time? The supply chain can account for as much as 75% of a product's cost. One company that is attempting to decrease this cost by manufacturing its product in direct proportion to actual consumer demand rather than forecasts is Proctor & Gamble (P&G). P&G has tested technology that will inform it the moment a customer lifts one of its products off the store shelf, whether it is Downy fabric softener, Tide laundry detergent, Crest toothpaste, or Charmin toilet paper (Dalton, 2001). A trial run was conducted in Baltimore, Maryland with an unidentified retailer.

This new technology could provide a wealth of data that consumer goods manufacturers could mine for predictive patterns and, rather than reacting to sales, they could foresee peaks and valleys in demand. It costs approximately $10 each for the circuit boards for store shelves and five cents apiece for the chips for individual packages (Dalton, 2001). The hope is to reduce this latter price to one cent each. When a consumer picks up a product, it signals the shelf. It also signals if it is put back on the shelf. The shelf transmits the data to a computer which then periodically, but frequently, transmits it to P&G. P&G can then adjust its manufacturing plans accordingly. Currently, a few large suppliers like P&G wait only a few (four or five) days to obtain data collected at checkout. Most companies wait from 20 to 30 days to obtain checkout data. Therefore, even if this technology proves too expensive for widespread deployment, it can be used at a few select locations to test consumer response to new products and predict demand for existing products. Hence, what benefits could P&G accrue from such technology? It could obtain sales data in practically real time, which would in turn decrease pipeline inventories. This would also increase working capital, and give P&G a greater ability to deliver the right products to the right place at the right time – ultimately benefiting consumers in the form of lower costs and less stockouts.

Record Matching: Most data is never used. Data warehouses are often data tombs. However, data-mining techniques make this data more useful and meaningful. Another area in which data mining might be used in a positive social manner is where "fuzzy set logic" is used. When analyzing data, it is important to weed out "matches" or duplicate entries. Data mining helps determine if you have a match, whether it matches well, matches fairly well, matches somewhat, matches poorly, or there is a complete mismatch (Bell & Sethi, 2001). For example, if you were analyzing records, and the social security number matches but nothing else matches, then the records associated with one of the two individuals might possibly indicate fraud. The logic associated with matching records from a number of sources can take into account events that naturally occur in one's life. For example, the rule:

> If the first name matches well and the last name is a mismatch, and the subject is a female, and date of birth matches, and social security number matches, and the maiden name matches well, and the place of birth matches well, and marital status of the old record is single or divorced, and marital status of the new record is married, then the record probably matches [Marriage]. (Bell & Sethi, 2001, p. 88)

Targeting Audiences: Instead of bombarding consumers indiscriminately, smart, technologically savvy corporations use advanced data warehousing and data-mining techniques to target their marketing efforts. Managing specialized customer knowledge allows businesses to respond to customer needs even before these needs are expressed. David Diamond is the President of Catalina Marketing, a Florida firm that operates customer loyalty programs for 14,000 supermarkets in the United States. Through data mining, he stated that one chain had searched through customer purchases data finding low-fat-food buyers who never bought potato chips. Using this data, the company offered these customers a coupon for a new brand of low-calorie chips. Diamond stated that 40% responded, which is much higher than the typical 1 or 2% you get from coupons in the mail ("Selling is getting personal," 2000).

Web Mining: One of the benefits of data mining, based on clickstream analysis, is that you can remove inventory from your product line that is not enhancing profitability. Another benefit is the ability to enhance product exposure through better marketing. With the widespread use of the Internet, we cannot talk about data mining without looking at Web mining. Specifically, we will look at "clickstream analysis." Companies with a Web presence that concentrate on content— rather than on the medium for distributing that content— will be those that thrive and survive on the Internet. But how does a company know what content is important? One answer is by analyzing clickstream data. Clickstream data is much more than just tracking page hits. As a consumer traverses a website, a trail of activity reveals his or her browsing behavior and potential interest in a corporation's products and services. Clickstream data captures data such as which links are clicked by surfers, how long a surfer spends on each Web page, and what search terms are used. Furthermore, if visitors fill out a profile or survey, even more information can be gleaned by matching these with surfing behavior. Lastly, if the site belongs to a third-party banner ad exchange, then the company might be able to track surfing behavior beyond its own site. This trail of activity is commonly referred to as clickstream data.

However, the sheer volume of data generated by consumers traversing a corporation's website requires that the data be condensed and summarized prior to its storage in the corporate data warehouse (Inmon, 2001). As a consumer journeys through a corporation's website, many of the pages displayed have dynamic content. Capturing this dynamic content in such a way that the user's experience can later be analyzed is a time-consuming and expensive endeavor. What often happens is that companies have the capability to gather the data, but fail to act upon it because of the cost associated with analyzing it. As analysis tools simplify, more and more corporations will be mining their clickstream data for patterns that might indicate answers to a number of questions.

Some issues that clickstream data can shed light on are (Inmon, 2001, p. 22):

1. What items did the customer look at?
2. What items did the customer not look at?
3. What items did the customer purchase?
4. What items did the customer examine and not purchase?
5. What items did the customer buy in conjunction with other items?
6. What items did the customer look at in conjunction with other items, but did not purchase?
7. What advertisements or promotions are effective?
8. What advertisements or promotions are ineffective?
9. What advertisements or promotions generate a lot of attention but few sales?
10. What advertisements or promotions are the most effective at generating sales?
11. Are certain products too hard to find?
12. Are certain products too expensive?
13. Is there a substitute product that the customer finds first?
14. Are there too many products for the customer to wade through?
15. Are certain products not being promoted?
16. Do the products have adequate descriptions?

Clickstream data allows an unprecedented analysis of consumer behavior. Obviously, when a consumer enters a store at a traditional physical location such as a mall, it would be a very time-consuming process to analyze every product a consumer picked up, every department he or she entered, and every interaction he or she had with a sales clerk. Theoretically, you could do that, but, in essence, you would be conducting surveillance on individuals. If the public found out such activity was being conducted, clearly there would be a public outcry. On the other hand, on the Web, such analysis is much easier. As time goes by, more and more companies are going to be turning to their clickstream data and creating profiles based on customers' online shopping data. Of course, with this increased scrutiny should come increased protections, whether through self-regulation or laws. This leads us to the issue of whether data mining benefits or harms society.

Customer Satisfaction: Over the past few years, companies have learned that they need to interact with customers in new ways. Customers are not brand loyal like they once were. Hence, companies need to better understand their customers and quickly respond to their wants and needs. The time frame for a company to respond is also shrinking with our "need it now" society. Businesses can no longer wait until the signs of customer dissatisfaction are obvious before corrective action is taken. Businesses must now anticipate customer desires. Given all of this, data mining is an obvious choice that businesses must use to gain a strategic advantage, to maintain their customer base, and to attract new customers.

It is often useful to examine a topic from several different perspectives. With respect to data mining, three obvious perspectives are (1) businesses, (2) individuals, and (3) society. Table 1 provides a list of benefits of data mining from each of these perspectives. The list is not meant to be comprehensive, but rather illustrates how each of these groups

Table 1: Benefits of data mining

For Businesses
• Tailor offerings to specific customer needs
• Determine product and service features that are important to customers
• Better customer relationship management
• Money and time savings
• Find, attract, and retain the best customers
• Distinguish preferred from marginal customers
• Customize marketing plans to specific markets
• Identify customers who may be planning to defect to competitors
• Identify new market opportunities
• Enhance productivity
• Develop insight into changing customer requirements
• Find out what customers will be interested in the company's new products or services
• Reduce risk
• Analyze delivery channels
• Manage portfolios
• Target pricing
• Identify patterns showing which customers are open to cross-selling
• Identify customers that have a high rate for purchasing particular products or services
For Individuals
• Can reach conclusions that are beyond simple human analysis
• Companies will understand the needs of consumers better
• Companies can react to customers faster
• Customers receive more customized products
• Customers get better prices, better deals, better facilities
• Better customer relationships
• Treat the more valuable customer differently
• Rapid access to integrated systems and information increases the number of choices for consumers
• Customers get exactly what they need
For Society
• Gaining intelligence information, such as information that might lead to terrorist activity
• Identifying criminal activity

Table 2: Drawbacks of data mining

For Businesses
• Open themselves up to possible lawsuits
• Data may be flawed, resulting in inaccurate conclusions
• With respect to information gathered via the WWW, many people enter false information
• Cost of setting up data warehouses
For Individuals
• Invasion of privacy
• Conclusions can be made about individuals that are not necessarily true
• Information gathered could be used inappropriately to the detriment of an individual
• When a large quantity of information is distributed, data errors can greatly affect and even destroy the lives of individuals
For Society
• Ethical questions about what is appropriate to mine

benefits from data mining. Table 2 provides some representative drawbacks of data mining, once again from the three different perspectives.

Does Data Mining Benefit or Harm Society?

How can governments take data from a number of different sources and mine it for possible suspects associated with terrorist acts? In the aftermath of the World Trade Center tragedy, governments will be seeking new broad powers to monitor electronic communications in an effort to identify and locate potential terrorists. One of the means at their disposal is to gather data from a number of different sources and use data mining to identify suspect financial transactions, which it is hoped will ultimately lead back to those who sponsor terrorism.

Shari Steele, an executive director of the San Francisco-based Electronic Frontier Foundation, a special interest group that aims to keep the Web as free and democratic as possible, is concerned about potential new powers for the government to invade personal privacy (Swisher, 2001):

"Now it looks like the government will be able to know that and a whole lot more, such as from where you surf, patterns of your e-mail use, what you buy. The ability to learn these patterns has been the dream of marketers and the rallying point for privacy advocates, who have fought successfully since cyberspace's earliest days to prevent such snooping." (p. B1)

Prior to the World Trade Center disaster, it would have been impossible for the government to put legislation in place that would allow it to monitor behavior on such an individual basis. In the aftermath, it is not clear whether those who are in society who are clamoring for restraint and a reasonable response will be heard. More than likely, their calls for a reasoned response will be drowned out by the cries of the masses for measures to safeguard society.

Another drawback is that there can be flaws in the data-mining process. There are a number of reasons why records in different databases—even though they actually contain information about the same person or entity—may not "match up" through the data-mining process. Some of the difficulties that arise might be through letter, field, or word-related mismatches. Bell and Sethi (2001), in their article, "Matching Records in a National Medical Patient Index," examine some of the reasons why data from a number of different sources may have difficulty matching records. Under the letter-related mismatches, transposition of letters, omission of letters, misspellings, and typing errors can occur during data entry. With respect to word- or field-related mismatches, maybe the person whose data is contained in two different databases may have had a change of address or a change of name. There is always the possibility of fraud, as well as change of ZIP code or change of phone number. So, one of the concerns that consumers must have is the accuracy of mined information. And that data from another person's history is not accidentally—through improper matching—coupled with their own legitimate data. In addition to the letter- and field-related mismatches, there are a number of other issues that might create inaccuracies. For example, Asian names often have surname and given name reversal. If someone is not aware that this is the case, then upon data entry, the names may be switched. Another example where names may appear differently for the same individual is when a person may be named William, but is going by Bill. Hence, through the data-mining process, these types of possibilities must be taken into account. Another problem is misspelling, e.g., when a last name might be Cook and is entered as Cooke. Another similar example is the name Smith, which can be mistakenly spelled Smith, Smithe, or Smyth.

Having examined ethical and social implications, we now turn our attention to legal issues. It is important that companies protect sensitive data while allowing key decision-makers access to real-time information online. This next section discusses legal matters and their role in data mining. Laws dictate what kind of data can be mined. It is important to understand some of the federal laws currently related to privacy to understand their impact (or lack thereof) on how data is currently mined. Following are brief descriptions of many federal laws that are important when dealing with privacy. While reading this section, keep this in mind: if you collect, manipulate, disseminate, and mine data, investing in legal advice is a smart decision.

LEGAL ISSUES

What is legal and what is wise often are two different things. Given the rapid advance in technology, it is likely that laws to protect against abuses will not be able to keep up. However, there are existing laws that apply in specific situations, and IS professionals must be aware of these. Sadly, many of these issues are not brought up in formal IS education and training. It is important to remember that ignorance of the law does not constitute a defense in a court of law. Therefore, IS professionals must educate themselves concerning existing laws, and be aware of potential future regulation so that they not only prepare their systems for such regulation, but also do not contribute to the social pressure for further government-imposed restrictions, as shown previously in Figure 1.

Lawmakers show little interest in passing a comprehensive privacy law but rather legislate each information source separately. Table 3 provides a brief overview of U.S. Federal regulations that both protect privacy and provide circumstances under which it may be invaded. An interesting point to make is that, prior to September 11, 2001, if the USA Patriot Act of 2001 had been before Congress, it would have probably been considered too invasive. However, the 9/11 attacks have changed that perception and the need for privacy in terms of balancing it with the ability to eliminate terrorism. In the following section, a representative sample of Federal acts is discussed. A complete and thorough discussion of all regulations concerning data collection and use is beyond the scope of this chapter. We begin our examination of U.S. Federal regulations with the Fair Credit Reporting Act and end with a brief discussion of the USA Patriot Act of 2001. Afterwards, we briefly explore legal issues in jurisdiction outside of the United States.

Fair Credit Reporting Act

Many people are concerned about using their credit card online for fear that their card information will be stolen. Another fear with the Internet is that a person's credit

*Table 3:   U.S. Federal Regulations that impact privacy (Adapted from Caudill &
Murphy, 2000)*

Laws Protecting Privacy		
Act	Year	Description
Fair Credit Reporting Act	1970	Allows consumers to correct errors in their credit reports.
Privacy Act	1974	Government officials may not maintain secret files or gather information about people irrelevant to a lawful purpose.
Right to Financial Privacy Act	1978	Government officials need a warrant to obtain a bank's copies of checks.
Electronic Funds Transfer Act	1978	Banks must notify customers when disclosing records to third parties.
Privacy Protection Act	1980	Government officials are restricted in their ability to seize records of the print media.
Cable Communications Act	1984	Cable companies may not disclose choices consumers make or other personal information without consent.
Family Education and Privacy Right Act	1984	Government officials are restricted in their ability to reveal to third parties information gathered by agencies or educational institutions.
Electronic Communications Privacy Act	1986	Prohibits telephone, telegraph, and other communications services from releasing the contents of messages they transmit (only the recipient of the message can be identified).
Computer Security Act	1987	All government agencies develop safeguards for protecting sensitive data stored in their computers.
Video Privacy Protection Act	1988	Video rental companies may not disclose choices customers make or other personal information without consent.
Computer Matching and Privacy Protection Act	1988	Allows governmental officials to increase the amount of information they gather if the safeguards against information disclosure also increases.
Telephone Consumer Protection Act	1991	Prohibits telemarketers from using automatically dialing telephone calls or facsimile machines to sell a product without obtaining consent first.
Drivers' Privacy Protection Act	1993	Places restrictions on state government agencies and their ability to sell driver's license records.
Health Insurance Portability and Accountability Act (HIPAA)	1996	Designed to reduce inefficiencies in the healthcare industry by reducing paperwork, controlling abuse in the system, providing privacy protection for individuals, and ensuring health care coverage for even those with pre-existing conditions.
The Gramm-Leach-Bliley Act	1999	Financial institutions can share information with affiliate companies, and with nonaffiliated companies after giving customers the option to "opt-out" of certain disclosures.
Children's Online Privacy Protection Act (COPPA)	2000	Sets rules for online collection of information from children.
Laws Invading Privacy		
Foreign Intelligence Surveillance Act (FISA)	1978	Provides law enforcement special authority when investigating terrorism or espionage.
Communications Assistance for Law Enforcement Act (CALEA) of 1994	1994	Guarantees law enforcement agencies access to telecommunications carriers' networks.
USA Patriot Act of 2001	2001	Enacted as a result of the September 11 attack on the World Trade Center and was signed by President Bush on Oct. 26, 2001. Grants law enforcement agencies the right to use Carnivore.

history can be easily accessed or obtained. With data mining, consumers are scared that
their credit card information and credit history will become even more vulnerable.
However, the Fair Credit Reporting Act (FCRA) of 1970 already protects consumers
against illegal use of credit information:

"Congress passed the Fair Credit Reporting Act in 1970, in recognition of the fact that false or inaccurate information on a credit report can have serious (and embarrassing) consequences for an individual. The act regulates the kind of information that can appear in credit reports, allows individual access to their reports, and sets up a system for an individual to contest the contents of their credit reports." (Alley & Harvey, 1998)

The FCRA applies to situations other than the loan- or credit-application process, such as employer background checks, court records, and motor vehicle reports, anytime the data was provided in a consumer report by a consumer-reporting agency as defined by the Act.

Just about every aspect of the FCRA and the amendment (which went into effect in October 1997) can apply to data mining. If a company participates in data-mining activities, it must carefully review how it uses the information in regards to the FCRA or face potential lawsuits. A company must also be careful that the information it obtains through data mining is accurate. Privacy is protected by the FCRA to a certain degree. This act affects data mining when the organization selling or obtaining the information can be defined as a credit-reporting agency according the FCRA. The entire Fair Credit Reporting Act may be obtained at http://www.ftc.gov/os/statutes/fcra.htm.

Right to Financial Privacy Act

An individual's rights in guarding his or her financial information are protected by The Right to Financial Privacy Act of 1978. Most people are concerned about their financial privacy and believe it is imperative that federal law protects it. Because of this law, procedures must be followed by banks, credit unions, credit card companies, savings and loan associations, and other financial institutions before any information about you is given to a Federal agency. Protecting their financial information is probably one of the areas about which individuals are most concerned. They do not want others to store and/ or analyze this type of data. As technology becomes increasingly more sophisticated, data-mining techniques will challenge this privacy act and threaten the protection it currently provides.

Electronic Funds Transfer Act

The Electronic Funds Transfer (EFT) Act of 1978 was designed to give customers protection by assigning liability to banks that allowed electronic access to customer accounts. There are many benefits to both the bank and individuals from the use of EFT. This act also states that customers must be notified about third-party access to their information on electronic funds transfer, either at the time that the consumer contracts for electronic funds transfer or before the first transfer is made. ATM and debit cards have since flourished, and the flow of data and access to your finances worldwide has increased. By taking the liability off of the consumer, the Electronic Funds Act made it possible for consumers to feel comfortable using ATM, debit cards, and, more recently, electronic funds transfer to pay almost any type of bill.

Electronic Communications Privacy Act

The Electronic Communications Privacy Act (ECPA) addresses the legal privacy issues involved with the use of computers and other new technology in electronic communications. This act updated 1968 legislation that clarified invasion of privacy with the use of electronic surveillance. This law was primarily aimed at preventing invasions of privacy by government. However, it has not been updated to reflect the technological advancements made possible through widespread use of the Internet. Technologies such as Carnivore collect more information than protected under the authority of this law.

Video Privacy Protection Act

The Video Privacy Protection Act of 1988 states that video store owners cannot divulge information about the videos rented or personal information about the consumers who rent them to the general public. This law was enacted to protect the privacy of consumers, in particular so that they would not be ashamed about or prosecuted for renting videos considered adult material. The beneficial result of this law is that people feel free to rent whatever they would like, without fear. Without this act, for example, homosexuals who are not public about their sexuality could fear that friends or employers could find out they are renting gay materials. This law protects them from such discrimination or public ridicule. Without this Act, individuals in high-profile jobs could reasonably fear their renting habits might be released.

Health Insurance Portability and Accountability Act (HIPAA)

The ability to compile, store and cross-reference personally identifiable health information easily is becoming technologically feasible. Unfortunately, patients must worry, and rightly so, about confidentiality. Furthermore, the healthcare industry is so competitive and medical information so valuable that information that should be shared often is not.

On August 21, 1996, U.S. President Bill Clinton signed the Health Insurance Portability and Accountability Act (HIPAA). HIPAA is designed to reduce inefficiencies in the healthcare industry by reducing paperwork, controlling abuse in the system, providing privacy protection for individuals, and ensuring health care coverage for even those with pre-existing conditions. A provision of HIPAA required Congress to enact medical privacy protections by August of 1999. The law also included a provision that gave the Secretary of the U.S. Department of Health and Human Services (HHS) the authority to write medical privacy regulations if Congress missed its self-imposed deadline (Leahy, 2001).

Concerned about the loss of personal privacy and fear that if medical records were not protected from unauthorized disclosure, it would deter people from seeking medical treatment, Senator Patrick Leahy of Vermont, in March of 1999, introduced comprehensive medical privacy legislation entitled, the Medical Information Privacy and Security Act (MIPSA). However, it was not enacted and Congress missed the August, 1999 deadline specified in HIPAA. Therefore, in October 1999, President Clinton and Secretary Donna Shalala unveiled their medical privacy proposal.

The final ruling for the HIPAA was in April 2001 under President George Bush. Most covered entities have two years (until April 2003) to comply with the final revisions of this law. This final law requires that all health organizations— including health care providers, insurers, and transaction processors— come into compliance with HIPAA by the April 2003 date.. However, it does not cover health-oriented websites that may collect personal data.

Under this law, patients have the right to control how their personal health information is used and must be able to get access to their own medical records if desired. Of course, patients must sign a release before records can be given to any party. However, patients do have the right to limit or withdraw this release of information. Health care organizations are required to have written privacy procedures detailing how information is used and disclosed and are required to provide this information to patients upon request.

The Gramm-Leach-Bliley Act of 1999

The Gramm-Leach-Bliley Act became federal law in November 1999, and states were ordered to comply (although the law did not preempt states from adopting more strict privacy standards). In general, this law states that financial institutions can only share information with affiliates and nonaffiliated companies after giving customers the option to "opt-out" of certain disclosures. Personal information can only be shared only after a consumer has had an opportunity to opt-out. Therefore, organizations must notify individuals when they are planning to share private information outside the scope of typical financial transactions; e.g., selling it to others who plan on using it for data-mining purposes. Enforcement began July 1, 2001. When financial institutions sent out federally mandated privacy notices in the summer of 2001, only 2% to 3% of all consumers opted out (Thibodeau, 2002).

The privacy provisions of Title V of the Act apply only to non-public personal information about individuals who obtain financial products or services for personal, family, or household purposes, and not to companies or individuals obtaining products or services for business purposes (Hirsch, 2000). In addition, this law requires that both stored and transmitted information be encrypted if security cannot be guaranteed. The following federal agencies have responsibility for enforcing the Act: the Federal Trade Commission (FTC), the Department of the Treasury, the Comptroller of the Currency, the Federal Reserve System, the Federal Deposit Insurance Corporation, the National Credit Union Administration, and the Securities and Exchange Commission. "Because the Gramm-Leach-Bliley Financial Services Act opened the door for banking and insurance markets to enter one another's business, both industries were compelled to gain more information about their customers to cross-sell banking, investment and insurance services" (Ruquet, 2000).

The state of Vermont has taken a much stronger position than the Federal statute by requiring (as of February 15, 2002) financial institutions to acquire affirmative customer consent (opt-in) of its citizens before personal data about customers from Vermont can be shared with others. Insurance trade groups retaliated by filing suit on

January 30, 2002, and threatening price increases (Thibodeau, 2002). In response to industry complaints, Elizabeth Costle, Commissioner of the Vermont Department of Banking, Insurance, Securities, and Health Care Administration, stated, "The industry can just assume that everyone with a Vermont ZIP code has opted out. That's the easy way to fix your computers" (Thibodeau, 2002, p. 16). Vermont's rules are a broader application of the state's existing banking privacy laws and not a result of legislature action (Thibodeau, 2002, p. 16). The insurance industry argues in its suit that the banking commission usurped legislative authority. Opt-in requires companies to convince consumers of the benefits of sharing their personal information with others. Vermont is not alone concerning "opt-in." According to the Internet Alliance, 13 states have pending opt-in privacy bills: Arkansas, California, Florida, Hawaii, Illinois, Iowa, Massachusetts, Minnesota, Missouri, North Dakota, New Hampshire, New Jersey and New York (Thibodeau, 2002). New Mexico is considering regulatory action similar to Vermont's. When acquiring data to mine, differences in state laws and regulations like Vermont's opt-in policy will play a role in acquiring data that can be legally used.

Children's Online Privacy Protection Act (COPPA)

To protect children's privacy online, the Children's Online Privacy Protection Act (COPPA) was created, with final legislation going into effect on April 21, 2000. It regulates the collection of personal information from individuals under the age of 13. The Federal Trade Commission (FTC) has been charged with issuing and enforcing rules concerning COPPA. COPPA was the first act involving government regulation solely for the Internet. Because of this law, websites must get parental permission before collecting or using personal information from children. Websites must have a privacy policy that explains what information is collected, how it is collected, and how it will be used. This privacy policy must be in plain view on the website. If a company makes a material change in its privacy policy, it must obtain consent from all parents again. COPPA applies to commercial websites and online services that target and collect information from children. The Act also applies to operators of general sites who have actual knowledge that they are collecting information from children under 13 years of age. Under the COPPA guidelines, operators of such sites must adhere to the following guidelines (FTC Website, http://www.ftc.gov/privacy/coppafaqs.htm):

1. post clear and comprehensive Privacy Policies on the website describing their information practices for children's personal information;
2. provide notice to parents, and with limited exceptions, obtain verifiable parental consent before collecting personal information from children;
3. give parents the choice to consent to the operator's collection and use of a child's information while prohibiting the operator from disclosing that information to third parties;
4. provide parents with access to their child's personal information to review and/or have it deleted;
5. give parents the opportunity to prevent further collection or use of the information; and
6. maintain the confidentiality, security, and integrity of information they collect from children.

In addition, operators are prohibited from conditioning a child's participation in an online activity on the child providing more information than is reasonably necessary to participate in that activity.

After a three-year effort by the FTC to identify and educate the industry and the public about privacy issues, the FTC recommended that Congress enact legislation protecting children. A March 1998 survey of 212 commercial children's websites found that "while 89% of the sites collected personal information from children, only 24% posted privacy policies, and only 1% required parental consent to the collection or disclosure of children's information" (FTC, 1999).

Ignorance of the law is not a defense in a court of law. If you are caught violating COPPA, you can be fined up to $11,000 per child per incident. Non-profit organizations, however, are exempt from COPPA. For more information about COPPA, you can visit the following sites: http://www.ftc.gov/kidzprivacy, http://www.kidsprivacy.org, and http://www.cdt.org.

USA Patriot Act of 2001

The Uniting and Strengthening America by Providing Appropriate Tools Required to Intercept and Obstruct Terrorism (USA Patriot) Act of 2001 is not a single new law but rather an omnibus piece of legislation that amends dozens of existing laws (Fausett, 2001, p. 10). Hence, if you read the text of the Act without a copy of the *United States Code* close at hand, it will make no sense whatsoever. According to M. Scott (2001), the act:

"greatly expands the right of law enforcement officials to wiretap the Web, including information transmitted over the Internet, corporate in-house networks and voice mail systems. It also lets them search stored e-mails and voice mails to collect evidence that may be useful in prosecuting criminals, including terrorists." (p. 82)

Unlike the Electronic Communications Privacy Act that requires a subpoena or search warrant, Section 212 of the Patriot Act "lets a system operator voluntarily disclose customer information along with the content of stored e-mail messages to a governmental entity if the provider reasonably believes that an emergency involving immediate danger of death, or serious physical injury to any person justifies disclosure." (M. Scott, 2001, p. 82). Section 210 of the Act requires an e-mail system operator to disclose the means or source of payment for the provider's services, records of session times and durations, and any temporarily assigned network addresses. The hope is that such information may help locate terrorists and those who fund them. This Act can provide a wealth of information on suspected criminals and terrorists that law enforcement agencies can merge with other data overlays to data mine in order to better identify candidates for intense scrutiny.

International Laws

Many nations have data protection laws that attempt to ensure an individual's privacy rights. These include but are not limited to:

- The Russian Federation Law on Information, Informatization, and Information Protection of 1995
- The U.K. Data Protection Act of 1998
- The New Zealand Privacy Act of 1993
- The 1995 EU Data Protection Directive
- The Hong Kong Personal Data (Privacy) Ordinance of 1996 (see http://www.pco.org.hk/)
- The Estonia Personal Data Protection Act in June 1996

The Electronic Privacy Information Center (EPIC) and Privacy International reviewed the state of privacy in over fifty countries around the world ("Privacy & Human Rights, 2000," 2000). The report found many countries around the world are enacting comprehensive data protection laws.

Other nations, such as China and India, have no general data protection laws enacted, although data privacy is referred to in a few regulations in both countries. Interestingly, however, the Chinese Constitution proclaims citizens have limited rights to privacy even though few laws limit government actions. For example, Article 37 of its constitution provides that the freedom of citizens of the People's Republic of China is inviolable, and Article 40 states: "Freedom and privacy of correspondence of citizens of the People's Republic of China are protected by law." However, whenever technological advancements seem on the brink of loosening the government's grip over its citizens, the Chinese government uses all its power to either suppress the technology or mold it to fit its own political agenda. For readers who are interested in exploring international laws pertaining to privacy and data protection, see http://www.privacyinternational.org/survey/.

Table 4: Issues surrounding data mining that are open for debate despite legal developments

- Society has a right and an obligation to protect itself, even if this results in violating an individual's privacy. However, what is required for society to adequately and irrepressibly protect itself?
- At what level are people willing to give up privacy for the sake of security?
- If an organization purchases data from another organization that gathered it illegally and then mines that data, what are the legal and ethical ramifications for that organization?
- When an organization must share data with a third party in order to provide an individual goods or services, to what extent is that organization legally obligated to ensure that the third party does not mine that data?
- With the increased value and usage of data by organizations, what legal mechanisms should be in place to enforce laws and regulations?
- Can a video store mine the rental transaction data of its customers to create customer profiles that could then be sold to others?
- If a company voluntarily discloses in good faith (under Section 212 of the USA Patriot Act of 2001), customer information along with the content of stored e-mail messages to a government agency when it reasonably believes an emergency exists, does the law give that organization immunity from a subsequent lawsuit from the e-mail user?
- What legal obligation does an ISP have if, through mining its own logs, it believes it has identified either criminal or terrorist activity?

Laws and Data Mining

The majority of laws that safeguard the privacy of consumers are positive for society because they make people feel comfortable providing information as well as purchasing or renting material, and this helps the economy. However, the downside of any database is that it is never totally secure from "the outside." Many of these laws pertain to the collection and dissemination of data. Companies interested in data mining must respect these restrictions. Despite these legal developments, there are still questions that remain open for debate. Table 4 lists some of the more pertinent questions.

FUTURE TRENDS

As our world becomes more interconnected, it will be possible to create detailed profiles on practically anyone. "According to one estimate, there are now 2.5 million surveillance cameras in Britain, and the average Briton is now thought to be photographed by 300 separate cameras in a single day" (Rosen, 2001, p. 24). The line between private and public information continues to shift with time (Figure 2). What was once considered private is now more likely contained in the public domain. The shift can greatly be attributed to the increased use of databases and the more recent use of the Internet as a way to collect and manipulate information (Caudill & Murphy, 2000). In a recent article, legal scholar Jeffrey Rosen (2001) stated that:

"At the beginning of the 21st century, however, thanks to the Internet, and the September 11 attack on the World Trade Center – which gave rise to the new antiterrorism law that gives authorities far more latitude to inspect logs of Internet use – we have vastly expanded the aspect of private life that can be monitored and recorded. As a result, there is increased danger that personal information originally disclosed to friends and colleagues may be exposed to, and misinterpreted by, a less-understanding audience." (p. 19)

As shown in Figure 2, the events of September 11, 2001 (which prompted new legislation and concern) have greatly excelled the rate at which information is changing from the private domain to the public domain. Looking back at Table 3, we may see more future legislation that will in fact invade privacy rather than protect it.

Relating back to Figure 1, at some point, enough individuals will be negatively impacted so that society will react by implementing legal countermeasures that prohibit and restrict all aspects of the data industry. It is in businesses' best interest to behave in the most ethical manner possible, so as not to create an environment in which lawmakers feel compelled to act. What does the future hold for data mining? After the events of September 11, 2001, society will more than likely demand that government institute anti-terrorist measures in which data mining will play a fundamental role. However, "Britain's experience in the fight against terrorism suggests that people may give up liberties without experiencing a corresponding increase in security" (Rosen, 2001, p. 24). Businesses will continue to encroach on personal privacy. Therefore, it is up to individuals to guard their personal data.

Figure 2: The line dividing public and private consumer information continues to shift.

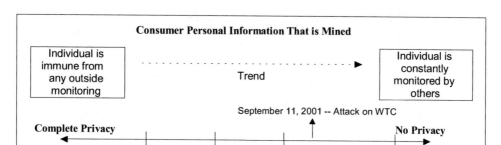

Currently, a number of researchers are investigating the use of distributed data-mining systems that operate over large-scale networks spanning several companies (K. Scott, 2001). Such systems could be used by the financial industry, for example, to detect fraud and intrusions. Luckily for consumers, companies historically have not collaborated nor shared data. Instead, security has been achieved primarily by limiting access via virtual private networks using passwords and firewalls. As companies collaborate, special care must be taken to protect the privacy of those whose data is shared.

Application Service Providers (ASPs) hosting Internet-based data-mining services are emerging as an attractive alternative for organizations needing such services who are reluctant to incur the high cost of buying, installing, training, and using data-mining software (Krishnaswamy, Zaslavsky, & Loke, 2001). These researchers propose a new multiple ASP model for the Internet delivery of data-mining services. This model has several advantages over the currently predominant, single-server provider model that requires a client to send its data to the service provider with whom it has a long-term service level agreement (SLA): (1) wider variety of options, (2) choice of service providers, and (3) the benefits of a more competitive marketplace (Krishnaswamy, et al.). However, some ethical concerns arise. For instance, consider the situation where the data to mine is sensitive and disclosure of any sort would cause grave harm. In that case, the client will not want to transport the data, but would rather have the ASP use mobile agents to perform the data mining on the client's server and destroy itself upon completion. Furthermore, confidentiality agreements would need to be signed each time an ASP is contracted to perform data mining. A multiple ASP model greatly complicates the possibility for ethical and legal dilemmas in the future.

CONCLUSION

It is important to note that the benefits of data mining are numerous, not only for businesses, not-for-profits, and governments, but also for individuals and society as a whole. "Mining for gold is only successful if you're sitting on a gold mine. And unlike a real gold mine, this one you can create yourself" (Maciag 2001, p. 37). Unfortunately, the social, ethical, and legal concerns created by data mining and the associated fears often raise questions about its use. If a middle ground can be reached that protects customers' privacy and ensures security without limiting the power of data mining, both consumers and business could enjoy substantial benefits.

With increasing ease, companies are able to collect vast quantities of data on current and potential customers. Data collected online can now tell decision-makers how customers search for products and services, how they navigate and traverse the Web and what products and services they purchase or fail to purchase. Coupling this data with information from legacy systems provides decision-makers with information concerning trends and patterns previously untapped. The advent of data mining opens up a number of interesting prospects to increase the competitiveness of a firm. In this volatile time, to remain competitive, a corporation must strategically manage its information and react quicker than its competitors. However, this information must be kept secure, but accessible. Every organization must be held responsible for ensuring that its data is being used in a legal and ethical manner. At the same time, organizations must remain competitive, and transforming their data into knowledge is a way to better serve their customers. As it becomes increasingly easy for businesses to gather personal information, individuals must demand and use information countermeasures to control who has access to their information and how it is used. After having read about the social, ethical, and legal issues of data mining, one should understand that there are a number of policy decisions that must be made prior to data mining.

REFERENCES

Alley, J. & Harvey, D. (1998). Disclosure and approval: The New Fair Credit Reporting Act. *Florida business insight*, July/August. Available online at: http://flabusinessinsight.com/1998Issues/july&august98/julyemployeerel.htm Retrieved July 29, 2001.

Bell, G. & Sethi, A. (2001). Matching records in a national medical patient index. *Communications of the ACM, 44*(9): 83-88. New York: Association for Computing Machinery, September.

Brandel, M. (2001). Spinning data into gold. *ComputerWorld,* March 26, p. 67.

Cannon, R. (2001). Coping with COPPA: Children's privacy in an online jungle. *WebTechniques*, August, pp.34-38.

Caudill, E. & Murphy, P. (2000). Consumer online privacy: Legal and ethical Issues. *Journal of Public Policy & Marketing*, Spring, pp.7-19.

Ceruti, M. (2000). The relationship between artificial intelligence and data mining: Application to future military information systems. *Proceedings of 2000 IEEE International Conference on Systems, Man, and Cybernetics, Nashville, TN, 3*, 1875.

Clifton, C. & Gengo, G. (2000). Developing custom intrusion detection filters using data mining. *21ˢᵗ Century Military Communications Conference Proceedings, Los Angeles, CA, MILCOM2000, 1*, 440-443.

Dalton, G. (2001). If these shelves could talk, *The Industry Standard.* April 2, www.theindustrystandard.com/article/display/0,1151,23090,00.html.

Direct Marketing Association, The (2002, April). http://www.the-dma.org/library/guide-lines/ethicalguidelines.shtml#6.

Fausett, B. (2002). Becoming a patriot, *Web Techniques.* February, pp.10-12.

Fayyad, U. (2001). The digital physics of data mining. *Communications of the ACM.* 44(3),62-65.

Glode, M. (1997). Most valuable programmer. *Wired,* , July 7, Archive 5.

Hirsch, R. (2000) The other privacy law: Preparing for the Gramm-Leach-Bliley Act. Available online at Davis Wright Tremain LLP, http://www.dwt.com/related_links/adv_bulletins/HLABMarch2001.htm. Retrieved August 1, 2001

In praise of privacy. (2000). *Canadian Banker*, Fall, pp.14-19.

Inmon, B. (2001). Why clickstream data counts. *E-Business Advisor*, April, pp.18-22.

Krishnaswamy, S., Zaslavsky, A., & Loke, S. W. (2001). Towards data mining services on the Internet with a multiple service provider model: An XML based approach. *Journal of Electronic Commerce Research (Special Issue on Electronic Commerce and Service Operators), 2*(3), August. ISSN 1526-6133.

Leahy, P. (2001). Medical privacy. Available online at: http://leahy.senate.gov/issues/medprivacy/. Retrieved September 10, 2001

Maciag, G. (2001). Who's mining the agency? *National Underwriter*, pp.35-37.

Markoff, J. (1999). The privacy debate: Little Brother and the buying and selling of consumer data. *Upside,* pp.95-106.

McCarthy, J. (2000). Phenomenal data mining. *Communications of the ACM,* 43(8):75-79.

Mearian, L. & Rosencrance, L. (2001). Police policed with data mining engines. *ComputerWorld,* April 4, p.6.

New rule will protect privacy of children online. (1999). *Online from the Federal Trade Commission (FTC)*, October 20. Available online at: http://www.ftc.gov/opa/1999/9910/childfinal.htm. Retrieved September 10, 2001

Privacy & human rights 2000: An international survey of privacy laws and developments. (2000). Available online from Privacy International: http://www.privacyinternational.org/survey/. Retrieved February 16, 2002

Rosen, J. (2001) Privacy, reconsidered. An interview with Jeffrey Rosen. *CIO Insight*, Dec. 2, pp.18-24.

Ruquet, M. (2000) Data mining challenges. *National Underwriter*, December 4, pp. 3-16.

Scheier, R. (2001). Finding pearls in an ocean of data. *ComputerWorld*, July, pp. 48-49.

Scott, K. (2001) Zeroing in. *Information Week*, November 5, 862:50.

Scott, M. (2001) War's new front. *CIO Insight*, December, pp.82-83.

Selling is getting personal. (2000) *Consumer Reports*, 65(11), 16.

Swisher, K. (2001). Will the hunt for terrorists target privacy? *Wall Street Journal*, September, 24, pp. B1, B6.

Thibodeau, P. (2001). FTC examines privacy issues raised by data collectors. *ComputerWorld,* March 26, 36, http://www.computerworld.com/news/weekinprint/0,10878,DAY03-26-2001,00.html.

Thibodeau, P. (2002). Vermont opt-in rules spur suit, *Computer World*, 36(7):1,16.

Waldrop, M. (2001). The technology review ten: Data mining. *Technology Review, 104*(1): 101-102, January/February.

Wilder, C. & Soat, J. (2001) The ethics of data. *Information Week*, May 14, pp. 37-48.

Chapter XIX

Data Mining in Designing an Agent-Based DSS

Christian Böhm
GIDSATD–UTN–FRSF, Argentina

María Rosa Galli
GIDSATD–UTN–FRSF and INGAR–CONICET, Argentina

Omar Chiotti
GIDSATD–UTN–FRSF and INGAR–CONICET, Argentina

ABSTRACT

The aim of this work is to present a data-mining application to software engineering. Particularly, we describe the use of data mining in different parts of the design process of an agent-based architecture for a dynamic decision-support system.

The work is organized as follows: An introduction section defines the characteristics of a dynamic decision-support system and gives a brief background about the use of data mining and case-based reasoning in software engineering. A second section describes the use of data mining in designing the system knowledge bases. A third section presents the use of data mining in designing the learning process of the dynamic decision-support system. Finally, a fourth section describes the agent-based architecture we propose for the dynamic decision support system. It implements the mechanisms designed by using data mining to satisfy the system functionality.

INTRODUCTION

Enterprise management involves making many different decisions. An enterprise can be generally considered as being organized in several domains in which different types of activities are performed and decisions are made. These decisions are associated to their corresponding activities but are usually closely related to decisions already made in other domains of the enterprise; that is, the different decision points of an organization often need information to be available in other enterprise domains. The enterprise integration systems provide the automatic communication among these points by transferring previously specified data (Shen & Norrie, 1999). These systems are designed based on the habitual requirements of each domain. But there exist non-foreseen situations that require information exchange. This occurs whenever new or non-habitual decisions must be made. In these cases, it is necessary to use a dynamic Decision-Support System (DSS) (Cabral et al., 2000).

A dynamic Decision Support System is a system able to look for information, analyzing where it is available or can be generated.

A dynamic DSS establishes contact among domains for the acquisition of necessary information for decision making. This implies that the information to be transferred and the domains to be communicated with are not specified on the system design time. The DSS itself should interpret the information requirement and infer which domain can answer it on the run time.

A dynamic DSS must operate in the following way: When a user of the system needs some information, he/she makes a query in natural language, and the dynamic DSS transfers that information requirement to a domain that can satisfy it. For that purpose, the system determines the sites that offer a greater possibility of providing the required information and those are targeted first. This defines the main functionality of this information system. Then, when it gets the answer from a domain, it takes this information to the domain that asked for it.

To develop a system with the aforementioned functionality, it must be provided with: (1) knowledge about the information that can be provided by domains; and (2) the capacity for updating that knowledge, learning from the cases that result from its operation. This chapter will present a description of how data-mining techniques have been used for designing a system with the aforementioned characteristics.

Dingsoyr (1998) presents several possible uses of data mining and case-based reasoning. He classifies these uses into two groups: data mining in case-based reasoning, and case-based reasoning in data mining. He sketches the following six possible uses:

1)   *Data mining search is the case.* That is, the information about the search results and the whole knowledge discovery in database process might be stored in a case so that extra time will not be spent on mining the same information more than once. Rodriguez, Ramos, and Henriques (2000) presented a heterogeneous architecture for knowledge extraction from data. The architecture combines the knowledge discovery in database process with a case-based reasoning system intended to record the successful knowledge extraction experiments to be shared later.

2)   *Case-based reasoning provides information* that can be used in providing some background knowledge about features in a database, for instance, the weight of features for a classifier can be learned.

3)   *Find features from cases base for a case.* It might be valuable for classifying the cases in the cases base. This might speed up the computation of similarity metrics in the *retrieve* step.

4)   *Find features from a database for a case* to supplement the information given in it.

5)   *Find domain knowledge* by mining a database or a cases base in the form of functions, rules, or causal graphs that can be used later to identify features and explain away unimportant features.

6)   *Construct artificial cases from a database* that are not present in a cases base. This would require a tight integration where the data-mining algorithm would search for patterns in the form of cases that could be evaluated by a novelty function that gives high values to cases not present in the base.

Ruiz, Fisler, and Cole (2001) describe a project of data-mining application on software engineering. Specifically, they propose to simulate the designed system to generate cases. Such cases are mined to detect possible behavioral patterns of the design.

It is necessary to highlight that data mining and case-based reasoning applications on system design offer a still little developed potential. On the other hand, in designing an information system, it is possible that several of the alternatives sketched by Dingsoyr (1998) are simultaneously used. In this work, we describe the use of data mining in different parts of the design process of a dynamic decision-support system architecture. By using data mining, we could define the structure of the system knowledge base, the data structure of the system cases base, and the rules of relationships among cases that were used to design the system learning mechanism.

USE OF DATA MINING IN DESIGNING THE SYSTEM KNOWLEDGE BASE

The main function of the system to be developed is to guide information requirements from users to the domains that offer the greatest possibility of meeting them. The purpose of this functionality is to prevent each query from being systematically directed to all domains, increasing the traffic in the net and interfering with the normal operation of domains. For that purpose, it is necessary to develop a strategy that provides the system with capacity for analyzing an information requirement and determining to which domains it will be directed. This can be formalized as follows:

Let D be the set of all domains being part of the system, given an information requirement q_i, the system must define the subset of domains $D_p \subset D$, that has the potential for answering the information requirement. Let d_R be the domain that can provide the required information, the system will be effective if $d_R \in D_p$; and the lower the number of domains included in D_p, the greater the system efficiency.

Then, for each information requirement q_i there will be a set of domains D_p that has the potential for providing the required information, and a set of domains D_N that are not able to provide the required information. In this way, the process can be seen as a classification of domains into: domains with potential for providing the required information, and domains without potential for providing the required information.

Table 1: Data associated with each query

Query	*Domain*	*ValuationAnswer*	*P₁*	...	*Pₖ*	...	*Pₙ*
q_i	d_j						

To carry out such a classification, a discriminating analysis can be employed (Kachigan, 1991). The needed data for the posed classification process could be hypothetically obtained allowing the system to initially operate without a process to drive queries to potential domains. Instead, it systematically sends each query to all domains. As it was specified in the previous section, queries are formulated by the user in his natural language, then the text is cleaned, deleting connectors, pronouns, articles, etc., just leaving the words considered as key for the query. Thus, the set of keywords Kq_i of query q_i is obtained. In this way, for each query q_i the data presented in Table 1 will be obtained.

The first field of Table 1 is called Query. It identifies the query q_i sent by the user. The second field called Domain identifies each consulted domain d_j. The third field, which is called ValuationAnswer (VA), contains the valuation of the result to a query. ValuationAnswer identifies a qualitative variable $va\ (d_j,\ q_i)$ that can take [Positive, Negative, Null] values. The Positive value indicates that the required information q_i was provided by the consulted domain d_j. The Negative value indicates that the consulted domain d_j answered the information query q_i in a negative way, and the Null value indicates that domain d_j did not provide any answer to query q_i.

Each of the remaining fields of Table 1 represents a keyword of the set of all keywords Kq of queries. Each field is named by a keyword and represents a binary variable p_k that takes 1 as its value if the keyword is stated in the query, and 0 if it is not stated in that query.

Once a considerable amount of data is stored, these data can be used to define a discriminating function that allows classifying the domains for each query. It should be said that domains are the objects subjected to analysis. We infer that the keywords included in the queries that have been positively answered (va =[Positive]) by a domain allow us to classify the latter. Then, we define variables p_k as predicting variables. The criterion variable is a qualitative one defined by the classification labels [Potential domain] and [Non-potential domain]. Then, we define the discriminating function as follow:

$$RSV\ (d_j) = w_1 p_1 + ... + w_k p_k + ... + w_n p_n$$

where w_k are the weights associated with each respective predicting variable, and RSV is the resulting domain's discriminating score. Each domain (object) $d_j \in D$ will have a value on this discriminating function depending upon its values on the predicting variables $p_1, ... p_k, ... p_n$.

The criterion variable is qualitative, and thus it will be necessary to define a cutoff score. The cutoff score will be equal to or greater than zero. Domains with RSV equal to or greater than the cutoff score are assigned to the D_p criterion set (Potential domain set), and domains with a RSV lower than the cutoff score are assigned to the D_N criterion group (Non-potential domain set).

On the other hand, given an information requirement q_i the RSV value of each domain classified into the D_P criterion set can be used to rank these domains. That is, the domain $d_j \in D_P$ with the greatest RSV will be ranked first, the domain $d_j \in D_P$ with the second greatest RSV will be ranked second, and so forth.

Initial Definition of the Discriminating Function Weights

An alternative for calculating the weights of the above-described discriminating function would be to implement a system without the main functionality (capacity for orienting user's query to the domains with the greatest possibility to answer that query) and to operate it for the time enough to store the necessary data to calculate such weights.

Another alternative would be to carry out an initial estimation of the discriminating function weights, so that the main functionality of the system can be developed. For this purpose, our proposal consists of working with experts of each domain, so that they provide an initial set of keywords (predicting variables) that can characterize the information that could be provided by that domain. This set of keywords we represent as Kd_j defines a taxonomy of domain d_j. Then, using the Analytical Hierarchy Process or AHP method (Saaty, 1970), support is provided so that experts of each domain, according to their expertise, can define the weights of the discriminating function associated to its domain (Stegmayer, Taverna, Chiotti, & Galli, 2001).

One initial discriminating function is defined for each domain; the former can be used to define a knowledge base about the information that can be provided by the different system domains. Such a knowledge base could be used to provide the system with capacity for guiding the user's information requirements to the domains with the greatest possibility of answering that query.

Since discriminating functions have been defined by experts of domains, it is not strange that classification errors do not affect the system efficacy. That is to say, domain d_R that can answer to such a query obtains a RSV(d_R, q_i)>cutoff score and comes to be classified into the D_P criterion set (Potential domain set). Nevertheless, classification errors may affect the system efficiency, and thus other domains d_j whose RSV(d_j,q_i)>cutoff scores are assigned to the D_P criterion set. In fact, this classification error only affects the system efficiency when RSV(d_j, q_i) > RSV(d_R, q_i). In that case, domain $d_R \in D_P$ but it does not have the first place in the ranking.

Classification errors of the initial discriminating function may be due to two main causes:

1) the value of weights w_k is not the right one, or
2) not all keywords (predicting variables) characterizing the domain are included.

It is necessary to highlight that these errors can be caused by the experts themselves in the discriminating function-definition process, but they could also originate from the evolution of domains that can take place as time goes by. Anyway, it will be necessary to update the system knowledge base to avoid these errors. This updating can be carried out by analyzing the results of all those cases in which there were classification errors.

In other words, domain d_R that answered to the respective query q_i did not have the greatest RSV(d_R, q_i), and therefore it was not ranked first. This process can be defined as a learning process that must be structured so that it can be automatically developed by the system. In the following section, we describe the use of data mining for designing the learning process.

USE OF DATA MINING IN DESIGNING THE LEARNING PROCESS

The learning process conceptually consists of analyzing the data of the stored cases to infer information that allows updating the discriminating function of the system domains. As it was previously indicated, this discriminating function defines the system knowledge base. This updating is necessary to avoid possible classification errors as described in the previous section. To carry out this task, data mining is the suitable technology (tool).

The first step in designing the learning process is to design a cases base in which data of queries and their respective results are stored. Conventional data-mining processes are carried out on a database whose structure was designed without taking into account such a process. For this reason, at their initial stages, these processes involve tasks such as selection, preprocessing, transformation, etc., that are needed to generate a convenient data structure to be analyzed. A way of simplifying the mining process is to take into account these tasks while designing the data structure to store cases in the cases base.

Structure of Data Associated with a Query

As it has been described, whenever a user performs a query, the system classifies domains according to its knowledge base. Then, the query is sent to domain $d_j \in D_p$ having the greatest discriminating score RSV(d_j, q_i). If the query is not positively answered, it is sent to domain $d_j \in D_p$ having the following lower discriminating score RSV(d_j, q_i) and so forth, till one of the domains positively answers the query. In general, if the classification error does not affect the system efficacy, some of the $d_j \in D_p$ should answer positively.

The data associated with each information requirement q_i, which are necessary for the learning process, will be stored as a case. Taking into account the possible classification errors previously discussed, it will be necessary to store the following data: the query q_i, the RSV(d_j,q_i) (discriminating function value) of domains classified into the D_p criterion set (Potential domain set), the taxonomy Kd_j of each domain $d_j \in D_p$, and the valuation of the answer $va(d_j, q_i)$ emitted by the user of domain d_j answering to query q_i. It should be stressed that from the learning point of view, the information in the answer to the query does not matter, but what does matter is whether the required information was provided by a domain or not. Therefore, the variable called valuation of the answer $va(d_j, q_i)$, which was described in previous sections, was introduced.

The logical structure of data to be stored for a specific query is summarized in Table 2.

Table 2: Logical structure of data for a query q_i

Domain	ValuationAnswer	RSV	wp1	...	wpn
dⱼ					

The first field, which is called **Domain**, stores the name that identifies each domain $d_j \in D_p$. The second field, called **ValuationAnswer (VA)**, stores the value of the qualitative value $va(d_j, q_i)$. In the third field, the RSV(d_j, q_i) is stored. This is the value of the discriminating function that helps to determine the position of the domain $d_j \in D_p$ in the ranking.

In the remaining fields, the values of the discriminating function weights are stored, w_{pk} $\forall p_k \in Kq_i \cap Kd_j / d_j \in D_p$. These are the weights of keywords that appear in the query and belong to the domains classified into the D_p criterion set. A field value equal to 0 indicates that the keyword associated to this field is not stated in the taxonomy of the respective domain.

Let us consider the following example:

Query: How many items of product X were for sale in promotion?
Filtered Query: $Kq_i = \{\text{items, product, X, sale, promotion}\}$

This example shows that four domains of the system were classified as potential, $D_p = \{\text{Marketing, Production, Forecast, Sales}\}$.

The Marketing domain presents the smallest RSV value, and therefore is the fourth one in the ranking. Moreover, this domain answers the consult in a positive way, *va(Marketing, q_i)* = Positive.

Forecast and Sales domains, which are second and first in the ranking, respectively, answer the consult in a negative way, *va(Forecast, q_i)* = *va(Sales, q_i)* = Negative. The Production domain presents a *va(Forecast, q_i)* = Null, since it exceeded the time period it had to answer the consult.

Finally, the intersection set between the set of keywords of the query and the set of keywords that define the taxonomy of Marketing domain is integrated by the following keywords: product and promotion. Thus, $Kq_i \cap K(\text{marketing}) = \{\text{product, promotion}\}$. For

Table 3: Logical structure of data for the example

Domain	VA	RSV	Wproduct	Wsale	Wpromotion
Marketing	P	1.0	0.4	0	0.6
Production	Null	1.1	0.9	0.2	0
Forecast	N	1.2	0.5	0.7	0
Sales	N	1.6	0.3	1.0	0.3

that reason, the respective weights of the discriminating function are higher than zero. As the keyword Sale is not include into Marketing taxonomy, the weight factor associated to the discriminating variable Sale is $w_{sale} = 0$.

The logical structure of data represented in Table 2, which is defined to store a case, allows easily visualization of the results associated to a query q_i. In other words, it is a visualization of data in the queries or cases dimension. From the point of view of the need for learning that has been posed, this is not a convenient structure, since in order to evaluate possible domain classification errors, it is necessary to visualize data from the domains dimension.

Visualization of Data of the Cases Base in the Domains Dimension

Table 4 presents a logical structure of data in the cases base that allows observing a domain's behavior before the various queries. This structure will store, for a given domain d_j, all queries q_i, for which RSV(d_j, q_i) > cutoff score. Essentially, this data structure uses binary fields to represent the relationship between a query q_i, which is defined by the set of keywords Kq$_i$, and the domain taxonomy Kd$_j$.

In Table 4, the first field, **Query**, stores the name that identifies each query q_i. The second field, called **VA**, stores the qualitative variable value $va(d_j, q_i)$. According to what has been described in previous sections, in order to determine possible errors in the classification efficiency, the RSV(d_j, q_i) value itself does not matter, but the relative position of each domain $d_j \in D_p$ does. Therefore, the third field (**Order**) stores the order that domain obtained in the ranking of domains classified as potential to answer to the query q_i. The remaining fields are divided into two groups. In the first group, each field represents a keyword of the domain taxonomy. Each field is designated with a keyword $p_k \in$ Kd$_j$, and represents a binary variable p_k that takes 1 as its value if the keyword p_k of the domain taxonomy is in the query q_i, and takes 0 as its value if p_k is not stated in that query.

$$p_k = \begin{cases} 1 & if \quad p_k \in Kd_j \wedge p_k \in Kq_i \\ 0 & if \quad p_k \in Kd_j \wedge p_k \notin Kq_i \end{cases}$$

In the second group, each field represents a keyword stated in query q_i that does not belong to the domain taxonomy. Each of these fields is designated with a keyword p'_k and represents a binary variable p'_k that takes 1 as its value if the keyword p'_k is stated in the query q_i but does not belong to the domain taxonomy d_j, and takes 0 as its value if p'_k is not in that query.

Table 4: Logical structure of data for the domain d$_j$

Query	VA	OR	P₁	...	Pₖ	P'₁	...	P'ₘ
q$_i$								

$$p'_k = \begin{cases} 1 & if \quad p'_k \notin Kd_j \wedge p'_k \in Kq_i \\ 0 & if \quad p'_k \notin Kd_j \wedge p'_k \notin Kq_i \end{cases}$$

Let us consider the previous example. Let us suppose that it is the first case for which the domain is classified as having potential for answering to the query:

Query: How many items of product X were for sale in promotion?
Filtered query: $Kq_1 = \{items, product, X, sale, promotion\}$

Marketing Domain

Query	VA	OR	marketing	product	promotion	items	x	sale
q1	P	4	0	1	1	1	1	1

Production Domain

Query	VA	OR	production	product	machine	items	x	sale	promotion
q1	Null	3	0	1	0	1	1	1	1

Forecast Domain

Query	VA	OR	forecast	age	sale	product	items	x	promotion
q1	N	2	0	0	1	1	1	1	1

Sales Domain

Query	VA	OR	sale	product	customer	promotion	items	x
q1	N	1	1	1	0	1	1	1

Thus, we have a structure for each system domain. Each structure stores the way in which the domain behaved for the different queries for which it has been classified as potential.

In the following section, we will see how this logical data structure meets the posed learning needs.

Application of Data Mining to the Learning Process Design

Once the logical data structure is designed and the cases are stored, the latter must be analyzed using data mining. The object is to analyze the data kept in the cases base so as to identify relationships among the data from which possible behavior patterns of cases can be defined. Such patterns are used to define rules for updating the discriminating function of each domain, which is stored in the knowledge base. This requires working with the cases data associated to the involved domain. For this purpose, the logical data structure presented in Table 4 of the previous section will be used. According to what has been discussed, the updating can be performed in two ways: either updating the weights of the keywords (predicting variables) that define the domain taxonomy or modifying the domain taxonomy by adding new keywords.

Patterns Obtainment

Once a significant number of cases q_i are stored, we can perform a mining of these data to look for patterns. For that purpose, we define Q_{dj} as the set of stored cases q_i associated to d_j. That is, $Q_{dj} = \{q_i / RSV(d_j, q_i) > cutoff\ score\}$.

To start with, cases $q_i \in Q_{dj}$ are classified into four groups: a first group formed by cases in which no classification error occurred; a second group of cases in which the domain provided a positive answer, but it was not the first one in the ranking of potential domains (these are cases in which the classification error affected the system efficiency); a third group of cases, in which the domain provided a negative answer; and, finally, a fourth group of cases in which the query was not answered.

To carry out this classification, $va(d_j, q_i)$ and $or(d_j, q_i)$ are defined as predicting variables.

Group of efficient cases Q^+_{dj}: integrated by those cases that present $va(d_j, q_i)$ = positive and $or(d_j, q_i) = 1$

$$Q^+_{dj} = \{q_i \in Q_{dj} / va(d_j, q_i) = \text{positive} \wedge or(d_j, q_i) = 1\}$$

Group of non-efficient cases Q^*_{dj}: integrated by those cases that present $va(d_j, q_i)$ = positive but $or(d_j, q_i) > 1$

$$Q^*_{dj} = \{q_i \in Q_{dj} / va(d_j, q_i) = \text{positive} \wedge or(d_j, q_i) > 1\}$$

Group of negative cases Q^-_{dj}: integrated by those cases that were answered in a negative way.

$$Q^-_{dj} = \{q_i \in Q_{dj} / va(d_j, q_i) = \text{negative}\}$$

Group of Null cases Q^0_{dj}: integrated by those cases in which an answer was not provided.

$$Q^0_{dj} = \{q_i \in Q_{dj} / va(d_j, q_i) = \text{null}\}$$

Once $q_i \in Q_{dj}$ cases are classified into one of the four defined groups, the purpose is to infer rules to update the discriminating function of each domain that is stored in the knowledge base. The action of these rules will be to:

- Modify the cases belonging to Q^+_{dj} to the lowest extent.
- Determine the weights w_{pk} of the keywords (predicting variable) of the domain taxonomy. These weights must be increased in order to correct the classification error produced in the cases of group Q^*_{dj}. These rules will operate on keywords $p_k \in Kd_j$ that are frequently present in queries $q_i \in Q^*_{dj}$, since it can be inferred that these predicting variables are more important to classify domains than what their associated weights really reflect. In other words, the current weight factors w_{pk} are low.
- Encourage the incoming of new keywords into the domain taxonomy. This means including new predicting variables in the discriminating function of domain d_j. These rules will operate on keywords $p'_k \notin Kd_j$ that are frequently present in queries $q_i \in Q^*_{dj}$. In other words, it is inferred that these predicting variables are important to classify domains. However, if those words are also frequently present in queries answered by most of the remaining domains, these keywords would not be useful to distinguish among domains and thus they should not be incorporated.
- Another possibility is that a domain presents many cases in which it answered in a negative form although appearing as better positioned in the ranking than the domain that actually provided a positive answer. This means that this domain taxonomy has words whose weights are too high when compared to their importance in the domain. Therefore, there should be a rule that diminishes the weights of these words.

With the aim of interpreting the relationships among variables, we present three main rules obtained by the mining process that will be used to develop the system learning process:

Given Q_{dj}, to classify:

$$Q^*_{dj} = \{q_i \in Q_{dj} \; / \; va(d_j,q_i) = \text{positive} \wedge or(d_j,q_i) > 1\}$$
$$Q^-_{dj} = \{q_i \in Q_{dj} \; / \; va(d_j,q_i) = \text{negative}\}.$$

Set

$p \in Kd_j$

n_P^*: frequence of p in queries of Q^*_{dj}.

n_P^-: frequence of p in queries of Q^-_{dj}.

α_1 and α_2: system parameters

IF $\quad \#Q_{dj} > \alpha_1 \; \wedge \; \dfrac{n_P^*}{\#Q_{dj}} > \alpha_2 \; \wedge \; n_P^* \gg n_P^-$

THEN $\quad p$ is a candidate for increasing its weight w_p

In the condition of this rule, we are saying that a word belonging to the domain taxonomy is a candidate for increasing its weight if:

a)   more than α_1 cases are stored in Q_{dj} and

b)   the number of times in which p is stated in queries of Q^*_{dj} is greater than α_2 and

c) n_p^* is much more higher than n_p^-

Now, we present the rule for the incoming of new words into the domain taxonomy.

Given Q_{dj}, to classify:

$$Q^*_{dj} = \{q_i \in Q_{dj} \,/\, va(d_j, q_i) = positive \wedge or(d_j, q_i) > 1\}$$
$$Q^-_{dj} = \{q_i \in Q_{dj} \,/\, va(d_j, q_i) = negative \}$$

Set

$p \notin Kd_j$

n_p^*: frequence of p in queries of Q^*_{dj}.

n_p^-: frequence of p in queries of Q^-_{dj}.

dn_p: number of domains in which p is stated or is a candidate for entering.

$D = \{d_1, d_2, ..., d_n\}$ set of system domains

IF $\#Q_{dj} > \alpha_3 \wedge \dfrac{n_p^*}{\#Q_{dj}} > \alpha_4 \wedge n_p^* \gg n_p^-$

THEN p is a candidate for entering Kd_j

p can enter Kd_j if it is not a candidate for entering the taxonomy of several domains and/or it does not belong to the taxonomy of several domains

$\dfrac{dn_p}{\#D} \cong 0 \Rightarrow p$ can be used to discriminate the domains, to which it is a candidate,

from the remaining domains. Then, p must enter the taxonomy of domains to which it is a candidate.

$\dfrac{dn_p}{\#D} \cong 1 \Rightarrow p$ can not be used to discriminate, then it can be included as stopword.

In the first condition of this rule, we say that a word is a candidate for entering a Kd_j if:

a)   more than α_3 cases are stored in Q_{dj} and

b)   the proportion between the number of times in which p is stated in queries of Q^*_{dj} in respect to the number of cases stored in Q_{dj} is greater than α_4.

c) n_p^* is much higher than n_p^-.

A word can enter Kd_j if the amount of domains in the system is much higher than the quantity of domains in which p is stated or is a candidate.

Set

d_R the domain that positively answer the query,

$Q^+_{dj} = \{q_i \in Q_{dj} \ / \ va(d_j,q_i) = \text{positive} \wedge or(d_j,q_i) = 1\}$

$Q^*_{dj} = \{q_i \in Q_{dj} \ / \ va(d_j,q_i) = \text{positive} \wedge or(d_j,q_i) > 1\}$

$Q^-_{dj} = \{q_i \in Q_{dj} \ / \ va(d_j,q_i) = \text{negative}\}$

$Q^\wedge_{dj} = \{q_i \in Q^-_{dj} \ / or(d_j,q_i) < or(d_R,q_i) \}$

$Q^\wedge_{dj}$ set of cases of domains that bring a negative answer to the query q_i and are best ranked than d_R

Set

$p \in Kd_j$.

n_P^+: frequence of p in queries of Q^+_{dj}.

n_P^*: frequence of p in queries of Q^*_{dj}.

$n_P^\wedge$: frequence of p in queries of $Q^\wedge_{dj}$.

IF $\quad \#Q_{dj} > \alpha_5 \wedge \dfrac{n_P^\wedge}{\#Q_{dj}} > \alpha_6 \wedge n_P^\wedge \gg n_P^+ + n_P^*$

THEN $\qquad$ p is a candidate for diminishing its weight

In the condition of this rule, we are saying that a word p is a candidate for diminishing its weight if:

a)   more than α_5 cases are stored in Q_{dj} and

b)   the proportion of the number of times in which p is stored in queries of $Q^\wedge_{dj}$ in respect to the number of stored cases Q_{dj} is greater than α_6 and

c) $n_p^\wedge$ is much greater than the number of times in which p is stated in queries with positive answer $(n_p^+ + n_p^*)$

MULTIAGENT-BASED ARCHITECTURE FOR THE DYNAMIC DSS

According to what has been described in the previous sections, we may distinguish various activities that must be carried out during the dynamic DSS operation. This system should work in the following way.

When an enterprise domain requires some information, a user of that domain gets into the dynamic DSS and formulates a query in natural language. The system interprets that query, compares the contents of the query with its knowledge about the type of information each domain can provide, and identifies the domains to which the information requirement must be derived. Then, the system communicates with this domain and waits for an answer. In case it does not obtain a positive answer, it communicates with the other domains. Once the pursued answer is obtained, this is transferred to the domain of origin and, if necessary, the knowledge updating is also done.

A system that operates in the described way can be implemented using the mobile agent technology (Rus, Gray, & Kots, 1998).

An agent is a software component that performs specific tasks in an autonomous, intelligent, and collaborative way in order to achieve its design objectives. Two classes of agents may be identified: static agents, which stay in their respective computers; and mobile agents, which are able to migrate among different locations of the network in order to perform their tasks locally.

A multiagent system consists of a set of software agents, each performing a specific activity but behaving as an organization, i.e., in a coordinated way. The main activities this system must perform are:

- transferring queries to different domains of the system;
- communicating with domains (either for capturing the query or answer or for delivering the answer or information requirement); and
- identifying the domains able to provide an answer.

Each of these activities requires a different type of software agent. A multiagent architecture for this dynamic DSS should be made up of three main kinds of software agents:

a) *Collecting Agents*: mobile agents that visit the different domains to find out which of them can give the appropriate answer.

b) *Domain Representative Agents*: static agents that act as mediators between a domain and the mobile agents. They send the queries coming from users of the domain to the collecting agents and also transmit the answers to queries of the mobile agents that arrive asking for information.

c) *Router Agent*: an intelligent agent, which, interpreting the query, decides where the collecting agents should look for the answer. It is an agent that centralizes the knowledge about the system and whose main responsibility is the system efficiency. It owns the system knowledge base that stores each domain taxonomy and the associated weight factors. The router agent calculates the value of the discriminating function for each domain whenever an information requirement is presented to the system. It is also responsible for updating that knowledge base. In other words, the router agent performs the learning process, and thus it is responsible for managing the cases base.

Figure 1 is a schematic representation of the multiagent architecture for the dynamic DSS.

This multiagent system, as depicted in Figure 1, works as follows:

When a decision-maker needs specific information, the former, being helped by an assistant, expresses the information he/she would like to receive (1). Then, the assistant passes it to the Domain Representative Agent (2), which changes the query into a format accepted by the mobile agents and sends it to the Collecting Agent Server (3). The Collecting Agent Server gives the query to a domain Collecting Agent, and it goes to a special agent server—the Router Agent (4). It receives the Collecting Agent that has just left its domain, reads the formulated query, filters it, and according to the information kept in its knowledge base (5), it computes the discriminating function of each domain and gives the Collecting Agent a ranked list of domains that would provide the searched

Figure 1: Multiagent architecture for the dynamic DSS.

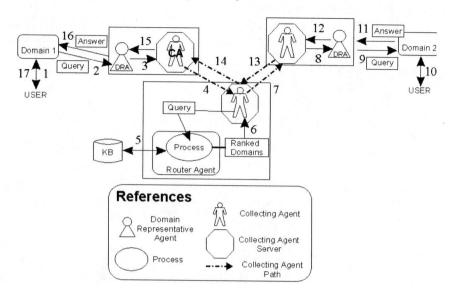

information (6). The Collecting Agent visits these domains with its query (7). Once it has found the answer and is about to go back to the original domain (8-12), it visits the Router Agent again to inform it of the obtained results, allowing it to have new information to update its knowledge base for future queries (13). That information is stored in the cases base to be used in the learning process. Finally, the Collecting Agent goes back to its domain, delivers the information and destroys itself (14-17).

CONCLUSIONS

A dynamic DSS that works efficiently, i.e., that does not constantly interrupt users with information requirements they cannot satisfy, must be able to identify the relationship among the characteristics of consults and domains. By using data-mining techniques it was possible to define a discriminating function to classify the system domains into two groups: those that can probably provide an answer to the information requirement made to the system, and those that can not do that. From this discriminating function, the system knowledge base was designed, which stores the values of the parameters required by such a function.

On the other hand, the system needs to learn from the errors it could make during its operation so that it can decrease the number of consulted domains in each information requirement presented to the system. The use of data mining allowed the definition of a data structure that is convenient for analyzing the system operation results and, according to that, for designing a cases base to store the information associated to the quality of each performed search.

Moreover, the application of data mining to the cases base allowed the specification of rules to settle relationships among the stored cases with the aim of inferring possible causes of error in the domains classification. In this way, a learning mechanism was designed to update the knowledge base and thus improve the already made classification as regards the values assigned to the discriminating function.

The selection mechanism designed using data-mining techniques is feasible to be implemented by means of agents technology. For this purpose, the roles required to operate the system have been identified (Jennings, 2000), and each of them was assigned to be under the responsibility of different software agents. Mobile agents take consults to the domains identified by an intelligent agent called a router agent. This agent is responsible for the classification and learning mechanism designed in this work.

In this way, it has been possible to design an agent-based architecture of a dynamic DSS that satisfies the main functionality specified for this system, i.e., to guide information requirements from users to the domains that offer the greatest possibility of answering them.

REFERENCES

Cabral, L., Caliusco, M., Nissio, H., Villarreal, M., Galli, P., Taverna, M., & Chiotti, O. (2000). Use of agents technology to support distributed decision processes. In J. A. Dominguez Machuca & T. Mandakovic (Eds.), *Proceedings of the First World Conference on Production and Operations Management, POM Sevilla 2000.* Sevilla, Spain, August , pp.1-10, Paper 2071.

Dingsoyr, T. (1998). Integration of data mining and case-based reasoning. Available online at: <http://www.idi.ntnu.no/~dingsoyr/diploma>. Jennings, N. (2001). An agent-based approach for building complex software systems. *Communications of the ACM*, 44 (4), 35-42.

Kachigan, S. K. (1991). Multivariable statistical analysis. A conceptual introduction. New York: Radius Press.

Rodriguez, F., Ramos, C., & Henriques, P. (2000). A case-based reasoning framework to extract knowledge from data. In N. Ebecken & C.A. Brebbia (eds.) *Data Mining II* .Southampton, Boston, MA:WIT Press.

Ruiz, C., Fisler, K., & Cole, C. (2000). "KDDRG – Data mining for software engineering". Available online at: <http://www.cs.wpi.edu/~ruiz/KDDRG/dm_for_se.html >.

Rus, D., Gray, R., & Kots, D. (1998). Transportable information agents. In M. Huhns & M. Singh (Eds.). *Reading in Agents*. San Francisco, CA: Morgan Kaufmann Publishers, Inc., pp. 283-291.

Saaty, T.L. (1980). *The analytical hierarchy process*. New York: McGraw-Hill.

Shen, W. & Norrie, D.H. (1999). Agent-based systems for intelligent manufacturing: A state-of-the-art survey. *Knowledge and Information Systems,* 1 (2), 129-156.

Stegmayer, G., Taverna, M.L., Chiotti, O., & Galli, M.R. (2001). The agent routering process of dynamic distributed decision support system. *Journal of Computer Science & Technology*, 2 (5), 30-43. Available online at: <http://journal.info.unlp.edu.ar>.

Chapter XX

Critical and Future Trends in Data Mining: A Review of Key Data Mining Technologies/ Applications

Jeffrey Hsu
Fairleigh Dickinson University, USA

ABSTRACT

Every day, enormous amounts of information are generated from all sectors, whether it be business, education, the scientific community, the World Wide Web (WWW), or one of many readily available off-line and online data sources. From all of this, which represents a sizable repository of data and information, it is possible to generate worthwhile and usable knowledge. As a result, the field of Data Mining (DM) and knowledge discovery in databases (KDD) has grown in leaps and bounds and has shown great potential for the future (Han & Kamber, 2001). The purpose of this chapter is to survey many of the critical and future trends in the field of DM, with a focus on those which are thought to have the most promise and applicability to future DM applications.

MAJOR TRENDS IN TECHNOLOGIES AND METHODS: WEB MINING

Web mining is one of the most promising areas in DM, because the Internet and WWW are dynamic sources of information. Web mining is the extraction of interesting and potentially useful patterns and implicit information from artifacts or activity related to the WWW (Etzioni, 1996). The main tasks that comprise Web mining include retrieving Web documents, selection and processing of Web information, pattern discovery in sites and across sites, and analysis of the patterns found (Garofalis, Rastogi, Seshadri & Shim, 1999; Kosala & Blockeel, 2000; Han, Zaiane, Chee, & Chiang, 2000).

Web mining can be categorized into three separate areas: web-content mining, Web-structure mining, and Web-usage mining. Web-content mining is the process of extracting knowledge from the content of documents or their descriptions. This includes the mining of Web text documents, which is a form of resource discovery based on the indexing of concepts, sometimes using agent-based technology. Web-structure mining is the process of inferring knowledge from the links and organizations in the WWW. Finally, Web-usage mining, also known as Web-log mining, is the process of extracting interesting patterns in Web-access logs and other Web-usage information (Borges & Levene, 1999; Kosala & Blockeel, 2000; Madria, Bhowmick, Ng, & Lim, 1999).

Web-content mining is concerned with the discovery of new information and knowledge from web-based data, documents, and pages. According to Kosala and Blockeel (2000), there are two main approaches to Web-content mining: an information retrieval view and a database (DB) view. The information retrieval view is designed to work with both unstructured (free text, such as news stories) or semistructured documents (with both HTML and hyperlinked data), and attempts to identify patterns and models based on an analysis of the documents, using such techniques as clustering, classification, finding text patterns, and extraction rules (Billsus & Pazzani, 1999; Frank, Paynter, Witten, Gutwin & Nevill-Manning, 1998; Nahm & Mooney, 2000). The other main approach, which is to content mine semi-structured documents, uses many of the same techniques as used for unstructured documents, but with the added complexity and challenge of analyzing documents containing a variety of media elements (Crimmins & Smeator, 1999; Shavlik & Elassi-Rad, 1998).

There are also applications that focus on the design of languages, which provide better querying of DBs containing web-based data. Researchers have developed many *web-oriented query languages* that attempt to extend standard DB query languages such as SQL to collect data from the WWW, e.g., WebLog and WebSQL. The TSIMMIS system (Chawathe et al., 1994) extracts data from heterogeneous and semistructured information sources and correlates them to generate an integrated DB representation of the extracted information (Maarek & Ben Shaul, 1996; Han, 1996; Meldelzon, Mihaila, & Milo, 1996; Merialdo, Atzeni, & Mecca, 1997).

Other applications focus on the building and management of *multilevel or multi-layered DBs*. This suggests a multilevel-DB approach to organizing web-based information. The main idea behind this method is that the lowest level of the DB contains primitive semistructured information stored in various Web repositories, such as hypertext documents. At the higher level(s), metadata or generalizations are extracted from lower levels and organized in structured collections such as relational or object-oriented DBs. Kholsa, Kuhn, and Soparkar (1996) and King and Novak (1996) have done research in this area.

Web-structure mining. Instead of looking at the text and data on the pages themselves, Web-structure mining has as its goal the mining of knowledge from the structure of websites. More specifically, it attempts to examine the structures that exist between documents on a website, such as hyperlinks and other linkages. For instance, links pointing to a document indicate the popularity of the document, while links coming out of a document indicate the richness or perhaps the variety of topics covered in the document. The PageRank (Brin & Page, 1998) and CLEVER (Chakrabarti et al., 1999) methods take advantage of the information conveyed by the links to find pertinent Web pages. Counters of hyperlinks, into and out of documents, retrace the structure of the Web artifacts summarized.

Web-usage mining. Yet another major area in the broad spectrum of Web mining is Web-usage mining. Rather than looking at the content pages or the underlying structure, Web-usage mining is focused on Web user behavior or, more specifically, modeling and predicting how a user will use and interact with the Web. In general, this form of mining examines secondary data, or the data that are derived from the interaction of users (Chen, Park, & Yu, 1996). There are two main thrusts in Web-usage mining: general access-pattern tracking and customized-usage tracking. General access-pattern tracking analyzes Web logs in order to better understand access patterns and trends. Customized-usage tracking analyzes individual trends. Its purpose is to customize websites to users. The information displayed, the depth of the site structure, and the format of the resources can all be dynamically customized for each user over time, based on their patterns of access (Kosala & Blockeel, 2000).

Srivastava, Cooley, Deshpe, and Tan. (2000) have produced a taxonomy of different Web-mining applications and have categorized them into the following types:

- *Personalization.* The goal here is to produce a more "individualized" experience for a Web visitor, including making recommendations about other pages to visit based on the pages he/she has visited previously.

- *System improvement.* Performance and speed have always been important factors when it comes to computing systems, and through Web-usage data, it is possible to improve system performance by creating policies and using such methods as load-balancing, Web caching and network transmission.

- *Site modification.* It is also possible to modify aspects of a site based on user patterns and behavior. After a detailed analysis of a user's activities on a site, it is possible to make design changes and structural modifications to site to enhance a user's satisfaction and the site's usability.

- *Business intelligence.* Another important application of Web-usage mining is the ability to mine for marketing intelligence information. Buchner and Mulvenna. (1998) used a data hypercube to consolidate Web-usage data together with marketing data to obtain insights with regards to e-commerce.

- *Usage characterization.* There is a close relationship between DM of Web-usage data and Web-usage characterization research. This area is focused more on such topics as interaction with the browser interface, navigational strategies, the occurrence of certain types of activities, and models of Web usage. Studies in this area include Catledge and Pitkow (1995), Doorenbos, Etzioni, and Weld (1996), and Arlitt and Williamson (1997).

Yet another area that has been gaining interest is agent-based approaches. Agents are intelligent software components that "crawl through" the Internet and collect useful information, much like the way a virus-like worm moves through systems wreaking havoc.

Generally, agent-based Web-mining systems can be placed into three main categories: information categorization and filtering, intelligent search agents, and personal agents.

Information filtering/categorization agents try to automatically retrieve, filter, and categorize discovered information by using various information-retrieval techniques. Agents that can be classified in this category include HyPursuit (Weiss et al., 1996) and Bookmark Organizer (BO). *Intelligent search agents* search the Internet for relevant information and use characteristics of a particular domain to organize and interpret the discovered information. Some of the better known include ParaSite, and FAQ-Finder. *Personalized Web agents* try to obtain or learn user preferences and discover Web information sources that correspond to these preferences, and possibly those of other individuals with similar interests, using collaborative filtering. Systems in this class include Netperceptions, WebWatcher (Armstrong, Freitag, Joachims, & Mitchell, 1995), and Syskill & Webert (Pazzani, Muramatsu & Billsus, 1996).

TEXT DATA MINING (TDM)

The possibilities for DM from textual information are largely untapped, making it a fertile area of future research. Text expresses a vast, rich range of information, but in its original, raw form is difficult to analyze or mine automatically. TDM has relatively fewer research projects and commercial products compared to other DM areas. As expected, TDM is a natural extension of traditional DM, as well as information archeology (Brachman et al., 1993). While most standard DM applications tend to be automated discovery of trends and patterns across large DBs and data sets, in the case of text mining, the goal is to look for pattern and trends, like nuggets of data in large amounts of text (Hearst, 1999).

Benefits of TDM

It is important to differentiate between TDM and information access (or information retrieval, as it is better known). The goal of information access is to help users find documents that satisfy their information needs (Baeza-Yates & Ribeiro-Neto, 1999). Text mining focuses on how to use a body of textual information as a large knowledge base from which one can extract new, never-before encountered information (Craven, DiPasquo, Freitag, McCallum, Mitchell, Nigam & Slattery, 1998). However, the results of certain types of text processing can yield tools that indirectly aid in the information-access process. Examples include text clustering to create thematic overviews of text collections (Rennison, 1994; Wise, Thomas, Pennock, Lantrip, Pottier, & Schur, 1995), automatically generating term associations to aid in query expansion (Voorhees, 1994; Xu & Croft, 1996), and using co-citation analysis to find general topics within a collection or identify central Web pages (Hearst, 1999; Kleinberg, 1998; Larson, 1996;).

Methods of TDM

Some of the major methods of TDM include feature extraction, clustering, and categorization. Feature extraction, which is the mining of text within a document, attempts to find significant and important vocabulary from within a natural language text document. From the document-level analysis, it is possible to examine collections of documents. The methods used to do this include clustering and classification. Clustering is the process of grouping documents with similar contents into dynamically generated clusters. This is in contrast to text categorization, where the process is a bit more involved. Here, samples of documents fitting into pre-determined "themes" or "categories" are fed into a "trainer," which in turn generates a categorization schema. When the documents to be analyzed are then fed into the categorizer, which incorporates the schema previously produced, it will then assign documents to different categories based on the taxonomy previously provided. These features are incorporated in programs such as IBM's Intelligent Miner for Text (Dorre, Gerstl, & Seiffert, 1999).

DISTRIBUTED/COLLECTIVE DM

One area of DM that is attracting a good amount of attention is distributed and collective DM. Much of the DM that is being done currently focuses on a DB or data warehouse of information that is physically located in one place. However, the situation arises where information may be located in different places, or in different physical locations. This is known generally as distributed-data mining (DDM). Therefore, the goal is to effectively mine distributed data that are located in heterogeneous sites. DDM is used to offer a different approach to traditional approaches to analysis, by using a combination of localized data analysis together with a "global data model." In more specific terms, this is defined as performing local data analysis for generating partial data models, and combining the local data models from different data sites in order to develop the global model. This global model combines the results of the separate analyses. Often the global model produced may become incorrect or ambiguous, especially if the data in different locations have different features or characteristics. This problem is especially critical when the data in distributed sites are heterogeneous rather than homogeneous. These heterogeneous data sets are known as vertically partitioned data sets. An approach proposed by Kargupta, Park, Herschberger, and Johnson (2000) speaks of the collective data-mining (CDM) approach, which provides a better approach to vertically partitioned data sets using the notion of orthonormal basis functions, and computes the basis coefficients to generate the global model of the data.

UBIQUITOUS DM (UDM)

The advent of laptops, palmtops, cell phones, and wearable computers is making ubiquitous access to large quantity of data possible. Advanced analysis of data for extracting useful knowledge is the next natural step in the world of ubiquitous computing. However, there are challenges that exist for UDM. Human-computer interaction and data management are challenging issues. Moreover, the sociological and psychological aspects of the integration between DM technology and our lifestyle are yet to be explored. The key issues to consider include theories of UDM, advanced algorithms for mobile and distributed applications, data management issues, markup languages, and other data representation techniques; integration with DB applications for mobile environments, architectural issues (architecture, control, security, and communication issues), specialized mobile devices for UDM, software agents and UDM (agent-based approaches in UDM, agent interaction-cooperation, collaboration, negotiation, organizational behavior), applications of UDM (in business, science, engineering, medicine, and other disciplines), location management issues in UDM, and technology for web-based applications of UDM (Kargupta & Joshi, 2001).

HYPERTEXT AND HYPERMEDIA DATA MINING

Hypertext and hypermedia DM can be characterized as mining data that includes text, hyperlinks, text markups, and various other forms of hypermedia information. As such, it is closely related to both Web mining and multimedia mining, which are covered separately in this section, but in reality are quite close in terms of content and applications. While the WWW is substantially composed of hypertext and hypermedia elements, there are other kinds of hypertext/hypermedia data sources, including online catalogues, digital libraries, online information DBs, and hyperlink and inter-document structures.

Some of the important DM techniques used for hypertext and hypermedia DM include classification (supervised learning), clustering (unsupervised learning), semistructured learning, and social network analysis. In the case of classification, or supervised learning, the process starts off by reviewing training data in which items are marked as being part of a certain class or group. This data are the basis from which the algorithm is trained (Chakrabarti, 2000). Unsupervised learning, or clustering, differs from classification in that while classification involves the use of training data, clustering is concerned with the creation of hierarchies of documents based on similarity and organizes the documents based on that hierarchy. Semi-supervised learning and social network analysis are other methods that are important to hypermedia-based DM. Semisupervised learning is the case where there are both labeled and unlabeled documents and there is a need to learn from both types of documents. Social network analysis is also applicable because the Web is considered a social network that examines networks formed through collaborative association (Larson, 1996; Mizruchi, Mariolis, Schwartz, & Mintz, 1986). Other research conducted in the area of hypertext DM includes work on distributed hypertext resource discovery (Chakrabarti, van den Berg, & Dom, 1999).

VISUAL DM

Visual DM is an emerging area of explorative and intelligent data analysis and mining, based on the integration of concepts from computer graphics, visualization metaphors and methods, information and scientific data visualization, visual perception, cognitive psychology, diagrammatic reasoning, visual data formatting, and 3-D collaborative virtual environments. Research and developments in the methods and techniques for visual DM have helped to identify many of the research directions in the field, including visual methods for data analysis, visual DM process models, visual reasoning and uncertainty management, visual explanations, algorithmic animation methods, perceptual and cognitive aspects, and interactivity in visual DM. Other key areas include the study of domain knowledge in visual reasoning, virtual environments, visual analysis of large DBs, collaborative exploration and model building, metrics for evaluation, generic system architectures and prototypes, and methods for visualizing semantic content (Han & Kamber, 2001).

MULTIMEDIA DM

Multimedia DM is the mining and analysis of various types of data, including images, video, audio, and animation. The idea of mining data that contains different kinds of information is the main objective of multimedia DM (Zaiane, Han, Li, & Hou, 1998). As multimedia DM incorporates the areas of text mining as well as hypertext/hypermedia mining, these fields are closely related. Much of the information describing these other areas also applies to multimedia DM. This field is also rather new, but holds much promise for the future. A developing area in multimedia DM is that of audio DM (mining music). The idea is basically to use audio signals to indicate the patterns of data or to represent the features of DM results. It is possible not only to summarize melodies based on the approximate patterns that repeatedly occur in the segment, but also to summarize style based on tone, tempo, or the major musical instruments played (Han & Kamber, 2001; Zaiane, Han, Li, & Hou, 1998; Zaiane, Han, & Zhu, 2000).

SPATIAL AND GEOGRAPHIC DM

Aside from statistical or numeric data, it is also important to consider information that is of an entirely different kind-i.e., spatial and geographic data that could contain information about astronomical data, natural resources, or even orbiting satellites and spacecraft that transmit images of earth from out in space. Much of this data is image-oriented and can represent a great deal of information if properly analyzed and mined (Miller & Han, 2001). Analyzing spatial and geographic data includes such tasks as understanding and browsing spatial data, uncovering relationships between spatial data items (and also between non-spatial and spatial items), and also analysis using spatial DBs and spatial knowledge bases. The applications of these would be useful in such fields as remote sensing, medical imaging, navigation, and related uses. Some of the techniques and data structures that are used to analyze spatial and related types of data include the use of spatial warehouses, spatial data cubes, and spatial On Line Analytic Processing (OLAP). Spatial data warehouses can be defined as those that are subject-oriented, integrated, nonvolatile, and time-variant (Han, Kamber, & Tung, 2001). Aside from the implementation of data warehouses for spatial data, there is also the issue of analyses that can be done on the data. Some of the analyses that can be done include association analysis, clustering methods, and the mining of raster DBs. There have been a number of studies conducted on spatial DM (Bedard, Merritt, & Han 2001; Han, Kamber & Tung, 1998; Han, Koperski, & Stefanovic, 1997; Han, Stefanovic, & Koperski, 1998; Koperski, Adikary, & Han, 1996; Koperski & Han, 1995; Koperski, Han, & Marchisio, 1999; Koperski, Han, & Stefanovic, 1998; Tung, Hou, & Han, 2001).

TIME SERIES/SEQUENCE DM

Another important area in DM centers on the mining of time-series and sequence-based data. Simply put, this involves the mining of a sequence of data that can either be referenced by time (time-series, such as stock market and production process data), or is simply a sequence of data that are ordered in a sequence. In general, one aspect of mining time-series data focuses on the goal of identifying movements or components that exist within the data (trend analysis). These can include long-term or trend movements, seasonal variations, cyclical variations, and random movements (Han & Kamber, 2001).

Other techniques that can be used on these kinds of data include similarity search, sequential-pattern mining, and periodicity analysis. *Similarity search* is concerned with the identification of a pattern sequence that is close or similar to a given pattern. *Sequential- pattern mining* has as its focus the identification of sequences that occur frequently in a time series or sequence of data. *Periodicity analysis* attempts to analyze the data from the perspective of identifying patterns that repeat or recur in a time series (Han, Dong, & Yin, 1999; Han & Kamber, 2001; Han, Pei, & Yin, 2000; Kim, Lam, & Han, 2000; Pei, Han, Pinto, Chen, Dayal, & Hsu, 2001; Pei, Tung, & Han, 2001).

DM TRENDS: METHODS AND TECHNIQUES
Constraint-Based DM

Many of the DM techniques that currently exist are very useful but lack the benefit of any guidance or user control. One method of inserting some form of human involvement into DM is in the form of constraint-based DM. This form of DM incorporates the use of constraints that guide the process. Frequently, this is combined with the benefits of multidimensional mining to add greater power to the process (Han, Lakshamanan, & Ng, 1999). There are several categories of constraints that can be used, each with its own characteristics and purpose. These include *knowledge-type constraints,* that specify the "type of knowledge" that is to be mined, and are typically specified at the beginning of any DM query. Some of the types of constraints that can be used include clustering, association, and classification. *Data constraints* identify the data that are to be used in the specific DM query. Since constraint-based mining is ideally conducted within the framework of an ad hoc, query-driven system, data constraints can be specified in a form similar to that of a SQL query. Because much of the information being mined is in the form of a DB or multidimensional data warehouse, it is possible to specify constraints that identify the levels or dimensions (*dimension/level constraints)* to be included in the current query. It would also be useful to determine what ranges of a particular variable or measure are considered to be particularly interesting and should be included in the query (*interestingness constraints*). Finally, *rule constraints* specify the specific rules that should be applied and used for a particular DM query or application.

One application of the constraint-based approach is in the Online Analytical Mining Architecture (OLAM) developed by Han, Lakshamanan, and Ng (1999), which is designed to support the multidimensional and constraint-based mining of DBs and data warehouses. In short, constraint-based DM is one of the developing areas that allow the use of guiding constraints, which should make for better DM. A number of studies have been conducted in this area (Cheung, Hwang, Fu, & Han, 2000; Lakshaman, Ng, Han, & Pang, 1999; Lu, Feng, & Han, 2000; Pei & Han, 2000; Pei, Han, & Lakshaman, 2001; Pei, Han, & Mao, 2000; Tung, Han, Lakshaman, & Ng, 2001; Wang, He, & Han, 2000; Wang, Zhou, & Han, 2000).

Phenomenal DM

Phenomenal DM is not a term for a DM project that went extremely well. Rather, it focuses on the relationships between data and the phenomena that are inferred from the data (McCarthy, 2000). One example of this is that by using receipts from cash supermarket purchases, it is possible to identify various aspects of the customers who are making these purchases. Some of these phenomena could include age, income, ethnicity, and purchasing habits. One aspect of phenomenal DM, and in particular the goal to infer phenomena from data, is the need to have access to some facts about the relations between this data and their related phenomena. These could be included in the program that examines data for phenomena or in a kind of knowledge base or DB that can be drawn upon when doing the DM. Part of the challenge in creating such a knowledge base involves the coding of common sense into a DB, which has proved to be a difficult problem so far (Lyons & Tseytin, 1998).

DM FOR BIOINFORMATICS

Bioinformatics is the science of storing, extracting, organizing, analyzing, interpreting, and utilizing information from biological sequences and molecules. It has been fueled mainly by advances in DNA sequencing and mapping techniques. The Human Genome Project has resulted in an exponentially growing DB of genetic sequences. KDD techniques are playing an increasingly important role in the analysis and discovery of sequence, structure, and functional patterns or models from large sequence DBs. High performance techniques are also becoming central to this task (Han et al., 2001; Han & Kamber, 2001).

Bioinformatics provides opportunities for developing novel mining methods. Some of the main challenges in bioinformatics include protein structure prediction, homology search, multiple alignment and phylogeny construction, genomic sequence analysis, gene finding and gene mapping, as well as applications in gene expression data analysis, and drug discovery in the pharmaceutical industry. As a consequence of the large amounts of data produced in the field of molecular biology, most of the current bioinformatics projects deal with the structural and functional aspects of genes and proteins. Many of these projects are related to the Human Genome Project. The data produced by thousands of research teams all over the world are collected and organized in DBs specialized for particular subjects; examples include GDB, SWISS-PROT, GenBank, and PDB. Computational tools are needed to analyze the collected data in the most efficient manner. For example, bioinformaticists are working on the prediction of the biological functions of genes and proteins based on structural data (Chalifa-Caspi. Prilusky, & Lancet1998). Another example of a bioinformatics application is the GeneCards encyclopedia (Rebhan, Chalifa-Caspi, Prilusky, & Lancet 1997). This resource contains data about human genes, their products and the diseases in which they are involved.

Since DM offers the ability to discover patterns and relationships from large amounts of data, it seems ideally suited to use in the analysis of DNA. This is because DNA is essentially a sequence or chain of four main components called nucleotides. A group of several hundred nucleotides in a certain sequence is called a gene, and there are about 100,000 genes that make up the human genome. Aside from the task of integrating DBs of biological information noted above, another important application is the use of comparison and similarity search on DNA sequences. This is useful in the study of genetics-linked diseases, as it would be possible to compare and contrast the gene sequences of normal and diseased tissues and attempt to determine what sequences are found in the diseased, but not in the normal, tissues. There are a number of projects that are being conducted in this area, whether on the areas discussed above, or on the analysis of micro-array data and related topics. Among the centers doing research in this area are the European Bioinformatics Institute (EBI) in Cambridge, UK, and the Weizmann Institute of Science in Israel.

SUMMARY

This chapter has discussed a number of technologies, approaches, and research areas that have been identified as having critical and future promise in the field of DM. For instance, with the Web becoming such as important part of the computing community, it is not surprising that Web mining is one of the most promising areas in DM. There are several areas of Web-based mining, all of which can bring about exciting new knowledge about information on the Web, Web- usage patterns, and the intricacies of how the Web has been "woven." Coupled with this is the explosion in the amount of information that we now produce and have access to—much in the form of electronic and hard-copy text documents. Mining information from these text sources can uncover important information that had previously been buried in all of our reports, correspondence, memos, and other paperwork. The extensive use of handheld, wireless, and other ubiquitous devices is another developing area, since a lot of information being created and transmitted would be maintained and stored only on these kinds of devices. Among the other areas that have been developed, investigated, and identified are hypertext and hypermedia DM, which involves the processing and analysis of varying kinds of data; phenomenal DM, which looks at identifying phenomenon associated with a set of data; the mining of visual-oriented information; and the mining of other kinds of specialized information.

Another issue to look at is the social impact of mining for knowledge from data. This includes whether DM can be considered a threat to data security and privacy. In fact, there are daily instances where data is being collected on individuals, in effect "profiling users." Consider the many transactions that one conducts on a daily basis; it would not be difficult to understand the concerns that some have about the potential dangers of misuse of information, e.g., surfing the Web, replying to an Internet newsgroup, subscribing to a magazine, renting a video, joining a club, or making a purchase/ transaction with a credit card, supermarket loyalty card, or frequent flyer card-all of these are opportunities for someone to collect personal information.

In closing, it would not be overly optimistic to say that DM has a bright and promising future, and that the years to come will bring many new developments, methods, and technologies. While some analysts and experts in the field caution that DM may go the way of artificial intelligence (AI) and end up not having the commercial success which was predicted, the field of DM is still young enough that the possibilities are still limitless. By expanding applications that can use it, integrating technologies and methods, broadening its applicability to mainstream business applications, and making programs and interfaces easier for end-users to use, it is quite possible and likely that DM will rapidly become one of the most important and key areas of research and technology.

REFERENCES

Arlitt, M. & Williamson, C. (1997). Internet Web servers: Workload characterization and performance implications. *IEEE/ACM Transactions on Networking*, 5,5. Stanford, CA: AAAI, pp. 76-89.

Armstrong, S.,Freitag, D., Joachims, T., & Mitchell, T. (1995). Webwatcher: A learning apprentice for the World Wide Web. In *Proceedings of AAAI Spring Symposium on Information Gathering from Heterogeneous, Distributed Environment.*

Baeza-Yates, R.& Ribeiro-Neto, B. (1999). Modern information retrieval. Boston, MA: Addison-Wesley Longman.

Bedard, Y., Merrett, T., & Han, J. (2001). Fundamentals of geospatial data warehousing for geographic knowledge discovery. In H. Miller & J. Han (eds.), *Geographic data mining and knowledge discovery*. London: Taylor and Francis.

Billsus, D. & Pazzani, M. (1999). A hybrid user model for news story classification. In *Proceedings of the Seventh International Conference on User Modeling*, Banff, Canadaz: Springer, pp. 127-139.

Borges, J. & M. Leveen, (1999). Mining of user navigation patterns. In *Proceedings of WebKDD '99*, New York, NY: ACM, pp. 23-29.

Brachman, R.J., Selfridge, P.G., Terveen, L.G., Altman, B., Borgida, A., Halper, F., Kirk, T., Lazar, A., McGuinness, D.L., & Resnick, L.A. (1993). Integrated support for data archaeology. International Journal of Intelligent and Cooperative Information Systems, 2 (2), 159-185.

Brin, S. & Page, L. (1998). The anatomy of a large scale hypertextual Web search engine. *Seventh International World Wide Web Conference*, Brisbane, Australia: WWW Consortium, pp. 107-115.

Buchner, A. & Mulvenna, M. (1998). Discovering marketing intelligence through online analytical Web usage mining. *SIGMOD Record*, 27:4.

Catledge, L. & Pitkow, J. (1995). Characterizing browsing behaviors on the World Wide Web. *Computer Networks and ISDN Systems*, 27:6.

Chakrabarti, S. (2000). Data mining for hypertext. *SIGKDD Explorations*, 1 (2).

Chakrabarti, S., Dom, B. E., Gibson, D., Kleinberg, J. M., Kumar, S. R., Raghavan, P., Rajagopolan, S., & Tomkins, A. (1999). Mining the link structure of the World Wide Web. *IEEE Computer*, 32,8: 60-67, August.

Chakrabarti, S., van den Berg, M. H., & Dom, B. E. (1999). Distributed hypertext resource discovery through examples. In *Proceedings of the 25th VLDB (International Conference on Very Large Data Bases)*, Edinburgh, Scotland, pp. 375-386.

Chalifa-Caspi, V., Prilusky, J. & Lancet, D. (1998). The Unified Database. Weizmann Institute of Science, Bioinformatics Unit and Genome Center (Rehovot, Israel). Retrieved on January 12, 2002 from http://bioinfo.weizmann.ac.il/.

Chawathe, H., Garcia-Molina, J., Hammer, K., Irland, Y., Papakonstantinou, J.D., Ulman, J., & Widom, J. (1994). The tsimmis project: Integration of heterogeneous information sources. In *Proceedings of the IPSJ Conference*, Tokyo: Information Processing Society of Japan, pp. 114-133.

Chen, M., Park, J.S., & Yu, P.S. (1996). Data mining for path traversal patterns in a web environment. In *Proceedings of the 16th International Conference on Distributed Computing Systems*, ICDCS, pp. 385-392.

Cheung, D., Hwang, C., Fu, A., & Han, J. (2000). Efficient rule-based attributed-oriented induction for data mining. *Journal of Intelligent Information Systems*, 15 (2), 175-200.

Craven, M., DiPasquo, D., Freitag, D., McCallum, A., Mitchell, T., Nigam, K., & Slattery, S. (1998). Learning to extract symbolic knowledge from the World Wide Web. In *Proceedings of AAAI Conference*, AAAI.

Crimmins, S. & Smeator, A. (1999). Information Discovery on the Internet, *IEEE Intelligent Systems*, 14, 4.

Delmater, R. & Hancock, M. (2001). *Data mining explained: A manager's guide to customer-centric intelligence*. Burlington, MA: Digital Press.

Doorenbos, R.B., Etzioni, O., & Weld, D.S. (1996). A scalable comparison shopping agent for the World Wide Web. Technical Report 96-01-03, University of Washington, Dept. of Computer Science and Engineering, Seattle, WA.

Dorre, J., Gerstl, P., & Seiffert, R. (1999). Text mining: Finding nuggets in mountains of textual data. In *KDD-99 Proceedings*, San Diego, CA: ACM, pp. 398-401.

Dyche, J. (2001). *The CRM handbook*. Reading MA: Addison-Wesley.

Etzioni, O. (1996). The World Wide Web: Quagmire or gold mine. *Communications of the ACM*, 39, 11.

Frank, E., Paynter, G.W., Witten, I.H., Gutwin, C., & Nevill-Manning, C.G. (1998). Domain-specific key phrase extraction. In *Proceedings of 16th Joint Conference on AI*. pp. 668-673, Stockholm, Sweden.

Garofalis, M.N., Rastogi, R., Seshadri, S. & Shim, K. (1999). Data mining and the Web. *Workshop on Web Information and Data Management*, Workshop in Data Mining WIDM'99, 43-47.

Greenberg, P. (2001). *CRM at the speed of light.* New York: McGraw-Hill.

Han, J., Dong, G., & Yin, Y. (1999). Efficient mining of partial periodic patterns in time-series database. In *Proceedings International Conference on Data Engineering ICDE'99*, Sydney, Australia: IEEE, pp. 45-52.

Han, J., Jamil, Y., Lu, L., Chen, L., Liao, Y., & Pei, J. (2001). DNA-Miner: A system prototype for mining DNA sequences. In *Proceedings of the 2001 ACM-SIGMOD*, Santa Barbara, CA: ACM, pp. 211-217.

Han, J. & Kamber, M. (2001). *Data mining: Concepts and techniques*. San Mateo, CA: Morgan Kaufmann.

Han, J., Kamber, M., & Tung, A.K.H. (2001). Spatial clustering methods in data mining: A survey. In H. Miller & J. Han (eds.), *Geographic data mining and knowledge discovery*. London:Taylor and Francis.

Han, J., Koperski, K., & Stefanovic, N. (1997). GeoMiner: A system prototype for spatial data mining. In *Proceedings of SIGMOD '97*, Tucson, AZ: ACM, pp. 189-207.

Han, J., Lakshmanan, L.V.S., & Ng, R.T. (1999). Constraint-based, multidimensional data mining. *COMPUTER (Special Issue on Data Mining)*, 32 (8), 46-50.

Han, J., Pei, J., & Yin, Y. (2000). Mining frequent patterns without candidate generation. In *Proceedings of 2000 ACM-SIGMOD Int. Conf. on Management of Data (SIGMOD '00)*, Dallas, TX: ACM, pp. 109-114.

Han, J., Pei, J., Mortazavi-Asl, B., Chen, Q., Dayal, U. & Hsu, M.-C. (2000). FreeSpan: Frequent pattern-projected sequential pattern mining. In *Proceedings of the KDD '00*, Boston, MA: ACM, pp. 88-97.

Han, J., Stefanovic, N., & Koperski, K. (1998). Selective materialization: An efficient method for spatial data cube construction. In *Proceedings Pacific-Asia Conference in Knowledge Discovery and Data Mining, PAKDD '98*, Melbourne, Australia: ACM, pp. 295-303.

Han, J., Zaiane, O.R., Chee, S.H.S., & Chiang, J.Y. (2000). Towards online analytical mining of the Internet for e-commerce. In W. Kou & Y. Yesha (eds.), *Electronic commerce technology trends: Challenges and opportunities*, IBM Press, 169-198.

Hearst, M.A. (1999). Untangling text data mining. In *Proceedings of ACL '99: The 37th Annual Meeting of the Association for Computational Linguistics*, University of Maryland, June 20-26, Association for Computational Linguistics, pp. 123-129.

Kargupta, H. & Joshi, A. (2001). Data mining to go: Ubiquitous KDD for mobile and distributed environments. Presentation at *KDD-2001*, San Francisco.

Kargupta, H., Park, B., Herschberger, D., & Johnson, E. (2000). Collective data mining. In H. Kargupta & P. Chan (eds.), *Advances in distributed data mining*. Boston, MA:MIT Press.

Kholsa, A., Kuhn, B., & Soparkar, N. (1996). Database search using information mining. In *Proceedings of the 1996 ACM-SIGMOD International Conference on Management of Data, Montreal, Canada*: ACM, pp. 201-209.

Kim, E. D., Lam, J. M. W., & Han, J. (2000). AIM: Approximate intelligent matching for time- series data. In *Proceedings of the 2000 International Conference on Data Warehouse and Knowledge Discovery* (DaWaK'00), Greenwich, U.K.: IEEE, pp. 36-49.

King & Novak, M. (1996). Supporting information infrastructure for distributed, heterogeneous knowledge discovery. In *Proceedings of the SIGMOD 96 Workshop on Research Issues on Data Mining and Knowledge Discovery*, Montreal, Canada: ACM, pp. 123-130.

Kleinberg, J. (1998). Authoritative sources in a hyperlinked environment. In *Proceedings of the 9th ACM-SIAM Symposium on Discrete Algorithms*, pp. 114-119.

Koperski, K., Adhikary, J., & Han, J. (1996). Spatial data mining: Progress and challenges. *ACM SIGMOD '96 Workshop on Research Issues in Data Mining and Knowledge Discovery* (DMKD'96), Montreal, Canada: ACM, pp. 80-87.

Koperski, K. & Han, J. (1995). Discovery of spatial association rules in geographic information databases. In *Proceedings of ACM SIG Conference on Management of Data 1995*, Portland, Maine: ACM, pp. 31-39.

Koperski, K., Han, J., & Marchisio, G.B. (1999). Mining spatial and image data through progressive refinement methods. *Revue internationale de gomatique (European Journal of GIS and Spatial Analysis)*, 9 (4), 425-440.

Koperski, K., Han, J., & Stefanovic, N. (1998). An efficient two-step method for classification of spatial data. *International Symposium on Spatial Data Handling SDH'98*, Vancouver, Canada: ISSDH, pp. 32-37.

Kosala, R. & Blockeel, H. (2000). Web mining research: A survey. *SIGKDD Explorations*, 2 (1).

Lakshmanan, L.V.S., Ng, R., Han, J. & Pang, A. (1999). Optimization of constrained frequent set queries with 2-variable constraints. *Proceedings of the ACM Special Internet Group on Management of Data 1999*, Philadelphia, PA: ACM, pp. 287-293.

Larson, R. (1996). Bibliometrics of the World Wide Web: An exploratory analysis of the intellectual structure of cyberspace. In ASIS '96: Proceedings of the 1996 Annual ASIS Meeting, Baltimore, MD: American Society for Information Science and Technology, pp. 65-71.

Lu, H., Feng, L. & Han, J. (2000). Beyond intra-transaction association analysis: Mining multi-dimensional inter-transaction association rules. *ACM Transactions on Information Systems, 18,* 4, October.

Lyons, D. & Tseytin, G. (1998). Phenomenal data mining and link analysis. In B. Jensen & F. Goldberg (eds.), *Proceedings of the Artificial Intelligence and Link Analysis Fall Symposium*, Phoenix, AZ: American Association for Artificial Intelligence, pp. 123-127.

Maarek, Y. S., & Ben Shaul, I. (1996). Automatically organizing bookmarks per content. In *Proceedings of the 5th International World Wide Web Conference/Computer Networks 28* (7-11): 1321-1334, Boston, MA.

Madria, S., Bhowmick, S., Ng, W. K., & Lim, E. P. (1999). Research issues in Web data mining. In *Proceedings of Data Warehousing and Knowledge Discovery, First International Conference, DaWaK '99,* Florence, Italy, pp. 303-312.

McCarthy, J. (2000). Phenomenal data mining, *SIGKDD Explorations*, 1 (2).

Mendelzon, A., Mihaila, G., & Milo, T. (1996). Querying the World Wide Web, In *Proceedings of Conference on Parallel and Distributed Information Systems PDIS'96*, Miami, FL, pp. 45-57.

Merialdo P., Atzeni, M., & Mecca, G. (1997). Semistructured and structured data in the Web: Going back and forth. In *Proceedings of the Workshop on the Management of Semistructured Data* (in conjunction with ACM SIGMOD), ACM, pp. 196-201.

Miller, H. & Han, J. (eds.).(2001). *Geographic data mining and knowledge discovery.* London:Taylor and Francis.

Mizruchi, M. S., Mariolis, P., Schwartz, M., & Mintz, B. (1986). Techniques for disaggregating centrality scores in social networks. In N. B. Tuma (ed.), *Sociological Methodology*, pp. 26-48, San Francisco, CA: Jossey-Bass.

Nahm, U. Y., & Mooney, R. J. (2000). A mutually beneficial integration of data mining and information extraction. In *Proceedings of the Seventeenth National Conference on AI (AAAI-00)*, Austin, TX: AAAI, pp. 627-632.

Pazzani, M., Muramatsu, J., & D. Billsus. (1996). Syskill & Webert: Identifying interesting websites. In *Proceedings of AAAI Spring Symposium on Machine Learning in Information Access*, Portland, OR: AAAI, pp. 54-61.

Pei, J. & Han, J. (2000). Can we push more constraints into frequent pattern mining? In *Proceedings of the ACM Conference on Knowledge Discovery for Databases, KDD'00*, Boston, MA, pp. 196-207.

Pei, J., Han, J., & Lakshmanan, L.V.S. (2001). Mining frequent item sets with convertible constraints. In *Proceedings of the 2001 International Conference on Data Engineering (ICDE'01)*, Heidelberg, Germany: IEEE, pp. 82-90.

Pei, J., Han, J., & Mao, R. (2000). CLOSET: An efficient algorithm of mining frequent closed itemsets for association rules. In *Proceedings of the ACM SIGMOD Workshop on Research Issues in Data Mining and Knowledge Discovery, DMKD'00*, Dallas, TX: ACM, pp. 21-30.

Pei, J., Han, J., Pinto, H., Chen, Q., Dayal, U., & Hsu, M.-C. (2001). PrefixSpan: Mining sequential patterns efficiently by prefix-projected pattern growth. In *Proceedings of the 2001 International Conference on Data Engineering (ICDE'01)*, Heidelberg, Germany: IEEE, pp. 245-259.

Pei, J., Tung, A., & Han, J. (2001). Fault-tolerant frequent pattern mining: Problems and challenges. In *Proceedings of the 2001 ACM-SIGMOD*, Santa Barbara, CA: ACM, pp. 33-40.

Rebhan, M., Chalifa-Caspi, V., Prilusky, J., Lancet, D. (1997). GeneCards: Encyclopedia for genes, proteins & diseases. Weizmann Institute of Science, Bioinformatics Unit & Genome Center (Rehovot, Israel). Retrieved on January 13, 2002 from http://bioinfo.weizmann.ac.il/.

Rennison, E. (1994). Galaxy of news: An approach to visualizing and understanding expansive news landscapes. In *Proceedings of UIST 94, ACM Symposium on User Interface Software and Technology*, pp. 3-12, New York: ACM.

Shavlik, J. & Eliassi-Rad, T. (1998). Intelligent agents for Web-based tasks. In *Working Notes of the AAAI/ICML-98 Workshop on Learning for Text Categorization*, Madison, WI: AAAI, pp. 111-119.

Srivastava, J., Cooley, R., Deshpe, M., &Tan, P. (2000). Web usage mining. *SIGKDD Explorations*, 1 (2).

Swift, R.S. (2000). *Accelerating customer relationships : Using CRM and relationship technologies*. Upper Saddle River, NJ: Prentice-Hall.

Tung, K.H., Han, J., Lakshmanan, L.V.S., & Ng, R.T. (2001). Constraint-based clustering in large databases. In *Proceedings of the 2001 International Conference on Database Theory (ICDT'01)*, London, U.K.: ACM, pp. 23-31.

Tung, K. H., Hou, J., & Han, J. (2001). Spatial clustering in the presence of obstacles. In *Proceedings of the 2001 International Conference on Data Engineering (ICDE'01)*, Heidelberg, Germany: IEEE, pp. 96-102.

Voorhees, E. M. (1994). Query expansion using lexical-semantic relations. In *Proceedings of the 17th Annual International ACM/SIGIR Conference*, pp. 61-69, Dublin, Ireland.

Wang, Zhou, S., & Han, J. (2000). Pushing support constraints into association mining. *International Conference on Very Large Data Bases (VLDB'00)*, Cairo, Egypt.

Wang, W., Zhou, S., & Han, J. (2000). Pushing support constraints into association mining. *International Conference on Very Large Data Bases (VLDB'00)*, Cairo, Egypt: Morgan Kaufmann, pp. 87-96.

Wang, K., He, Y., & Han, J. (2000). Mining frequent itemsets using support constraints. In *Proceedings of the 2000 International Conference on Very Large Data Bases (VLDB'00)*, pp. 43-52, Cairo, Egypt, 43-52.

Weiss, F., Velez, B., Sheldon, M.A., Namprempre, C., Szilagyi, P., Duda, A., & Gifford, D.K. (1996). Hypursuit: A hierarchical network search engine that exploits content-link hypertext clustering In *Hypertext'96: The Seventh ACM Conference on Hypertext*, ACM, pp. 211-218.

Wise, J. A., Thomas, J. J., Pennock, K., Lantrip, D., Pottier, M. & Schur, A. (1995). Visualizing the non-visual: Spatial analysis and interaction with information from text documents. In *Proceedings of the Information Visualization Symposium 95*, pp. 51-58, IEEE Computer Society Press.

Xu, J. & Croft. W.B. (1996). Query expansion using local & global document analysis. In SIGIR '96: Proceedings of the 19th Annual International ACM SIGIR Conference on Research & Development in Information Retrieval, 4-11.

Zaiane, O., Han, J., Li, W., & Hou, J. (1998). Mining multimedia data. In *Proceedings of Meeting Of Minds, CASCON '98*, Toronto, Canada: IBM.

Zaiane, O., Han, J., & Zhu, H. (2000). Mining recurrent items in multimedia with progressive resolution refinement. In *Proceedings of the International Conference on Data Engineering ICDE'00*, San Diego, CA: IEEE, pp. 15-28.

About the Authors

John Wang is a professor in the Department of Information and Decision Sciences at Montclair State University (MSU), USA. Having received a scholarship award, he came to the USA and completed his Ph.D. in Operations Research from Temple University in 1990. He worked as an assistant professor at Beijing University of Sciences & Technology, China, for two years. In the fall of 1992, he transferred to MSU. Dr. Wang received his tenure in 1997 and was promoted to full professor in 2000 for his outstanding and extraordinary contributions. Dr. Wang has published 72 papers in refereed journals and conference proceedings, as well as two research books. He has been an active member of five renowned professional organizations. He has served as session chairman and track chair seventeen times on the most prestigious international and national conferences. His research activities and articles have been well received, enabling him to build a reputation with other significant professionals in his field. He was further invited to serve as a referee for *Operations Research* (a flagship journal) and *IEEE Transactions on Control Systems Technology* (a very prestigious journal). He has also developed several computer software programs based on his research findings. Dr. Wang is a highly accomplished and well-established operations research scholar. His current research interests include optimization, nonlinear programming, and manufacturing systems engineering. A long-term goal is to study the synergy of operations research and cybernetics.

*   *   *   *   *

Stefan Arnborg received his M.Sc.E. and Dr.Tech. in Engineering Physics from the Swedish Royal Institute of Technology in 1968 and 1972, respectively. In 1971, he joined the Swedish National Defense Research Institute and in 1979, Philips Elektronikindustrier AB. Since 1982, he is a professor in Computer Science at the Royal Institute of Technology. His interests are in education, operations research and defense systems, programming systems, algorithms, biomedical informatics, verification, inference, and uncertainty management. He is chairman of the Computer Engineering program at the Royal Institute of Technology and scientific advisor to the Swedish Institute of Computer Science.

Barbro Back is professor in Accounting Information Systems at Åbo Akademi University in Turku, Finland. Her research interests include accounting information systems, intelligent systems in business, neural networks, and data mining. She has presented her research in the *Journal of Management Information Systems, Accounting Management and Information Technology, European Journal of Operations Research, International Journal of Intelligent Systems in Accounting, Management and Tax, Advances in Accounting*, and other journals. She currently serves on the editorial boards of *The New Review of Applied Expert Systems and Emerging Technologies*, and *The International Journal of Accounting*.

Christian Böhm was born in Argentina in 1980. He is pursuing his Information Systems Engineering degree at Universidad Tecnológica Nacional- Facultad Regional Santa Fe, Argentina. He holds a fellowship of UTN-FRSF and has been working for GIDSATD (Group of Research and Development in Decision Support Systems) since 2001. His research interest is related to data mining.

Marvin L. Brown is an assistant professor in the School of Business Administration at Hawaii Pacific University, USA. He holds a B.S. from Shepherd College, an M.B.A. from Morehead State University, and is A.B.D. in Computer Information Systems from Cleveland State University. He has several years of industrial experience in database management and information technology as a consultant to NASA, the U.S. Federal Energy Regulatory Commission, and the U.S. Federal Department of Transportation. He is also a former partner in the consulting firm, Mardale Consulting LLC.

Robin Burke is an associate professor in the Department of Information Systems and Decision Sciences at California State University, Fullerton. He received his Ph.D. in 1993 from the Institute for the Learning Sciences at Northwestern University. In 1996, he was co-founder of the Intelligent Information Laboratory at the University of Chicago. His research is on the application of artificial intelligence to electronic commerce and digital libraries, particularly recommender systems, integrating a variety of natural language, information retrieval, machine learning, and artificial intelligence techniques, with an emphasis on case-based reasoning.

Yao Chen is an assistant professor of Manufacturing and Information Systems in the College of Management at the University of Massachusetts, Lowell, USA. Her current research interests include efficiency and productivity issues of information systems, information technology's impact on operations performance, and methodology development of Data Envelopment Analysis. Her work has appeared in such journals as *European Journal of Operational Research, International Journal of Production Economics, Information Technology & Management Journal* and others. She is a member of the Institute for Operations Research and Management Sciences (INFORMS).

Omar Chiotti was born in Argentina in 1959. He received his degree in Chemical Engineering in 1984 from Universidad Tecnológica Nacional and his Ph.D. in Engineering from Universidad Nacional del Litoral, Argentina, in 1989. Since 1984, he has been working for CONICET (Consejo Nacional de Investigaciones Científicas y Técnicas), currently as a researcher. He is a professor of Information Systems Engineering at Universidad Tecnológica Nacional – Facultad Regional Santa Fe, Argentina, since 1986. Currently, he teaches Management Systems. He is the director of the GIDSATD (Group of Research and Development in Decision Support Systems) since 1994. His current research interests are focused on decision-support systems engineering.

Jack S. Cook is an associate professor of Information Systems at the Rochester Institute of Technology (RIT), USA. His specialties are Electronic Commerce, Information Systems and Production/Operations Management. Dr. Cook has extensive experience in teaching and training experience in these fields that spans over two decades and includes over 50 conference presentations and numerous journal articles. Dr. Cook is a Certified Fellow in Production and Inventory Management (CFPIM). His education includes a Ph.D. in Business Administration, an M.S. in Computer Science, an M.B.A., an M.A. in Mathematics, and a B.S. in Computer Science.

Laura L. Cook works for the Computing & Information Technology Department at the State University of New York at Geneseo, USA. She is currently a graduate student in Information Technology at the Rochester Institute of Technology. Laura has four journal publications and has given numerous presentations. She also volunteers as the Publicity Director for the Rochester, NY, Chapter of APICS. Laura has taught Electronic Commerce for the Jones School of Business and Computers in Education for the School of Education at SUNY-Geneseo. She has also taught many technology workshops on various topics.

Massimo Coppola (1969) is a Ph.D. candidate in Computer Science at the Department of Computer Science of the University of Pisa, Italy. He received his master's in C.S. in 1997, and works with the Parallel Architecture Research Group. He is a member of the ACM SIG on Knowledge Discovery and Data Mining. His research interests also include parallel architectures and programming languages for parallel computation. The research topic of his Ph.D. studies is the application of structured parallel programming to high-performance data mining, out-of-core and data-intensive algorithms.

Sorin Draghici has obtained his B.Sc. and M.Sc. degrees from Politehnica University in Bucharest, Romania, followed by a Ph.D. degree from the University of St. Andrews (third oldest university in UK after Oxford and Cambridge). He has published over 50 peer-reviewed journal and conference publications, as well as three book chapters. He is co-inventor on four patent applications and a frequent journal reviewer and NSF panelist. Currently, Dr. Draghici is the head of the Intelligent Systems and Bioinformatics in the Department of Computer Science at Wayne State University, USA (http://vortex.cs.wayne.edu).

Tomas Eklund received an M.Sc. (Econ.) in Information Systems from Åbo Akademi University, in Turku, Finland, in 2001. He is currently working as a researcher and is pursuing a Ph.D. at the Department of Information Systems at Åbo Akademi University. His primary research interests include data mining, knowledge discovery, and neural networks.

Farshad Fotouhi received his Ph.D. in Computer Science from Michigan State University in 1988. He joined the faculty of Computer Science at Wayne State University in August 1988, where he is currently an associate professor and associate chair of the department. Dr. Fotouhi's major area of research is databases, including relational, object-oriented, multimedia/hypermedia systems, and data warehousing. He has published over 80 papers in refereed journals and conference proceedings, served as a program committee member of various database-related conferences, and he is currently a member of the Editorial Advisory Board of the *Journal of Database Management*.

María Rosa Galli was born in Argentina in 1958. She received her degree in Chemical Engineering in 1983 from Universidad Nacional de Mar del Plata, Argentina and a Ph.D. in Chemical Engineering from Universidad Nacional del Litoral, also in Argentina. Since 1984, she has been working for CONICET (Consejo Nacional de Investigaciones Científicas y Técnicas), currently as a researcher. She is a professor of Operation Research of Information Systems Engineering at Universidad Tecnológica Nacional – Facultad Regional Santa Fe, Argentina, since 1989 and co-director of GIDSATD (Group of Research and Development in Decision Support Systems) since 1995. Her current research interests are focused on decision-support systems engineering and multiagent systems.

Donald W. Gribbin is an associate professor of Accountancy at Southern Illinois University at Carbondale, USA. He received a Ph.D. in Business Administration from Oklahoma State University. He has published papers in *Decision Sciences*, *Journal of Management Accounting Research*, *Journal of Business Finance & Accounting*, and *The British Accounting Review*. His research interests include the distributional properties of financial ratios and the modeling of various types of cost data.

Jerzy W. Grzymala-Busse (M.S. in Electrical Engineering, Technical University of Poznan, Poland, 1964; M.S. in Mathematics, University of Wroclaw, Poland, 1967; Ph.D. in Engineering, Technical University of Poznan, Poland, 1969) is a professor of Electrical Engineering and Computer Science at the University of Kansas, USA. His research interests include data mining, knowledge discovery from databases, machine learning, expert systems, reasoning under uncertainty, and rough set theory. He has published three books and over 150 articles in the above areas, mostly in data mining. He has presented numerous invited presentations on international scientific conferences and has served as a session chair and in steering committees, advisory committees, and program committees of various international and national scientific and technical conferences.

Jeffrey Hsu is an assistant professor of Information Systems at the Silberman College of Business Administration, Fairleigh Dickinson University, USA. His research interests include human-computer interaction, e-commerce, groupware, distance learning, and data mining. He is the author of six books and numerous papers and articles, and has professional experience in the IT industry. Hsu holds a Ph.D. in Management Information Systems from Rutgers University, three master's degrees, and several professional certifications. Dr. Hsu is always interested in discussing opportunities for research and other scholarly activities, and can be reached via e-mail at jeff@fdu.edu.

William H. Hsu received B.S. degrees in Computer Science and Mathematical Sciences and a Master of Science in Engineering in Computer Science from Johns Hopkins University in May 1993. He received his Ph.D. degree from the University of Illinois at Urbana-Champaign in 1998. He is currently an assistant professor of Computing and Information Sciences at Kansas State University, USA, and a visiting research scientist at the National Center for Supercomputing Applications. His research interests include machine learning and data mining, probabilistic reasoning, decision support and sensor fusion in automation, learning spatial and temporal models from data, and soft computing.

Michael Johnson obtained his B.S. in Computer Engineering from the University of California, San Diego, in 1987. After working in industry at GTE Communications and AT&T Bell Labs for four years, he returned to school and obtained his M.S. in Computer Science at Michigan State University in 1993. For the past eight years he has been an assistant professor and head of the Computer Science Department at Madonna University in Livonia, Michigan, USA. Mr. Johnson is currently completing his Ph.D. studies at Wayne State University.

YongSeog Kim received an M.S. degree in 2000 in Computer Science, and a Ph.D. in Business Administration in 2001 from the University of Iowa. He is currently a post-doctoral student in the Management Sciences Department at the University of Iowa, USA. His research interests are in machine learning and data mining including feature selection in supervised and unsupervised learning, evolutionary algorithms, neural networks, and ensemble methods. In particular, he is interested in applying data-mining algorithms to real-world business applications. He is a member of INFORMS, IEEE, ACM, and AAAI.

John F. Kros is an assistant professor in the Decision Sciences Department, School of Business Administration at East Carolina University, USA. He holds a B.B.A. from the University of Texas, Austin, an M.B.A. from Santa Clara University, and a Ph.D. in Systems Engineering from the University of Virginia. He has several years of industrial experience in electronics manufacturing, specifically in operations management, and is a member of INFORMS, DSI, and ASQ.

Vladimir A. Kulyukin is an assistant professor of Computer Science at the School of Computer Science, Telecommunications and Information Systems of Utah State University, USA. He received his Ph.D. in Computer Science from the University of Chicago in 1998. His research interests are information retrieval and robotics.

Eitel J.M. Lauría has worked in the IT arena for over 15 years and has consulted with many multinational corporations across a wide range of industries, advising on such topics as Decision-Support Systems, Business Intelligence, Client/Server Technology and Web-Based Applications. He holds an M.S. in Electrical Engineering from the University of Buenos Aires, Argentina, and an M.B.A. from Universidad del Salvador (USAL), Argentina. A former faculty member at USAL, he is currently a lecturer at the School of Business, University at Albany, while completing his Ph.D. in Information

Science. His teaching and research interests cover the fields of Information Technology, Information Decision Systems and Statistical Data Mining.

Chung-Hong Lee received an M.Sc. in Information Technology for Manufacture from the University of Warwick in 1994. He has been awarded a Ph.D. in Computer Science from the University of Manchester in 1997. He currently is an assistant professor at the Chang Jung University, Taiwan. He has worked at Chang Jung University since 1998, prior to which he was a postdoctoral fellow at Institute of Information Science, Academia Sinica, Taiwan. Current research interests include multilingual text mining, automatic ontology acquisition, computational linguistics, and information retrieval. He is both members of ACM and IEEE.

Lori K. Long is a doctoral student in the Department of Management & Information Systems, the College of Business, Kent State University in Kent, Ohio, USA. Her concentration is Human Resources Management, and her current research interests include the role of technology in effective human resources management, e-learning, and computer-based employee assessment.

Filippo Menczer is an assistant professor in the Department of Management Sciences at the University of Iowa, USA. He received a Laurea in Physics from the University of Rome in 1991, and a dual Ph.D. in Computer Science and Cognitive Science from the University of California at San Diego in 1998. Dr. Menczer has been a Fulbright, Rotary Foundation, NATO, and Santa Fe Institute fellow. He pursues interdisciplinary research spanning from ecological theory to distributed information systems; these contribute to artificial life, agent-based computational economics, evolutionary computation, neural networks, machine learning, and adaptive intelligent agents for Web, text, and data mining.

Alan Oppenheim obtained his B.S. in Mechanical Engineering and his M.S. in Industrial Management from the Polytechnic Institute of Brooklyn (now the Polytechnic University), and his Ph.D. in Business Administration from New York University. He is dean of the School of Business and professor of Information and Decision Sciences at Montclair State University, USA. He is an active member of several professional organizations, has consulted on quality and productivity with various firms, and has presented seminars nationwide. He has published many articles, contributed to several texts, and is the co-author of the book *Quality Management: Tools and Methods for Improvement* published by Richard D. Irwin, which is about to enter its third edition and which has received widespread industrial and academic acceptance.

Eric Paquet has a Ph.D. in Computer Vision from Laval University, and he is currently working with the Visual Information Technology Group at the National Research Council of Canada. He is working in collaboration with various enterprises, research institutes, and universities. He is representative at the Web3D Consortium and MPEG. He is the author of numerous publications and has won many international awards. His research activities include content-based management of multimedia information, virtual environments, collaborative virtual environments, and anthropometric databases.

Fay Cobb Payton is an assistant professor of Information Technology at North Carolina State University, USA. She earned a Ph.D. in Information Systems from Case Western Reserve University. She holds a B.S. in Industrial and Systems Engineering from Georgia Institute of Technology and an M.B.A. in Decision Sciences from Clark Atlanta University. Her research interests and projects include healthcare, information privacy, supply chain management, data warehousing/mining, diversity, and systems implementation. She has published in *Communications of the ACM*, *Health Care Management Review*, *Information and Management*, and *International Journal of Technology Management*. Dr. Payton is also on the editorial board of *IT Professional* - an IEEE publication.

Gys le Roux is a lecturer at the Department of Informatics, University of Pretoria, South Africa. He holds an M.Com. in Informatics and a B.Sc. (Hon.) in Computer Science. His research interests include data mining, data warehousing, and data visualization.

Murali S. Shanker is an associate professor in the Department of Management and Information Systems at Kent State University, USA. He received a Ph.D. from the Department of Operations and Management Science, University of Minnesota. His research interests are knowledge management and data mining, simulation, and distributed processing. His papers have appeared in journals such as *INFORMS Journal on Computing*, *IIE Transactions*, *Omega*, and *Annals of Operations Research*. His current research includes developing tools to optimize web-server performance, and in conducting a statistical analysis of the behavior of neural networks as applied to classification and prediction problems.

W. Nick Street is an assistant professor in the Management Sciences Department at the University of Iowa, USA. He received a Ph.D. in 1994 in Computer Sciences from the University of Wisconsin. His research interests are machine learning and data mining, particularly the use of mathematical optimization in inductive-learning techniques. His recent work has focused on dimensionality reduction (feature selection) in high-dimensional data for both classification and clustering, ensemble prediction methods for massive and streaming data sets, and learning shapes for image segmentation, classification, and retrieval. He has received an NSF CAREER award and an NIH INRSA postdoctoral fellowship.

Giri Kumar Tayi is a professor in the Department of Management Science and Information Systems in the School of Business at the State University of New York at Albany, USA. He obtained his Ph.D. from Carnegie-Mellon University, Pittsburgh, USA. His teaching and research interests are interdisciplinary and cover the fields of Information Systems and Technology, Service and Operations Management, and Operations Research. He has published over 30 scholarly papers in academic and refereed journals and has been the guest editor of several journal special issues on topics such as Data Quality, Operations Management, Communication Networks: Design and Management, and Mobile Computing.

Marvin D. Troutt is a professor in the Department of Management & Information Systems and in the Graduate School of Management at Kent State University, USA. He received a Ph.D. in Mathematical Statistics from the University of Illinois at Chicago. He is an associate editor of *Decision Sciences* Journal and a Fellow of the Decision Sciences Institute. His publications have appeared in *Decision Sciences, Management Science, Journal of the Operational Research Society, European Journal of Operational Research, Operations Research, Decision Support Systems, Naval Research Logistics, Statistics*, and others. His current research interests include the statistics of performance data with application to data mining and decision support.

Hannu Vanharanta began his professional career in 1973 as technical assistant at the Turku office of the Finnish Ministry of Trade and Industry. Between 1975 and 1992, he worked for Finnish international engineering companies, i.e., Jaakko Pöyry, Rintekno, and Ekono as process engineer, section manager, and leading consultant. His doctoral thesis was approved in 1995. In 1995-1996, he was professor in Business Economics in the University of Joensuu. In 1996-1998, he served as purchasing and supply management professor in the Lappeenranta University of Technology. Since 1998, he has been Professor of Industrial Management and Engineering at Pori School of Technology and Economics, Tampere University of Technology, Finland. He is a member of IPSERA and a Research Fellow at the Institute for Advanced Management Systems Research, Åbo Akademi.

Marco Vanneschi is a full professor in Computer Science at the Department of Computer Science of the University of Pisa, Italy. His research and teaching activity has been developed in the area of high performance computing, systems architecture, and programming models. He has coordinated national and international projects. He has been member of the official Working Group of MURST on High Performance Computing, and of several international committees (IFIP, IEEE, EuroPar, ParCo, international journals and conferences). He is author of more than 150 scientific papers, three books on computer architecture and parallel programming, and he is scientific editor of six international books.

Herna Viktor is an assistant professor at the School of Information Technology and Electrical Engineering (SITE) of the University of Ottawa, Ottawa, Ontario, Canada. She holds a Ph.D. in Computer Science. Her research interests include data mining, multi-agent learning systems, and data warehousing. Professor Viktor is also a visiting professor at the Department of Informatics, University of Pretoria, Pretoria, South Africa.

Ari Visa received his M.S. in Computer Science and Technology from Linköping University of Technology, Sweden, in 1981. The Licentiate and the Doctor of Technology degrees in Information Science he received from the Helsinki University of Technology, Finland, in 1988 and 1990, respectively. Since 1996, he has been a professor, first at Lappeenranta University of Technology and from the beginning of 2000 at Tampere University of Technology in Finland. He is currently a professor in Digital Signal Processing at Tampere University of Technology, and a docent in Image Analysis at HUT. His current research interests are multimedia and multimedia systems, adaptive systems, wireless communications, distributed computing, soft computing, computer vision, knowledge mining, and knowledge retrieval. Professor Visa is the former president and vice president of the Pattern Recognition Society of Finland.

Hsin-Chang Yang received his B.S. degree in Computer Engineering in 1988 from the National Chiao-Tung University, Hsin-Chu, Taiwan, and M.S. and Ph.D. degrees in Information Science and Computer Engineering in 1990 and 1996, respectively, from the National Taiwan University, Taipei, Taiwan. Since 1998, Dr. Yang has been an assistant professor of Information Management at Chang Jung University, Tainan, Taiwan. Dr. Yang's research interests include pattern recognition, neural networks, knowledge discovery, and information retrieval. He is a member of both ACM and IEEE.

Aimao Zhang received her Bachelor of Science from Indiana University of Pennsylvania in 1990. She earned her master's of Business Administration in 1991 from Indiana University of Pennsylvania. She was awarded a Doctor of Philosophy in 2001 from Southern Illinois University at Carbondale, with a major in Management Information Systems and a minor in Production/Operations Management. Zhang has broad interests in teaching and research. She has taught and is teaching courses in Information Technology. Zhang's publications include book chapters, papers in refereed journals, and national conferences.

Joe Zhu is an assistant professor of Operations, Department of Management at Worcester Polytechnic Institute, Worcester, MA. Professor Zhu is an expert in methods of performance measurement and his research interests are in the areas of information technology and productivity, and performance evaluation and benchmarking. He has published a book focusing on performance evaluation and benchmarking using *Data Envelopment Analysis* (DEA) and developed the *DEAFrontier* software. With more than 150 DEA models, this software can assist decision-makers in benchmarking and analyzing complex operational efficiency issues in manufacturing organizations as well as evaluating processes in banking, retail, franchising, healthcare, e-business, public services and many other industries. His research has appeared in such journals as *Management Science, Operations Research, Annals of Operations Research, Journal of Operational Research Society, European Journal of Operational Research, Computer and Operations Research, OMEGA, Socio-Economic Planning Sciences, Journal of Productivity Analysis, INFOR*, and *Journal of Alternative Investment*.

Wojciech Ziarko received an M.Sc. degree in Applied Mathematics from the Faculty of Fundamental Problems of Technology of the Warsaw University of Technology in 1975. In 1980, he received a Ph.D. degree in Computer Science at the Institute of Computer Science of Polish Academy of Sciences. In 1982, he joined the University of Regina, Canada, where he is now a professor in the Computer Science Department. His research interests include knowledge discovery, machine learning, pattern classification, and control algorithm acquisition. These research interests are largely motivated by the theory of rough sets. He is one of the pioneers of this research area.

Index

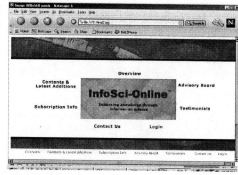